Workers on the Nile

Workers on the Nile

Nationalism, Communism, Islam, and the Egyptian

Working Class, 1882–1954

By Joel Beinin and Zachary Lockman

The American University in Cairo Press

Published in Egypt in 1998 by
The American University in Cairo Press
113 Sharia Kasr el Aini, Cairo, Egypt
420 Fifth Avenue, New York, NY 10018
www.aucpress.com

Copyright © 1998 by Joel Beinin and Zachary Lockman

All rights reserved. No part of this publication may be reproduced, stored in a retrieval system, or transmitted
in any form or by any means, electronic, mechanical, photocopying, recording, or otherwise, without the
prior written permission of the publisher.

Dar el Kutub No. 4080/98
ISBN 978 977 424 482 7

2 3 4 5 6 7 8   14 13 12 11 10 09

Printed in Egypt

For our parents

Contents

List of Tables   xi

List of Abbreviations   xiii

Preface   xvii

Part One
The Emergence of the Egyptian Workers' Movement,
1882–1942

I   Introduction   3

The Egyptian Working Class
The Development of Capitalism in Egypt
The Wafd
Class and Nation in Colonial Countries
The Historiography of the Egyptian Workers' Movement

II   The Formation of the Egyptian Working Class   23

Peasants into Workers
The Coalheavers of Port Said
From Guild Members to Wage Workers
Immigrant Workers
A Working Class in Formation
Continuity and Change in the Interwar Period

viii Contents

III. The Emergence of Labor Activism, 1899–1914 48

Cigarette Workers: An Embattled Elite
The Tramway Workers of Cairo
The Nationalist Party and the Workers
Struggle at the 'Anabir
The First Wave in Perspective

IV 1919: Labor Upsurge and National Revolution 83

The Revival of Labor Activity
Egyptian Workers and Egyptian Nationalism
The Cairo Tramway Workers in the Revolution
Railway Workers and the Revolution
Patterns of Participation and Leadership
Radicalism and Nationalism at the Suez Canal
August 1919: "Il Pleut des Syndicats!"
Dénouement: The Cairo Tram Strike

V The Unions, the Left, and the Wafd, 1920–1924 121

The Tramway Workers on the Defensive
The Left and the Labor Movement
The Wafd and the Workers
The Wafd's Conception of the Working Class
Promises and Results of Wafdist Hegemony

VI Workers, Effendis, Pashas, and a Prince 171

The Pashas of Labor
Aborted Hopes
From Nahhas Pasha to Sidqi Pasha
Prince of the Workers
The Repression of the Labor Movement
The Resurgence of the NFTUE
The Struggle for Power in the Labor Movement

VII Toward an Independent Workers' Movement 218

The Wafd Restored
A New Departure
The Wafd in Crisis and the Workers
The Coalescence of a New Leadership
Egypt and the World War
The Cairo Tramway Workers, 1939–1942

Contents ix

Part Two
Class Conflict and National Struggle
1942–1954

VIII The Formation of an Industrial Proletariat 257

The Growth of the Industrial Working Class
Contradictory and Uneven Development
"The Labor Question"
Textiles: The Leading Sector

IX The Struggle for the Trade Unions During the War 285

The Wafd and the Shubra al-Khayma Textile Workers
The Legalization of Trade Unions
Reassertion of Wafd Leadership over the Trade Union
Movement
Resistance to Wafd Domination
Announcement of the Cadre for Government Workers
'Abbas Halim Returns to the Labor Movement
British Attempts to Co-opt the Labor Movement

X Communism and the Egyptian Workers' Movement,
1942–1948 310

New Dawn and the Shubra al-Khayma Textile Workers
Beyond Trade Union Politics: Workers in the Electoral Arena
The Egyptian Movement for National Liberation
Communist Factionalism and the Workers' Movement
The Congress of the World Federation of Trade Unions
The Workers' Committee for National Liberation
The National Committee of Workers and Students
February 21, 1946: Problems and Prospects
The Attempt to Establish Trade Union Unity
Repression and Reorganization
Strike at Misr Spinning and Weaving Company
The Strike Wave Continues

XI The Muslim Brothers and the Egyptian Workers'
Movement 363

Muslim Brothers and Communists in Shubra al-Khayma
The Great Confrontation
The Muslim Brothers' Vision of a "Moral Economy"
Methods of Trade Union Struggle

x Contents

Local Strength in the Canal Zone
Dissolution, Reformation, and Radicalization

XII The Labor Movement and the Crisis of the Old Regime 395

The Labor Movement and the Final Wafd Regime
Broadening Communist Influence in the Workers' Movement
Toward a National Trade Union Federation
From the Cairo Fire to the Military Coup

XIII The Free Officers and the Labor Movement 418

Kafr al-Dawwar: A Turning Point
Trade Unions and the Military Regime After Kafr al-Dawwar
The RCC's Labor Policy: Corporatism and Paternalism
The Crisis of March 1954
March 1954: An Assessment

XIV Conclusion 448

Bibliography 463

Index 479

List of Tables

1   Distribution of Labor Force by Sector   38
2   Membership of the MTWU by Craft   69
3   Wholesale Prices of Basic Food Items, Cairo   86
4   Number of Factories and Employees, 1945–1951   262
5   Concentration of the Egyptian Industrial Work Force   265
6   Cost of Living Index, 1939–1954   267
7   Daily Industrial Wage Rates, 1937–1945   268
8   Union Membership as of December 31, 1943   294

List of Abbreviations

I. Bibliographical Citations

'Izz al-Din I — Amīn 'Izz al-Dīn, *Ta'rīkh al-ṭabaqa al-'āmila al-miṣriyya mundhu nash'atihā ḥattā thawrat 1919* (Cairo, 1967).

'Izz al-Din II — Amīn 'Izz al-Dīn, *Ta'rīkh al-ṭabaqa al-'āmila al-miṣriyya, 1919–1929* (Cairo, 1970).

'Izz al-Din III — Amīn 'Izz al-Dīn, *Ta'rīkh al-ṭabaqa al-'āmila al-miṣriyya, 1929–1939* (Cairo, 1972).

'Amara, T — Muḥammad Ḥasan 'Amāra, "Min mudhakkirāt niqābī qadīm," memoirs serialized in *al-Thaqāfa al-'ummāliyya* published by the Workers' Education Association.

AP — "Rapports du jour" from Branch B, Public Security Department, Commandant of the Alexandria City Police to Sa'īd Pasha Dhū al-Faqār, Grand Chamberlain of the Royal Dīwān, June 1923–April 1929.

AS — *Annuaire Statistique*, followed by year.

'Askari, U — Maḥmūd al-'Askarī, "Min Ta'rīkh al-ḥaraka al-'ummāliyya al-miṣriyya," memoirs serialized in the weekly *al-'Ummāl* published by the General Federation of Egyptian Trade Unions.

BE — *La Bourse Égyptienne* (daily newspaper).

Belgium, MAE — Belgium, Archives du Ministère des Affaires Étrangères, Brussels: files marked "AF 10" and others.

xiv Abbreviations

CP	Reports from the Office of the Commandant, Cairo City Police to the Undersecretary of State for Public Security at the Ministry of the Interior, July 1923–November 1924.
CSB	Reports from the Special Branch, Cairo Police to the Undersecretary of State for Public Security at the Ministry of Interior, February 1940–December 1941.
CSP	Reports from the Special Branch, Cairo Police to Saʿīd Pasha Dhū al-Faqār, Grand Chamberlain of the Royal Dīwān, designated *sirrī siyāsī* ("secret/political"), August 1926–November 1926.
EG	*Egyptian Gazette* (daily newspaper).
ESR I	Egypt, Maḥfūẓāt majlis al-wuzarā', niẓārat al-ashghāl, maṣlaḥat al-sikka al-ḥadīd (records of the Egyptian State Railways), carton marked "28 February 1910–November 1923."
ESR II	Egypt, Maḥfuẓāt majlis al-wuzarā', niẓārat al-ashghāl, maṣlaḥat al-sikka al-ḥadid, carton marked 2 January 1882–22 December 1918.
F	France, Archives of the French Embassy in Cairo, followed by carton number.
FO	Great Britain, Foreign Office, Archives in the Public Record Office, London.
ICC 1927	Egypt, Ministry of Finance, *Industrial and Commercial Census 1927* (Cairo, 1931).
ICC 1937	Egypt, Ministry of Finance, *Industrial and Commercial Census 1937* (Cairo, 1942).
IM	*al-Ikhwān al-muslimūn*, official publication of the Society of Muslim Brothers. Frequency varies.
M	Minutes of the meetings of the executive board of the Cairo Tramway Workers' Union, November 1939–August 1942.
Mudarrik, TU	Muḥammad Yūsuf al-Mudarrik, "Ṣafḥa min ḥarakat al-ʿummāl qabla al-thawra," memoirs serialized in *al-Thaqāfa al-ʿummāliyya*.
ʿUthman, K	Ṭaha Saʿd ʿUthmān, "Mudhakkirāt wa-wathā'iq min ta'rīkh al-ṭabaqa al-ʿāmila," memoirs and documents serialized in the monthly *al-Kātib*.
WM	*al-Wafd al-miṣrī* (daily newspaper).

Abbreviations **xv**

II. Trade Unions, Political Organizations, and Government Agencies

CETU	Congress of Egyptian Trade Unions
CGT	Confédération Générale du Travail
COWM	Commission to Organize the Workers' Movement
CPE	Communist Party of Egypt
CTC	Cairo Tramway Company
CPSTU	Congress of Private Sector Trade Unions
CTUE	Congress of Trade Unions in Egypt
CTWU	Cairo Tramway Workers' Union
DMNL	Democratic Movement for National Liberation
EFI	Egyptian Federation of Industry
EMNL	Egyptian Movement for National Liberation
ESP	Egyptian Socialist Party
ESR	Egyptian State Railways, Telegraphs and Telephones
EWU	Egyptian Workers' Union
FCGFETU	Founding Committee for a General Federation of Egyptian Trade Unions
GCMTWU	Greater Cairo Mechanized Textile Workers' Union
GFLUKE	General Federation of Labor Unions in the Kingdom of Egypt
GUMTPWGC	General Union of Mechanized Textile and Preparatory Workers of Greater Cairo
GUMTWSKC	General Union of Mechanized Textile Workers of Shubra al-Khayma and Cairo
GUW	General Union of Workers
IFTU	International Federation of Trade Unions
JTF	Joint Transport Federation
LCB	Labor Conciliation Board
MTWU	Manual Trades Workers' Union
NCWS	National Committee of Workers and Students
NFTUE	National Federation of Trade Unions in Egypt
PCETUC	Preparatory Committee for an Egyptian Trade Union Congress
PCGFETU	Preparatory Committee for a General Federation of Egyptian Trade Unions
PSD	Public Security Department, Ministry of Interior
RCC	Revolutionary Command Council
SCC	Suez Canal Company

xvi Abbreviations

SKMTWU	Shubra al-Khayma Mechanized Textile Workers' Union
SLAC	Supreme Labor Advisory Council
TUC	Trades Union Congress
TUCDL	Trade Union Committee for the Defence of Liberties
WCNL	Workers' Committee for National Liberation

Preface

Although this book is a collective work for whose entire contents both authors are jointly responsible, it grew out of two separate research projects embodied in our respective dissertations. Those dissertations were conceived and completed separately, and only later were their findings integrated and reworked into this study. We felt that publication of our research in one book made the most sense intellectually as well as in terms of the book's probable audience. Joint publication also benefited our work by encouraging the exchange of ideas and mutual criticism and by allowing us to overcome the isolation and privatization of knowledge which are potential hazards of academic life. We want this work to be treated as an organic whole, but we would also like to note that each of us took primary responsibility—subject to mutual criticism and redrafting—for writing the segment with which our own separate research made us most familiar. Thus Part One was written by and based on the research of Zachary Lockman, while Part Two was written by and based on the research of Joel Beinin; the Introduction and Conclusion were jointly written.

This book is a collective work in another sense as well. It owes a great deal to the support and assistance of many individuals who helped make it what it is without, of course, their having any responsibility for its shortcomings. Our primary debt is to those Egyptian trade unionists and political activists, retired or still active, who gave of their time for interviews and shared source materials in their possession. We would especially like to thank Abu al-Wafa' 'Afif, Alfi Zaki Bisali, Fathi Kamil, Jamal al-Banna and Taha Sa'd 'Uthman. They

xviii   Preface

aided and encouraged us to record the history of the workers' movement to which they dedicated their lives. We hope that this book, by making that history accessible to a wider audience, can in return make some contribution, however modest, to the ongoing struggle of Egypt's people for a better life.

We would also like to thank by name at least some of those, in Egypt and elsewhere, who contributed to our research efforts, improved this book by their criticism, or provided support and guidance. Among the Egyptian scholars and friends to whom we owe a debt of gratitude are Amina Shafiq, Mohamed Sid Ahmed, Rif'at al-Sa'id, Ra'uf 'Abbas, 'Afaf Mahfuz, 'Asim al-Disuqi and Nawla Darwish. Thanks are also owed to Albert Hourani, Roger Owen, Talal Asad, David Landes, Louise Tilly, Ronald Suny, and Jerrold Green.

The personal and intellectual example of the late Richard P. Mitchell deserves special mention as an important source of inspiration. His profound knowledge of Egypt, deep sympathy for the Egyptian people, and personal support for our research contributed greatly to this work. We would also like to thank Ellis Goldberg, fellow student of Egyptian labor history, whose intellectual stimulation and friendship have been invaluable. In addition, he contributed to this book by participating in several of the interviews that were an important source for Part Two.

The staffs of a number of institutions in Cairo—Dar al-Watha'iq, Dar al-Kutub, Mu'assasat al-Thaqafa al-'Ummaliyya and the Ministry of Manpower and Training—also facilitated the research embodied in this book. Our research also benefited from the innovative explorations in Middle East studies and the critical intellectual climate promoted by the Middle East Research and Information Project (publisher of MERIP Middle East Report) and by local study groups of the (now defunct) Alternative Middle East Studies Seminar (AMESS).

The research and writing of this book were made possible by funding from the following sources, which we gratefully acknowledge: the Fulbright-Hays program, the American Research Center in Egypt, the Foreign Language and Area Studies fellowship program, the National Endowment for the Humanities, the Mrs. Giles Whiting Foundation, the Rackham School of Graduate Studies of the University of Michigan, and the Stanford University History Department. Susan Riecken prepared the maps for this book and we thank her for her painstaking labors.

We would also like to thank the many unnamed friends whose support and affection sustained us during the years we worked on this project. We have both dedicated the book to our respective parents. Joel would also like to pay special tribute to Miriam, without whose

Preface **xix**

constant support it would not have been possible for him to undertake this effort. Miriam and Jamie traveled to Egypt and Europe, and lived patiently with this project from its inception to its completion.

In this book we have adopted a system of transliteration based on that used in the *International Journal of Middle East Studies*. The symbol ' is used to indicate an *'ayn*, and ' is used for a *hamza*. The diacritical marks indicating long vowels and emphatic consonants have not been included because they are largely unnecessary for those who know Arabic and irrelevant for those who do not. They are supplied in the Bibliography to facilitate the identification of the Arabic sources on which this study is based.

Joel Beinin
Zachary Lockman
April 1986

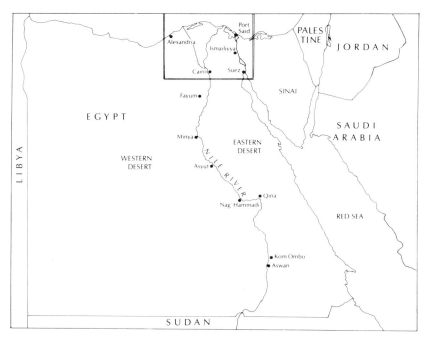

Egypt

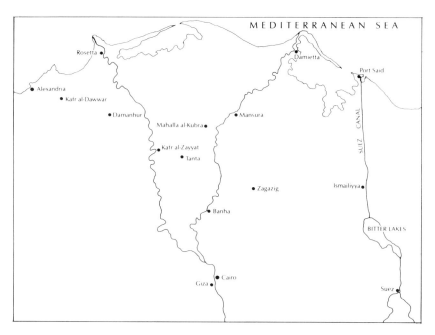

The Nile Delta

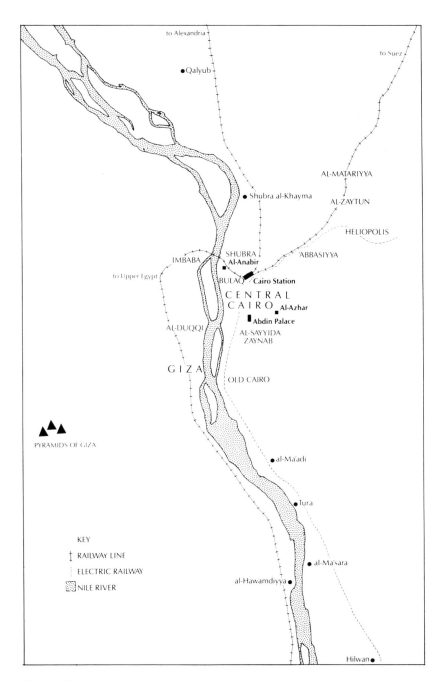

Greater Cairo

Part One

The Emergence of the Egyptian Workers'

Movement, 1882–1942

Chapter I

Introduction

This book is a study of the development of a working class and labor movement in Egypt from the end of the nineteenth century until the consolidation of power by the regime of Jamal 'Abd al-Nasir in 1954. Its central problematic is the dialectic of class and nation: the formation of a new class of wage workers as Egypt experienced a particular kind of capitalist development, and these workers' adoption of various forms of consciousness, organization, and collective action in a political and economic context structured by the realities of foreign domination and the struggle for national independence.

Until quite recently the hegemonic scholarly interpretations of Middle Eastern history rejected the idea that the process by which various parts of the region became part of the world capitalist market and continued to develop on that basis might be relevant for understanding the modern history of the region. That class analysis might shed light on the economic and political dynamics of these societies was also denied. In the last few years this nearly total rejection has given way to grudging acceptance and even new interest as some noteworthy attempts have been made to apply the insights of political economy to Middle Eastern history.[1] Our treatment of the history of the Egyptian workers' movement is based on the premise that analysis of the process of capitalist development and the emergence of new

1. Among these are Hanna Batatu, *The Old Social Classes and the Revolutionary Movements of Iraq* (Princeton, 1978); Peter Gran, *Islamic Roots of Capitalism* (Austin, 1979); Roger Owen, *The Middle East in the World Economy, 1800–1914* (London, 1981); Ervand Abrahamian, *Iran Between Two Revolutions* (Princeton, 1982); and Eric Davis, *Challenging Colonialism: Bank Misr and Egyptian Industrialization, 1920–1941* (Princeton, 1983).

4 Introduction

social classes as part of that process is essential to understanding the history of modern Egypt.

The Egyptian Working Class

In recent years the concepts of class and class consciousness have been greatly enriched by the debate between the English school of "cultural" Marxism, whose leading labor historian is E. P. Thompson, and the French school of "structuralist" Marxism under the influence of Louis Althusser.[2] Both of these approaches build on the foundations laid by Antonio Gramsci, the first scholar-politician in the Marxist tradition to examine the role of politics and culture in class formation and class consciousness. This debate has advanced our understanding of class far beyond the boundaries imposed by the mechanical determinism and economism which characterized the Marxism of the Second and Third Internationals. It is now clear that an adequate conception of class must involve both objective and subjective factors. In this study, therefore, we do not argue that relation to the means of production uniquely determines whether a given group of people will emerge as a class conscious of its own interests and acting in the economic and political spheres to further those interests. Rather, location in the system of production determines the range of courses of action and perspectives likely to be adopted by individuals who share the same objective relationship to the means of production. Objective economic relations constitute the basis for a certain configuration of political and ideological relations in a given society, and it is in the matrix of this structured totality that class struggle takes place.

To put it another way, the process of capital accumulation creates the objective matrix within which human agency operates, limiting and thus to some extent determining the choices real people can make in a given situation. Class formation is a perpetual process: as capitalism develops, as the relations of production are continuously restructured, and as the political and ideological framework changes, classes are perpetually reshaped. Classes as historical actors are thus the "effects" of struggles which are structured by the totality of eco-

2. It is impossible to summarize this complex debate here. We note only some of the most salient contributions that have influenced our understanding of this question: E. P. Thompson, *The Making of the English Working Class* (New York, 1963), especially the preface, and *The Poverty of Theory and Other Essays* (New York, 1979); Nicos Poulantzas, *Classes in Contemporary Capitalism* (London, 1978), and *Political Power and Social Classes* (London, 1978); Perry Anderson, *Arguments Within English Marxism* (London, 1980), especially chapter 2.

Introduction 5

nomic, political, and ideological-cultural relations. They should therefore not be regarded as entities which exist independently of political and ideological practice. Rather, classes are formed in the course of social and political conflicts in which multiple historical actors seek to organize a given group of people as members of a particular class, as citizens of a nation, as adherents of a religious group, or around some other pole of identity. Objective conditions may make some outcomes more likely than others, but no single outcome is automatic or entirely predictable. This conceptualization of class demands investigation of real historical conjunctures and of the role of politics and ideology as autonomous factors in the formation of consciousness and behavior.[3]

The principal aspect of the formation of the Egyptian working class with which we are concerned in this study is the emergence of a new group of urban wage workers, from the end of the nineteenth century onward, employed in relatively large, modern industrial and transport enterprises, owning no means of production, and earning their livelihood solely from the sale of their labor power. These proletarians do *not* constitute the whole of the Egyptian working class whose other components are elaborated upon below. But in the course of the period covered by this study, they became the best organized, most politically conscious workers, and came to constitute the active core of the working class. This justifies our focusing on them. We also pay special attention in this study to transport workers (tramways and railways) and to textile workers who assumed in turn the leading role in the labor movement before and after the Second World War respectively.

Although the use of abstract and ahistorical criteria might require that the growing stratum of landless agricultural wage workers be included in the working class, it would be difficult in the context of Egyptian culture and economy to treat urban and rural wage workers in the same category either analytically or empirically. Because of the vast differences in the historical conditions of development of the urban and rural working class, rural wage earners receive little attention in this study. The large numbers of peasants who worked on a casual or seasonal basis in industry or transport must, however, be considered a segment of the urban working class. Those craftsmen who owned some means of production but were in practice completely dependent on merchants or factory owners (such as workers in the

3. See Adam Przeworski, "Proletariat into a Class: The Process of Class Formation from Karl Kautsky's *The Class Struggle* to Recent Controversies," *Politics & Society* 7 (1977):343–401.

6 Introduction

leather shoe industry, for example), as well as many working foremen, should also be regarded as part of the working class. Wage workers employed in small workshops also constituted a component of the Egyptian working class. But as this study will show, though workers from small workshops often participated in the political movement of the working class through organizations dominated by their employers, they rarely engaged in struggles against those employers in the workplace or organized themselves independently. In many respects their political consciousness was shaped by their employers' class situation.

In addition to this working class, there were (and still are) in Egypt a number of social strata accounting for a large proportion of the urban population which, using objective criteria, can be said to constitute a broadly-defined urban petty bourgeoisie. Although these strata have been an extremely important social category in modern Egyptian history, they have been difficult to define precisely because of their heterogeneity. Their relations with the working class are complex and will be dealt with when appropriate to the focus of this study, but we cannot here provide the detailed analytical treatment these strata certainly merit. For our purposes it must suffice to say that people in this category can be distinguished from members of the working class and the more well-to-do middle strata by their possession or lack of some means of production, capital, or education. These urban petty bourgeois strata encompassed traditional and modern occupations and included independent craftsmen and artisans, proprietors of small workshops and of service enterprises such as laundries and barbershops, owner-operators of motor vehicles, pushcart vendors, low-level white collar employees in the private sector, and low-level government functionaries. Very successful independent producers and those with sufficient education or skills tended to blend into the social status group of the *effendiyya* (on whom more later) and to distance themselves from the working class. Although from our standpoint even the poorer elements of these strata were set apart by their possession of some means of production, some small amount of capital, or some education, their economic and social status was in reality nearly indistinguishable from that of skilled proletarians. Despite the fact that we do not categorize them as members of the working class, many members of the lower levels of these strata perceived of themselves and were perceived by others as workers. During the interwar period the Arabic term "*al-'ummal*" often referred to an undifferentiated category of urban "working people," encompassing all those performing manual labor or lower level clerical tasks.

The lower strata of the petty bourgeoisie often acted in concert with workers, formed unions, played an important role in the Egyptian labor movement well into the interwar period, and even influenced the political consciousness and actions of workers, especially in the earlier period covered by this study. As a group they were particularly receptive to the appeals of those forces (the Wafd, Prince 'Abbas Halim, the Muslim Brothers) seeking to dominate the workers' movement on the basis of ideologies which denied the existence of antagonistic classes in Egypt. We have termed these ideologies "corporatist," not in the specific Italian Fascist sense, but in the more general sense of an ideology which denies the reality of class conflict in society, rejects an independent role for the working class, and projects the state as the benevolent guardian of workers' interests. This perspective was shared by all the political forces that contended for leadership of the workers' movement except the communists and their supporters. The low level of social differentiation between the lowest of the urban middle strata and the working class, largely a product of the retarded and uneven development of capitalism in Egypt, played a large part in sustaining corporatist ideologies in the labor movement.

It was only with the growth of large-scale mechanized factory production, especially in the textile sector, during and after the Second World War that the center of gravity within the labor movement shifted, and the proletarian component of the working class sought to assert its political leadership over the entire workers' movement. At the same time, despite the general decline in the influence of older, paternalistic forms of consciousness in the labor movement as a whole, it must be acknowledged that not all industrial workers shared the new vision put forward by the textile workers' leaders or shared their high capacity for independent organization. Even in highly capitalized, large-scale industries such as cigarettes and oil, a variety of factors, especially the ability of multinational capital to grant certain concessions to workers and the local strength of an outstanding social democratic or anticommunist labor leader, allowed a paternalistic business unionism or the Islamic vision of the Muslim Brothers to exert a significant influence over workers and their leaders. Although the working class and the labor movement were changing, this was a complex, contradictory, and uneven process rather than a smooth and unilinear one, as the events of 1952–1954 demonstrate.

As the following chapters will show, the political orientation and behavior of the workers' movement was also a product of the inextricable interlocking of class and national consciousness among the vast

8 Introduction

majority of Egyptian workers during the period of this study. We will thus try to explain how, within a matrix shaped by the ongoing process of capitalist development in Egypt, the social structure it produced and specific political conditions, a number of political forces expressing various forms of consciousness, various visions of society and of identity, emerged and contended for the allegiance of the working class. These struggles determined the role of the new working class as a historical actor. In Egypt as elsewhere, before there could be a struggle *among* classes there had to be a struggle *about* class.

The Development of Capitalism in Egypt

The process by which capitalism emerged in Egypt can only be briefly outlined here and will be dealt with only peripherally in this book.[4] The premise underlying this book's theoretical approach is that the central problematic of modern Egyptian history is the integration of Egypt into the world capitalist system on a subordinate and dependent basis, and the consequent growth of a capitalist mode of production and class differentiation. This process of integration was driven in the nineteenth century largely by the cultivation of cotton and its export to Europe. The rapid expansion of cotton cultivation provided much of the impetus for the transformation of agricultural land into private property, a transformation that resulted in the restructuring of agrarian social relations. The great majority of the peasantry was by the end of the nineteenth century either landless or land-poor, while a new class of large landowners—an agrarian bourgeoisie—had emerged and would remain the dominant class until the land reform of 1952.

Egypt's social transformation and the creation of the foundations of capitalism in the country were facilitated by an influx of foreign capital. Most of it went directly or indirectly into agriculture. Foreigners directly invested their capital in land companies, established mortgage and credit companies and banks, and gained control of the im-

4. For various perspectives on capitalist development in Egypt see Davis, *Challenging Colonialism*; Owen, *The Middle East*; Anouar Abdel-Malek, *Egypt: Military Society* (New York, 1968); Shuhdi 'Atiyya al-Shafi'i, *Tatawwur al-haraka al-wataniyya al-misriyya* (Cairo, 1957); Mahmud Mutawalli, *al-Usul al-ta'rikhiyya l'il-ra'smaliyya al-misriyya wa-tatawwuriha* (Cairo, 1974); Robert L. Tignor, *State, Private Enterprise, and Economic Change in Egypt, 1918–1952* (Princeton, 1984); and Alan Richards, *Egypt's Agricultural Development, 1800–1980: Technical and Social Change* (Boulder, CO, 1982).

Introduction 9

port and export trade. European banking houses also lent vast sums of money to the Egyptian state, which used most of it to develop the country's infrastructure—irrigation, railroads, port facilities—in order to facilitate the cultivation and export of cotton and enhance Egypt's prosperity. Heavy borrowing abroad led to a downward spiral of indebtedness that culminated in bankruptcy in 1876. Foreign financial controls were imposed on the Egyptian government which in turn stimulated a nationalist reaction and led to Egypt's occupation by British forces in 1882.

Whereas the land itself was largely in the hands of an Egyptian agrarian bourgeoisie, then, the country's economy as a whole was by 1914 largely controlled by foreign interests. Some of these were European companies that had invested in Egypt, and others were *mutamassirun*; that is, people of foreign origin who had become permanent residents and had been "Egyptianized." The economy was largely geared toward the production and export of a single crop, cotton, which accounted for 93 percent of exports in the period just before the First World War. Credit, foreign trade, and shipping were almost entirely in non-Egyptian hands. A small modern industrial and transport sector had emerged and consisted mainly of enterprises processing agricultural products, producing limited kinds of goods for the European and Europeanized segments of the urban population, and providing such public services as light, gas, and mass transit (tramways) in a few of the major cities and towns. A small working class was employed in these enterprises, on the railways, at the Suez Canal, and in government enterprises. Virtually all of Egypt's industrial and transport enterprises were either owned, or in the case of state enterprises like the railways, managed by non-Egyptians. And of course, effective state power was in the hands of Great Britain, whose officials protected the interests of metropolitan capital and of the legally privileged foreigners.

In the countryside where the great majority of Egyptians lived and worked, there was relatively little use of wage labor in agriculture until the interwar period. The large estates were usually worked by peasants who received a plot of their own in return for labor service, or were rented out to small tenants. There was little investment, even by wealthy landowners, in either mechanization or in other means of raising productivity. The majority of the urban population was engaged in small-scale crafts and services, but the guilds, which had previously constituted the framework of urban economic life, had ceased to exist. There were very few Egyptian entrepreneurs who owned medium or large-scale industrial, commercial, or financial en-

10 Introduction

terprises. Out of the "traditional" urban and rural middle classes there emerged by the beginning of the twentieth century a new social group, the *effendiyya*. These men were the product of modern education, wore western-style clothing, emulated European lifestyles, and worked in the new occupations to which capitalist development had given rise. This category included secondary and university students, teachers, lawyers, journalists, and other professionals, white-collar employees, and lower and middle-level government functionaries. These effendis would, despite their relatively small numbers, play a central role in Egypt's political life before 1952.

The period leading up to the First World War thus witnessed Egypt's integration into the world market and the far-reaching transformation of its social structure, a classic case of dependent capitalist development. There emerged from this uneven and distorted process what Anouar Abdel-Malek has termed a "backward capitalism of a colonial type, predominantly agrarian."[5] It was characterized by a monoculture economy oriented toward and dependent on the world market, the absence of a significant industrial base or the impetus for industrial investment, an extreme concentration of wealth in the hands of the indigenous agrarian bourgeoisie and foreign and *mutamassir* capital coupled with extreme deprivation of the masses, and an apparently limited capacity for self-sustaining economic growth.

Despite the contention of some proponents of dependency theory, however, the subordination of Egypt's economy to the dictates of metropolitan capital did not permanently preclude industrial development. As James Petras and Kent Trachte have argued, imperialism should be seen as "the international expression of capitalism's historical mission to develop the forces of production" in the peripheral societies however "uneven, exploitative and contradictory" the process.[6] After the First World War significant industrial development began to take place under the aegis not only of foreign and *mutamassir* capital but also of a new group of indigenous industrialists. The establishment of Bank Misr in 1920 in the midst of—and in some sense as part of—the struggle for national independence symbolized the organizational consolidation of an aspiring Egyptian industrial bourgeoisie.

Bank Misr's capital was largely drawn from an agrarian bourgeoisie

5. Anouar Abdel-Malek, *La Formation de l'idéologie dans,la renaissance nationale de l'Égypte (1805–1892)* (Paris, 1969), p. 112, and *Egypt: Military Society*, p. 401 n. 72.
6. James Petras, *Critical Perspectives on Imperialism and Social Class in the Third World* (New York, 1978), p. 40.

anxious to diversify the sources of its wealth and develop alternatives to foreign control of credit and trade, and it took on itself the task of creating a purely Egyptian-owned industrial sector. The bank was in fact responsible for establishing a large number of industrial enterprises in the four decades before its nationalization in 1960. Although originally opposed to collaboration with foreign and *mutamassir* capital, however, it was ultimately not strong enough to survive on its own. Bank Misr's compromises with foreign capital culminated in its entry into joint ventures with British corporations in the late 1930s, and the Misr group ceased to be "national" in character. Whereas a completely independent national industrial bourgeoisie had been envisioned when Bank Misr was first established, this project never materialized.

By the Second World War there was therefore no sharp division between a "comprador" and a "national" bourgeoisie in Egypt, for the leading indigenous industrialists found common ground for cooperation with foreigners and *mutamassirun* involved in industrial development. There was likewise no sharp distinction between the agrarian and industrial sections of the bourgeoisie. Although many large landowners had no interest in industry or in state support for industrialization, a section of the agrarian bourgeoisie did actively participate in industrial development. There were divisions and conflicts among landed, financial, commercial, and industrial interests as well as among foreign, *mutamassir*, and Egyptian capital before 1952, but there was also considerable overlap and a fair degree of common interest. For this reason some Egyptian historians'[7] search for a "national bourgeoisie" based on indigenous industrial interests whose historical task was to establish a modern capitalist order in Egypt in opposition to "feudal" landed interests has been misguided. The Egyptian industrial bourgeoisie that actually emerged was not particularly nationalist, nor was it very interested in breaking the power of the large landowners. It was also generally hostile to the Wafd (the party that did in fact lead the struggle for independence) though there were some exceptions to this tendency, such as the entrepreneur Ahmad 'Abbud, who was a major financial supporter of the Wafd.

7. See for example al-Shafi'i, *Tatawwur*, and Fawzi Jirjis, *Dirasat fi ta'rikh misr al-siyasi mundhu 'asr al-mamalik* (Cairo, 1958). Muhammad Anis and 'Abd al-'Azim Ramadan have also developed this theme in several works some of which are discussed in Peter Gran, "Modern Trends in Egyptian Historiography: A Review Article," *International Journal of Middle Eastern Studies* 9 (1978):367–71.

12 Introduction

The industrial development Egypt underwent in the three decades that followed the First World War did not resolve the structural economic problems faced by Egyptian society. Indeed, by 1952 the old political and social order was suffering from an acute and prolonged crisis and was on the verge of collapse. The domination of the countryside by the large landowners and their suppression of all attempts at agrarian reform had resulted in the further impoverishment of the peasantry and a massive exodus to the cities in search of work. The pace of industrial growth remained far too slow to meet the need of the country's rapidly expanding population for jobs. Structural changes—land reform to help the peasantry and free capital for industrial investment, a state-sponsored development program, a commitment to improving the standard of living of the workers and peasants, complete sovereignty in both the political and economic spheres—were essential to removing the barriers to further economic development. Not only were these basic reforms not forthcoming, but the political parties, the monarchy, and the parliamentary system itself were also discredited by corruption, the abuse of power, the defeat in Palestine, and the failure either to resolve the social crisis or end British military occupation. While the industrial interests would have benefited from such measures as land reform, they were generally too closely tied to conservative agrarian interests to take the initiative.

It was in order to forestall more radical challenges to the prevailing social order, to resolve the political and social crisis, to remove the obstacles to development by enacting basic reforms and allowing Egyptian capitalism to realize its full potential that the Free Officers seized power in July 1952. They hoped that by carrying out land reform, restoring order and stability, and encouraging the private sector (as well as foreign investment) they could get the Egyptian economy back on track. The disappointment of their hopes would eventually lead them to more radical structural reforms as they searched for a way out of underdevelopment and dependency that would not require mass mobilization and social revolution.

The Wafd

The national question, Egypt's struggle for complete independence, was central to the country's political life from the early years of the twentieth century until after the Anglo-French-Israeli invasion of 1956, and the political formation that virtually embodied this strug-

Introduction   13

gle from 1919 to 1952 was the Wafd. Because of this party's key role in the labor movement, it is important to understand its class character.

What was the social base and orientation of the Wafd which allowed it to retain enough mass support to win every free election held in Egypt before the 1952 military coup? Ten of the fourteen original members of the Wafd's high command were large landowners. Although the political weight of this social class within the Wafd diminished in the 1920s, its power increased again from the late 1930s as large landowners (such as Fu'ad Siraj al-Din) became more influential in the party apparatus. Yet the Wafd was not the representative of the agrarian bourgeoisie. That role was played by the Liberal Constitutionalist party. Although the Wafd supported industrial development, it was not the party of a mythical "national industrial bourgeoisie" determined to achieve complete political as well as economic independence. The elements within the Wafd most closely linked to industrial interests split in 1937 to form the Sa'dist party, and Egyptian industrialists soon developed close links with *mutamassir* and metropolitan capital. The Wafd can best be characterized as a bourgeois nationalist party, representing most directly the interests of the urban and rural middle classes: the owners of medium-sized agricultural properties and the urban *effendiyya*. It was from the latter group that the party's political activists were drawn, although wealthier elements continued to dominate the top leadership. Although the influence of the large landowners tended to impose a conservative social orientation on the Wafd, the party's populist rhetoric allowed some of the *effendiyya* in mid-level leadership positions to play an important role in the labor movement during the interwar period. Despite its generally conservative outlook, the Wafd enjoyed massive support among the rural masses, the urban working class, and the *effendiyya* as the leading party of the national movement.[8]

This amalgam of constituencies and interests both shaped the Wafd's political practice and raised several difficulties. Although the Wafd first won mass support in the course of a violent popular uprising against British rule in 1919, the party's leaders feared autonomous popular action and generally sought to constrain the struggle for independence within the boundaries of legal and peaceful protest.

8. See 'Asim al-Disuqi, *Kibar mullak al-aradi al-zira'iyya wa-dawruhum fi al-mujtama' al-misri, 1914–1952* (Cairo, 1975) and Marius Deeb, *Party Politics in Egypt: The Wafd and Its Rivals, 1919–1939* (London, 1979).

14 Introduction

The Wafd was not prepared to mobilize the people for a militant and uncompromising struggle for national liberation because its leaders feared losing control of such a struggle and having it threaten their own interests. Ultimately the Wafd did not envision a complete political and economic break with British imperialism, but sought to negotiate a transfer of power from the British, their allies among the large landowners, and the Palace to the more nationalist segments of the bourgeoisie, hence securing for Egypt the status of junior partner rather than that of a powerless subordinate in the imperial political and economic order. The demands of the Wafd's increasingly assertive mass base, however, required it to temper its social conservatism with a populism generally couched in paternalistic terms. The Wafd's failure to realize the dreams of 1919, its inability to achieve complete political and economic independence or resolve the country's urgent social problems, eventually discredited it (along with the parliamentary system whose chief defender it was), and opened the way for the military coup.

Class and Nation in Colonial Countries

This book is about the development of the Egyptian working class and its role in the national political arena, and it must therefore respect the specificities of Egypt's history, society, and culture. At the same time, however, Egyptian labor history shares a problematic common to many colonies and semicolonies where foreign rule coincided with the development of capitalism and the growth of a working class. In these countries European political domination was inextricably intertwined with economic exploitation by foreign capital. In the historiography of their anticolonial national liberation movements, therefore, the same set of questions can be posed: To what extent did the indigenous working class participate in the national movement? What impact did it have on that movement and on the struggle for independence? Did workers and their organizations raise independent class-based demands? Or were such demands suppressed and the autonomy of the labor movement subordinated to a nationalist leadership drawn from other strata? What were the relations among the working class, the state, and the new indigenous ruling class after independence?

Many of the earliest Western academic efforts to address these questions were rooted in the modernization theory approach then prevalent in American social science. Formulated under the influ-

Introduction **15**

ence of Africa's "decade of independence" and reflecting apprehension about the political instability that might result from decolonization, this literature tended to portray anticolonial nationalist movements as narrowly political manifestations of indigenous middle class discontent.[9] From this perspective, urban workers did not play a significant role in the national struggle or in determining the character of the postcolonial state. Ironically, this insistence on the minor or even negative role of organized urban workers in the struggle for national liberation can also be found in the work of Frantz Fanon, who described such workers as a labor aristocracy, bought off by the relatively high incomes they enjoyed as a result of regular employment.[10] Both the liberal and radical variants of this view of the working class have been largely discredited, however, by the extensive research in labor history undertaken in many parts of Asia, Africa, and Latin America in recent years. Modernization theory has been largely abandoned, though some revised versions can still be found in Middle East studies, and even a leading scholarly proponent of the Fanonist view of the working class, John Saul, has criticized his former position.[11]

Scholarly discussion has therefore turned away from the question of *whether* workers participate in the national movement, and has focused on *how* they do so and on what impact they have. Thomas Hodgkin was one of the first to address these questions in a balanced and sober manner that opposed the prevailing wisdom of modernization theory.[12] He argued that the emergence of an African working class was an important social and political phenomenon, and whereas African workers might not assume the leadership of the national struggle, they would tend to raise social and economic demands that could radicalize the national movement by pointing beyond the simple goal of political independence envisaged by most middle class nationalist leaders.

Studies of the working class and the national movement in Ja-

9. See, for example, Martin Kilson, "Nationalism and Social Change in British West Africa," *The Journal of Politics* 20 (1958):368–387, and Elliot J. Berg and Jeffrey Butler, "Trade Unions," in James S. Coleman and Carl G. Rosberg (eds.), *Political Parties and National Integration in Tropical Africa* (Berkeley, 1964), pp. 340–381.
10. Frantz Fanon, *The Wretched of the Earth* (New York, 1968), especially pp. 108–109.
11. John Saul, "The Labour Aristocracy Thesis Reconsidered," in Richard Sandbrook and Robin Cohen (eds.), *The Development of an African Working Class* (Toronto, 1975), pp. 303–310.
12. Thomas Hodgkin, *Nationalism in Colonial Africa* (New York, 1956), especially chapter 4.

16 Introduction

maica,[13] Nigeria,[14] Kenya,[15] Senegal, and Mali[16]—to name a few of the non-Middle Eastern examples which could be cited—as well as the countries of the Maghrib[17] along with Sudan,[18] Iran,[19] Iraq,[20] Syria,[21] and of course Egypt have shown that despite significant local variations a common historical pattern can be discerned. In these coun-

13. Ken Post has written extensively on labor and politics in Jamaica which is a particularly important case because the Jamaican "emergency" of 1938 was a major factor in reshaping British imperial policy toward labor movements in the colonial countries after World War II from one of repression to reform and cooptation. For a succinct introduction to Post's work, see "The Politics of Protest in Jamaica, 1938: Some Problems of Analysis and Conceptualization," in Robin Cohen, Peter Gutkind, and Phyllis Brazier (eds.), *Peasants and Proletarians: The Struggles of Third World Workers* (New York, 1979), pp. 198–218.

14. Robin Cohen, *Labor and Politics in Nigeria, 1945–1971* (New York, 1974), and "Michael Imoudou and the Nigerian Labor Movement," *Race and Class* 18, no. 4 (1977):345–362. See also A. G. Hopkins, "The Lagos Strike of 1897: An Exploration in Nigerian Labor History," in Cohen, Gutkind, and Brazier (eds.), *Peasants and Proletarians*, pp. 87–106. Although Hopkins' article is not specifically about labor and the national movement, which had not yet emerged, it illuminates the very early link between collective action for economic objectives and the anticolonial struggle, and has parallels with some of the matters discussed in chapters II and III.

15. Sharon Stichter, "Workers, Trade Unions and the Mau Mau Rebellion," *Canadian Journal of African Studies* 9, no. 2 (1975):259–275.

16. The best study of these themes in these countries is Ousmane Sembene's historical novel, *God's Bits of Wood* (New York, 1970), which concerns the strike on the Dakar-Niger railway line in 1947–1948. This edition also has a good introduction by A. Adu Boahen.

17. Eqbal Ahmad, "Trade Unionism," in Leon Carl Brown (ed.), *State and Society in Independent North Africa* (Washington, D.C., 1966), pp. 146–191. This is a good comparative study of the labor movements in Morocco, Algeria, and Tunisia. For a more detailed study of Morocco see Abdeltif Menouni, *Le syndicalisme ouvrier au Maroc* (Casablanca, 1979). For Algeria see François Weiss, *Doctrine et action syndicales en Algérie* (Paris, 1970), Ian Clegg, *Workers' Self-Management in Algeria* (New York, 1971), and Marnia Lazreg, *The Emergence of Classes in Algeria* (Boulder, CO, 1976).

18. We do not know of a first-rate study of the Sudanese labor movement despite its prominence and close links with the Egyptian situation. For basic information see Saad ed Din Fawzi, *The Labour Movement in the Sudan, 1946–1955* (London, 1957).

19. For Iran, see Abrahamian, *Iran Between Two Revolutions*, and "The Strengths and Weaknesses of the Labor Movement in Iran, 1941–1953," in Michael Bonine and Nikki Keddie (eds.), *Modern Iran: The Dialectics of Continuity and Change* (Albany, 1981).

20. Batatu, *The Old Social Classes*; Kamal Mazhar Ahmad, *al-Tabaqa al-'amila al-'iraqiyya: al-takawwun wa-bidayat al-taharruk* (Baghdad, 1981); Marion Farouk-Sluglett and Peter Sluglett, "Labor and National Liberation: The Trade Union Movement in Iraq, 1920–1958," *Arab Studies Quarterly* 5, no. 2 (1983):139–154.

21. 'Abd Allah Hanna, *al-Haraka al-'ummaliyya fi suriyya wa-lubnan, 1900–1945* (Damascus, 1973). For a study of the contemporary Syrian working class which does not pay much attention to politics see Elizabeth Longueness, "La classe ouvrière au Proche Orient: La Syrie," *La Pensée*, no. 197 (January–February, 1978), pp. 120–132, and "The Syrian Working Class Today," *MERIP Reports*, no. 134 (July–August, 1985), pp. 17–24.

Introduction   **17**

tries foreign capital and the requirements of the colonial power bring an urban working class into existence. These workers organize themselves in various forms, including trade unions, and engage in different kinds of collective action against foreign capital, the colonial state (which directly controls certain sectors of the economy, typically the railways), and the foreign managerial personnel who dominate their working lives. The fact that economic and social grievances are directed against a foreign-run state apparatus as well as a foreign-dominated economy creates the basis for close links between indigenous workers and the emerging nationalist political movement. Workers participate in that movement largely through their unions which are often brought under the tutelage of nonworker nationalist politicians and activists. The socially conservative nationalist leaders willingly countenance worker militancy against foreign employers and the colonial state as long as such militancy can be controlled and serves as an instrument of pressure for achieving their political goals.

In time, some sections of the workers movement come to reject the leadership of nonworker elements and seek to build an autonomous labor movement; some even insist that workers should play an independent or leading role within the broader national movement. The workers are supported in this demand by radicalized members of the urban intelligentsia who join with the workers' movement and promote it both for its own sake and because they believe that the potential militancy of the working class makes it the best leadership for the nationalist movement. (Communists were often, but not necessarily, associated with this development.) At the same time, nonworker elements in alliance with the more privileged or more dependent sectors of the working class attempt to restrain the social demands of the more radical workers and to minimize the potentially radicalizing effect of the presence of the working class within the national movement. These elements seek to preserve or restore the tutelary relationship between nonworker patrons and the organized workers that prevailed when the two movements first established links.

Once it becomes clear that the colonial power will be compelled to grant independence, or at least move toward sharing power with the nationalist leadership, that leadership seeks to attenuate or entirely break its alliance with the workers' movement and lay the basis for a new relationship of domination of the indigenous working class. After independence the erstwhile nationalist leadership or its successors in most of these countries suppresses the workers' autonomous political activism and transforms itself into a new ruling elite. This elite's policies may promote capitalist development through further

18 Introduction

integration into the world market and increase the exploitation of workers and peasants, or may promote a statist path of development involving significant, though not revolutionary, structural reforms imposed from above as well as some improvement in the standard of living for the masses. In either case trade unions are often incorporated into the state apparatus either directly or through the official ruling party. It was this second, statist pattern that prevailed in Egypt, Algeria, Iraq, and Syria where the postindependence regimes came to be dominated by army officers who displaced colonial or indigenous bourgeois elites and adopted some variant of what came to be known as "Arab socialism."

Of course, not all the examples cited above fit this pattern completely, and in each case particular circumstances determine relations among the social forces which significantly alter the outcome of both the national and the class struggle. Moreover, an important variation in the pattern occurs when the weakness of the middle class nationalists results in the communists' or other left-wing radicals' assuming leadership of the entire nationalist movement as occurred in China, Vietnam, Cuba, Nicaragua, and several southern African countries.[22] Obviously cases such as Kenya and Algeria, in which the expropriation of considerable agricultural land by European settlers drove large numbers of peasants into wage labor, and cases such as Nigeria, Iran, and Egypt, where this factor is nearly absent, differ significantly. Many other differences could be noted, and the specificities of each country's history must be taken into account. Still, we are convinced that these differences do not outweigh the importance of the similarities. Whereas in Egypt the working class may not have been as strong, as radical, or as influential a factor in the nationalist movement as it was in Iran or Iraq, for example, it would nonetheless be a serious error to ignore its role altogether as most Western and many Egyptian historians have done. Comparisons between the Egyptian case and other countries reveal important similarities that not only put Egyptian labor history in a broader context, but also highlight the role of Egyptian workers in their country's modern history.

22. The Chinese example is a significant one in our context because unlike the other cases in this group, the original political base of the Communist Party was among urban workers. Although the party lost this base when it was driven out of Shanghai, the political perspective that grew out of that experience (broadly speaking) subsequently won leadership of the national movement. See Jean Chesneux, *The Chinese Labor Movement, 1919–1927* (Stanford, 1968).

Introduction 19

The Historiography of the Egyptian Workers' Movement

In 1964 the Egyptian economist Samir Amin noted, "Nothing serious has been published in any foreign language on Egyptian trade unionism."[23] He might have also added that little had been published within Egypt itself on the history of the country's working class or labor movement. The mid-1960s saw the publication of a number of studies by Egyptian intellectuals which reinterpreted their country's modern history in class terms, breaking with older schools that had explained that history in terms of the actions and ideas of "great men," or as the inexorable unfolding of the national will to freedom. These were the years when Nasserism, "Arab socialism," had reached the limits of its radicalism. Since the regime's official line proclaimed that the new revolutionary order in Egypt was based on a bloc of the "popular forces"—peasants, workers, soldiers, intellectuals and "national capitalism"—it was only fitting that historians should investigate and highlight the struggles of the oppressed classes. Several pioneering works on the history of the Egyptian workers' movement were published in Egypt in that period which both constituted the first attempts at synthesis and today remain essential secondary sources. Other works have since appeared in Egypt and abroad.

Most of the studies hitherto published can be roughly divided into two distinct, yet overlapping, analytical tendencies. The first, typified by the work of Ra'uf 'Abbas, Sulayman al-Nukhayli, Nawwal 'Abd al-'Aziz, and Marius Deeb,[24] can be characterized as Nasserist or nationalist. The work of 'Abbas and al-Nukhayli reflects the perspective of Nasserism in that the history of the workers' movement is treated as an integral part of the national movement, of Egypt's long struggle for full political and economic independence. That struggle is seen as culminating in the "July revolution" of 1952 and Egypt's entry into the era of Arab socialism. The approach of 'Abd al-'Aziz

23. Hassan Riad (pseudonym of Samir Amin), L'Égypte nasserienne (Paris, 1964), p. 214.
24. Ra'uf 'Abbas, al-Haraka al-'ummaliyya fi misr, 1899–1952 (Cairo, 1967), and al-Haraka al-'ummaliyya al-misriyya fi daw' al-watha'iq al-baritaniyya, 1924–1937 (Cairo, 1975); Sulayman al-Nukhayli, al-Haraka al-'ummaliyya fi misr wa-mawqif al-sihafa wa'l-sultat al-misriyya minha min sanat 1882 ila sanat 1952 (Cairo, 1967); Nawal 'Abd al-'Aziz Radi, Adwa' jadida 'ala al-haraka al-'ummaliyya al-misriyya, 1930–1945 (Cairo, 1975), as well as her unpublished Ph.D. dissertation; Marius Deeb, "Labor and Politics in Egypt: 1919–1939," International Journal of Middle East Studies 10 (1979):187–203.

20 Introduction

and Deeb tends to glorify the Wafd, and treats the workers' movement as little more than an auxiliary of that party. While these historians made important contributions to the field, their approaches were ultimately unsuccessful in explaining the close yet complex, contradictory, and shifting relationship between the working class and the nationalist movement.

The second tendency is Marxist in orientation, and includes the work of Amin 'Izz al-Din, 'Abd al-Mun'im al-Ghazzali, and Jacques Couland.[25] The forerunner of this tendency was Shuhdi 'Atiyya al-Shafi'i, a communist activist whose *Tatawwur al-haraka al-wataniyya al-misriyya, 1882–1956*, first published in 1957, initiated the reinterpretation of his country's history as one of its peasants and workers propelling from below the struggle for social as well as national liberation. The Marxist school of Egyptian labor history, especially 'Izz al-Din's three-part synthesis, realized a major advance by emphasizing the reality and importance of class antagonisms within Egyptian society as well as the struggles between contending tendencies within the workers' movement.

The analyses of this school, however, are informed by a rather mechanistic Marxism that often reduces historical process to economic determinism. These analyses tend to utilize concepts and categories uncritically borrowed from a European context, and not always appropriate to the specific circumstances of Egypt's historical development. Their economistic and reductionist version of Marxism assumes that the Egyptian working class was inexorably propelled forward by objective economic developments toward the realization of revolutionary class consciousness. Al-Ghazzali and Couland disagree, however, about which postwar communist organization most fully expressed that consciousness, and by concluding their discussions with the military coup of 1952, these authors avoid the crucial question of how the post-1952 military regime was able to suppress the independent left-wing tendencies in the workers' movement with relative ease and eventually to coopt the trade unions into the state apparatus. In short, despite notable contributions, the Marxist school has not grappled adequately with a number of important historical problems. But there can be no doubt that the field of Egyptian labor history has made great strides forward in the past two dec-

25. 'Izz al-Din I, II, III (see List of Abbreviations); 'Abd al-Mun'im al-Ghazzali, *Ta'rikh al-haraka al-niqabiyya al-misriyya, 1899–1952* (Cairo, 1968); Jacques Couland, "Regards sur l'histoire syndicale et ouvrière égyptienne (1899–1952)," in René Gallisot (ed.), *Mouvement ouvrier, communisme et nationalisme dans le monde Arabe* (Paris, 1978).

Introduction **21**

ades both in empirical knowledge and in theoretical sophistication, and further advances can be expected.[26] Having set out the theoretical framework of this study, we feel it important to acknowledge that this book's focus on organized workers, on labor politics, and on the "institutional" history of the Egyptian working class is not unproblematic. The role of women in the workplace, in labor organizations and in the private sphere, working-class family life, the composition and structure of workers' neighborhoods, popular culture, and religion are aspects of the history of the working class that have received relatively little attention in this study. It is clear that Egyptian workers—male and female, adult and child—were not just wage workers who sometimes organized unions and went on strike, but also belonged to families, worshipped in mosques, churches, or synagogues, patronized coffeehouses and public baths, had ties to particular villages, regions or even foreign countries, and lived in complex communities. Like all of us, they were involved in a dense web of social relations both within and without the workplace that certainly affected their perceptions, consciousness, and behavior.

The fact that many of these aspects receive limited attention here should not be taken to reflect a lack of interest or a belief that they are unimportant to a deeper understanding of the political-institutional issues under examination, but rather is a result of the scarcity of the kinds of source materials that would shed light on those areas of workers' lives outside the sphere of production and of formal organization. The illiteracy and extreme poverty of most Egyptian workers, the social segregation of women, and the limited documentary evidence available required us to limit our focus in certain ways.

These same limitations on the available evidence have also meant that certain innovative theoretical approaches—the analysis of strike patterns, labor market segmentation, the structure and transformation of the labor process, and the "language of labor"—which have been fruitful for historians of European and North American labor and with which we are in principle sympathetic have proven impossible to apply.[27] We certainly do not deny that these theoretical ad-

26. The reader's attention is especially directed to the recent book by Ellis Goldberg, *Tinker, Tailor, and Textile Worker: Class and Politics in Egypt, 1930–1954* (Berkeley, 1986).

27. On strikes, see Edward Shorter and Charles Tilly, *Strikes in France, 1830–1968* (London, 1974); on labor market segmentation, see Charles Sabel, *Work and Politics* (Cambridge, 1982); on labor process, see Harry Braverman, *Labor and Monopoly Capital* (New York, 1974), and Victoria Bonnell, *Roots of Rebellion: Workers' Politics and Organizations in St. Petersburg and Moscow, 1900–1914* (Berkeley, 1983); on lan-

22 Introduction

vances might have been potentially illuminating, and we have used such insights as we could, but the character of the evidence at our disposal leads us to believe that any sustained effort to structure a book around such concepts would require more speculation than our historical training allows us to feel comfortable with.

The present study is, therefore, more traditional and circumscribed than we would wish because of the evidence available to us and the current state of the literature. Nonetheless, we hope that this study elucidates some of the main problems in Egyptian labor history, and will stimulate others to address the questions we leave unasked or unanswered not only for Egypt but for other Middle Eastern countries as well. It has given us great pleasure to learn that some of the veteran Egyptian trade union leaders we interviewed have published new memoirs and historical studies since we carried out our research. These efforts are testimony to their deep conviction that the working class has been an important social force in twentieth-century Egypt and that its history is worth studying. We hope that our own work contributes to validating that conviction, and more generally, demonstrates the utility of the theoretical approach on which it is based for the study of modern Middle Eastern history.

guage, see William G. Sewell, *Work and Revolution in France: The Language of Labor from the Old Regime to 1848* (Cambridge, 1980), Gareth Stedman Jones, *Languages of Class: Studies in English Working Class History, 1832–1982* (Cambridge, 1983).

Chapter II

The Formation of the Egyptian Working Class

In April 1882 several thousand Egyptian coalheavers at Port Said on the Suez Canal went on strike for higher wages, an event that appears to have been the first major manifestation of collective action by indigenous workers in modern Egyptian history. This episode, whose causes and character will be examined below, was followed at the very beginning of the twentieth century by a rising tide of labor activism, including strikes, the formation of trade unions, and the establishment of links between Egyptian workers and the nationalist movement. The years leading up to the First World War thus witnessed the emergence in Egypt of an embryonic labor movement which was to make its presence increasingly felt, politically as well as economically.

While workers in small-scale handicrafts enterprises played a part in this movement, members of an emerging class of wage workers employed in relatively large-scale, modern, industrial, and transport enterprises were also involved. These enterprises were, as noted in the Introduction, established from the second half of the nineteenth century, and especially in the two or three decades before the First World War, by foreign and *mutamassir* capital or by the Egyptian state. The specific form taken by Egypt's integration into the world capitalist system had led to a limited but nonetheless significant influx of investment in such sectors as the processing of agricultural raw materials, the provision of goods and services for the European and Europeanized segments of the urban population, and the transport infrastructure. It was in these sectors therefore that a modern working class first emerged, and soon began to engage in collective action along with some of the craftsmen and artisans.

24 Formation of the Working Class

At the beginning of the twentieth century, and indeed until the Second World War, wage workers in large enterprises constituted only a minority of the labor force in Egyptian manufacturing, construction, and transport. As Table 1 shows, that labor force of half a million persons—a figure that includes a great many large and small proprietors together with the self-employed and wage workers in tiny workshops as well as those in sizeable factories—was in 1907 itself far outnumbered by the millions of Egyptian peasants. Yet the existence even at this early date of a new and growing social stratum composed of propertyless laborers available as wage workers in modern industry and transport was indisputable. Over the decades that followed, the numbers and social weight of wage workers employed in large-scale manufacturing industry would increase both absolutely and in relation to the small-scale crafts sector. In its early stages of development, the members of this new "class in formation" were for the most part drawn from the Egyptian peasantry, from among urban artisans and workers in the traditional trades, and from foreign immigrants. The specific characteristics of each of these sources of recruitment will be examined in this chapter as an introduction to an analysis of the character of the Egyptian working class in the first four decades of the twentieth century.

Peasants into Workers

The sweeping transformation of agrarian relations in nineteenth-century Egypt adversely affected many peasants. Landholdings once largely controlled by peasants eventually passed into the hands of a new class of indigenous large landowners through a variety of ways that included outright seizures, peasant flight to evade heavy taxation, conscription or corvée, failure to pay taxes, or foreclosure for nonpayment of debt. In addition, the Muslim law of inheritance, by tending to fragment holdings beyond the point of viability, and a rapid population growth contributed to this process of dispossession so that by 1907, over 90 percent of Egypt's 1.6 million rural families owned too little land for even subsistence, or no land at all. To survive, these peasants would have to rent land, work on the estate of a large landowner, or hire themselves out as wage laborers.[1]

Most peasants compelled to turn to wage labor in the late nineteenth and early twentieth centuries could find work in the agricultural sector either as cultivators or as workers hired for such tasks as

1. See Richards, *Egypt's Agricultural Development*, and Owen, *The Middle East*, especially pp. 216–33.

Formation of the Working Class   **25**

maintaining irrigation canals. There were however a number of sectors outside agriculture proper in which peasants could also hope to find jobs. These were primarily those sectors requiring a great deal of cheap, heavy physical labor and little skill or training. The demand for labor in these branches of industry or transport often fluctuated seasonally or even daily. Although mechanized industry was slow to develop in Egypt, the orientation of the country's economy toward export agriculture and transport drew an increasing number of landless peasants into wage labor outside of agriculture: into jobs as coalheavers (on whom more below), dockworkers, and construction workers, as workers in cotton ginning and packing plants, sugar crushing mills and the Hawamdiyya sugar refinery, and as casual laborers of all kinds. An important component of the emerging working class thus consisted of these "peasant workers" who retained a variety of ties to their villages and to rural ways of life.

Peasants were usually recruited for industrial jobs by a labor contractor (*khawli* [in colloquial Egyptian Arabic *kholi*] which means "supervisor," "overseer," though *shaykh, ra'is*, and in construction *mu'adhdhin*, were also used) who would contract to provide a certain number of workers for a specific period of time at a fixed rate of pay, for which service he would receive a fee. The *kholi* was also responsible for both supervising the work and paying the workers after deducting his commission. A contractor might also enhance his income by acting as a moneylender, advancing money at high rates of interest to his workers, and deducting what he was owed from their pay. In this way workers were often kept in virtual debt peonage. This system of labor recruitment and control, found almost everywhere a large, unskilled work force was employed, had definite advantages for the managers of large enterprises, especially those that were foreign-owned. Their unskilled laborers were hired and supervised by a native familiar with local conditions who could be held responsible for ensuring that the work was properly done and for resolving any problems that might arise. Contracting allowed them maximum flexibility in adjusting to seasonal or conjunctural fluctuations in their labor requirements and permitted them to circumvent the establishment of a stable, more or less permanent, and directly-employed work force which might eventually make claims for higher wages and better working conditions.

Some peasant families were able to find seasonal work for one or more of their members near their villages, processing locally-grown crops. At one plant north of Cairo—and many similar enterprises could be found in the Nile Delta provinces and in Middle Egypt—some three hundred peasants from nearby villages (half of them chil-

26 Formation of the Working Class

dren) fed cotton into gins, while others, including women, sorted the raw cotton and tended the pressing and baling machines. During the season for processing cotton, from September to February or March, the men could expect to earn as much as six to eight piastres for a fifteen-hour workday, the women and children half that amount. In the sugar cane crushing mills scattered across Upper Egypt (the Saʻid), the peasant workers were frantically driven between December and May to process the ripe cane before its sugar content dropped. The work was intensive, exhausting, and sometimes dangerous, but the peasants desperately needed these jobs to supplement meager family incomes from agriculture. Rural industrial employment was shortterm, but wages were usually substantially higher than those normally paid for agricultural labor in the prewar period.[2]

Jobs near home were, however, difficult to find for most peasants, who were compelled to migrate to find temporary work in large-scale construction projects (for example, railway roadbeds, irrigation canals, barrages, and the first Aswan Dam, completed in 1902), in urban construction, in port cities, or in the rural processing plants of other regions. A disproportionate number of the peasants who migrated long distances in search of work came from the Saʻid rather than from the Nile Delta, which reflected the uneven manner in which different regions were affected by the country's new economic orientation. While the Delta had been converted to the perennial irrigation required for the expansion of cotton cultivation during the nineteenth century, the Saʻid was not converted to this system until after the First World War. Although sugar cane cultivation was greatly expanded in the region and the extension of the railway system allowed easier access, the Saʻid was at the end of the nineteenth century significantly less developed than the more prosperous and populous north. The seasonal rhythms of life set by the Nile still persisted here, allowing many thousands of impoverished Saʻidis, desperate for additional income, to seek work in the fields of the Delta, but also in industry and transport, during the few months each year that they were not needed for fieldwork.

For these reasons many Saʻidis worked at the Suez Canal, on the docks of Alexandria, and at construction sites in Cairo. They were reputed to surpass *fallahin* from the Delta in stamina and physical strength, and monopolized some of the more strenuous, better-paid jobs such as weighing and transporting raw cotton at many Delta ginning plants. The Saʻidis' reputation probably owed something to eco-

2. See Jean Vallet, *Contribution à l'étude de la condition des ouvriers de la grande industrie au Caire* (Valence, 1911), pp. 86–94.

Formation of the Working Class   **27**

logical factors. The peasants of the Delta were more prone to such strength-sapping parasitic diseases as bilharzia and ankylostoma, which thrived in the region's perennial irrigation system, whereas under the system of basin irrigation still prevalent in the Sa'id disease vectors were controlled by the heat of the sun in the dry fallow soil.[3]

The Coalheavers of Port Said

One particular group of migrant Sa'idi workers made a place for themselves in the annals of Egyptian history, and shed light on the character of early labor activism, by launching what was probably the country's first large-scale strike in modern times. By 1882, several thousand Sa'idi laborers were employed at Port Said, site of the Suez Canal Company's main workshops and maintenance facilities. Port Said was the only important coaling station along the vital waterway, and these Sa'idis were hired to offload the coal brought from abroad onto barges, and to refuel ships transiting the canal. One British official later wrote of them:

> In the old days of basin irrigation, Middle and Upper Egypt produced the finest manual labour in the whole of Egypt or perhaps anywhere. Port Said had the reputation of being the fastest coaling station in the world with its thousands of Sa'idi labourers swarming like ants up the ships' gangways and tipping the coal into the bunkers.[4]

Like many peasant workers, these coalheavers were not employed directly by the foreign-owned companies, but through intermediaries ("shaykhs") who paid the coalheavers their wages. A "government head sheikh" was responsible for deducting the *firda* (capitation tax) from their pay. Given this arrangement, as a British observer noted in 1880, that official acquired "many opportunities of defrauding the poor collier, who seldom receives his due." In fact, the shaykhs may have kept for themselves as much as 30 percent of the coalheaver's

3. Gabriel Baer, *Studies in the Social History of Modern Egypt* (Chicago, 1969), pp. 215–16; Thomas Russell, *Egyptian Service, 1902–1946* (London, 1949), pp. 38–39. It is interesting to compare the role of the Sa'idis with that of the migrant Irish workers who in nineteenth-century England often performed the heavy physical labor for which, according to E. P. Thompson, the English worker was no longer suited by physique or temperament. See *The Making of the English Working Class* pp. 432–35.
4. Russell, *Egyptian Service*, pp. 38–39. The introduction of perennial irrigation into Upper Egypt eventually sapped the working energy of the Sa'idis as earlier it had made many Delta peasants incapable of sustained strenuous labor.

28 Formation of the Working Class

nominal wage of one franc per ton.[5] The role of the shaykhs led the late Gabriel Baer to refer to the Port Said coalheavers as having constituted a guild, and to argue that the series of labor disputes that began in 1882 were manifestations of "a class struggle [which] developed between the workers and their shaykhs who had become contractors."[6] It does not, however, seem possible to sustain the claim that the coalheavers and their shaykhs constituted a guild in any meaningful sense of the term. The British and other sources on which the accounts of this episode rely make no mention whatsoever of a guild.[7] Certainly coalheaving was a very new occupation at Port Said, because the city itself had only been founded in 1859 and the Canal had only opened in 1869. Moreover, the workers themselves were recent migrants from the Saʻid who had left their families at home and may well have worked at Port Said for only part of the year. Finally, there is no evidence of any guild structure or ritual among the coalheavers.

For these reasons it would seem that this was not a case of guild shaykhs transforming themselves into labor contractors and thereby provoking a conflict with former guild members who had now become oppressed wage workers. The implicit analogy with the internal conflicts engendered by the rise of capitalism which destroyed many West European guilds is not appropriate in this case. The foundations of capitalism in Egypt had not emerged organically out of an indigenous precapitalist social order but had been largely "imposed" from without by the impact of the world market and the action of foreign capital. This combined and uneven process of development destroyed certain features of the old order and preserved others while introducing new forms of social organization. Rather than being a remnant of the traditional guild system, labor contracting was in fact a new form of labor exploitation engendered by the development of capitalism in Egypt. This form suited the need of many new industrial and transport enterprises for unskilled workers. The coalheavers were subject to a system of labor contracting in which shaykhs recruited, paid, and controlled the work force on behalf of the coaling

5. Wolff (Acting Consul in Port Said) to Malet, May 25, 1880, Egypt no. 3 (1880), C. 2606, p. 11 (in House of Commons, *Accounts and Papers 1880*, LXXV); FO 141/160, Wolff to Malet, May 18, 1882.

6. Baer, *Egyptian Guilds in Modern Times* (Jerusalem, 1964), p. 136. Professor Baer was the first to bring these workers and their conflicts to scholarly attention.

7. See the Wolff-Malet correspondence cited above, as well as FO 141/160 (April–May 1882) and FO 141/165 (October–November 1882), and *al-Ahram*, April 25, May 24, 1882, quoted in al-Nukhayli, *al-Haraka al-ʻummaliyya*, pp. 15–16.

Formation of the Working Class   **29**

companies. The Egyptian government also played a role in this system by supervising the appointment of the shaykhs. Although no guild seems to have been involved at Port Said, they did exist in the urban craft and service trades, and the specific role and significance of these organizations in the context of modern Egypt will be discussed in more detail later.

The coalheavers began their strike on April 1, 1882. Edward Royle of the Port Said & Suez Coal Company claimed that the strike was instigated

> by some Higher Authority in Cairo as our men were perfectly contented with their pay, and on the day of the Strike they were simply driven, by force, away from their work by some ringleaders whom the Governor [of the Canal Zone] did not even think of punishing.[8]

This was indeed a period of political turmoil in the country. A nationalist military-civilian coalition led by Colonel Ahmad 'Urabi was in control in Cairo, and the Khedive Tawfiq was seeking foreign support to regain power. In July the crisis would come to a head and the British occupation would begin. Although the coalheavers may have been taking advantage of the unsettled situation, their grievances were essentially local and economic: they wanted a doubling of their piece rate, and refused to return to work at the old rate of one franc per ton even under the "protection" of government troops. The employers claimed that the coalheavers' wages were already very high, indeed higher than the wages paid their counterparts in Malta, Marseilles, or even London. Whereas they admitted that the cost of living was higher in Port Said than elsewhere in Egypt, the companies asserted that "thanks to a genial climate and a low order of civilization, the wants of an Arab are comparatively almost Nil . . . for the Arabs who live in a state of nature the difference [in the cost of living] is not great at all."

Early in the strike, in which the shaykhs apparently played no role, the employers proposed a new payment scheme that would have kept the old piece rate but reduced the contractors' commissions. But very few of the strikers returned to work, indicating their continued insistence on a general increase in the rate that would benefit both workers and shaykhs. With pressure mounting from ship captains unable to take on coal, the companies threatened to bring in Maltese

---

8. This quotation and most of the other information on the events of 1882 are from the sources cited in the previous footnote.

30 Formation of the Working Class

and Armenian laborers from Istanbul, and asked for the protection of a British warship in case of clashes. The local and central governments were sympathetic to the strikers, in keeping with their nationalist orientation. Two commissions, one "mixed" (Egyptian and European) and one purely Egyptian, were sent from Cairo to look into the dispute. The first was unfavorable, but the second rejected the contention that the men were "already too well paid" and called for a 13 percent raise. The companies rejected this, claiming that "the Employers instead of being the oppressors as the Arab Commission [sent by the government] would have it are really the oppressed." Still, the strikers returned to work in May satisfied that they had won. Their employers were in fact compelled to accept the raise under threat of a second strike. In the following months the coalheavers made further gains, getting as much as three to four francs per ton for coaling steamers and one franc per ton for the lighter work of unloading the coal ships.

The coalheavers' victory had been made possible mainly by the national political situation in the spring and early summer of 1882. Once the British occupation was an accomplished fact, the employers took the offensive. In October 1882, citing the "arrogant stubbornness of the misguided men," the nine coaling firms locked out all the coalheavers, and demanded that they accept the old piece rate. The workers resisted, but they were in the end defeated. Some were reported to have left Port Said during the lock-out, presumably to look elsewhere for work or to return to their villages in the Sa'id. There is no further record of the Port Said coalheavers until 1896, when Lord Cromer, the British Agent and Consul-General in Egypt and the country's de facto ruler, received a "very numerously signed petition" from them. The workers complained of ill-treatment by the contractors, who "buy and sell us like slaves . . . taking away most of our wages by force." To get a job one had to bribe a shaykh, and anyone who complained was fired and forced to leave the city. Furthermore, some of the shaykhs had opened shops where the workers had to buy everything they needed and pay high prices for goods of poor quality, especially before Muslim holidays. The whole corrupt and oppressive system was run by Muhammad Effendi Labib, the chief clerk at the Governorate for twenty-nine years and the person from whom the shaykhs took their orders.[9] Cromer acknowledged receipt of the petition in a letter to the coaling companies, and remarked that the work-

9. On this episode see FO 141/322 (May 1896) and FO 633/8 (Cromer Papers, May 1896).

Formation of the Working Class **31**

ers "seem to have some real grievances, notably in connection with the truck system." When the employers rejected the allegations as groundless and asked that the petition be turned over to them so that "its Fabricators may be brought to light and punishment," Cromer refused, though he also failed to intervene to correct the alleged abuses.

The system of labor contracting was increasingly resented and challenged by the coalheavers. When they again went on strike in April 1907, it was to win not only a higher piece rate but the abolition of contracting, that is, direct employment and payment by the coaling companies.[10] Such a status would have greatly enhanced the workers' bargaining power, hence it was demanded by many Egyptian workers who were employed through contractors at the Suez Canal and elsewhere. But the Port Said coalheavers were not to win their struggle against contracting. In fact, their jobs ceased to exist as the world's shipping and navies gradually shifted from coal to oil in the interwar period, and they disappeared from the industrial scene. The contracting system would prevail in many branches of industry and transport for several decades to come because the foreign-owned companies were strongly opposed to eliminating a method of labor recruitment and control that served them so well.

A very important component of the emerging Egyptian working class thus consisted of peasants who were no longer able to subsist from agriculture alone and had to sell their labor power for wages in the new industrial and transport sectors. These workers usually found temporary employment in those branches where cheap unskilled labor was in demand. By becoming seasonal wage workers they did not however sever their ties to their villages or rural ways of life, and in fact preserved them in various ways. Many peasants returned to their homes to work on family plots when their labor was needed, or the men in the cities would send part of their wages home while the women looked after the household and continued to work in agriculture. Some combination of men, women, and children in the family would work in both rural industry and agriculture depending on the season and the availability of work. Whatever the form, there was in most cases no sharp break between agrarian and industrial modes of life or work, no immediate and radical transition on the part of peasants working more or less temporarily and provisionally in non-agricultural jobs to a new urban, industrial mode of existence. The implications of this continuity for the behavior of these peasant workers are significant, and will be discussed later.

10. 'Izz al-Din I, pp. 78–81.

32 Formation of the Working Class

From Guild Members to Wage Workers

Until the latter part of the nineteenth century, those urban Egyptians engaged in production, commerce, and service activities of every kind were organized into guilds. Every trade from prostitutes to beggars, water-carriers, servants, weavers, goldsmiths, and merchants had its guild or guilds. Well into the post-Mamluk era, the guild shaykh had some power to restrict entry into the trade, set maximum wages, participate in the setting of prices, and arbitrate internal disputes. But his chief function was to serve as the government's administrative and fiscal link with the guild's members. Indeed, the guild itself seems to have been primarily an administrative unit, established and recognized by the state in order to facilitate tax collection, regulate economic life, and maintain public order. Parallels between the Egyptian guilds and those of medieval Europe with their substantial corporate autonomy, their rich spiritual life and their strong social identity reinforced by ritual are misleading, for the evidence suggests that the Egyptian guilds never really had a great deal of social content or a corporate existence independent of the state. There is therefore little reason to believe that the very limited scope of guild activity in late nineteenth-century Egypt was the result of a process of decline in which the guilds had lost their complex structure and rich social significance. In the two or three decades before the First World War, when the state developed other means of taxing and regulating urban artisans, merchants, and service providers even the formal-legal semblance of a "guild system" disappeared.[11]

The disappearance of the guilds by the early twentieth century was not unconnected with the changes experienced by the traditional urban trades in the same period. Many writers have suggested that Egypt's integration into the world market and the influx of foreign manufactures that accompanied it simply wiped out the traditional urban trades. There is, for example, Cromer's vivid and often-quoted passage, written in 1906:

> Quarters that were formerly hives of busy workmen—spinning, weaving, braiding, tassle-making, dyeing, tent-making, embroidering, slipper-making, gold and silver working, spice crushing, copper-beating, water-skin making, saddle making, sieve mak-

11. See Baer, *Egyptian Guilds*; Claude Cahen, "Y a-t-il eu des corporations professionelles dans le monde musulman classique?" and S. M. Stern, "The Constitution of the Islamic City," in A. H. Hourani and S. M. Stern (eds.), *The Islamic City* (Oxford, 1970); and André Raymond, *Artisans et Commerçants au Caire au XVIIIe Siècle* (Damascus, 1973–1974), II, pp. 503–585.

Formation of the Working Class **33**

ing, wooden-mold making, lock making, &c.—have shrunk to attenuated proportions or have been entirely obliterated.[12]

In reality the situation seems to have been much more complex. First it is essential to distinguish among the craft industries, commerce, and services. It is undoubtedly true that many crafts seem to have died out, contracted drastically as their products were replaced or undersold by imports, or became obsolete as local tastes and consumption pattern changed. In some trades Egyptian craftsmen were replaced by European and Levantine immigrants who came to monopolize production for their fellow foreigners. It was just when the impact of foreigners and foreign goods was at its greatest, and the local crafts and craftsmen at their nadir, that Cromer wrote.

Yet, in a broader perspective it becomes clear that many craft industries were transformed rather than obliterated. Whereas Europeans resident in the country as well as wealthy Egyptians may have preferred imported goods or turned to non-Egyptian artisans, most Egyptians continued to patronize local craftsmen who produced the kinds of items they preferred at low cost. Many of the foreign-owned workshops employed Egyptians to actually perform the work according to new methods and to new specifications. In many cases local artisans were eventually able to adapt, learn new styles and techniques, and cater to new tastes. The furniture industry is a case in point. Cromer wrote that the upholsterer, "who could cover a divan to meet the needs of the last generation, finds himself unequal to the new demand for Louis XV brocaded chairs and couches. In furniture, clothing, and all necessities, the upper classes are now supplied almost entirely with European goods, and the tendency is working downwards."[13] Furniture-making had by that time become almost the exclusive province of Italian artisans. But after the First World War Egyptian artisans mastered the craft in its new form, and were able to compete with the foreigners for a significant share of the local market. Other crafts underwent a similar transformation as craftsmen began to make new products in new ways. Spinning and weaving, for example, were undoubtedly hurt by imports but did not disappear; instead, local weavers began to use imported yarns, and retained a sizable share of the market.[14]

12. Great Britain, *Reports by His Majesty's Agent and Consul-General on the Finances, Administration, and Condition of Egypt and the Soudan in 1905*, Egypt no. 1 (1906), C. 2817, pp. 89–90.
13. *Ibid*.
14. Between 1897 and 1907 the number of persons engaged in the textile industry rose by 40 percent. See Pierre Arminjon, *La Situation économique et financière de l'Égypte*

34 Formation of the Working Class

This is not to say that many artisans were not displaced and impoverished, but the decline of the small local industries and their inability to adapt to changing conditions should also not be exaggerated. The mass of small Egyptian wholesale and retail merchants was similarly affected. Many indigenous merchants were hurt or altogether displaced by the transformation of urban commerce in the late nineteenth century, though as a group they would make something of a comeback in the interwar years. Some of the service trades, such as the cereal measurers and most of the water-carriers, became obsolete.[15] For others, demand may have increased as the urban population grew (doorkeepers, barbers, domestic servants), or as the economy developed (stevedores, porters). In short, the economic changes Egypt underwent during the period of British occupation had profound though varied effects on the traditional urban petty bourgeoisie and those employed by it. Certain trades were adversely impacted or even disappeared; others were little or even positively affected; and still others adapted or were transformed to meet the requirements of changing conditions. Although in nearly all cases the guilds disappeared, former guild shaykhs made the transition to a new role as labor contractors in only a few instances. The guilds were an essentially precapitalist institution, whereas contracting was an integral part of an emerging capitalist order in Egypt.

In the course of this transition to capitalism, a great many people, both small proprietors and their workers, must have been uprooted. Some probably reestablished themselves as self-employed artisans, small merchants, or wage workers in the petty trades, whereas others were integrated as laborers or as skilled workers in the new large-scale industrial sector. It seems likely that the relatively skilled indigenous workers in this last sector were drawn from among former members of the urban artisanate. They usually learned their trades as apprentices, often of family members. Later, however, the ranks of the more highly skilled Egyptian workers in large enterprises were augmented by those who had received some formal vocational education. The Egyptian government had established an industrial school in Bulaq (Cairo) in 1839 which closed a decade later but reopened in 1876. It trained skilled workers and technicians for government service, the army, and private industry, and was supplemented after 1900

(Paris, 1911), pp. 182–83, 186–87, and Jacques Berque, *Egypt: Imperialism and Revolution* (London, 1972), pp. 328–31.

15. Great Britain, *Reports by His Majesty's Agent and Consul-General on the Finances, Administration, and Condition of Egypt and the Soudan in 1904*, Egypt no.·1 (1905), C. 2409, p. 74.

Formation of the Working Class **35**

by privately funded Muslim and Coptic industrial schools and state-sponsored "model workshops" and apprenticeship programs.[16]

Unlike the peasant workers discussed earlier, this component of the working class consisted of relatively skilled and thoroughly urbanized workers who in earlier times would have been members of a craft guild. They had no ties to agriculture, but were not thereby necessarily committed to a lifetime of wage work in large industry. Many could have easily returned to work in a small handicraft enterprise. The dream of amassing enough capital to set up one's own small business, to be an independent artisan, remained strong, and for a few, attainable. Yet, the realities of life in capitalist Egypt compelled most of them to eventually face the prospect of becoming permanent members of the working class, wage workers in a new system of industrial production. Their role in that new system influenced the forms of organization and action they soon developed. This role will be discussed in some detail below.

Immigrant Workers

A small but significant part of the great wave of migration that swept southern Europe in the decades before the First World War flowed into Egypt. The rapid development of the Egyptian economy created lucrative opportunities for foreigners, while the difficulty of making a decent living in their countries of origin was an incentive to emigrate. The establishment of cheap steamship service among the countries of the Mediterranean littoral made the move an easy one, and by 1907 there were some 147,000 Europeans residing in Egypt, including 63,000 Greeks, 35,000 Italians, 21,000 British subjects (among them 6,000 Maltese), and 15,000 French subjects (one-fifth of them North Africans). Some 34,000 immigrants from geographical Syria (comprising the present-day states of Syria, Lebanon, Jordan, and Israel), 7,700 Armenians, and 18,000 Sudanese were also resident in Egypt. Finally, many Jews of various nationalities had settled in Egypt in previous decades and added to the long-established Egyptian Jewish community of 30,000.[17]

Only a minority of those who came to Egypt in these years were workers in industry. Most sought jobs in commerce or services, and used what capital they had brought or could save to establish small

16. *Ibid.*, p. 75; Vallet, *Contribution*, pp. 17–23, 118; F/172, Ministère de l'Instruction Publique, "Note concernant l'École d'Ar's-et-Métiers de Boulaq", and Emile Fahmi Hanna Shanuda, *Ta'rikh al-ta'lim al-sina'i hatta thawrat 23 yulyu 1952* (Cairo, 1967).
17. Egypt, Ministry of Finance, *The Census of Egypt taken in 1907* (Cairo, 1909); Charles Issawi, *Egypt at Mid-Century* (London, 1954), p. 43.

36 Formation of the Working Class

businesses of their own. Of those who found jobs in industry, only few intended to settle permanently in the country. These often became foremen and supervisory personnel or worked at highly skilled trades. A much larger group consisted of less-skilled workers who generally came without their families to make some money and then move on, but of course some of them eventually brought their families and stayed for years.

We have the story of one construction worker from Sicily which may well be fairly typical. R.'s father owned a flour mill near Syracuse which had to be sold to pay the inheritance taxes after his father died in 1903. The sons left the country; R. went to Egypt to look for work, leaving his wife and six children behind. After six months in a carpentry shop in Alexandria, R. worked in construction and learned masonry. His higher wages allowed him to bring his family to settle in Cairo where he worked as a stonecutter at the British army barracks in 'Abbasiyya.[18] Although R. and those like him became long-term residents, the cheap fares across the Mediterranean allowed seasonal migration as well: from about 1906, for example, poor peasants from Puglia and Calabria began coming to Egypt to work in construction from November to March each year.[19]

These foreigners, generally poor peasants or workers in their countries of origin, filled the upper ranks of the working class in Egypt and occupied a highly disproportionate share of the skilled, supervisory, and technical positions. The Europeans among them also shared the special rights and privileges enjoyed by most foreigners (but not by Ottoman subjects), and generally received much higher wages than Egyptians for the same skilled jobs on the grounds that the foreigners were more efficient and able. There were foreign workers in all the large enterprises, though certain branches of industry were associated with workers from particular countries. The Greeks, for example, dominated the cigarette industry; Italians construction; and the Suez Canal enterprises recruited most of their skilled workers from both these groups. Syrians and Armenians often worked in the cigarette factories; East Europeans (including Russians) in the Alexandria cottonseed oil plants; and recently arrived Jewish immigrants in the needle trades.

Although the foreign workers were relatively few in number, enjoyed a status superior to that of the indigenous workers, and often had little long-term stake in the country, they were for a time to play

18. Vallet, *Contribution*, pp. 128–34.
19. *Ibid.*, p. 117; Bent Hansen, *Wage Differentials in Italy and Egypt: the Incentive to Migrate before World War I* (Working Paper no. 164, Department of Economics, University of California, Berkeley, October 1982).

Formation of the Working Class   **37**

an important role in the development of trade unionism in Egypt. Their privileges, higher wages, higher rate of literacy, and prior experience of both industrial life and industrial conflict allowed them at the turn of the century to engage in forms of organization and action that were new to Egypt and which indigenous workers were quick to emulate. As will be seen later, their role in the Egyptian labor movement was significant during the early years.

A Working Class in Formation

From the last decades of the nineteenth century until well unto the 1930s, the Egyptian working class was still in the early stages of formation. Many of its members were employed in the modern industrial and transport sectors only provisionally, and considered industrial employment a temporary expedient rather than a permanent status. The work force at many of the major enterprises consisted largely of peasants who retained strong ties to the land, and because they were employed on a seasonal and indirect basis, they had little reason to see themselves (or to be regarded by others) as part of a distinct new class in Egyptian society whose size and weight would continue to grow as capitalist development inexorably proceeded. Furthermore, skilled foreign workers often had little intention of remaining in Egypt indefinitely, even if for economic reasons that was what in fact happened, and ethnic differences divided them from their indigenous co-workers.

Only a relatively small number of enterprises had large, permanent work forces consisting mostly of indigenous workers. These included the Egyptian State Railways (ESR), the tramway companies of Cairo and Alexandria, and later the Suez Canal Company and the cigarette factories. This component of the working class remained a small minority of the labor force well into the interwar period. While the number of Egyptians engaged in manufacturing, construction, and transport grew between 1907 and 1937 (as Table 1 shows) much of the increase was due to the establishment of a large number of very small enterprises. As late as 1937, over half of Egypt's industrial establishments employed no staff, and 92 percent had fewer than five employees. Only 3 percent employed more than ten workers, though these "large" firms accounted for a total of some 140,000 workers.[20] There had certainly been significant industrial development in Egypt, especially in the late 1920s and the 1930s, but it was only toward the

---

20. *ICC 1937*; Samir Radwan, *Capital Formation in Egyptian Industry and Agriculture, 1882–1967* (London, 1974), p. 191.

38 Formation of the Working Class

Table 1 Distribution of the Labor Force by Sector

	1907	1917	1927	1937	1947
Total[a]	9,510,920	10,964,064	12,147,169	13,813,120	16,381,950
Agriculture	2,440,030	4,044,458	3,526,036	4,038,201	4,244,951
Mining & extraction	4,112	2,693	9,741	10,828	12,965
Manufacturing	281,416	423,109	482,681	478,199	708,776
Construction	94,925	66,586	125,272	120,706	113,361
Transport & communication	101,136	150,633	130,935	138,911	203,335
Commerce	161,210	280,562	407,560	460,075	620,288
Personal services	94,294[b]	204,041[b]	284,076[c]	256,099	392,151
Public administration & social services	192,966	186,332	283,563	321,963	515,414
Unproductive & unknown occupations	3,449,694[d]	1,037,298[d]	595,801	1,327,203	1,572,232
Without occupation	105,325[e]	372,289[f]	6,301,504	6,390,935	7,998,477

SOURCES: 1907: *1907 Census*; 1917: *1917 Census*; 1927–1947: *AS 1951/1954*
NOTE: The last two categories are vague and ill-defined, and those included changed from census to census.
[a] Children under the age of 5 are excluded from the totals for 1927–1947.
[b] Category is designated "Domestics" and excludes family members.
[c] Includes servants in agricultural households; in 1937–1947 these are included in "Agriculture."
[d] Excludes most children.
[e] Designated "General designation without indication of a determinate occupation."
[f] Designation as in e; includes 308,816 workers engaged by the British Army.

end of the 1930s that there emerged a sizable body of workers who were completely dependent on industrial wage labor for subsistence and had no choice but to make a permanent place for themselves in the framework of the new capitalist industrial system.

Until that time they were outweighed by, and in many respects not highly differentiated from, the great mass of what we earlier termed the urban "working people"—owners of and workers in small workshops, independent and semi-independent artisans, those self-employed in marginal occupations, and casual laborers. The social relations that prevailed in the small enterprise where proprietor and employee worked side by side, lived in close proximity, and may have been kin—that is, the traditional world of the artisan—continued to have a great deal of meaning, and helped shape the social identity and vision of the world shared by many members of the urban lower classes including those here defined as working class. The ethos of the independent (or formally independent, because many

Formation of the Working Class **39**

such people were in fact subordinate to wealthy merchants or other middlemen) artisan or shopkeeper, still clinging to the vision of a world of small, more or less equal economic units linked organically to a community, a common culture, and a way of life, remained strong. Some decades were to pass before capitalist development and the social differentiation it generated gradually led Egyptian workers to adopt forms of consciousness and a social identity more congruent with their real (and permanent) conditions of work and life and increasingly distinct from those of the urban petty bourgeoisie.

As a result of the complex and uneven pattern of industrial development in Egypt, this embryonic working class was very heterogeneous. The members of its proletarian core were united by the fact of their employment in large-scale enterprises, but divided by their varying origins and commitment to industrial life, modes of employment, income levels, degree of job security and benefits, and skill levels. This heterogeneity was to be expected, given the recent emergence of this social group and the underdevelopment of large-scale, mechanized mass production industry.

The most privileged stratum of the working class consisted of such highly-skilled workers as electricians, machinists, plumbers, and for a time at least, cigarette rollers—trades that were much in demand. Few Egyptians were to be found in these trades before the First World War. These workers were generally European or Levantine immigrants who, if part of the permanent staff of a large company, could earn from twenty to forty piastres a day. The larger category of skilled workers—which included the skilled building trades (joiners, carpenters, masons, glaziers, tile-layers, painter, and so on), mechanics, iron-workers, turners (in the railway and tramway workshops, sugar mills and cotton gins, engineering firms and Suez Canal enterprises), and some cigarette workers—consisted mainly of Egyptians though the best jobs were held by foreigners. Wages for these kinds of work ranged from fifteen to thirty piastres a day. Below this group was a mass of mostly indigenous, less well-paid (usually eight to fifteen piastres a day), semi-skilled workers such as tram drivers and conductors, workers in the cigarette industry and the public utilities, a small number of mechanized textile factory workers, railway workers, machine-tenders, stokers, and building workers. At the bottom of the working class were the unskilled laborers, mostly peasants and the urban poor; women and children workers were also concentrated in this stratum. These jobs—on the docks, in construction, as guards and attendants, in domestic service, in the sugar mills, cotton gins,

40 Formation of the Working Class

and at every form of manual labor—paid no more than eight piastres a day.[21]

This admittedly schematic description of the early Egyptian working class nevertheless shows that its centers of gravity lay in the transport sector (railways, tramways, marine services) and in cigarette factories. Indeed, the greatest numbers of permanently employed workers concentrated in large workplaces were found in these industries, and not surprisingly, the first manifestations of labor organization appeared among these workers. The working conditions these workers experienced were an important stimulus to collective action. In 1900 the normal working day ranged from ten to fifteen hours: cigarette workers were at the lower end of the scale; tram, railway, and construction work in the middle; and cotton ginning and sugar crushing at the high end. Whereas some enterprises shut down one day a week or gave employees a day off—the particular day chosen might reflect the religion of the owner, of the individual workers, or of the majority of the work force—this was not the general rule: for most Egyptian workers the seven-day work week was the norm, although work was suspended on a number of religious holidays.

Only a very small proportion of workers enjoyed benefits such as regular paid vacations, medical care, a fixed wage scale graduated to account for seniority and aptitude, pensions, or severance pay in case of dismissal. Those who did enjoy such benefits were usually foreign workers employed on a permanent basis and designated as "cadre" by the larger companies or state agencies. Workers classified in other ways had few or no rights, even if employed by the same enterprise. The state railways, for example, had three categories of employees, the highest of which consisted of the permanent, pensionable, disproportionately European employees who enjoyed extensive benefits and numbered 2,335 in 1907. The second category consisted of 4,905 non-pensionable but permanent employees paid monthly. The great bulk of this work force was made up of nearly 15,000 "temporary" workers, many of whom had worked for the ESR for years, but nevertheless were paid on a daily basis, could be fired without cause or compensation, and had no right to paid days off or medical care. Similar conditions prevailed at the Suez Canal Company, one of the largest private firms. In 1900 this company directly employed only 1,661 men, two-thirds of them foreigners, who were entitled to a pension plan, vacation rights, medical care, and even a profit-sharing scheme. Much of the work, however, was performed by several thousand

21. Vallet, *Contribution*, passim; F. Legrand, *Les Fluctuations de prix et les crises de 1907 et 1908 en Égypte* (Nancy, 1909), p. 29; AS 1914, pp. 376–80.

Formation of the Working Class   **41**

Egyptians (many of them skilled) employed through a labor contractor under what was known as the *tâcheron* system. Although many of these workers had in fact worked for the company for long periods, they received much lower wages and had none of the benefits or job security of the cadre workers. So while the skilled and semi-skilled workers employed by large enterprises were generally better off than those employed in small workshops, and certainly privileged in comparison to the mass of peasants hired through contractors for unskilled labor, there were nonetheless important cleavages even within this section of the working class that often coincided with ethnic divisions.

These ethnic divisions between Egyptian workers and foreign (European, Syrian, and Armenian) workers, foremen, supervisors, and owners were an extremely important factor in shaping the character and behavior of the early working class. Not only were virtually all the large private companies owned by foreigners, whether resident abroad or in Egypt (*mutamassirun*) but the Egyptian state, its agencies and departments, were controlled by a foreign power, and the managers, supervisory personnel, and technical staff who oversaw the work force were also usually foreigners. Even at the workshops of the ESR, the chief engineers, their deputies, and other managerial personnel were English, whereas the foremen and the most highly skilled workers were usually Europeans. The Egyptian's working life was thereby controlled by a non-Egyptian whose authority was backed by the foreign manager or owner of the enterprise.

Not only were the better-paid jobs to which the Egyptians might aspire usually held by foreign workers to whom the employer gave preference, but even when the Egyptian held the same job he was often paid less than his European counterpart. This wage differential was sometimes justified by employers on the grounds of the European's allegedly superior speed and workmanship, but a contemporary observer gave other reasons:

> This difference is realized in practice and justified not only by the industrial law of supply and demand, a great number of natives seeking every day to be employed by the [Suez Canal] Company, but also by the fact that, living in his country of origin and accustomed since infancy to a frugal existence, which a hot climate requires, the natives spend on their subsistence the equivalent of about half of the costs of subsistence of a European worker in the same trade.[22]

22. J. Charles-Roux, *L'Isthme et le canal de Suez* (Paris, 1901), p. 241.

42 Formation of the Working Class

Not surprisingly, this subordinate position created real grounds for resentment among Egyptian workers against foreign workers, managers, and owners, and when combined with a sense of humiliation and wounded self-esteem, helped make the Egyptian worker receptive to a nationalism which tended to blend national and class consciousness.

The methods by which management sought to control the work force also strengthened the workers' sense of grievance. The chief means of enforcing labor discipline in the large enterprises that employed their workers directly were fines and the threat of suspension or dismissal. A *kholi* could simply get rid of a worker at his pleasure. But the railways, the tram companies and other large-scale, highly articulated, and hierarchical organizations had a system of sanctions that could be applied to workers who were late, insubordinate, negligent, or violated the rules in other ways. Management deemed these sanctions as indispensable in its struggle to control a work force unaccustomed to the demands and rhythms of industrial life, and shape it in accordance with the imperatives of production. Summing up the views of many foreign employers at the beginning of the century, views which underpinned their insistence on the importance of instilling discipline in their workers, Pierre Arminjon wrote:

> Vigor, activity, endurance, sobriety, an alert and lively intelligence—these are the natural gifts and innate qualities of the fellah and the Egyptian worker; improvidence, thoughtlessness, lack of perseverance, disorder, superstitious credulity, routine apathy, these are the faults. . . . The urban worker is naturally at least as thoughtless as the peasant. In the opinion of the industrialists whom I asked about this, this defect would be a serious obstacle to the formation of work teams capable of tending machinery without themselves being supervised by Europeans. "The native worker," they state, "manages to carry out his work well, he is extremely resistant to fatigue, but he has no notion of time nor any feeling of responsibility." It must be added that the lively, easy and extensive intelligence of the Egyptian is equalled neither by his good sense nor by his judgement nor by his firmness of character, probably because these qualities depend much less on nature than on education.[23]

23. Arminjon, *La Situation économique*, pp. 152, 155. It is interesting to compare these views with those of English employers in the 1830s concerning immigrant Irish workers: "In general the Irish labourers are faithful, steady to their work, and almost invariably honest. They are much trusted about houses, and I have seldom had any complaints against them. They are usually very intelligent; they are remarkably quick and

Formation of the Working Class **43**

These sanctions, and the manner in which they were applied, were to be a very important cause of industrial conflict in Egypt, reinforcing as they did workers' resentment over low wages, poor working conditions, and abusive treatment.

Continuity and Change in the Interwar Period

Some of the important characteristics of the early twentieth-century working class were to persist through the interwar period and even beyond. Although industry did grow through the 1920s and 1930s, and with it the working class, it was only in the late 1930s that this growth amounted to a qualitatively new stage in Egypt's economic development. Yet those decades also witnessed important shifts in the composition and social weight of the working class, shifts that pointed toward very significant future developments.

The first noteworthy aspect of this change was the gradual decline in the number of foreigners in the working class: by 1937 foreigners constituted only 0.5 percent of employees in industry. In Egypt's two largest cities, the foreign presence was of course greater—5.2 percent of the workers of Cairo and 12.7 percent in Alexandria were still foreign—but these figures did represent a decline from previous years and reflected a general, long-term drop in the size of the foreign communities in the country. The slow but real expansion of industry and the development of technical education allowed more Egyptians to move up into the skilled, technical and supervisory positions formerly monopolized by foreigners, though large wage differentials persisted. In 1930 a European mason might earn sixty to one hundred piastres a day to an Egyptian's thirty-five to forty-five and a European mechanic might be paid from one-quarter to one-third more than an Egyptian.[24]

In terms of overall wage levels there was more continuity than change during this period, for most Egyptian workers lived at the edge of subsistence. Wage gains won through industrial action between 1908 and 1919 had been severely eroded in subsequent years.

---

sharp, especially in manner and conversation. They scarcely ever make good mechanics: they do not make good millwrights or engineers, or any thing which requires thought: they do not even make good bricklayers. . . . If a plan is put in an Irishman's hands, he requires looking after continually: otherwise he will go wrong, or, more probably, not go on at all." Testimony of Samuel Holme, in Great Britain, *Report on the State of the Irish Poor in Great Britain* (Parliamentary Papers, 1836, vol. 34, p. 28).

24. See FO 141/658/164/18/30, letter from C.C.M. Brooks, structural engineers, to the Residency, March 17, 1930, and Hoare to the Foreign Office, April 26, 1930; and Hasan el-Saaty and Gordon K. Hirabayashi, *Industrialization in Alexandria: Some Ecological and Social Aspects* (Cairo, 1959), p. 17.

44 Formation of the Working Class

Indeed, a government study conducted in 1936 reported that the average daily wage in industry was 7.8 piastres: for male workers the average was 8.4, for women 5.5.[25] However, these averages were greatly affected by the very low wages paid to the large numbers of workers employed in small workshops, and therefore do not provide a good indication of the real level of wages in large enterprises. Unskilled workers in such enterprises generally earned about 8 piastres a day in the mid-1930s, compared to 4 piastres for agricultural labor. Semi-skilled workers, including construction, railway, cigarette, and by this time a fairly substantial body of textile workers, usually earned from 7 to 15 piastres daily. The next higher stratum (15 to 25 piastres daily) included such groups as tramway workers (who had made significant gains as the result of labor struggles discussed below), gas and electricity workers, the Suez Canal Company's permanent workers, and other skilled laborers such as handloom weavers employed in large factories. The most highly skilled workers of course earned even higher wages.[26]

These data would seem to show that whereas some workers had been able to win higher wages, others were earning at or below prewar levels given the 25 percent increase in the cost of living between 1913 and 1933. Overall, the real wages of most industrial workers seem to have risen very little, if at all, and there is some reason to believe that they actually fell. Standards of nutrition and housing were very poor, contributing to a life expectancy of 35.6 years for Egyptian men and 42.1 years for women in 1937. Meat and eggs were luxury items for most workers, 95 percent of whose caloric intake came from cereals and vegetable oils.[27] At the same time, Egyptian workers continued to work long hours with few rest days. Workers in 40 percent of the industrial firms which supplied the relevant information to the government had a workweek of seventy or more hours in 1937 and 43 percent of reporting firms had no weekly day of rest.[28] The larger

---

25. Published in 'Abd al-Mun'im Nasir al-Shafi'i, Ba'd mashakil al-'amal fi Misr (Cairo, 1939).

26. Marcel Clerget, Le Caire: Étude de géographie urbaine et d'histoire économique (Cairo, 1934), II, pp. 155–56; André Eman, L'Industrie de Coton en Égypte: Étude d'économie politique (Cairo, 1943), passim; Report of Harold Butler of the International Labor Office, 1932, p. 6, hereafter cited as "Butler Report."

27. See Charles Issawi, Egypt, pp. 85, 170; Khaireya Khairy, "The Nutritive Aspects of Egyptian Labor" (Unpublished B.A. Thesis, American University in Cairo, March 1946); Zaki Badaoui, Les Problèmes du travail et les organisations ouvrières en Égypte (Alexandria, 1948), p. 62. For data on retail food prices, see Clerget, Le Caire, pp. 157–58.

28. ICC 1937, p. 410. About half of those enterprises that did close down one day a week chose Friday to do so, the other half chose Sunday.

Formation of the Working Class **45**

firms tended to have shorter workdays, usually nine to ten hours, as well as a regular weekly holiday, but paid vacations, sick pay, and compensation for work-related accidents were still not common. One observer writing in the early 1930s summed up his description of the squalid state of the working poor of Cairo in the following lurid but not inaccurate manner:

> The *Description d'Égypte* [researched during the French occupation of 1798-1801] estimated that in 1800 two-thirds of the working proletariat of Cairo lived in foul huts, slept on mats, nourished themselves on raw vegetables and let their progeny run about in a state close to that of nudity; the situation has not changed much.[29]

Conditions in the 1930s, as at the beginning of the century, were worst for the workers to whom this passage primarily refers: those employed in small workshops and casual or seasonal laborers, especially migrant workers. Women workers, even in the new factories, were also disadvantaged because they continued to be concentrated in the low-skill, low-wage jobs. In the mechanized textile mills, for example, they wound bobbins, and earned only four to six piastres a day, far below the daily wage rate for men, and the same differential prevailed in other industries.[30] The tens of thousands of children employed in small workshops, ginning plants, and textile factories were usually paid three to four piastres a day. Foreign visitors in the 1930s were quite horrified by the exploitation, abusive treatment, and poor working conditions they endured even in modern, foreign-run enterprises despite the protective legislation enacted as early as 1909.[31] In general, however, workers in many of the large enterprises continued to be at least somewhat better off than those in small workshops or marginal occupations, largely as a result of the higher wages and better benefits they had been able to win through organization and mu-

29. Clerget, *Le Caire*, p. 159.
30. Eman, *Coton*, p. 102; Aziz el-Maraghi, *La Législation du travail en Égypte* (Paris, 1937), p. 8. There is unfortunately little information available on the specific conditions of women's labor in Egyptian industry. The very fact of such employment, far from home and outside the direct supervision of the male head of household, contravened social norms and received relatively little attention however essential it was to the economic survival of many thousands of peasant and poor urban families.
31. See al-Maraghi, *Législation*, pp. 9, 127; FO 141/658/164/19/30, Report of Adelaide Anderson, "Employment of Young Workers in Industrial Occupations in Egypt," April 1930; Butler Report, pp. 13, 26. A law prohibiting the employment of children below the age of nine in certain industries and requiring factory inspections was widely acknowledged to be completely ineffective; see Chapter VI.

46 Formation of the Working Class

tual aid. But their position was only relatively better, always precarious, and still below the standards of a decent existence.

The onset of the economic depression of the 1930s exacerbated this deplorable state of affairs by causing widespread unemployment as well as wage cuts. The persistent agrarian crisis, compounded by a high birth rate, led peasants in massive numbers to migrate to the cities in search of work: while Egypt's total population grew by 25 percent between 1917 and 1937, the population of Cairo grew by 66 percent (to 1.3 million) and that of Alexandria by 55 percent (to 686,000). Indeed, the total population of the twenty largest cities grew by 55 percent, and by 1927, 34 percent of the population of Cairo had been born elsewhere in Egypt.[32]

Industrial employment in large, modern enterprises therefore continued to be a very new experience for most workers, especially for newly recruited peasants, and only a minority of them had grown accustomed to it, had been compelled to accept it as their lot, or had sought ways of improving conditions within the new industrial framework. Although the strength of the working class and of the labor movement was gradually shifting in the direction of mechanized factory production, especially textiles, the petty bourgeois and peasant presence in the working class and the ethos it bore with it remained quite strong well into the 1930s. The existence of a large reserve of unemployed peasants, their lack of prior industrial experience, and their limited commitment to industrial life were real and strong barriers to effective organization and activism by workers. Large employers were not unaware of this, and sometimes took advantage of the steady influx of peasants to hinder the emergence of a conscious and organized work force capable of making demands.

These factors meant that a cohesive and experienced working class was slow to emerge, even at the largest and most modern industrial complexes such as those of Misr at Mahalla, Kafr al-Dawwar, and elsewhere, because the work force through the 1940s might be largely composed of peasants with only a few months or years of industrial experience. For many of these peasants, factory employment was a short-term way of earning a living that might be given up when other opportunities presented themselves, and for this reason they were less likely to engage in sustained, organized industrial action. Whereas the weight of experienced production workers in the working class and their participation in industrial conflict was on the rise by the 1930s, they would only come to play a central role during the

32. Issawi, *Egypt*, p. 60; Janet Abu Lughod, *Cairo: 1001 Years of the City Victorious* (Princeton, 1971), pp. 125–29.

Formation of the Working Class **47**

following decade. After four decades the working class as a whole was still quite heterogenous in its origin and composition, still rooted in other forms of production, and still struggling to develop its own identity and vision of society. Yet, as we will see in Chapter III, this emerging class and the labor movement to which it gave birth at the beginning of the twentieth century had already experienced and been shaped by a long history of industrial and political struggle.

Chapter III

The Emergence of Labor Activism, 1899–1914

Egyptian workers were making use of the strike as least as early as 1882, but substantial and sustained labor activism culminating in the formation of trade unions began only at the turn of the century. There were certainly instances of industrial conflict in the intervening period, but none of them seem to have involved large concentrations of permanently-employed workers in a major urban center, or to have produced any form of ongoing labor organization.[1] However, the period of economic expansion that began in the mid-1890s and gathered momentum after the Anglo-French *entente cordiale* of 1904 created new conditions that spurred labor activism. Whereas the first decade of the British occupation had been characterized by a more or less constant state of fiscal instability and little foreign investment, the subsequent decade and a half saw a great influx of foreign capital. The paid-up capital of companies operating only in Egypt rose from £E 7,326,000 in 1892 to £E 26,280,000 in 1902, then to £E 87,176,000 in 1907—almost all of it raised abroad.[2] Most of this capital flowed into mortgage and land companies as well as commercial enterprises, but

---

1. Muhammad Farid, later the leader of the Nationalist party, recorded the occurrence in April 1894 of a strike for higher wages by "wheat transport workers" (*'ummal naql al-qamh*) at Port Said; see 'Abbas, *al-Haraka*, p. 49. There was another strike that same year by European workers on the dredges and "bateaux-porteur" of the Suez Canal Company. Employed seasonally through a contractor, the strikers demanded a guarantee of ten months' work a year. The strike failed and its leaders were deported, but the Company's chief engineer was subsequently assassinated outside his home in Isma'iliyya, presumably as an act of revenge. See Charles-Roux, *L'Isthme*, pp. 258–60. Other conflicts of the period probably went unrecorded or have not yet come to light.
2. Arthur E. Crouchley, *The Economic Development of Egypt* (London, 1938), pp. 179–80.

Labor Activism, 1899–1914   **49**

some part of it financed expansion in the country's industrial and transport sectors. By 1911 industry and transport (excluding the Suez Canal Company) accounted for over 10 percent of the capital of all Egyptian joint-stock companies.[3] A growing stream of foreigners entered the country attracted by the opportunities offered by Egypt's political stability and apparent prosperity, and some of them joined the ranks of the emerging working class.

The economic boom created a wave of inflation, however, which was perhaps exacerbated by the fact that the expanded cultivation of cotton and rapid population growth forced Egypt to become a net importer of foodstuffs. Reliable indices of prices are nonexistent for this period, but a contemporary study estimated that food prices rose from 1 to 1.8 between 1882 and 1907, while rents rose from 1 to 2.5, with most of the increases occurring in the period after 1900.[4] In some industries, such as construction, wages rose as well, without any apparent evidence of industrial conflict.[5] In general, however, wages failed to keep up with prices, and the resulting drop in real wages became a persistent source of working class grievance as the cost of living climbed steadily. In these circumstances many workers were compelled to seek some means of defending their already meager standard of living, and some form of organization, mutual aid, and collective action was the logical solution. It was the skilled cigarette workers, predominantly Greeks, who first followed this path at the turn of the century, and set an example that would be quickly emulated by others. An examination of the specific situation that prevailed in the cigarette industry and of the forms of activism in which these workers engaged can shed light on the origins and characteristics of the embryonic labor movement in Egypt.

Cigarette Workers: An Embattled Elite

The Egyptian cigarette industry was originally established by Greek entrepreneurs who transferred their businesses from Istanbul after the establishment of an Ottoman state tobacco monopoly in 1875. The industry soon flourished, even though the raw tobacco used in cigarette production had to be imported: the Egyptian government had outlawed its cultivation in 1890 to benefit from the customs revenue.

3. Owen, The Middle East, p. 236.
4. Yacoub Artin, Essai sur les causes du renchérissement de la vie matérielle au Caire dans le courant du XIXe siècle (1800 à 1907) (Cairo, 1907), p. 131. Cromer also reported in 1904 that the cost of living had risen substantially; see Great Britain, 1904 Report, p. 62.
5. See Legrand, Les Fluctuations, p. 29, and AS 1914, pp. 376ff.

50 Labor Activism, 1899–1914

At the turn of the century, the cigarette industry consisted of two branches: the companies producing for export (which accounted for half of the country's output), and those producing for local consumption.

The export market had been undergoing rapid expansion since 1895. Exports of Egyptian cigarettes, which at that time enjoyed an international reputation for quality, rose from 230,000 kilograms in 1895, to 446,861 in 1900, and 702,813 in 1905. Production for export was dominated by five large, Greek-owned firms that together employed some 2,200 workers and accounted for nearly 80 percent of the business. With the exception of one French-owned company located in Alexandria, the export-oriented firms were all based in Cairo. By contrast, the branch of the cigarette industry producing for the local market was dominated by Armenian firms (Matossian foremost among them), though a few Greek houses, the English-owned firm of Maspero Frères Limited, a Belgian company, and numerous small firms also flourished, and experienced a moderate expansion at the turn of the century.[6]

In this period the cigarette industry had the largest concentrations of workers engaged in the actual production of commodities. The work force within each factory, some of which employed several hundred workers, was stratified along craft lines determined by the division of labor prevailing in the manufacturing process. The best paid and most highly skilled workers in the industry were those who rolled individual cigarettes by hand and were paid by the piece, though there were relatively few of them in each factory because employers increasingly preferred to divide the labor process further by employing "macaronistes" to roll the paper tubes into which other skilled workers stuffed the tobacco. Below this elite of rollers, composed mainly of Greeks but also including some Armenians, Syrians, and even a few Egyptians, stood the rest of the work force: quality control inspectors, cutting machine operators, packers, and at the bottom, the sorters (most of them Egyptian women) who sorted the tobacco leaves according to grade.[7]

Exactly when the mainly foreign cigarette rollers began to organize themselves and press for higher wages, shorter hours, and better conditions is uncertain. But there must have been a considerable degree of agitation and informal organization among the rollers of Cairo at the very end of the 1890s, because the refusal of several of the large

6. On the Egyptian cigarette industry, see Roger Owen, *Cotton and the Egyptian Economy, 1820–1914* (London, 1969), p. 158; Athanase G. Politis, *L'Hellénisme et l'Égypte moderne* (Paris, 1930), II, pp. 330ff; Vallet, *Contribution*, p. 96.
7. Vallet, *Contribution*, pp. 96–100.

Labor Activism, 1899–1914   **51**

employers to grant wage increases to their workers led to a sudden, coordinated, and apparently widespread strike in December 1899 spearheaded by the Greek rollers. Deprived of the labor of those who performed the most highly-skilled and crucial segment of the production process, many cigarette factories were forced to shut down. Some of the manufacturers sought to resume production using Egyptian strikebreakers, a tactic to which the workers responded by demonstrating en masse outside the factories and parading through the streets of Cairo in a bid for public sympathy. The strikers were able to hold out until their employers' inventories were depleted, and the latter were forced to enter negotiations (mediated by the Greek consul) and make significant concessions. Ultimately a settlement was reached, and the strike ended on February 21, 1900.[8]

While it is clear from their conduct during the strike that the cigarette workers from different factories must have been coordinating their common struggle, negotiations on the exact terms of the final settlement were carried on separately between each employer and his employees. One result of the strike was that there emerged a craft association of Cairo cigarette rollers, nominally led by a Greek physician, though it played no effective role and was apparently defunct by 1902. There are some indications that the association was undermined and ultimately destroyed by the companies' harassment. The role of the Egyptian workers employed in the struck plants is not entirely clear. In general it would seem that this strike was largely a struggle between Greek craft workers and Greek capitalists, an instance of class conflict within the Greek community in Egypt. The skilled Greek cigarette rollers who fomented and led the strike may well have come to Egypt with some knowledge of, or even direct experience with, trade unionism. Presumably literate, they would also probably have had access to up-to-date information about labor, syndicalist, and socialist movements in their homeland and elsewhere.[9] Given their superior status and power in the work place and their experience of labor activism, they were best suited to take the lead in initiating struggles for higher wages as well as shorter hours and better working conditions.

The first strike the Greeks organized (December 1899–February 1900) had taken the factory owners by surprise, won considerable

---

8. *Ibid.*, p. 101; 'Abbas, *al-Haraka*, p. 50ff; *al-Muqattam*, February 6, 1900; Badaoui, *Problèmes*, p. 21.

9. That there were radical currents already present within the foreign communities in Egypt is shown by the existence in Alexandria of an anarchist newspaper and a "people's free university" run by Italian radicals for their compatriots as early as 1901. See Berque, *Egypt*, p. 241.

52 Labor Activism, 1899–1914

public support, and culminated in victory, but further gains were to be much more difficult. The Cairo cigarette rollers went on strike for a second time at the very end of 1903, but this time the stoppage was preceded by lengthy negotiations so that the employers were far better prepared than four years earlier. Determined to reverse the gains the workers had won, the owners not only rejected demands for higher wages and the removal of despotic foremen, but also declared a general cut in wages. The resulting strike was long and bitter, and led to considerable violence as the employers managed to keep production going with the help of the police. Many of the Egyptian and Syrian workers did not join the strike, and were eventually quartered inside the factories for their protection. The militant Greek workers were isolated, the strike was broken, and with the approval of the Greek consul, some of the strike leaders were arrested, tried, and deported. The owners then imposed a uniform and lower wage rate that prevailed for some years thereafter.[10]

This defeat apparently demonstrated to the workers the urgent need for a strong and permanent organization of cigarette workers. A union did emerge at the Matossian factory but remained weak for several years. In October 1908, however, after a brief and unsuccessful strike in Cairo, this union became the core of a new and broader grouping, the Ligue Internationale des Ouvriers Cigarettiers et Papetiers du Caire. The use of the term "international" in the union's name indicated that it was open to workers of all nationalities, Egyptians as well as foreigners, and apparently included production workers other than the skilled rollers. In 1910 the Matossian union had some 200 members, the Cairo union over 1,500; the latter even had a mutual aid fund supported by a proportion of the members' dues of 5 piastres a month.[11] The establishment of these relatively stable and popular organizations was spurred by the fact that the cigarette rollers were faced with a grave new threat not only to their wages but to their very jobs.

The series of strikes that began in 1899 made the cigarette factory owners much more attentive to ways of reducing the rollers' control of the labor process, and hence their own vulnerability to stoppages, as well as their wage bills. One way of limiting the rollers' autonomy

10. 'Izz al-Din I, pp. 64–66; Vallet, Contribution, p. 102. There were also several smaller and less significant strikes by cigarette workers in these years in Alexandria as well as Cairo.
11. Vallet, Contribution, pp. 142–43; Badaoui, Problèmes, p. 21. The term "mixed" was used in the same sense as "international." On the emergence of the cigarette workers' union, see also the account given by the prominent trade unionist Sayyid Qandil, in his memoirs Niqabiyyati: al-risala al-'ummaliyya al-'ula (Cairo, 1938).

and power and raising productivity was to further divide their work into its component parts. This was accomplished by gradually replacing the hand roller with two somewhat less-skilled workers (a "macaroniste" and a paper tube stuffer) for all but the finest grades of cigarettes. The decline of the export market after 1905 strengthened the manufacturers' incentive to cut costs. New protective tariffs on some of the most important foreign markets, a flood of imitations fraudulently sold abroad as Egyptian cigarettes (which damaged the reputation of the authentic product), the Egyptian government's lack of support for export sales—these factors all contributed to a decline in exports from a 1905 high of over 700,000 kilograms to an annual average of just 487,171 kilograms between 1907 and 1913.[12] These changes prompted some of the export-oriented firms to move into the domestic market, thereby sharpening competition throughout the industry.

These market pressures as well as the threat of labor militancy in an industry highly vulnerable to paralysis by a small number of skilled workers stimulated an interest in mechanization. The introduction of cigarette rolling machines imported from the United States began on a small scale after 1905. These machines could produce cigarettes in greater numbers and at a lower cost than skilled rollers, and could be operated by semi-skilled workers, though the high initial costs, the uncertainty of consumer preferences, and worker resistance all slowed mechanization, and only after the First World War was mechanization fully implemented. Until that time the threat mechanization posed stimulated workers to organize in defense of jobs, though organization had already begun as a response to adverse economic conditions and workplace grievances.

The early history of labor activism among the cigarette workers can be taken as typical of this stage in the history of the Egyptian labor movement as a whole. The years from 1899 to 1907 witnessed the emergence of labor militancy and organization among several groups of skilled, mainly foreign workers. Apart from the Cairo, and later Alexandria, cigarette rollers, the groups that organized themselves in this period included workers in the garment industry, printing workers, metal workers, barbers, and lawyers' clerks. The organizations these workers created were usually small craft unions, generally known (after French usage) as "associations" or "leagues." The presidency of these unions was sometimes conferred on sympathetic notables prominent in the workers' ethnic community. This was particularly true of the Greeks, who chose Dr. Kyriazi to lead the first

12. Politis, *L'Hellénisme*, pp. 339–41.

54 Labor Activism, 1899–1914

cigarette rollers' union and Dr. Pastis to lead the clothing workers, and may well have been a way of enhancing the respectability of, and thereby winning broader support for, the new unions. Mutual aid was a very important function of these unions, and particularly for new immigrants often crucial. The unions may also have had a social function, providing a framework in which workers could gather outside the purview of the wealthy and powerful. A sense of labor solidarity beyond the narrow confines of their crafts was however also present. For example, when the garment workers (among them some Egyptians) struck in November 1901 for a higher piece rate, a large meeting was held in their support at a Cairo cafe. The agenda included a speech by the president of the cigarette rollers' union on the reciprocal rights and obligations of workers and employers, a reading of the workers' demands in Italian, Greek, Arabic, Hebrew, and Austrian [sic], and a nighttime march through the streets of Cairo by some 3,000 chanting workers.[13]

Relations between the foreign workers, their craft unions, and Egyptian workers were not always friendly in this period. In some cases, as in the garment workers' strike just referred to, foreign and Egyptian workers cooperated in struggles at the workplace and in the new labor organizations. In other cases, as in the Cairo cigarette rollers' strike of 1903–1904, Egyptians were used as strikebreakers, and incurred the hostility of the militant foreign workers. Of course, specific circumstances determined what action might be deemed appropriate by Egyptian workers. They often shared the grievances of their foreign co-workers about problems such as low wages, long hours, and oppressive supervisors, and so possessed the basis for solidarity across ethnic lines. At the same time, the foreign workers were usually privileged by comparison with the indigenous workers: they monopolized the better jobs, enjoyed higher wages and better benefits, and often displayed an attitude of superiority and contempt toward the natives. With their own grievances ignored or neglected and often discouraged or even prohibited from joining the craft unions, Egyptian workers sometimes opted for loyalty toward employers who could skillfully manipulate tensions among the workers rooted in real positional differences within the workplace. The potential costs of militant action were also higher for Egyptians than foreigners: a Greek strike leader might be deported, but an Egyptian would face a

13. *al-Muqattam*, November 5, 1901, in 'Izz al-Din I, pp. 69–72. It is possible that what the correspondent took for either Hebrew or "Austrian" (*nimsawiyya*) was in fact Yiddish, spoken by many Jews newly arrived from Eastern Europe.

Labor Activism, 1899–1914   **55**

heavy fine, perhaps imprisonment, and have a much harder time finding another job.

At the same time, it was not uncommon for the foreign worker, who shared bonds of religion, nationality, language and legal status with the employer, to turn his back on the demands of his Egyptian co-workers in order to protect his privileged position. Indeed, it is likely that in certain cases it was the desire of foreign workers to protect their jobs and wages by excluding cheaper Egyptian labor from their trades that stimulated unionization. The stratification of the labor force along ethnic lines and the superior status enjoyed by the foreign workers, as well as the inexperience of many Egyptian workers new to industry and industrial conflict, thus hindered cooperation between indigenous and foreign workers. It was therefore the latter who, as a result of these factors as well as of their greater experience, literacy and resources, played in these years the leading role in industrial conflict and the organization of the first trade unions in Egypt.

At first these new phenomena were seen by many members of the upper and middle classes in Egypt as deleterious and alien, as imports from Europe. "This European disease has spread to Egypt," wrote the future nationalist leader Muhammad Farid of an early strike, implying that class conflict was an avoidable malady afflicting an essentially stable and cohesive social order, rather than a manifestation of tensions inherent in capitalist industrialism.[14] This view was to prove very influential and persistent over the following decades, and only slowly and painfully did an awareness emerge that a distinct working class with its own interests and demands was in the process of formation.

The Arabic terms used to denote the new phenomena were at first not specific to labor. *Jam'iyya* was used for the early trade unions, a direct translation of the foreign terms "association" and "league." For "strike," early accounts used the term *i'tisab*, from a root connoting tying or wrapping, and by extension, banding together: the workers had formed a cohesive group and stopped work. Only in the 1920s did *idrab*, the standard term today and intrinsically closer to our own "strike," come into general use. By contrast, *jam'iyya* was replaced by another term considerably earlier, reflecting the dramatic entrance of Egyptian workers and their organizations onto the scene.

Despite the clear preeminence of skilled foreign workers, of course, Egyptian workers had not been entirely invisible in the early years of the twentieth century. There had been several episodes of unrest, and

14. 'Abbas, *al-Haraka*, p. 49.

56 Labor Activism, 1899–1914

even strikes, by unskilled Egyptian workers: the Alexandria coal-heavers in 1900, the Port Said coalheavers in 1907, sugar mill workers and others. However, none of these more or less spontaneous explosions by peasant workers (followed by lengthy periods of quiescence) resulted in the formation of unions or other organizations. Of the more skilled and permanent Egyptian workers employed in large enterprises, only the telegraphists and the Alexandria tramwaymen were active in this period. The former, government employees suffering inflationary pressures on their already low wages and discontented about their long hours, agitated for relief in the fall of 1903, and later went on strike.[15] The tramwaymen were one of the first groups of indigenous workers to engage in sustained collective action because they were both highly-concentrated and directly experienced the consequences of colonial domination in the workplace. These circumstances reflected the uneven nature of capitalist development in Egypt and its differential impact on various segments of the working class. Several years were to pass before other Egyptian workers would emulate the example of the cigarette rollers and other activist foreign workers by organizing themselves and confronting their employers.

This relatively short delay is not really surprising. The factors that enabled foreign workers to engage in struggles with their employers with some likelihood of success have already been noted: they were simply better placed and better equipped, at least initially, to take the lead. In addition, most Egyptians even in the largest and most modern industrial enterprises were very new recruits to the working class with little or no experience of this new mode of life and labor. However oppressive these workers soon felt their new situation to be, they were nonetheless usually better off than their compatriots employed in the craft industries, the petty trades, or agriculture. The fear of losing their new jobs, apathy born of oppression and poverty, illiteracy, the daily grind required merely to survive and support their families, an understandable lack of trust in fellow workers who were still strangers because they were drawn from diverse strata and locales—all these factors worked against the development of a sense of common interests and a capacity for joint struggle. Inevitably, however, like other workers thrown together in the same workplace, confronting the same working conditions, feeling the same grievances, and taught to act in common by the collective character of the production process and the failure of individual efforts, some Egyptian workers soon assimilated and adapted models of activism and organization

15. See Great Britain, *1904 Report*, Enclosure no. 5, pp. 103–104.

first employed by foreign workers. The first major group to accomplish this were the tramway workers of Cairo, who for much of the following three decades would play a leading role in the Egyptian working class and labor movement.

The Tramway Workers of Cairo

In 1894 the Egyptian government granted Baron Edouard Empain of the Société Générale des Chemins de Fer Économiques a concession to build and operate a tramway system in Cairo. This Belgian company operated the Metropolitain of Paris as well as the tramway systems of Geneva, Marseilles, and Naples. The first sections of the new system, operating as the Société des Tramways du Caire (Cairo Tramway Company, henceforth CTC) began to function two years later. By 1914 it had over sixty-three kilometers of track and 498 tramcars in service, and was carrying some fifty-three million passengers a year.[16] The tram system had a profound impact on the city because it sharply reduced travel time within Cairo and allowed easy access to, and the development of, areas outside the old central city.

The CTC employed over 2,000 workers in the first decade of the twentieth century, most of them tramway drivers and conductors. Although there had been a brief and unsuccessful strike in 1900 by workers operating the Alexandria and suburban Ramleh tram lines, the Cairo tramwaymen were not heard from before the summer of 1908. Then we see that the demands raised by the Alexandria strikers—a shorter workday and higher wages, but also the opening of the better-paid jobs to Egyptians and an end to abusive treatment of Egyptian workers by foreign inspectors and supervisors—certainly reflected the concerns felt by the Cairo tramway workers. Inflation had caused a drop in the real wages of the tramwaymen, and though the economic boom had come to an abrupt end with the crash of 1907, prices remained high. Like many other workers, these too worked a twelve-hour day, and received no paid vacations, sick pay, compensation for accidents, or other benefits.

Just as important as these economic grievances, however, was the resentment Egyptians felt about their subordinate status in the workplace. Whereas the drivers and conductors were usually Egyptians, the inspectors were generally foreigners, mainly Greeks and Italians, and held great power over the workers: the inspectors could arbitrarily impose fines or other disciplinary sanctions against which the

16. Émile Boulad, *Les Tramways du Caire en 1919* (Cairo, 1919), p. 2; *AS 1916*, pp. 208–209; Abu Lughod, *Cairo*, pp. 132–39.

58 Labor Activism, 1899–1914

worker had no right of defense or appeal. These fines could amount to a significant portion of the worker's wages, which were only about eight piastres a day. Petty tyranny and verbal abuse by the inspectors must have been frequent causes for grievance, as a contemporary foreign observer noted:

> It must be admitted that the men are not infrequently subjected to undeserved abuse on the part of inspectors. . . . When, then, they are subjected to unnecessary and undeserved abuse by an inspector in the full hearing of every passenger on the tram they must feel that life is not worth the living. A specific case came under my notice recently. I had travelled from Opera Square to Abbassia on a tram car, and certainly upon this occasion the conductor was lacking neither in zeal nor in energy in the performance of his duties. At a certain corner of the line the guide left the overhead wires and the tram of course stopped. An inspector—presumably an Italian—was at hand and in shouting orders, he confused the conductor who was doing all he could to replace the guide as quickly as possible, with the result that he let the rope go at the wrong moment. The language which the inspector hurled at the unfortunate man was such as is fortunately not often heard in our streets, donkey, pig, and gammous [water buffalo] being the least of the epithets applied. The conductor was silent for some minutes but eventually he could stand it no longer and he returned the abuse with interest. And not only this, for the rest of the time that I was on the car he made no further attempt to collect fares; he stood the picture of misery on the footboard thinking the matter over.[17]

At the same time, the tram company discriminated against Egyptians in promotions so that it was rare for them to become inspectors or skilled workshop workers themselves.

These grievances surfaced in a rising tide of unrest in the summer of 1908, and were reflected in a flurry of articles and letters in the local press, especially the nationalist newspapers, on the plight of the Cairo tramwaymen.[18] By the fall the more militant workers among the drivers and conductors had begun to organize, formulate demands, and seek public support. Workers dismissed for their role in the agitation played a key role in carrying on the struggle. In early October the first open meetings of tram workers were held, and on October 13,

17. *EG*, October 20, 1908.
18. See Belgium, MAE, J. de Villenfaquy to Davignon (Minister of Foreign Affairs), October 24, 1908, hereafter cited as the Villenfaquy Report.

Labor Activism, 1899–1914   **59**

1908, a group of drivers and conductors sent a letter to the Cairo manager of the CTC (whose head offices were in Brussels) and to the press, listing their demands and threatening a strike. The demands including the following:

> (1) the eight-hour day; (2) a 40 percent increase in wages, so that even after the deduction of fines a worker would earn enough to support his family; (3) a choice of a month's vacation per year or a month's extra pay; (4) inspectors should be prohibited from hitting, humiliating or abusing workers; (5) the reinstatement of workers unjustly fired; (6) the establishment of a committee, composed of equal numbers of worker and company representatives, to investigate alleged infractions of work rules, decide on penalties and determine compensation for accidents at work; (7) the payment of half of all fines into a fund for the workers' benefit and of the rest as bonuses to outstanding workers; (8) no dismissals without good cause, and a month's severance pay when justified; (9) the provision of work uniforms at company expense; (10) the removal from their posts of several disliked company employees.[19]

This comprehensive list of demands reflected the core grievances not only of the Cairo tramwaymen but of many groups of Egyptian workers employed in large, foreign-run enterprises. These workers sought to defend, and if possible improve, their standard of living while reducing the length of the workday. At the same time, however, they demanded that they be treated with dignity and respect by their superiors, and to realize this sought to impose restrictions on the absolute power of management in the workplace. A joint labor-management committee was to investigate and rule on alleged violations of work rules, protect workers from arbitrary harassment and thereby considerably enhance their own power in the workplace. Empowering this same committee to set compensation for accidents would, it was hoped, compel the company to take financial responsibility for its employees when they were killed or injured at work. The Cairo tramwaymen were the group of Egyptian workers best-suited to take the lead in struggling for these demands primarily because they constituted the largest concentration of indigenous workers employed by a privately owned enterprise located in a major urban center. By 1908 many of the tram workers had considerable experience on the job, and had been able to watch the emergence of activism and organization among foreign workers. Finally, the tramwaymen operated the

19. *al-Mu'ayyad*, October 18, 1908; 'Izz al-Din I, pp. 85–87.

60 Labor Activism, 1899–1914

mass transit system of Egypt's capital, and this gave them considerable leverage to compel not only the CTC but also the central government to respond favorably to their demands.

The letter containing these demands was not signed by the workers themselves but by a lawyer of Lebanese Christian origin named George Sidawi, acting as president of the "Committee to Defend the Workers' Rights." The choice of a sympathetic middle-class individual to represent the workers preserved the anonymity of the militant tramwaymen and protected them from company harassment. It also meant that negotiations on the workers' behalf would be carried out by someone who possessed not only the skills and education to do an effective job, but also the social status to deal directly with company and government officials as an equal.[20] The Cairo Tramway Company, however, refused to negotiate with Sidawi, who it claimed did not really represent the workers. The company declared that if the latter were discontented, they should deal directly with management. The efforts of officials at the Governorate of Cairo to mediate failed: company officials claimed they had to consult with Brussels, whereas the workers demanded a response within twenty-four hours. As the strike deadline approached, the police called in reinforcements, and the CTC recruited strikebreakers. On Saturday night, October 17, the drivers and conductors met and agreed to strike the following morning.[21]

The strike was initially quite successful; some 1,600 workers participated. The few hundred who did not join were largely inspectors or mechanics in the repair shops. The strikers gathered very early in the morning, and lay down in large numbers on the tracks in front of the tram depots in Bulaq, Shubra, 'Abbasiyya, and Giza, effectively blocking the efforts of employees loyal to the company to drive the cars out onto the street. When the police dispersed them, the workers simply lay down at other places along the tracks. The first day of the strike passed peacefully with the exception of the arrest of several workers who tried to sabotage electric lines near Bulaq, and many strikers spent that night as well as the following night sleeping on the tracks, joined in some cases by their families. On the following day, Monday, the CTC was able to run a few cars on some lines, but it was clear that the strike was solid and would not soon die a natural death.

20. Villenfaquy Report; *EG*, October 19, 1908.
21. *al-Mu'ayyad*, October 17–18, 1908; *EG*, October 17, 1908. The same Belgian capitalists who owned the Cairo tramway system also owned the tram system that served the new Cairo suburb of Heliopolis, which they had developed. The Heliopolis tram workers, always close to their colleagues in Cairo proper, apparently participated in the agitation and the strike that ensued.

Much of the press sympathized with the workers, despite the inconvenience they were causing the public, and funds were collected on their behalf. Announcing that any worker who did not report to work would be fired, the CTC and the police decided on harsher measures. On Tuesday, October 20, mounted police under Mansfield Pasha, police commandant of Cairo, charged the strikers at Bulaq to clear the tracks; many were injured and arrested. At Giza, fire hoses were used to disperse the workers. These measures succeeded: threatened with dismissal and the full force of police power, with many of their leaders arrested and the Bayram holiday approaching, the strikers began to return to work on Wednesday the 21st. The company promised to consider their demands seriously, and took most of them back with the exception of those identified as militants, and those detained by the police.[22]

Although the CTC was able to break the strike with the help of the police, it had been evident early on that some concessions would have to be made to conciliate the disaffected workers and forestall future strife. Late in October management unilaterally reduced the workday to ten hours, raised the starting wage to 10.5 piastres and the maximum to 14 piastres (after eight years' service), agreed to pay compensation to injured employees, took back all the strikers, and made several other less significant concessions. Management avoided, however, making any concessions that might have entailed the dilution of its direct and absolute control over the work force such as the creation of a joint labor-management grievance committee, or recognition of Sidawi as a negotiating partner. "Certainly it is necessary to make concessions," an official at the Belgian Consulate in Cairo, which had monitored events closely and pressured the British authorities to support the CTC fully, wrote shortly after the strike ended; "but it is a great achievement to have excluded from the talks the dismissed workers, M. Sidawi and everyone outside the company."[23]

With this strike Egyptian workers made their first major appearance as independent actors on the industrial scene, and the event had a considerable public impact.[24] As had been the case with the cigarette workers and others, formal organization followed, rather than preceded, a major strike or surge of unrest. Therefore, it was only on March 8, 1909, that the Cairo tramway drivers and conductors established a union. Membership was apparently open to all tramway

22. al-Mu'ayyad, October 19–23, 1908; EG, October 19–23, 1908; Villenfaquy Report.
23. Villenfaquy Report.
24. For a survey of the attitude of the Egyptian press toward the strike see al-Nukhayli, al-Haraka, pp. 23–28.

62 Labor Activism, 1899–1914

workers regardless of nationality, at least in principle, but given the ethnic composition of the traction department, the union must have largely if not entirely consisted of Egyptians. The early emergence of close links between the nationalist and labor movements will be discussed later, though it should be noted here that Nationalist party leaders supported the establishment of the tramwaymen's union and some of them became directly involved in its leadership. These included the lawyer 'Umar Bey Lutfi, founder of the cooperative movement in Egypt, and his brother Ahmad Bey Lutfi, also a lawyer and from 1909 vice-president of the Nationalist party, as well as George Sidawi.[25] It seems however that the union never really got off the ground, and a foreign observer wrote two years later that because of threats of dismissal and other forms of harassment by the CTC the organization existed only on paper.[26]

Although the tram workers still found it difficult to form a strong, stable union, they were nonetheless willing and able to fight for their demands in the course of the next few years. In November 1910 the predominantly foreign workers at the tramway repair shops, led by militant Italians, struck for the ten-hour day (already achieved by the traction workers) and for higher wages. They were unsuccessful, but the defeat apparently taught them that they could not win on their own and that unity with the drivers and conductors was essential.[27] Thus when agitation again boiled over in the summer of 1911, the CTC confronted a united and determined work force for the first time. The issues that fueled the workers' militancy were similar to those of 1908, but the demands went considerably further and included a nine-hour workday, higher wages with double pay for overtime, a paid day off every ten days, full pay while sick, an end to harassment by foremen, the abolition of fines, the provision of work uniforms at company expense, and permanent status after one month's probation. In order to discourage the company from dismissing workers, as well as to cushion the often catastrophic impact of unemployment, the tramwaymen also demanded that any worker who had lost his job be entitled to one month's severance pay for each year of service, and that disputes over dismissals be referred to a judge for arbitration.[28] This last demand was intended to draw the state into the arena of labor-management relations. Given their weakness relative to their em-

25. Badaoui, *Problèmes*, p. 22; Salama Musa, "Harakat al-'ummal fi misr," *al-Majalla al-jadida* (February 1935), p. 21; 'Izz al-Din I, p. 120.
26. Vallet, *Contribution*, p. 143.
27. EG, November 3–5, 1910.
28. Belgium, MAE, Charles de Royer to Davignon, August 7, 1911 (hereafter Royer Report); EG, July 24, 1911.

Labor Activism, 1899–1914 **63**

ployer, the workers felt that it could only be to their advantage to involve this powerful outside party, sensitive to public opinion and political pressures, anxious to avoid any disruption of public order, and capable of compelling the CTC to make concessions.

The Egyptian government had of course already involved itself in the conflict between the tramwaymen and the CTC in 1908, first by trying to mediate, then by sending in the police to break the strike. Three years later state intervention took place at a higher level when M. de Lancker, the Cairo director of the company, again refused—despite anxious appeals from both British and Belgian consular officials to avoid a strike—to hold direct talks with the workers' legal counsel, Ahmad Lutfi and a Maltese lawyer named Gresh Mifsud. Prime Minister Muhammad Sa'id Pasha agreed to mediate, and a number of meetings were subsequently convened in Alexandria (the summer seat of the Egyptian government) in which CTC officials negotiated with a delegation of Cairo tramwaymen (including Egyptian, Italian, Greek, Austrian, and Armenian workers) and their lawyers. These talks were unsuccessful because the company was unwilling to concede the workers' key demands on a shorter workday, paid sick leave, and perhaps most important of all, severance pay. The workers believed that only a strong financial disincentive could dissuade the company from arbitrary or punitive dismissals. Management was of course well aware of the danger this demand posed to its control over the work force. "The Company would never again be master of its employees," a Belgian consular official warned Brussels, "who after spending several years in its service would get themselves fired in order to receive this indemnity, which after a few years at the Company would amount to what is for them a small fortune."[29]

The threatened strike began on the morning of Sunday, July 31, 1911, with the participation of nearly all the company's employees. During the first three days of the strike the CTC made no effort to run tram cars, and there was no violence. The strikers camped peacefully outside the depots, keeping in touch with each other by means of bicycle messengers, and organized processions through Cairo to publicize their cause and solicit donations. The latter were given profusely (in one day over £E 600 was collected) and the public was, as one newspaper put it, "astonished at the appearance of complete unity among the tramway workers despite their different nationalities and their large numbers."[30] But as the days passed, British officials became increasingly concerned about the strike, fearing it might take on

29. Belgium, MAE, van Grootnen to Davignon, October 24, 1911.
30. *al-'Alam*, August 1, 1911. See also *EG*, July 27–August 2, 1911.

64 Labor Activism, 1899–1914

a political character given public sympathy and the Nationalist party's active support. It was therefore deemed necessary to break the strike as a warning for the future. The CTC began to run cars on August 2 under heavy police protection which led to escalating clashes between strikers and the police, the sabotage of tram equipment, and the use of fire hoses against crowds of strikers. As in 1908 the massive intervention of the police proved decisive: after more than two days of often violent resistance the tramwaymen decided to accept the company's final offer, and returned to work. Nearly all the strikers were reinstated with the exception of a few militant Italian and Greek inspectors. Eleven workers were convicted of assaulting policemen or damaging tram cars and were given short prison terms or fines.[31]

While the tramwaymen of Cairo were on strike, unrest was on the rise among the tramway workers of Alexandria. The latter had apparently been inspired by the example of Cairo, and it is also likely that relations between militants from the two cities were established during the repeated visits of the Cairo negotiating team to Alexandria in late July. After negotiations failed, workers on the Alexandria and suburban Ramleh tramway lines struck on August 7. The strike was quite brief (only the militant Armenian workers remained on strike for more than a day and even they returned to work soon thereafter), but it led to a settlement which won the tramwaymen far-reaching concessions. The agreement reduced the workday to nine hours in Alexandria and eight in Ramleh, provided for one day off at half pay every fortnight, guaranteed a half month's severance pay for each year of service, and allowed the workers to form a union.[32]

After a brief, disunited, and unsuccessful strike, the Alexandria tramwaymen had been able to make gains that were in many respects much greater than anything their counterparts in Cairo had been able to achieve, despite their solidarity and militancy. The higher proportion of foreigners among the tramway workers as well as among the general population of the port city may have been a factor in this outcome. Alexandria at this time enjoyed a limited but significant degree of municipal self-government in which the city's foreign residents played an important role. This may account for the more flexible labor policy of the local and national authorities and the Alexandria Tramway Company. There was a greater willingness and capacity to respond to the demands of the tram workers, many of them foreigners with strong links to their ethnic communities in the city. Alexandria was in many ways a more "European" city than Cairo which perhaps

31. Royer Report; *EG*, August 3–7, 1911.
32. *EG*, August 2, 7, 1911; 'Izz al-Din I, pp. 108–113; al-Ghazzali, *Ta'rikh*, pp. 47–48.

Labor Activism, 1899–1914 **65**

engendered a somewhat easier recognition of the legitimacy of labor's demands. The capital was by contrast ruled much more directly by the central government. There the British were much more concerned about the strength of nationalist sentiment in a tense political climate, and feared that agitation by a largely Egyptian work force might get out of hand. The directors of the tramway company and the local authorities in Alexandria also had the example of the bloody tramway strike in Cairo to graphically illustrate the costs of taking a hard line and encourage them to be generous with their own workers.

Their defeat in Cairo notwithstanding, the tramway workers had come by 1911 to constitute—along with the railway workshop workers (on whom more below), and the gas and electric workers also active in this period—an elite of sorts among the great mass of Egyptian workers. Before 1908 they had been subject to conditions not unlike those of many semi-skilled indigenous workers. During the subsequent three years they won gains that would be beyond the reach of most Egyptian workers for many years to come. Indeed, they were in certain respects in advance of some of their counterparts in the industrialized countries.[33] These achievements were made possible by the high degree of organization and unity they forged in the course of their struggles, and it was clear that the militant tramwaymen of Cairo had come to the fore as the vanguard, the pace-setter of the Egyptian labor movement. They very quickly developed a strong trade union consciousness, learning from their experiences in the workplace that only unity across craft and ethnic lines and a willingness to struggle offered them some hope of improving their standard of living, winning some measure of job security, and compelling their bosses to treat them with respect and dignity.

The latter two goals were often as important as the first. Higher wages, shorter hours, sick pay, days off, and other economic demands were naturally of vital importance. But the tramwaymen's insistence on the prohibition of abusive and insulting treatment by foremen and inspectors, the abolition of arbitrary punishments, and their right to defend themselves against management's charges indicates the depth of the resentment these workers felt, and the strength of their desire to be treated like human beings. The struggle to end abusive treatment was also bound up with the struggle to enhance the workers' control over the labor process and their power within the workplace. Economic necessity and difficult working conditions certainly moti-

---

33. Until a successful strike in 1919, for example, the Boston carmen worked ten hours a day, seven days a week, with no vacations, holidays, or benefits. See James R. Green and Hugh Carter Donahue, *Boston's Workers: A Labor History* (Boston, 1979), p. 95.

66   Labor Activism, 1899–1914

vated these workers to put themselves on the line and take risks in order to improve their lot and that of their families. But Egypt's subjection to colonial domination, and the impact of that domination on the daily lives of these Egyptians inside and outside the workplace, must also be recognized as factors that moved them to collective action and gave specific political and cultural meaning to their struggles.

The Nationalist Party and the Workers

Labor activism among indigenous workers was almost from the start closely linked to the Egyptian nationalist movement. That movement had been revived in the mid-1890s, after more than a decade of quiescence, by a small group of mainly middle-class activists led by the young orator and publicist Mustafa Kamil and at various times backed by the new khedive 'Abbas Hilmi (1892–1914). These activists pursued a two-pronged strategy. They sought to instill nationalist sentiment among members of the emerging *effendiyya* stratum from which they themselves were drawn: secondary and university students, lawyers, journalists, teachers, government functionaries, and other professionals. Often the sons of urban or rural small or medium property owners, these *effendis* had received an essentially European-style education, dressed in the European manner, and whether employed or self-employed earned their living by mental rather than physical labor. This was the political class from whose ranks the activists of the Egyptian nationalist parties, and later of other political tendencies, were to be drawn for decades to come. The other major focus of nationalist activity was a campaign for public and governmental support abroad, especially in the Ottoman Empire (which until 1914 retained nominal sovereignty over Egypt), and in France, toward which many young nationalists were culturally drawn and which, along with the other European powers, did not recognize the British occupation of Egypt as legitimate. The nationalists' goal was to undermine Britain's position by means of international pressure.

The new nationalist movement initially showed little interest in domestic social issues, except when they could be used to discredit the occupation regime, or in organizing the urban and rural masses. This attitude changed only after 1904, when the Anglo-French *entente cordiale* secured European recognition of Britain's control of Egypt and rendered the nationalists' strategy for winning independence unrealistic. The enormous impact on Egypt of the 1906 incident at Dinshawai, where four villagers were executed and others punished in reprisal for the death of a British officer in an altercation with

Labor Activism, 1899–1914 **67**

local peasants, pointed to an alternative strategy for the movement. It was however only in 1908, after the formal establishment of the Nationalist party (al-Hizb al-Watani), and the sudden death shortly thereafter of Mustafa Kamil, that a new orientation was adopted. Under the leadership of Muhammad Farid efforts were made to build a base among the Egyptian masses which could be mobilized to compel the British to leave the country.[34]

A key component of the new strategy was the development of ties with, and the organization of, urban workers. As early as June 1908 Farid was publicly criticizing the absence of labor legislation in Egypt and the terrible conditions prevailing in many workplaces.[35] The Nationalist party's newspaper *al-Liwa'* vigorously supported labor struggles, especially the 1908 Cairo tramway strike. Later that same year a more concrete step was taken: party activists and members of the Higher Schools Club (Nadi al-Madaris al-'Ulya), founded in 1905 to mobilize advanced students and alumni, set up a network of "people's night schools" (*madaris al-sha'ab al-layliyya*). These schools were the primary means by which the party's educated, middle-class activists were to reach out to the urban working people. By 1909 four schools were functioning in Cairo, and by the following year there were eight in the Cairo area and others in provincial cities. These schools provided instruction in literacy as well as the rudiments of arithmetic, hygiene, history, geography, religion, and ethics. Courses were usually taught by nationalist students from the Cairo schools of law and medicine, or the polytechnic, though senior party leaders also participated and often delivered the regular Friday lectures at which, a foreign observer reported, speakers "exalted the virtues of the Arab race and the advantages of free government."[36]

Several thousand workers and artisans had some connection with these schools in their first two years of operation, and the Nationalist party soon sought to organize this potential base of support. The party had already given active support to the Cairo tramwaymen, and even played a role in the formation of their union, but early in 1909 it went a step further by sponsoring the establishment of the "Manual Trades

34. See Arthur Goldschmidt, Jr., "The Egyptian Nationalist Party," Ph.D. diss., Harvard University, 1968; Mustafa al-Nahhas Jabar Yusuf, *Siyasat al-ihtilal tijah al-haraka al-wataniyya* (Cairo, 1975); 'Abd al-Rahman al-Rafi'i, *Muhammad Farid: ramz al-ikhlas w'al-tadhiyya* (Cairo, 1962: Third Printing).
35. al-Rafi'i, *Farid*, p. 110. The nationalists' agitation around this issue was widely credited with inducing the government to promulgate the 1909 law on child labor mentioned earlier.
36. Vallet, *Contribution*, pp. 153–54; al-Rafi'i, *Farid*, p. 109; Congrès National Égyptien, *Oeuvres du Congrès National Égyptien ténu à Bruxelles le 22, 23, 24 Septembre 1910* (Bruges, 1911).

68 Labor Activism, 1899–1914

Workers' Union" (Niqabat 'Ummal al-Sana'i' al-Yadawiyya (henceforth MTWU) headquartered in Bulaq. Leadership was provided by a group of party leaders, notably 'Umar and Ahmad Lutfi (both of whom were also involved in the tramway workers' union founded at about the same time) and 'Ali Bey Tharwat, the new organization's first president and formerly superintendant of the Mansura industrial school. The leading role of notables was enshrined in the new union's statutes which (like the tramwaymen's union) gave "contributing" members (who paid double the regular monthly dues of five piastres a month) and "honorary" members (who contributed some capital to the organization) ten of the twenty-five seats on the MTWU's executive board. These statutes were reportedly modelled on those of an Italian mutual aid society, and mutual aid was certainly a very important aspect of the union's activities. Dues were pooled into a fund out of which small payments to sick and unemployed members were made. The MTWU also offered its members legal advice, libraries, lectures, and perhaps most important, free medical care donated by physicians sympathetic to the national cause. By far the best known of these was Dr. Mahjub Thabit, a graduate of the medical school of the University of Paris. He had returned to Cairo in 1906 and was the first Egyptian to teach at the Qasr al-'Ayni medical school. Thabit was a very popular figure among the workers, and after the war would play a prominent role in the labor movement.[37]

The establishment of the MTWU seems to have been one of the first occasions on which the term *niqaba* was used to denote a labor organization. The Arabic noun had earlier possessed guild-related connotations, and its adoption for this new nationalist-led organization may have represented an attempt to "Egyptianize" the idea of labor unions by linking it with older, indigenous forms of organization by the urban working people. The MTWU thus made a break with the use of *jam'iyya* which may have been regarded as too imitative of the French *ligue* or *association* and too closely identified with the craft unions recently established by foreign workers. The transition from one usage to another (*niqaba* would gradually become the standard term for trade union) would seem to have reflected the assumption, from 1908 onwards, of the leading role in industrial conflict by indigenous rather than foreign workers. However, *niqaba* could be as

37. Amin 'Izz al-Din, "Mahjub Thabit," *al-Hilal* (June 1969), and "Ba'kukat Mahjub Thabit," *al-'Arabi* (May 1975). Ibrahim Wardani, the young pharmacist who in 1910 assassinated the detested Prime Minister Butrus Ghali Pasha, had also been among the young professionals involved in the Higher Schools Club, the night schools and the MTWU. See FO 141/802/022, Report of Dr. Nolan, controller of the Public Security Department of the Ministry of the Interior; al-Rafi'i, *Farid*, p. 186.

widely applied as *syndicat* (its best equivalent), and after the First World War many social groups would use it to denote their own organizations. The social composition of the MTWU, whose first six or seven hundred members were recruited from among those enrolled in the night schools, was quite diverse and consisted (as Table 2 shows) of Egyptians engaged in a variety of trades. Some of its members were workers in large enterprises, notably the Egyptian State Railways (ESR), but most were employed in small workshops or were independent artisans. The MTWU was in reality more an organization of the urban working people, comprising small proprietors, the self-employed, and wage workers, than a union or a federation of crafts workers. This characteristic reflected the continuing predominance of craft industry over modern mechanized industry, hence the low level of social differentiation between the new working class, whose members were employed in large-scale enterprises, and the traditional *artisanat*. It was therefore not surprising that the bourgeois nationalists who created and led the MTWU should have considered anyone who worked with his hands at a skilled trade as part of a single social group, "the workers." This conception also coincided with their own class outlook which stressed nationhood as the primary category of social identity and subsumed therein social strata which

Table 2 Membership of the MTWU by Craft

Craft	1909	1910	1912	1919	1921
Carpenters	130	335	378	95	83
Blacksmiths and metal workers	250	670	739	209	188
Mechanics and stokers (at ESR)	100	289	276	105	90
Shoemakers, workers in leather	85	137	218	90	77
Cigarette workers	36	167	560	110	85
Painters	95	139	158	112	65
Printers	18	121	91	75	4
Masons	65	65	193	105	75
Weavers	58	95	193	101	79
Railway workers	60	64	87	18	9
Barbers	—	—	49	45	79
Other trades	80	283	197	148	209
TOTAL	979	2365	3139	1213	1043

SOURCES: Malika 'Aryan, *Markaz misr al-iqtisadi* (Cairo, 1923), p. 88; Vallet, *Contribution*, p. 159.

70 Labor Activism, 1899–1914

might have significant differences or even conflicts among themselves. These attitudes were manifested in the very name of the organization, and in the fact that members belonged to the local branch regardless of the industry they worked in, and were listed by trade rather than by industry or place of employment. These attitudes were also manifested in the writings and public utterances of Nationalist party leaders, as in Muhammad Farid's address at the party's 1910 annual meeting:

> There is no way to establish this blessed [trade union] movement in Egypt, so that the craftsman and the farmer (*al-sani' wa'l-muzari'*) might be safe from poverty and destitution when they are old or sick, or to improve their standard of living, except by opening more night schools in the cities and villages, to teach them their rights and obligations and to make them understand the importance of unions and cooperative societies. Our blessed party has already begun to implement this idea [by founding night schools whose students are] of different crafts and trades. We find the carpenter next to the shoemaker and the stonecutter next to the cook. . . . In al-Khalifa [party activists] founded a society for oratory (*jam'iyya lil-khitaba*) which holds its sessions every Thursday evening, at which the teachers lecture, and workers themselves also lecture, with almost perfect style. I attended one of these sessions with some of my colleagues and we heard two members speak, both of them shoemakers; their address concerned the necessity of protecting the industry from the competition of foreigners.[38]

From such evidence it can be seen that the nationalists' attitude toward labor related more to the world of the independent artisan or craftsman than to that of the wage worker in one of the new industrial or transport enterprises. It was certainly the former who set the tone of the MTWU. The concern about competition from foreign artisans and products, the stress on the reciprocity of rights and obligations between employer and worker, the bringing together of the different trades into one organization—all point to the prevalence among the nationalist activists, and probably among many workers as well, of a social consciousness still rooted in the old craft system of production. Labor organizations structured on the MTWU model were to play a major role in the Egyptian workers' movement for close to two decades. The craft and industrial union models were only gradually ac-

38. al-Rafi'i, *Farid*, pp. 150–51.

Labor Activism, 1899–1914   **71**

cepted by all wage workers as the most appropriate forms of self-organization.

The Egyptian nationalist movement's turn toward the workers may have been influenced by the example of, and contacts with, European socialism and trade unionism. The many Egyptian students and others who spent time in Europe before the First World War were certainly exposed to the ideas of the left, even if it may have been the anti-imperialist motif which most interested them. Educated Egyptians were at least vaguely familiar with socialist principles, and a contemporary observer went so far as to assert that many of the students and lawyers active in the MTWU displayed Marxist tendencies and believed in the necessity of the class struggle.[39] Keir Hardie, leader of the Independent Labor party, attended the Egyptian Youth Congress held in Geneva in 1910 together with a number of his English and Irish comrades and met Farid, and the latter often held up the European labor movement as an example for Egyptians to emulate.[40] The main motive for the Nationalist party's interest in labor was however the national cause rather than any inclinations toward socialism. Yet the nationalists were quite prescient in their grasp of the fact that Egyptian workers would become a significant social force, however unclear their conception of exactly who those workers were. "Your cause," the Nationalist party's organ al-Liwa' told the Cairo tramwaymen after their strike in August 1911,

> is the cause not only of the tramway workers but of all the workers in Egypt. Your strike coming after that of the [railway workshop] workers is proof that a new power has emerged in Egypt that cannot be ignored—the awakening of the power of the working class (tabaqat al-'ummal) in the countries of the East and their becoming conscious of their interests and rights and desire to be men like other men. . . . Let the earlier massacre at the [railway shops] and the 'Abbasiyya [tram depot] massacre be a lesson to you. Unite and strengthen yourselves and increase your numbers through combination and through unity with the European workers, your comrades; form unions and bestow upon them funds, providing a large permanent capital from which you will benefit in time of need.[41]

The breakdown of MTWU membership by trade given in Table 2 shows that a significant proportion consisted of railway workers.

39. Germain Martin, Les Bazars du Caire et les petits métiers arabes (Cairo, 1910), pp. 86–87.
40. al-Rafi'i, Farid, p. 134, 150.
41. August 5, 1911, quoted in al-Ghazzali, Ta'rikh, pp. 45–46.

72 Labor Activism, 1899–1914

This category included not only those listed as such and as ESR mechanics and stokers, but also many of the blacksmiths and metal workers. The railway workers, and especially those employed at the sprawling locomotive and passenger car repair and maintenance workshops located about a mile from Cairo's central station and known as al-'Anabir (the "warehouses" or "depots"), were the one group of workers in a large, modern enterprise who were recruited directly into the MTWU. The Cairo tramwaymen had their own union, whereas the MTWU's cigarette workers were generally employed in small workshops rather than large factories. These railway workers were quite active and militant in the period before the First World War and merit special attention because of the close and direct links they developed early on with the nationalist movement.

Struggle at the 'Anabir

The development of Egypt's railway system began in the 1850s and proceeded rapidly thereafter. By 1914 the country had over 1,700 miles of main track and the Egyptian State Railways, which operated the system, was the largest single employer with some 12,000 workers. Although there are records of grievances raised by individual workers dating back to the very inception of the system,[42] there is no evidence of significant collective action until 1906. Like other Egyptian workers, the railwaymen were at that time agitated by inflationary pressures on wages, poor working conditions, and what was perceived as management's oppressive, arbitrary behavior. Many indigenous railway workers were denied benefits and job security by their exclusion from the "cadre" under the system of classification described in the previous chapter. Egyptian railway workers also resented the gradual Europeanization of the ESR work force, as foreign workers took an increasing proportion of the jobs to which Egyptians might otherwise have aspired.[43]

As early as February 1906 there were reports of widespread unrest over low wages among workers at stations throughout Egypt. The Supreme Railway Board promised to try to find the money in its severely-constrained budget to raise wages, but in the absence of substantial improvement discontent festered. Agitation erupted in the summer of 1908 after management issued a decree establishing a

42. See Egypt, Mahfuzat majlis al-wuzara', nizarat al-ashghal, maslahat al-sikka al-hadid, "mawdu'at mutanawwa'a" (in the Dar al-Watha'iq, Cairo).
43. Great Britain, *Report of His Majesty's Agent and Consul-General on the Administration, Finances and Condition of Egypt and the Soudan in 1906*, Egypt no. 1 (1907), C. 3394, p. 40.

Labor Activism, 1899–1914   **73**

workday of at least twelve hours at busy stations and up to twenty-one hours (followed by an equal number of hours off) at secondary stations. Harsh penalties for infractions of work rules were also announced, and these measures led to a wave of protest and secret meetings of workers' delegates to draw up a list of demands. These included an eight-hour workday, an increase in wages, the establishment of a regular system of pay raises by merit ("There is absolutely no system," claimed the workers; "the energetic worker is denied all rights and the bootlicking fool rises quickly"), and an end to arbitrary and illegal fines and punishments and to maltreatment by supervisors.[44] Through the pages of a largely sympathetic press, the anonymous leaders of the railwaymen's movement exhorted their fellow workers to action:

> Until when will they beat us with sticks? Right backed by demands will not be denied. Our misery is known to one and all, and it is no wonder that we have risen to rid ourselves of this misery. Nowhere in the world is there anyone who would rebuke a human being for demanding his due when the cause is so obvious. . . . Have you lost what distinguishes a man from an animal, namely courage and culture and concern for your happiness and your future?[45]

Although a strike was threatened it never materialized. But the threat, the scale of the protests, and widespread press criticism impelled the ESR to promise to ask the government for additional funds with which to meet some of the workers' demands. The ESR also announced that Egyptians would once again be appointed stationmasters and inspectors, and that it would stop seeking candidates for these posts in Europe. The wave of unrest and agitation subsided, but what was perceived as management's tyrannical behavior kept workers' grievances alive. A secret Railway Workers' Association, probably sponsored by the Nationalist party, continued to voice those grievances, and placed special stress on the prevalence of favoritism in promotion as one of the evils of managerial oppression and arbitrariness.[46]

After 1908, however, the focus of activity among the railway workers shifted to those employed at the 'Anabir in Cairo. In 1909 the MTWU began recruiting among the thousands of workers employed at the workshops and the main Cairo rail yards nearby. The many work-

---

44. *al-Mu'ayyad*, August 12, 1908.
45. *Ibid.*, August 13, 15, 1908.
46. See for example *Majallat 'ummal al-sikka al-hadid*, March 15, 1909.

74 Labor Activism, 1899–1914

ers who joined affiliated themselves to the MTWU branch in the Bulaq neighborhood of al-Sabtiyya near the 'Anabir, which soon became known as the "railways club." The MTWU appears to have been most successful in recruiting relatively skilled 'Anabir workers, especially metal workers. These were the best-paid of the manual laborers, and because of their skills were potentially in the best position to exercise some power on the shop floor. The grievances of the 2,400 'Anabir workers centered on their supervisors' abusive treatment. Pay had been docked week after week for the slightest alleged infraction of work rules, as determined arbitrarily by R. G. Peckitt, the English assistant chief engineer; a half-day's wages might be withheld for five minutes' lateness. Peckitt also ordered the installation, early in October 1910, of chronographs on the doors of the workshop's toilets to keep track of how long each worker took, and pay was docked if the permitted maximum of five minutes was exceeded. The workers' resentment was compounded by the ESR's failure to resolve the chronic issue of low wages, a problem exacerbated by a cut in the piece rate for each passenger or freight car repaired.[47]

For some months the workers' unrest was manifested through petitions, the MTWU branch serving as the focal point of the agitation. But when the workers received their pay on October 17, 1910 only to find that many had been docked for no apparent reason and had not received a promised bonus, the accumulated anger exploded.[48] A riveter active in the MTWU exhorted the workers to strike as they left work, and a union meeting that night ratified the strike decision. The workers' demands included regular increases in wages, the dismissal of the detested Peckitt, the revocation of the humiliating latrine rules and the appointment of a permanent committee of workers and managers to examine grievances and review disciplinary sanctions. These demands were of course very similar to those raised by the tramwaymen and other workers in this period, and included the insistence on the prohibition of abusive treatment and the institutionalization of a means of resolving conflicts with management which again reflected the Egyptian workers' concern with being subordinated to foreigners in the workplace.

The strike that ensued was short but violent. The thousands of

47. Vallet, *Contribution*, pp. 42–43; ESR I, Report of October 19, 1910.
48. A major railway strike, widely reported in the Egyptian press, had begun in France on October 11. The pro-British *Egyptian Gazette* reported on October 18 that "the trouble [in Cairo] is said to have been caused by the men reading highly coloured accounts of the strike riots in France, published in some of the Nationalist papers." Although the 'Anabir workers' grievances were of course local in origin, they may have been inspired to militant action by the example of the French railway workers.

workers who gathered at the 'Anabir on the morning of October 18 were reinforced by an even larger number of people from the neighborhood. The rail line from the yards to Upper Egypt was cut and all work stopped. The crowd invaded the workshops and promptly destroyed not only the offensive chronographs but also the latrines, and repeated efforts by the police and army units to dislodge them were repelled. Many were injured and arrested in the clashes, which prompted the less militant foreign and Coptic workers to leave the scene of battle. The anger of the remaining workers also soon subsided, and within a day or two most of the strikers had peaceably returned to work. The Supreme Railway Board eventually made some minor concessions. Although it rejected demands for the establishment of a grievance committee and Peckitt's dismissal, penalties for infractions were somewhat eased, the latrine restrictions were cancelled, there were promises to seek more money for wages and to open more jobs to Egyptians, and Peckitt was quietly transferred to another department.[49]

The earthquake of October 1910 produced a number of weaker aftershocks among the locomotive firemen and the mechanics in the weeks that followed, but there were no further large-scale eruptions of militancy on the part of the 'Anabir workers in the prewar period. The MTWU, however, retained and even strengthened its following among the railway workers, who joined in large numbers immediately after the strike. The episode elicited an outpouring of labor support for the railwaymen, and especially for those subsequently victimized by the ESR and the police for their role in the strike. A large number of Cairo workers offered to join the MTWU on condition that their first month's dues be allocated to aid the families of imprisoned workers, but the MTWU refused, perhaps because of bureaucratic rigidity and a lack of initiative.[50]

The strong base of support the MTWU enjoyed at the 'Anabir was something of an anomaly, given that most MTWU members were artisans or craftsmen in small workshops. The presence of many skilled workers in the 'Anabir who may still have identified themselves primarily as craftsmen, and despite their belonging to a large work force felt themselves to have much in common with other craftsmen, may help explain this. It is also significant that much of the work in the shops was apparently carried on by work teams, each of which was paid in accordance with the amount of work it performed (that is, a

49. *EG*, October 18–27, 1910; ESR I, October 19, 1910, and Macauley (ESR general manager) to the prime minister, October 27 and November 28, 1910; Vallet, *Contribution*, pp. 57–59.
50. Vallet, *Contribution*, p. 59.

76 Labor Activism, 1899–1914

piece rate) rather than on a daily basis. This method of production and the highly stratified character of the work force might have made organization on the MTWU model, rather than through an industrial union comprising all the railway workers, seem well suited to the workers' needs. The question of who held state power was also crucial to these workers and gave them a special affinity for nationalism, thereby enhancing the attractiveness of the Nationalist party-sponsored MTWU beyond its value as a labor organization. Nationalism held out the prospect of limiting or even eliminating the power of foreign foremen, managers, and senior officials, of improving conditions on the shop floor, and of opening more jobs to Egyptians. Wage increases and the extension of benefits had to be paid for out of an ESR budget approved by the government, thus making labor demands into a political issue. Indeed, the ability of railway workers to paralyze the country's main means of internal transport now made them an object of special interest to government.

The 'Anabir was to remain a bastion of support for the nationalist movement through the 1920s and 1930s. The 'Anabir workers would display considerable militancy, but were rarely able to build a strong, stable union of their own, and remained dependent on outside forces that propagated an ethos not always suited to the workers' long-term needs and aspirations. This pattern, which contrasted with that of the much more independent Cairo tramway workers, had its origin in the prewar period. While the MTWU played a central role in mobilizing the 'Anabir workers in 1909 and 1910, their integration into this organization dominated by artisans and craft workers precluded their development of a potentially more powerful and independent industrial union based in the workshops. This was in keeping with the perspective of Nationalist party leaders, who regarded the working class primarily as a component of the Egyptian nation whose strategic social location and persistent grievances could be successfully utilized to further the struggle for national independence.

The First Wave in Perspective

The support that Nationalist party activists could give Egyptian workers in the course of the prewar "first wave" of labor activism was of great value, and contributed significantly to their ability to organize. As nonworkers they were not subject to the same pressures as those they represented and could therefore present demands with impunity and conduct negotiations as social equals. The lawyers and other professionals who played leading roles in the new unions the party helped establish provided these organizations with continuity,

Labor Activism, 1899–1914   77

stability, and in some cases, financial support. Their legal skills were invaluable in defending the workers in the courts as well as in formulating demands, drawing up union statutes, and evaluating proposals from management. As important, if not more so, were the ties these notables had with the national movement. These gave the workers a major base of support, both moral and material, and opened to them the pages of a sympathetic press. They encouraged both the workers and nationalist sympathizers to regard the struggles of Egyptian workers as an integral part of Egypt's struggle for respect, dignity, and self-rule. These nationalist activists were also the means by which a variety of important services—medical, educational, legal, and financial—were provided to workers. The organizational ties that developed underpinned the ideological convergence between the workers' economic interests and their nationalist orientation. This convergence was reinforced by repeated confrontations with the repressive power of an Egyptian state controlled by the English occupiers and protecting the property and privileges of other foreigners dominant in the workplace.

Although there was much that workers could and did gain from ties to the bourgeois nationalist movement, there were also potentially negative aspects to this relationship. For all their sympathy and support, these lawyers, students, and other nationalist activists were not workers. Their goals may have partly coincided with those of the emerging labor movement, but there might very well arise situations in which the aims, means of struggle, and strategies of the two movements might conflict. In fact, the social perspective of such organizations as the MTWU would ultimately prove inappropriate to the needs of industrial workers because of its roots in precapitalist forms of production and consciousness. Furthermore, the influence of the nationalists was always in danger of becoming a form of paternalistic control (organizational and ideological) over the working class. In their writings, their speeches, and above all in their organizational practice, the bourgeois nationalists involved in labor affairs articulated a particular conception of the workers and their identity, and of the very nature of Egyptian society. This conception tended to lump together as "workers" small proprietors, skilled and unskilled wage workers, artisans, and casual laborers. The grievances of Egyptian workers were regarded not as inherent in a particular form of social organization but as the result of foreign political and economic domination. Support for the struggles of those workers was therefore largely a means to an end, that of an independent Egypt ruled by its indigenous elite.

The contradictions inherent in bourgeois leadership of the labor

78 Labor Activism, 1899–1914

movement, however, would emerge only after the war. Before that time union membership was small—one observer estimated the total at 4,600 in Cairo in 1911—and only a few of the unions were strong enough to compel employers to bargain with them.[51] In these circumstances the support the Nationalist party extended the workers was of the utmost importance in enabling them to stand up to the power of the employers and the police. The ability of the nationalists to foster union activity was however severly limited after 1911 by adverse political conditions. By 1909 the occupation regime had already begun taking measures to suppress the growing nationalist movement. The government first sought to muzzle the often vociferous opposition press by reviving the rarely applied 1881 Press Law, which allowed the temporary or permanent suspension of newspapers without trial. This action aroused considerable protest, including a demonstration in Cairo by some 4,000 workers most of whom were typographers and printers. On this issue, nationalist and democratic sentiment coincided with self-interest: jobs would be lost if newspapers were shut down. Later that same year the government promulgated a new law providing for the internal exile by administrative order of any person believed to constitute a danger to public security. In 1910 Muhammad Farid, the president of the Nationalist party, was imprisoned for six months for having written the introduction to a book of nationalist poetry the courts found objectionable.[52]

It was in this climate of increasing repression that police intervention against the 'Anabir strike of October 1910 and the Cairo tram strike of July–August 1911 took place. Whereas in the latter case the Egyptian prime minister—widely regarded as sympathetic to nationalist aspirations—had sought to settle the dispute peaceably, the British officials in charge of the security apparatus at both the national level (the Public Security Department of the Ministry of the Interior) and the local level (the commandant of the Cairo police) decided to use force to break the strike. This decision was motivated by concern about the dangerous political implications of labor activism in key foreign-controlled industries which was abetted by the nationalists and enjoyed a great deal of popular support. The mobilization of the repressive powers of the state against striking workers, the suspension of newspapers, the prosecution of opposition publishers, and the jailing of Farid must have all had a chilling effect on labor activity.

51. Apart from the MTWU and the tramwaymen, the most important unions were those of cigarette workers, printing workers, bakery workers, and retail sales employees. *Ibid.*, p. 146.
52. Lord Lloyd, *Egypt Since Cromer* (London, 1933), I, pp. 93–94; al-Rafi'i, *Farid*, p. 128.

Labor Activism, 1899–1914 **79**

This political climate and the relative stabilization of the economic situation explains the apparent passivity that characterized the fledgling workers' movement from the second half of 1911; the tram strikes of that year marked the high-point of the prewar workers' movement and a period of quiescence, if not retreat, followed.

The labor organizations linked to the Nationalist party were particularly susceptible to the effects of the repression, but all forms of labor activism and organization were affected. It was evident that strikes in sensitive sectors would have to confront the police in unequal battle, while harassment by employers made mere membership in unions (which enjoyed no defined legal status or protection) seem not only unattractive but very risky to many workers. The MTWU did not disappear, but the scope of its activity as well as that of other labor organizations was severly curtailed. Unable to recruit aggressively or take the offensive against employers, even the strongest unions were forced to turn inward and try to preserve themselves by focusing on their mutual aid functions. Other unions went out of existence, or barely held on with only a small core of loyal members. Those best equipped to survive were the craft unions of skilled foreign workers which had no links to politics and restricted themselves solely to craft issues.

In these circumstances of heightened repression, the Nationalist party was unable to devote as much energy and resources to labor affairs. Some nationalists active in labor left the party, and others turned to other, apparently more pressing issues such as resistance to government repression. The intensified pressure to which the party was subjected and the increased cost of maintaining its mass base while it was on the defensive led to some dissension within the Nationalist party about the proper course to follow. At the party's March 1912 general meeting some argued that the party's human and financial resources should be devoted primarily to work in the schools where students had always constituted a strong and secure base of support. Others wanted to continue building a base among the lower classes, especially among workers employed at the foreign-owned public utilities, by linking the national cause with social issues. Farid strongly supported the latter course as the only way of resisting government efforts to isolate the party. "You have no alternative but to concern yourselves with the workers' unions, with spreading the principle of solidarity among them and defending their rights," he argued, and stressed the important role of the night schools and the agricultural cooperatives.[53] Within a week of this meeting, however, the

53. al-Rafi'i, *Farid*, pp. 318–20; Yusuf, *Siyasat al-ihtilal*, pp. 167–68.

80 Labor Activism, 1899–1914

party leader was forced into exile in order to escape a year's imprisonment for allegedly inciting antipathy toward the government in the same speech in which he had called for continuation of the party's labor work. Muhammad Farid was never to return to Egypt. He died in Berlin in November 1919, a few months after the upsurge of popular opposition to the occupation for which he had hoped and worked so long.

The exile of the Nationalist party's leader, continued repression, and intraparty factionalism effectively paralyzed much of the Nationalist party's work in the subsequent two years. With the outbreak of war in 1914, all oppositional political activity and all labor activity that might threaten public order came to an end. In October controls were imposed on public gatherings, and the following month martial law and press censorship were proclaimed. The Nationalist party and its affiliated organizations were dissolved, their assets and papers were seized, and their activists were harassed, imprisoned, or exiled. The proclamation of a British protectorate over Egypt in December 1914 put an end to the pretense that Egypt retained even nominal sovereignty over her own affairs.

Egypt's involvement in the war led to the nearly complete (if temporary) eclipse of the fledgling workers' movement. The preceding fifteen years, however, had seen the first sustained manifestations of large-scale collective activity among workers in Egyptian industry and transport. Some of the patterns set in this embryonic stage in the development of the Egyptian working class and labor movement would persist in the following years. Although the emergence of a new class of industrial wage workers distinct from the traditional *artisanat* had only just begun to impinge on the consciousness of most of Egyptian society before the war, and though these workers were still largely subsumed in older social categories, it was evident that industrial conflict and labor activism had become part of the Egyptian scene. Foreign workers were the first to strike and unionize, but Egyptians employed in the large enterprises capitalist development had generated in this period were quick to follow their lead, and learn their techniques and forms of organization and struggle. The indigenous workers may have been inspired by the example of the foreigners, but the impulse to respond collectively derived from their own grievances as well as from the very structure and logic of the industrial experience itself.

That experience was to a considerable degree determined by Egypt's semicolonial status. The country's political domination by an occupying power facilitated economic domination by foreign capitalists resident abroad or in Egypt itself, and as a result the workplaces in which Egyptian workers found themselves employed in large numbers were almost without exception owned or managed by foreigners. Ethnic, cultural, and religious differences further compounded the inequalities inherent in the capitalist workplace, and created grievances and resentments rooted not only in economic exploitation but also in what many Egyptian workers perceived as an assault on their humanity and dignity. This is not to say that foreign employers were inherently oppressive or Egyptian employers more humane, rather that the logic of the colonial encounter inevitably created a situation in which conflicts over wages, hours, and working conditions became bound up with the subordinate status and maltreatment of Egyptian workers, resulting in the conflation of class conflict with ethnic and national conflict. This set the stage for bourgeois nationalism to emerge as the primary political, ideological, and organizational influence on the Egyptian workers' movement for many decades to come.

The Nationalist party thus found many workers ready to accept its involvement in and leadership of their struggles and organizations. Certainly, one way to understand the workers' acquiescence in the tutelage of notables, of members of superior social strata, is in terms of traditional relations of patronage and deference, though a more satisfactory explanation would see colonialism's impact on Egypt as the key factor in the relationship between the bourgeois-led nationalist movement and the labor movement. That relationship was already evident in 1908 in the Nationalist party's support for the tramway and railway workers, which resulted in the establishment of what were, from one perspective, party "front organizations" for workers. Yet, the relationship was in many respects functional for both the party and the workers, and for this reason persisted in different forms and changed circumstances for a long period of time.

The complex and problematic labor-nationalist relationship will be discussed more fully below, but one significant aspect of it should be noted here. Both artisans and wage workers were recruited into the MTWU, the labor organization that before the First World War most clearly embodied that link. It was however the MTWU members employed in large enterprises—specifically, the railway workers—who became involved in industrial conflict. Except for some of the skilled foreign workers employed in small workshops, those who took the lead in the labor struggles of the prewar period were not artisans fighting foreign competition or craft workers demanding higher wages from the small proprietors who employed them, but workers in workplaces with large concentrations of wage labor. Yet despite their relative passivity, it was the artisans and craftsmen who, in the MTWU

82 Labor Activism, 1899–1914

and later in many other labor organizations, often set the tone and determined the prevailing ethos. Their social identity and outlook was closest to that of the middle-class nationalists who often ran these unions and, as noted earlier, they were as a group not yet highly differentiated from the emerging working class. They were therefore able to play an important ideological and organizational role in the labor movement for a long time, a role already foreshadowed in the structure and make-up of the MTWU, even as the weight of the working class employed in large, modern enterprises slowly but steadily increased.

In one sense the events of the prewar period constitute the "prehistory" of the Egyptian workers' movement—a period of embryonic development preceding and making possible the real birth of the movement in 1919—though this period should also be regarded as important in its own right. For the first time Egyptian workers emerged as the subjects of the historical process and not only as its objects, as agents acting on their own behalf despite adverse circumstances. The course of this first wave of labor activism was aborted by the war, but its imprint did not entirely disappear. The experiences and lessons of the prewar years were not forgotten, and this ensured that the workers' movement would soon re-emerge at a considerably higher level of consciousness and organization.

Chapter IV

1919: Labor Upsurge and National Revolution

The Egyptian working class was quiescent during the early years of the First World War, and the nationalist movement that had provided it with much of its leadership had apparently been suppressed. A more direct form of British rule was imposed on Egypt in 1914, and colonial planners looked forward with confidence to the country's smooth postwar integration into the empire. But in Egypt as in so many other countries, from the heartland of Europe to the colonies of Asia, the war and its turbulent aftermath were to mark one of the great turning points of modern history. While the old order crumbled in much of the European metropole, many of the peoples subject to colonial domination rose up in militant and sometimes violent struggles for independence. Egypt in 1919 was part of the great wave of nationalist upsurge that engulfed India, China, Ireland, Turkey, and the Arab East. The political, social, and economic conditions that characterized the Egypt that emerged from the war were the tinder the spark of nationalist agitation ignited, producing the popular uprising against British rule that came to be known as the 1919 revolution.

In the course of that revolution, and during the protracted period of unrest and nationalist struggle that followed it, working class activism and organization became significant and permanent features of the country's economic and political life. The year 1919 thus witnessed not only the rebirth of the nationalist movement and the involvement of broad sections of the indigenous population in the struggle for Egypt's independence, but also the birth of a labor movement which, despite defeats and long periods of weakness, would make its presence increasingly felt during the interwar years. The emergence of this movement at a time of nationalist upsurge was no

84 1919: Upsurge and Revolution

coincidence. Given Egypt's semicolonial status and the form of capitalist development it had experienced, the national question could not be easily separated from the social and economic grievances felt and expressed by working people. For this reason the 1919 revolution also marked the first full articulation of the special labor-nationalist relationship which had already been foreshadowed by the Nationalist party's prewar role in labor affairs and would significantly shape the Egyptian union movement in the following decades.

The Revival of Labor Activity

By the end of the First World War, nearly every segment of Egyptian society had reason to resent British rule and be receptive to renewed nationalist agitation. The war had disrupted the country's economy. Although large landowners had generally benefited from high cotton prices, they resented official agricultural policies designed to serve British interests rather than their own. The bulk of the peasantry suffered from the requisitioning of their animals and their grain and, later in the war, from being drafted by the hundreds of thousands for forced labor with the Allied armies in the Middle East and Europe. The temporary weakening of ties with the European economy stimulated significant growth in those industries that produced substitutes for imports unavailable during the war or which catered to the needs of wealthy Egyptians as well as the very large Allied forces stationed in Egypt. Total industrial employment increased substantially (see Table 1), though some industries—cigarettes, for example—were hard hit by the loss of export markets and sources of raw materials, and laid off many workers.[1]

Any gains in employment or wages made by the urban working population, in particular by the growing working class, were soon eroded by two interrelated factors that defined the context for the rising tide of labor discontent in 1917–1918 and set the stage for the social explosion of 1919. The first of these factors was the appearance of severe food shortages, especially in the large cities. Heavy demand by the Allied forces, the cut-off of foreign supplies, and an increase in the area planted in cotton when restrictions were lifted led to serious shortfalls in the food supply by the end of 1917. This gave rise to and was compounded by the second factor, a high rate of inflation. The prices of many food items had been rising slowly but steadily through

1. On the war's impact on various classes, see 'Abd al-'Azim Ramadan, *Tatawwur al-haraka al-wataniyya al-misriyya min sanat 1918 ila sanat 1936* (Cairo, n.d.), pp. 66–82, and the classic nationalist account of the revolution, 'Abd al-Rahman al-Rafi'i, *Thawrat 1919* (Cairo, n.d.: Third Printing), I, pp. 40–44.

1919: Upsurge and Revolution   **85**

1915 and 1916, after which they began to skyrocket, as Table 3 shows. Retail prices rose even faster than wholesale prices, while government measures to set maximum prices for basic commodities and to import wheat from Australia, to be distributed below cost as bread, were ineffective. The combined impact of shortages and inflation was devastating to the standard of living of wage workers and salaried employees, many of whom were driven to the very edge of subsistence. The British authorities calculated for example that the monthly expenses for food of a typical Cairo family "of the poorest class" rose from 109 piastres a month in February 1914 to 305 piastres in 1919.[2] The rapid decline in the real wages of many Egyptian workers, which produced widespread suffering, largely accounts for the revival of labor activism during the last year of the war.

Under conditions of martial law, Egyptian workers had been able to voice their grievances only by means of petitions to the authorities. Their complaints were similar to those heard before the war: low wages, long hours of work, abusive treatment, and unjust dismissals. The humble, indeed, self-effacing and obsequious tone of some of these petitions, however, reflected the debilitating effects of wartime repression.[3] But as the battle front receded eastward, away from Egypt's borders, and the regime relaxed its grip somewhat, workers began to resume organized activity and confront their employers more forcefully. The threat of repression seemed less serious, while the accelerating inflationary spiral made action imperative.

The first group of workers to take the initiative were the original pioneers of the labor movement, the cigarette workers. Their already precarious situation before 1914 had been made even more difficult by wartime dislocation because wages were cut and unemployment rose. As early as August 1917 a strike broke out at the Coutarelli factory in Alexandria, and the following February a series of larger strikes began in both Alexandria and Cairo. The cigarette workers in Alexandria were able to win a modest wage increase because of their high level of organization and discipline, and the sympathy of the press, whereas the strikers in Cairo were less united and faced vigorous police repression. T. R. Russell, then assistant commandant of the Cairo police, reported in a letter to a friend:

2. FO 407/186/325. According to Issawi, war-related malnutrition had a major impact on the death rate in Egypt as the total number of deaths per year rose from 300,000 before the war to 500,000 by 1918. *Egypt*, p. 41.
3. See for example ESR II, "Iltimas kalimat haqq awhat bi-nashriha 'awatif al-ikhlas'' and "Sadan iltimas kumsariyyat al-sikka al-hadid,'' two pamphlets published anonymously by railway workers sometime between November 1916 and October 1917.

86 1919: Upsurge and Revolution

Table 3 Wholesale Prices of Basic Food Items, Cairo
(1 January 1913–31 July 1914 = 100)

	Local wheat	Sa'idi beans	Shami maize	Sugar	Wheat flour
Avg. 1915	112	82	77	132	116
Avg. 1916	123	111	91	144	135
Jan. 1917	172	165	102	152	182
July 1917	204	192	167	160	229
Avg. 1917	199	162	138	179	211
Jan. 1918	266	145	138	248	277
July 1918	225	174	170	250	248
Avg. 1918	242	165	164	271	265
Jan. 1919	221	170	166	294	248
March 1919	221	170	166	294	248
Aug. 1919	257	247	189	294	239

SOURCE: *AS 1923/1924*, pp. 212–15.

I've been having a busy four days with some cigarette-rollers on strike. We've got very strict laws of course on illegal assemblies and this morning about five hundred of the strikers refused to accept the very good terms the Governor [of Cairo] had got for them out of the Company. They came here *en masse* and I told them off, but they then announced their intention of marching on the Abdin Palace. I let them start and then sent word after them that I would see them again. They all came back to Headquarters and when I got them all in the yard I locked the gate and put a strong guard over them, searched and listed the lot of them, read them the riot act and then let them go. I hear they have accepted the terms since.[4]

In fact, the Cairo strike was finally broken with the help of the police only after violent clashes and numerous arrests.

The fact that it was the cigarette rollers who were the first to resume open and militant activity after three years of silence is not surprising. These workers had remained part of the elite of the working class—highly paid, relatively well-educated, and with a high proportion of foreigners among them. Their long history of struggle and organization made it possible for them to move quickly from the limited and largely unsuccessful stoppages of 1917 to the more general and fruitful strikes of 1918. They were able with little difficulty to revive the unions they had first established more than a decade earlier. In-

4. Quoted in Ronald Seth, *Russell Pasha* (London, 1966), p. 130. See also 'Izz al-Din I, pp. 161–74.

Onions	Oil	Eggs	Lentils	Weighted avg.
108	96	103	109	103
94	119	133	125	128
114	136	130	131	150
111	207	136	167	193
149	165	159	139	176
228	171	209	127	208
70	196	192	169	206
101	232	210	158	211
87	296	231	167	215
90	314	215	167	216
129	318	178	230	239

deed, this step was a vital necessity for them because they were threatened not only by conjunctural unemployment and declining real wages, but also by the looming threat of mechanization. Within a few months other groups of workers cautiously began to become more active. Among these were the Cairo tramwaymen, who by December 1918 had begun to raise many of the same demands for which they had fought in 1908–1911. At this point they still lacked any form of union organization, and limited themselves to petitioning management because a strike would certainly have led to an immediate confrontation with the authorities which the workers were in no position to win. By the beginning of 1919, however, it was apparent that the union movement had begun to revive, and signs of life and movement were visible among workers in many trades.

One of these signs was the reappearance of the MTWU in Alexandria, henceforth its main base of support. This organization was revived by unionists who had been active in the local branch before the war and with the cooperation of the Nationalist party, which was also slowly coming back to life. As before the MTWU sought to unite all Egyptian workers and artisans, regardless of trade or relationship to ownership of the means of production, into one citywide organization. This was in contrast to the industrial and craft unions which were at this time being reestablished or being newly formed by Egyptian and foreign workers. The MTWU was well aware of this contrast and insisted that its model was the most appropriate one for the labor movement. A statement it issued several days after its formal re-establishment at the beginning of March 1919 argued:

88   1919: Upsurge and Revolution

The Union in Alexandria calls on all workers outside its ranks to join, because this would bring unity and strengthen the Union in its course. We warn the workers against those who are infiltrating among them in order to agitate for the creation of a new union, which would destroy their unity. There is no need for the existence of several unions in a single city like Alexandria.[5]

This warning certainly reflected the desire of the MTWU and its Nationalist party patrons to monopolize the organization of the Egyptian working class of Alexandria, though as we have seen in the previous chapter, the warning also reflected a form of consciousness still rooted in the social milieu of petty-commodity production and in the low level of differentiation between wage workers on the one hand and artisans, small proprietors and their employees on the other hand. This perspective blurred real and potential differences among these groups by subsuming all of them in the ideological category of "workers in the manual trades." Although the Nationalist party and the labor organizations under its influence were to remain loyal to this perspective for some years, it became increasingly less appropriate to the realities of the postwar working class and labor movement. Yet in 1919 the MTWU in Alexandria was quite successful in its efforts to organize among railway workers—its traditional base of support among workers in modern industry. The MTWU was the first organization to reappear on the local labor scene; it had an established labor record and solid political credentials; and its leadership was in the course of that eventful year assumed by Dr. Mahjub Thabit, a veteran of the prewar labor-nationalist upsurge and a popular figure among the workers.

Egyptian Workers and Egyptian Nationalism

The revival of the labor movement at the end of 1918, and especially during the first two months of 1919, must be seen in the context of political developments. The war had come to an end in November 1918, and the question of Egypt's future status immediately came to the fore. A group of nationalist politicians and notables, most of them large landowners, formed a delegation (wafd) under the leadership of Sa'd Zaghlul Pasha which demanded the right to put forward Egypt's claim to full independence at the Peace Conference. The British authorities, however, refused to recognize the Wafd or permit it to travel to Europe to press its case. The Wafd responded by launching a campaign to gather the signatures of former elected officials, notables, and

5. al-Muqattam, March 6, 1919, quoted in 'Izz al-Din I, p. 184.

1919: Upsurge and Revolution **89**

other members of the upper and middle classes deputizing it to act as the sole legitimate representative of the nation in striving peacefully for complete independence. Two representatives of the Nationalist party—chosen not by that party but by Zaghlul who was emerging as the forceful and popular leader of the new nationalist movement—were added to the Wafd, together with representatives of the Coptic community. The growing popularity of the Wafd and the spreading agitation associated with it led to the resignation of the Egyptian government, which unlike the Wafd was not opposed in principle to protectorate status, and had thereby lost its credibility as spokesman for the nation. In an effort to resolve the ensuing political crisis and squelch the nationalist upsurge, the British arrested Zaghlul and three of his colleagues on March 8, 1919 and deported them to Malta.[6]

There is no evidence of any direct connection between the Wafd's political agitation at the beginning of 1919 and the rising tide of labor unrest. The members of the Wafd leadership had little interest in the problems of the urban working class, or indeed in social issues in general. Rather they were seeking, at least initially, to mobilize upper and middle-class opinion for a peaceful campaign for Egyptian independence—a struggle to compel the British to transfer power to the indigenous elite. The Wafd's activists and organizers were, to be sure, drawn from the same *effendiyya* strata which had been attracted to the Nationalist party before the war. That party, however, though much weakened by wartime repression, held to its uncompromising demand for immediate and unconditional independence, and had shown an interest in social problems. The Wafd by contrast was initially quite uninterested in, or at best conservative on, social issues. Its leaders were committed to legal methods of struggle, and before March 1919 had no expectation of, and no desire to encourage, mass popular agitation, much less a revolution.

If the leadership of the postwar Egyptian nationalist movement was generally upper-class and conservative—even by comparison with other contemporary nationalist movements, for example the Indian National Congress or the Kuomintang—this is not to say that its demands did not represent the interests of other classes as well, at least up to a point. The vast majority of the country's population responded to the Wafd's appeal in 1919 for a variety of reasons. The struggle against the foreign occupier and the goal of that struggle (complete independence) meant different things to different segments of Egyptian society.

6. For a more detailed account of these events see al-Rafi'i, *1919*, Ramadan, *Tatawwur*, or Deeb, *Party Politics in Egypt*, ch. 2.

90 1919: Upsurge and Revolution

The sources of urban working class support for the national cause in 1919 were essentially those that underlay the labor-Nationalist party link in 1908–1911 discussed in the previous chapter. For most Egyptian workers, class divisions coincided with ethnic or national divisions in the workplace. The poor conditions of labor and the abusive treatment at the hands of foreign employers and foremen which they experienced were quite naturally linked to foreign domination of the economy and to British rule. The occupation regime protected the power and privileges of the foreigners who controlled their working life and whose arbitrary and high-handed behavior was so bitterly resented. When workers sought to organize and improve their lot, the role of the British-controlled police in strikebreaking and repression was certainly evident enough. It was therefore inevitable that the sense of oppression felt by workers subject to deteriorating working and living conditions at the hands of foreign employers or a foreign-controlled government would converge with these same workers' sense of humiliation as Egyptians subject to foreign rule in their own land. There were thus concrete reasons for Egyptian workers to wholeheartedly support a nationalist movement aimed at ending British rule (itself a desirable goal) but which might, by restoring Egypt's sovereignty, also create more favorable conditions in which to seek a better life for themselves. Segments of the Egyptian bourgeoise had their own reasons and projected advantage for wanting to end foreign domination of the country's economy, so that the nationalism of the upper and middle classes possessed an economic component with which Egyptian workers could identify. Nearly all classes shared, up to a point, a common set of enemies and goals, such that the young working class supported and participated in the national cause and accepted its bourgeois leadership.

Labor activity was already on the rise before March 1919, stimulated by inflation, rising unemployment resulting from the postwar contraction of industry, and accumulated wartime grievances. But under the martial law regime it remained quite difficult for workers to organize and especially to strike with much hope of success, as the experience of the Cairo cigarette rollers had shown. The popular nationalist revolution that was to erupt in March–April 1919 shook the occupation regime to its foundations and created political conditions in which workers, whose numbers had increased during the war, could quickly organize themselves and launch strikes for economic demands which blended completely into the national struggle. The popular uprising, spontaneous and massive, incorporated and sustained this new social movement, and made possible its rapid growth and quick victories. In this period of political and social turbulence the tramway and railway workers were once again in the vanguard of the labor movement. An examination of their involvement in the first phase of the 1919 revolution, in a sense the formative experience of the Egyptian workers' movement, will illustrate that interaction of class and national dimensions so crucial in much of subsequent Egyptian labor history.

The Cairo Tramway Workers in the Revolution

The work force that operated the tramway system of Egypt's capital consisted of just over 2,000 workers in 1918, a decline of about 10 percent from the prewar level. In that same period, however, ridership had gone up by over 30 percent. Overall fewer workers were conveying many more passengers in more crowded cars running on a reduced schedule, all of which pointed to speed-up by management and a deterioration in working conditions.[7] The demands the workers formulated and presented to the company at the end of 1918 included an eight-hour workday, a substantial wage increase (drivers and conductors earned ten to fifteen piastres for a ten to twelve-hour day, a rate essentially unchanged since 1908), paid days of rest, better treatment by supervisors, a more rational and equitable system of disciplinary penalties, severance pay based on length of service, and free uniforms.[8] These demands were similar to those raised before the war, and indicated the absence of any improvement in relations between workers and supervisors, but they also reflected the impact of the war-related drop in real wages and intensified exploitation on the job. The CTC failed to accede to the demands, and in the first months of 1919 the tram workers began to organize. When the revolution broke out, they were ready to seize the opportunity.

Zaghlul and his three colleagues were arrested on March 8. The following day saw peaceful protest demonstrations by students, and by the 10th, all of the capital's students, including those of al-Azhar, the great mosque and center of Islamic learning, were on strike. On that day a large demonstration clashed with security forces, causing the first casualties of the revolution. The following days and weeks witnessed a veritable explosion of popular protest with almost daily demonstrations in the streets of Egypt's cities and bloody clashes with British military forces. This was accompanied throughout the country by attacks on British installations and personnel, the cutting of railway lines, and other forms of popular revolutionary violence.

7. *AS 1914*, pp. 218–19; *AS 1919*, pp. 138–140.
8. Muhammad Zaki ʿAli, *Taqrir ʿan halat ʿummal al-tram bi'l-qahira* (Cairo, 1920); ʿIzz al-Din II, p. 16.

92 1919: Upsurge and Revolution

One of those forms was the destruction of tram cars—from this time forward a standard feature of outbreaks of popular protest. Overturning and wrecking tram cars was an effective means of paralyzing mass transit in the capital as well as a way of venting popular anger at a very visible symbol of foreign economic power. This anger may also have been stimulated by the fact that with even second-class fares at five milliemes (one-half piastre), a tram ride was still too expensive for many poor Egyptians. By March 11, the Cairo tram system was no longer functioning, and the public at first supposed that the company had suspended operations to protect its vulnerable property from the demonstrators. It soon became clear, however, that though the demonstrations and attacks may have disrupted service, the tramways of Cairo had stopped running altogether because the tram workers had gone out on strike. The taxi drivers also stopped work, and within a few days other forms of public transport such as hackney cabs and mule-drawn omnibuses had virtually ceased to circulate.[9]

The British authorities were certainly soon aware of the tramway workers' strike, because on March 12 the High Commissioner received a telegram from one Yusuf Khalil announcing the strike and demanding on behalf of the tramwaymen that the British authorities intervene with the CTC. The Residency, however, was not interested in playing the role of mediator. Indeed, one official commented that the workers were adequately paid and worked reasonable hours, and another that "as things stand—a foreign company with no labour clauses in their contract [that is, the concession agreement]—Eg. Govt. could only really interfere if the Co. appealed for assistance in settlement of difficulties with their employees."[10]

The legal niceties of the situation were quite beside the point, however. In reality the British authorities were in no position to intervene as decisively as they had in 1908 and 1911. The revolutionary situation that prevailed in March–April 1919 made it very difficult for them to attempt to break the strike. Army and police forces in the capital and elsewhere in Egypt were stretched thin in trying to contain the more immediate and dangerous threats to British authority and the established order. At the same time, the tram workers' strike enjoyed widespread public support. The indigenous population of Cairo perceived the strike as an important part of the national struggle and displayed sympathy and support for the workers as fellow Egyptians oppressed by foreign bosses. Even when the tram company was

9. al-Rafi'i, *1919*, I, pp. 117–19; *al-Watan*, March 14, 1919, quoted in 'Izz al-Din II, p. 16. On the poor public reputation of the tramway company, see Boulad, *Les Tramways*, pp. 14–19.
10. FO 141/748/8839/1, notes by Thomas and Moesworth.

1919: Upsurge and Revolution **93**

able to run a few cars under heavy British guard, a general boycott left them empty. As the weeks passed, other means were employed to keep the transport system shut down. The London press reported early in April that non-striking tramway and railway personnel and shopkeepers had been attacked with sulfuric acid by unknown assailants, presumably striking workers or members of one of the secret nationalist organizations. The use or threat of violence must certainly have intimidated the company and those loyal to it, and a martial law decree promulgated on April 16 made such acts punishable by death.[11]

The Wafd opposed these attacks and, in the midst of a popular revolution, publicly denounced all forms of violence. Although some of its leaders had secret links with the underground terrorist organizations, most of the prominent Wafdists were genuinely fearful of popular violence, and worried that once unleashed, the masses might threaten property and social order. In a statement issued on March 24, the Wafd leadership in Egypt warned the people that

> the Military Authorities have issued a warning that they will employ the most harsh military means as punishment in dealing with attacks on means of transport and public property. It is obvious to everyone that attacks on persons or on property are forbidden by divine law and by positive law, and that sabotage of the means of transport clearly harms the people of our country. . . . Therefore the undersigned see it as their sacred national duty to refrain from any attack and ask that no one violate the law, so as not to obstruct the path of all those who serve the nation by legal means.

This appeal was in response to official proclamations imposing the death penalty on anyone found guilty by a British military court of interfering in any way with the normal operation of the railway, telegraph, or telephone systems. Precisely this kind of sabotage by peasants was widespread in the countryside. Although the Wafd's appeal was signed by a host of pashas as well as by Muslim and Christian religious leaders, it did little to stem the tide of popular violence. That would require severe measures of repression, including the burning and aerial bombardment of villages, and eventually political concessions by the British.[12]

11. al-Rafi'i, 1919, I, p. 126; Michael Messiri, "Tnu'at hapo'alim bazira hapolitit bemitzrayyim, 1919–1936—l: Tza'adim rishonim," *Hamizrah Hehadash* 21 (1971):148; Seth, *Russell Pasha*, p. 146.

12. al-Rafi'i, 1919 pp. 168–69. On the links between the secret groups and certain key Wafdists, notably 'Abd al-Rahman Fahmi, who was then general secretary of the Wafd-

94 1919: Upsurge and Revolution

The Cairo tram strike continued through March and into April while the workers and the CTC negotiated but failed to reach a settlement. Under pressure from a British Residency anxious to end the dispute and return the capital to normalcy, the company did make some concessions. On March 28, for example, management announced the creation of an investigations panel to examine charges brought against workers by their supervisors. But the workers believed that such a body would be a creature of management unless worker representatives participated on an equal basis, and the company's offers were rejected. It was only in mid-April, after the new Prime Minister Husayn Rushdi Pasha took an active role in the talks, that an agreement was reached on all but one of the issues in dispute. The main features of the settlement were a workday of eight-and-a-quarter hours, a general and permanent raise of one piastre a day as well as the incorporation of the two piastre wartime cost of living allowance into the regular wage, half-pay for sick workers, one paid day of rest every twelve days, and the establishment of an investigations panel to resolve differences between workers and inspectors over penalties. The one major issue left unresolved was that of severance pay. The workers still insisted on compensation of at least one month's pay per year of service as a deterrent to arbitrary or mass firings and as a cushion against the vicissitudes of unemployment. The two sides agreed to defer the issue while the CTC director in Cairo consulted with the head office in Brussels, but the prime minister promised that the question would be resolved to the workers' satisfaction.[13]

The settlement of the Cairo tramway strike was part of a general subsidence of the revolutionary upsurge in late April. Rushdi Pasha, whose resignation on March 1 had precipitated the political crisis that had led to the arrest of Zaghlul, had resumed the post of prime minister on April 9 after the British agreed to release the Wafd leaders and allow them to travel to Europe. This was seen as a great defeat for the occupation regime and a victory for the Wafd. The Residency made these political concessions in order to restore calm and public order, and the settlement of the tram strike should be seen as a step in the same direction. The Rushdi government was, however, brought down twelve days later by a political strike of government employees which marked the culmination of the much broader strike wave in which the tramwaymen had participated. The end of the government

---

ist central committee in Cairo, see Muhammad Anis, *Dirasat fi watha' iq thawrat 1919, I: al-murasalat al-sirriyya bayna Sa'd Zaghlul wa-'Abd al-Rahman Fahmi* (Cairo, 1963); and Ramadan, *Tatawwur,* pp. 158–75.

13. 'Ali, *Taqrir,* p. 12; 'Izz al-Din II, pp. 26–27.

employees' strike on April 23 was followed by the return to work of many other groups of strikers, including the tram workers, and the wave of popular protest and violence finally petered out. The very end of April thus witnessed the end of the first, militant phase of the 1919 revolution, and in the months that followed the focus of the struggle for independence shifted from the streets and countryside of Egypt to the ministries and conference rooms of Europe.

The tram workers owed the major gains they won in April 1919 to their own militancy and solidarity, but more to the extraordinary political conditions of that turbulent spring. The state had found itself temporarily unable to intervene forcefully and break the strike, the workers had enjoyed broad public support, and the Egyptian government, backed by the British authorities, had for political reasons been willing to pressure the CTC to make concessions. Motivated by a desperate economic situation and by their solidarity with the national cause, the tramwaymen were able to take advantage of the unique situation that prevailed in March–April 1919 to win many of their demands. This unprecedented victory was achieved in the absence of a union, but there must have been informal structures, such as mass meetings, through which the workers chose delegates to negotiate with management and heard their reports. Still, the gains achieved in April were not entirely secure. Without a union recognized by the company and the government as the workers' representative and empowered to monitor implementation of the agreement, it was likely that in more favorable circumstances the CTC would regain the upper hand. The high rate of inflation persisted, and a number of issues were still not definitively or satisfactorily resolved. It was therefore not surprising that labor relations at the Cairo Tramway Company remained unsettled in the following months, and 1919 would see still further instances of industrial conflict in this key enterprise.

Railway Workers in the Revolution

Unrest had been growing among the railway workers too in the early months of 1919. This was especially true at the 'Anabir in Bulaq, where some 4,000 workers were now employed, and at the Jabal al-Zaytun repair shops at al-Qabbari in Alexandria. The 'Anabir had of course been the scene of industrial conflict before the war, and both workshops were strongholds of nationalist sentiment. Indeed, as has already been noted the MTWU was busily recruiting among the Jabal al-Zaytun workers before March 1919. In February the Jabal al-Zaytun workers, represented by a MTWU lawyer named Husayn al-'Ararji, sent a petition to Brigadier General Macauley, director of railway

96 1919: Upsurge and Revolution

traffic, demanding a doubling of wages, an end to arbitrary dismissals and fines, leaves of absence for the *hajj*, and time off for Friday prayer. As with the tramwaymen and many other Egyptian workers, low wages and maltreatment by foremen were central issues.

Macauley himself considered the pay issue as most important, and though he recognized that some of the workers had not had a raise in a long time, a doubling of wages was simply out of the question. In any event, he saw the pay demand as a symptom of a peculiarly "Oriental" attitude toward work and wages.

> The native way of looking at such matters differs entirely from the European; the native considers that he is entitled to pay in proportion to his expenses, whatever these latter may happen to be; and the European expects to give and receive pay according to his skill and efficiency. These two views can never be reconciled.[14]

Macauley's analysis reflected a belief widespread among British colonial officials and others that non-Western peoples were incapable of rational thought, the opposite of Europeans in all respects, and not only backward but incomprehensible.[15] Yet workers' insistence that they are entitled to a living wage is not a particularly "Oriental" phenomenon, and it is clear that the railway workers who petitioned Macauley really were suffering from a sharp decline in real wages. In this same period output per worker was reported to have dropped sharply because of widespread malnourishment in the work force.[16] In truth, the workers' demands about wages and other issues must be understood as rational responses to concrete circumstances, and not as the product of some inherent defect of the "native mind."

In any event ESR management regarded the discontent as potentially dangerous and responded by transferring seven workers allegedly active in the agitation. Workers loyal to management had already claimed in a counterpetition that the troublemakers were a small group of "notorious men known for their revolutionary ideas arising from reading newspapers & their inclination to Bolshevist principles." Despite the failure of MTWU lawyer al-'Ararji to get the seven

14. FO 141/687/8705/2.
15. See for example the Earl of Cromer, *Modern Egypt* (London, 1908), I, ch. 1, II, chs. 34, 61–62. This book was standard reading for British officials in Egypt and was taken as gospel, a distillation of the wisdom and experience of Egypt's de facto ruler for over two decades.
16. Messiri, "Tnu'at hapo'alim," I, p. 145.

1919: Upsurge and Revolution **97**

reinstated, the organization continued to recruit at Jabal al-Zaytun and elsewhere in Alexandria.[17]

The demands raised by the 'Anabir workers in Cairo in these months also focused on higher pay, but included shorter hours and other issues as well. One grievance unique to the 'Anabir was the stationing of a contingent of British soldiers in the workshops, obstensibly to acquire industrial skills. The workers feared that management was preparing to replace them with soldiers. On March 15, as the revolution erupted in full force, the 'Anabir workers went on strike, and this brought most maintenance and repair work on the ESR's locomotives to a halt. The workers also destroyed switches and cut the railway lines near Imbaba, which prevented trains from leaving for Upper Egypt. These acts of sabotage, coming just two days after the imposition of the death penalty for such offenses, indicate that alongside their grievances in the workplace the 'Anabir workers were motivated by support for the revolution and saw their strike as an integral part of the struggle for independence. In fact, throughout the country peasants were taking identical steps to sabotage rail transport as well as the communications system.

The British authorities responded by dispatching army units to occupy the 'Anabir and the surrounding neighborhood in force, and they also sought to seal the Bulaq district off in order to prevent contact between the large, staunchly nationalist populace of one of the country's oldest and most important industrial zones and the mass demonstrations and clashes taking place elsewhere in the city. Prevented from participating en masse in the huge demonstration at al-Azhar on March 17, the railway workers planned their own march for the following day in order to break the blockade of their neighborhood. Joined by the striking workers of the Government Press and many residents of Bulaq, they marched, carrying banners, toward the center of the city. Near the Abu al-'Ala bridge British troops opened fire on the crowd and dispersed it, killing and wounding many.[18]

The railway workshop workers (Jabal al-Zaytun had been struck on March 16) were joined by many traffic department workers and remained on strike well into April. As with the tramwaymen, intimidation was used to prevent employees loyal to management from returning to their jobs. Twenty-six ESR employees were said to have been the victims of acid attacks by mid-April, but there can be no

17. FO 141/687/8705/3, 4.
18. FO 141/687/8705/28, Blakeney to Cheetham, October 23, 1919; al-Rafi'i, 1919, I, pp. 125–26, 131–32, 141; memoirs of 'Abd al-Rahman Fahmi Pasha (at the Dar al-Watha'iq, Cairo), p. 122.

98 1919: Upsurge and Revolution

question that the great majority of workers supported the strike and the national struggle to which it contributed.[19] With the aid of soldiers and loyal staff, the British were ultimately able to restore railway operations, though on a much-reduced scale, and it was only after the release of Zaghlul and his colleagues that the railway workers slowly returned to work. In a sense their strike petered out rather than ended, and this reflected the general downturn in mass mobilization, though there was no immediate resumption of normal service. Slowdowns and brief stoppages persisted, and the ESR clerical staff struck in mid-month as part of the general strike of government employees. Citing their "bad records," management did not permit some 155 strikers to return to their jobs, and unrest continued at Bulaq and elsewhere into May.[20]

The railway workers had won at least some of their demands, the most important of which was a substantial increase in wages, but these gains were achieved through the decrees of ESR officials rather than through any form of collective bargaining, another indication of the difficulty which even the militant 'Anabir workers were to experience in creating their own stable and independent organizations. Apart from the MTWU in Alexandria, there is no evidence that the railway workers established or participated in any union in the course of March–April 1919, though they did have links with the nationalist movement led by the Wafd—links which were to form the basis for a long-lasting and important relationship.

Patterns of Participation and Leadership

Tramway and railway workshop workers were not the only ones to strike during the spring of 1919. The workers at the ESR printing press, the Government Press, the Arsenal and the government workshops, the Alexandria tramways, the Hilwan electric railways, the Cairo electric company, postal, port, lighthouse and customs employees, taxi and carriage drivers—these and others also went on strike within days of the outbreak of the revolution. Peasants working in industry were also involved. On the night of March 15-16, for example, a large band of "pillagers" (probably local peasants) attacked the railroad station near the Hawamdiyya sugar refinery on the western bank of the Nile just south of Cairo. Many of the refinery's 1800 workers (recruited from local villages) left to join the rioters who threatened

19. FO 141/687/8705/8, Macauley to General Officer Commanding Forces in Egypt, March 22, 1919.
20. FO 141/781/8915, General Staff Intelligence, April 10, 28, 1919; FO 141/687/8705/14; FO 407/184, Allenby to Curzon, no. 277, May 1–2, 1919.

1919: Upsurge and Revolution **99**

to attack the refinery, itself. Local police and notables reinforced by Australian troops prevented this, but the refinery was idled through April because most of its workers were absent.[21] Many workers who did not actually strike in this period seized the opportunity to begin organizing themselves, present their demands to their employers, and prepare for future action. These demands almost always included higher wages to offset inflation, the eight-hour day, improvements in oppressive working conditions (especially abuse by foreign supervisors), and compensation for illness and dismissal. Few workers actually realized any of these demands in March and April 1919, and none achieved nearly as much as the tramwaymen or even the railway workers. Nonetheless, these months saw a wave of strikes and industrial unrest involving many thousands of Egyptian workers that was unprecedented in Egyptian history.

The great majority of the strikers were employed either by the government or by the foreign-owned public utilities, the most heavily Egyptian sectors of the labor force and ones that included the greatest concentrations of workers. Their combined ethnic identity and concentrated force were stimuli to these workers' collective experience and action in both class and nationalist dimensions. For them as for a general population supportive of the national cause, strikes that raised economic demands were regarded as an integral part of the broader struggle of the Egyptian people for independence and dignity. The workers were Egyptians, their oppressive bosses were foreigners, and the work stoppages contributed materially to the campaign against the occupational regime. This explains the public support for the strikers manifested in the boycott of the Cairo tramways, and also explains both why the Wafd's leaders acclaimed the strikers as patriots and the secret nationalist groups were ready to use violence against strikebreakers.

The massive strike wave was sparked off by, and can be understood only in the context of, the even more massive explosion of popular protest against British rule. The contribution of the working class in the 1919 revolution was nonetheless significant in its own right, despite the limited size and social weight of this social group. It should not be overestimated—labor activism never reached the point of a coordinated nationwide general strike, for instance—but neither should it be underestimated. The disruption caused by the strikes and the participation of workers in demonstrations certainly gave added force to the national struggle and increased the pressure on the oc-

21. F/512, Henri Naus (general director of the sugar company) to the French minister in Cairo, April 30, 1919.

100 1919: Upsurge and Revolution

cupation regime. Without the paralysis of key government institutions and of the country's transportation systems, largely the result of strikes, the events of 1919 would have had far less impact and been much easier for the British to contain.

In this upsurge of mass mobilization, wage workers in large enterprises were only one of several groups to stop work, motivated at least partly by solidarity with the national cause. Students, lawyers, shopkeepers, and even the normally docile government employees went on strike in March–April, and members of nearly every class marched in demonstrations demanding the release of Zaghlul Pasha and complete independence. This wave of popular action was accompanied by a wave of organization in which many sectors of the population participated. Students, lawyers, teachers, 'ulama, and others created new organizations or mobilized existing ones in support of the national struggle. The term niqaba, generally used by this time for labor unions, was also widely used by nonworkers to denote their own organizations; even large landowners referred to their organization, established in 1921, as a niqaba. This flexible usage reflected the perception of workers as just another occupationally differentiated section of the Egyptian nation rather than as a distinct class. The labor strikes and unionization were thus only part of a nationwide upsurge of militancy and association in which many different groups organized themselves by trade. In this process the sectional interests of the workers were seen as identical to the national interest, whereas the Wafd, until this time a small group of wealthy notables making extravagant claims to speak for Egypt, really did come to be perceived as the embodiment of the national cause.

In these same months the first organizational links were forged between workers and nationalist activists. Where workers had already established ties with the Nationalist party or the MTWU before the war, persons associated with that party emerged as leaders of or spokesmen for the new unions or pre-union formations. This was the case in Alexandria where Dr. Mahjub Thabit came to lead the MTWU, whose base was among the railway workers. Ahmed Bey Lutfi, who had served as a leader of the Nationalist party, the MTWU, and the Cairo tramway workers before the war, now reemerged as counsellor to the Heliopolis tram workers. Muhammad Kamil Husayn and Muhammad Zaki 'Ali, both lawyers linked to the Nationalist party, led the Cairo tramwaymen at different times. The ease with which these men assumed leading roles in labor affairs was the result of the Nationalist party's long history of involvement in this sphere and the contacts they had established before the war. Another contributing

1919: Upsurge and Revolution   **101**

factor was the relative absence of rivalry between the Nationalist party and the Wafd in the first months of the revolution. In March and April all factions in the national movement were united in rejecting protectorate status or anything less than complete independence, and it was not felt to be important that some of the activists who were organizing workers in the national cause were linked to the Nationalist party rather than to the newer and broader Wafd. Furthermore, the Wafd had neither the organizational infrastructure nor sufficient cadre of its own to involve itself directly in labor affairs as a distinct political tendency. The Wafd only gradually transformed itself into an organized movement complete with a central staff, effective methods of developing and maintaining ties with its various constituencies and a nationwide network of local committees. In later years, having been eclipsed and reduced to a politically marginal position by the vast popularity of Zaghlul and his movement, the Nationalist party would become the Wafd's bitter rival. But in 1919 the two were part of the same revolutionary tide, and the Wafd functioned as more of a national front than a party.

Most workers had, however, no prewar connection with a middle-class nationalist leader that could serve as the basis for a new relationship, and it was in the heat of the revolutionary upsurge itself that these links were forged. A group of militant workers might approach a lawyer or notable known for his nationalist activism, and possibly also his interest in labor affairs, or alternatively, such a figure might seek out and cultivate contacts among a particular group of workers. In either case he would then lend his skills, connections, and prestige to the workers and their emerging union as part of his nationalist activism.

The framework in which these first links were often forged, where workers and the lawyers who would help them create and lead their unions made initial contact, was the mass meeting or rally frequently held in one of the larger mosques. Before the Wafd formalized its organization and developed institutionalized links with the masses, especially during the stormy first weeks of the revolution, the mass meeting was a key instrument of communication and mobilization for the urban population. Thousands or even tens of thousands of people, including workers, artisans, shopkeepers, students, and professionals, would gather almost daily to hear speeches and reports from the Wafd's leaders, exchange information, and coordinate the national struggle. On special occasions, such as the April 16 rally in support of the striking government employees, a crowd of 80,000 could jam the precincts of the al-Azhar mosque complex and the sur-

102 1919: Upsurge and Revolution

rounding streets.[22] From these meetings demonstrations would depart to wend their way through the city's streets, to be dispersed eventually by British gunfire. The great mosques had for centuries been vital centers of civil society, and as enclosed sanctuaries were relatively safe from the incursions of British forces. Usually situated in the older, less Europeanized sections of the cities, the mosques served as great social and cultural symbols of Egypt's distinct identity and nationhood, and together with the palatial homes of the members of the Wafd were the nerve centers of the revolutionary movement.

This is not to suggest that the primary motivation of those who gathered at al-Azhar was some antiforeign or anti-Christian fervor supposedly inherent in Islam. Both the crowds and the orators at al-Azhar and elsewhere included Copts as well as Muslims, and the whole tone of the 1919 revolution was resolutely secular. The Wafd consistently propounded a purely ethnic Egyptian identity, and denounced all forms of sectarianism as harmful to the cause of national independence. Religion was regarded as a private matter to be entirely separated from public affairs and the political struggle, though of course, not all Egyptians may have drawn these distinctions as finely as the bourgeois and rather Europeanized nationalist leaders. Some Muslims may indeed have seen the struggle for Egypt's independence as a campaign for the defense of Islam, and the removal of oppressive Christian rule over a Muslim land, but for the great majority the central issue was self-rule for an Egypt in which all Egyptians regardless of their faith could live together in peace and share in a common culture and destiny. It is a fundamental misreading of modern Egyptian history to attribute mass support for the national movement of 1919 to an Islamic xenophobia allegedly ingrained in the belief system of Egypt's Muslim majority. The absence of any evidence of sectarian strife in 1919 disproves this interpretation, as do the instances of class conflict among Muslims—attacks by Muslim peasants on the estates of Muslim large landowners, for example—that occurred in March–April 1919 and terrified the upper class. In Egypt's large industrial and transport enterprises, where Muslims and Copts worked side by side and went on strike with apparently total unanimity, religious differences played no role in this period.

Once initial contact had been made between workers and their bourgeois patrons, more tangible links quickly developed. There is some evidence, based on British intelligence reports, that some nationalist activists were distributing, or promising to distribute, money to striking workers from funds raised by the Wafd's extensive

22. al-Rafi'i, *1919*, pp. 138–39.

canvassing campaign among the country's prosperous strata. On April 26, for example, a tailor named Ahmad Bahnasi, claiming to be on the run from the British because he had incited the people of his home village to destroy the railway line, spoke to a crowd at the ibn Tulun mosque in Cairo. He said that the nationalist lawyer Muhammad Kamil Husayn "had asked him to ask the strikers to go and take strike money from him" and gave out slips of paper with Husayn's name and address. A British intelligence report of early May stated that the railway workers at the 'Anabir, at Zagazig and at the Tanta locomotive works were disgusted with strikes because they had received many promises from Wafdist agitators but no strike pay. To survive during the strikes of March–April the railwaymen had had to sell their wives' jewelry, gold ornaments given as wedding presents which were poor people's only store of wealth, and even their families' clothing in order to buy bread. They were not about to strike again unless they received some tangible support beforehand.[23]

It is likely that there is more involved here than an effort by British intelligence to attribute the militancy of the workers to bribery by outside agitators. It is quite plausible that some money was paid out or at least promised to workers because it was certainly in the interests of the nationalist leadership to provide workers the means to endure lengthy strikes or even to initiate strikes in sectors that the leadership wished to have paralyzed for political reasons. With no strike fund or savings, the workers themselves might have felt that the sacrifices they were making for the national cause entitled them to some material support from wealthier compatriots, though this is not to say that the workers who participated in the events of March–April 1919 did so because they were "bought" by the Wafd. Any material or moral support extended to the workers by the Wafd came only after the workers had already gone on strike, motivated by both economic and political grievances. In any event the amounts of money involved were probably not large and can have been small recompense for the sacrifices of the strikers, very few of whom received any money at all.

After the first phase of the revolution had come to an end and the strike wave had subsided, a period characterized by consolidation and organization rather than conflict ensued. In May and June 1919, many groups of workers formally established unions, often with the support or under the leadership of nationalist notables. The Cairo tramway workers, for example, formed their union on June 15, some two months after their strike had been settled. Many of these new organizations were industrial unions made up of all those employed for

23. FO 141/781/8915, Reports of April 28, May 7, July 8, 1919.

104 1919: Upsurge and Revolution

wages at a particular large enterprise. But there was also a wave of unionization among craft workers as well as employees in retail shops, restaurants, cafes, and other small establishments. The Wafd leadership in Egypt—Sa'd Zaghlul and other top leaders were still in Europe at the time—was very supportive of this development, and regarded the new unions of Egyptian workers as an important asset of the national cause. In the fall of 1919 'Abd al-Rahman Fahmi described the emergence of a labor movement in Egypt in a secret report sent to Zaghlul:

> I will explain to you the results of the efforts made to spread unions (ta'mim al-niqabat) throughout the length and breadth of the land. These efforts have, praise be to God, borne fruit: a union has been formed for every craft (hirfa), and there remains in Egypt no craft or trade (san'a) without a union. It is true that the government has not recognized these unions up to now, and it is not anticipated that it will recognize them in the present circumstances. But they are in any case very useful to the nationalist movement and a powerful weapon which should not be underestimated. In time of calamity they will respond to the call of patriotism as quickly as possible.[24]

In many of these new unions, bourgeois lawyers or notables played leading roles and constituted the link between the labor movement and the nationalist movement. The relationship between unionized workers and these middle or upper-class personalities could take various forms. Where there was a membership with extensive experience of unionism, and was militant, independent, or relatively well educated, the outsider holding a high union post—generally that of honorary president, president, counsellor (mustashar) or treasurer—might be merely a respected figurehead or some combination of advisor, patron, negotiator, and link to the national movement. In these cases it was the members of the executive board and the union's officers, elected at regular general meetings of all paid-up members, who actually ran the organization on a day-to-day basis, though outsiders may have had significant influence on major policy decisions. In other unions, however, the lawyer or notable made the decisions himself and ran the union, by acting through a coterie of worker activists loyal to him. This was especially true where a small or weak union depended on the leader and his party connections for organizational continuity, money, and protection from harassment by employers or the police. Even in such cases, however, the potential for

24. Quoted in Anis, *Dirasat*, p. 154.

1919: Upsurge and Revolution **105**

conflict existed between the workers and their counsellors, which indicated that union members were not passive when they felt their interests were being neglected or harmed.

The reasons that induced many Egyptian workers to seek or accept leadership from members of the middle and upper classes were discussed in the previous chapter with reference to the prewar Nationalist party, and these factors were in general still at work in 1919 and later years. For many unions, there were concrete practical benefits to be derived from a relationship with a politically influential or legally talented patron, though such relationships reflected, and in later years would tend to perpetuate, the relative weakness and dependent status of the young working class and labor movement. The country's subjection to foreign rule was also a crucial factor in subordinating the union movement to the bourgeois-led national movement. The key issue of Egyptian political life from 1919 until 1956 was British domination and the struggle for complete independence, and as a result the central dynamic governing labor's political role was for much of this period its relation to the national movement. The control of many unions by outsiders, usually lawyers linked to the Wafd, was in this sense a manifestation of their incorporation into the national movement. On the other hand these professionals and notables were accepted as leaders at least in part because the unions thereby became an integral component of the broader struggle for Egypt's independence and dignity. The events of 1919 had fused national and class consciousness into one composite world-outlook for most Egyptian workers, an alloy which was to be reinforced by the course of political and economic life in subsequent years.

The complex patron-client relationship between the Wafd and the labor movement, which will be examined in greater detail below, was based on a degree of common interest in opposing imperialism and the foreign interests it protected. This relationship operated on both the practical-organizational level (skills, resources, publicity, popular support, control of unions) and the ideological level (the conception of the workers' movement as lacking legitimate goals and interests of its own, as essentially one component of the national movement embodied in the self-proclaimed representative of the entire nation, the Wafd). In the interwar period this special relationship developed and changed in form and content, though nationalism continued to play a central role in shaping the workers' movement. Indeed, the subsumption of labor's own interests in a national struggle whose tone was set by other social strata would have profound and long-lasting effects.

The British authorities had ultimately been able to contain the pop-

106 1919: Upsurge and Revolution

ular uprising of March–April 1919, but only at the price of releasing Zaghlul and allowing him to make his case. In the following months the Wafd enhanced its prestige and consolidated its support among the masses. Although the Peace Conference rejected Egyptian demands for independence and recognized the British protectorate, the Wafd's success in mobilizing the people in demonstrations and the near-total boycott of the Milner Mission proved its growing strength. Although nationalist agitation and British repression continued through 1919, this was a period of political rather than violent struggle, of unionization among workers in the aftermath of the firestorms of March and April, and of a decline in the level of industrial conflict. The relative calm of late spring and early summer, however, was broken by an important strike at the Suez Canal which indicated that even foreign workers in Egypt had been deeply affected by the local and global upheavals that characterized the immediate postwar period.

Radicalism and Nationalism at the Suez Canal

The work force of the Suez Canal Company was divided into two segments of unequal size. One was made up of a small number of mainly foreign workers, relatively well-paid and permanently employed. The other was much larger and consisted of workers, mostly Egyptian, employed provisionally or indirectly at lower wages and lacking any job security. Wartime inflation and other grievances had led to unrest among both foreign and Egyptian workers at the SCC and the other foreign-owned firms serving the waterway before March 1919. Greek workers, who constituted the largest single ethnic group among the SCC's permanent cadre, formed the core of a new union in Port Said early in 1919, and were led by a lawyer named Zizinia. In its petition to the canal company the union, known as Le Phénix, asked for the eight-hour day, the permanent addition of all temporary wartime raises to the official wage scale, extra pay for work on Sundays and holidays, and the automatic granting of permanent status to all workers after a certain number of years' service.[25]

This last demand was especially important to the many SCC workers who despite years of employment were still considered provisional employees, were paid less for the same work, and enjoyed no benefits. That the cadre workers took up this issue is very significant, for it constituted an effort by the most privileged segment of the work

25. F/510, Services des Informations de la Marine dans le Levant (hereafter SIML), no. 198-CE, Port Said, March 30, 1919, "Rapport de l'agent D."; FO 141/487/7392/7-9.

force to reach across ethnic lines to their disadvantaged Egyptian fellow workers. The Greek workers may have been motivated not only by abstract principles of class solidarity but perhaps also by a recognition that their own status and jobs were vulnerable as long as the company was allowed to maintain a large reserve of cheap Egyptian labor. Rather than seeking to exclude the nonpermanent workers and fight to defend their own privileges, the organizers of Le Phénix resolved to compel the Suez Canal Company to treat all its workers equally.

The new union did not call a strike during March–April 1919, though once the situation grew more settled, the union stepped up its organizing efforts and attracted many of the scc's Egyptian workers. 'Ali Bey Lahayta, a local nationalist notable who had been arrested earlier for fomenting a strike, cooperated with Zizinia behind the scenes, and gave Le Phénix the seal of approval of the nationalist movement. A hitherto separate organization of Italian workers also merged with Le Phénix, which grew rapidly among the canal workers in Port Said and, to a lesser extent, in Suez and Ismailia. The Italians in particular had a well-deserved reputation for militancy, perhaps because of their relatively longer industrial experience and their exposure to trade unionism and socialist or anarchist politics in Italy.

There was another factor, however, that in 1919 helped create what might seem a rather unlikely alliance between Italians in Egypt and the Egyptian nationalist movement. An Italian of radical convictions would presumably be opposed to British rule in Egypt on grounds of anti-imperialist principle, but many other Italians felt great resentment after the war toward what they believed had been Britain's treacherous refusal to allow Italy the rewards of her wartime sacrifices. In particular the British had upheld Greek over Italian territorial claims, and this had engendered Italian hostility toward both the Greeks and the British—attitudes shared by many Egyptians. Indeed Italian workers and radicals in Egypt would play a key role in the labor movement in the summer of 1919, prompting General Allenby, the British High Commissioner in Egypt, to assert that the union movement "commands the support of the natives, who however do not appear to appreciate its real meaning, and of the Italians in Egypt, who, in this movement, are making common cause with the Egyptians against the present regime, which they hope to embarrass in this way."[26]

26. FO 407/185/27, Allenby to Curzon, July 1, 1919; FO 407/185/36, Allenby to Curzon, July 12, 1919; F/512, SIML, no. 210-CE, May 6, 1919. Within Le Phénix Greek and Italian workers cooperated closely, except for Greeks from the Dodecanese Islands (then under Italian rule) who were hostile toward their Italian co-workers.

108 1919: Upsurge and Revolution

By May 1919 Le Phénix felt strong enough to risk a confrontation with the powerful Suez Canal Company. Having failed to get a satisfactory response to its demands, the union called a general strike of all canal workers, and on May 13 work stopped at the SCC and all shipping companies. The next day the coalheavers also stopped work, and the strike spread slowly throughout the Suez Canal region, affecting even cigarette and electric company workers. The striking workers were led by a committee composed of three Greeks, two Italians, a Frenchman, and an Egyptian, and enjoyed considerable public support. Large sums were contributed to aid the strikers, mainly by European residents of the canal cities. French intelligence sources claimed that the donations were made by wealthy persons in order to forestall the emergence of Bolshevism among the workers, whereas the British asserted that Egyptian merchants were promoting the strike as a means of taking over the positions and profits of the local labor contractors. Neither of these allegations is supported by the evidence. The grievances of the Suez Canal Company's workers were unquestionably authentic, and the coalheavers and other area workers simply seized the opportunity offered by Le Phénix's strike to improve their own wages and working conditions. The coalheavers returned to work by June 1 after the contractors had agreed to supplement their piece rate out of their own pockets, but the other strikers remained out.[27]

Nonetheless, the Suez Canal continued to function in late May and early June despite the strike because British naval personnel took over key positions. The French government, pressured by SCC officials and shareholders in Paris, grew increasingly nervous, and demanded that the British authorities take action to break the strike. Allenby refused because (according to the French) he worried that "once drawn into such affairs he might find himself much more involved than he would have wished; every step on his part must be well-considered if he wishes to avoid compromising his authority." The French Minister in Egypt insisted that the strike was political in character, because it had been fomented by foreigners and was supported by the nationalists, and the protectorate must therefore intervene. The French were quite disturbed by what they regarded as the reluctance or inability of their obstensible ally to protect their investments and interests in Egypt forcefully. Still, Allenby continued to reject French demands, and argued that the strikers were not disturbing public order and the canal was functioning. The British authorities

27. FO 141/781/8915, May 14, 26, June 4, 1919; FO 141/487/7392/2, 3, 4, 5; F/510, SIML, no. 213-CE (May 17, 1919) and no. 214-CE (May 22, 1919).

1919: Upsurge and Revolution **109**

had enough problems elsewhere and were not anxious to dispatch military forces to break a popular strike at a delicate political juncture.[28]

Because British intervention was not forthcoming and the strikers remained united, the SCC was eventually forced to make concessions. The cadre workers won some of their principal demands, including the eight-hour day and a fortnight's paid leave with passage to and from Europe so that foreign workers could visit their homelands, and returned to work on June 10. It is not clear what if anything the noncadre SCC workers, and those employed at other companies, won as a result of the strike. Certainly such practices as maintaining a reserve of nonpermanent workers and contracting work out were not abolished at this time, and yet, the partial success of the strike was to provide the impetus for the emergence of the International Workers' Union of the Isthmus of Suez in the following months. Led by the radical Greek Dr. Skouphopoulos, this union sought to unite all those who worked at Canal-related enterprises into one organization around a core of SCC workers.

The Suez Canal workers' four-week strike was characterized by an unprecedented degree of unity between foreign and indigenous workers, and this unity resulted from the convergence of the militancy (and in some cases political radicalism) of the European workers and the nationalism of the Egyptian workers. This kind of organization across ethnic lines and common struggle had been rare in Egypt, and was facilitated by the fact that the Suez Canal area labor force included Europeans influenced by left-wing ideas and leaders and unsympathetic to the occupation regime. Their willingness to take risks in order to help their Egyptian co-workers opened the way to cooperation with local nationalist leaders and the formation of a strong union of all Suez Canal Company workers.

The summer of 1919 marked the limit of cooperation between Egyptian and foreign (especially Italian) workers elsewhere in Egypt as well, though it did not always take the form of joint organization. The strike wave of March–April had largely involved Egyptian workers and been inextricably linked with the nationalist upsurge. During the following three months the young labor movement began to emerge in its own right, and appear as a distinct phenomenon. Egyptian nationalism was of course a key factor in this process, but foreign workers became much more active and militant as well, often in cooperation with indigenous workers. It was this unprecedented devel-

28. F/39, P. Lefevre-Pontalis to S. Pichon, Minister of Foreign Affairs, June 5, 1919. See also FO 141/787/7392/23, June 23, 1919.

110   1919: Upsurge and Revolution

opment that led General Allenby to comment in July 1919 that "the foreign and native working classes have apparently identified in their own minds the Syndicalist [that is, trade union] movement and the Extremist [that is, nationalist] agitation."[29] In that sense the Suez Canal strike in May–June foreshadowed another explosion of industrial conflict in the summer. That explosion unavoidably had a nationalist dimension, but its class dimension was more crucial and more pronounced than that of any previous upsurge of the Egyptian labor movement. If the spring of 1919 had seen the birth of a workers' movement in the midst of national revolution, then the summer of that year saw the working class find its own distinctive voice and come out fighting for its own demands.

August 1919: "Il Pleut des Syndicats!"

As early as June there had been signs of increasing unrest in many sectors of the working class. There were real reasons for labor dissatisfaction. Whatever wage gains had been made in the spring were rapidly being eroded by renewed inflation as prices began to leap upward again after March (see Table 3). In addition, specific groups of workers had their own particular grievances. The tramway workers, for example, wanted higher wages, but they also felt that the CTC was reneging on the concessions it had made in the spring. The panel the company had created to investigate sanctions against workers was composed of white-collar employees loyal to management and approved whatever punishments supervisors imposed. Promised pay raises had not been implemented, the issue of severance pay remained unresolved, and other company obligations provided for in the April agreement had not been fulfilled. Early in August the tram workers presented the CTC a list of demands to definitively settle these issues. The workers also insisted that the company formally recognize the new union as their bargaining agent. The head of the union was the nationalist lawyer Muhammad Kamil Husayn, recently released from internment and once again in the thick of labor affairs.[30] On all sides, Egyptian and foreign workers (many of them now unionized) began pressing their demands.

The first week of August saw a brief strike by dockworkers at the port of Alexandria, but what really set off the explosion was the sudden strike on August 10 of the Cairo tramway workers. Apparently

29. FO 407/185/57, Allenby to Curzon, July 22, 1919.
30. FO 141/781/8915, June 3, 1919; FO 141/748/8839/12, Dr. Granville, "Note on the Strike of the Cairo Electric Tramways," October 6, 1919; 'Ali, *Taqrir*, p. 12; al-Rafi'i, *1919*, II, p. 29.

1919: Upsurge and Revolution 111

fearing that the company was about to fire a large number of workers in order to preempt a strike, the union chose to act first. The tram system was completely shut down, and negotiations began under government auspices. The bold action of the tramwaymen, who had in the past often set the pace for the entire workers' movement, broke the dike of passivity. Within a few days many of the Egyptian and foreign workers of Cairo and Alexandria were on strike. The great strike wave of August 1919 included the tramways of Cairo, Helipolis, and Alexandria, omnibus drivers, the 'Anabir and Jabal al-Zaytun railway workers, numerous cigarette factories, the Abu Qirqas sugar mill, the Hawamdiyya refinery, waiters and kitchen workers in the major cafes, restaurants, and patisseries of Cairo and Alexandria, shop and bank employees, bakery workers, the Ma'asara quarrymen, the Candida engineering works in Alexandria, Bonded Stores warehouses and the Spathis soda factory. There were also strikes in Suez, Tanta, and Mansura. The strike wave was accompanied by a wave of unionization which largely though not exclusively affected relatively skilled or educated foreign workers and white-collar employees. During these weeks, for example, new unions were established by bank, hotel, and shop employees, journalists, tailors, carpenters, electricians (foreign and native), lithographers, bakery workers, waiters, chauffeurs, automobile mechanics, lawyers' clerks, cabdrivers, painters, and hairdressers. It was the sudden mushrooming of labor unions that prompted the daily newspaper *La Bourse Égyptienne* to proclaim in its headline of August 21: "Il pleut des syndicats!"

The spread of strike fever from the Cairo tramwaymen to other workers was apparently not entirely spontaneous. When the tram strike first began, British intelligence reported rumors that certain nationalists and European workers were trying to bring other public utility workers out on strike as well. These rumors had some basis in fact, for a group of Italian radicals, with the tacit support of the Wafd, was indeed trying to generalize the strike wave and encourage the formation of unions. Two individuals played important parts in this agitation. One was Max di Collalto, proprietor of the Italian-language Cairene daily *Roma* and leader of the Societé Internationale des Employés du Caire, which claimed over a thousand members. His role was mainly that of propagandist. A second Italian, Guiseppe Pizzuto, was more directly active in labor struggles. An Italian subject born in Egypt, Pizzuto had served in the Italian army during the war, then returned to become president of the printers' union. Although his precise political affiliations cannot be determined, he was certainly a revolutionary socialist and much affected by the radical upsurge then taking place in Italy. He took his internationalist principles seriously,

112 1919: Upsurge and Revolution

for he convinced the printers' union (hitherto an exclusive European preserve) to accept Egyptians as members on equal terms. Workers in the printing trades were for a time among the most radical segments of the working class, a phenomenon found in many countries.[31]

Pizzuto went into action at the earliest opportunity. He attended the first meeting of the striking tramwaymen accompanied by 60 Italian workers to express support for their struggle, and broached the idea of a government takeover of the tramways. On their way home the Italians were reported to have shouted "Long Live Bolshevism!" Shortly thereafter Pizzuto established a "Bourse de Travail" in Cairo and served as its secretary. The Bourse functioned during August as a sort of trade union center, sponsoring the formation of new unions (most of them craft unions of skilled foreign workers), assisting in talks with employers, and issuing almost daily bulletins to the press about strikes, disputes, demands, and union activities. The Bourse claimed that it had 15,000 members in twelve affiliated unions, but this seems an exaggeration.

The August strike wave had two distinct but overlapping components. The predominantly Egyptian workers in the transport sector and a few other large enterprises touched off and constituted the core of the upsurge of class conflict. At the same time, the mainly foreign workers in the skilled and service trades also went on strike or at least formed unions, and in these sectors the struggles were coordinated by the Bourse de Travail set up by the Italian radicals. Unity seems to have been strong across ethnic, national, and religious lines with no reports of internal conflicts among the strikers. Within a few weeks, however, the strike wave among the foreign workers subsided, for many of them had won substantial gains from the small proprietors who employed them, their unions were firmly established, and they returned to work. The British authorities also moved against the Bourse de Travail which they saw as a dangerous center for radical agitation linked to the nationalist movement. Allenby sought to have Collalto deported to Italy, but was initially unsuccessful. When the pro-occupation *Egyptian Mail* launched a press campaign against the Bourse and its leader Pizzuto, the linotypists at the newspaper agreed not to set in print any article hostile to the organization of which their own union was an affiliate. It was only at the end of September that Collalto and Pizzuto were deported, a step that offended public opin-

31. FO 141/748/8839, Department of Public Security/Military Intelligence, August 10, 1919; FO 407/185/57, Allenby to Curzon, July 22, 1919; FO 407/185/171, Cheetham to Curzon, September 8, 1919; FO 141/779/9065/12.

1919: Upsurge and Revolution **113**

ion and prompted a brief protest strike by Cairo printing workers.[32] The removal of the two Italian activists from the scene resulted in the demise of the short-lived but influential Bourse de Travail.

Dénouement: The Cairo Tram Strike

Even while the Bourse had been active, the main focus of both official and public concern were the tram strikes in Cairo, Alexandria and Heliopolis. The strikes involving foreign workers had in general been brief and most of the stoppages involving Egyptian workers had ended in August, but the tram strikes continued. In Cairo it had become evident shortly after the strike began that the central issue was that of union recognition. The CTC claimed to be willing to negotiate with its workers, but it adamantly refused to negotiate with Muhammad Kamil Husayn or anyone else as the representative of a tramway workers' union. The tramwaymen were quite determined that their union be recognized, as they demonstrated at a meeting of nearly 2,000 strikers—essentially the entire work force—on August 15, five days after the strike began. Muhammad Kamil Husayn chaired this meeting as president of the union, and rank and file workers were represented in the leadership by delegates elected from the various branches of the company. These delegates represented a fair cross section of the CTC work force: those elected by the drivers and conductors in the three depots were mainly Egyptian Muslims; the two representatives of the inspectors and station chiefs were foreigners; and the delegates from the workshops consisted of a Jew, an Italian, an Egyptian Muslim, and a Syrian Christian. The nonsectarian character of the union and the strike was further demonstrated when the opening benediction was given by a priest, Father Zakhari al-Antuni, who spoke of the benefits of unity and concord. At this meeting the workers voted (with only one dissenting ballot) to reject a proposal by the prime minister that the president and delegates of the union agree to negotiate with the tram company not as representatives of the union but as representatives of the company's employees.[33]

Another mass meeting held three days later at the American Cosmograph movie theater reaffirmed this decision and also adopted a new and unprecedented tactic devised by the union's president. In order to compel the company to recognize the union, the workers agreed to assign the union all back wages still owed them from before

32. *BE*, August 21, 1919; FO 407/185/137, 171, 215; FO 141/781/8915; F/39, Alexandria, September 20, 1919.
33. *BE*, August 18, 1919.

114   1919: Upsurge and Revolution

the strike, and they signed forms requesting the company to deposit their wages in the union's account at the Banco di Roma. Not surprisingly the CTC refused to cooperate, and the workers refused to draw their wages directly from the company. The stalemate was broken after the governor of Cairo stepped in to mediate and the workers backed down, but the tactic was one Muhammad Kamil Husayn would employ again.[34]

The nationalist press was of course strongly supportive of the strike, and the British believed that the Wafdist central committee was distributing large sums of money to the tramway workers in the capital. The nationalists were also said to have imposed a special levy of fifteen piastres a day on every cabdriver in Cairo for the benefit of the strikers.[35] Support for the tram workers and criticism of the Cairo Tramway Company also came from circles beyond those with a purely political interest in undermining British authority. Muhammad Tal 'at Harb, for example, the apostle of Egypt's economic independence and later the founder of Bank Misr, was motivated by the long strike to write a series of articles in September 1919 on the question of the tramways. Critical of foreign domination of Egypt's economy and anxious to promote indigenous capitalist development, Harb sharply attacked the tram company's corporate structure and the easy concession terms granted it by the Egyptian government. The CTC was now claiming that it could not afford to raise its workers' wages unless it was allowed a fare increase, but Harb argued that an increase would only benefit the company's founders and directors. Harb's articles were sympathetic to the workers, and epitomized the convergence of the interests of the young working class and a nascent Egyptian industrial bourgeoisie, both fighting the power of foreign capital in their country.[36]

Much of the middle-class European and Levantine tram-riding public also expressed resentment toward the CTC and sympathy for

---

34. *BE*, August 19, 27, 1919; FO 141/748/8839/3a, August 19, 1919. The Banco di Roma seems to have served as a repository and conduit for nationalist and labor funds, a manifestation of the special relationship between some segment of the Italian community in Egypt and the independence movement. British and tramway company officials were of course well aware of the bank's role; see for example FO 141/748/8839/7, Secretary of State for Foreign Affairs to the High Commissioner, September 5, 1919, which includes a copy of a letter on this matter from Gaston Ithier, director of the CTC's parent company in Brussels.

35. FO 407/185/205, Cheetham to Curzon, August 18, 1919; FO 141/781/8915, August 26, September 6, 1919.

36. These articles originally appeared in *al-Ahram* ending on September 17, 1919, and were also published in Hafiz Mahmud et al., *Tal'at Harb* (Cairo, 1936), pp. 74–82. On Tal'at Harb and the early history of Bank Misr, see Davis, *Challenging Colonialism*.

the workers. Their viewpoint was represented by Emile Boulad, a lawyer of Syrian origin who practiced in both the Mixed and National Courts. His pamphlet *Les Tramways du Caire en 1919* was published during the strike, for which Boulad held the company to blame. Boulad believed that by granting a minimum wage of fifteen piastres, free uniforms, a workday of eight or nine hours, reasonable provision for days of rest, severance pay, and sick pay the company's labor troubles would end. He also criticized management for poor service, dirty and overcrowded cars, a shortage of first-class seats, and untrained workers. Boulad denounced the company's plan to raise fares, and advocated special trams at half-fare for workers during certain times of the day. This last proposal, however, seems to have been due less to a concern for the plight of poor workers than a desire to segregate them from the middle classes. In order to protect the public interest and prevent continual labor strife, Boulad proposed that an independent and impartial lawyer be appointed to the company's departments that handled the recruitment and disciplining of workers. His proposals were submitted to a public meeting of tram passengers held at the Cinema Obelisk on September 28. Four delegates were chosen to help mediate the strike which by that time had gone on for more than seven weeks.

The British authorities did not intervene directly to break the strike—an indication of how much the revolution had weakened their grip on Egypt—but they were quite concerned about the dangerous political implications of the simultaneous tramway strikes in Cairo, Alexandria, and Heliopolis. One official wrote:

> If the strikers should succeed in enforcing all their demands, their success would not only be considered as a triumph for them, but would also be looked upon by the natives as a defeat of both the employers and the Authorities, a fact which will probably encourage the mass of the population to make trouble.[37]

Therefore, two measures were taken in late August to quell the strike wave spearheaded by the Cairo tramwaymen. First, Muhammad Kamil Husayn was arrested, allegedly for trying to organize the 'Anabir workers and bring them out on strike. The railway workshop workers had struck briefly in mid-August, but then returned to work, and were not heard from again until the autumn. Despite Husayn's arrest the tramwaymen's union continued to function and the workers stayed out on strike.[38]

37. FO 141/781/8915, August 18, 1919.
38. *Ibid.*, August 25, 1919.

116   1919: Upsurge and Revolution

The other measure was more far-reaching in its consequences. Until this time there had existed no institutionalized system of mediating labor disputes. If a dispute or strike were significant enough, the governor of the city concerned or even the prime minister might bring the two parties together, and try to resolve the conflict. This informal system was overwhelmed and collapsed during the August strike wave, and so the government of Muhammad Sa 'id Pasha, with General Allenby's encouragement, announced the creation of a Labor Conciliation Board (LCB) on August 19. This body was to investigate disputes between workers and employers, appoint mediators to convene negotiations, propose measures to resolve disputes, and participate in the development of representation for workers and employers. The first president of the LCB was Dr. Alexander Granville, who was also serving at that time as president of the Quarantine Board, vice-president of the Alexandria Municipal Commission, and head of the Red Cross. Its other members were Rafla Tadrus Bey, a government official; Muhammad Sadiq Bey, chief of the Alexandria prosecutor's office; and William Hornblower, a British official who soon resigned.[39]

The establishment of this specialized body to deal with labor disputes is a clear indication of how seriously British colonial officials and the Egyptian government took the new phenomenon of class conflict. Clearly, the time had come to develop some means of lessening the impact of industrial strife which might boil over and threaten the political stability of the occupation regime and the interests of foreign capital. Yet in keeping with the principles of classical liberalism, the LCB was granted only very limited powers, for it could not impose binding arbitration, or enforce compliance with agreements reached under its auspices, but merely report its findings and make recommendations. Furthermore, given the scale of industrial unrest, the Board was incapable of handling every dispute, and once again the job of mediation generally devolved on the local governors. Nonetheless, the creation of the Labor Conciliation Board was a significant first step by the Egyptian state in recognizing the importance of the working class and labor movement, and in deploying methods of control other than the police.

British officials had considered going even further that autumn. Sir Miles Cheetham, who replaced Allenby during the latter's absence in England, discussed with the Foreign Office a draft decree officially recognizing trade unions for workers other than white-collar civil servants, subject to approval in each case by the minister of the interior.

39. *BE*, August 19, 1919.

1919: Upsurge and Revolution   **117**

The Egyptian government was desperate to enhance its popularity, and reportedly favored the idea. The power to deny formal legal status to unions whose charters the government did not approve would constitute a powerful means of control, while the courts could dissolve any union whose conduct contravened public policy. But the Residency was worried about the public perception of such a step at a time of widespread labor militancy and nationalist agitation. Cheetham cabled Curzon that

> Government recognition would give impetus to [the trade union movement] and be regarded as a victory of Extremists, and it is doubtful if, in present circumstances, Government policy, as proposed, would be immediately effective. . . . I think that law may be interpreted as a sign of weakness at present moment and increase influence of Extremists.[40]

In the end the proposal was shelved, and many years were to pass before legal recognition of unions won a serious place on the government's agenda. In 1919 the British officials who directed Egypt's affairs were not surprisingly too fearful that the new unions would be an instrument with which the Wafd, and perhaps radical elements as well, could mobilize the working class to take this step. The creation of a mediation board with limited powers was the furthest they were willing to go in confronting the emergence of an active Egyptian workers' movement.

The first major task of the new Labor Conciliation Board was the settlement of the Cairo tram strike, which remained difficult. The company claimed it could not afford to make any substantial concessions unless tram fares were increased, though the government's accountants who examined the CTC's books ultimately rejected this contention. It was only at the beginning of October that an agreement was finally achieved, and tram service was resumed on October 5 after fifty-six days. The October agreement gave the drivers and conductors a wage increase that brought their pay scale to between sixteen and twenty-one piastres a day when counting the supplement for inflation. The other CTC workers also won increases. The company agreed to rehire all the strikers and not oppose union activity, though it continued to refuse to actually recognize or deal with the union. All penalties imposed by inspectors had to be approved by the head of the traffic department after consultation with the investigations panel, which was to include an Arabic-speaking representative of

---

40. FO 407/185/181, 202, 208, Cheetham to Curzon, September 25, 26, October 6, 1919; /219, Curzon to Cheetham, October 13, 1919.

118   1919: Upsurge and Revolution

management, a clerical employee to act as recorder, and a worker appointed by the company. Also important was the company's promise to publish (in both French and Arabic) and distribute copies of its work rules and conditions of service (*la'ihat al-khidma*) to the workers. The strikes on the Heliopolis and Alexandria tram systems also came to an end on the basis of agreements similar to that reached in Cairo. In Alexandria, however, the strike was settled only after the Municipal Commission, exasperated by the tram company's intransigence and its plans to double fares, threatened to buy out the tram concession and run the system itself.[41]

The settlement of the tram strikes marked the end of the great strike wave that had erupted in mid-August. Unrest among the 'Anabir workers had fluctuated during the summer and fall, and a strike had seemed imminent in late October. But in the end the railwaymen contented themselves with a twelve-hour protest strike for higher wages, and on the whole the 'Anabir workers were only marginally involved in the labor militancy of the second half of 1919.[42] It was the tram workers, especially those of Cairo, who had touched off the explosion of industrial unrest, and it was they who stayed out on strike long after the many Egyptian and foreign workers who had initially followed their lead returned to work. The agreement of October 1919 which ended the Cairo tram strike embodied substantial gains for the workers, especially with regard to wages, but it also involved compromises. The workers did not win recognition for their union or severance pay, and the composition of the investigations panel still did not give them the strong protection against managerial abuse they had sought. Nonetheless the bargain was seen as a victory for the workers, and the agreement of October 1919 served as a point of reference in numerous struggles in the following years. It is a measure of the degree to which favorable political circumstances allowed the Cairo tramwaymen to win important gains in 1919 that decades would pass before the promise of the October agreement would be fully realized.

The strike wave of August 1919 was made possible by the popular uprising of the preceding spring. The national revolution against Brit-

41. FO 141/748/8839/12, Granville, "Note," October 6, 1919; Belgium, MAE, N. Leysbeth (consul in Alexandria) to Paul Hymans, Foreign Minister, September 22, October 10, 1919; *BE*, August–October 1919, passim.

42. FO 141/687/8705/17, Macauley to the Residency, September 1, 1919; /27, Major Courtney, Intelligence, to the Residency, October 22, 1919; /28, Blakeney (ESR general manager) to Cheetham, October 23, 1919; FO 407/186/325; FO 141/781/8915, Intelligence, October 27, 1919. The passivity of the 'Anabir workers may be explained by such measures of intimidation as the arrest of M. K. Husayn and government threats to militarize the railways as well as by the fact that they had already won substantial wage increases earlier in the year.

1919: Upsurge and Revolution **119**

ish rule opened the floodgates of labor organization and militant action, while the persistence of high inflation rates ensured that worker activism would continue. In 1919 a specific conjuncture of political, social, and economic factors not only propelled workers in large industrial and transport enterprises into action but won their struggles popular legitimacy and material support. Workers' efforts to improve their lot were seen as an integral part of the struggle of the whole Egyptian nation to free itself of foreign domination. This identification continued to earn the workers popular sympathy on into the summer and fall, even while they were fighting to achieve more purely economic demands. Those demands were also taken up by foreign workers in Egypt who took advantage of the opportunities opened up by the weakening of the colonial regime to form new unions and confront their employers. Many of the foreign workers were influenced by the Italian socialists who, along with their internationalism and anti-imperialism, stressed a new and radical notion of class identity and unity across ethnic and occupational lines. It may seem paradoxical that it was just when Egyptian nationalism was at its most militant and vigorous that foreign workers joined with their indigenous co-workers in common struggle against their employers, though in fact it was the resurgence of nationalism that facilitated the emergence of a workers' movement that could temporarily encompass workers of many nationalities. In a period of political struggle involving the broad masses of the population, common ground was established on which Egyptian workers motivated both by their own grievances in the workplace and by patriotic sentiment could cooperate on a relatively equal basis with their foreign counterparts.

By the end of 1919 there were an estimated twenty-one unions functioning in Cairo, seventeen in Alexandria, and others in the Suez Canal cities, the Delta towns, and elsewhere.[43] This momentous year had witnessed the birth of an Egyptian workers' movement closely linked to the simultaneous upsurge of nationalism. That movement would bear marks of the circumstances of its birth for a long time in the form of a special relationship with the Egyptian nationalist movement. This is not to say that the subsequent history of Egyptian labor was already determined in 1919, but in many ways the 1919 revolution was the formative experience of the Egyptian union movement— an experience that played a large part in molding the ideological perspective and organizational practice of both unionized workers and

43. A.A.I. El-Gritly, "The Structure of Modern Industry in Egypt," *L'Égypte Contemporaine*, no. 241-242 (November–December 1947).

120 1919: Upsurge and Revolution

bourgeois nationalists active in labor affairs. The "lessons" learned in 1919 would be reinforced by the daily experiences and struggles of Egyptian workers inside and outside the workplace. This helped foster continued dependence on bourgeois nationalists as leaders or patrons and on bourgeois nationalism as the dominant ideological framework. Countervailing tendencies were of course also at work which would in time lead Egyptian workers to see the disadvantages and contradictions in the labor-nationalist relationship and increasingly question it. But in 1919 this was all far in the future. In the course of a few stormy months the indigenous working class had emerged, forcefully and irrevocably, onto the stage of history with its own forms of organization and struggle. Egypt would never again be without a union movement which, however weak and divided at times, would nevertheless retain strong roots among the workers, and remain a significant factor in industrial and political life.

Chapter V

The Unions, the Left, and the Wafd, 1920–1924

The five years that followed the upheavals of 1919 were important ones in the history of Egyptian labor. After making substantial gains in the spring, summer, and fall of 1919, many unions found themselves unable to make further headway, or were forced onto the defensive. Despite the use of aggressive and innovative methods of struggle even such militant groups as the Cairo tramwaymen could not gain any new ground and were unable even to secure what they thought they had won in 1919. In part this resulted from the fact that the conjuncture of widespread class conflict with popular nationalist agitation did not recur on the same scale in 1920–1924 as it had in the revolutionary year 1919. Economic conditions also played a part, as did the Wafd's ambivalent attitude toward popular and worker struggles.

The attitude of the Wafd was important because in this period Wafdist lawyers and other bourgeois elements assumed leading roles in the major Egyptian unions and the party consolidated its hegemony over the organized working class. This hegemony was strengthened during the brief period in 1924 when the Wafd held the reins of government under a limited form of independence, and used its power and prestige to bring the unions directly under its control. For a few years a small but vigorous Egyptian communist movement with strong roots in certain segments of the trade union movement challenged the Wafd's influence and projected another conception of class identity and struggle, but the leftist challenge was ultimately defeated and bourgeois nationalism firmly established as the dominant organizational and ideological influence on Egyptian labor. In many respects the patterns set in the first half of the 1920s would shape the course of labor politics until the Second World War.

122 Unions, 1920–1924

This period was characterized by continued struggle, usually political but sometimes violent, for Egyptian independence. Resistance to British rule took the form of demonstrations, boycotts, and sporadic acts of terrorism against English officials and Egyptian collaborators. Sa'd Zaghlul Pasha, the tribune of the national movement, returned to Egypt in the spring of 1921 after two years of fruitless campaigning and negotiating in Europe. The tumultuous welcome he received demonstrated once again the degree to which the Wafd had won massive popular support. In order to preempt the Wafd and reach a compromise with the British, Prime Minister 'Adli Yakan Pasha asserted his claim to lead the Egyptian delegation in a new round of talks in London. Zaghlul rejected this claim because he regarded the Egyptian government as essentially a tool of the British, and insisted that he head the delegation as leader of the Wafd, the sole legitimate representative of the Egyptian nation. The ensuing conflict led to a split in the Wafd's leadership. The more conservative members had no stomach left for militancy and struggle and favored a compromise with 'Adli and the British. They would later form the Liberal Constitutionalist party, dominated by and championing the interests of the large landowners. The Wafd's majority led by Zaghlul was against compromise, and insisted on the termination of the British protectorate, the abolition of martial law, and complete independence. This split was the first major crack in the facade of national unity. Although large landowners would retain considerable influence in the Wafd's leadership, the split helped transform the Wafd into a party of the democratic nationalist urban and rural middle classes, supported by the masses, and acting in the name of the entire nation.

After 'Adli Pasha's departure for London, the Wafd sought to mobilize its constituencies in order to undermine his legitimacy and demonstrate its own. The British eventually responded to this renewed upsurge of nationalist agitation by again arresting Zaghlul and other Wafd leaders and deporting them. This of course led to further unrest and violence and discredited 'Adli, who resigned after the collapse of the London talks. By the end of 1921 it had become clear to the British that the protectorate they had imposed on Egypt in 1914 could not be maintained, and on February 28, 1922, they unilaterally declared Egypt an independent state except for four areas over which the British retained control: the security of imperial communications, the defense of Egypt, the protection of foreign interests and minorities, and the Sudan.

The Wafd's political rivals accepted the unilateral declaration and began to draft a constitution, whereas the radical nationalists rejected it as a disguised protectorate. The government, backed by the British, responded to continued nationalist opposition with increased repression, and Zaghlul remained in detention abroad until March 1923. The Wafd eventually went along with the British *fait accompli* despite its dislike of the limited independence Egypt had been granted and the extensive powers the new constitution gave King Fu'ad, who had authoritarian ambitions. In the first elections under the 1923 constitution (January 1924) the Wafd won 195 of 214 seats, the Liberal Constitutionalists and Nationalists two seats each, and independents the rest. Zaghlul had conclusively demonstrated that he was in fact regarded by the masses as "leader of the nation," and shortly thereafter he formed the first elected government of a semi-independent Egypt.

Economic conditions from 1920 to 1924 stimulated continued labor unrest. Unemployment rose at the beginning of the decade as certain industries contracted because of the loss of artificial wartime protection and changes in the world market. Inflation remained high, with 1920 the worst year: the weighted wholesale price index rose from 239 in August 1919 to 261 in December, then to a high of 375 in February 1920. Thereafter prices declined gradually, and approached the levels of the early war years by 1922 or 1923.[1] The real wages of many workers were still below prewar levels, however, and price deflation was accompanied by a business slump that resulted in higher unemployment and wage cuts. For these reasons many of the struggles of the early 1920s were the result of the erosion of whatever gains had been won earlier, of continued downward pressure on real wages, and of the improved bargaining position of the employers. However, the years 1920 and 1921 saw more industrial unrest and conflict than 1922 or 1923. This was due both to the relative economic stabilization that began after 1921 and to changing political conditions whose relation to labor activism will be discussed below.

The labor movement that emerged from the tumult of 1919 consisted of several components. The Labor Conciliation Board reported in 1921 that there were thirty-eight unions in Cairo, thirty-three in Alexandria, eighteen in the Suez Canal area, and six elsewhere in Egypt. Some of these existed only on paper or functioned only when economic conditions allowed. For example, severe unemployment in Port Said was reported to have resulted in the paralysis of the unions of tailors, bootmakers, and bumboatmen for lack of funds. These figures also include a number of workers' mutual aid societies as well a

---

1. *AS 1923–1924*, pp. 212–17. These figures do not include rents, which rose rapidly, and probably underestimate the impact of inflation.

124 Unions, 1920–1924

few *syndicats* of bakery, restaurant, and shop owners.[2] Total union membership is difficult to determine but was probably no more than twenty thousand. Nonetheless, an active trade union movement was in existence.

The strongest unions were those formed by workers in the public utilities: the tramway, gas, electric, and water companies. The authorities generally sought to mediate disputes and strikes in this sensitive sector in order to avoid the disruption of services, and this intervention could benefit the workers by putting pressure on the companies to make concessions. The employers were also often able to pass the costs of concessions on to their customers because the services they provided had a low elasticity of demand. As noted earlier, many of these workers had in 1919 won higher wages, improved benefits, and a workday of close to eight hours. However, these gains proved inadequate in the following years, prompting continued agitation and conflict. Moreover, the workers had not been able to compel either the companies or the state to recognize their unions as bargaining agents, or to grant them a defined legal status, and this also led to conflict. In the early 1920s the employers regained the superior bargaining position they had temporarily lost in 1919, and this would make industrial conflict long, bitter, and often unsuccessful for the workers.

In contrast with these industrial unions, which however embattled remained vigorous, the MTWU was clearly on the decline by 1921. Although it represented workers at twenty-six different enterprises in Alexandria, its total membership had dropped to about one thousand. In Cairo a smaller MTWU branch continued to exist but was less active because most workers preferred to be part of a union that comprised all the wage workers in the workplace or all the workers employed in their trade in their locale.[3] The 'Anabir workers in Cairo, who tended to be organized into unions which followed the MTWU model, constituted the major exception to this pattern. Even in their case, however, the exception was usually more formal than real, for though these unions included workers from various trades, the great majority of their members were 'Anabir employees which in effect made them railway unions. The MTWU lingered on for some years in its original form, but it was no longer an important force on the labor scene. As its patron the Nationalist party had been eclipsed in political life by the Wafd, so the MTWU was eclipsed by the new union

---

2. FO 141/779/9321, "VIIe Rapport de la Commission de Conciliation de Travail" (July 1921–March 1922), hereafter cited as LCB VII. On Port Said see FO 407/185/12, June 22–30, 1922.
3. 'Aryan, *Markaz*, p. 88; LCB VIII.

movement that emerged in 1919 under the influence of the Wafd and other new political forces.

The many unions formed by skilled foreign and Egyptian workers before or during 1919 generally continued to function. Some concentrated solely on narrowly-defined union issues, whereas others played important roles in labor politics and were frequently involved in industrial conflict. Among the latter were the unions affiliated with the socialist-led labor federation established in 1921 which will be discussed in detail below, and the Suez Canal workers' union led by the radical Dr. Skouphopoulos. In contrast the skilled cigarette rollers, the first workers in Egypt to organize and often in the vanguard of the labor movement, found themselves facing extinction in the early 1920s. The threat of mechanization that had been hanging over their heads for a decade finally materialized. Sharpened competition in the industry and the world market impelled the cigarette companies to replace workers with machines. Once the process began it proceeded very rapidly. In January 1920 the twelve largest Egyptian cigarette firms employed 1,519 rollers; eighteen months later only 318 still had jobs. Layoffs continued apace, and soon reached other categories of skilled cigarette workers while the wages of those still employed were cut sharply. By 1921 these workers, only recently the elite of the working class, were in a state of extreme distress, destitute and unemployable.[4]

The cigarette rollers sought to resist the introduction of machinery by industrial action, but they were in no position to win. Although the Labor Conciliation Board agreed that many had received little or no severance pay, it could not compel the companies to do anything. Despite numerous public meetings, demonstrations and petitions, the government refused to take any measure to discourage mechanization or relieve the workers' misery. There was, of course, no provision for unemployment benefits in Egypt at that time, and well-paid jobs were hard to find. Other workers and unions, especially those influenced by the left, contributed funds to help the cigarette rollers, but as the years passed the tone of their petitions and supplications for assistance grew ever more desperate. A petition presented to the prime minister in August 1926 and preserved by the secret police lists the names of 28 workers (Greeks, Syrians, and Egyptians), who had fallen into depression and despondency because of their poverty and degradation and had finally killed themselves. This appeal, like

4. See Politis, L'Hellénisme, pp. 341–45; Dr. I. G. Levi, "Le Commerce et l'industrie de l'Égypte," L'Égypte Industrielle III, 4 (April 4, 1927); FO 141/779/9321, "The Cigarette-making Industry in Egypt," July 19, 1921, LCB VII; FO 141/814/10464, E. Homan Mulock, "Report on the Economic and Financial Situation of Egypt," April 1922.

126 Unions, 1920–1924

all the rest, fell on deaf ears, and the once proud elite of skilled cigarette workers ceased to exist.[5]

The Egyptian cigarette industry was itself completely reorganized in the late 1920s as the huge British-American Tobacco Company invaded the local market. In 1927 British-American bought out nine of the largest firms and transformed them into a modern, integrated, highly mechanized enterprise known as the Eastern Tobacco Company. In this way the technical and organizational transformation the industry underwent in the 1920s eliminated the jobs of the most skilled cigarette workers and much reduced the bargaining power of those who remained. Their once powerful unions declined and in some cases disappeared; over a decade was to pass before new organizations arose to take their place. The tragedy of the cigarette rollers demonstrated to other Egyptian workers the fragility of their livelihoods, the importance of unions strong enough to match the employers' power, and the need for a benevolent state willing and able to intervene and legislate on behalf of the disadvantaged.

In this period there were also strikes by workers not organized into unions, many of them seasonally-employed peasants. In the fall of 1919, for example, 1,800 workers struck at cotton ginning plants in Fayum and Buhayra, and two years later there was a brief stoppage at Zifta. The carters and coalheavers of Port Said, workers at the sugar mills at Kom Ombo and Hawamdiyya, and a thousand workers employed at the Suez petroleum refinery also struck in the early 1920s. Strikes among these peasant workers were usually brief and often involved violence or threats of violence. This was especially true in the sugar industry where the seasonal character of the work and the unskilled peasant composition of the work force made sustained organization and struggle difficult to achieve. Early in 1922, for example, the director of the Hawamdiyya refinery told the police that agitators among the workers had hung pictures of revolvers around the premises in order to intimidate the illiterate workers into joining a threatened strike. Tensions between foreign employers and indigenous workers could also explode into violence, as in November 1923 when a European engineer at the Armant sugar mill in Upper Egypt shot and killed a worker during a strike.[6]

Outbreaks of violence could also reflect a convergence of class and national conflict reminiscent of the 1919 revolution. In May 1921, for example, a large Alexandria soap and vegetable oil factory managed

5. See CSP, August 24, 1926.
6. *BE*, January 10, 1922; F/233, Gaillard (French diplomatic agent in Cairo) to the Foreign Minister, November 21, 1923.

by a Greek was attacked by several thousand rioters among whom were former workers. This attack took place during several days of bloody clashes between Egyptians and Greeks in the port city in a period of acute political crisis. This particular factory was a target because it was associated with Greeks, because it was foreign-owned, and because its workers had specific grievances against its management.[7] Egyptian workers also continued to express nationalist sentiments by more peaceful means, as unions, for example, took up collections among their members to send collective telegrams of protest to the British and of support to the Wafd.

A relatively small number of lawyers served as counsellors or presidents of one or more of the unions listed by the LCB in 1921. Muhammad Kamil Husayn, whose career will shortly be examined in some detail, was for example counsellor of the tram workers, the gas and electrical workers and the cigarette workers in Cairo. In Alexandria Sayyid Khadr and the same al-'Ararji who had first appeared on the labor scene at Jabal al-Zaytun in February 1919 represented many of the affiliates of the MTWU as well as the tramwaymen. Two other lawyers who were later to play key roles in the Wafdist labor movement were also already connected with unions, Hasan Nafi' as counsellor of the Heliopolis company's workers, and 'Aziz Mirham as *mustashar* (along with M. K. Husayn) of the cigarette workers. The roles these men and others played in the union movement of the 1920s embodied the developing relationship between the bourgeois nationalism of the Wafd and the emerging working class.

In the first half of the decade two poles of attraction, of very unequal strength, existed in the labor movement. On the one hand was the Wafd, which was closely linked to many unions and enjoyed vast popular support. Although it was only able to seek direct hegemony over the labor movement for a brief period in 1924, its influence was strong even earlier and can be studied in the forms of organization and struggle that characterized one of its most loyal constituencies, the 'Anabir workers. Second, an organized revolutionary left had emerged and struck roots in certain unions. Between those two poles and steering an independent course under a forceful and ambitious leader were the Cairo tramwaymen, who had continued to justify their reputation in these years as the most militant section of the working class. The following sections will discuss the Cairo tram workers, the communist presence in the labor movement, and the role of the Wafd in labor affairs in the first half of the 1920s, culmi-

7. F/40, letter from the Société des Huileries et Savonneries du Delta, May 24, 1921.

128   Unions, 1920–1924

nating in the Wafd's victory at the polls in January 1924 and the establishment of a Wafdist government.

The Tramway Workers on the Defensive

The Cairo tramwaymen quite rightly regarded the October 1919 agreement that ended their eight-week strike as a major step forward. But during the following years they found that their victory had been a largely empty one. Despite a series of bitter strikes and the employment of other means of collective struggle, it proved very difficult for them to hold the ground they thought they had won in 1919, much less gain new ground.

The tramwaymen's gains of October 1919 were eroded away almost immediately. The rate of inflation escalated at the end of 1919 and the beginning of 1920 so that the wage increases won in the autumn were no longer adequate. Furthermore, even though the Cairo Tramway Company had established a panel to investigate disciplinary charges and appointed a worker to it, the tramwaymen felt that the appointee was a puppet of management, "a negligible quantity who had no idea of what was going on around him, so that his presence was purely formal and the situation did not improve."[8] The company also fired numerous workers early in 1920 in what the workers saw as an attack on their union. Even the strike that ensued in February 1920 after unsuccessful negotiations was quickly and easily broken by the police and the army, for not only were the British authorities far better prepared than the previous year, but they did not have to contend with widespread strikes and disturbances and could turn their full might and attention to this struggle. Public and press sympathy for strikes had been eroded by the month-long gas workers' strike just ended, and after four days the tramway workers agreed to resume work. This defeat was a major blow for the Cairo Tramway Workers' Union (CTWU) and signalled that the company now had the upper hand.[9]

In the months that followed management stepped up its efforts to break the union and fired numerous activist workers. These policies, together with declining real wages, set the stage for further conflict at the CTC, but until Muhammad Kamil Husayn was released from detention on September 9, 1920 the catalyst would remain absent. He had long been connected with the Cairo tramway workers and until his arrest by the British had led their union in the first weeks of their

8. 'Ali, *Taqrir*, p. 14.
9. *BE*, February 12, 1920; FO 407/186/121, Allenby to Curzon, February 28, 1920. See also FO 141/748/8839/16, Russell (police commandant of Cairo) to the Advisor, Ministry of the Interior, February 23, 1920.

Unions, 1920–1924 **129**

ultimately successful strike the previous year. Husayn was a popular figure among the workers, a strong, ambitious leader with a forceful personality, and within a few weeks of his release he emerged as the union's *mustashar*. Indeed, it seems as though the lawyers and notables who headed the CTWU while he was in prison were merely filling in for him in his absence. The British regarded him with great suspicion and believed that he wanted to become Egypt's "labor dictator."[10]

Under Husayn's leadership, the CTWU immediately took the offensive by issuing a list of demands that include recognition of the union as bargaining agent, appointment of a union representative to the investigations panel, publication of the long-awaited work rules, and the permanent addition of the cost of living bonus to the wage scale. These demands were intended to secure the gains supposedly won in October 1919 by establishing the union as a recognized and institutionalized force in the CTC's relations with its workers. The company of course rejected these demands, and through the following year Husayn and the tramwaymen were to employ a variety of methods, some of them quite innovative, to achieve their goals.

The first new tactic the Cairo tramwaymen employed was sabotage. In November 1920, recognizing that a strike would have little likelihood of success, the tram drivers simply began to neglect the controls on their cars and allow them to derail, while the repair shop workers went on a slow-down strike. The tactic was very effective: within ten days service had been either stopped or severely reduced on many lines because of a shortage of rolling stock. Yet the tramwaymen continued to report for work and draw their wages, and the CTWU blamed the disruptions on poor management practices. Normal service was restored in January 1921 only after the government threatened to take forceful action against the union, which did not ultimately win any concessions by means of this clear demonstration of its power.[11]

Muhammad Kamil Husayn had other weapons in his arsenal, however. A few weeks after the end of the sabotage campaign the CTWU threatened that unless its demands were met the conductors would collect only enough fares to pay their own wages. This novel idea might have both hurt the company and pleased the tram-riding public, but for some reason it was never implemented. Instead, Husayn revived a tactic he had tried to use in August 1919 to compel the CTC to recognize and bargain with his union. In January 1921 the manager

10. FO 407/187/289, 340, 395.
11. FO 371/E9982/1364/16, "Fifth Report of the Labour Conciliation Board" (October–December 1920), hereafter cited as LCB V; FO 141/748/8839/17, M. Dauge of the CTC to the High Commissioner, December 16, 1920.

130 Unions, 1920–1924

of the tram company was notified that some 800 employees had irrevocably assigned all their wages to what was in effect their union. General Allenby, the British High Commissioner, was quite alarmed. "This extraordinary device is without precedent," he wrote the Foreign Office; it would "place this important Public Service Company entirely at the mercy of Kamel Effendi Hussein, the ambitious lawyer who is fomenting the movement." In the British view "the Tramway Company had been selected by political agitators [that is, the nationalists] as a fruitful ground on which to operate and to create trouble, so a series of minor conflicts were constantly arising between the Company and the men." When they felt that political stability and the security of their regime—as opposed to strictly economic issues—were at stake, the British were prepared to intervene. Allenby therefore immediately issued a martial law decree prohibiting the assignment of wages to a trade union or similar association as a threat to public order.[12]

The wage assignment tactic, then, proved a failure because of the prompt action and extraordinary legal powers of the British authorities. While Husayn's abortive maneuver was certainly clever, it also indicated the weakness of the CTWU in 1921 as compared to 1919. Less than a third of the CTC's 2,600 employees had agreed to assign their wages. Indeed, those who went along with the counsellor's plan were all Egyptians whereas the foreign workers were more cautious, which pointed to a breakdown in the unity and solidarity that had characterized the tramwaymen's struggles in 1919. The LCB, the British, and the CTC repeatedly claimed that the CTWU was dominated by Muhammad Kamil Husayn and a handful of followers who "terrorized" the peace-loving and hard-working majority. It does in fact seem that by 1921 the union was largely run by Husayn and by tramwaymen who had been fired for their activism. This does not however validate the "outside agitator" theory propagated by those who had an interest in suppressing and downplaying worker militancy. The harassment and dismissal of union activists and members had made it impossible for any tramway worker who wanted to keep his job to support the union openly, and for this reason the leading role in agitation devolved on the fired activists. Nonetheless, a gap may have developed between the activists and those still employed at the CTC because the latter still had something to lose and were vulnerable to victimization by management. The workers were also demoralized by

12. FO 407/188/70, January 12–19, 1921; FO 141/779/9321, Allenby to the Foreign Office, January 27, 1921; LCB V; FO 371/E2811, Granville to the Residency, February 23, 1921.

the series of defeats the union had suffered since the end of 1919, and by its inability, even under the leadership of Muhammad Kamil Husayn, to successfully confront management and win some concessions. There were, then, objective reasons for the decline in the tramwaymen's enthusiasm and support for the CTWU, a decline reflected in their hesitation about joining the wage assignment scheme and in a drop in the number of dues-paying members. Yet, as the events of 1921 were to make clear, there still existed among the rank and file a great reservoir of anger and frustration which could be tapped and channeled into militant action under the right circumstances.

This was manifested first in a number of brief and partial strikes that erupted over conflicts in the workplace in the spring of 1921, then in a prolonged and violent general strike by the Cairo tramway workers that began at the end of April. In the latter conflict the question of discipline was central. The workers demanded that a union appointee sit on the investigations panel along with the representatives of management as well as of the government. This was the only means through which they felt they could secure protection from abusive treatment and harassment. It would also give the workers some voice in controlling the work process through their union, and prevent intensified exploitation by means of speed-up, compulsory overtime, and the like. In addition the union demanded that all workers fired since October 1919 (by now some 337) be rehired.

The strike dragged on for weeks amidst sporadic clashes with police and company loyalists. Negotiations were held but foundered over the issue of rehiring workers accused of assaulting company employees during the strike. By the middle of May rank and file support for the strike was clearly wavering, and Muhammad Kamil Husayn became the target of open hostility from workers who felt the strike was lost. It was briefly given new life by the violent nationalist upsurge that erupted in May over the question of who would represent Egypt in negotiations with the British, but once the demonstrations and riots had subsided, the tram strikers again found themselves fighting a losing battle. At the end of May they returned to work, having won nothing for their efforts except further firings of union activists.[13]

This defeat demoralized the tram workers and undermined Husayn's position. He had now led the union to a series of defeats, the last of which had been a long and debilitating strike that had accomplished nothing. He had also failed to secure strike pay for the workers as he had apparently promised. Husayn still enjoyed enough sup-

13. FO 407/188/107, 185; /189/90, 161.

132   Unions, 1920–1924

port to retain control of the organization in the union elections held in the fall of 1921, defeating a challenge by Amin 'Izz al-'Arab, a Wafdist lawyer. This electoral challenge may have been an early attempt by the Zaghlulists to gain control of this key union and eliminate the influence of the ambitious and unruly Husayn who was linked to the Wafd's political rivals. It certainly reflected rank and file discontent with Husayn, and perhaps an incipient inclination to join the Wafdist camp motivated by both patriotism and a hope that the establishment of links to the popular and powerful Wafd might enhance the union's strength. That discontent with Husayn and support for the Wafd were not unconnected is suggested by the refusal of tram drivers and conductors to heed their leader's call for a strike in October 1921 on the grounds that a strike might embarrass Zaghlul who was visiting Giza. M. K. Husayn's own base of support lay increasingly among the activists who had been fired rather than among the rank and file workers still employed, and the latter were increasingly alienated from their counsellor and his style of leadership.[14]

Muhammad Kamil Husayn made however one last attempt to launch a strike. On November 11, 1921, what the authorities described as "malcontents"—presumably dismissed tram workers—boarded tram cars, expelled the drivers, and disrupted tram service. It is not clear whether this was an attempt by Husayn and his followers to force a strike against the will of the reluctant majority of the workers, or whether it was a ruse to absolve the workers of responsibility for stopping work. In any event, given that the action occurred during the period of rising tensions that preceded November 13, the anniversary of the Wafd's original call for Egyptian independence, the British authorities were unwilling to tolerate any agitation. The oriental secretary at the Residency immediately wrote directly to Muhammad Kamil Husayn to say that unless the strike ended promptly, he would be detained and deported to Malta. Husayn had no desire to spend more time in prison, and normal service was soon restored.[15]

The following two years were a period of quiescence and passivity for the Cairo tramwaymen. Repeated defeats had taken their toll, and M. K. Husayn dropped out of sight. Tram company management worked closely with the security agencies to suppress labor activism. In the first three months of 1922 alone, some sixty "troublemakers" from among the tram workers were exiled to their villages of origin under martial law decrees, and others were fired. The authorities forbade the union from collecting membership dues near the pay win-

14. FO 407/190/41, 84; 191/32, 36; EG, November 8, 1921.
15. FO 141/748/8839/33.

dows or on the streets on the pretext that union toughs were coercing workers into paying dues. This seems unlikely because the union appears to have been moribund. The company claimed that calm had returned because "the hard-working employees [who] form a majority [had been] finally liberated from the terror that had been imposed on them."[16] The passivity of the workers and the decline of the union should however be attributed mainly to the heightened repression and demobilization of the popular nationalist struggle that characterized 1922 and 1923. The unilateral grant of limited independence by Britain had changed the terms of the political struggle. Zaghlul was in detention abroad while in Egypt the Wafd's enemies, with British support, were molding a constitution that would suit their own interests. As always, labor activism rose and fell with the tide of the national struggle and popular protest. This had been the case before the war, and the pattern would recur throughout the 1920s and 1930s. When the general political climate improved, the national movement stirred, and repression eased, the workers would also revive their unions and seek to make gains. But when the grip of the occupying power or an authoritarian regime was tight, and the Wafd was in the political wilderness, the labor movement lost ground and was weak.

With their union inactive and conditions unsuitable for collective action, some of the Cairo tram workers apparently turned to terrorism. An Italian tram inspector was shot by an unknown assailant, and in January 1922, Van der Hecht, the tram company's manager in Cairo, was assassinated. The police claimed to have foiled other conspiracies.[17] These incidents could not of course compensate for the union's weakness and the demoralization of the tramwaymen, but they did give the authorities a further pretext to crack down on union activists. It should be noted that in this period of demobilization, secret nationalist organizations also used terrorist methods to harass the British and keep the spirit of national resistance alive.

It was only from the summer of 1923 that the political climate began to improve. Zaghlul was allowed to return to Egypt, and the Wafd and its rivals began to mobilize for the upcoming elections. Martial law was lifted in July and gradually the tramway workers began to stir. Muhammad Kamil Husayn reappeared on the scene, anxious to use his former ties with the Cairo tram workers as the basis for a political career, but he had lost nearly all his support among the rank and file by the latter half of 1923. Although dismissed workers still loyal to him had returned to Cairo from their places of exile after mar-

16. FO 141/748/8839/33, 35, 37.
17. *BE*, January 3, 1922, February 19, 1924.

134 Unions, 1920–1924

tial law had been lifted, intent on restoring Husayn to the leadership of a revived union, the tram workers still employed no longer wanted him and were moving into the orbit of the Wafd. Husayn had alienated them by his failures, by his dictatorial manner, and by the coercive means he and his partisans had employed to maintain control of the union. He had also become openly identified as an ally of the Liberal Constitutionalist party at a time when the urban and rural masses, including the tramway workers, were solidly behind the Wafd in the electoral campaign. Within a few months the tramway workers' public opposition to their former counsellor's coercive and manipulative machinations to get on the ballot had foiled his political ambitions.[18]

After the Wafd's overwhelming victory at the polls in January 1924, Husayn made a last attempt to assert his influence over the workers. His agents began agitating for a strike on February 18 in the guise of a congratulatory procession of tram workers to the Bayt al-Umma ("House of the Nation"), residence of the newly elected Prime Minister Sa'd Zaghlul Pasha and headquarters of the Wafd. But a delegation of rank and file tramwaymen who went to see Zaghlul were told that he wanted no processions and no strikes, just work as usual and public order so that the Wafd might continue to seek Egypt's full independence. The prestige of Zaghlul and of the Wafd were such that despite Husayn's efforts at the depots to incite a strike, only in Giza did a small number of workers leave their jobs and try to march into Cairo. Their leaders were quickly arrested for violating public order, as was Muhammad Kamil Husayn himself, who was also charged with insulting the prime minister.[19]

This ended the long reign of the ambitious and unscrupulous lawyer. He had emerged in 1919 as the popular and successful leader of the Cairo tramway workers and reappeared a year later, still genuinely popular, as the man who could reverse the union's declining fortunes. Despite clever and innovative tactics, however, he could not prevail in the adverse political and economic conditions of the time, and by 1922 the union had become weak and ineffectual. Husayn himself had also alienated many rank and file workers by his reliance on strong-arm methods and his style of leadership. That leadership had become increasingly authoritarian in character, to the point where he was running the union with the support of a small number of cronies and former workers, at times against the wishes of the majority of the members. When he returned in 1923 to reclaim his

18. FO 407/196/172; FO 407/197/17.
19. CP, February 17, 18, 1924; F/42; *al-Ahram*, February 18, 19, 1924.

position of leadership over the tramwaymen and use it to win election to Parliament, he discredited himself completely by opposing the party most Egyptians regarded as the embodiment of the national cause, and by his use of intimidation and cynical manipulation. Muhammad Kamil Husayn died in July 1924, under investigation by the public prosecutor's officer on charges of embezzlement of union funds.[20]

In the course of 1924 the Wafd, now the ruling party, moved to gain direct control over the labor movement. In the case of the Cairo tramway workers this entailed the Wafd's establishment of an advisory council consisting of Shafiq Mansur, Mahmud 'Allam, and William Makram 'Ubayd. The first two were Wafdist labor lawyers, and 'Ubayd was a key figure in the Wafd organization and later a member of the top leadership and a minister. The functions of this council reflected the Wafd's paternalistic attitude toward the working class in that it supervised the union's executive committee elected by the workers themselves, and asked the Governorate and the CTC to grant it responsibility for disciplinary action against workers accused of wrongdoing. The company, however, which had fought for so long to retain exclusive control over discipline, was not at all interested in this proposal.[21]

Although the Wafd was paternalistic and sought to control the tram union for its own ends, the tramwaymen saw it as sympathetic, likely to defend the interests of Egyptian workers oppressed by a foreign-owned monopoly, and therefore gained renewed confidence. Although the tram workers heeded Zaghlul's admonition to remain at their jobs in February, the secret police reported them saying that the strike Husayn had tried to foment had been postponed rather than abandoned. In the fall of 1924 there were several incidents in the workshops which indicated this increased self-assurance. In October, for example, the chief engineer was compelled by the "menacing attitude" of the other workers to reinstate an employee he had just fired, and a month later the shop workers stopped work briefly to compel the rehiring of a co-worker fired for his militancy.[22] Yet in general the workers were willing to give the new government time to get the company to accede to their demands. Despite years of accumulated grievances there were no major tram strikes in Cairo during 1924; this reflected the extent to which the workers were willing to accept the Wafd's counsel of patience and the peaceful resolution of social con-

20. al-'Ummal, June 24, 1924; Ittihad al-'ummal, June 26, 1924; CP, July 22, 1924.
21. CP, July 9, August 6, 9, 1924.
22. CP, February 19, October 11, November 18, 1924.

136 Unions, 1920–1924

flict. Another factor was that for much of the year public attention was focused on the new government's negotiations with Britain aimed at concluding a treaty that would resolve the issues left open in 1922. This, the Wafd argued, was the country's highest priority, and domestic issues would have to wait. The tram workers found this argument plausible, and despite their discontent and high expectations they refrained from industrial action. In November 1924, however, after the Wafd had been in power only ten months, a crisis in relations with Britain forced the Wafd from power, and destroyed the tramwaymen's hopes for the support of a sympathetic government.

Several aspects of the experience of the tramway workers in the 1920–1924 period are worthy of note, especially as they were shared by other groups of Egyptian workers. These years were characterized by setbacks and by an inability to challenge successfully the power of the CTC. In the absence of a broader upsurge of popular mobilization to support them, the tramwaymen were not strong enough to compel the company to fully honor the 1919 agreement, make concessions on various issues, or recognize the union as their bargaining agent. They could not even prevent management from systematically firing activists, thereby undermining the union and raising the costs of resistance to its dictates. The British authorities were ready to intervene to break strikes whenever they thought that security mandated it, and the police cooperated closely with the company to ferret out and eliminate those workers suspected of being troublemakers. In these circumstances the CTWU was barely able to hold its own, and indeed lapsed into inactivity during the worst years of repression.

This experience served to strengthen the affinity of Egyptian workers and their unions for the national movement and its vanguard, the Wafd. The latter appeared as the champion of the Egyptian people against the foreign oppressor and its local collaborators. When the masses were mobilized, when the repression eased, and a freer political climate prevailed, the workers could act with greater hope of success. However, when political forces that were socially reactionary or linked to the British were firmly in power, the workers could expect the worst. It was therefore logical to see the attainment of favorable conditions of struggle as linked to the triumph of the national cause and to seek a place in the Wafdist camp. The Cairo Tramway Workers' Union, along with many other Egyptian unions, adopted this perspective in this period. Because of the repression it was not until 1924 that the Wafd could exert direct control over key unions, though Wafdist counsellors were active from 1919 on. Once martial law ended and the election campaign got underway, the union movement was increasingly taken under the wing of the Wafd, encouraged but also controlled in ways that will be examined below. It is not surprising that Egyptian workers had great expectations of the new Wafd government, and were willing to defer strikes while they awaited the support of the newly Egyptianized state in resolving their grievances. For years they had been accustomed to seek the mediation of the government in their conflicts with employers, and it was only natural to assume that with the self-proclaimed "party of the people" finally in power things would improve through action from above.

Still, the Cairo tramway workers had learned something from their experiences in 1920–1923. Although they had accepted the tutelage of Wafdist lawyers in 1924, and later of other nonworker elements out of patriotism, personal loyalty, or expediency, they retained a capacity for autonomous action and decision-making rarely found in other unions until much later. By the mid-1920s they were too large, experienced, stable, and concentrated a work force to easily acquiesce in the kind of organizational and political dependency that characterized relations between the Wafd and certain other groups of workers, as we shall see below. The experiences of these years demonstrated something else, too. Despite the defeats, repression, and demoralization of the early 1920s, the union established by the Cairo tram workers had survived, had struck deep roots among the workers, and played a vital role in the working lives of these men that nothing else could fill. The union could be suppressed and driven almost out of existence, it could be weakened and even suffer a loss of support among the rank and file workers because of poor leadership and disunity, it could be reduced to a small but faithful core of true believers. But when circumstances changed, it was quickly reconstituted and once again attracted the support of the bulk of the work force. For the tramwaymen as for other Egyptian workers, the trade union had become the only viable instrument of collective action, the only means by which they could hope to achieve unity and fight to improve their lives.

The Left and the Labor Movement

Prior to the First World War educated Egyptians were not unaware of socialist ideas and the existence of powerful European social democratic parties, and foreign workers in Egypt had often acquired some familiarity or even personal experience with socialism, syndicalism, or anarchism in their countries of origin. But no distinct socialist tendency emerged in Egypt until after the war, when a small number of foreigners, later joined by Egyptians, established the first socialist organizations. A socialist party, which was soon transformed into a

138 Unions, 1920–1924

communist party, was formed and developed close ties with a number of unions through its affiliated trade union federation. This radical tendency in the Egyptian labor movement had a limited but nonetheless important influence on the movement as a whole. It projected conceptions of Egyptian society and of working class identity that challenged those of the Wafd whose bourgeois nationalism the left criticized. The early communist movement was eventually suppressed and the labor movement purged of leftist influences, but the communists' labor work had an impact that was felt beyond the circles in direct contact with it.

The key figure in the socialist wing of the labor movement and in the early socialist movement in general was Joseph Rosenthal, a Jew born in Palestine, and a jeweller by profession. Rosenthal had come to Egypt at the turn of the century, had been a socialist since his youth, and soon began to work with the unions organized by foreign workers in Alexandria. Many years later he would recall this early activism:

> I began to strive for the formation of unions. The first union in whose organization I participated was the cigarette workers' union, and after that I participated in the formation of other unions for the tailors, metal workers and printers. These unions were almost entirely made up of foreign workers, because the Egyptian workers were at that time a minority in all the trades and occupations relative to their foreign colleagues.[23]

Rosenthal soon became a well-known figure among the radical foreigners in the port city, and the police regarded him as a man "holding very advanced ideas on social questions."[24]

The waves of strikes and unionization among both foreign and Egyptian workers in 1919 led Rosenthal to begin working toward the creation of a general federation of labor which would unite all the existing unions, organize the unorganized workers, and establish a socialist presence in the labor movement. In 1920 he published a call for the formation of such a federation, and talks were begun by union leaders. But, Rosenthal claimed, "the union chiefs who were saturated with [nationalist] political ideas felt that the establishment of real unions that would look out for the workers would result in the loss of their power and obstruct the achievement of their political goals. They therefore worked very hard to keep their unions out of the federation, and continued to prolong the preliminary steps for an ex-

23. *al-Ahram*, March 7, 1924.
24. FO 141/779/9065/87, Public Security Department to the Residency, July 21, 1921.

tra year." Finally, in late February 1921, a meeting was held in Alexandria at which the Confédération Générale du Travail (CGT)—as it was known to its contemporaries—was founded. Dr. Skouphopoulos, the radical leader of the Suez workers' union, presided at the meeting which was attended by Rosenthal, the left-wing Egyptian lawyer Amin 'Azmi, and several other leading socialists.[25]

At its formation the CGT—clearly modelled on the socialist-led European union federations—represented only a small fraction of even the organized working class. Twenty-one unions affiliated to the new federation, and most of their 3,000 members were foreign workers in Alexandria. The important Egyptian unions led by the "chiefs" Rosenthal criticized did not join in. For example, the Wafd had no intention of allowing the labor organizations within its orbit to come under the influence of radical foreigners, nor did such independent leaders as Muhammad Kamil Husayn of the Cairo tramwaymen see anything to be gained by affiliating.

The formation of the CGT was followed in August 1921 by the establishment of the Egyptian Socialist party (ESP). Talk of socialism and projects to form a socialist party in Egypt had been in the air since the end of the war, and it was socialist activists involved in these projects who helped launch the CGT. Some Egyptians had been much influenced by European socialism, and the Bolshevik revolution in 1917 had had a further radicalizing effect on both Egyptians and foreigners. A number of Egyptian intellectuals, of whom the best known is Salama Musa, began to propagate socialist ideas, although they were often inspired more by Fabianism than by Marxism. The more radical foreigners, including Rosenthal, Skouphopoulos, and Yanakakis began to organize preparty groups, the first of which was the Groupe d'Études Sociales established in 1920 which held lectures and discussions and was composed mainly of Greeks. Somewhat later the Clarté group, modelled on the French communist clubs of the same name, began to meet. Its membership was also largely Greek and overlapped with that of the Études Sociales group. The two organizations were a means by which socialist ideas could be publicized and contact made with sympathetic individuals, both foreign and Egyptian.

The activity of small circles of intellectuals reflected a broader public interest in communism. The victories of the Bolsheviks were widely applauded as defeats for the imperialist powers, including Britain, and the British authorities sought to counter this by launch-

25. F/42. Minute. Afrique n. 33. March 12, 1921; EG. March 2, 1921; al-Ahram. March 7, 1924.

140   Unions, 1920–1924

ing an anti-Bolshevik propaganda campaign which included distribution of a *fatwa* by the Grand Mufti of Egypt condemning Bolshevism. The campaign was so clumsy that it was ridiculed in the press and increased public interest in communism. Early in 1920 the Cairo police reported:

> It is noteworthy that coffee-house talk of Bolshevism continues to be reported. It is entirely vague, and is probably an indirect result of alarmist leaders in the "Times" rather than of Bolshevist propaganda. Its general tendency is that the Bolshevists are coming to take Egypt, and it will be a fine thing for Egypt when they do. Then if a poor man wants money he will just take it from the rich. Vague as it is, it has its importance as a symptom of economic unrest.[26]

The Egyptian Socialist party founded in 1921 represented the convergence of two groups: Egyptian left-wing intellectuals, and Greek, Jewish, and other foreign radicals some of whom identified completely with the Bolshevik revolution and the new Communist International.[27] The new party's program called for the liberation of Egypt from foreign rule, a new society based on the common ownership of the means of production, free compulsory education, the improvement of the lot of the workers through the formation of unions and the election of labor representatives to Parliament, and the emancipation of women. These goals were to be achieved by peaceful means, and reflected the extent to which at least some of the ESP's founders were following the example of the European social democratic parties, especially the British Labor party.

But the differences between social democrats and revolutionaries within the party were too great to ignore. By the middle of 1922 the leadership of the ESP had been transferred from the inactive and moderate Cairo branch to the more radical and worker-oriented Alexandria branch. This led to the departure of Salama Musa and some of the

26. FO 141/779/9065/2–17; FO 141/779/9065/41, Commandant, Cairo City Police to General Staff Intelligence, G.H.Q., Egyptian Expeditionary Forces, February 21, 1920. Some British officials in Egypt had an extremely paranoid notion of the Bolshevik threat and saw evidence everywhere of a Bolshevik-German-pan-Islamic conspiracy about to engulf the Middle East. But even the more sober officials felt threatened enough, as early as March 1920, to send police officials to England for special training in "anti-Bolshevik methods." FO 141/779/9065/43–44.

27. On the history of the early communist movement, discussed here only as it relates to the labor movement, see Rif'at al-Sa'id, *Ta'rikh al-haraka al-ishtirakiyya fi misr, 1900–1925* (Cairo, 1975); Suliman Bashear, *Communism in the Arab East, 1918–1928* (London, 1980); and Selma Botman, "Political Opposition in Egypt: The Communist Movement, 1936–1954," Ph.D. diss., Harvard University, 1984.

Unions, 1920–1924 **141**

other Egyptian intellectuals influenced by Fabianism and opposed to Bolshevism. The party, now led by Mahmud Husni al-'Arabi, an Egyptian lawyer, by the Syrian lawyer Antun Marun, and by Rosenthal, who with the other foreigners kept out of the limelight, began to openly identify itself as a communist party. Al-'Arabi was sent to Moscow for the Fourth Congress of the Communist International and returned at the end of 1922 to oversee implementation of the three conditions imposed on it for Comintern membership. The party became officially known as the Communist Party of Egypt (CPE), a program for work among the peasants was prepared, and Joseph Rosenthal was expelled. This last step was apparently taken because of Rosenthal's unwillingness to accept Moscow's line without question, and perhaps also his opposition to changes in the party's line. The CPE published a new program in line with the Comintern's Twenty-One Points, and in 1923 entered a new phase characterized by more intensive activity and greater flexibility.

Between its establishment and the end of 1922 the CGT, the labor federation first of the ESP and then of the CPE, played a relatively minor role in the labor movement. It had close ties to the Alexandria cigarette workers, whose counsellors were Rosenthal and Amin 'Azmi, the European and Egyptian secretaries of the CGT respectively. The federation sponsored meetings on behalf of the unemployed workers and pressed for government action to relieve their suffering. The CGT also organized a May Day celebration in Alexandria, and an enthusiastic Rosenthal later told a journalist that the Cairo tramway workers had shown that Egyptian workers were capable of militancy. "You may rest assured," he said, "that we are on the eve of great days here and that the dead bones of this old place are going to get pretty severely shaken in the next few years."[28] But the CGT's growth was slow partly because of the general decline in labor activism during 1922, but also because the CGT leadership was predominantly foreign and more radical than much of the rank and file. In November 1921 when Rosenthal read a letter from the Profintern—the Comintern's international trade union federation—inviting the Egyptian CGT to join, many of those present at the federation's weekly meeting protested. Rosenthal was criticized for even contacting the Bolsheviks, some of the union leaders asked that the CGT issue a statement denying any connection with Bolshevism, and the proposal to affiliate was shelved.[29]

28. FO 371/E6878/260/16, unpublished interview with *EG* correspondent.
29. FO 407/191/24; F/42, French Consulate in Alexandria to Gaillard, November 12, 1921.

142 Unions, 1920–1924

The left's attitude toward Egyptian nationalism and the Wafd also limited its attractiveness for Egyptian workers. This attitude is illustrated by an incident that took place at an ESP meeting in Alexandria attended by some seventy people in June 1922. Rosenthal had just delivered a lecture on patriotism, the British report relates.

> An Egyptian workman dressed in a gallabieh asked to be allowed to speak. He was given permission by El Orabi, who did not know him personally and who told the audience that he (the workman) would be responsible for his own words. The workman then spoke in poetical form of his misery at the commencement of the war and of his career in the Egyptian Labour Corps, where he had been obliged to work to keep his family, although he hated the English. He ended his poem by two verses about Zaghlul Pasha, at the mention of whose name the audience broke into cheers for Zaghlul. Husni-el-Orabi did not hide his annoyance caused by the fact that members of the Egyptian Socialist Party should so compromise their principles of Socialism by cheering a Nationalist leader.[30]

Al-'Arabi had by his own lights good reason to be annoyed. But in a situation where Zaghlul's Wafd was overwhelmingly popular, and the question of national independence foremost in the public mind, it is not surprising that the party alienated Egyptian workers when it downplayed the importance of the national struggle and criticized the bourgeois character of the nationalist leadership.

The question of how communist parties in what are today called Third World countries should relate to bourgeois-led nationalist movements preoccupied Comintern strategists in the 1920s. The issue was both theoretical and practical, and had consequences of the utmost importance for fledgling communist movements in such countries as China, where the rival Kuomintang was trying to unify the country, eliminate foreign domination, and break the power of local warlords and remnants of the old regime. The question was whether the communists should reject any alliance with bourgeois nationalist forces and fight independently on an explicitly communist program, or whether they should form a united front with sections of the bourgeoisie in order to end imperialist domination and defeat local reactionary forces. The second option of course required that the communists defer the revolutionary struggle and if necessary dampen the class struggle in order to preserve their alliances. This option raised a new set of difficult questions about the form such al-

30. FO 407/194/12.

liances might take, the strategy and tactics to be adopted, and the class forces involved.

Before al-'Arabi's return from the Fourth Comintern Congress, the Egyptian communist movement had taken the position that cooperation with bourgeois nationalism was neither possible nor desirable. The party's main thrust was anticapitalist rather than anti-imperialist; that is, it saw the class struggle of Egyptian and foreign workers as primary and the bourgeois-led struggle for independence as secondary. The Wafd was regarded as the party of the nationalist bourgeoisie whose goal was to compel the British to turn control of Egypt over to the indigenous elite so that it could more effectively exploit the workers and peasants.

For its part the Wafd was not averse to cooperating with the left when it was to its advantage. When for example six Labor members of Parliament sympathetic to the Wafd visited Egypt in September 1921, Zaghlul invited Rosenthal as secretary of the CGT to participate in the welcoming ceremonies. The shrewd Wafd leader apparently wanted to impress the MPs by demonstrating the support of the left-wing unions for the national cause. Rosenthal, however, refused to be associated with "capitalism" even in its Egyptian nationalist form and later met with the MPs separately. A few months later a police agent reported that Makram 'Ubayd and Rosenthal had discussed the possibility of the CGT's participating in the campaign of popular resistance the Wafd was planning to bring down the 'Adli government.[31] It would certainly have been to the Wafd's advantage to involve the radical unions in the national struggle, and the nationalists had nothing to lose from such cooperation. A more formal alliance, the formation of a united front between the Wafd and the CPE, was, however, entirely out of the question even if the communists had been interested before 1923. The Wafd leadership was socially conservative and anticommunist, and it had no reason to share control of the national movement: it already enjoyed the overwhelming support of Egyptian workers and regarded itself as not merely the representative but the embodiment of the Egyptian nation. During a period of repression and weakness the Wafd's leaders were willing to cooperate with the left when it served their interests, but in the long run they viewed the communists as a potential threat to their hegemony and the social order.

Mahmud Husni al-'Arabi's return from Moscow at the very end of 1922 brought about a change in the CPE's attitude toward the nation-

31. FO 407/191/10; FO 371/E336/189/16, Alexandria City Police report, December 22, 1921.

144 Unions, 1920–1924

alists and relations with other political forces in general. At its Fourth Congress the Comintern had recommended that affiliated parties in colonial and semicolonial countries seek alliances with bourgeois nationalist forces and adopt more flexible tactics to overcome their isolation from the masses. The improvement in the political climate that began in 1923, the easing of repression, and the revival of the labor movement provided a context well-suited to the CPE's implementation of this new approach. The CGT, the party's link with the workers, would have a key part to play in this new course. In any event the federation's leadership was by this time almost identical with that of the party. Al-'Arabi served as general secretary of both the CPE and the CGT, his deputy at the CGT Mustafa Abu Harja was a party leader, and Antun Marun served as CGT counsellor and later as CGT secretary as well as a party deputy secretary. The two organizations shared the same offices along with the Études Sociales, Clarté, and Jewish Goldfaden groups.

The CGT played an important role in one of the first and largest strikes of 1923, that of the Alexandria gas and electric workers in February. The following month the CGT organized a demonstration against the Labor Conciliation Board, which it regarded as an instrument serving the interests of the employers by deceiving the workers. This demonstration provided the authorities with the opportunity they had been waiting for to move against the party. Al-'Arabi and Marun were arrested, the party's headquarters were raided and shut down, and its papers were seized. The crackdown on the CPE was ordered by Alexander Keown-Boyd, the most powerful figure in the British security apparatus in Egypt. At that time he was director-general of the Public Security Department at the Ministry of the Interior and later chief of its European section; he was notorious as a hardliner and for many years the nemesis of the left and the labor movement. He expected that the British military court trying the two communist leaders would punish them severely for organizing a forbidden demonstration, but he was to be disappointed. "Unfortunately," he lamented, "this Court, imbued with the British idea that all persons are at liberty to express their opinions and that you cannot do anything to them for such opinions until they convert them to direct action, acquitted these gentlemen."[32]

Keown-Boyd's sarcasm notwithstanding, the Egyptian state was hardly defenseless against the threat of subversion. In order to control political opposition and labor unrest after the end of martial law, the

---

32. FO 371/E6287/85/15, report by Keown-Boyd, May 23, 1923; FO 141/779/9065/201, report by Keown-Boyd, "The Communist Movement in Egypt," June 22, 1925.

Unions, 1920–1924   **145**

British-controlled Egyptian government had by the end of 1923 promulgated a series of repressive laws. One required that the police be notified before any public meeting was held, and they could prohibit or dissolve such meetings if they saw fit to do so. A second law, designed to target the communists, set prison terms of up to five years for anyone who fomented hatred or contempt against the government, propagated subversive ideas contrary to the new constitution or advocated the alteration of fundamental institutions by illegal means. The courts could suspend or permanently close newspapers which contravened these prohibitions. Two other measures were intended to control the working class. A law enacted in July 1923 permitted the expulsion from the cities of persons defined as vagrants, police supervision of suspects and ex-criminals, enforced residence, and other measures of control. This decree was particularly galling to workers because it established in law the right of the police to round up and expel the unemployed. For workers without jobs this was a very real fear. In periods of high unemployment such as 1921 hundreds of laborers in Alexandria had been sent back to their home villages in Upper Egypt against their will. Fear of arrest for vagrancy (*tasharrud*) was widespread among Egyptian workers and served to dampen labor and political militancy. Another law promulgated in September 1923 prohibited workers in the railways, tramways, and public utilities from striking unless fifteen days' prior notice had been given.[33]

After the release of their leaders the CPE and CGT resumed activity on the basis of their new and more flexible strategy. Al-'Arabi began to assert openly that instead of attacking the Wafd, the party should start working with the nationalist leaders to end the British occupation and win full independence for Egypt. Once that was accomplished the communists could resume the fight for a socialist Egypt. At the same time the CGT called on all unions, affiliated or not, to form a united front around a common program it had formulated. The program incorporated the key demands of the Egyptian labor movement: the eight-hour day, a paid weekly day of rest, higher wages, paid vacations, pensions, equal pay for Egyptian and foreign workers, protection for women and children workers, and official recognition of trade unions. The program also rejected any role for the Labor Conciliation Board, proposing instead that councils representing employers and workers be set up to resolve disputes.[34]

The CGT's appeal for unity was not successful in attracting the ma-

33. F/41, June 1, 1923; FO 141/767/886/13/31; FO 407/190/16, 191/32.
34. FO 407/197/36, 67; CP, July 15, 1923.

146 Unions, 1920–1924

jor Egyptian unions. The Alexandria tramwaymen's union unanimously rejected the federation's invitation to affiliate and expelled union members who had joined the communist-led organization. The other tramway, railway and utility workers' unions also remained loyal to their nationalist leaders and refused to affiliate. But the new emphasis on solidarity and cooperation seems to have attracted members from other quarters, so that by the beginning of 1924 the CGT was reported to have had from 15,000 to 20,000 members in Alexandria, its main sphere of influence. If this estimate is accurate, the CGT was by far the largest labor organization in Egypt and comprised a substantial proportion of the country's organized workers. Many of its members were relatively skilled foreign workers in small enterprises, but the CGT had affiliates at several large workplaces as well.

Notable among these were the Suez Canal Company (whose predominantly European permanent employees were still led by the radical Dr. Skouphopoulos) and the Kafr al-Zayyat, Abu Shanab, and Egolin vegetable oil factories in or near Alexandria. The communist presence at the Egolin factory was particularly strong. Many of its 750 workers were Russian Jews who were politically conscious and had built a strong union affiliate, though indigenous Muslim workers were also involved. At one of the oil extraction plants the proprietor employed a "green shaykh" who would tell injured workers that they should not seek compensation. The CGT union countered this with its own "red shaykh" who encouraged the workers to press for their due. The federation's close ties with the Alexandria cigarette workers had important consequences for the communist movement in the Middle East. Fu'ad al-Shimali, a Lebanese cigarette worker who learned his communism from Rosenthal and was active in the CPE while working in Egypt in the early 1920s, returned to his native country in 1924, and was the founder of its communist movement which was initially based among the tobacco workers.[35]

By the beginning of 1924 the CGT was the major force in the Alexandria labor movement. In January the electoral victory of the Wafd elevated Sa'd Zaghlul to the post of prime minister, arousing great expectations among the masses. The communists sought to take advantage of the new political circumstances by encouraging labor activism, for example in the campaign for shorter hours launched by the CGT union of sales personnel at the big department stores in Alexandria. The left took further heart from the formation of a Labor gov-

35. AP, August 18, 1923; FO 407/197/136, November 14–27, 1923; FO 371/41380, Muhammad Zein el-Din, "Report on Trade Unionism in the Middle East," 1944. On the origins of Lebanese communism, see Hanna Batatu, The Old Social Classes and the Revolutionary Movements of Iraq, p. 382.

Unions, 1920–1924   **147**

ernment in Britain. The CPE leadership decided to convene a party congress on February 23 to discuss the party program, modify it to suit current conditions, and elect delegates to the forthcoming Comintern congress.[36] The events that followed must be seen in the context of several industrial conflicts of long standing.

The large work force at the Filature Nationale in Alexandria had gone on a slowdown strike the previous November to protest a 10 percent wage cut imposed by management, only to be met with a lockout. Other unions, including the CGT, rallied to the textile workers' support, but early in February 1924 the strikers were forced to return to work and accept the cut. The union at the Filature, Egypt's only large mechanized textile factory, was affiliated to the MTWU and represented by Sulayman Hafiz of the Nationalist party. Relations between that party and the Wafd had deteriorated sharply since the heady days of 1919. The Nationalists had been humiliated by their crushing defeat at the polls, and bitterly attacked the Wafd for its willingness to form a government despite the limitations on Egypt's sovereignty. Given this hostility, Zaghlul not surprisingly saw in the labor agitation of late February evidence of a politically motivated campaign against his new and still untested government: Muhammad Kamil Husayn had tried to bring out the Cairo tram workers on February 18; there was unrest among the railway workers at Jabal al-Zaytun, another Nationalist stronghold; and on February 22 the Filature workers struck suddenly because of their employer's failure to ratify the agreement that had ended their last strike or to resolve other outstanding issues.

Determined not to be locked out again, the Filature workers refused to leave the factory until their demands had been met. Emulating their example the Egolin workers also struck and occupied the premises, citing long-standing grievances. For months, management had been laying off workers on the ground of poor business conditions. The workers, represented by Antun Marun, had volunteered to work fewer hours (thereby earning lower wages) in order to prevent further layoffs, but management had refused. The wave of strikes and occupations spread to the Kafr al-Zayyat and Abu Shanab oil factories, whose workers Marun also represented, to the Salt and Soda Company and to the Vacuum Oil plant. Anxious to demonstrate its authority, the central government responded forcefully to this outburst

36. AP, February 4, 1923; FO 371/E1914/193/16. Al-'Arabi had travelled to Berlin late in 1923 to confer with communist leaders and request financial assistance for the CPE, long promised but never sent. After his return Rosenthal was reportedly readmitted to the party under circumstances that remain obscure. FO 371/E1916/16, Allenby to MacDonald, February 23, 1924.

148 Unions, 1920–1924

of militancy among the workers of Alexandria. Zaghlul immediately sent Keown-Boyd and Deputy Minister of the Interior 'Ali Jamal al-Din Pasha to Alexandria to restore order with a battalion of Egyptian infantry. These officials were able to settle the dispute at the Filature quickly and work resumed on February 25. They then turned their attention to Egolin where, with the cooperation of Antun Marun, an agreement was reached a few days later. At the other oil plants the workers agreed to end their occupation after the companies promised to pay them directly rather than through contractors.[37]

Thus far the disputes seem to have been settled rather easily and with the cooperation of CGT leaders, but the wave of unrest surged again. At Kafr al-Zayyat the workers reoccupied their plant on March 1, and were removed by the police a few days later. The Abu Shanab workers also reoccupied their plant, on March 3, after learning that their grievances had been referred to the LCB in which they had lost all confidence. This time the disgusted Marun refused to counsel them to leave, and they vacated the premises only in response to a direct threat from the prime minister:

> If you respect the property of others and leave the company's premises voluntarily, you will be considered loyal to the law and the nation. But if you insist on occupying the property of others in your strike you will be treated as usurpers who have put themselves outside the law.[38]

Work resumed at the two factories a few days later and the unrest gradually subsided.

When the strikes and occupations first erupted, the government began to claim that they were political rather than economic in origin. The Nationalist party was said to be behind the Filature strike, while the communists had allegedly engineered the strikes at Egolin and Abu Shanab. The government had prohibited the convening of the CPE congress scheduled for February 23, and the strikes of late February and early March were alleged to have been launched in retaliation and as a direct challenge to the authority of the Wafd government. On this pretext the police were ordered to arrest the leaders of the Communist party and the CGT. The party's offices were searched and sealed, and a campaign of vilification began in the pro-Wafd press. Within a matter of weeks the fledgling communist movement had been smashed.

---

37. See *al-Ahram* of February–March 1924; Fo 407/198/7, 94, 108, 139; and FO 141/779/9065/152–155.
38. *al-Ahram*, March 5, 1924.

Careful examination of the facts suggests that the government's allegations were probably false and that the communist leaders were not in fact guilty of irresponsible adventurism. The strike that had touched off the wave of agitation, at the Filature, had nothing to do with the communists. Keown-Boyd claimed that at Egolin the workers had understood the need for layoffs, but had been pushed into a strike by Marun. This factory was indeed a center of communist activity, but given their militancy, their long-standing grievances, and the fact that many of the workers were experienced East European radicals themselves, it seems unlikely that they had needed Marun to convince them to strike. In any case Marun was quite cooperative in settling the first strike, and had convinced the occupiers at Egolin and Kafr al-Zayyat to leave the factories when negotiations had been concluded. The second wave of occupations seems to have been more the product of the workers' anger at the lack of progress in resolving their grievances than of Marun's machinations. Indeed, his actions do not give the impression of a man deliberately challenging the government by engineering and prolonging labor strife. Similarly, the tactic of occupying the workplace was a very effective means of putting pressure on employers to negotiate seriously and one the workers need not have learned from the communists, so that even if the communists were undoubtedly involved in the unrest and may have been angry at the government for prohibiting their congress, the strikes and occupations were primarily the result of worker dissatisfaction. When Jamal al-Din Pasha asked several workers how they had learned of factory occupations he was told that "we have only repeated what the workers of Milan and other Italian cities did before Mussolini came to power."[39]

It would seem, then, that the Egyptian government used the events of February–March as a pretext to destroy the communist movement, especially its base in the labor movement. Once in power Zaghlul Pasha was not prepared to countenance any extraparliamentary opposition from any quarter or the infringement of property rights. The strikes and occupations were perceived as a threat to public order and an embarrassment to the new government, especially because the involvement of foreign-owned enterprises raised the possibility of British intervention on the eve of delicate negotiations with the Mac-

---

39. *BE*, February 29, 1924. This analysis of the events of February–March 1924 differs substantially from the version presented in Bashear, *Communism*, pp. 63–65, Ramadan, *Tatawwur*, pp. 538–542, and Walter Laqueur, *Communism and Nationalism in the Middle East* (London, 1956). Although these three authors disagree among themselves about various aspects of this episode, they all suggest that the CPE deliberately defied the government by engineering the strikes and occupations.

150 Unions, 1920–1924

Donald government on the question of full independence. From this point of view the suppression of the communist movement was a practical necessity for the Wafd, and the CPE, with no more than 1,500 members nationwide, was far too weak to resist. The British were understandably quite pleased with Zaghlul's forceful actions. An official at the Foreign Office noted: "In Austria during the last few years it has been the Social Democrats & not the Right who have kept the Communists in order. It is to be hoped that Zaghloul will deal as faithfully with the Communist party in his country; he seems to be starting well."[40]

As the wave of arrests continued, the Wafd mobilized its supporters in the labor movement to publicly denounce the communists and purge leftist counsellors from the unions. Rallies were held at which Wafdist dignitaries vehemently attacked the communists as foreign troublemakers who had tried to mislead Egypt's workers.

> The communists are people who fled their own countries after having ruined them. If they had truly been reformers, they would have begun by reforming their own countries. The communists are people who came from abroad, deceived the workers and came to an agreement with several unions, collecting the workers' money under the pretext that they were working in the interests of the workers against the capitalists and improving their wages. These are nothing but deceptions and lies.[41]

Unions loyal to the Wafd joined the chorus of condemnation and expressed their support for the measures taken by the "people's government." Mahjub Thabit convened the executive board of the MTWU to declare its members innocent of any taint of communism, though he made a point of expressing sympathy for the workers' just demands so long as they were achieved with discretion and patience. The overwhelming popularity of the Wafd and the isolation of the communists made resistance virtually impossible even among the unions affiliated to the CGT. On March 9 the Plumber's Union in Alexandria publicly reaffirmed its allegiance to the CGT and denounced the arrest of its leaders, but thereafter the voices of protest ceased.[42] The risks of police harassment and the loss of their jobs were too great for workers to bear, and even left-wing unions quickly understood that the price of their survival was silence, the severing of connections with the accused communists, and withdrawal from political

40. FO 37/E1916/16.
41. *BE*, March 4, 1924.
42. CP, March 9, 1924.

Unions, 1920–1924   **151**

involvement. The mass base of the CGT evaporated and the federation, along with the Communist party that had led it, ceased to exist. The communist leaders were imprisoned until their trial at the end of September. The eleven defendants—Mahmud Husni al-'Arabi, Antun Marun, Shaykh Safwan Abu al-Fath, Al-Shahhat Ibrahim, 'Abd al-Hamid Tura, Mahmud Ibrahim al-Samkari, Sha'aban Hafiz, Muhammad al-Saghir, 'Abd al-Hafiz 'Awwad, Abraham Katz, and Hillel Zanburg—were charged with conspiracy to overthrow the government and establish a communist regime. The accused admitted that they were communists but denied they advocated or employed violent means. On October 6 the court sentenced the top leadership (al-'Arabi, Marun, Abu al-Fath, Ibrahim, Katz, and Zanburg) to three years' imprisonment, and the rest to six months, most of which they had already served. Communists who were not Egyptian nationals were deported. The authorities especially wanted to be rid of Joseph Rosenthal, the founder of Egyptian communism. He had been questioned in the spring and released for lack of evidence, though in the following months the government sought to deport him, only to discover that no other country would grant him a visa. A British official finally obtained a Rumanian visa through bribery, but when Rosenthal arrived there, the Rumanian authorities would not let him disembark, and he was returned to Alexandria. A legal battle then ensued as the Egyptian government tried to prevent him from landing and Rosenthal insisted in court that as an Egyptian citizen he could not be departed. Only after Labor party leaders took an interest in the case did the Egyptian government relent and allow Rosenthal to remain in Egypt on condition that he stay out of politics.[43]

Efforts were made to reconstitute the Communist party in 1925 with the assistance of militants sent from Palestine and England. The communist group led by Rafiq Jabbur, a Syrian who held Egyptian citizenship, published a newspaper for a short time as a means of reestablishing a presence in the labor movement, but the British-run secret police were quite effective at infiltrating and exposing the communist cells, and further arrests and deportations followed. Other attempts to revive the communist movement were made in the later 1920s and 1930s, but all were quickly suppressed. Indeed, official vigilance went to great lengths to prevent any renewal of communist activity. For example, Shapurji Saklatvala, the communist member of Parliament for North Battersea, was not even allowed to land in Egypt on his way to India in 1927, and the British embassy in

43. *al-Ahram*, September–October 1924; F/42, d'Aumale to Herriot, August 13, 1924; FO 371/J3654/1153/16.

152 Unions, 1920–1924

Rome insisted that the Fascist government certify that each Italian worker sent to the Sudan for a dam construction project was free of communist tendencies.[44] After a brief interlude in 1921–1924, communism ceased to exist as a functioning political movement in Egypt and was confined to a few scattered and isolated cells until the Second World War.

The failure of the early communist movement in Egypt to survive and develop into a significant political force can be attributed to both historical circumstances and political errors. The central issue of Egyptian political life in this period was the struggle for independence, and the leadership of that struggle was firmly in the hands of the Wafd. Unlike Vietnam or China in the interwar period, a strong nationalist movement rooted in an established indigenous bourgeoisie existed in Egypt, its popular mandate won in protracted and often violent struggle. The communists were therefore unable to assume leadership of the national movement, and mobilize the masses by linking the cause of national liberation with the struggle for social transformation. The open hostility the communists expressed toward the party most Egyptians regarded as the vanguard of the national cause also alienated many Egyptian workers. Whereas radical social ideas and the CGT's vision of a united and militant working class appealed to at least some Egyptian workers, the communist movement's abstract internationalism can have held little attraction in a semicolonial situation, and for this reason not only was the CGT's base of support predominantly among foreign workers in Egypt's most cosmopolitan city but militant Egyptian unions kept clear of the radicals.

The centrality of the national issue also had the effect of subordinating social issues. Despite the emergence of a labor movement and the very real grievances of the country's peasant majority, public attention was focused on the question of independence as the sine qua non for the resolution of Egypt's other problems. Zaghlul himself expressed this attitude in a 1923 interview:

> For the moment we are only preoccupied with independence. It will be time enough to consider domestic policy when the fiction of our independence, which is purely nominal, has been ended. Then, doubtless, there will be a separation into parties—Conser-

44. FO 141/779/9065/200, 201; FO 371/J2372/16/16, August 26, 1927. Some of the Russians identified by police informers as communist agents and deported to the Soviet Union were shot on arrival in Odessa as Whites and monarchists, which led the police to the belated conclusion that some of their informers had been unreliable. See FO 141/779/9065/220, R. M. Graves to the Residency, September 21, 1925.

vatives, Progressives, Radicals—when the followers of the Wafd will not all be found in one camp.[45]

The clear implication was that until complete independence was achieved all Egyptians must subordinate their personal and class interests for the good of the nation as interpreted by the Wafd.

The small size of the working class, its poverty, illiteracy, and peasant origin made it difficult for the communists to establish a secure base among Egyptian workers. The fact that many of the communist activists were foreigners did not help either. Even with the best of intentions it was not easy for foreigners who enjoyed a privileged status to overcome barriers of ethnicity, language, religion, and culture, and establish close ties with Egyptian workers. The educated Egyptians who joined the Communist party were far removed from the indigenous masses and too oriented toward Europe (particularly toward Moscow) to really analyze and understand their own society, and develop a program suited to Egyptian realities. Little effort was made to reach the peasants, though it is unlikely that the communists would have been able to make much headway among them without many years of patient work.

In short, it is difficult to see how the communists could have achieved greater success in the early 1920s even if they had made no mistakes. Given the short period in which they were able to operate, they managed to establish a substantial (if not durable) presence in the labor movement in spite of their being closely monitored by the security agencies. Moreover, they had little chance of striking roots strong enough to withstand the repression that was bound to come once they became a significant force and hence a significant threat. There was simply neither enough time nor, given the ideological hegemony of the Wafd, a real opportunity to recruit enough members and develop enough committed Egyptian cadre to ensure the party's survival.

The short period of communist activity left few enduring traces on the Egyptian workers' movement. The radical unions were crushed or cowed into submission and the leftist counsellors were deposed. A few Egyptian socialist intellectuals remained on the scene, and sought to share their vision with worker activists during periods of labor resurgence, but socialism, much less communism, was not to be a powerful intellectual force in Egypt for two decades. Perhaps the early communists' most lasting legacy was the conception of class unity and solidarity the CGT had promoted. By emphasizing the need for workers' solidarity, by actively encouraging workers and unions

45. *Journal du Caire*, September 21, 1923, in FO 407/197/97.

154 Unions, 1920–1924

to support one another in their struggles, by building an organization which ideally would unite all the workers in Egypt, and by fighting for the common interests of the entire working class the communists introduced a new and potentially powerful vision into the Egyptian labor movement. The perspective of a workers' movement independent of other class forces and oriented toward social transformation through political and industrial power was crushed along with the CGT and the Communist party in 1924, and the struggle to revive it was to be long and arduous. But even at that early date it was sufficiently powerful that even the communists' enemies, including the Wafd, felt compelled to seize on and employ it, albeit in a distorted form, when they set out to organize the trade union movement. As the years passed this vision would continually reappear in new forms to inspire Egyptian unionists because it reflected a new reality coming into being, a growing and ever more vigorous working class.

The Wafd and the Workers

Soon after it took up the reins of government in January 1924, the Wafd moved to consolidate its control over the urban working class. The arrest of Muhammad Kamil Husayn, the takeover of the key Cairo Tramway Workers' Union and the suppression of the CGT and the Communist party were crucial first steps toward the elimination of the influence the Wafd's rivals exercised over sections of the labor movement. Immediately thereafter the Wafd went on to the next phase—the creation of mechanisms by which the party could supervise the unions already in its sphere of influence and further expand its base of support. The Wafd's brief tenure in power in 1924 witnessed the party's first open and direct entrance into the labor movement. Although the form the Wafd's hegemony over the labor movement took and the attitudes of its bourgeois nationalist leaders toward the workers would eventually prove to be highly problematic, the Wafd's enormous prestige and its genuine popularity among the mass of Egyptian workers made its first efforts quite successful. This was the first full expression of the Wafd-labor relationship that was to be such a powerful ideological and organizational influence on the workers' movement for the next twenty years.

The Wafd had of course been very involved in the union movement since 1919. As noted earlier, lawyers active in or associated with the Wafd served as counsellors for many of the most important unions of Egyptian workers in the four years before Zaghlul came to power. During moments of upsurge in the national struggle, these links were utilized to mobilize this important constituency against foreign capital and the occupation regime. The workers at the 'Anabir in Cairo, who combined shop floor militancy with patriotic fervor, provided the best example of both the positive and negative aspects of this relationship.

Although the 'Anabir workers had played an important role in the 1919 revolution, they did not really participate in the August strike wave that followed. The Bulaq railway workshops, however, remained both the largest single concentration of industrial workers in the country and a bastion of Egyptian nationalism. In fact, some of those who worked there were involved with the secret terrorist groups linked to members of the Wafd's leadership, and for that reason, and because the 'Anabir was still run by English managers, class and national grievances intersected quite naturally and often took violent forms. In December 1919, for example, a worker fired for having participated in a brief strike called to protest the arrival of the boycotted Milner Mission tried to shoot R. G. Peckitt, chief engineer at the 'Anabir. This was the same Peckitt whose abusive and arbitrary behavior had so angered the workers in 1910 and whose removal had been one of the main demands of the strike initiated that year. Not surprisingly, someone else, either a worker or a member of one of the terrorist groups, made another attempt to assassinate Peckitt less than a year later.[46]

Individual acts of terrorism were most frequent however when collective action was unfeasible. When circumstances permitted, the 'Anabir workers expressed their grievances about declining real wages and maltreatment by supervisors through militancy on the shop floor. From the end of April to the beginning of June 1921 these workers successfully used a variety of tactics, including short sudden stoppages, sit-down and slowdown strikes, and finally a full-scale walkout, to challenge management's control at the point of production. Things reached the point where even railway officials acknowledged they had lost control of the shop floor to the militant and determined workers. This extraordinary state of affairs was closely connected with the contemporaneous upsurge in the national movement triggered by the struggle between Zaghlul and his Wafd loyalists, and the Wafdist dissidents and the government of 'Adli Pasha.

Although the workers raised their own economic demands, it is clear that they were also motivated by patriotism, and as in 1919 were quite willing to take on the authorities. They demonstrated this con-

46. *Journal du Caire*, December 23, 1919; FO 407/186/14A–C, December 29, 1919. On the secret societies see Ramadan, *Tatawwur*, pp. 169–75 and Nawal 'Abd al-'Aziz, ''al-Haraka al-'ummaliyya wa-atharuha fi tatawwur al-ta'rikh al-siyasi fi misr,'' M.A. Thesis, Department of History, Cairo University, 1973.

156 Unions, 1920–1924

clusively when the students at the nearby Bulaq Technical School went on strike and marched into the streets to demonstrate on May 19, 1921. The police were called in and drove the students back into the school, but on their way back to the station the police contingent passed the 'Anabir. Someone had evidently alerted the workers there, for they came out in force, attacked the policemen, and injured forty-two of them. The crowd that gathered cheered the workers and joined in by taking the policemen's uniforms and equipment.[47]

After the popular mobilization of May 1921 subsided, ESR management was able to confront and defeat the 'Anabir workers by locking them out until they agreed to return on its terms. The workers nonetheless remained loyal to their union (led by the MTWU veteran Dr. Mahjub Thabit), and acts of terrorism against the English officials who ran the workshops continued even after the union had become defunct during the year and a half of repression that followed. Limited government budgets made it impossible for the ESR to raise its workers' admittedly inadequate wages and so discontent festered, and as soon as martial law was lifted the railway workers revived their union and again chose Thabit, just released from detention, to lead it. Expectations of the new Wafd government were high and were expressed through vocal protests and a march to the Bayt al-Umma by 8,000 railway workers which manifested both loyalty to the Wafd and discontent over its inaction. Zaghlul's government clearly regarded the railway workers as an important constituency, and sought both to pacify them by promising a 20 percent cost-of-living increase and to bring them under its control by incorporating them into the new union movement it was building and appointing Egyptians to replace senior English railway officials.

The railway workers, especially those at the 'Anabir, were for many years among the Wafd's most loyal supporters in the labor movement. As government employees whose wages and benefits were dependent on the budget, they had a strong material interest that a sympathetic party, which could only be the Wafd, remain in power. Furthermore, they had a strong interest in the Egyptianization of all levels of the state apparatus (including the ESR) which was also a popular nationalist demand. Indeed, while the gradual replacement of foreign by Egyptian supervisors might afford them some relief from what they had long felt to be oppression and discrimination, this action would inevitably also open up greater opportunities for advancement. For

---

47. On developments at the 'Anabir see FO 141/687/8705/51, 52, 55; FO 141/782/12709; and FO 407/189, report of May 19–21, 1921.

all these reasons, as well as their long history of involvement in the national cause, the railway workers linked themselves to the Wafd far more closely than many other groups of Egyptian workers. Even when led by Wafdist counsellors, most other unions sought to preserve at least some degree of independence and ensure that the workers played some role in setting policy. By contrast the close identification of the railway workers with the Wafd fostered dependence on outside personalities and hindered the development of a strong, stable, and self-reliant union. Even the 'Anabir workers were unable to sustain such an organization over long periods, much less serve as the core of a powerful industrial union of railway workers. They tended instead to be organized into unions established on the MTWU model which, though made up largely of 'Anabir and sometimes other railway workers, also included workers employed elsewhere.

If the relationship between the Wafd and the railway workers did not necessarily serve the long-term needs of the latter, it was certainly in keeping with the former's conception of the working class and its project for the organization of the labor movement. That project got underway in the spring of 1924, just two months after the Wafd came to power. The first step was apparently initiated by a group of trade unionists who had left the MTWU because of its ineffectiveness and its lack of ties to the Wafd. Led by Muhammad Fu'ad, these unionists approached 'Abd al-Rahman Fahmi Pasha in March 1924 and asked him to assume the leadership of the four unions they represented. The linkage of workers with the national movement (and now the government) by having a Wafdist notable become the patron of their unions had become a common phenomenon by this time. Fahmi, it may be recalled, had been the secretary of the Wafd's central committee in Cairo in 1919 and in that capacity had encouraged the formation of unions. He had been arrested by the British authorities in 1920 and sentenced to death for involvement in terrorist activities, but his sentence had been commuted to fifteen years' imprisonment. Elected to Parliament in 1924, he was released by order of the new government.

According to his memoirs, Fahmi declined to accept the leadership of such a small segment of the labor movement and called on the unionists to expand their base of support. Thereupon they founded the General Union of Workers (al-Niqaba al-'Amma li'l-'Ummal) with Fahmi as president, and Muhammad Fu'ad as the organization's secretary and Fahmi's chief aide. The General Union was modelled on the MTWU, in the sense that it organized Cairo workers in different trades into a single union. At first it was headquartered in Fahmi

158 Unions, 1920–1924

Pasha's own luxurious residence, but it was soon able to rent its own offices and grew rapidly, claiming some 12,000 members by June.[48]

The General Union was the first instrument by means of which the Wafd, acting through Fahmi, sought to establish control over the labor movement, though it was not well-suited to this purpose. First, Fahmi did not trust some of the people who had organized it, perhaps because they had had ties to the Nationalist party, but more important, he envisioned the establishment of a national labor federation which would organize and include unions composed strictly of workers in the same trade or industry. He thus rejected the MTWU model the General Union had emulated in favor of the model the recently-destroyed CGT had pioneered in Egypt. For this reason Fahmi created an entirely new organizing committee consisting of prominent Wafd activists involved in labor affairs such as Hasan Nafi' (counsellor of the Heliopolis workers and a Wafd radical), 'Ali Bey Lahayta of Port Said, Makram 'Ubayd and 'Ali al-Shamsi (leading Wafd politicians), Shafiq Mansur (a prominent labor lawyer active in the nationalist movement), and Sayyid Khadr of Alexandria. With the skeleton of his apparatus in place Fahmi abandoned the General Union and in April–May 1924 laid the foundations for a new Wafd-led labor federation.

The new organization's formal name was the General Federation of Labor Unions in the Nile Valley (al-Ittihad al-'Amm li-Niqabat al-'Ummal bi-Wadi al-Nil), with the term "Nile Valley" intended to demonstrate the nationalists' conviction that the Sudan was an integral part of Egypt. The organization attracted many workers because it was openly linked to the Wafd, was led by well-known and popular personalities, and had adequate funding and press promotion. In Alexandria a newspaper named al-'Ummal (The Workers) began to appear in April attacking communism and publicizing the activities and outlook of Fahmi and his associates. Early in June the Federation began to publish its own weekly newspaper, Ittihad al-'Ummal (Workers' Unity or Labor Federation). Finally the Federation benefited from the noninterference, or even sympathy, of local officials now subject to orders from the Wafd government.

Nearly all the major Egyptian unions affiliated themselves to the Federation, and many hitherto unorganized workers formed unions and joined as well. Branches were established not only in Cairo and Alexandria but in provincial towns as well. In Fayum, for example, the local branch was headed by a Wafdist notable, and included various skilled trades, workers on the agricultural railways, and drivers.

48. Fahmi Memoirs, 2815; Ittihad al-'ummal, June 12, 1924.

Another example is that of the workers at the Kom Ombo land company's estates in Upper Egypt who also joined. For years they and their union had been persecuted, they said, because "we are supporters of the Wafd and men of the Wafd" while "the Wafd was suppressed." Union activists had been fired because of their politics and their union work, but after the Wafd's electoral victory the union had revived and was affiliated with Fahmi's federation.[49]

By December 1924 Muhammad Fu'ad, who had abandoned his former colleagues in the General Union to become the tireless secretary of the Federation, claimed that over one hundred unions with a total membership of 150,000 had affiliated. This figure seems much too high, but there can be no doubt that the Wafd had built a labor movement of significant proportions in only a few months' time.[50] The Federation had by that time developed a centralized and hierarchical organizational structure. Its president—titled "leader of the workers" (za'im al-'ummal) in emulation of Zaghlul, who was often called "leader of the people" or "leader of the nation"—enjoyed broad powers, and no member union could strike without the approval of the Federation's executive board. A special role was created for the Wafdist lawyers and other notables who ran most of the affiliated unions.

The Wafd's Conception of the Working Class

The way in which the new General Federation was structured reflected the Wafd's attitude toward the working class. The party's leaders realized that the urban working class was an important social force and a key constituency of the Wafd. At the same time, the propertied classes had been frightened by the events of February–March 1924 and the Wafd wished to keep a firm ideological and organizational grip on the labor movement. The Wafd's populism was therefore always tempered with paternalism. Fahmi and his fellow pashas, beys, and effendis demonstrated the Wafd's populism when they expressed their love and concern for the oppressed workers in the most lofty rhetoric they could dredge up. "It is my belief," said Fahmi, "that the worker is the foundation of everything and the source of all good. . . ." He condemned "those people who say that the worker should toil day and night for a pittance while the capitalist amasses gold; they are people corrupt in reason and religious faith."[51] Raghib

49. Ittihad al-'ummal, October 26, November 16, 1924.
50. Ibid., December 7, 21, 1924.
51. Fahmi Memoirs, 2842 (interview with al-Ahram, September 6, 1924); Ittihad al-'ummal, November 16, 1924.

160   Unions, 1920–1924

Iskandar, another wealthy Wafdist, addressed the workers in an article entitled "My Brother the Worker":

> Permit me, my brother the worker, to talk with you a little. For you are the enterprising and gentle-hearted person whose hands have exerted themselves and tired in order to complete the hard and exhausting labor you are charged with and brought forth all the manifestations of civilization and prosperity we see around us.[52]

Zaghlul Pasha himself set the tone for the party's populist rhetoric at a tea party hosted by the Heliopolis workers' union when he praised the workers for their loyalty and patriotism. The real Egyptians, he said, are those who are called "the rabble" (al-ra'a'), "and I am proud to be from the rabble like yourselves."[53]

At the same time the workers were continuously told that they must accept the wise and benevolent guidance of their social superiors, respect the rights of property, and eschew violence and communism. These themes were stressed repeatedly during 1924 in speeches and articles by Wafd leaders. "Know, O my sons," 'Abd al-Rahman Fahmi told the government workshops workers in Bulaq, "that if it is my duty to defend your rights, it is also my duty to defend the rights of others, whether or not they ask me to do so. I will not permit any of you workers to take more than you are due...." At Fayum, he noted that "many of the capitalists in Egypt are observing this new movement of ours with vigilant watchfulness, fearing that their property will be subject to loss after the foreign hand has been removed. ... We absolutely do not want anything like that said of us." If the property owners were reassured they would "broaden the scope of their investments with security and trust, as befits a people as peaceful as the Egyptian people."[54] The attacks on communism were particularly vehement.

> On this occasion, esteeming your pure and innocent souls, I warn you against polluting yourselves with the filth of communism, which knows no right and no law. Beware of its intrigues, reject its propaganda, and know that it is the doctrine (madhhab) of ruin and destruction, leading the world to anarchy and returning it to the first days of ignorance (jahiliyya). Law! Law! (al-qanun! al-qanun!)—that is my message and my recommendation to you.

52. *Ittihad al-'ummal*, January 11, 1925.
53. Fahmi Memoirs, 2819.
54. *Ittihad al-'ummal*, November 9, 1924; Fahmi Memoirs, 2869–71, 2859.

By respecting it you will win the sympathy of all men and by it you will realize the hopes for which you are yearning.[55]

Muhammad Bey Basyuni, member of Parliament for Hawamdiyya, invoked religious themes at the opening of the sugar company workers' club there.

> Know that the Islamic religion is a religion of equality and justice and will not permit injustice. It will also not allow the seizure of the property of others, whatever their religion. The traditions of us Orientals (*sharqiyyin*) are not like those of the other nations and you must adhere to religion and our Oriental traditions.[56]

This message was further buttressed by the use of patriotic appeals to convince the workers to rally behind the Wafd.

In the course of this campaign to eliminate any influence but that of the Wafd from the labor movement, Fahmi expressed the bourgeois nationalist conception of the ideal Egyptian worker. "We know that the Egyptian worker is patient, loyal and diligent," he said, "but can he be better?"

> We want the worker in his factory to be like a soldier on the field of battle. There is a time for work and a time for leisure. At work there should be devotion, diligence and sacrifice; at leisure freedom and renewal. We want him properly behaved, moderate in his habits, sincere in his desires and relationships, pious in all situations, pure and clean in his actions. He should respect law and order and preserve peace and public security, meritorious in the eyes of men and rewarded by God.[57]

This conception was shared by other Wafd leaders and was obviously rooted in an ethos and a vision of society very different from that which had motivated the activists of the CGT. For the Wafd the primary category of social identity was the nation, composed not of potentially antagonistic classes but of a variety of strata united by their common ethnicity and their participation in the struggle for independence. Most if not all of Egypt's problems were seen as resulting mainly from foreign domination; all other issues were secondary and could not be allowed to divide the nation or hinder its struggle for independence.

From this perspective the workers' grievances about exploitation were generated not by any systemic or structural forces but by the op-

55. Speech by Fahmi, Memoirs, 2817.
56. *Ittihad al-'ummal*, October 26, 1924.
57. *Ibid.*, June 19, 1924.

162 Unions, 1920–1924

pressive behavior of employers, most of them foreigners. Even those economic nationalists most enthusiastic about industrialization as the solution to Egypt's economic and social problems were only dimly aware of the impact capitalist development would have on their society. In terms of their conception of their own society, most of the bourgeoisie was unprepared to deal with the full implications of rapid social transformation, growing class differentiation, and all their contradictory and disruptive consequences. The workers were not conceived of as a distinct social class of propertyless wage laborers, as the usage of the term "worker" by the bourgeois leaders and activists of the Wafd makes clear. For them, "the workers" constituted a vaguely-defined conceptual category still rooted in an environment dominated by small-scale production and service enterprises. The Wafd's social outlook, like that of the prewar Nationalist party, blurred the distinction between the proletarian and the small proprietor as both worked with their hands. Some of the unions affiliated to the General Federation were made up of genuinely propertyless wage workers, whereas others were composed of artisans who owned their means of production, taxi owners, small shopkeepers, and proprietors of service establishments. The latter type of "unions" were especially predominant in the provinces where they depended for patronage on, and were a base of political support for, local Wafdist notables.

To a considerable extent this ideological conception reflected the still limited development of large-scale capitalist production in Egypt, the small size of a modern working class, and the low level of social differentiation between it and the petty bourgeoisie. This conception also coincided with the social interests and outlook of the nationalist bourgeoisie who were property-owners or professionals themselves, and therefore had no interest in class conflict. In their vision of society the workers were to work diligently for their employers, respect the existing social order, cause no trouble, and depend upon their social betters to resolve their grievances, yet stand ready to answer the battle cry of the Wafd when necessary. There was much genuine interest in bettering the lot of the poor unfortunate workers, and some sense of responsibility for fellow Egyptians, but also much concern that labor activism promote rather than hinder the struggle for independence as the Wafd determined it should be waged. Disruption of public order was therefore to be condemned and avoided, except when required by the exigencies of the national cause. Furthermore, and this was particularly crucial in 1924 when the communist threat seemed to loom so large, the workers were to respect the rights of property and accept the guidance of the middle and upper-class Wafd leaders.

The populism and paternalism toward the workers rooted in the Wafd's conception of Egyptian nationalism were components of a broader perspective here termed "corporatism." We use this term neither in its specific Italian Fascist sense nor precisely as it is employed by political scientists, but in the more general sense of an ideology which denies the reality of class conflict in society, rejects an independent role for the working class, and projects the state as the benevolent guardian of the workers' interests. This perspective was shared by all the political forces which attempted to gain hegemony over the workers' movement, except for the communists. In the case of the Wafd, which was the only one of these forces to actually control the government, this was often accompanied by aspirations for the incorporation of the labor movement into the state apparatus. These aspirations were never fully realized by the Wafd, whose control of the state was limited and sporadic as a result of the countervailing power of the British and the Palace. In fact, it was only fully realized during the regime of Jamal 'Abd al-Nasir, through this corporatist perspective consistently characterized the attitude of all the noncommunist political forces toward the Egyptian working class.

Promises and Results of Wafdist Hegemony

Its paternalistic declarations notwithstanding, however, the Wafd government did little to benefit the workers during its ten months in power in 1924. Most of the Wafd's leaders were socially conservative, the government wished to reassure foreign investors and attract additional foreign capital, and the cabinet was preoccupied with the negotiations with Britain over a treaty that would complete the realization of independence. Labor legislation had been promised in the speech from the throne when Zaghlul assumed office, but the only measure taken was the replacement of the Labor Conciliation Board by a system of local boards in May 1924. The strikes and occupations of the spring had convinced Zaghlul that a single nationwide board was incapable of dealing effectively with industrial conflict. A new system was devised whereby *ad hoc* boards were to be constituted as necessary in each urban governorate and in the provinces. These mediation boards were to be composed of the provincial governor as president, a representative of the local prosecutor's office, a judge appointed by the minister of justice, and representatives of the employer and the workers involved in the dispute.

The Zaghlul government avoided intervention in the many labor

164   Unions, 1920–1924

disputes unleashed by its own presence in power, ignored the increasingly desperate pleas for relief of the unemployed cigarette workers, and enacted no labor legislation. Even the Wafd's own union federation was dissatisfied with this record, and Fahmi warned the government that without official recognition the unions were at a grave disadvantage and might lose control of the workers.

> For the unions cannot lead the workers unless the government assists them morally and helps them to protect the workers' rights and achieve their just demands. If the union is unable to win the sympathy (*'atf*) of the government or the government cannot convince the employers, the workers will turn against the union and throw off the oath of obedience to it; for one who is needy is heedless and cares only about his own satisfaction.[58]

The government's inaction made life difficult for workers who had taken heart from the Wafd's promises and put themselves at risk. The Kom Ombo workers mentioned earlier found their newly revived union under attack by the same Ahmad Bey Mustafa—supervisor of the estates project, powerful local notable, and member of the Senate—who had destroyed their first union, formed in 1919. As long as he lived, he threatened, there would be no union; he was above the law. The beleaguered workers appealed to Fahmi for help, then struck to protest the firing of their leaders. Ahmad Bey controlled many of the local village headmen and brought in guards to intimidate the workers. The dispute was eventually referred to a conciliation board and the Federation supplied a lawyer to represent the workers. But complaints of harassment continued, and 1924 ended without any definitive resolution of the conflict. It would seem likely, given subsequent developments in the political arena, that Ahmad Bey got his way in the end.[59]

Official inaction had similar consequences at the largest strike of the summer of 1924, at the Belgian-owned Ma'sara cement factory south of Cairo on the east bank of the Nile (opposite the Hawamdiyya sugar refinery). Some 400 of the workers there lived in the nearby villages of Tarfaya and Hawamdiyya and supported the demands for a shorter workday, higher wages and some provision for sick pay and compensation for injuries. The other 300 workers employed at the factory were mainly Beduins or Sa'idis and opposed the militants. When management fired the ringleaders of a threatened strike on June 9, the factory was occupied for thirty-six hours. Muhammad Fu'ad

58. *Ibid.*, June 19, 1924.
59. See *ibid.*, October–December 1924.

hurried to the scene and convinced the workers to leave peaceably, and the grievances were referred to a conciliation board. But the company refused to rehire the militants and a new strike began on July 3. This time Fahmi's deputy Fu'ad was cursed and abused by the workers who accused his boss of making promises while doing nothing to help them. Although the government prohibited the police from taking "stern measures of repression," the workers were eventually compelled to end their strike.[60]

In these cases as in many others, the political connections, famous leaders and large membership of the Wafd's General Federation did not translate into an enhanced bargaining position for the workers in the face of determined opposition by employers, and in the absence of supportive legislation and government action. The Wafd's emphasis was on harmony and cooperation between workers and employers, and the Federation sought to avoid strikes by having disputes handled through the lengthy and still ineffectual conciliation process. And because the employers continued to be intransigent, this amounted to disarming the workers after raising their hopes and expectations. Although Wafdist labor activists must have had misgivings about this policy, neither the Federation nor the loyal unions ever contemplated any action or public protest to pressure the government to act. There were no illusions about the Federation's independence: it was not an autonomous entity defending the interests of the workers, but rather an instrument of the Wafd to organize and control the workers. In August for example, it planned a large demonstration to protest British suppression of nationalist agitation in the Sudan, but Zaghlul was afraid the demonstration would be infiltrated by "rifraff" and degenerate into rioting, and therefore ordered it cancelled. Fahmi complied immediately and directed the unions to send written protests instead.

Yet despite the Wafd's paternalistic attitude, its failure to take positive action on the workers' behalf and its determination to rid the labor movement of all traces of radicalism, it is nonetheless true that the positive climate engendered by the Wafd's presence in power and its encouragement (within limits, of course) of labor activism created new opportunities for workers to organize, if not to make significant gains. The labor movement gained new legitimacy under the direct patronage of the Wafd, and reached workers who had never before been organized or whose unions had faded away in the lean years following the upsurge of 1919. Paternalism from above was also often

60. *Ibid.*, June 19, 1924; EG, July 29, 1924; FO 141/583/9321/123, 172; CP, July 2, 3, 5, 6, 1924.

166 Unions, 1920–1924

complemented by deference from below. Many Egyptian workers accepted, indeed sought, the patronage and guidance of Wafdist notables. Apart from the material and ideological factors discussed earlier, and even more potent in 1924 with the Wafd in power, it seemed only natural that the party of the people, led by patriotic members of the nation's elite, should take the labor movement in hand and guide it for the sake of the movement and Egypt. The argument that patience and respect for the law would bring results was a powerful one, and was reinforced by the Wafd's being in power, while the view that the attainment of complete independence took priority over everything else was also widespread. At the same time, the destruction of the left meant that there was no alternative movement putting forth another perspective and advocating another course for the labor movement, though it would probably not have been heard in any case when the Wafd's prestige among the masses was at its height and a new and better day seemed about to dawn.

The weekly labor newspapers that were published in 1924 helped reinforce the Wafd's hegemony at the same time as they provided a forum in which literate workers could voice their grievances and share their experiences. The pages of *Ittihad al-'ummal* and *al-'Ummal* constitute a rich source of information on disputes, unionization, and the internal functioning of some of the Federation's unions. They show, for example, that even some of the "mixed" unions affiliated with the General Federation. For example, the union of workers in the *franji* (European-style) bakeries of Cairo had an executive board composed of seven Egyptians and four Europeans. Many unions provided their members with important social welfare and mutual aid services that neither the government nor the employers would undertake. These included sick pay, funeral expenses, and short-term interest-free emergency loans. The labor movement expanded rapidly as established unions grew and new unions were organized. Whatever the attitudes of their bourgeois leaders, the climate of 1924 helped consolidate a sense of common identity among the workers, however vague and ill-defined, and a certain feeling of self-esteem as a patriotic and productive part of society with its own organizations.

For the first time, too, the labor movement now paid explicit attention to at least some women's issues. Most women workers were employed in unskilled occupations, at cotton gins, in construction, and in textiles, and they were poorly paid and often had no contact with the trade union movement. There is certainly no mention in the press of their concerns or activities in this period, but *Ittihad al-'Ummal* did take an interest in the problems of educated women employed outside the home, specifically schoolteachers. In February 1925 the newspaper began to publish a women's page edited by a women who called herself Najah. She had begun to write articles about women during January and elicited such a response that she was given a regular column. The women teachers she communicated with complained about having to teach too many classes, long hours, low pay, and maltreatment by supervisors, and some even talked of forming a union for women teachers. Articles were published on "The Renaissance of the New Woman in China," "The Emancipation of Women and their Equality with Men," women school principals in New York City, "What I Love in My Husband," women factory workers in Japan and so forth.

That such issues should have been taken up in this forum is perhaps not surprising. As early as 1919 a group of middle and upper-class women had organized themselves to take an active part in the national movement. Led by Huda Sha'rawi, the wife of one of the original members of the Wafd, they demonstrated in the streets and helped promote the anti-British boycott of 1922. They also laid the foundations of the movement for women's emancipation in Egypt, calling for the improvement of the legal, social, and economic status of women, and the expansion of educational opportunities. Just as the postwar national movement had stimulated the rebirth of a labor movement, so it had facilitated the appearance of a women's movement. The concerns of the two movements first overlapped where the interests of middle-class professional women met, whereas working class and peasant women remained outside the purview of the editors of these labor newspapers.

Even as the General Federation expanded its constituency, its growth was not entirely trouble-free. Although eclipsed by the Wafd's new federation, the General Union of Workers which 'Abd al-Rahman Fahmi had first encouraged, then abandoned, continued to exist and consisted largely of workers at the 'Anabir. Relations between the two organizations deteriorated and by the fall they were openly attacking each other. Fahmi ordered the General Union disbanded, while its leader Shafiq Mansur had Fahmi deposed from the presidency and severed all ties to the Federation. The two organizations carried their conflicts into the workplace, as when Fahmi sought to undermine the General Union's base of support at the Hawamdiyya sugar refinery by reporting to the company's director about the doings of several rival activists there.

Personal conflicts between Fahmi and Shafiq Mansur seem to have been involved in this schism, though certainly resentment in the General Union at the high-handed behavior of the self-styled "leader of the workers" also played a part. There is also evidence of political en-

168 Unions, 1920–1924

tanglements, for the opposition Liberal Constitutionalist party apparently backed the General Union as part of its campaign against the Wafd government, and this prompted some General Union members to seek out a prominent Wafdist notable in order to profess their continued loyalty to the Wafd and deny any connections with its enemies.[61] Whatever its causes the episode was accompanied by barrages of mutual recrimination in the press, unsavory tactics, public misrepresentation, and political intrigue, and foreshadowed some of the afflictions suffered by the weak and factionalized labor movement of the later 1920s. The absence of any clearly articulated and positive program for the workers' movement, and the scarcity of experienced and committed leaders drawn from among the workers, corollaries of labor's dependence on the Wafd and other external forces, made such painful and disruptive episodes possible.

Before the end of 1924, national political developments once again intervened to alter the course of the labor movement. The negotiations between Zaghlul and Ramsay MacDonald ended in failure in October. The limitations on Egypt's sovereignty remained in force, leaving the Wafd in a very difficult position and without a clear sense of what course to follow. King Fu'ad was hostile to the populist Wafd, and joined forces with the British to bring down the Zaghlul government and replace it with a more pliable one. Their opportunity came on November 19, 1924, when Sir Lee Stack, commander of the Egyptian Army and governor-general of the Sudan, was assassinated in Cairo, apparently by a secret nationalist cell operating on its own. Several days later, unable either to accept a harsh British ultimatum or resist British threats of military intervention, Zaghlul resigned. Egypt's first democratically-elected government was deposed by undemocratic means, setting a precedent which would be repeated often through 1952. The president of the Senate, Ahmad Ziwar Pasha, assumed the post of prime minister. Through a series of repressive and antidemocratic measures the Ziwar government sought to undermine the Wafd's strength and break the resistance of the popular nationalist movement.

'Abd al-Rahman Fahmi's General Federation of Labor Unions, closely linked to the Wafd, could not long survive the fall of Zaghlul. As always, the advance of the workers' movement was closely correlated with the upsurge in the national movement and periods of democratic or at least less repressive government. Fahmi himself was arrested (along with hundreds of other leading Wafdists) immediately

61. CP, September–November 1924; FO 141/583/9321/125, note by Keown-Boyd; *al-Ahram*, September 9, 1924; Fahmi Memoirs, 2853-2855.

after the assassination as an alleged former terrorist, and was released only in January 1925. At the end of that month he resigned as "leader of the workers," ostensibly for reasons of health. In fact, as he wrote in his memoirs, he feared that the British-controlled secret police would manufacture some conspiracy involving workers in order to implicate him. He therefore severed his connections with the labor movement.[62] Shafiq Mansur, who had also had long-standing ties to the terrorist underground, was also arrested and eventually executed for complicity in Stack's murder along with two 'Anabir workers. The other patrons of the labor movement had of course lost their positions of power. The Federation's newspaper ceased publication in February 1925, and the organization itself disappeared virtually without a trace.

That this large organization could fade away so rapidly once deprived of the support of a sympathetic government was due less to the repressiveness of the new Ziwar regime than to its own inherent defects. The Federation had been created from above and always remained a superstructure imposed on the workers rather than a living movement arising organically from among them. Leadership was concentrated in the hands of a small coterie of Wafd politicians who saw their main task as the organization of the labor movement in the interests of their party. Satisfaction of the workers' own demands, or the encouragement of self-reliant and independent trade unionism were not priorities. Strike action and militancy were discouraged as the leaders preached patience, social harmony, and deference. Many of the new unions, especially in provincial towns, were completely dependent on the patronage and financial support of a local Wafdist notable, and when this personality lost his status because of the deposition of Zaghlul in Cairo they ceased to exist. In general, although unionization was broad and rapid in 1924, it was not deep and did not put down strong roots among the workers because it was not an organic process. The unions that survived best in the hard times that followed were those that had emerged through their own efforts and enjoyed a real base of support among their workers.

The Wafd's expulsion from power brought to a close a momentous chapter in the history of Egypt's struggle for independence, and not only constituted a major defeat both for the nationalist movement and the labor movement but inaugurated a period of repression and reaction. The great hopes aroused by the popular uprising of 1919 and ap-

---

62. Fahmi Memoirs, 2876–2879; Anis, *Dirasat*, pp. 28–29. After his resignation Fahmi's relations with Zaghlul deteriorated and he was not nominated for Parliament by the Wafd in 1926. He returned to political life briefly in 1936 and died ten years later.

170   Unions, 1920–1924

parently realized with the triumph of the Wafd in 1924 were dashed less than a year later. The bullying behavior of the British, determined to maintain their dominant position in the country despite the formal grant of independence, contributed to this disillusioning setback. The intrigues of a king who wished to rule absolutely a country whose language he could not even speak properly must also share in the blame. The vacillation of the Wafd, its commitment to playing the political game according to rules rigged against it, and its social conservatism undermined its ability to fulfil the mandate with which the Egyptian people had entrusted it. Thus were the hopes of an independent, democratic, and progressive Egypt betrayed, and herein lie the origins of the crisis that would undermine and eventually destroy the old order three decades later.

For the working class, and especially its unionized component, the five years preceding Zaghlul's resignation were marked by defeats, or at least by an inability to capitalize on the breakthrough of 1919. The employers had regained the upper hand, few groups of workers were able to make significant gains, and during periods of intensified repression many unions were forced into passivity or even dissolution. The Wafd's brief tenure in power aroused the workers' hopes, and the Wafd sought to channel and shape them for its own ends through the imposition of its organizational control and its ideological outlook on the labor movement. These months in 1924 witnessed a resurgence in labor's fortunes and the organization of the largest and broadest trade union federation Egypt had yet seen. But the Wafd's caution and restraining influence prevented the achievement of many lasting gains by the workers, and the period ended in a grave setback for labor as well as for the national movement. Nonetheless, the experiences of many Egyptian workers in the first half of the 1920s had reinforced rather than weakened their conviction that unions were a necessary instrument of self-defense and progress. Despite adverse political and economic circumstances, the strong and less dependent unions persevered and survived employer and police harassment. They would endure difficult times through much of the next decade and face great trials, but their members and leaders would also continue to learn from experience and draw conclusions for the future. This process of maturation, reflective of the growing size and social weight of the industrial working class, would gradually spread throughout the labor movement, and create tendencies within it that would eventually counter the evils of dependence on outside forces, deference, and disunity.

Chapter VI

Workers, Effendis, Pashas, and a Prince

Between the 1924 elections that first brought the Wafd to power and the Anglo-Egyptian treaty of 1936, the recurrent pattern of Egypt's political life provided the context for labor politics. Reasonably free elections would bring the Wafd a substantial parliamentary majority, reflecting its continuing popularity among the urban and rural masses. The Wafd government formed on the basis of that electoral victory would then enter into negotiations with the British in order to conclude a treaty that would resolve the problem of the four spheres reserved to British control in the 1922 unilateral proclamation of independence. The negotiations, however, would soon founder because the British were unwilling to compromise on what they regarded as their vital security interests, or surrender their preeminent position in the country, whereas the Wafd was unable to accept the limitations on Egypt's sovereignty on which Britain insisted. Relations between the two countries would deteriorate, and the British would then lend support to behind-the-scenes schemes to bring down the Wafd government and install a more amenable regime. The king and the Wafd's rivals, including the Liberal Constitutionalist party and various groups controlled by the palace or by powerful politicians, were happy to cooperate with the High Commissioner. The Wafd's enemies would then orchestrate a political crisis in which the king could plausibly intervene and dismiss the Wafd cabinet.

The reactionary new cabinet would do its best to suppress the popular nationalist movement by weakening and isolating the Wafd. Parliament would be prorogued or dissolved and an authoritarian regime deriving its support mainly from the Palace and the Residency would be established. Recognizing the inevitability of a Wafd victory in any

172 Workers, Effendis, Pashas, Prince

fair election, the government would revise the electoral laws to make them less democratic and, with the help of the security apparatus, hold rigged elections to produce a docile Parliament. The 1923 constitution might even be revised or replaced with another, more authoritarian constitution. The opposition press would be muzzled, civil liberties restricted and critics harassed.

The Wafd leadership would meanwhile struggle to maintain its links with its mass base and, in the face of official repression, try to rouse the country against the government through demonstrations, election boycotts, and press campaigns. Eventually it would become clear that the popular national movement could not be destroyed and that no Egyptian government without popular support could hope to negotiate and implement a treaty with Great Britain that would have any legitimacy or durability. The High Commissioner would begin pressing for a return to authentic parliamentary government; free elections would be held in accordance with the 1923 constitution and democratic electoral laws; and the Wafd would again win a majority, whereupon the whole cycle would begin again.

It is in the context of this pattern that the development of the Egyptian labor movement in this period must be considered. In the second half of the 1920s, and to some extent in the first half of the 1930s, the fortunes of the workers' movement would rise and fall in accordance with the general political situation. When the Wafd was in power trade unionism revived, labor militancy rose and links were reestablished between the major unions and the nationalist leadership. When the Wafd was removed from power and a period of reactionary and authoritarian government ensued, unions were suppressed, harassed, or taken over by anti-Wafd notables. It became much more difficult for workers to achieve substantial gains through militancy in the workplace, or even to defend themselves against the employers' ongoing offensive, and the cohesion of the labor movement declined. It was therefore natural for the major Egyptian unions, many of which had already forged strong ties with the Wafd from 1919 onward, to see their destinies as closely linked to the destiny of the national and democratic movement as a whole. Egyptian workers continued to support the Wafd as the champion not only of the national cause but of democracy and constitutionalism as well. Indeed, only when the Wafd was in power could most workers even hope to wage a successful struggle to improve wages and working conditions, to organize strong unions, and to exert significant pressure for favorable legislation. Yet these hopes were generally unfulfilled, for even when the Wafd was in power workers' gains were often more illusory than real.

This linkage between labor activism and the fortunes of the Wafd

Workers, Effendis, Pashas, Prince **173**

was quite strong in the second half of the 1920s, but weakened and was transformed in the first half of the 1930s. The latter period witnessed the emergence of a labor movement progressing toward organizational autonomy from the Wafd, a development that reflected changing social realities and the spread of new forms of consciousness. The workers continued to suffer under anti-Wafdist regimes and persisted in supporting the Wafd, though there were also signs of a new desire for independence and an increasing awareness of labor's own interests that foreshadowed the overt and conscious struggles for independence of the post–1936 period. This chapter will examine the complexities of labor politics from 1925 to 1930 and the emergence of new personalities and new orientations in the half-decade preceding the 1936 treaty, which was regarded at the time as a major turning-point in Egypt's political history.

The Pashas of Labor

The regime of Ahmad Ziwar Pasha, which assumed power after the downfall of Zaghlul's government in November 1924, lost little time in consolidating its power and striking out on a course antithetical to that of the Wafd. The Wafd-dominated Parliament elected at the beginning of 1924 was suspended, then dissolved, and new laws were promulgated which provided for multistage elections and gerrymandered districts. Despite these measures and other machinations carried out under the able direction of Isma'il Sidqi Pasha, minister of the interior, the Wafd managed to win a majority when new elections were held in February 1925. The king dissolved the new Parliament nine hours after it convened, and the Ziwar regime remained in power in contravention of the 1923 constitution. The regime grew increasingly repressive and increasingly isolated, especially after the Liberal Constitutionalist ministers quit the cabinet in the middle of 1925. This left the government in the hands of the Ittihad (Unity) party created early in 1925 as an instrument of the Palace and composed of the king's favorites, high-ranking army officers, government officials, and various notables.[1]

The reactionary and repressive political climate led to a sharp decline in labor activism in 1925. Confronting management now clearly carried much higher risks than had been the case just a few months earlier, risks few workers could afford to take. The labor movement

1. On the politics of the period see Ramadan, *Tatawwur*, pp. 567–606; 'Abd al-Rahman al-Rafi'i, *Fi a'qab al-thawra al-misriyya* (Cairo, third printing: 1969), I, chs. 10–11; and Afaf Marsot, *Egypt's Liberal Experiment* (Berkeley, 1977).

174 Workers, Effendis, Pashas, Prince

shared in the general demoralization and decline afflicting the popular national movement as a result of the defeat it had suffered. Many unions saw their membership drop, and in some cases organizational continuity became difficult or impossible to sustain. After the uncertainties and fears of the previous year, some employers, encouraged by a government sympathetic to business interests, took the offensive once again. The shift in the balance of power was certainly evident to the 1,800 workers (300 of them women) at the Gamsaragan cigarette company which was soon to be absorbed into the Eastern Tobacco empire. They had refused to draw their pay for March 1925 after learning that the company would henceforth consider them day laborers, and unilaterally revoked their pension and severance pay rights. Locked out of their jobs, the workers appealed in vain to the authorities. In some cases, the employers turned to the police for assistance in controlling their work force. In January 1925, for example, the management of the Kom Ombo sugar mill fired Hasan 'Ali Nasr as the alleged instigator of unrest among the workers. When Nasr tried to organize a strike, the company called in the police who returned Nasr to his village of origin and warned the workers to cease their agitation.[2]

The defeat suffered by the Wafd and the repressive policies of the Ziwar regime weakened the links between the Wafd and the unions. The Wafd's leading labor activists were either no longer on the scene or were preoccupied with the political struggle, and the labor federations which the Wafd had created in 1924 no longer functioned. A vacuum was thus created into which the governing parties were quick to move. The Wafd had already demonstrated the value it placed on control of the labor movement, and the Ziwar regime could not afford to ignore this sphere, if only to preempt its rivals. From early 1925 the Ittihad and Liberal parties sought to take over the most important unions by having their leaders, nearly all of whom held the title of pasha, installed as president or *mustashar* in place of the Wafd's men, who were mostly effendis.

The Palace played a direct role in initiating this scheme. In March 1925 King Fu'ad announced a grant of £E 3,000 to the union of railway and government workshop workers which adopted a new name: the Egyptian Workers' Union (Niqabat 'Ummal al-Qatr al-Misri). The workers were expected to show their gratitude for this huge sum of money by choosing as their president al-Sayyid Pasha Abu 'Ali, minister of agriculture in the first months of the Ziwar regime, a rich landowner, a leader of the Ittihad party and a man the British privately

2. Al-Ghazzali, *Ta'rikh*, p. 148; FO 141/583/9321.

characterized as "a stupid boor." Al-Sayyid Pasha replaced Dr. Mahjub Thabit, the long-time leader of the railway workers who had gone into exile in Syria to escape government harassment. Mahmud Fu'ad Pasha, a retired major general (*liwa'*) in the Egyptian Army, was chosen as treasurer. The larger General Union of Workers, which had its base among the 'Anabir workers but also included men at the Government Press and elsewhere, was taken over by 'Ali Shawqi Pasha, also a retired major general. Given that these workers were government employees, other means of pressure were presumably available to induce them to "elect" progovernment personalities. But private-sector unions were also taken over. In March 1925, the Cairo Tramway Workers' Union chose as its *mustashar* Wahid Bey Duss, a relative of the Liberal leader Tawfiq Bey Duss. Their former counsellor, the Wafdist Makram 'Ubayd, had allegedly been neglecting his duties, and Shafiq Mansur was in prison. By the middle of 1925 the energetic 'Ali Shawqi Pasha had taken over the CTWU and become its president.[3]

The rapid takeover of many hitherto pro-Wafd unions by the Ittihadists and their Liberal allies can be explained by several factors. First, there were the incentives offered by the Palace: for £E 3,000 some union leaders and workers were more than willing to choose a favorite of the king as union president or counsellor. Second, King Fu'ad still retained some degree of personal prestige, and sought to identify patriotism with loyalty to his person, which gave the Ittihadists an important ideological weapon. Third, there was the power of the police and the fragility of the unions, which enjoyed no recognized legal status. The fate of many unions which had emerged in 1919 or 1924 only to fade away under the blows of official harassment and the employers' offensive was well known to the workers. Finally, the Wafdist labor apparatus had never struck deep roots, and had made little apparent effort to protect its ties to the unions. In these conditions it is not surprising that the unions sought to survive and protect their members by accepting Ittihad and Liberal pashas as patrons. There is little doubt that in their hearts the workers remained as strongly pro-Wafd as ever, but in the absence of some realistic alternative prudence dictated that they bend with the prevailing wind in the hope of better times to come.

Even as they adapted to the new situation, however, the submissiveness of at least some workers had its limits. For example, when

3. FO 141/583/9321/143, "Report on the Labour Situation," January 1925-September 1926; /151, February 20, 1928; /152, Graves to Smart, February 25, 1928; FO 407/210; FO 141/748/8839/38, Keown-Boyd to the Residency, March 30, 1925.

176 Workers, Effendis, Pashas, Prince

the Cairo tramwaymen elected a new counsellor in March 1925, they stipulated that he was not to conclude any agreement without the approval of the union's executive board. In the following months there was also talk among the tramwaymen of replacing their proregime counsellors with new counsellors drawn from the opposition Nationalist party. Ironically, the Ittihadist and Liberal pashas leading the unions were, in spite of the reactionary attitudes they and their parties held, compelled by virtue of their new positions to resist management attempts to destroy the unions. They had to maintain their organizational bases and the loyalty of their constituents, or the prize (control of the unions) was not worth having. Nonetheless, many workers responded to the takeover of their unions by these pashas by abandoning them, by failing to pay their monthly dues, which further contributed to the decline of the labor movement in 1925.[4]

As so often before, labor's situation would only improve as the political climate eased, democracy was restored, and workers regained control of their unions and again acted without fear of immediate repression. Toward the end of 1925 the reactionary tide began to ebb. The united opposition of Wafdists, Liberals, and Nationalists began to assert itself with increasing vigor. The country had been particularly stirred to outrage by a decree of the Ziwar cabinet which raised the voting age and imposed property and educational qualifications for electors. A "national congress" was convened in February 1926 to unify the opposition forces and demonstrate their strength. The organized workers' movement was represented at this event mainly by the Wafd's labor lawyers, though each union also received three extra tickets to the congress. By the spring of 1926 the Ziwar regime was clearly losing its grip on power. Village chiefs resigned rather than implement the amended election law, the opposition parties agreed to boycott the forthcoming elections, and the new British High Commissioner, Lord Lloyd, counselled political reconciliation. Politically isolated, the Ziwar government announced that it would not implement the amended election law, thereby guaranteeing the victory of the opposition at the polls. The three opposition parties agreed to divide up the parliamentary districts among themselves, and when national elections were held in May 1926, the Wafd again emerged the overwhelming victor. The Ittihad party elected only five deputies compared to 165 Wafdists, twenty-nine Liberal Constitutionalists, and five Nationalists. The British, however, would not allow Sa'd Zaghlul to become prime minister. He was therefore forced to serve as president of the Chamber of Deputies while coalition Wafd-Liberal

4. FO 141/748/8839/39–41.

cabinets were headed by the independents 'Adli Yakan Pasha (June 1926–April 1927) and 'Abd al-Khaliq Tharwat (April 1927–March 1928).

Wafdist influence in the labor movement had revived even before the fall of the Ziwar government when a number of labor lawyers, notably Hasan Nafi' in Cairo and Ja'far Fakhri in Alexandria, had begun to reestablish contacts with the unions in the course of organizing the national congress. As soon as political conditions allowed, union members were quick to depose their Ittihadist leaders and replace them with Wafdists. In August 1926 the Egyptian Workers' Union, the centerpiece of the Ittihad party's attempt to take over the labor movement, was reported to be nearly defunct because many members had stopped paying dues. Its president, al-Sayyid Pasha Abu 'Ali, was said to have "lost interest in the union since the election results were announced." Members of the union's executive board were already approaching Wafdist leaders and seeking their help in finding new patrons. Other union members were at the same time pressing al-Sayyid Pasha to turn the king's £E 3,000 gift over to them. Finally, at the beginning of October, the Ittihadist president was deposed, and a general assembly of union members unanimously restored their old leader Mahjub Thabit to the presidency.[5] A similar process was simultaneously underway in the General Union of Workers. This organization's leader, 'Ali Shawqi Pasha, had anticipated the downfall of Ziwar early in 1926, and sought to ingratiate himself with the opposition. Nonetheless, a struggle had erupted within the union's leadership between 'Ali Pasha's supporters and those who wanted to install a new president and new counsellors. In October 'Ali Pasha was removed and after lengthy factional disputes Hasan Nafi' was elected to replace him.[6]

The restoration of Wafdist influence in the Cairo Tramway Worker's Union was a more complex and problematic process involving both internal factional struggles and conflict with the Cairo Tramway Company. As usual the tramwaymen were among the first to resume activity as soon as political conditions allowed. Petitions listing their grievances and demands were presented to management as soon as it became feasible to do so. Although the company had renounced the agreement of October 1919, it agreed to begin negotiations when a sympathetic Wafdist deputy used Parliament as a forum to air the workers' grievances and thereby put pressure on both management

5. CSP, February 19, August 7, 19, September 30, October 3, 1926; AP, January 14, 18, 27, 1926.
6. CSP, October 8, 21, 26, November 3, 7, 1926; FO 141/583/9321/149, Report by Graves, May 3, 1927 (hereafter cited as Graves Report, 1927).

178 Workers, Effendis, Pashas, Prince

and the government.[7] The ensuing negotiations undermined worker support for the leadership of 'Ali Shawqi Pasha, still president of the CTWU, and of the *mustashar* Ahmad Muhammad Agha, another Wafdist lawyer. According to a secret police report, the two leaders had concurred in a conciliation board proposal that would

> make the 1919 agreement applicable only to the traction workers, to the exclusion of the rest. Ahmad Effendi Muhammad Agha, one of the union's counsellors, tried to make the workers understand the gains that this [conciliation board] meeting had won for them, but they would not listen to him. These workers spread the word that the incumbent president and counsellors of the union had sided with the company and were no longer trustworthy. 'Abd al-'Aziz Sayf [the union's secretary] and a group of the workers tried to convince the rest to elect Zuhayr Sabri as their counsellor. We have also heard that another group of workers from the 'Abasiyya and Shubra depots will go this afternoon to see Fakhri 'Abd al-Nur Bey, member of the Chamber of Deputies, to ask him to accept the presidency of the union.[8]

At its meeting on September 30, the union's executive board voted to depose 'Ali Shawqi Pasha from the presidency, dismiss all the counsellors except the treasurer, and elect the Wafdist Zuhayr Sabri as the new *mustashar*.

The tram worker's decision was clearly rooted in the work-related grievances 'Ali Pasha and Agha had failed to resolve, though politics also played a role in this change of leadership. 'Ali Pasha was a relic of the dark days of the Ziwar regime and he was deposed from the presidency of the General Union at virtually the same time as he was repudiated by the CTWU. The election of Sabri represented not only discontent with the old leadership's apparent capitulation to management but also a return to the Wafdist fold. Although Agha was himself a Wafdist and would serve his party well in labor politics, he was discredited in the eyes of the Cairo tramwaymen through his association with 'Ali Pasha and his attempt to "sell" the conciliation board's proposal to the workers.[9] In speeches to his new clients im-

---

7. See Majlis al-Nuwwab, *Majmu'at madabit dawr al-in'iqad al-awwal al-'adi*, session of August 22, 1926.

8. CSP, September 25, 29, 30, 1926.

9. Ahmad Muhammad Agha and his associates never recognized their removal and Sabri's election as legitimate, and the events of September-October 1926 led to the emergence of two organizations which claimed to be the legitimate CTWU. Although Agha's faction won the union's funds and property after protracted court battles, it had only 200 members in the spring of 1927 as compared to 800 in Sabri's union. See Graves Report, 1927.

Workers, Effendis, Pashas, Prince **179**

mediately after his election, Zuhayr Sabri was quite explicit about the association of the workers' cause with the national cause and the linkages between the workers' political and economic enemies.

> It is impossible to achieve independence without the participation and organization of the workers in the political movement when necessary. For we must have two perspectives (*madhhabayn*): the political perspective outside the union to implement as necessary, and the economic perspective inside the union to help one another. . . . Then Zuhayr Sabri Effendi explained to the workers about the Ittihad party and the circumstances of the former counsellors' entry among the workers. He said that the Itthihad party had always worked against the national movement. . . . He is against this party to the end, because it works for the benefit of the English and the foreigners against his country.[10]

Aborted Hopes

By the fall of 1926, then, most of the major unions had reverted to their Wafdist allegiances and Palace influence had been largely eradicated: the Wafdist effendis had replaced the Palace-backed pashas. This was accompanied by a surge of activity throughout the labor movement as old unions resumed activity and new unions were formed. A survey prepared in the spring of 1927 by the British security officer responsible for monitoring the labor scene reported sixty-two unions in Egypt with a total membership estimated at 25,665: Cairo had twenty unions with 13,650 members and total funds of £E 8,708; Alexandria had twenty-one unions with 5,541 members and £E 4,216; Port Said (with Isma'iliyya) had eight unions with 4,227 members; and the rest of the country (mainly Delta towns) 2,247 union members.[11]

These figures seem reasonably accurate, with certain exceptions, though not all the "unions" listed were in fact composed of wage workers. For example, among the 2,500 members of the Cairo drivers' union there were probably some who owned their own vehicle and were really independent entrepreneurs. Many of the 2,000 members of the Cairo weavers' union were independent artisans who owned at least some of the means of production with which they worked, rather than wage workers. Low-level government functionaries (*muwazzafun*) were also included in the totals, as were "unions" of cafe owners, brewers, and dragomen. In the provincial cities class lines

10. CSP, October 1, 2, 4, 1926.
11. Graves Report, 1927.

180 Workers, Effendis, Pashas, Prince

were even more blurred. Damietta, for example, had a union comprised of both shoemakers and shoe merchants, and as will be discussed in more detail later, the "labor organizations" in some provincial centers included both employers and the self-employed along with wage workers in various trades.

As the deposition of the anti-Wafd leaders imposed under the Ziwar regime showed, the larger and stronger unions were no longer entirely dominated by middle and upper-class patrons. The activists who had risen from the rank and file to positions on the executive boards of the major unions were not passive tools in the hands of scheming lawyers. They were increasingly willing and able to challenge their counsellors in order to defend their own interests. The Ciaro tramwaymen had demonstrated this when they got rid of 'Ali Shawqi Pasha and Ahmad Muhammad Agha, and elected Zuhayr Sabri who was more militant in both nationalist and industrial terms. The tramwaymen of Alexandria showed similar independence when in 1927 most of them turned to 'Abd al-Hamid al-Sanusi, a lawyer whom the police regarded as a dangerous radical with communist connections, for leadership in their struggles with the tram company. Al-Sanusi himself would later come under attack from a group of dissident workers who felt that their counsellor had failed to defend the workers' interests energetically enough and sought to elect a new *mustashar.*[12]

While very little biographical information is available about these proletarian trade unionists of the 1920s, their contribution to the labor movement is clear. Their increasingly assertive behavior refutes the notion that the Egyptian union movement was completely subservient to the will of outside forces, especially the Wafd and its agents. The situation was clearly much more complex: there were pressures from below, from among the workers, as well as from outside the unions, from the counsellors and the politicians. A stratum of worker militants was emerging which was increasingly determined at least to share control of their own unions with their social superiors. They could still only replace one set of counsellors with another, and apparently still felt the need for the patronage of notables or a link with the Wafd through their counsellors. But the events of the latter half of the 1920s foreshadowed a new stage in the long struggle of the Egyptian workers' movement to chart an autonomous course.

12. On the Alexandria tram workers, see AP, 1927–1928, passim, and *al-Muqattam*, March 1927.

Bourgeois labor activists continued however to play a considerable role in these years, and several names stand out. Mahjub Thabit was very active in the union movement of the late 1920s. He had been trained as a physician in Europe and had been active in the MTWU and the Nationalist party before 1914. After the war he had been active in the national movement, maintaining close ties with the Wafd leadership despite his affinity for the Nationalist party, and had led the MTWU for some years. He had especially close ties with the Cairo railway workers, and won widespread popularity by providing free medical care for workers and the poor at his Cairo clinic. The French diplomatic staff in Cairo considered him a socialist, perhaps because of his friendship with leftist intellectuals, and saw him as a threat to foreign economic interests in Egypt. In fact, Thabit was really a political maverick: he defeated a Wafdist candidate in a by-election for Parliament early in 1927 in a working-class district of Alexandria only to cooperate with the Wafd in Parliament. From 1926 to 1928 he was a leading figure on the labor scene, serving as president of several unions, trying to resolve the problems of many others and attempting to build union federations independent of political parties, including the Wafd.[13]

'Aziz Mirham was another labor politician active in these years, and indeed well into the 1930s. Scion of a wealthy Coptic landowning family, he had studied law in Egypt and France, and returned to his native land in 1918. He was among the founders of the short-lived Democratic party, composed of left-leaning Egyptian intellectuals, then became involved in labor affairs under the aegis of the Wafd. He was elected to the Senate in 1926 and served as *mustashar* of the cigarette workers' union, the tramway workers' union, and the union of Model Workshops graduates. He was atypical of the Wafd's labor chiefs in that he was of upper-class rather than middle-class origin and (probably for that reason) a member of the upper rather than the lower chamber of Parliament. Although not a first or second-line leader of the Wafd, Mirham seems to have functioned as the senior member of the Wafd's labor apparatus, which was not formally structured at this time, and as such played a leading role in parliamentary

---

13. On Thabit see FO 407/221/5, "Leading Personalities in Egypt," 1937; F/43, Report to Paris, February 2, 1927, no. 43; Salih 'Ali 'Isa al-Sudani, *al-Asrar al-siyasiyya li-abtal al-thawra al-misriyya wa-ara' al-duktur Mahjub Thabit* (Cairo, n.d.); and 'Izz al-Din, *Marahil*, pp. 19–37. On the attempt to unify labor, see CSP, August 21, September 13, 1927; 'Izz al-Din II, pp. 185–87; memoirs of Muhammad Hasan 'Amara, pp. 31–32 (typewritten form), found at Mu'assasat al-Thaqafa al-'Ummaliyya, Cairo (also published in serial form in *al-Thaqafa al-'ummaliyya*).

182 Workers, Effendis, Pashas, Prince

efforts to enact social legislation in general and labor legislation in particular.[14]

Two other Wafdists active in the labor movement are also worthy of note. Hasan Nafi' had been a member of Parliament since 1924, and from 1926 served as counsellor or president of the drivers' union, the Heliopolis tramwaymen, the General Union of Workers, and the cigarette workers' union. Zuhayr Sabri was also a lawyer, but not a member of Parliament, had long been active in the nationalist movement, and also had ties to the socialists. The British authorities displayed considerable paranoia about Sabri, and regarded him as a very dangerous man, even a member of the Communist party. Although he appears to have been a friend of Joseph Rosenthal, there is no evidence that he was ever a member of any communist organization. Sabri was particularly close to the Cairo tramwaymen but also worked with the drivers, the Heliopolis tramwaymen, the cigarette workers, and the barbers.[15]

These sketches make it clear that there was a great deal of overlap in the spheres of activity of each of the Wafd's labor activists. The major unions each had several counsellors, and some also had honorary counsellors and an honorary president. For example, when Zuhayr Sabri became *mustashar* of the Cairo Tramway Workers' Union, he secured the election of over a dozen honorary counsellors, all prominent Wafdist members of Parliament with the title of bey, and through this step was apparently recreating the advisory council the Wafd had set up in 1924 to oversee the activities of this key union. Although these counsellors were all Wafdists, there were a significant number of cases in which rivalries among counsellors attached to the same union erupted into factional disputes. In some cases personality conflicts seem to have been involved, in others rivalry among the counsellors for the power base and perhaps the financial gain that association with an important union might bring. These struggles among counsellors were not of course conducive to the emergence of a strong and united labor movement. Notwithstanding the manifestations of workers' growing determination to run their own unions, the labor movement remained divided and unable to fully capitalize on the presence in power of a sympathetic government by taking the offensive against the employers.

The years 1926 and 1927 therefore saw few successful strikes and little progress made in negotiations over long-standing grievances.

14. FO 141/583/9321/161, Keown-Boyd to Smart, July 19, 1928. See also 'Izz al-Din's brief treatment in *Marahil*, pp. 55–67.
15. *al-Ittihad*, July 19, 1924; Graves Report, 1927; FO 371/J3023/213/16, Henderson to Chamberlain, October 27, 1926.

Workers, Effendis, Pashas, Prince **183**

Most workers sought higher wages, compensation for work-related injuries, and in some cases the opening of the better-paid jobs to Egyptians. For the Cairo tramwaymen discipline was still a key issue, and they were still demanding implementation of the 1919 agreement. Their new *mustashar* Zuhayr Sabri had promised a militant stand toward the CTC ("I know of nothing called the 'conciliation board'; we demand the convening of the cabinet itself to look into our demands, just like the workers of England") and threatened to call a strike of all the transport unions if the tramwaymen's demands were not met. But when the required fifteen days' strike notice was given in March 1927, the police cooperated with the CTC to forestall any stoppage. Alexander Keown-Boyd, the notorious chief of the security apparatus, called in Zuhayr Sabri and warned him that the police would use any means necessary to keep the tram lines running. The police official also sought to bring psychological pressure on the union leader. Sabri, Keown-Boyd boasted in a report, "had previously been shaken by the fact that most of the vernacular newspapers had talked of him as a Communist—this was previously arranged." Under duress Sabri withdrew the strike notice and accepted terms which won for the workers only the appointment of a government representative to the disciplinary investigations panel.[16]

This had in fact been one of the tramway workers' long-standing demands. They saw it as a means of weakening or at least counterbalancing management's power by involving what they hoped would be a sympathetic or at least neutral state in labor relations. Although the achievement of this goal was a step forward, the settlement as a whole must be seen as a disappointment given the high hopes and militancy the restoration of the Wafd had aroused. Other groups of workers were similarly disappointed by their inability to make up for ground lost since 1924, whether due to factionalism or the unions' weak position vis-à-vis the employers.

It was in order to remedy this weakness that the labor movement had long been pressing for the enactment of legislation that would grant unions a defined legal status and give workers statutory rights to healthy and safe working conditions, compensation for injuries at work, sick pay, and severance pay. The need for such legislation, promised .but never enacted by the Wafd in 1924, was widely acknowledged and again became a public issue with the Wafd's return

16. FO 141/748/8839/42, 43; 'Izz al-Din II, pp. 178–9. Sabri had warned the tram workers of the dangers of red-baiting when he first took office. Sa'd Zaghlul himself had been accused of communism by the British because he praised the workers, Sabri claimed. "Know that anyone who joins the workers' movement will find the government accusing him of being a communist." CSP, October 2, 1926.

184 Workers, Effendis, Pashas, Prince

to power in 1926. Union meetings, delegations of workers and sympathetic Wafdist deputies raised the question repeatedly.

The employers were of course strongly opposed to the very idea of such legislation. The Egyptian Federation of Industries (EFI), founded in 1921 and consisting mainly of several hundred large foreign-owned and *mutamassir* companies, used its organ *L'Égypte Industrielle (Misr al-Sina'iyya)* to campaign against the proposed laws. "It must not be forgotten," the industrialists' monthly warned, "that most of the provisions of these laws could not be applied in Egypt, because they presuppose a different degree of economic and social evolution." Egyptian industry was in a precarious state, the EFI argued, and the government's priority should be supporting industrial development rather than further burdening companies by increasing their labor costs.[17]

Despite opposition from the industrialists, the Wafd-led government appointed a commission to study the question of labor legislation in July 1927. Its president was 'Abd al-Rahman Rida Pasha, undersecretary of state at the ministry of justice, and it included Dr. Levi, secretary of the EFI and of the Société Royale d'Économie Politique, de Statistique et de Législation; two senators, including 'Aziz Mirham; Mahjub Thabit; a Wafdist deputy; and several government officials. The commission took a long time to carry out its work: it only got around to visiting workplaces and union offices in the fall of 1928, and presented its report in April of the following year. The scope of the Rida commission's mandate was restricted to industrial labor, which led to protests from the unions of sales workers. The EFI also argued forcefully against the focus on industrial workers. The industrialists hoped that if the large landowners who dominated Parliament could be made to fear that labor laws might be extended to agricultural wage workers, they would surely scuttle the whole project.

The Rida commission's final report set forth a comprehensive program of labor legislation. Specific provisions included a uniform nine-hour work day, restrictions on child and female labor, conciliation boards composed of judges, recognition of labor unions, employer responsibility for sick pay, compensation for injuries, and the creation of a Labor Office in the Ministry of the Interior. It is significant that these proposed laws covered both manual workers (*sunna'*, laborers) and those who performed mental labor (*mustakhdimun*, employees), the two categories that comprised "the workers" (*al-*

17. See *L'Égypte Industrielle* (hereafter *EI*) 2 (December 1926), 3 (January and March 1927). An article in the issue of January 1927 reported sympathetically on the way the fascist regime in Italy had resolved the "imaginary conflict" between capital and labor.

'ummal).[18] Had these proposals been enacted into law and implemented, they would have given an enormous boost to the labor movement and the working class generally. Indeed, the workers were themselves quite aware of this. At one "very important" factory in Alexandria, *L'Égypte Industrielle* reported with alarm, the workers presented management with a copy of the draft proposals, "adding in a menacing tone that things would change when the proposals were enacted into law."[19] But the report of the Rida commission, quite enlightened and progressive for its time, remained a dead letter. By the time it was completed the political climate had changed once again. By failing to move expeditiously while it was in power, the Wafd ensured that no labor legislation would be forthcoming for some years.

When Sa'd Zaghlul died in August 1927, leadership of the Wafd passed to Mustafa al-Nahhas, who became prime minister of a Wafd-Liberal coalition government in March 1928, after a draft Anglo-Egyptian treaty presented to the Egyptian Parliament by the independent Tharwat Pasha had been rejected. The favorable political climate encouraged the Wafd's labor activists to seek once again to unite the unions under their control. Early in 1928 a new General Federation of Labor Unions in Egypt was set up with Ahmad Muhammad Agha as president and Ahmad Isma'il as secretary. This Federation had little real support among the trade unions, but it did for the first time establish contacts with labor organizations outside Egypt. Ahmad Isma'il (formerly secretary of the General Union and brother of Mahmud Isma'il, who had been executed along with Shafiq Mansur for complicity in the Lee Stack assassination) travelled to Europe in 1928 and met with officials of the social-democratic International Federation of Trade Unions based in Amsterdam. Contacts were also made with the International Labor Office in Geneva.

This Federation was however never more than a pale shadow of 'Abd al-Rahman Fahmi's organization of 1924 and proved even more short-lived. After only three months in power, Nahhas Pasha was forced to resign because of a financial scandal in which he was allegedly involved (he was later cleared) and because of British disapproval of a draft law easing restrictions on public meetings. The king and the British were once again determined to rule without the Wafd, that is, without a popular or constitutional mandate, and hence instituted what amounted to a dictatorial regime. To that end Muhammad Mahmud, leader of the Liberal Constitutionalist party and one of

18. FO 141/583/9321/163, 178a; *EI*, IV, 2 (February 1928) and IV, 7 (November 1928). The full text of the report can be found in *al-Tali'a* (May 1965), pp. 153–62.
19. *EI*, V, 2 (February 1929).

186 Workers, Effendis, Pashas, Prince

Egypt's largest landowners, was designated prime minister. Mahmud's regime lasted until October 1929, and was similar to that of Ahmad Ziwar (1925–1926). Parliament was dissolved, rule by decree instituted, political liberties curtailed, and opposition newspapers harassed.

The new prime minister professed interest in labor's problems and allocated some funds for the construction of workers' housing. The sixty-one units actually completed in the Sayyida Zaynab section of Cairo were however too few to even begin to alleviate the severe shortage of affordable housing, and ultimately they were rented out to government employees because the rents were too high for workers. The social demagogy of the Mahmud government notwithstanding, this was a bleak period for the labor movement. Repression once again undermined even the strongest unions, while the working class as a whole suffered from depressed economic conditions reflected in falling cotton prices and declining real wages. A report to the Residency by a British security official noted that 1929 had been "singularly free" of labor unrest. This was attributed to the government's housing scheme, which the report claimed "has had a very settling effect, and the personal interest His Majesty [King Fu'ad] has shown in the matter has caused the workers to feel that the Government is really interested in their welfare." A much more likely cause for the low level of industrial conflict was alluded to later in the same report: "Conciliation Boards have not been much in request because of the close personal touch kept up between the Public Security Department and various large business concerns. This has enabled causes of unrest to be dealt with in their early stages."[20]

The fledgling General Federation established by the Wafd did not long survive that party's fall from power. Its secretary Ahmad Isma'il sought to secure the favor of the new government by replacing Ahmad Agha with Mahjub Thabit, who was considerably more acceptable to the authorities, and the organization disintegrated in a welter of splits and mutual recriminations. Thabit himself played a curious role in this period. Although he had cooperated with the Wafd, he was an independent whose desire to rid the unions of control by politicians and other outsiders seems to have been sincere. He was however also a close personal friend of Muhammad Mahmud, and the prime minister sought to use him to establish Liberal control over the labor movement. The Wafdist press bitterly attacked Thabit for alleg-

20. FO 141/649/268, "Report on Labour during 1929," Major E. Anson, European Department of the Ministry of the Interior, to W. A. Smart, Oriental Secretary, January 14, 1930.

edly collaborating with the unconstitutional regime and implied that he had been bought off. Thabit denied these charges and claimed that he was using his access to the prime minister to press for social programs and labor legislation. Although he often accompanied Muhammad Mahmud on his tours through the country, Thabit insisted that he disapproved of the government's antidemocratic measures. In a message to the workers he called on them to stay out of politics.

> Keep away from the parties, for your own good and the good of the country. Don't be tools of the [prominent] personalities, beware of leaders·and would-be leaders and their exploitative agents. Don't be partisan; rather take a negative attitude toward the parties: support any party which works in your interest and your country's interest. Support whoever does well by you, and abandon whoever tries to exploit you.[21]

While ostensibly a call for the independence of labor, this advice was generally taken as a veiled attack on the Wafd, the party that was dominant in the union movement and whose activists were Thabit's chief rivals. The call to support whomever did well by the workers was seen as an appeal to support the Mahmud government, which at that time was promising much-needed reforms in an effort to win popular support. Whatever Thabit's real motives and intentions, his activities in 1928 and 1929 discredited him in the eyes of the Wafd and its supporters and eroded his base among the workers. Thabit played only a very minor role in the labor movement in the 1930s, and financial difficulties compelled him to leave politics and take up a position as chief medical officer at Cairo University.

In sum, the second half of the 1920s was a difficult time for the Egyptian labor movement. Adverse political and economic circumstances diminished the ability of workers to develop or even maintain their organizations and to wage successful struggles for improved wages and working conditions. Repression and the apparent inability of the nationalist leadership to effectively resist the British and the king left the workers weak and isolated. At the same time the Egyptian economy was on the verge of the world depression of the 1930s.

Factionalism was rife in this period as both Wafdists and anti-Wafdists vied for control of the major unions in order to gain personal or political advantage. Union members could and did play a role in initiating and deciding these contests, but the alternatives available to them were quite limited. They still depended on the link to an influential lawyer or other patron and deferred to outside leadership.

21. Al-Sudani, *Asrar*, p. 132.

188 Workers, Effendis, Pashas, Prince

The labor organizations which fared best were the unions of skilled craftsmen, sales, and clerical workers. They were generally composed of better-paid, better-educated workers, many of them foreigners. These workers could develop experienced and stable leadership, sustain mutual assistance schemes, and avoid control by the political parties. The more politically and economically sensitive Egyptian unions were not so lucky, and the price they paid in disunity and ineffectiveness was therefore quite high.

Nonetheless, Egyptian workers were quite capable of learning from their experience and drawing conclusions as to a more effective course for the union movement. The struggles within the tram unions have already been cited as evidence of the increasing awareness among trade unionists of the costs of deference and dependence, and of their growing willingness to fight for what they saw as the best interests of their fellow workers. Mahjub Thabit's repeated calls for a labor movement independent of the parties were reaching receptive ears among the workers active in union politics, a theme made explicit in a letter published in *al-Muqattam* in June 1929. Entitled "The Workers Must Themselves Take Control of the Leadership of Their Unions," and written by Ahmad 'Ali Badawi, a leader of the printing workers' union, the letter notes that after the successes of 1919 "individuals who were not workers [began to] meddle in the unions to serve their own interests."

> As a worker and a member of one of the unions and as someone in a position which allows broad contacts, I can confirm that most of these bosses [of unions, *ru'asa'*] know nothing of their union's affairs. They don't attend meetings except if they have some selfish interest or if it touches on things that concern them personally. And if you will permit me I will note with great sorrow that splits among members of some of the unions have been caused by these bosses. . . . They get some members of the union to support them and incite them to opposition toward those of their colleagues who already know the truth about [the boss'] aims. The members of the union then split, and another union is formed.

Badawi cites the examples of the tramway and railway unions and calls upon the outsiders to leave the workers alone.

> I do not think that these are my personal feelings alone; rather they are natural feelings which are widespread in all the unions. We see the unions try from time to time to get rid of these alien leaderships (*ri'asat ghariba*) in order to assume responsibility for

their affairs themselves, without any need for foreign hands to lead them or outside minds to direct them. There are among the workers many of superior capabilities and intelligence who can assume the leadership of their unions and guide them on the right path.[22]

Badawi was certainly correct in his assertion that he was not alone in his views. Other workers who had risen from the rank and file to take over the day-to-day leadership of their unions were coming to a similar understanding of the experience of the labor movement since 1919. The struggle of this new worker leadership for an independent and militant course would be long, difficult, and often contradictory, as the events of the early 1930s would show. The emergence of this new perspective can first be glimpsed toward the end of the 1920s, and it was facilitated by the growing size and social weight of the working class, the spread of mechanized industry, and changing political conditions.

From Nahhas Pasha to Sidqi Pasha

The new decade of the 1930s opened with yet another repetition of the now familiar political cycle. The authoritarian government of Muhammad Mahmud was ultimately no more successful than that of Ahmad Ziwar had been. The prime minister had negotiated a draft treaty with the British, but it was clear that only ratification by a freely elected Parliament on the basis of the 1923 constitution (which Mahmud had been planning to revise) would be accepted as legitimate and binding by the Egyptian people. The new British High Commissioner, Sir Percy Loraine, therefore moved to have Muhammad Mahmud resign after some fifteen months in power. The Wafd won an overwhelming majority in the elections that followed, and by January 1930 Mustafa al-Nahhas Pasha was prime minister once again.

As had been the case in 1919, 1924, and 1926–1928, the upsurge in the national-democratic movement manifested in 1930 in the Wafd's return to power was accompanied by a dramatic rise in the level of worker activism and organization. Once again many groups of workers revived their unions, renewed their ties with their Wafdist counsellors, and raised demands. Long-standing grievances were exacerbated by the effects of the world depression whose impact was now beginning to be felt in Egypt. Employers sought to cut costs by speeding up work, laying off workers, and reducing wages and benefits.

22. June 17, 1929, quoted in 'Izz al-Din II, pp. 189–90.

190   Workers, Effendis, Pashas, Prince

With democracy restored workers were somewhat better able to resist these measures, though solid victories were still few and far between. The workers at the 'Anabir, for example, still a hotbed of labor as well as nationalist militancy, found themselves in open conflict with their English chief engineer. Management attempts to cut labor costs by firing workers and compelling the rest to work harder were met with a brief and inconclusive strike in February 1930. Negotiations between the workers and ESR officials were begun, but conditions in the 'Anabir did not improve. Months later protests were still being ignored and agitators punished, transferred, or dismissed. The workplace grievances of the 'Anabir workers would contribute to their political militancy after the Wafd's fall from power.[23] At the Suez Canal Company, the Egyptian *tâcheron* workers—employed indirectly through labor contractors and paid far less than the SCC's permanent workers, most of them foreigners—took advantage of the improved political climate and formed a union. They demanded equality of rights and benefits with the cadre workers, and especially permanent status. Once again the existing unions of SCC workers demonstrated their progressive and internationalist attitude by cooperating with the new union in a federation of all Canal Company workers. Despite their unity, however, these workers were to make little headway against their very powerful and determined adversary in 1930.[24]

The revival of labor activity in 1930 was encouraged by and covered in the pages of two new weekly publications. The first of these, *al-'Amil al-Misri (The Egyptian Worker)*, began publication in February 1930. Edited by the Wafdist labor lawyer Husni al-Shantanawi, it was in fact the Wafd's labor organ, so it supported that party's effort to organize the union movement, and also published reports on union meetings and industrial conflicts. The weekly was explicitly anti-communist and "moderate" in tone with a stress on the patriotic obligations of the workers' movement. Some unions sent representatives to regular meetings with the paper's editors, and *al-'Amil al-Misri* claimed to be not only "the workers' spokesman" but also "published by the labor unions." The very fact that such a claim was expressed is significant because it indicates the extent to which the ideas of an autonomous labor movement run by the workers themselves had caught on by 1930 and had to be formally acknowledged.

23. FO 141/649/268, European Department, Ministry of the Interior, to Smart at the Residency, January 14, 1930; *Ruh al-'asr* (hereafter cited as *Ruh*) and *al-'Amil al-misri* (hereafter cited as *AM*), February–March 1930, passim.
24. *Ruh*, February–July 1930, passim; FO 141/689/610, reports by Graves to the Residency, March–June 1931.

Yet *al-'Amil al-Misri* remained in essence a Wafdist publication in the tradition of 'Abd al-Rahman Fahmi's *Ittihad al-'Ummal* of 1924. The other labor weekly was by contrast a genuinely new phenomenon. *Ruh al-'Asr (Spirit of the Age)* also began to appear in February 1930, but explicitly described itself as socialist, by which it meant social democratic. It was ably edited by a physician, 'Abd al-Fattah Muhammad al-Qadi, and contributors included Mahmud Husni al-'Arabi, the former communist leader; Sayyid Qandil, a self-educated printing worker; and 'Isam al-Din Hifni Nasif. Like al-Qadi, Nasif had been a young Wafd activist in 1919, then joined the Nationalist party and finally became a socialist, at least partially as a result of his contact with the left in Berlin in the 1920s.[25] *Ruh al-'Asr* was regarded by its publishers as a vehicle for the propagation of progressive ideas, and in the long run, as a step toward the establishment of a socialist movement in Egypt. To that end the weekly published articles explaining socialism and how it differed from both Soviet communism and anarchism. The state-owned Egyptian railway and telegraph systems and the city-owned Ramleh tram system were cited, in the best German social democratic tradition, as examples of authentic socialism. Husni al-'Arabi translated Ramsey MacDonald's history of the socialist movement into Arabic, and short biographies of Fourier, Lasalle, and Saint-Simon were published along with stories by Strindberg, Dostoyevsky, and Gorky. In the issue of May 2, 1930, *Ruh al-'Asr* proudly featured what it claimed was the first photograph of Karl Marx—*mu'allimuna al-akbar*, "our greatest teacher"—ever published in Egypt. The weekly's cover often carried topical cartoons criticizing the exploitation of the peasants and workers of Egypt.

Ruh al-'Asr took a strongly prolabor stance, carrying news of union activities, reports of strikes and grievances, letters and opinion pieces from workers, and interviews with labor politicians. Unlike its Wafdist counterpart, *Ruh al-'Asr* presented all sides of the conflicts within the labor movement, forcefully criticized the role of political parties and middle-class lawyers in that movement, and encouraged workers to take full control of their unions. The need for workers' unity and solidarity was a theme stressed over and over again.

What impact *Ruh al-'Asr* actually had even on the literate minority of trade union activists is uncertain. Some of its contents were probably too European and too high-brow to appeal to more than a very few Egyptian workers. Yet its open call for social reform, its vigorous assertion of the rights of the workers and peasants, and its insistence

25. See Rif'at al-Sa'id. " 'Isam al-Din Hifni Nasif," in *al-Mu'allafat al-kamila* (Cairo, 1977). I, pp. 450–530.

192 Workers, Effendis, Pashas, Prince

on the need for a strong and united labor movement appealed to precisely that emerging group of worker activists seeking a new perspective for their movement. The association of workers with the weekly and the fact that both union leaders and rank and file workers wrote to it indicate that it did in fact have an impact on the workers' movement of the time. However short-lived, *Ruh al-'Asr* served as an independent forum through which workers could express not only their grievances but their developing ideas as well, and thereby both reflected and stimulated alternative perspectives in the labor movement. The vision of the left-wing intellectuals who founded it was at least to some extent realized, and the weekly constituted the first public expression of the connection between socialism and the Egyptian working class since the suppression of the communist movement in 1924–1925.

The Wafd, however, remained the most powerful organizational and ideological force in the labor movement, and even before it resumed power, the party had moved to regain its influence over the unions by promising to take action on labor legislation and workers' grievances. But once Nahhas Pasha was in office, the government was preoccupied with the treaty negotiations and no legislation was forthcoming. In any case many of the Wafd's leaders were very conservative on social issues, and extremely reluctant to enact legislation that would in any way limit the prerogatives of property owners.

There was, however, a growing clamor from the unions for immediate action on labor's legislative agenda, and 'Aziz Mirham and his colleagues in labor affairs had to face down worker dissatisfaction. By now the workers had considerable experience of the government's broken promises, and they responded with bitterness. "I will repeat what I have said," wrote the unionist Ahmad Mustafa in a letter to *Ruh al-'Asr*, "that in the view of every government that assumes power the workers are nothing but a negligible quantity that they exploit for their own ends as it suits them." A conference attended by representatives of the major Cairo unions in May 1930 rejected a proposal by 'Aziz Mirham to set up an "advisory council" composed of Wafdist members of Parliament and counsellors to guide the labor movement, and instead called on the Wafd government to expedite the enactment of labor legislation. These resolutions undoubtedly discomfited the Wafd's labor lawyers, but the unions did not go beyond protesting government inaction. They resented the Wafd's failure to fulfil its promises, but they also knew that it was only when the Wafd was in power that they enjoyed some freedom to organize and

Workers, Effendis, Pashas, Prince **193**

that only from the Wafd could they expect sympathy for their demands.[26]

The Wafd, however, was not alone on the labor scene. Some of the leaders of the General Federation of 1928 who had collaborated with the Mahmud regime were trying to revive their organization. This federation's influence was limited to the Mechanized Transport Worker's Union (Cairo automobile, taxi, bus and truck drivers and mechanics who had left the older Chauffeurs' Union) led by Muhammad Ibrahim Zayn al-Din; the public works department union; and the barbers led by Muhammad Hasan 'Amara. To compensate for its weakness, this group found itself a patron in Da'ud Ratib, a wealthy member of an aristocratic Egyptian-Turkish family and a leader of the Liberal Constitutionalist party. The Wafd found it easy to attack this "fake federation" as a tool of the Liberals. Although largely discredited at home, the federation's leaders were able to use Ahmad Isma'il's earlier contacts with the European labor movement and Ratib's money to sent two representatives to the 1930 Congress of the International Federation of Trade Unions in Stockholm.[27] The Liberal-backed federation and a rival organization established by the Wafd wasted much of their energy attacking each other.

In June 1930 the Wafd, having again failed to negotiate a treaty with the British, was expelled from power. King Fu'ad, with the tacit support of the British, managed to oust Nahhas Pasha and install Isma'il Sidqi as prime minister. Sidqi Pasha had been the strongman of the Ziwar regime and could be relied on to crush the Wafd and institute an authoritarian regime. He was also one of the top leaders of the Egyptian Federation of Industries, whose interests were always close to his heart. Sidqi followed the same antidemocratic path as his predecessors Ziwar and Mahmud, but he was determined to say the course this time. The repression that characterized his regime was far more severe and effective than that of the preceding interludes of dictatorship. Parliament was suspended and dissolved, and the press subjected to censorship and harassment. Demonstrations by opponents of the regime were violently suppressed by the police, resulting in numerous casualties. The Wafd's leaders were restricted to Cairo to cut them off from their bases of support in the provinces. Finally, Sidqi scrapped the 1923 constitution, and replaced it with an entirely new document which drastically reduced the powers of Parliament and increased those of the monarchy. A new electoral law gave the

26. *Ruh*, May 9, 1930; *AM*, April 4, May 26, 1930.
27. See *AM* and *Ruh*, March–June 1930.

194 Workers, Effendis, Pashas, Prince

government the means of ensuring the election of its candidates. These measures aroused violent opposition among the Egyptian people, including the workers.

Sidqi Pasha, a shrewd and Machiavellian politician, did not neglect the labor movement. With close ties to foreign, *mutamassir* and Egyptian industrialists, and a great interest in using the state to promote industrial development, he understood the potential significance of the working class better than most upper-class Egyptians. In general the repression his regime unleashed was highly debilitating to the labor movement, but there were two measures Sidqi took that were specifically aimed at controlling the workers. First, the government acquired the allegiance of Da'ud Ratib and his organization by offering a subvention to its leader. More important, the government established a Labor Office in the Public Security Department of the Ministry of the Interior in November 1930. The conciliation board system had long been ineffective, and it was felt that a permanent agency with a trained staff was required to monitor labor affairs, gather data, and intervene in disputes. The Public Security Department had for some years played this role, and it was therefore natural that the new Labor Office should be part of the British-run security apparatus. This relationship reflected the view of the government and the employers that labor affairs were less a social than a police problem. The new office was headed by R. M. Graves, who had been Keown-Boyd's deputy at the European Department of the Ministry of Interior for many years, and its staff was in large part drawn from and paid by the security agencies.[28]

The downfall of the Wafd, and Sidqi's institution of a dictatorship, were clearly severe blows to the workers' movement. Intense repression, a regime openly sympathetic to the industrialists, and the effects of the economic slump all undermined the unions and made struggle in the workplace very risky. The Wafd was preoccupied with its struggle to survive, and was unable to maintain its links with the workers. Neither *al-'Amil al-Misri* nor *Ruh al-'Asr* were able to publish after the summer of 1930, and Husni al-'Arabi fled into exile in Berlin to escape arrest.[29] Yet the labor movement did not quickly and easily fade away as had been the case in 1925 and 1928. Under the leadership of a prominent nonworker personality new to Egyptian labor politics, a cadre of dedicated unionists were able to make the first months of 1931 a period of brief but significant revival.

28. FO 141/658/164/27/30, Loraine to the Foreign Office (draft), December 27, 1930.
29. See Mahmud Husni al-'Arabi, *89 shahran fi al-manfa* (Cairo, 1948).

Prince of the Workers

On December 17, 1930, the executive board of what had up to that point been a weak and discredited federation of unions deposed their organization's incumbent president and elected 'Abbas Ibrahim Halim in his place. 'Abbas Halim was a member of Egypt's royal family, a great-grandson of the founder of the dynasty, Muhammad 'Ali, and a cousin of King Fu'ad. Peculiar as it might seem for a prince[30] to assume a position of leadership in an authentic labor movement, 'Abbas Halim would be central to Egyptian labor politics for nearly a decade. He played a complex and often contradictory role in the trade union movement, using it to further his own ambitions while being used by genuine worker activists to build a labor federation independent of the Wafd and other political parties. 'Abbas Halim became seriously involved in labor affairs as a result of the political struggles of 1930, and once involved contributed greatly to the emergence of the strongest and most autonomous union federation Egypt had yet seen. He also contributed to its disintegration in 1935 in the course of a paralyzing split in the fledgling labor movement. The cadre of dedicated trade unionists who had worked with 'Abbas Halim in that period endured, however. Learning from both the positive and negative experiences of the first half of the 1930s, when the twists and turns of labor's political and industrial struggles were bound up with this forceful personality, they would reemerge after 1936 as a distinct and independent voice charting a new course for the Egyptian working class.

'Abbas Halim was born in 1897. Like many princes of the Egyptian royal family he spent much of his childhood in Europe and was educated mainly in Germany; only the winter months were spent in Egypt. As a result 'Abbas Halim's command of Arabic was never perfect. In his teens he entered Germany's Imperial Horse Guard and served as an *aide-de-camp* to Kaiser Wilhelm II. During the First World War he fought with the German forces in Belgium, France, and Russia, was wounded several times and won the Iron Cross First Class. He then turned to flying and served in the squadron of the German ace and later Nazi chieftain Herman Goering. When the war ended he was an officer in the Turkish Air Force. He spent the next few years travelling in Europe and big game hunting in Africa. After

---

30. 'Abbas Halim's formal title was *nabil*, which was used for members of the royal family who were not full princes (*amir*), though contemporary English-language sources generally used the term "prince," which was itself sometimes transliterated back into Arabic (*al-birins*). For that reason, as well as for convenience's sake, 'Abbas Halim will be referred to here as a prince.

196 Workers, Effendis, Pashas, Prince

the British authorities allowed him to return to Egypt, 'Abbas Halim became a leading patron of sports, founded numerous sports associations, and served as president of the Royal Automobile Club and the Royal Flying Club. Indeed, it was through his interest in promoting sports among the poor that he first came into contact with the labor movement. In the 1920s he was the patron of a small union of chauffeurs and auto mechanics in Alexandria but played no active role in its affairs.[31]

It was the political crisis of 1930 that brought him to the attention of the Egyptian public and propelled him into the leadership of the labor movement. The young prince had long been on bad terms with his cousin King Fu'ad and sympathetic to the popular democratic cause led by the Wafd. In October 1930, soon after Sidqi Pasha announced his plans for a new constitution and electoral law, 'Abbas Halim published an appeal to the Egyptian people in which he warned that the antidemocratic measures taken by the government were leading to civil war. Openly siding with the Wafd, he called on the king to change course and prevent catastrophe.[32] Whether 'Abbas Halim's defiance of the king was motivated by sincere distress at the subversion of constitutional government or (as the British believed) by his ambitions to succeed the ailing and much-disliked Fu'ad cannot be determined. In any case the prince's actions infuriated the king, who promptly deprived him of his titles, his royal prerogatives, and his allowance from the civil list. This only further enhanced the popularity of the young, vigorous, and handsome 'Abbas Halim, who had already shown his concern for the people and had now lost his title in defense of democracy. For some weeks in the fall of 1930 'Abbas Halim's appeal was the talk of the country and the prince was the hero of the Wafdist press.

These developments set the stage for 'Abbas Halim's assumption of a leading role in the labor movement. Many of the unionists who ran Da'ud Ratib's labor federation had come to feel they had reached a parting of the ways with their patron. Their organization was weak, lacked credibility, and was tainted with Ratib's Liberal and pro-Sidqi connections. The leadership of Ratib was no longer an asset, yet the unionists who had struggled for so long to avoid Wafd domination could not now dissolve their organization and accept the tutelage of 'Aziz Mirham and his colleagues. The solution was to find another patron under whose protection the federation's work could proceed, someone with solid patriotic, democratic, and labor credentials who

31. F/44; FO 407/221/25, "Personalities"; *EG*, February 5, 1931.
32. *La Patrie*, October 8, 1930, in FO 371/14621.

also possessed financial resources. 'Abbas Halim fit the bill perfectly, and when secretly offered the post the prince expressed his willingness to accept. Thus on December 17, 1930, the executive board voted to depose Ratib and elect 'Abbas Halim as their president. The deposed leader's loyalists called in the police in an effort to prevent his overthrow, but the dissidents managed to seize the organization's papers and take refuge in 'Abbas Halim's palace in Qasr al-Dubara, in the Garden City section of Cairo.[33]

'Abbas Halim threw himself into his new job in the first months of 1931. The federation he headed—hereafter referred to as the National Federation of Trade Unions in Egypt (NFTUE), as it called itself in English—opened new offices in Cairo and launched a campaign to win over the existing unions and organize new ones. The Wafd, on good terms with 'Abbas Halim and anxious to present a united front to the Sidqi regime, soon joined forces with the dissident prince by merging its own federation into the NFTUE. This added to the momentum and prestige of the new federation, and many new unions and workers affiliated. An *Egyptian Gazette* reporter visited the NFTUE offices early in February 1931 and saw "hundreds of labourers waiting to enroll."[34] From its original base among the barbers and mechanized transport workers in Cairo, the NFTUE rapidly expanded to organize workers in a broad range of trades and in many parts of the country. Each affiliated union was required to have a minimum of fifty members and could then choose at least one representative (who had to be literate) to the NFTUE Executive Board. By March–April 1931 the Federation was claiming over thirty union affiliates with some 30,000 members, which seem more or less reasonable figures.[35]

'Abbas Halim was determined to keep nonworker elements, especially Wafdist lawyers and politicians, out of positions of power in his movement, which had quickly become the leading force in the Egyptian labor movement. The Federation's rules stipulated that member unions not have a general counsellor but only a legal counsellor who could not speak in the union's name and whose opinion was purely advisory. Union presidents and executive board members had to be workers, and in fact, 'Abbas Halim's own staff, the leadership of the NFTUE, was made up of committed unionists drawn from the working class: Ibrahim Zayn al-Din, Muhamad Hasan 'Amara, Kamil 'Izz al-Din, and Ahmad al-Masri. While lawyers and politicians

33. 'Amara Memoirs, pp. 12–13; 'Amara, T, December 1, 1975. The memoirs of Muhammad Hasan 'Amara, leader of the Cairo barbers' union and a labor movement activist for many years, are the primary source for these events.
34. *EG*, February 5, 1931.
35. FO 141/763/506/5/31, April 14, 1931; *al-Safa'*, passim.

198 Workers, Effendis, Pashas, Prince

continued to play a role in many unions, they were noticeably absent from the Federation's national leadership. The NFTUE published a weekly newspaper called *al-Safa'* ("clarity," "felicity," "candor"), which carried news of the labor movement, articles by 'Abbas Halim, and such features as a weekly recipes column by Ahmad Zaki, treasurer of the Hilwan regional federation and restaurant owner. 'Abbas Halim spent thousands of pounds out of his own pocket to support the Federation's work, for the dues (two piastres a month) were entirely insufficient to finance the movement.

The attraction of the new National Federation of Trade Unions for Egyptian workers in the early months of 1931 is easily explained. The organization was headed by a popular member of the royal family, a dashing figure who was a symbol of devotion to constitutional government. His wealth sustained the Federation and his personal status gave some measure of protection to his associates. 'Abbas Halim's intervention in labor disputes on behalf of the workers had a powerful effect on employers, an effect which it was rumored the prince heightened on occasion by administering a good thrashing to a stubborn employer. He seems not to have put on aristocratic airs, and came across instead as a "real man."

Furthermore, 'Abbas Halim's efforts were supported (but not controlled) by the Wafd. The NFTUE not only enjoyed impeccable patriotic credentials but also the aura of independence, of a movement run by and for the workers themselves. The Federation united both Wafdist and non-Wafdist unions and unionists, and was organized around an explicit and comprehensive set of goals that included the unity and improvement of the working class (referred to explicitly as such: *tabaqat al-'ummal* or *al-tabaqa al-'amila*), labor legislation, better wages and working conditions, equality with foreign workers in Egypt, more housing, educational and social facilities for workers, and government programs to aid the unemployed. The Federation also made a concerted effort to expand the union movement by organizing the unorganized, and realized some success in this effort.[36]

Although the NFTUE to some extent represented a new tendency toward independence in the labor movement, important elements of continuity with past practices could be found as well. The explicit effort to build a union movement run by workers constituted an important step beyond the Wafd's more openly paternalistic approach. Still, 'Abbas Halim's attitude toward the working class was also patronizing and paternalistic, and reflected the same corporatist outlook that characterized the Wafd. Political ambitions aside, his moti-

36. See *al-Safa'*, April 3, 19, 1931.

vation for involvement in labor affairs was rooted in the same sense of noblesse oblige that had led him to promote sports for the poor. Like the Wafd, the prince did not believe in the existence of classes with fundamentally conflicting interests in Egypt. The working class itself was defined in *al-Safa'* as being composed of "the industrial and agricultural workers and of every person who works and earns his living with his brain or his intellect . . . the overwhelming majority of the nation."[37] Some NFTUE unions continued to include small proprietors and independent owner-operators alongside wage workers, as had been the case with the Wafd's unions and federations.

It is also significant that the core leadership of the NFTUE, 'Abbas Halim's closest associates, was generally made up not of workers from large industry but rather semi-autonomous workers, skilled artisans, or small proprietors. Zayn al-Din and Kamil 'Izz al-Din were chauffeurs, 'Amara and Ahmad al-Masri were barbers who may well have owned their own shops, and Ahmad Zaki owned a restaurant. The leading role such men played in labor affairs can be explained by their relatively high level of education and income. Yet while production and transport workers were exercising a greater degree of control over their own unions than ever before, the relative absence of these kinds of workers in 'Abbas Halim's inner circle suggests that the social vision that inspired the NFTUE had still not fully come to grips with the consequences of Egypt's transition to capitalism, however incomplete, and the emergence of a new working class.

The Repression of the Labor Movement

The resurgence of the labor movement in early 1931 was perceived by the Sidqi regime as a threat, a conspiracy organized by its enemies, and the regime responded in typical fashion. On March 15, 1931, the police closed down the headquarters of the NFTUE, whereupon the organization's offices were transferred to the basement of 'Abbas Halim's palatial residence and work continued, though in subsequent weeks union activity became increasingly difficult. Repression took a variety of forms. At the Hawamdiyya sugar refinery, for example, where 750 workers who earned seven piastres for an eleven-hour day were enrolled, the police shut down the union's office and turned the names of members over to the company. In Damanhur the police issued 200 violations against members of the NFTUE-affiliated drivers' union in two days' time in order to induce them to leave the union. At the same time the police set up a rival organization which drivers

37. *Ibid.*, May 28, 1931.

200 Workers, Effendis, Pashas, Prince

were forced to join. In Kafr al-Zayyat a union meeting was called, but broke up in an uproar when the workers realized that the organizers had no connection with 'Abbas Halim but were in fact police agents. Even 'Abbas Halim was subjected to harassment. Late in March he went to Alexandria to oversee the establishment of a regional federation there. The police sought to prevent him from preceeding on to Damanhur, but 'Abbas Halim managed to avoid their roadblocks and reach his destination.[38]

The NFTUE leader protested that his organization was not involved in politics and was not a threat to the government.

> I have the honor to be a Wafdist outside the Federation because I believe that the Wafd is the faithful servant of Egypt as regards her freedom, her constitution and her independence. That is my belief and it is the religion to which I adhere after Islam. Does this prevent me from taking up other work that does not involve politics?[39]

This was obviously not a very credible position, and the repression continued. Unable to defend his organization against government attacks, he sought help in the international arena.

Early in April 1931 'Abbas Halim wrote to Arthur Henderson, the British foreign secretary and a leader of the Labor party. He appealed to the British labor movement to help the Egyptian unions by sending a delegation to study their situation, while his lieutenant Ibrahim Zayn al-Din went to England to talk with leaders of the Trades Union Congress. After some discussion Walter Citrine, the general secretary of the TUC, wrote to Henderson asking that he use his influence with the Egyptian authorities to ensure the workers' freedom of association. Citing information supplied by the High Commissioner in Cairo, Henderson downplayed the scale of repression and refused to take any action. The British government in this period was not displeased with the policies of the Sidqi regime, especially its campaign to isolate and weaken the Wafd.[40]

'Abbas Halim's envoy also made contact with the International Federation of Trade Unions and was invited to address the meeting of its General Council in Madrid. After hearing his report on conditions

38. *Ibid.*, April–May 1931. At the same time the government not only tolerated but encouraged the rump federation of Da'ud Ratib and another entirely bogus organization created and controlled by the Palace.
39. *Misr*, March 25, 1931.
40. FO 141/763/506/5/31; TUC archives, file T1903, parts I and II. The International Committee of the TUC General Council considered Henderson's reply unsatisfactory and continued to press for action.

Workers, Effendis, Pashas, Prince **201**

in Egypt, the Council adopted a resolution protesting the Sidqi regimes's suppression of trade unionism and calling on the British Labor government to press that regime to restore the workers' right to organize.[41] This resolution had little immediate impact on government policy in Egypt, but Zayn al-Din's trip did lead the TUC and the IFTU to take an interest in Egyptian labor affairs, and eventually to send a delegation whose visit will be discussed below.

In the interim the wave of repression intensified. Early in May 1931 the Wafd and the Liberal Constitutionalist party had issued a joint appeal demanding the restoration of the 1923 constitution, a boycott of the elections scheduled for mid-May, and an end to the repression. In cities and towns across Egypt, demonstrations against the Sidqi regime turned into bloody riots. Workers and the poor had particular cause to oppose the new constitution and electoral law. The latter abolished direct elections, raised the voting age, imposed property and educational qualifications, and added other provisions that would allow the government to determine the outcome of any election. Meanwhile, political grievances acquired a social dimension as the poor felt the impact of falling cotton prices, foreclosures against debtors, rising unemployment, and wage cuts. The Federation participated actively in publicizing the electoral boycott, but once again it was the 'Anabir workers who put themselves in the forefront of resistance to the regime.

The work-related grievances of the 'Anabir workers had been festering since the beginning of 1930, while its 4,000 workers continued to be a bastion of nationalist sentiment. With the proper spark this volatile mixture had exploded several times in periods of popular upsurge, and 1931 would be no exception. The first part of May saw a mounting tide of violence, but only on the ninth did it reach the 'Anabir. A group of women demonstrating against the Sidqi regime drove by the railway workshops in the afternoon; the workers inside heard their shouts, took up their slogans, and eventually walked off the job to join the demonstration. The police were summoned and clashed with the workers and the students who had joined them. Eventually the workers were persuaded by their foremen to return to work, but tensions remained high.[42]

When the workers arrived the following morning they found police units stationed at the entrance of the 'Anabir and demanded successfully that the police be withdrawn. Another clash erupted during the

41. TUC, file T1903.
42. This account is based on *al-Ahram*, May 1931, passim; see also Radi, *Adwa'*, pp. 42–45.

202 Workers, Effendis, Pashas, Prince

lunch break when the locomotive shop workers left the 'Anabir and began to cheer the leaders of the Wafd and the 1923 constitution. Numerous small demonstrations and disturbances in the working class and pro-Wafd district of Bulaq took place in the following days. These often took the form of stoning the modern buses that had recently been introduced in Cairo. The buses were operated by the Egyptian General Omnibus Company, which was owned by its ostensible competitor the Cairo Tramway Company and managed by Ahmad 'Abbud Pasha, one of Egypt's leading industrialists. Both the buses and the company were popularly known as Thornycroft (after the English vehicle manufacturer) and like tram cars were targets of popular anger.

May 14 was the day on which the first stage of Sidqi's elections was to take place. The 'Anabir workers had been paid the previous day, and the authorities were not expecting trouble. But the workers from the Arsenal and the Government Press left work to demonstrate that morning and together with students from the nearby industrial school marched to the 'Anabir. The workers inside took up the chant and stopped work. Army units standing by surrounded the shops and opened fire, killing and wounding many. The workers inside and the crowds outside resisted with whatever weapons they could find, and there was considerable damage to locomotives and equipment. The official toll for the incident was seven killed and ninety-three wounded, but the true numbers were certainly much higher. Across the country at least a hundred people were killed by the police and army on May 14 as Sidqi proceeded to suppress all opposition to his fraudulent elections.[43]

In the aftermath of these bloody events, the government shut down the 'Anabir completely. After a few weeks the more docile workers were allowed to return and work resumed, but as of August 458 workers were still forbidden to return and over a hundred were in prison awaiting trial. As in previous years, the suppression of the popular movement led to a resurgence of terrorism which only intensified the repression, and the following years, characterized by further layoffs, short hours, and wage cuts, were bleak ones for the workers.[44]

---

43. Ramadan, *Tatawwur*, p. 750.

44. FO 371/J2481/26/16, Hoare to Henderson, August 1, 1931; FO 371/J2583/49/16, Hoare to Henderson, August 15, 1931; FO 371/J587/587/16. It is interesting to note that when new locomotive repair and maintenance facilities were built in 1932, they were sited at Abu Za'bal, then a relatively isolated town some twenty miles from Cairo. Since suitable land was available near the 'Anabir, it is possible that the Abu Za'bal site was chosen in order to avoid creating another concentration of militant workers in the heart of the capital.

Workers, Effendis, Pashas, Prince **203**

The possibilities for active trade union work diminished sharply after May 1931: the police stood ready to intervene on the side of the employers, as they did for example in a strike against cuts in the piece rate launched in September 1931 by some 15,000 contracted workers at the port of Alexandria, most of whom were seasonally employed peasants. The NFTUE was unable to function much beyond the confines of 'Abbas Halim's mansion, which was under constant police surveillance, and many of the newly formed affiliates succumbed to police pressure and disintegrated. The older and larger unions were compelled to sever their ties to 'Abbas Halim and the Wafd as the price of survival. Deprived of the strike weapon and unable to organize aggressively, they could not protect their members against the layoffs, wage cuts, and speedup that accompanied the depression in both the public and private sectors.

The paralysis of the NFTUE prompted 'Abbas Halim to undertake a new initiative in June 1931. He announced the formation of an Egyptian Labor party (Hizb al-'Ummal al-Misri) with himself as president, the labor lawyer Ramsis Jabrawi as vice-president, and a staff drawn from the NFTUE leadership. In his memoirs 'Amara asserted that Halim's motivation was to avoid prosecution and possible exile for conspiracy to overthrow the regime by forming a legal political party protected by Sidqi's own constitution. But in a 1964 interview 'Abbas Halim told the Egyptian historian Ra'uf 'Abbas that he had wanted to frighten the Wafd by showing it that the labor movement could be politically independent.[45] The most probable explanation, however, is 'Abbas Halim's desire to transform the labor organization he controlled, paralyzed by the repression, into a political movement which could function effectively and realize his ambitions. The Labor party's platform called for the complete independence of Egypt, democratic government, social reform, and labor legislation, but it was in no sense socialist or social democratic, and its membership consisted largely of people who were also NFTUE members.

Soon the Labor party found itself in serious trouble, because as Graves reported to the Residency, despite 'Abbas Halim's personal popularity the "syndicates and responsible bodies of the workmen realise that he is in strong and somewhat dangerous opposition to the present Government and that support of him might involve them in certain risks." At the same time the Wafdist press launched a vigorous attack on the new party which, it argued, divided the ranks of the nation in its hour of crisis and thereby aided the government. The regime extended its campaign against the NFTUE to the Labor party. Un-

---

45. 'Amara Memoirs, p. 16; 'Abbas, al-Haraka, p. 211.

204 Workers, Effendis, Pashas, Prince

der pressure from all sides, 'Abbas Halim met with Nahhas Pasha in July, and agreed to restrict his activities to the trade union sphere and leave politics to the Wafd. The Labor party was never formally dissolved, but it quickly faded out of existence.[46] Although the idea of such a party was to surface again and eventually acquire some real political and social content, its brief appearance in 1931 had no lasting impact on the workers' movement or Egyptian politics.

Two missions to Egypt in 1931–1932 by foreigners concerned with the country's labor problems also had only limited long-term impact, though they received considerable attention in that period of repression and paralysis. In October 1931 Walter Schevenels, the general secretary of the International Federation of Trade Unions, undertook a brief fact-finding trip to Egypt at the request of the TUC, which had been alarmed by reports about the suppression of the trade unions. The Egyptian authorities made considerable efforts to prevent his trip, and when that proved impossible, tried to control what he saw and heard, and limit the impact of his mission. Schevenels nonetheless managed to meet with authentic Egyptian trade unionists (as well as with government officials) and persistently stressed the importance of labor's independence and unity.[47] Schevenel's mission temporarily heartened Egyptian trade unionists during a bleak period, but its main effect was to compel Prime Minister Sidqi and R. M. Graves of the Labor Office to take action that would preempt criticism of the Egyptian government's labor policies. For this reason, at the very end of September 1931, even before Schevenels had arrived, Sidqi invited the International Labor Office in Geneva to send an advisory mission to Egypt to study industrial conditions, the organization of the Egyptian Labor Office, and proposed measures of social reform. In November the prime minister appointed a high-level committee to draft labor legislation, and included top Egyptian and British security officials as well as Graves among its members.[48]

The ILO mission to Egypt was carried out by Harold Butler, who spent some four weeks in the country in February–March 1932. Unlike Schevenels, who was a dedicated trade unionist wary of the government's claims and intentions and committed to labor's independence and progress, Butler was an outside expert invited by the government to provide advice on a narrowly defined set of problems.

46. See the manifestos preserved in the Wasif Ghali papers at the Society for Coptic Archaeology, Cairo, file 38; FO 141/763/506/22/31, Graves to the Oriental Secretary, June 30, 1931; FO 371/J2421/49/16, Hoare to Henderson, August 4, 1931.
47. Schevenel's report on his trip to Egypt can be found in the TUC archives, file T1903.
48. FO 141/770/361/10/31, Graves to Sidqi, September 30, 1931; FO 141/763/506/36/31, Graves to Smart, December 14, 1931; Butler Report, p. 1.

He apparently met only such "labor activists" as the police permitted, and acquired a rather one-sided perspective on Egyptian labor's problems and aspirations. Butler's thinking on Egypt's labor problems and the proposals he put forward in his report were in full accord with the perspective of the Sidqi government's own committee on labor legislation. Like the government and the employers, Butler recommended that labor legislation be promulgated in piecemeal fashion, beginning with laws regulating the employment of women and children and accident compensation. "To attempt a more ambitious programme in the present state of industrial and social development would be to court certain failure," he warned.

The upshot of his mission and report was the promulgation of two new laws in the summer of 1933. The first, regulating women's labor, established a nine-hour working day for women, restricted their night work, required a weekly day of rest, and excluded them from certain dangerous industries. The second law regulated the employment of children. In general, twelve years was established as the minimum age of employment, but children over nine years of age could work in certain industries (including textiles, carpet weaving, and furniture) provided that certain standards were met.[49] These were the first laws regulating the conditions of work to be enacted since 1909, and fell far short of what the workers and sympathetic observers felt necessary. The laws were deemed too favorable to the employers, and in any case were widely ignored and inadequately enforced. The section of the Labor Office responsible for implementing them employed only three inspectors, two inspectresses, and one clerk for all of Egypt.

Sidqi Pasha made one additional gesture of concern for labor during his tenure in office. In December 1932 a Supreme Labor Advisory Council was set up to advise the government on labor affairs: its members were all government officials or employers, with the exception of two workers chosen on the advice of the police, and its chairman was Ahmad Ziwar Pasha, the former prime minister who now served as a director of many leading financial and industrial companies. This new body made little positive contribution to resolving labor's problems and was moribund for long periods.

The missions of Schevenels and Butler in 1931–1932 neither stimulated the revival and reorganization of the union movement, nor produced labor legislation on a scale significant enough to enhance the bargaining power of the organized workers. The Sidqi years were marked by repression and a low level of worker activism. Some

49. See FO 141/617/237/13/35, report by Graves, April 10, 1935.

206 Workers, Effendis, Pashas, Prince

groups of workers in the private sector, made desperate by wage cuts and sharply deteriorating working conditions, did take action. The Thornycroft bus workers in Cairo stopped work several times in the spring of 1933, and in June shut down the bus system for three weeks, but their strike was ultimately broken, and it was clear that while the Sidqi regime remained in power labor militancy was unlikely to succeed. Moreover, the new Labor Office was of little help. Workers frequently complained that it had repeatedly failed to defend them, or resolve their grievances, and usually sided with the bosses.[50] Indeed, at this point the agency was largely an organ of the security apparatus and its primary responsibility was the maintenance of peace and quiet on the labor scene.

Isma'il Sidqi Pasha remained in power until September 1933 when he resigned after a conflict with the king. Like Ziwar and Muhammad Mahmud before him, Sidqi had ultimately failed to subdue the Egyptian people while preserving good relations with the only other domestic source of power, the Palace. He was replaced by 'Abd al-Fattah Yahya Pasha, who was more pliant to royal dictates than Sidqi and lasted until November 1934. Although Yahya opposed the restoration of the 1923 constitution and tried to maintain the authoritarian regime Sidqi had established, the latter's departure from power led to an easing of the tense and repressive political atmosphere, and consequently, to signs of revival in the labor movement.

The Resurgence of the NFTUE

'Abbas Halim and his associates had been unable to carry on union work in public since the middle of 1931, but the labor federation they headed remained in existence, at least on paper. The very beginning of 1934 witnessed a marked resurgence of labor activism and the rapid revival of the NFTUE. The Federation's offices, still located in 'Abbas Halim's palatial residence, once again became a center of intensive activity as the organization renewed its ties to unions now resuming open activity, played a more vigorous role in disputes at the workplace, and encouraged the formation of new unions, many of which had their offices and meetings in the basement of 'Abbas Halim's home. The growth of 'Abbas Halim's support and influence among the workers was of increasing concern to the government, especially to Keown-Boyd, who was director of the European Department at the Ministry of the Interior and had consistently pressed for a hard line against the unions and the NFTUE. In June 1934 the deci-

50. See for example *Ibn al-Balad*, May 20, September 25, 1933.

Workers, Effendis, Pashas, Prince **207**

sion was taken to crush the revived Federation. The police were ordered to compel workers affiliated to 'Abbas Halim to abandon him "by means known to the Police"; to revise all agreements reached through his mediation and to draw up new agreements through the police; and to explain to the workers and employers that the Federation was unauthorized and without legal standing and should be shunned. On June 20 the police surrounded 'Abbas Halim's house while he was away in Alexandria and prevented unionists from entering it.[51]

The NFTUE leadership decided to organize a demonstration for the following day to protest, and if possible break through, the siege of their headquarters. A large crowd of workers assembled near 'Abbas Halim's residence and clashed with the police who killed one worker and wounded others. Numerous demonstrators were arrested including most of the NFTUE leadership. The funeral of the slain worker was attended by the leaders of the Wafd and the other opposition parties, and became a mass demonstration of protest against the Yahya regime's repressive policies. Workers carried out many brief protest strikes, and demonstrators smashed buses and tram cars.

At a meeting just after this incident with W. A. Smart, the Oriental Secretary at the Residency, 'Abbas Halim quite accurately blamed Keown-Boyd for trying to shut down his Federation. Whereas most British officials believed 'Abbas Halim to be harmless and not particularly anti-British, Keown-Boyd took a far tougher line. He claimed that 'Abbas Halim had involved himself in labor affairs "mainly to irritate and annoy the King and Sedky Pasha," and that he "openly says that he intends to be the next King of Egypt." 'Abbas Halim was not himself a communist, but "he is the kind of element which it is the Communist plan here to make unconscious use of in their anti-Imperialist campaign." On these grounds 'Abbas Halim was arrested at the end of June, and imprisoned for twenty-six days. The prolonged detention of a great-grandson of Muhammad 'Ali attracted considerable attention, especially after he went on a hunger strike for several days, and became an embarassment to the government. His release was popularly believed to have been due to the personal intervention of the High Commissioner, Sir Miles Lampson. The workers arrested at the June 21 demonstration fared less well, for all but five were sentenced to prison terms that ranged from two to six months.[52]

The crackdown of June 1934 failed to halt the resurgence of the la-

51. FO 141/713/259/1/35, copy of note to Salim Zaki, chief of the Special Branch, in Keown-Boyd, "Activities of Abbas Halim in Regard to Labour," December 23, 1934.
52. FO 141/733/894/1–15/34; FO 371/J2062/9/16; 'Amara Memoirs, pp. 32–33.

208 Workers, Effendis, Pashas, Prince

bor movement. Unpopular and discredited, the Yahya cabinet resigned in November, and Tawfiq Nasim Pasha, a veteran politician friendly to the Wafd, agreed to serve as prime minister on condition that progress be made toward the restoration of popular government. King Fu'ad, in failing health, was compelled to abolish the 1930 constitution imposed by Sidqi Pasha, and though the more democratic 1923 constitution was not immediately restored and no new elections were held, free political activity became possible once again. In these circumstances the NFTUE began to recruit aggressively and achieved some remarkable successes even before the end of 1934. In December 1934 the important unions of Thornycroft, Cairo tram, and Heliopolis tram workers decided to affiliate to 'Abbas Halim's Federation, and for the first time since March 1931 the NFTUE was able to leave the safety of its leader's mansion and set up its own offices. Several factors augured success.

The NFTUE now had a cadre of experienced trade unionists tested repeatedly during the Sidqi and Yahya years. These activists expounded a clear set of demands that summed up the workers' immediate goals: the legal recognition of trade unions, labor legislation, wage increases, action on the unemployment problem, repeal of the vagrancy law, removal of the Labor Office from police control, the establishment of a permanent conciliation mechanism in place of the cumbersome, slow and ad hoc system then in use, and the rehiring of the 'Anabir, Arsenal, and other workers dismissed for political reasons since 1930. Moreover, the popularity of the NFTUE's leader had been enhanced by his imprisonment and his willingness to intervene on the workers' behalf in the rising tide of labor unrest. Finally, the Federation was closely linked to the Wafd, which was itself reorganizing and reasserting its strength after the long years of repression.

One particular project heavily promoted and indeed underwritten by 'Abbas Halim in 1934 may also have made his organization more attractive to workers. 'Abbas Halim was active in an effort to establish a cigarette company which would provide jobs for cigarette workers displaced by machinery, and whose shares would be sold largely to workers on the installment plan. Such schemes to relieve unemployment had been frequently proposed but only rarely attempted. In fact, a factory was set up in Cairo, but foundered after a few months for lack of capital and because of the conflicts afflicting the labor movement in 1935. Given economic conditions in Egypt, the poverty of most workers, and the entrenched position of foreign capital, such projects were very unlikely to succeed. One group, the Muslim Brothers, did succeed in establishing a ramified network of economic institutions, including some small factories, to provide employment for their members and help finance the organization's other work, but the Brothers had a different social base and the sustained support of numerous wealthy contributors.

The resurgence of worker activism in the early months of 1935, including an increasing number of strikes, alarmed the British officials responsible for security and labor affairs. Those most directly involved in handling labor disputes, such as Graves of the Labor Office, believed that most of the incidents of industrial conflict were the result not of political agitation but of genuine grievances on the part of the workers. Graves argued that the Egyptian state should enact labor legislation and recognize labor unions which, he suggested, might lead to the emergence of a labor movement modeled on English trade unionism and eschewing politics. This approach called for a strategy of cooptation, and was opposed by Keown-Boyd and his fellow hardliners in the security agencies. These officials regarded 'Abbas Halim as a serious threat to British interests in Egypt, and thought his base among the workers should be eliminated through repressive measures. In place of the existing unions, the police and the employers would then establish docile benevolent societies and guild-like organizations. The Residency never conclusively adopted either of these two perspectives, which shared the goal of maintaining British preeminence in Egypt and controlling the workers' movement, and continued to treat the Egyptian workers' movement with a mixture of repression and cooptation.[53]

The Struggle for Power in the Labor Movement

Keown-Boyd did not have to worry about the growth of 'Abbas Halim's influence for long, for 1935 witnessed a crippling split in the labor movement which once again underscored the costs of domination by outside political forces. The Wafd took advantage of the freer political climate that characterized Tawfiq Nasim's tenure in office to revive its organizational apparatus and renew its links with its constituencies, among which was the labor movement led by its ally 'Abbas Halim since 1931. Feeling more sure of its popular base and anticipating a return to power at the next election, the Wafd began to prepare to reassert its tutelage over the union movement. The party's perspective was expressed in a speech delivered by 'Aziz Mirham to the "national congress" organized by the Wafd and attended by some 20,000 people in January 1935.

53. See FO 141/617/237/11,12,17,19,22/35 and FO 141/713/259/1,3,5,6/35.

210 Workers, Effendis, Pashas, Prince

As for Egypt, it is unnatural that the workers should constitute a political party while the nation is preoccupied—in its totality and in its parts—with its struggle for freedom and independence, in whose quest are united all Egyptians whether workers or not. . . . To this end the workers declare that they are Wafdists before they are workers; to this end the workers refuse to place their particular demands before the common demands of the nation.[54]

The implied criticism of 'Abbas Halim's abortive Labor party of 1931 and of the NFTUE's insistence on autonomy from the Wafd signalled that the party was ready to assume the direct control over the workers' movement it had been unable to exercise during the previous four years.

Although 'Abbas Halim had been an ally of the Wafd since 1930, he was not completely trusted. His brief foray into party politics was not forgotten, and at the beginning of 1935 he was flirting with Misr al-Fatat (Young Egypt). This organization had been founded two years earlier by Ahmad Husayn, who had been much influenced by the ethos of European facism, and appealed to educated youth with a program that called for complete independence, the Egyptianization of the economy, and a strong state. Under the slogan of "God, Fatherland, and King," Young Egypt rejected the gradualism, conservatism, and constitutionalism of the Wafd, which in turn perceived its new rival—one manifestation of the growing radicalization of the *effendiyya* which will be discussed more fully below—as a serious threat.[55] As the NFTUE continued to grow—it claimed from 300,000 to 400,000 members in fifty-eight unions, though 70,000 was probably closer to the truth—the possibility that 'Abbas Halim would use it to launch his own political ambitions also grew.[56] The Wafd leadership wanted 'Abbas Halim as a subordinate rather than as an ally of questionable loyalty leading an independent movement, while Wafdist lawyers and politicians who specialized in labor affairs and had close ties with many of the affiliated unions wanted to play a more direct role in running the NFTUE.

Secret negotiations to strengthen the Wafd-labor relationship were therefore begun with 'Abbas Halim, and culminated on February 11, 1935 with the Wafd's announcement (without prior consultation with the unions themselves) that it was creating the "Supreme Coun-

---

54. *al-Ahram*, January 9, 1935.
55. In January 1935 the secret police reported that 'Abbas Halim had met with Ahmad Husayn and agreed to hire Young Egypt lawyers as union counsellors. See FO 141/713/ 259/2/35, Report of the Special Section, January 24, 1935.
56. *al-Masa'*, March 19, 1935.

cil of the NFTUE." This body was to have 'Abbas Halim as president, the Wafdist Ahmad Hamdi Sayf al-Nasr as vice-president, 'Aziz Mirham as secretary, several other Wafdists as members, and eight worker delegates chosen by the executive board of the Federation. The new Supreme Council was clearly intended to be the instrument by which the Wafd assumed control of the labor movement, and it was vigorously opposed as such by the shocked and angry NFTUE leadership. The British High Commissioner wrote to the foreign secretary a few days later that "the workmen themselves are opposed to political control of their organisations, and at a meeting of the Federation held on February 12th the members expressed strong views to 'Abbas Halim regarding this declaration of the Wafd and insisted on maintaining themselves independent of that or any other political party."[57] The union leaders also reaffirmed their policy that no lawyers should preside over unions and that workers should elect their own representatives.

Attempts to implement the new arrangement soon ran into trouble and resulted in a grave crisis within the NFTUE. Under strong pressure from his associates, 'Abbas Halim resisted blatant attempts by Wafdist lawyers to take control of his organization, and by April the break between 'Abbas Halim and the Wafd was open and complete. 'Abbas Halim publicly accused the Wafd of trying to capture the workers' movement and exploit it for its own political ends, and he severed his connections with the Supreme Council. The Wafd responded by installing Sayf al-Nasr as president and launching a vicious press campaign against their erstwhile ally. From the bitter struggle for the allegiance of the unions and regional organizations that ensued, two distinct and mutually hostile federations emerged. While the evidence is not entirely clear, it seems that many if not most of the major unions severed their ties with 'Abbas Halim and affiliated to the Supreme Council. The core leadership of the NFTUE along with some of the unions remained loyal to 'Abbas Halim, though his influence was much diminished. To strengthen his position and offset the Wafd's campaign against him he began to cooperate more closely with Young Egypt and with the Palace.

The schism in the labor movement did not have a uniformly debilitating effect on the level of worker activism. Indeed, in some cases the split stimulated labor unrest. Where individual unions split or the Wafd set up a new union to compete with 'Abbas Halim's affiliate, the rivalry often touched off strikes as each side vied to win worker support. Both factions sought to take advantage of grievances over low

57. FO 141/713/259/6/35, Lampson to Simon, February 15, 1935.

212 Workers, Effendis, Pashas, Prince

wages and poor working conditions, and this led to a continuation of that wave of unrest that had so alarmed Keown-Boyd. In general Graves and his Labor Office tended to favor 'Abbas Halim, seeing him as a moderating influence and clearly preferable to Wafdist hegemony over the unions, though this policy was very much opposed by Keown-Boyd who would have liked to suppress both factions.[58]

The persistence of strikes should not however obscure the fact that the split precipitated by the Wafd's bid for complete control cost the workers' movement a great deal. Some unions were destroyed by the schism, while others were certainly weakened. Although many individual unions avoided being damaged by the split and remained as active as ever, British officials reported at the end of 1935 that both federations were in bad shape. 'Abbas Halim's organization was behind in the rent for its offices, and after an initial burst of energy the Supreme Council had run out of steam: Sayf al-Nasr was being criticized for his lack of initiative and 'Aziz Mirham had apparently quit as secretary. Indeed, a new epithet for those unionists and lawyers who ran the Wafd's federation gained currency: they were called *awantagiyya*, (from the French *avantage*), meaning "men on the make," "opportunists." Only Zuhayr Sabri, who was said to be genuinely interested in the workers' cause, was exempted from this characterization.[59]

Despite a decline in their level of practical activity, however, both organizations continued to speak out on issues of concern to workers. Both for example applauded the transfer of the Labor Office to the newly created Ministry of Commerce and Industry in the autumn of 1935, a step which removed the Office from the direct control of the police, and also expressed pleasure at its elevation to the status of a full department (*maslaha*) the following year. The two organizations also continued to demand the enactment of labor legislation and to criticize the government's failures in this area.

At the end of that year a new upsurge in the national movement paved the way for the Wafd's return to power. A speech in November 1935 in which the British foreign secretary advised against the restoration of the 1923 constitution, which he described as unworkable, outraged public opinion in Egypt and touched off massive popular demonstrations spearheaded by militant students. The protests were met with bullets, but eventually the students' pressure compelled the politicians to form a national front of all the political parties and unite around demands for independence, restoration of the 1923 con-

58. FO 371/J1043/2/16, Graves, "Note on Labour Developments in Egypt during 1935."
59. See FO 141/617/237/29/35, Graves, December 19, 1935.

Workers, Effendis, Pashas, Prince **213**

stitution, and parliamentary government. In December King Fu'ad agreed to restore the constitution he so detested and the Nasim cabinet resigned. The new prime minister, 'Ali Mahir, headed a transitional government that would oversee free elections and prepare for a new round of talks with Great Britain.

Although many workers participated in the demonstrations of November 1935, the students were much better organized and constituted the movement's vanguard. However, this upsurge, which finally eradicated the last vestiges of the Sidqi regime, strengthened the Wafd's popularity among the workers and gave it an opportunity to emphasize its leadership role. On December 15, for example, the Wafd's labor leadership attended the unveiling of a memorial to a painting worker and union member who had been "martyred in the nation's cause" on November 14. The spirit of national unity which the November uprising produced led to several attempts to overcome the divisions within the union movement, but all proved abortive. As the elections scheduled for May 1936 drew closer, the Wafd maintained its control of the unions loyal to it by convening meetings and labor conferences to demonstrate and strengthen its support among the workers. In December 1935 'Abbas Halim's federation announced its intention to run labor candidates for Parliament, but nothing came of this, though according to police reports 'Abbas Halim was discussing plans with the enemies of the Wafd to win support among the students and unemployed workers.[60]

Despite these schemes, 'Abbas Halim lost interest and withdrew from labor politics in the early months of 1936. He was no doubt discouraged by his defeat in the struggle with the Wafd for control of the majority of the unions. The approaching elections were certain to return the Wafd to power, and would leave him in an even weaker position. Moreover, public attention was increasingly focused on the new round of negotiations with Britain that would follow the elections, and these both displaced social issues from the agenda and further enhanced the Wafd's popularity. Labor could not have seemed to 'Abbas Halim a very fertile field in which to work at the moment, and he devoted himself instead to sports and foreign travel, justifying his withdrawal from the scene by reference to the priority of the national question and the time the Wafd government must be given to fulfil its promises to the working class.[61]

The NFTUE quickly faded out of existence, though the unions on

60. al-Muqattam, December 15–16, 1935; FO 371/J618,642,1463/2/16, Lampson to Eden, January 16, February 6, 1936.
61. al-Ahram, July 10, 1936.

214 Workers, Effendis, Pashas, Prince

which it had been based and the unionists who led it remained. In effect, the Wafd in the spring of 1936 emerged triumphant from its struggle with 'Abbas Halim, the only significant political force on the labor scene, just as it was poised to resume power after six long years in opposition. Yet in the years that followed its hegemony over the workers' movement would prove to be no more secure or enduring than its grip on power, so that 1936 would mark the end of one era in the history of Egyptian labor and the beginning of another.

The period between the fall of the first Wafd government in 1924 and the party's assumption of power in 1936 were tumultous ones in Egyptian political life and constituted an important stage in the development of the Egyptian working class and labor movement. Despite the world economic depression whose effects hit Egypt hard, the working class, especially that segment of it employed in large-scale mechanized industry, continued to grow in size and social weight, while those workers involved in trade unionism gained greater experience in unionism and labor politics. In 1924 the Wafd had been able to exercise a hegemony over the fledgling labor movement that was virtually unquestioned except by the scattered remnants of the communist movement. The half decade that followed Zaghlul's downfall had seen the movement often afflicted by factionalism and divisions and dominated by Wafdist and other labor politicians and lawyers. Yet by the end of the decade a significant tendency based in a new stratum of experienced and committed trade unionists had begun to emerge which rejected outside domination and sought to build a militant and independent labor movement.

From the time he began to play a major role in Egyptian labor politics late in 1930, 'Abbas Halim appeared as the symbol of those hopes again and again. It was not that his social thought was more advanced than that of the Wafd, for he too rejected the notion of class struggle and shared the Wafd's paternalistic outlook. And he certainly sought to use the labor movement to further his own political ambitions as much as the Wafd wished to use the workers to enhance its power and achieve its political goals, which it identified with those of the Egyptian nation as a whole. 'Abbas Halim's efforts to promote unionism, his talk of establishing a labor party, and his concern that the workers run their own unions did not derive from a commitment to the empowerment of workers, much less social transformation. Yet they served the purposes of a small group of worker-activists who took advantage of 'Abbas Halim's protection, status, and wealth to achieve their own. goals, and foster their own vision of independent trade unionism.

These men saw themselves as workers rather than Wafdists first and foremost, and their association with 'Abbas Halim in the first half of the 1930s allowed them to keep out of the clutches of that party. Certainly 'Abbas Halim was simultaneously exploiting their commitment and skills to win a base of popular support for himself. After 1936 many of these men would come to regard both 'Abbas Halim and the Wafd as major obstacles to labor's independence and unity, but at the time the bargain with 'Abbas Halim seemed worthwhile and the most realistic of alternatives. 'Abbas Halim, then, played a complex and contradictory role in the Egyptian labor movement in 1931–1936 which, whatever his own personal goals, served in the long term to protect and strengthen those elements that favored the elimination of all forms of control by outside parties and personalities, and a new focus on the workers' own interests.

That vision, however, was slow to emerge and even slower to prove of practical value. In the decade before 1936, Egyptian workers continued to be essentially on the defensive. Their struggle to regain the ground won in 1919 and lost in subsequent years took second place to a general struggle for survival in an era of widespread unemployment, drastic wage cuts, and sharply deteriorating working conditions. The best that most workers could hope for was to mitigate the worst effects of the depression and preserve their jobs in the hope of better times. Even the powerful Alexandria tramwaymen's union could achieve no more than a more equitable system of wage cuts in 1933. This did not however dampen workers' interest in, or enthusiasm for, organization and collective action. Indeed, the idea of trade unionism spread more widely among the Egyptian working class after 1924 than ever before, and whenever workers were able to organize and engage in industrial action freely they did so, often with a vengeance. It was clear by the 1930s that unions were the only means available by which the workers could hope to improve their lot in the workplace or as a vocal pressure group in the political arena. The workers' willingness to organize and resist was amply demonstrated by their enthusiastic response to 'Abbas Halim's NFTUE in 1931 and the wave of labor unrest and strikes in 1935.

Labor activism at the local and national levels and overt resistance to the employers' power, however, were made impossible for much of the decade by severe repression. With the police ready to enforce the dictates of management, there was little hope that the workers' standard of living could be successfully defended, and the obvious connection between periods of authoritarian rule and the suppression of labor strengthened the workers' identification with the broad popular democratic movement. The measures taken by the Sidqi regime in the labor field—the creation of the Labor Office, the 1933 laws

216   Workers, Effendis, Pashas, Prince

on female and child labor, the ILO mission, the creation of the SLAC— were perceived as camouflage for an essentially antilabor attitude, or as means to better control the working class. Sidqi's attempts to disenfranchise the workers and the poor brought the linkage between political rights and class interest into stark relief. That many workers understood this linkage was demonstrated by the open resistance of the 'Anabir, Arsenal, and Government Press workers in May 1931, and the further failure of the repressive governments to alleviate the suffering caused by the depression also helped strengthen that connection.

The British and the Palace were popularly and not inaccurately regarded as the main forces propping up the Sidqi and Yahya regimes, and the long years of struggle for the restoration of parliamentary democracy enhanced the prestige of the Wafd. During the brief periods it held office up to 1930, the party had repeatedly failed to fulfil its promises to the workers. Yet, as the only party that was at least theoretically solicitous of the workers' interests, had well-established and deeply rooted links with many unions, consistently defended the 1923 constitution, and continued to claim the leadership of the unfinished struggle for independence, the Wafd in opposition was more than ever the repository of the workers' hopes for change.

Continued support for the Wafd before 1936 was not incompatible with a desire to prevent Wafdist domination of the labor movement. The tendency in the union movement which advocated autonomy from all the parties and worker control of their own unions and coalesced around 'Abbas Halim remained by and large loyal to the Wafd as the leader of the national cause. Indeed, the NFTUE benefited greatly from the fact that it upheld the slogan of labor's independence while enjoying the blessing of the Wafd. This situation, however, could last only so long as the Wafd was on the defensive and unable to exert direct control over the unions, which muted the conflict between the independent tendency and the Wafd's desire for hegemony. The conflict emerged into the open in 1935 when the Wafd's return to power became a real if not yet imminent prospect, and 'Abbas Halim's independence was no longer seen as an asset to the party.

Although the Wafd ultimately prevailed in the struggle for control of most of the unions in 1935, it was able to do so only at the cost of severely weakening the movement as a whole. The federation controlled by the Supreme Council, dominated by Wafdist politicians and labor lawyers, soon became an empty shell, a mere fragment of what had been a strong and united union movement. The workers in the NFTUE leadership along with many other unionists rejected 'Abbas Halim's initial capitulation to the Wafd's dictates, and compelled him to defend the organization. Some may have merely wanted to avoid being displaced by the Wafd's agents, but many acted out of principle, which reflected a distinct weakening in the Wafd's ideological and organizational grip on the unionized workers since 1924 and the emergence of an alternative perspective. In the changed political and social conditions that characterized Egypt after the conclusion of the Anglo-Egyptian treaty that perspective would grow increasingly coherent and popular, which set the stage for the emergence of new, more radical political forces contending for the allegiance of the working class.

Chapter VII

Toward an Independent Workers' Movement

Although many contemporary observers regarded the year 1936 as a turning point in modern Egypt's political history, in retrospect the elements of continuity appear as significant as the elements of change. In April the ailing King Fu'ad finally died and was succeeded by his young son Faruq. The new monarch at first seemed everything his father was not—patriotic, vigorous, intelligent, and democratically-inclined—and so won immediate and widespread popularity. It was hoped that the repeated confrontations between the Palace and the Wafd that had marked Fu'ad's reign would not recur.

In May of the same year the Wafd returned to power with a solid majority in Parliament. The new prime minister, Mustafa al-Nahhas Pasha, headed a multiparty delegation in negotiations with Britain for an agreement that would resolve the issues left outstanding in 1922, and secure for Egypt full independence. Before the summer was out an Anglo-Egyptian treaty had been concluded, and was endorsed by all the leading politicians except the uncompromising Nationalists. While Egypt was to be fully independent, a member of the League of Nations, and entitled to secure the abolition of the capitulations, Britain would continue to maintain troops in the Suez Canal Zone for at least twenty years, and in the event of war would have full use of various installations. The Wafd justified these concessions by citing the growing danger of war—Italy had conquered Ethiopia the previous year and a European conflict was just over the horizon—and argued that Egypt should seize the opportunity to get the best terms it could.

With the Wafd firmly in power, a new and popular king on the throne, and the national question apparently resolved, it seemed that

An Independent Workers' Movement **219**

Egypt was about to enter a lengthy period of stability and progress, and could devote its attention to domestic problems. In reality the long-awaited treaty solved nothing. In the years that followed the structural crisis of the Egyptian economy deepened; the political system continued to operate much as it had before 1936 as the British, the Palace, and their allies sought to weaken the Wafd and exclude it from power. At the same time, new and more radical forces appeared on the scene to challenge not only the Wafd's political hegemony but the established order itself. The years between the Wafd's assumption of power in May 1936 and its return to power after several years in opposition in February 1942 were thus marked by turbulence and crisis.

This same period would be a very significant one in the history of the Egyptian workers' movement. The rapid growth of large-scale mechanized industry, discussed in the next chapter, led to a gradual shift in the center of gravity of the working class which had important consequences for the labor movement, and together with a new political climate in the country and the maturation of existing trends among trade unionists served to strengthen precisely that tendency that struggled for the independence of the unions from outside control. Although the Wafd and 'Abbas Halim retained considerable influence among the organized workers in the years leading up to 1942, a vigorous new labor organization determined to build a strong and fully independent trade union movement appeared on the scene. This development marked an important break with the previous history of the Egyptian workers' movement, and prepared the way for a new era during and after the war.

The Wafd Restored

Even before it returned to power the Wafd had reasserted its control over the labor movement and driven 'Abbas Halim from the scene. Once in power, the party moved quickly to consolidate its support among the workers. In the speech from the throne the government expressed its intention to "enact legislation for the workers which will provide for the reform of their condition, the recognition of their unions in accordance with the law and the regulation of relations between them and the employers. [The government] takes a special interest in questions of social insurance and action to combat unemployment by various means."[1] Concerned about the growing influence of Young Egypt, which had created a uniformed paramili-

1. *al-Ahram*, July 14, 1936.

220 An Independent Workers' Movement

tary organization (the Green Shirts) and was trying to attract workers to its ranks, the Wafd decided to recruit workers for its own new paramilitary organization (the Blue Shirts). Ahmad Husayn's movement had won support, especially among students and the *effendiyya*, by attacking the Wafd as corrupt and ineffective, and the Anglo–Egyptian treaty as a capitulation to imperialism. Clashes soon erupted between members of the rival uniformed groups, and the Wafd government used the Blue Shirts to drive Young Egypt's partisans off the streets.[2]

Despite the Wafd's efforts to defeat its rivals and keep the workers under control, it was unable to restrain workers impatient to redress their grievances. The Wafd's leadership was preoccupied in the summer of 1936 with the treaty negotiations, and was unable to do more than promise the workers that their self-restraint would eventually be rewarded with official action on issues of concern. The workers, however, had endured a long period of quiescence imposed by years of repressive government, then by anticipation of immediate action once the Wafd had returned to power, and in consequence their standard of living and working conditions had deteriorated sharply over the past years. Now, with a partial recovery underway and a government in power that though officially sympathetic was nonetheless slow in fulfilling its promises, the time seemed ripe for action. Egyptian workers were also inspired by the massive strike waves that swept across France, Belgium, Spain, and Greece in the spring and summer of 1936 and which were well covered in the Arabic-language press.

As a result the summer of 1936 saw an explosion of labor militancy on a scale not equalled for many years past. In May workers of every trade had already begun to flood employers and the government with petitions and demands, and by early June the strike wave began with a stoppage and brief occupation at the Kafr al-Zayyat Oil Company. In the weeks that followed industrial conflict spread in the Alexandria area and elsewhere, taking the form of strikes, occupations, and clashes with the police. On June 24, for example, after fruitless negotiations, the day shift at the Filature Nationale in Alexandria refused to leave the factory, and was joined by the incoming night shift. The police cleared the premises in the middle of the night and arrested 800 workers, but a new agreement was negotiated shortly thereafter. On July 5, the Alexandria tramwaymen decided to strike,

2. *al-Ahram*, March 31, 1936; FO 371/J6799/2/16, High Commissioner to Eden, July 24, 1936; FO 407/219/35, Kelly to Eden, October 24, 1936; Jankowski, *Young Rebels*, pp. 23–25.

An Independent Workers' Movement **221**

and shut the city's mass transit system down for six days. They returned to work only after the prime minister expressed his sympathy but refused to help the workers unless they ended their strike.[3] The British-run security agencies were quick to suspect that Italian agitation was behind at least some of the strikes, but the real factors were familiar enough. Demands for higher wages to offset the cuts or freezes imposed in previous years were most often heard, along with shorter hours, and a host of other unresolved issues. The Kafr al-Zayyat workers were resisting layoffs and speedup; the Filature workers demanded and won an eight-hour day and regular pay increases; and the Alexandria tramwaymen sought higher wages and full implementation of their 1919 agreement with management. The strike wave was clearly not the work of paid agitators but the genuine product of long-standing grievances which the changed political and economic climate had allowed open expression.

The labor resurgence of the summer of 1936 reached its peak in mid-July with a sudden strike and occupation at the Hawamdiyya sugar refinery near Cairo. The workers (most of them seasonally-employed peasants from nearby villages) had long-standing grievances: their wages had been cut to as little as four piastres a day; they worked fifteen-hour days at the height of the season; there was only one doctor to tend to the 3,000 workers at Hawamdiyya; and though Sunday was their day off, they preferred Friday so that they could pray. When the workers had organized a union in 1933 under the leadership of Hamid Salim, an associate of 'Abbas Halim, to replace one suppressed two years earlier, the sugar company had fired its leaders. 'Abbas Halim had been able to use his influence to get some of them rehired, but Hamid Salim and a number of his colleagues were not taken back and continued to agitate from the outside.

The course of events at Hawamdiyya well illustrates the volatile character of this segment of the working class. The workers had arrived at work as usual on the morning of July 13, but at 9:30 a.m. Hamid Salim and some of his associates who had also been dismissed entered the plant. The police later alleged that Salim had been armed with a revolver and his friends with iron bars, and that they began moving around the plant threatening the foremen and managers and calling for a strike. Salim himself claimed that he had come to see the director about getting his job back, and the workers had spontaneously gathered around him and demanded he take up their griev-

3. *al-Ahram*, June–July 1936, passim; *al-Muqattam*, July 7–11, 1936; FO 371/J6692/2/ 16, Fahmy of the Alexandria Labor Office to Graves, July 17, 1936; FO 371/J7698/2/16, Kelly to Eden, September 9, 1936.

222 An Independent Workers' Movement

ances and seek 'Abbas Halim's assistance. In any event the situation quickly got out of hand; the workers stopped production, harassed their foremen, and wrecked equipment with gusto. Police reinforcements were sent for and officials tried to convince the workers to leave peaceably. But the strikers refused, and insisted that action be taken on their grievances and 'Abbas Halim be called in to mediate on their behalf. As the day wore on army units arrived and surrounded the complex, and by early evening clashes had broken out in which one worker was killed and many wounded. The workers used what weapons they found at hand, including loaves of sugar which they threw at their besiegers. The wives and children of the strikers soon arrived on the scene, and camped outside the walls of the refinery all night long.

The occupation ended peacefully the next morning in anticlimactic fashion. Hamid Salim had fled the occupied plant during the night, and when a high-ranking army officer entered the plant alone and asked the workers to leave, they quickly agreed, provided that their grievances were brought to the attention of the prime minister. The crisis was over. What explains the sudden eruption of the Hawamdiyya strike and its equally sudden collapse is the composition of the work force. These peasant workers had only rarely been able to sustain a union on their own. Leadership had generally come from the outside, either from the Wafdist labor federation's organizers in 1924, or from men like Hamid Salim, who had close ties to 'Abbas Halim and the world of Cairo labor politics. When an outside stimulus was applied the Hawamdiyya workers' grievances could spontaneously explode into violent action, but without much cohesion within the work force or a sustained capacity for organization, the workers' anger quickly subsided and their militancy evaporated.

Hamid Salim and seventy-eight others stood trial in August for unlawful assembly and destruction of property. The team of lawyers for the defense was headed by the top leaders of Young Egypt, Ahmad Husayn and Fathi Radwan, who used the trial to undermine the Wafd and enhance their own standing among the workers. This ploy confirmed the Wafd in its perception of the strike wave as a conspiracy of its political rivals to sabotage the treaty negotiations by threatening foreign business interests, a perception which prompted quick and forceful official intervention to end the disturbances. The government's intervention would not have succeeded so easily, however, had not the Wafd still enjoyed a great deal of prestige among the workers. In several major strikes in the summer of 1936, at Hawamdiyya and also among the Alexandria tramwaymen—who had the experience of more than three decades of militancy and collective ac-

An Independent Workers' Movement   **223**

tion behind them—the workers agreed to resume work in return for nothing more than a vague promise that their demands would be looked into by the government. Clearly, the events of the previous half-decade had strengthened the Wafd's credit among many workers despite its earlier failures to fulfil its promises, the split it had engineered in the labor movement, and years of pent-up grievances.

The Wafd's return to power had thus unleashed a wave of worker activism while giving the government the popularity with which to temporarily pacify the discontent. But the summer of 1936 marked the highest point in the Wafd's standing among the workers: they were still willing to give the party time to firmly grasp the reins of power and complete negotiations on a treaty that would finally realize Egypt's dream of complete independence. But labor's support for and patience with the Wafd were much more provisional than had previously been the case, and demands for action and interest in alternative paths remained very much in the air.

Once the Anglo-Egyptian treaty had been ratified, the Wafd did for a time devote greater attention to its base constituencies among which were the workers. For example, most of the 'Anabir workers victimized in May 1931 were restored to their jobs and compensated. In September 1936 Parliament finally enacted a law that established workers' rights to monetary compensation from their employers for work-related injuries, and because unsafe conditions prevailed in most Egyptian workplaces and the impact even relatively minor accidents might have on workers with no savings could be catastrophic, this was a welcome if not entirely adequate piece of legislation. Some months later the vagrancy law, under which unemployed workers could be imprisoned, was amended to apply only to true vagrants.[4]

Soon after these measures had been instituted government action on behalf of workers ceased as the cabinet seemed to lose interest in labor issues. The Supreme Labor Advisory Council, still dominated by such champions of big business as Ahmad Ziwar Pasha and Henri Naus of the sugar company, did its best to block further legislative initiatives. In fact, despite the Wafd's overwhelming majority in Parliament, a bill recognizing trade unions introduced by Zuhayr Sabri got nowhere, and though Wafdists involved with the unions pressed for legislation, the top leadership continued to favor caution and conservatism concerning labor legislation and social reform in general.[5] De-

4. For data on the appallingly high accident rate in Egyptian industry see Radi Abu Sayf Radi, "Mushkilat al-'amil," *Majallat al-shu'un al-ijtima'iyya* 3 (March 1942):33–42.
5. Five years earlier Graves had reported receiving messages from three "fairly prominent Wafdists advising me most strongly to go slowly into the matter of Labour legis-

224 An Independent Workers' Movement

spite attempts to revive the Wafd's labor federation—led now by 'Aziz Mirham after Ahmad Hamdi Sayf al-Nasr resigned to become minister of agriculture—it remained weak and disorganized. Before the Wafd's return to power it had devoted considerable energy to establishing its hegemony over the union movement and mobilizing workers on its own behalf; once securely in control of the government, however, the Wafd's interest waned.

The neglect of issues of importance to labor led to considerable worker disillusionment with the Wafd by the end of 1936, and given the Supreme Council's lack of initiative, to renewed talk of independent labor organization. Zuhayr Sabri, the most progressive of the Wafd's labor activists, responded to this undercurrent of resentment in a speech he delivered in December 1936 at a meeting of the Wafd's Alexandria labor federation.

> If we do not arrive at an understanding with the Wafd, how do you want us to be able to achieve anything? Furthermore, up to now we have had nothing but praise for them. Your law on accidents at work was adopted in three days by the Chamber of Deputies and the Senate; the French parliament however took three years to adopt this bill. This means that the Wafdist deputies have a lot of sympathy for the labor movement.
>
> But, if we were to say tomorrow: "We are a labor party" or "We are socialists," that would mean that war was declared between the classes, between the capitalists and the workers. Where would we be going? You know well that the present number of workers is insufficient to elect one deputy. You should think about whether anything useful could be done.
>
> How long do you think it would take to have the necessary majority in Parliament to enact your demands? That is the principal question. Therefore I have come today to warn you, not at all for fear of a labor party or of socialism but for fear of a war which would seriously damage the workers' interests. How can you want to declare war against a government and against a parliament that offers us, every day, part of our demands?[6]

It is significant that Sabri's plea that the workers continue to trust in the Wafd was based not on patriotism or the need for national unity but on purely pragmatic grounds. A labor party or a socialist move-

---

lation and in particular to resist any movement in favour of recognising syndicates."
FO 141/506/23/31, Graves to the Residency, July 3, 1931.
6. Quoted in el-Maraghi, *Législation*, pp. 174–75.

An Independent Workers' Movement **225**

ment would not necessarily be bad, he implied, but the workers were at that point simply too weak to challenge the capitalists on their own and achieve a measure of political power, and for this reason they had to support the Wafd which would gradually satisfy their demands.

This new approach in seeking labor support reflected the changed political conditions that resulted from the 1936 treaty, as well as a growth in working-class awareness. By the Wafd's own claims the struggle for independence was over, and appeals for support on the grounds that the party embodied the national will to freedom, overriding the sectional interests of social classes, lost much of their force. Increasingly challenged by new, more radical, and more dynamic forces—Young Egypt, and later the Muslim Brothers and a new communist movement—the Wafd would henceforth be increasingly compelled to prove that of all the political parties it could best satisfy the demands of its constituents. Its monopoly of popular support had begun to erode, and this encouraged a revival, at a higher stage of organization and consciousness, of the tendency toward independent organization in the unionized working class.

A New Departure

Late in 1936 a number of veteran Cairo unionists began to meet informally to discuss the state of the labor movement and seek ways to revive it. Sometime in the first part of 1937 they constituted themselves formally as the Committee to Organize the Workers' Movement (Lajnat Tanzim al-Haraka al-'Ummaliyya), and began more intensive work aimed at supporting the creation of new unions, strengthening existing unions, and laying the basis for the eventual creation of a labor federation independent of all political parties. At a meeting in September 1937 attended by representatives of Cairo-area unions, the term "committee" in the organization's name was replaced by *hay'a*—"commission," "movement," "organization."

The president of the new group was Muhammad Yusuf al-Mudarrik. Relatively well-educated, al-Mudarrik had long been a leader of the shop clerks' union and was active in many of the efforts to achieve labor unity in the 1930s. Sayyid Qandil served as secretary. He had been a printing worker since 1928, had taught himself to read and write on the job, and had become the leader of the printing workers' union. He had published numerous articles on labor affairs and had been associated with the social democratic weekly *Ruh al-'Asr* in 1930. Among the other leaders of the new organization were such veterans as Muhammad Hasan 'Amara of the barbers' union, Kamil 'Izz al-Din (now of the Misr Airworks union), and Labib Tadrus of the tai-

226 An Independent Workers' Movement

lors. Relatively new faces included Mahmud al-'Askari of the mechanized textile workers and 'Abbas Yusuf of the carpenters.[7] In a word, this new movement consisted of people like al-Mudarrik and al-'Askari who were strongly committed to building a fully independent union movement, and of people like Qandil, 'Amara, and others who had for years been closely associated with 'Abbas Halim and saw his patronage as somehow different than subordination to the Wafd or other political parties.

This difference in perspective became a divisive issue almost immediately, for 'Abbas Halim was preparing to resume his involvement in labor affairs. In August 1937, just before departing on a lengthy trip to Europe, he had told the press that he would resume his leadership of the workers' movement and establish a labor party on his return.[8] His titles and prerogatives had been restored in 1936 by King Faruq with whom he was on good terms. After eighteen months 'Abbas Halim apparently felt it was time for him to reappear on the labor scene and reclaim his leading role. The Wafd's grip on power as well as its labor support had been slipping, his former lieutenants had already resumed activity with considerable success, and he had the backing of the Palace for this new project.

The return of 'Abbas Halim aroused considerable excitement among some of the unionists who led the new movement. Their motives for seeking or accepting his leadership varied. Some apparently felt that their careers and prospects were inextricably linked with his, whereas others believed that his prestige and past record of service to the workers would facilitate the growth of the labor movement. Some labor activists may have seen in 'Abbas Halim a source of protection from the Wafd as well as a link with the popular young king. More mercenary motives may also have played a part. 'Abbas Halim had subsidized the NFTUE with large sums of money, and it was not unreasonable to expect that if offered the nominal leadership of the new organization the prince could be induced to underwrite its projects.

Other leaders of the Commission to Organize the Workers' Movement, however, were less pleased, and at the organization's inaugural meeting there was a heated discussion about 'Abbas Halim's role. Al-Mudarrik and al-'Askari, for example, argued against any connection with 'Abbas Halim, but they were outvoted, and as a result the organ-

---

7. 'Askari, U, August 16, 29, 1976; 'Amara, T, May 1, 1976; 'Abd al-Warith 'Abd al-Halim 'Abd Allah, al-Wa'y al-niqabi fi misr (Cairo, 1957), pp. 34–37; al-Nahar, July 1, 16, 1941.

8. In the course of this trip 'Abbas Halim attended the Nuremberg Congress of the Nazi party. The German government provided him and his wife with a villa in Bayrouth and a valet. See Shubra, August 12, September 9, 1937.

An Independent Workers' Movement **227**

ization sponsored large receptions for the prince on his return in November 1937 and named him "leader of the workers" (*za'im al-'ummal*). Yet even those who supported the election of 'Abbas Halim as president did not really want him to exercise effective leadership over the movement. The real issue seems to have been whether 'Abbas Halim should be used as a figurehead or not at all. In the discussions that began after 'Abbas Halim's return concerning the foundation of a new federation, those who had opposed any ties with him as a matter of principle were quite successful in keeping his leadership role as purely nominal as possible, and in retaining all policy decisions in the hands of genuine trade union leaders.

The Wafd in Crisis and the Workers

The coalescence of this new tendency in the labor movement was aided by the erosion of the Wafd's grip on power in the second half of 1937. Like his father before him, young Faruq wanted to get rid of the Wafd cabinet and install a government that would be more responsive to his wishes. To that end the Palace helped organize, finance, and promote a variety of anti-Wafdist groups, such as the students at the university and at al-Azhar. The Palace's encouragement of 'Abbas Halim's renewed involvement in labor affairs should be seen as part of the same policy of undermining public support for the Wafd, which was in fact declining in popularity. That decline was exacerbated by a split in the Wafd leadership in the fall of 1937 and the departure of two of the Wafd's most capable and popular leaders—Mahmud Fahmi al-Nuqrashi and Ahmad Mahir—to form the Sa'dist party. Although the Sa'dist party—named after Sa'd Zaghlul, whose true political heirs its founders claimed to be—attracted only a small fraction of the Wafd's following and came to be regarded as the spokesman for the major Egyptian financial and industrial interests, the split damaged the Wafd's prestige and aided its enemies.

With its public support slipping and aware of the emergence of tendencies in the union movement that favored independence, the Wafd began to take a renewed interest in labor affairs in the second half of 1937. Many of the university and secondary students, once staunch supporters, had been won over by the Palace and its allies, but the workers were still by and large loyal. 'Aziz Mirham sought to have Parliament appropriate money to finance and thereby reinvigorate the Wafd's labor federation, which was disorganized and chronically short of cash. This blatant maneuver to strengthen the Wafd's support among the workers failed, and the government turned to more indirect means. For example, when a number of strikes broke

228 An Independent Workers' Movement

out in the summer of 1937 the attitude of the authorities toward the workers changed, according to the disgusted director of the Labor Department, from "inactive benevolence" to "open support." In October the government intervened in favor of the union during a strike at the Tura cement works. At the same time, the business-oriented Supreme Labor Advisory Council was bypassed while the Wafd sought to take direct control of the Labor Department by appointing its supporters to key positions and threatening to remove officials close to Graves. The director felt that his situation was "rapidly becoming untenable" and thought of resigning.[9]

The Wafd government's campaign to bolster its support among the workers was most successful with those employed by the government itself. Government workers had long had a special relationship with the Wafd, and Nahhas Pasha exploited that relationship as best he could in the fall of 1937. When a strike broke out at the Government Press in September, the cabinet settled it by granting all government workers a minimum of two weeks paid vacation a year as well as pay for public holidays, which amounted to an increase in wages of almost 10 percent. Relatively generous sick pay was also granted, and the unpopular acting director of the Government Press was replaced. Graves was quite right when he charged that, as he put it, the Nahhas government was "pandering to labor" to shore up its political position.

The dramatic concessions of September were accompanied by an intensified propaganda campaign aimed at workers. The prime minister visited the offices of the Wafd's labor federation in the Delta town of Tanta and declared: "I have already told you that I am the protector of the workers (nasir al-'ummal), and God willing I will remain the protector of the workers." Makram 'Ubayd, now the most powerful figure in the party and government after Nahhas Pasha, added in a rhetorical style which perfectly reflected the Wafd leadership's conception of the working class: "We have promised you that we will work for the workers' benefit; consider me a worker like you, for if I work on behalf of the workers I am one of them."[10]

Nahhas Pasha also vigorously denounced the idea of a labor party, revived in this same period by 'Abbas Halim, as a conspiracy by the enemies of the Wafd. In a speech to a Wafdist meeting in Alexandria, the prime minister said:

9. *Shubra*, June 24, July 15, 1937; FO 141/660/357/7/37, R. M. Graves, "The Egyptian Government's Attitude towards Labour," November 20, 1937.
10. *Nahdat al-'ummal*, September 12, 1937.

An Independent Workers' Movement **229**

Workmen: what you hear said about it's being desired to form a Labour Party to take you away from the Wafd, which is zealous on behalf of your interests and which works for your good, is treachery and intrigue against the Wafd. The Wafd will continue to labour on behalf of the workers' conditions by passing laws benefitting their standard of life and their syndicates. No intrigue that these people can start—and God is everywhere about them—will prevent us from labouring in the interests of the workers (cheers).[11]

In October, with the political situation worsening, Nahhas spoke at a Wafdist workers' rally held at the municipal stadium in Alexandria, talked of the labor laws already promulgated by the Wafd, and detailed a list of further measures that would soon be taken including the recognition of trade unions. "The realization of the legitimate interests of the workers," he asserted, "is in the employers' interest, just as ensuring the legitimate interests of the employers is in the workers' interest." Stressing the benefits the "people's government" had brought the workers, he again attacked the idea of a labor party and praised the workers' loyalty. "You understand that the Wafd government is the people's government, and that in the vanguard of this faithful people are her sons the workers, whom I know to be the trustworthy soldiers of the Wafd and its strong arm."[12]

These appeals had the greatest impact on the government workers who had tangible proof of the Wafd's concern, and they stood by the party. As the struggle between Nahhas Pasha and the Palace intensified in November and December 1937 and tensions rose, the government workers came out in defense of the Wafd. On November 15, for example, when the king returned to Cairo, pro-Wafd railway workers armed with crowbars overawed the anti-Wafd crowds waiting to greet Faruq. In December workers from the Arsenal and the Government Press demonstrated in front of the royal palace shouting "No Faruq without Nahhas Pasha!" The government workers' support could not avert the fall of Nahhas, but it stood in sharp contrast with the attitude of the students, many of whom had come to support the king or other anti-Wafd forces.

The unionized private sector workers in Cairo and Alexandria were in general less enthusiastic about the Wafd government by the end of 1937, an attitude demonstrated by the positive response many of them showed toward the return of 'Abbas Halim and the renewed ef-

11. *EG*, August 23, 1937.
12. *al-Muqattam*, October 4, 1937; FO 407/221/37, Kelly to Eden, October 8, 1937.

230 An Independent Workers' Movement

forts to build an independent labor movement. The Cairo tramway-men's union, for example, was nominally affiliated to the Wafd's Supreme Council federation, and its counsellor was 'Aziz Mirham. In June 1937 the union's executive board sent Nahhas Pasha a telegram congratulating him on the occasion of Egypt's entry into the League of Nations, though there soon followed a second set of telegrams calling on the government and Parliament to enact labor legislation. By September union leaders were expressing support for a labor party and criticizing the political parties for exploiting the workers' movement. There was clearly considerable latent support for a break with the Wafd and independent organization among the large, experienced, and well-established unions in Cairo and Alexandria.[13]

In the provincial towns, however, the Wafd retained much of its prestige and support. In many places labor organizations were an integral part of the local Wafd apparatus. Tanta is a case in point. Here the lawyer 'Abd al-Hamid Lutfi ran the Gharbiyya Federation of Labor Unions, affiliated with the Supreme Council. This federation included unions of drivers, barbers, nurses, gas workers, shop clerks, shoemakers, coppersmiths, tailors, tarbush makers, and butchers. Several of the unions included both workers and small proprietors: this was certainly true of the shoemakers, of those who ironed clothes (al-makwagiyya), and probably of the drivers, butchers, tailors, and barbers as well. In places like Tanta, economically less developed and somewhat isolated from the new political trends emerging in the two big cities, the craft ethos still persisted, linked to and encouraged by the local Wafd organization which was a vehicle and power base for local notables like 'Abd al-Hamid Lutfi. Here the union movement was primarily a means of organizing and mobilizing the workers and petty bourgeoisie of the town, suggesting that the distinction between small proprietors and wage workers, irrelevant in Wafdist ideology, was less socially apparent or significant in Tanta than in Cairo or Alexandria.

The Gharbiyya federation was in practice an arm of the local Wafdist committee, which still enjoyed mass support. 'Abd al-Hamid Lutfi published a biweekly newspaper called *Nahdat al-'Ummal (Workers' Renaissance)*, which carried news of local and national labor affairs, and was of course strongly pro-Wafd. This kind of labor organization, which flourished while the Wafd was in power in 1937, was however more or less confined to the provinces. It was already anachronistic and retrograde when measured against the new tendencies develop-

13. See *Shubra*, June 24, August 19, September 2, 9, 1937.

ing within the labor movements of Egypt's two largest cities. The blurred conception of what a union was for and who should belong, and the dependence of the unions on the Wafd apparatus, were no longer acceptable to most organized workers in Cairo and Alexandria. Social and political conditions in places like Tanta made this form of workers organization viable as long as a local notable was in a position to provide patronage and support.

This was not however to be the case for long, for the Wafd ultimately lost its struggle for power with the Palace. As usual the party was outmaneuvered and defeated because it continued to play by the rules of a game which were rigged against it. Having created the proper political conditions, Faruq dismissed the Nahhas government, and appointed Muhammad Mahmud of the Liberal Constitutionalists to form a new cabinet. The elections held in March 1938 were said by British officials to have been even more manipulated than Sidqi's, and as a result the Wafd retained only a few seats in Parliament. For the next four years, until the dramatic events of February 1942, the Wafd was to remain in the political wilderness, and Egypt was to be governed by a succession of politicians allied to or creatures of the Palace.

The Wafd was in office for twenty months in 1936 and 1937, the longest it had ever held power. Preoccupied with other matters and disinclined to alienate its more conservative constituencies, it managed to enact only a single piece of labor legislation. The Wafd had been victorious in its 1935 struggle with 'Abbas Halim for control of the bulk of the union movement, and still retained enough moral authority to quell the 1936 strike wave fairly easily, but over the following year it not only failed to consolidate its control over the unions by creating a strong, active national labor federation, but squandered its support by defaulting on its promises to the workers. The Wafd could still buy the allegiance of the government workers, but the organized workers in private-sector industry and transport grew increasingly disillusioned. Remembering earlier reactionary governments backed by the Palace, these workers cannot have been pleased with the Wafd's downfall, and most continued to support that party as the only populist alternative, though they no longer identified so closely with the Wafd to feel its defeat as their own. Meanwhile, an alternative pole of attraction had emerged within the labor movement, led by veteran unionists who had never accepted, much less sought, the tutelage of the Wafd. This tendency was determined to ensure that the union movement forged ahead with or without the Wafd in power, charting its own course, and fighting for its own goals.

232 An Independent Workers' Movement

The Coalescence of a New Leadership

In the latter part of 1937 and the first months of 1938, the Commission to Organize the Workers' Movement in collaboration with 'Abbas Halim laid the foundations of a new labor federation, which was formally established on March 1, 1938 at a meeting of representatives of thirty-two Cairo-area trade unions. Unions from other parts of the country affiliated in the months that followed. The new organization was called the General Federation of Labor Unions in the Kingdom of Egypt (GFLUKE). 'Abbas Halim assumed the presidency, Muhammad Yusuf al-Mudarrik the vice-presidency, and Muhammad Hasan 'Amara served as general secretary. The founders included many veterans of the NFTUE of 1930–1935, of which the GFLUKE was in some ways a reincarnation, but important new elements were also involved.

The leadership of the new Federation continued to be divided over the role nonworkers should play in the organization, and in fact this conflict surfaced a month after the Federation was formed, when 'Abbas Halim and his allies pushed for the appointment of Ahmad al-Damardash al-Shanadi as president. Al-Shanadi was an engineer at the Filature Nationale in Alexandria who had won election to Parliament from the district of Karmuz as a Sa'dist in April 1938. Although there existed a precedent for the election of a popular worker-identified candidate over a Wafdist—the victory of Mahjub Thabit in 1927—it is likely that al-Shanadi's victory owed less to his own popularity than to the government's fixing of the election to produce an anti-Wafd majority. In any event al-Shanadi regarded himself, and was regarded by such Federation leaders as 'Amara and Qandil, as a worker, indeed the first worker elected to the Egyptian Parliament, and on that basis they supported 'Abbas Halim's campaign to install him as president.

But other leaders such as al-Mudarrik rejected the underhanded and undemocratic way in which al-Shanadi's "election" as president had been engineered by 'Abbas Halim. They also did not consider this foreign-trained professional a genuine worker, and opposed the installation of someone so closely identified with the Sa'dist party as a violation of the principle of labor's independence from the government, the parties, and nonworker notables. Al-Mudarrik lost this battle as he had lost the battle to exclude 'Abbas Halim: al-Shanadi was eventually designated president and 'Abbas Halim assumed the title of "leader" (za'im). Yet, despite these defeats the role of these two outsiders in the actual leadership of the Federation was purely nom-

An Independent Workers' Movement **233**

inal, and the principle that genuine unionists should control their own affairs gained widespread support.[14]

The GFLUKE became the most important organization on the Egyptian labor scene in the course of 1938. The Wafd's Supreme Council lapsed into complete inactivity after the Nahhas cabinet was deposed, and affiliates that sought to continue their activities found themselves facing police harassment. The authorities banned and disrupted union meetings, encouraged splits in pro-Wafd labor organizations, and arrested activists.[15] Although the Palace sponsored the creation of a labor federation under its aegis and control, it failed to gain much worker support, and the way was thereby open for the General Federation, led by experienced and committed unionists prepared to try new methods, to take the lead.

There is some irony in the fact that the tendency within the Egyptian workers' movement that fought for labor independence could emerge only after the downfall of the Wafd and during the reign of parties historically hostile to the working class. Although the Wafd was the party popularly identified with democracy and nationalism, the leadership of the tendency fighting for an independent and militant stance developed in opposition to the Wafd, and was at times encouraged by reactionary forces hostile to the Wafd. The experience of unionists in the 1930s can explain this apparent paradox. The embrace of the Wafd in power or on the verge of power (as in 1935) was stifling to these unionists because it required their subordination to a coterie of politicians who put their party's interests first. At the same time the Wafd had repeatedly failed to make good on its promises, and was growing more conservative on social issues because of the rising influence of large landowning elements (typified by Fu'ad Siraj al-Din) within the party. Furthermore, the nationalist credentials of the Wafd were both less relevant and under sustained attack after the 1936 treaty whose chief architect it had been. The party's democratic pretensions had been damaged by its abuses of power in 1936–1937. In contrast the monarchy had gained considerably in prestige and popularity.

In the absence of a socialist or communist party that could provide a distinct ideology and political leadership for the workers' movement, the slogan under which the most advanced unionists organized was independence. In practice this meant rejection of unconditional

14. 'Askari, *U*, August 30, September 21, 1976; 'Amara, *T*, May 1, 1976; Qandil, *Niqabiyyati*, pp. 34–38.
15. See for example *Nahdat al-'ummal*, January 23, February 6, October 16, 1938.

234 An Independent Workers' Movement

support for or subordination to the Wafd or any other party. In their place came a policy of pragmatism, of making demands that served the special interests of labor, and of cooperating with any government that met those demands regardless of whether that government was anti-Wafdist, undemocratic, or reactionary in other respects. Given the experiences of the 1930s and the conditions that prevailed after 1937, this orientation was a rational and productive one, and represented an important step forward. In their hearts most workers and labor activists remained staunch patriots, and were probably sympathetic to the Wafd, but they were no longer willing to tie their fortunes exclusively to that party and its political destiny. Thus the close linkage once prevalent between labor activism and nationalist resurgence under the leadership of the Wafd continued to erode.

The new spirit that characterized the leadership of the General Federation was typified by its first public action. The organization had condensed the urgent concerns of the labor movement into five immediate demands: legal recognition for trade unions and the labor federation; a reduction in the work day; enforcement of Labor Department regulations; a solution to the unemployment problem; and revision of the weak accident compensation law of 1936. This program was brought to public attention by traditional means: delegations visited government officials and presented petitions urging immediate action on these demands. 'Abbas Halim even visited his cousin the king, who expressed his sympathy. At the same time, however, the Federation's leaders planned a public demonstration by workers in support of these demands. Despite the opposition of 'Abbas Halim and the police to such an open display of labor's discontent, the march went ahead as planned. On May 8, 1938, thousands of union members carrying signs and banners paraded past 'Abdin Palace, government ministries, Parliament, and the offices of the major newspapers. This unprecedented demonstration won considerable public attention and sympathetic press coverage, and marked a new tactical departure in the struggle for labor's demands.

In the months that followed the Federation busied itself with ordering its internal affairs and broadening its base. The labor group sponsored by the Palace was absorbed into the GFLUKE, but the Wafd refused to participate in efforts to unify the labor movement. The extent to which the principle of labor's independence and the rejection of deference to outsiders had begun to take hold was illustrated by the comments of a weekly sympathetic to labor on a report that a union counsellor had apologized for being unable to attend a particular conference. "We do not understand," *al-Shu'a'* commented, "how [the counsellor] presumes to apologize when he was not the one invited;

An Independent Workers' Movement **235**

rather it was the workers who were invited! But [the counsellor] is 'excused'. . . because he still thinks that he is counsellor to the workers and doesn't know that the workers have divorced the counsellors for good."[16]

The Federation's energies, however, were soon focused on a campaign to secure legal recognition of trade unions, an issue that by the spring and early summer of 1939 had begun to receive considerable public and parliamentary attention. The committee on labor and social affairs of the Chamber of Deputies had been discussing and revising a draft law introduced by Mustafa Ahmad al-'Assal. As modified, the bill allowed commercial employees as well as workers to form unions; women would however be barred from union membership (a prohibition allegedly required by religious law); and no federations were to be allowed. Even this weak bill, unsatisfactory to the union leaders, seemed unlikely to pass. The Federation's council therefore resolved to take the initiative in May 1939. Citing the procrastination of successive governments and the failure of the supplicatory approach used up to that point, the council decided that unless labor legislation, especially full legal recognition of unions, was enacted within fifteen days, Federation leaders would begin a hunger strike which would continue until their demands were met, or "they have the honor of martyrdom in the cause of serving the workers of the Kingdom of Egypt."[17]

The use of the hunger strike as a means of exerting political pressure was quite rare in Egypt, except for political prisoners. 'Abbas Halim had refused to take food for a time during his imprisonment in 1935, but the union militants were more influenced by Mohandes Gandhi's use of the tactic in India's struggle for independence, and al-'Askari described the hunger strikers as "the successors of Gandhi in Egypt." Certainly neither 'Abbas Halim or al-Shanadi seem to have had anything to do with the decision or its implementation. Careful preparations were made: government officials and the police were informed of the ultimatum, volunteers were signed up and prepared, and teams were set up which would carry on as the members of the first team collapsed or died. The first group consisted of eight unionists: Muhammad Yusuf al-Mudarrik, the Federation's vice-president and guiding force, and member of the retail clerks' union; Labib Zaki, secretary of the commercial workers' union; 'Abbas Yusuf of the furniture workers' union; 'Ali Rihan, also a furniture carpenter; 'Abd al-

16. *al-Shu'a'*, September 12, 1938.
17. See 'Abbas, *al-Haraka*, pp. 328–29; 'Askari, *U*, September 27, October 4, 1976; 'Amara, *T*, June 1976.

236 An Independent Workers' Movement

Maqsud Yusuf, a weaving worker; 'Abd al-Wahhab Muhammad, a leather worker; 'Ali Salih Darwish, of the drivers' union; and Labib Tadrus, a leader of the tailors' union.

The hunger strike began on June 12, in the small garden at the center of one of Cairo's main squares. The strikers refused police requests that they go home but in the evening were compelled to move to the nearby offices of the Peasants' party, a politically insignificant but sympathetic group. The police sealed off the building in an attempt to isolate the strikers and prevent access to supporters and the press. Thanks to a publicity campaign organized by 'Amara, the event caught the attention of the public, especially after unions began flooding the newspapers and the government with messages of support. Enterprising reporters got into the building and interviewed al-Mudarrik, the spokesman for the group. He stressed that the strikers represented different federations and trades but were united in their determination to win their demands. Every other method of struggle had been tried; now the eight men were ready to die for labor's rights.[18]

While supporters demonstrated outside, the strikers were visited during the following days by numerous public personalities. 'Abbas Halim turned up and tried to convince the strikers to quit, though he also accompanied union delegations to the Palace, ministries, and Parliament. Salih Ashmawi, a leader of the Muslim Brothers, sent a telegram that expressed sympathy for their grievances, but called on them to end their strike and trust the government. Ahmad Husayn, leader of Young Egypt, also came and advised the workers to quit. Finally, on June 15, Mustafa al-'Assal brought the strikers a copy of the printed agenda of the Chamber of Deputies, which included consideration of his bill on the unions. Having forced Parliament to take up their concerns and attracted public attention to the issue, the eight strikers ended their fast. However, they announced their intention to strike again if the bill were not enacted. They felt they had won a major victory, for not only had their cause been taken seriously but their bold action had galvanized and unified the labor movement as nothing else in recent years.

Yet despite the initiative of the General Federation, no law on trade unions was enacted in 1939. The government and its supporters in the Chamber procrastinated until the end of the parliamentary session. In August Prime Minister Muhammad Mahmud, who had often expressed interest in the workers' grievances and allocated funds for cheap housing, resigned and was replaced by 'Ali Mahir. Shortly

18. See *al-Ahram*, June 13–18, 1939.

An Independent Workers' Movement   **237**

thereafter the outbreak of war in Europe claimed the attention of the public and the government, and social issues again dropped to the bottom of the political agenda. The war, in which Egypt could not remain uninvolved, created new economic and political conditions with profound effects on the working class.

Egypt and the World War

The Second World War greatly stimulated the growth of large-scale industry in Egypt and the growth of the working class, developments that will be analysed in the following chapter. The immediate effects of the outbreak of war were, however, harmful to many Egyptian workers. The disruption of the sea lanes, increased costs, the loss of foreign markets, and decreased supplies of certain imported raw materials resulted in a wave of layoffs beginning in September 1939. The workers most affected by these events were in the ports, printing, and textiles. Some, especially the unionized textile workers of Shubra al-Khayma near Cairo, were able to successfully resist the layoffs, but many others lost their jobs. Although the unemployment caused by war-related economic dislocations remained a concern, it was overshadowed by an accelerating wave of inflation that began in 1940. A military decree of September 6, 1939 (martial law and press censorship had been imposed when the war began) had established a system of boards that were supposed to set maximum prices for foodstuffs and other essential commodities and prevent speculation and hoarding. Nonetheless, prices began to rise relentlessly; the cost-of-living index (based on official wholesale prices, hence an understatement of real market prices) went from 131 in 1939 to 156 in December 1940, to 195 in 1941, and 276 in December 1942.[19] (See Table 6 for more data on inflation.)

The resulting sharp drop in real wages led to widespread discontent among workers in every sector. The GFLUKE had joined the struggle for government action against the wave of layoffs in the fall of 1939, but though it sought to articulate the demand for a general wage adjustment in the following months, it was ineffective. The powers the government enjoyed through martial law made the Federation's work at first difficult, then impossible. Finally, the police shut down the organization's headquarters, and its leaders decided to suspend operations and work through the unions to which they belonged. In short, the General Federation was defunct by the beginning of 1941 if not earlier. Individual unions would now take the initiative in mobi-

19. *AS 1939/1940–1942/1943.*

238   An Independent Workers' Movement

lizing their increasingly hungry and desperate members in the rising tide of discontent that would crest in the fall of 1941.

Nonetheless, despite the fact that it was only active for a relatively short time and disappeared under wartime official pressure, the GFLUKE was a significant organization and left an important legacy. Although similar to 'Abbas Halim's federation in 1930–1935 in some respects—his role as well as that of some of his associates from that period, the emphasis on autonomy from the parties, especially the Wafd—the GFLUKE should be seen primarily as a labor formation of a new kind: it carried the principle of the independence of labor from outside control much further than its predecessor could have, for the former had been dominated by the ambitious 'Abbas Halim. Despite the presence in leadership positions of unionists who still believed 'Abbas Halim had a positive role to play, it was the more advanced group led by al-Mudarrik which increasingly set the tone. 'Abbas Halim and al-Shanadi chaired conferences and lent their names, but it was the executive board and council of the Federation, composed exclusively of union members, which not only ran the organization's day-to-day affairs but also made policy decisions. As the hunger strike of June 1939 showed, 'Abbas Halim was not even consulted about planned actions, much less heeded when he advised against them. Indeed, by the fall of 1939 the prince had apparently given up on the Federation and devoted his energies to developing another, less independent-minded base in the labor movement, among the Cairo transport workers.

The GFLUKE was significant because it was the framework within which the new stratum of trade unionists, which had been emerging in the 1930s, coalesced and sought to put their principles into practice. By 1938 these unionists had developed a coherent perspective on the nature of the working class and the authentic role of the union movement. This perspective was not explicitly socialist, though many of these unionists were certainly familiar with socialist ideas and intellectuals. It consisted rather of a militant trade unionism, a working class radicalism oriented less toward the acquisition of political power than toward organizing the working class, fostering a sense of class identity and self-reliance, and laying the foundations for a strong, united, and militant labor movement.

During the GFLUKE's brief lifespan, the organization had no public outlet through which this perspective could be expressed, and only for a few months in 1941, after the Federation's demise, were some of the unionists who adhered to this viewpoint able to gain editorial control of the weekly al-Nahar (The Day) and use it to set forth their views. Al-Nahar carried news of union meetings and activities, as

An Independent Workers' Movement   **239**

had previous publications with a labor focus, but it differed from its predecessors in that it was directly controlled and edited by unionists and stressed the perspective of the most advanced section of the labor movement. The new tone was unmistakable.

Sayyid Qandil, Yusuf al-Mudarrik, and others published articles that stressed the need for independence, unity, and a trade unionist perspective. An article signed " 'Antar" spoke of the vital importance of self-reliance: if the workers got rid of the elements which exploited them and achieved unity, they too could be represented in Parliament and obtain their objectives. Muhammad Hamdi of the Gharbiyya Committee to Defend the Workers' Interests wrote:

> In order for our movement to really succeed, we must rid it of those who exploit and manipulate it, and first of all those who have penetrated the labor movement but are not workers. . . . We as workers do not lack knowledge or experience, and we have already spent half our lives caring for this movement. So we must be men and defend our cause ourselves, without need of the intervention of patrons (*awsiya'*) who raise themselves upon our shoulders and are not of us.[20]

The workers were seen in this publication as members of a distinct class with interests and goals of its own, in contrast to the perspectives of both the Wafd and 'Abbas Halim.

The editors of *al-Nahar* and their colleagues, with years of experience in the union movement, had drawn important conclusions from the hard lessons of the 1920s and 1930s. While many of them were relatively young men, in their late twenties and thirties, they had, as Hamdi put it, spent "half their lives" in the labor movement and had developed a fierce loyalty and commitment to it. The industrial development of Egypt, however halting and uneven, could no longer be in doubt, and the emergence of a working class most of whose members would remain wage workers all their lives was an inescapable social reality. These phenomena had to be accommodated in a vision that reflected the urgent needs and long-term goals of that class, and that understood the working class not as a docile object of exploitation by employers or of manipulation by politicians but as a subject capable of action. Of course, these young unionists had also been formed by new political conditions. Most had been children in 1919, and the heroic role of the Wafd belonged less to living memory than to past history. Most had entered the work force in the 1930s, and their experience had been shaped by the political and economic

20. *al-Nahar*, May 31, 1941.

240   An Independent Workers' Movement

forces of that turbulent era. Blind loyalty to the Wafd or deference to a socially prominent individual were not responses that made sense to them, and they were aware of and affected by the challenges to the established political and social order that arose after 1936.

The family history and social background of some members of this new breed of labor activist may also have contributed to their ideological breakthrough. The depression of the 1930s had forced the sons of many petty bourgeois families into the proletariat, which transformation at least some of these new leaders had experienced. As a result, the generation of union leaders that emerged in the late 1930s and the 1940s had a level of education and a family background superior to those of the average Egyptian worker or even of the previous generation of union leaders. For example, Sayyid Qandil's father had been a small merchant, and when he died, Qandil had had to leave school, and so was largely self-educated. Taha Sa'd 'Uthman, a leader of the Shubra al-Khayma textile workers, was born in 1916, completed a vocational secondary school, and was eventually hired as a foreman. Ahmad Fahim also had a diploma from an industrial school and became a leader of textile workers' unions. Muhammad Ramadan 'Ali, a leader of the Shell Oil workers in the 1940s, graduated from a commercial institute; his father had been a book dealer. Anwar Salama (Muhammad 'Abd al-Latif Salama), another petroleum workers' leader, graduated from an industrial secondary school; his father had been a primary school teacher. Fathi Kamil, leader of the Eastern Tobacco Company union in the 1940s and 1950s, came from a middle peasant family and had completed his secondary schooling in Cairo. He worked for some years as a low-level government functionary before beginning at Eastern Tobacco as an assistant clerk.[21]

These examples may not be entirely representative, but it is a fact that many relatively educated or skilled Egyptians entered the industrial work force in the 1930s and during the war. Under the impact of changing political conditions and a new stage of industrial development, these better educated and more skilled workers found it easier to break free of dependence on nonworker patrons, demand control over their own organizations, and assert a new sense of class identity; indeed, it was often foremen or skilled independent workers who played a leading role in many of the unions in this period. To be sure, the leadership of the GFLUKE was still composed largely of artisans, owner-operators, petty proprietors, and white-collar workers, but

21. 'Abd Allah. *al-Wa'y*, pp. 25–34, 48–50; interviews with Taha Sa'd 'Uthman conducted by Joel Beinin on October 28, 1980, and with Fathi Kamil on November 29 and December 3, 1979.

An Independent Workers' Movement **241**

even unionists drawn from these categories were affected by the new perspective that emerged just before the war.

Nonetheless, the GFLUKE should be regarded as a transitional stage in the emergence of the labor movement, for while its social perspective looked toward the future and spoke to the kind of working class just emerging in Egypt its own base was still largely rooted in small-scale production and the *artisanat*. As subsequent chapters will show, however, a new element—the textile workers of greater Cairo—was coming to play an important role in the Federation in the late 1930s, and it was the textile workers who would constitute the bridge to the future and the new vanguard of the workers' movement.

The Cairo Tramway Workers, 1939–1942

Already before the First World War, the role of vanguard had often been played by the tramway workers of Cairo. They had been one of the first groups of indigenous workers to form their own union and to launch militant struggles to improve their lot. Both in 1919–1921 and at other times, they had been extremely active and were the model of organization other workers sought to emulate. They had also developed strong links with the national movement early on and generally remained within the orbit of the Wafd. Yet for most of the 1930s relatively little was heard of the Cairo tramway workers. Their union certainly continued to exist and function, but it was in no position to gain any new ground or even resist the employer's offensives of the 1920s and 1930s. Because of the depression and the competition of motorized buses, ridership on the capital's tram system peaked in 1930, then dropped off, and stagnated until the war. The tramway work force had fallen to 2,400 by the end of the decade; during these years wages were cut, the pace of work intensified, and working conditions deteriorated. The Cairo tramwaymen had seemingly lost their historic leadership role in labor's struggles.

Their eclipse, however, was only temporary. In September 1941 the Cairo tramwaymen and their allies, the bus drivers and conductors, were compelled to resort to militant and illegal measures when they decided to confront the martial law government and force concessions. Their return to the center of labor activism took place under the leadership of 'Abbas Halim, whose only secure base of support in the labor movement was among the Cairo transport workers. Recently discovered union documents as well as secret police reports make it possible to answer several important questions about how this union (and others) functioned during the first three years of the war; the character of 'Abbas Halim's role in the workers' movement;

242 An Independent Workers' Movement

and the inherent limits of the paternalism which the Cairo tramway workers found so difficult to overcome.[22]

The CTWU had affiliated to 'Abbas Halim's NFTUE for the first time in 1934, had followed the Supreme Council when the Wafd broke with 'Abbas Halim in 1935, and remained, at least nominally, a Wafdist union until 1939. Two years earlier, however, some tramway union leaders had been involved with the Commission to Organize the Worker's Movement and in 1938 were among the founders of the GFLUKE. By late 1939, two factions had developed within the CTWU. The incumbent leadership led by 'Ali Shahin was challenged by a group of dissidents who charged that Shahin and his cronies were running the union in a dictatorial manner, and demanded new leadership. The dissidents won the union elections held in November 1939, but because Shahin refused to accept the results, the CTWU split into two rival organizations. The group led by Shahin remained loyal to the Wafd's Supreme Council, but the great majority of the members supported the new leadership.

The split seems to have reflected not only the failure of the old leadership to restore the declining fortunes of the union but a growing discontent with the moribund Supreme Council. Excluded from all but the most nominal connection with the GFLUKE by this time, 'Abbas Halim took advantage of the schism in the CTWU (if he did not help instigate it) to gain control of the organization. When the newly elected delegates met in November to reorganize their union, they decided to get rid of their Wafdist *mustashar* 'Aziz Mirham. Rejecting Wafdist domination of their union but unwilling or unable to opt for complete independence, they turned to 'Abbas Halim as a symbol of autonomy from the political parties and as a powerful patron. The union's new counsellors were chosen from among his associates, and in December 1939 'Abbas Halim was elected "supreme president" (*al-ra'is al-a'la*) of the Cairo Tramway Workers' Union.

It may seem surprising that a union as old, large, and experienced as the CTWU should have felt the need at this late date to ally itself with 'Abbas Halim. Certainly its leaders were well aware that a vigorous tendency within the labor movement was arguing that the principle of independence required the exclusion of 'Abbas Halim as well as the Wafd. Yet, it would seem that having cut their ties with the

22. Unless otherwise specified, the chief source used in this section is the handwritten minutes-book of meetings of the union's executive board. The manuscript was found at the offices of the Cairo Tramway and Trolley-bus Workers' Committee, successor to the tramwaymen's union. It is the only record of their historic past that these workers were able to preserve from the vicissitudes of time and police repression. It will be cited here as M, followed by the date of the meeting.

An Independent Workers' Movement   **243**

Wafd, the union's leaders felt they required a patron who was on good terms with both the king and the prime minister and whose status and prestige could enhance their ability to negotiate successfully with the CTC. Indeed, the policy of accepting the patronage of a friend of the government seemed to bear fruit almost immediately, for in December the prime minister responded to union complaints about the institution of a split work shift and compelled the company to withdraw it.[23]

Although expediency may seem to have played a major role in the relationship between 'Abbas Halim (for whom involvement in the labor movement was a way of achieving his political ambitions) and the tramwaymen, it alone does not entirely explain the relationship. The tramway workers deferred to 'Abbas Halim's leadership and judgment to a surprising extent, in contrast to those unionists in the GFLUKE leadership who sought to exploit his name and status while denying him any policy-making or executive role. This difference may be attributable partly to the fact that when 'Abbas Halim had been the chief of a labor federation he had operated largely through his lieutenants. With the tramwaymen in 1939–1942 he was, by contrast, the head of an individual union and worked closely with the leadership of that union; hence his control was much more direct and immediate. 'Abbas Halim did use his base in the CTWU to extend his influence over all the other Cairo transport workers, but his close personal association with the tramway workers laid the basis for a unique relationship that was to endure for some years. As 'Abbas Halim's influence over the labor movement as a whole declined, his influence among the transport workers of Cairo grew, and this sector would in later years be the last in which he had direct links with the workers.

There was, of course, an ideological component to the tramway union's attitude toward 'Abbas Halim as well. Although still capable of militant action and still able at times to play a vanguard role in labor struggles, the Cairo tramwaymen never entirely emancipated themselves from the habits of deference and the acceptance of paternalism that had marked the early years of the workers' movement. In its formative years and at the height of its power, when transport workers had been the vanguard of the Egyptian labor movement, the union had been led by nonworker patrons. As the shape of Egyptian industry and transport changed, and with it the structure of the working class, new perspectives surfaced within the union movement

---

23. See *Nahdat al-'ummal*, December 24, 1939. Several of the tram workers had begun a brief hunger strike to pressure the government.

244 An Independent Workers' Movement

which reflected these changes and projected a different vision of the working class and its role in Egyptian society. Still, the tram workers kept to the old ways, continuing to believe in the necessity of a powerful patron even if that meant compromising their union's independence. They therefore remained intimately linked with, indeed under the control of, 'Abbas Halim until 1942, and were never again to be in the vanguard as they had once been.

The first task of the new union that emerged from the split at the end of 1939 was to set its own house in order. The CTWU's structure was similar to that of most major Egyptian unions. The rank and file workers in the various departments of the enterprise—in the case of the tramwaymen, the three tram depots and the workshops—elected representatives to an executive board that in turn elected a president. The thirty-two board members chose Salim Fuda, one of the union's oldest members and always referred to by the honorific shaykh. The board generally met on Fridays at the union's office and spent much of its time tending to internal affairs, especially the union's important social welfare functions. For example, the union's treasury paid benefits of £E 5 to the families of deceased paid-up members and to dismissed workers, and five piastres a day—about one-third of the starting wage—to imprisoned members and those unable to work for more than thirty days. The union also provided legal services to members and small loans or even special grants in cases of dire need. These services accounted for a large part of its budget: of a total of £E 489 spent in 1940, £E 128 went for illness and death benefits; £E 103 for legal fees (though some of the latter were incurred by the union's own court battles); and the remainder for administrative expenses, salaries, rent, and furniture. Income for that year, mainly from dues, amounted to £E 787, and left a healthy surplus deposited in Bank Misr under 'Abbas Halim's name.

The actual membership of the union is difficult to determine because not all the CTC workers—whose numbers rose as a result of the dramatic wartime increase in ridership to 2,800 in 1942—belonged to the union, because payment of dues was irregular, and because not all paid-up members voted in union elections. Some 1,600 members were said to have voted in the elections of January 1941, but smaller numbers showed up for general meetings. The union was sustained by a small core of leaders beyond which lay a large periphery of members more or less active in, or committed to, the union. Although not all CTC workers joined the union, the company negotiated with the union as the representative of all the workers and the agreements they reached covered the entire work force. When a strike was called virtually all the workers followed the union's lead, indicating a high de-

An Independent Workers' Movement **245**

gree of support for the union among the tram workers. The commitment of the union's leaders to the organization was publicly demonstrated and reinforced by the oath of allegiance required of all executive board members:

> I swear by Almighty God and his power, and by the noble Qur'an and its sanctity, that I will be faithful to the union and the workers and obedient to the charter (qanun) of the union, and that I will implement it as best as I am able, and that I will sacrifice life and property for the union and its welfare, so help me God.

An earlier version had contained no specifically Muslim references, and since some of the executive board members were Christians there must have been a slightly altered formula for their oaths.[24]

Once the procedures for the union's internal government and the administration of its social welfare functions had been set up, the leadership's main preoccupation was to make some progress in achieving the workers' demands. In pursuit of this goal they were much more active and militant than 'Ali Shahin had been. As early as January 1940, in an attempt to resist speedup, the union called on the workers to adhere strictly to work and traffic rules regardless of supervisors' orders to the contrary. In the weeks that followed a memorandum was drawn up detailing the demands of the Cairo tram workers and copies were sent to the prime minister, other government officials, and the CTC management. The most important of the twelve demands involved higher wages, a minimum starting wage of fifteen piastres, permanent status for new workers after six months, a day off every week rather than every twelve days, a month's vacation each year, and the rehiring of dismissed workers. Some of the demands—particularly those concerning regular wage increases and negotiated work rules published in Arabic and distributed among the workers—can be traced back to 1919 and the subsequent refusal of the company to implement the agreements it had signed at that time.[25]

Negotiations between the CTWU and the tram company got underway but failed to make much progress, so in February 1940 the union authorized 'Abbas Halim to issue the required fifteen days' strike notice whenever he came to the conclusion that further talks were pointless. Although the executive board thereby delegated a great deal of power to 'Abbas Halim, there were workers present at all the negotiating sessions and the board was kept informed of the progress

---

24. M, March 8, 1940, January 31, 1941.
25. On the demands see CSB, March 2, 1940.

246 An Independent Workers' Movement

of the talks. Not all board members, however, were entirely satisfied with this arrangement. Late in March, for example, one member pressed 'Abbas Halim for more information about the negotiations, and he seems to have taken this as an insult and exploded in colloquial Egyptian Arabic:

> You want to strike, it's clear from your words and your face. If they go along with you about this and strike and it fails, I will be blamed. If that is what you want I'm not with you . . . I will leave you.[26]

There was no breach and 'Abbas Halim's anger subsided, but the outburst points to the potential for conflict with the union's leaders inherent in 'Abbas Halim's leadership role.

March 1940, when the CTWU was raising and pressing its demands, was a time of widespread labor unrest, and 'Abbas Halim was involved in much of it. The scope of his influence in the labor movement at this time is indicated by the unions that sent representatives to a tea party held in his honor at the end of the month: the Cairo and Heliopolis tramwaymen, the Thornycroft bus drivers and conductors, the cooks' union, the chauffeurs' union, some printers, a few unions in Alexandria, and the Cairo gas and electric workers.[27] The number of workers in 'Abbas Halim's sphere of influence was small by comparison with that of the Wafd, or of the GFLUKE at the height of its influence in 1938–1939, but the concentration of these workers in the sensitive public transport and public utilities sectors of the capital made him a potentially powerful figure. Indeed, when the electric company's workers had struck for over a week in March, 'Abbas Halim had used his friendly relations with Prime Minister 'Ali Mahir, who by showing sympathy toward the workers hoped to enhance his popularity, to settle the strike as well as to pressure the tram company on behalf of his clients. The British, however, had become quite concerned about the influence of 'Abbas Halim and the pro-Axis inclinations of 'Ali Mahir, and they forced the king to replace 'Ali Mahir with the more pliant Hasan Sabri in June 1940, and after Sabri's death in November with Husayn Sirri. Soon after Sabri's accession to power a decree was promulgated prohibiting strikes in enterprises serving the public—government, public transport, and utilities—and providing for fines and prison terms for striking or inciting to strike. This decree was intended to prevent a recurrence of the March strike and limit 'Abbas Halim's ability to disrupt normal life in Cairo.

26. M. March 27, 1940.
27. CSB. March 31, 1940.

An Independent Workers' Movement **247**

In the interim some progress had been made in the tram talks, and in July an agreement was reached between the two sides which won for the workers modest but not insignificant gains. Several key issues, most importantly the question of a new schedule of disciplinary fines, remained unresolved and were to cause not only further conflict between the workers and management but dissension within the union itself. Husayn Ibrahim, the same executive board member whose questions had aroused 'Abbas Halim's wrath a few months earlier, was removed from office in August for openly expressing opposition to the new schedule of fines the board had approved earlier. The schedule was clearly unpopular with many rank and file workers, but it was considered a grave breach of discipline for a board member to talk publicly of his disagreement with the majority. Such an appeal, it was feared, might eventually lead to a split, and unity was to be maintained even at the price of curbing dissent and limiting the members' control over their own leaders.

The board's determination to safeguard its power and status was also displayed in its relations with the union's counsellors. In August the Labor Department had forwarded a letter from the CTC to the union's lawyer Murshid Amin, who had replied without consulting the executive board. This angered the union leadership which voted to send an official letter to the Labor Department warning it not to communicate with anyone other than the union's president and his staff. The lawyer was told that he was not "to reply on behalf of the union in the name of the workers in such cases to any official agency except after consulting the board."[28]

Once the agreement of July 1940 had been concluded, the executive board spent most of its time dealing with requests for aid and the workplace grievances of individual workers. 'Abbas Halim attended board meetings only rarely, though he still played a role in the inconclusive talks that dragged on with CTC management, and instead devoted his energies to the creation of a Joint Transport Federation (Ittihad al-Naql al-Mushtarik) that would include all the unions of Cairo-area transport workers. Such an organization would be able to paralyze the capital's mass transit system and give whomever controlled it great political power. The JTF was finally set up in the spring of 1941 and included the unions at Thornycroft, the Cairo and Kafouri bus companies, and the Cairo and Heliopolis tram companies.

The main concern of the JTF and its member unions, indeed of all Egyptian workers at this time, was the high cost of living, for skyrocketing prices were rapidly outstripping wages. In fact, the secret police

28. M, August 19, 1940.

248 An Independent Workers' Movement

reported the rapid spread of discontent about declining real wages among workers everywhere.[29] The economic crisis was exacerbated by the exodus of some 250,000 people from Alexandria after German bombing raids on the city in June 1941. The government, however, failed to respond to the very real suffering of the working people by ordering wage increases, and the crisis reached its peak when the Cairo transport unions organized in the JTF announced their intention to strike for a large wage increase on September 16, 1941.

Tensions rose as the strike date approached. The war was going badly for the British: Axis armies had reached the Egyptian frontier several hundred miles west of Alexandria, fifth columnists were active in the country, and social unrest was widespread. Workers in both the public and private sectors were following developments among the tram and Thornycroft workers closely, and it was feared that they might follow their lead.[30] 'Abbas Halim met with government officials, but when no results were forthcoming the strike threat was implemented: on the morning of September 16 a general strike of all the Cairo transport workers began. The strike finally forced the cabinet to take action. It was announced that efforts would be made to resolve the inflation problem, though the workers were also warned that their strike violated the decree of July 1940 and that they would be punished if they did not return to work.

At a meeting of the JTF leadership presided over by 'Abbas Halim that night, it was decided that in light of the promises made by the prime minister the strike would be called off the following day, but that unless the government took action by October 1, the strike would resume. The unions' willingness to resume work on the basis of some rather vague promises was probably enhanced by the fact that just as the strike was beginning, Cairo experienced its first major air raid of the war: thirty-nine people were killed and ninety-three injured. Continuation of the strike in the face of this disaster might have cost the workers public sympathy and brought down upon them the wrath of a government armed with full martial-law powers; so thirty-six hours after the transport strike began, 'Abbas Halim himself drove the first tram car out of the Giza depot.

Nonetheless, an atmosphere of crisis persisted during the next two

29. See CSB, February 1940–December 1941. Some workers complained not only about the high price of food but also about the high price of culture. On June 14, 1941, *al-Nahar* appealed to the management of the Metro cinema in Cairo and to MGM-Middle East to make it possible for workers to see the new hit film *Gone With the Wind*, either by arranging a special low-price showing or by giving union members a 50 percent discount. "Poverty is not an unforgiveable sin," *al-Nahar* noted.
30. CSB, September 15, 1941.

An Independent Workers' Movement **249**

weeks. The tram and bus companies asked for permission to raise fares, citing higher fuel and raw materials costs. Workers at the railway workshops, the Government Press, the electric and water companies, and elsewhere were reportedly thinking of joining the tram and bus workers if the latter struck again on October 1.[31] Thoroughly alarmed and aware of the critical military situation, the British Ambassador Miles Lampson urged the prime minister to take energetic action to control prices and compensate the workers. Something must be done, the British argued, not just out of a sense of "justice and humanity" but also for "stability and security."[32] Finally, on September 29, two days short of the strike deadline, the cabinet decreed a 10 percent wage increase for all workers.

Many transport workers were displeased with the government's decision, so clearly inadequate given the large rise in the price index. At a stormy meeting on September 29, the workers insisted that 'Abbas Halim press for a 50 percent increase, but at another meeting of transport and utility workers the following night, he called for a postponement of the strike pending further talks. It was only with difficulty that he prevailed upon them to wait by intimating that the cabinet was planning to decree another raise above the 10 percent already ordered. Because no further increase was in fact forthcoming until December, unrest continued and labor's discontent was bitterly expressed at meetings of the Joint Transport Federation and in the streets.

The brief strike of September 1941 was a success in that it compelled the government to take the problem of inflation seriously and do something about it. While the cabinet's response did little to alleviate the desperate situation of the workers, many of whom had to fight to make their employers actually pay the decreed increases, the transport workers' willingness to stop work in defiance of martial law proved an important breakthrough. It is not unlikely that a new wave of worker militancy would have arisen as prices continued to soar and German forces approached Alexandria, but in February 1942 the British intervened to install the Wafd in power, a move that helped shore up their control over the country. This act of armed intervention and, its consequences opened a new chapter in Egypt's political history, and in the history of the workers' movement as well.

Ironically, the months that followed the brief strike of September 1941 were for the Cairo tramway workers a period of dissension and

31. CSB, September 23, 1941.
32. FO 371/J3275/18/16, Aide-mémoire to the Prime Minister, September 8, 1941, and Lampson to Eden, September 26, 1941.

250 An Independent Workers' Movement

disunity. An internal conflict broke out which pitted the union's president, Salim Fuda, against a group of oppositionists who came to have the upper hand on the executive board. Fuda was accused of opposing the September strike and of secretly conspiring with management to sabotage it by trying to convince the strikers to resume work before their arrested colleagues had been freed. He was also accused of signing, on his own initiative and without consulting the board, an agreement with the Labor Department on the day the strike ended. Later, all sorts of other charges were also raised to discredit him, and though some were plausible, others were ludicrous. Underlying the conflict, which resulted in Fuda's removal from the presidency and his expulsion from the board, was a struggle for power among the different depots: Fuda was from Shubra, whereas many of his opponents were from 'Abbasiyya. Also, Fuda's ambivalence about the September strike had angered the rest of the leadership, and he appears to have had a falling out with 'Abbas Halim.

Yet, Fuda's long record of service to the union, his age and personal authority made him a formidable opponent even out of office. He continued throughout 1942 to agitate against the leadership that had deposed him by holding meetings of his supporters in a Shubra coffeehouse. It seems likely that by this time Fuda had allied himself with the Wafd, which was now back in power and anxious to break 'Abbas Halim's power over the transport workers. In any case, by the end of 1942, the long struggle had led to a split in the union between those backing 'Abbas Halim's leadership and those backing Fuda and the Wafd.[33] By that time, however, 'Abbas Halim was no longer on the scene. The British had long been concerned about him not only because of his power in the unions, but also because of his close ties to Germany. In August, despite protests from the Palace, the Wafd government arrested 'Abbas Halim and several of his associates and interned them in a government guest house. There he would remain for two years, while his followers sought to maintain control over his client unions.[34]

The two years that followed the break with the Wafd in November 1939 had witnessed a significant revival in the fortunes of the Cairo Tramway Workers' Union. The government of 'Ali Mahir was not unsympathetic to their demands and cannot have been displeased at the tramwaymen's defection from the camp of the Wafd. Their association with 'Abbas Halim had given the tram workers direct access to

33. See *Shubra*, December 2, 1942.
34. FO 371/J79/79/16; FO 141/829/1/60/42, Lt. Colonel R. J. Maunsell, February 6, 1942; FO 371/J3319, 3337, 3409, 3463/38/16, Lampson to the Foreign Office, July 27, 28, August 3, 9, 1942; M, August 3, 1942.

An Independent Workers' Movement **251**

top government officials and a spokesman who could negotiate with company officials as an equal, and his patronage had also helped protect the union and its activists against harassment by the company and the police. 'Abbas Halim's successful effort to win control of all the Cairo-area transport unions had been prompted by his own ambitions, but it had also served the interests of the tramway workers in that the threat of joint action by all the transport workers had to be taken much more seriously by the government. In contrast with the defeats of the 1930s, the tram workers won modest gains in July 1940, and led the struggle which in September 1941 had made it impossible for the government to ignore the suffering of the working people any longer. The economic boom and lower unemployment rate that had accompanied the war and the obvious profitability of the CTC had facilitated that struggle, while the intolerably high rate of inflation had made it vitally necessary.

Conflicts within the union make clear the fear of disunity and the preference for strong, centralized leadership that characterized the organization. Having broken with the former leadership themselves, the new leaders of the CTWU were well aware of the potential threat and the high costs of disunity. They could also not afford to take the stability of the union for granted in a turbulent political and economic situation. Hence, their sometimes excessive suspiciousness, their suppression of all hints of factionalism, and their concern for maintaining a strong, unified executive board. Preservation of the union was the supreme value, and all other virtues (free discussion, open meetings, and public disagreements over policy issues) might be sacrificed to it.

If the years of 'Abbas Halim's leadership had brought the tramwaymen some gains and internal cohesion, there had also been costs. The leadership's deference to 'Abbas Halim had robbed the union of the power of independent decision-making. 'Abbas Halim had had his own agenda, and had been fully prepared—and usually able—to check the militancy of the rank and file when this had been required to implement that agenda. The paternalistic relationship between the workers and 'Abbas Halim had not been confined to the industrial sphere, about which he continued to believe that "there does not exist in Egypt what is called a class system" or class struggle.[35] This viewpoint took on political dimensions as well, for 'Abbas Halim and his associates inculcated loyalty to the king, described as the "protector of the workers" (hami al-'ummal), and told the workers that their slogan should be "God, King and Country"—the same slogan em-

35. al-Ahram, June 16, 1939.

252 An Independent Workers' Movement

ployed by Young Egypt. 'Abbas Halim continued to style himself "leader of the workers," and his cronies announced that "he is the only person whom the workers should acknowledge as their leader."[36]

These attitudes, which were manifested in the deferential utterances of many tram union leaders, were in sharp contrast to the perspective of such unionists as al-Mudarrik and al-'Askari. Even Sayyid Qandil, though friendly with 'Abbas Halim, would never have let him take control of his printers' union or exercise real power within the GFLUKE, much less accept his political proclivities. As the events of September 1941 demonstrated, the Cairo tramwaymen could still at times take the lead in labor's battles. But their industrial militancy was not matched by adherence to a perspective that put their own interests first or insisted that they themselves run their union and choose their own course of action. There were clearly ways in which they benefited from their relationship with 'Abbas Halim, but not having broken with the old patterns of deference and clientage they ended up as a vehicle for his ambitions. As a result, despite their potential power and their willingness to fight, they were left ideologically disarmed—a retrograde element within the workers' movement. Their experience in the years before the Wafd's return to power in 1942 demonstrates the limits and pitfalls of dependency. The failure of the Cairo tram workers to break free and adopt the perspective spreading in other, newer, and more vigorous segments of the labor movement relegated them to a less prominent role. Other groups of workers, particularly in the rapidly expanding textiles sector, would in the following years assume the leadership of the workers' movement and provide models of organization, consciousness, and action.

The stage for the emergence of a new perspective and new leadership had already been set by the time of the Wafd's return to power in February 1942. The workers' movement had taken a great step forward in the previous six years. Recovering from and determined to avoid a recurrence of the disunity and political manipulation of the labor movement that had resulted in its disruption in 1935, a new group of union activists had emerged with a new program for the working class. Responding to new economic, social, and political conditions (examined more fully in the following chapter), they projected a vision of a united and independent labor movement based on strong, dynamic unions, and a conscious and militant working class. They instinctively recognized that the course of industrial development had produced a working class ready to come into its own and

36. See for example CSB, November 27, 1941.

An Independent Workers' Movement **253**

requiring new forms of organization, awareness, and identity. Their understanding of the history of the Egyptian labor movement and their own experiences led them to insist on the necessity for self-reliance, independence from all nonworker parties and personalities, and a new pragmatism in their dealings with government and political forces. This perspective allowed the workers' movement to remain viable and develop even when no upsurge in the national movement was under way and the Wafd was out of power, thereby breaking with the pattern that had prevailed into the 1930s.

This new brand of working class radicalism, of militant trade unionism, took on organizational expression in the GFLUKE. Its leadership, program, strategic vision, and tactical initiatives marked this organization as a departure from all previous attempts to create a national labor federation in Egypt, despite some continuity of personnel with the past. The perspective it developed and put forward clearly resonated with the needs and interests of significant segments of the organized working class and won widespread acceptance. Some groups of workers would certainly continue to cling to old patterns, to seek powerful patrons or the tutelage of the Wafd. Indeed, politically most workers still favored the Wafd which, however tarnished its image, could still claim the allegiance of the masses as the party of nationalism and parliamentary government. Yet, the logic of capitalist development in Egypt and its social consequences made the General Federation's perspective an increasingly powerful pole of attraction for many. Ultimately the GFLUKE found it impossible to survive in the harsh conditions of official repression bolstered by martial law. But it had prepared the ground for the further spread of its vision, and in that fertile soil new and vigorous ideas and tendencies would thrive.

It is in that sense that the years immediately preceding the return of the Wafd to power in 1942 can be said to constitute the end of the beginning of the history of the Egyptian workers' movement. Though still without any recognition in law, still small in size and relatively weak, still largely on the defensive in struggles with the employers, that movement had nonetheless become established as a distinct and legitimate force in the country's economic, social, and political life. A labor movement had emerged and matured to the point where it could begin to break away from deference to and dependence on outside elements, and assert its own self-defined identity and needs. During and after the Second World War the working class and its organizations would grow dramatically in size and social weight. Old and new political forces, each projecting their own program and definition (or negation) of class identity, would vie for the allegiance of

254 An Independent Workers' Movement

the workers in a complex, changing, and crisis-ridden matrix of economics and politics. New challenges would arise to confront Egyptian workers and be met by new responses. But these would be rooted in the struggles and experiences of the previous half-century of the emergence of a workers' movement, and more directly in the developments of the immediate prewar period.

Part Two

Class Conflict and National Struggle, 1942–1954

Chapter VIII

The Formation of an Industrial Proletariat

The 1930s bridge two stages in the development of Egyptian capitalism. Although some large-scale, heavily capitalized enterprises were established even before the First World War, small-scale artisanal production dominated the economy until well into the 1930s. During this decade Egypt experienced a spurt of industrial growth and capital formation. By decade's end, and even more so by the end of the Second World War, large-scale industry and transport, although still employing a minority of the work force, became a major component of the urban economy.

One of the factors facilitating this industrial growth was the gradual increase in Egypt's formal economic autonomy. The enactment of a series of protective tariffs for manufactured goods in the 1930s encouraged the growth of local enterprises engaged in import-substitution production. The decline of industrial imports as a consequence of the depression in the advanced capitalist world decreased competition for the products of Egyptian industry and allowed it to expand rapidly. In 1937 the Capitulations (judicial and economic privileges granted to foreigners) were abolished, allowing Egypt to increase taxes on foreign nationals and thus reduce the advantage of foreign capital over native Egyptian capital operating in the country.

The main stimulus for the growth of large-scale mass production industry, however, was World War II. Import-substitution industries flourished as a result of the sharp decrease in trans-Mediterranean trade. In addition, the presence of the Allied armies in Egypt temporarily created a vastly expanded internal market with sufficient cash to pay for Egyptian manufactures. Many new industries were established while older ones expanded dramatically. A well-informed es-

258 Formation of a Proletariat

timate of the increase in the output of large-scale manufacturing enterprises between 1939 and 1945 put the figure at 40 percent.[1] This figure is, of course, far less than the total increase in wartime production when smaller enterprises are included. Food processing, chemicals, textiles, sisal, jute, metals, dry batteries, paper, and cardboard were among the major growth industries during the war.[2] Industrial expansion was encouraged by the Middle East Supply Center, an agency established to organize production and procurement of supplies for the allied troops in the Middle Eastern theater. It established factories, imported capital equipment, and provided technical training and assistance.

Not only was there considerable growth in Egyptian industry from the mid-1930s to the end of the Second World War, but Egyptian capitalists came to play a larger role in the industrial sector than ever before.[3] The gradual expansion of a native Egyptian industrial bourgeoisie had begun in the period immediately following the First World War. The expansion of indigenous industrial capital during World War II was further stimulated by a law enacted in 1947 requiring that Egyptians own at least 51 percent of the capital of companies operating in Egypt. By the late 1940s, the proportion of the total capital invested in Egypt held by residents of the country had increased substantially as a result of the overall growth of the indigenous Egyptian industrial bourgeoisie and the application of the new law.

Yet, despite the impressive growth of native Egyptian industrial capital, foreign and *mutamassir* capital continued to play a major role in the development of Egyptian industry. Foreign participation in industrial development, though a minor share of total foreign investment, remained considerable. With few important exceptions, industrial enterprises owned by foreigners or *mutamassirun* were generally older, better established, and more heavily capitalized than those managed by Egyptians. Foreign and *mutamassir* capital also controlled some of the major monopolies or semimonopolies in key sectors of the economy. Because of the preponderant power of foreign capital, native Egyptian capital (represented by the Misr, 'Abbud, and

1. Robert Mabro and Samir Radwan, *The Industrialization of Egypt, 1939–1973: Policy and Performance* (Oxford, 1976), p. 82.
2. Great Britain, Department of Overseas Trade, *Commercial Conditions in Egypt* (May 1945), quoted in Mahmoud Anis, "A Study of the National Income of Egypt," *L'Égypte Contemporaine*, no. 261–62 (November–December 1950), pp. 778–82.
3. For a discussion of the formation of the Egyptian bourgeoisie see Tignor, *State, Private Enterprise, and Economic Change*. Although based on the same empirical data, this analysis of the continuing role of foreign capital in the Egyptian economy differs from the thrust of Tignor's work because he ignores the nuances in the relationship between foreign and indigenous capital emphasized here.

Formation of a Proletariat **259**

Yahya groups) had reached a compromise with *mutamassir* capital (represented by the Egyptian Federation of Industries) and foreign capital (for example, Calico Printers and Bradford Dyers). As a result, Bank Misr and its associated industrial enterprises, originally touted as Egypt's nationalist entrepreneurs *par excellence*, lost their purely Egyptian character, although this did not prevent the management of Misr's industrial establishments from invoking it when workers engaged in strikes. Despite the close links between indigenous, *mutamassir*, and foreign capital, most Egyptians continued to regard indigenous industrial enterprises as manifestations of Egypt's struggle for economic independence. At the same time, the continuing dominance of foreign capital in Egypt meant that nationalist sentiment would continue to play a major role as a justifying framework and ideology for workers' struggle, even as Egyptian workers increasingly came into sharp conflict with Egyptian capitalists.

The emergence of large-scale capitalist industry during the 1930s and 1940s had a decisive impact on the size, the character, the public perception, the modes of organization, and the political outlook of the working class. As the industrial working class became more sharply delineated as a specific social group with a particular role in the production process, workers began to see themselves and to be seen by others in a new light. During the interwar years there was usually no distinction made between small employers, owner-operators, and wage workers engaged in urban production and transport. All were considered part of what we have referred to as the urban "working people," and in many trades, including carpentry, upholstery, barbering, handloom weaving, motor transport, laundering, and others, were often members of the same organization calling itself a trade union. However, by the end of the Second World War, although workers in large-scale industry did *not* become a numerical majority of the working class, they became the leading element in the workers' movement, radically changing its character in the process. Nowhere was this process more clearly evident than in the mechanized textile industry.

The Growth of the Industrial Working Class

The increase in the number of enterprises and in the volume of industrial production was accompanied by an increase in the size of the urban wage labor force. Some estimates of the size and character of the Egyptian working class during the pre-World War II period have been given in Chapter II. During the war both British and Egyptian officials began to collect more reliable and differentiated statistics on

260 Formation of a Proletariat

industry and employment. Until then the official government statistical categories reflected and simultaneously reinforced the persistence of popular conceptions of the social division of labor which were rooted in precapitalist and simple commodity production relations and also in the low level of social differentiation between those occupying objectively distinct roles in the production process.

The Allied war effort generated a great demand for new wage labor. At the peak of the military production effort in November 1943, the British forces employed 263,080 Egyptians directly and through labor contractors. This·figure began to decline as the war wound down, and by May 1944 it had dropped to 243,496.[4] These figures understate the impact of the war on industrial employment because they do not include Egyptians employed by civilian suppliers of the military or an estimated 25,000 Egyptians employed by the American armed forces in 1944.[5] Most of the workers employed by the allied armies were unskilled recent migrants from the countryside who could not be expected to return there after the war because of the land shortage. Only among the minority of skilled workers, had a high proportion been urban dwellers before the war.[6]

By early 1944 it was apparent to British officials that the Egyptian economy would not be able to absorb this work force after the war. Some formal efforts were made to find a solution to this problem, including the appointment of Robert Peers as labor advisor to Lord Killearn, the British minister resident in the Middle East. But no concrete measures were adopted by either the British or Egyptian authorities to deal with the high level of unemployment foreseen by Peers. Consequently, postwar unemployment was indeed very high, and it was one of the principal factors shaping the demands and the tone of the postwar workers' movement.

Official government unemployment statistics are utterly unreliable and grossly underestimate the high level of postwar unemployment.[7] Several unofficial estimates agree on a figure of about 250,000 as the number of workers unemployed due to the closure of allied military production facilities and bases, and the withdrawal of military orders

4. FO 921/331 (1945), "Report of the Labour Advisor on Egypt."
5. Anis, "National Income of Egypt," p. 775.
6. FO 921/290/117(1)/44/5 (1944).
7. An official report issued to mark the tenth anniversary of the establishment of the Labor Department indicates that 11,502 workers registered in government employment bureaus in 1945 and 12,039 registered in 1946. Job interviews were arranged for 2,845 job seekers in 1945 and 1,392 in 1946. This less-than-impressive record may explain why so few unemployed workers bothered to register at all. See Egypt, Ministry of Social Affairs, Labour Department, *The Labour Department* (Cairo, 1951), p. 43.

Formation of a Proletariat **261**

from civilian-owned enterprises—a figure nearly equivalent to the total number employed by the allies.[8] This figure should be increased by an indeterminate number of workers who lost their jobs as a result of the resumption of the import trade and the reduction in the size of the local market created by the evacuation of most of the allied troops.

Widespread public concern about the level of industrial unemployment was one of the motivations for the institution of new statistical categories used by the government and a more persistent official interest in obtaining reliable data about industrial production and employment. The *Census of Industrial Production*, first taken in June 1945, is the first official statistical publication which attempts to make meaningful distinctions between those employed in large- and small-scale enterprises. A distinction is also made between factories engaged in producing of new commodities and factories engaged in repairing and servicing. Small shops with an indeterminate production are excluded from the census, (though no precise criteria for exclusion are indicated) and so are the remaining enterprises of the allied forces in Egypt. For the first time, the statistics distinguish between proprietors, monthly paid employees, and daily or piece-rate workers. This division is not entirely satisfactory for the purpose of determining class position because it does not always correspond to a distinction of function within an enterprise. Despite its inadequacies, the attempt of the designers of the *Census of Industrial Production* to develop some meaningful distinctions among those employed in industry is indicative that the existence of an Egyptian industrial working class was beginning to receive some official recognition.

The number of factory employees enumerated in Table 4 does not include those employed by the allied forces. Mahmoud Anis estimates that in 1945 there were 165,000 Egyptian industrial workers employed by the allied forces.[9] Additional Egyptians were employed as drivers, cooks and waiters in mess halls, and at other nonindustrial tasks. If this number is added to the number of industrial employees in all factories during 1945, the new total would be, according to Table 4, 623,000. It is clear from this figure that the total number of industrial workers did not increase between 1945 and 1948, but fell by some 45,000. This may be considered a rough indication of the number of industrial workers who were not integrated into the civil-

---

8. This is the figure given by Issawi, *Egypt*, p. 262. *IM*, May 10, 1946, reports that 206,233 workers formerly employed by the allies had requested unemployment assistance. *WM*, May 1, 1946 reports that nearly 250,000 workers were dismissed from employment by the allied armies.
9. Anis, "National Income," p. 786.

262 Formation of a Proletariat

Table 4 Number of Factories and Employees, 1945–1951

Year	All Factories		Productive Factories	
	Factories	Employees	Factories	Employees
1945	129,231	457,954	22,220	316,144
1948	133,619	577,506	26,743	367,336
1951	124,551	474,832	19,527	307,443

SOURCE: Egypt, Ministry of Finance, Statistical Department, *Census of Industrial Production, 1950.*
NOTE: Productive factories refers to enterprises engaging in manufacture of new products, while all factories includes servicing and repair shops.

ian economy after the war. Of course, the number would have been higher in 1945 and 1946 than in 1948, by which time some of the unemployed industrial workers did find new jobs. If those employed by the allied armies are counted, it is apparent that there was a steady decline in industrial employment between 1945 and 1951, despite the continuing growth of a small number of very large enterprises.

The decline in postwar industrial employment was the result of a conjunctural reduction in demand for war-related commodities—the immediate cause of the drop in industrial employment after 1944—and the simultaneous manifestation of a common structural tendency in the process of capitalist development. The nature of this structural tendency was not understood by Egyptian labor experts, who expected capitalist industrialization to absorb large numbers of peasants leaving the land. The public tended to identify the unemployment problem as principally due to the shutdown of the allied war factories, thus politically the struggle against unemployment was assimilated into the anti-British national struggle. While the closure of war industries was clearly the immediate cause of unemployment, the structural component of the crisis was ultimately much more powerful and long-term.

As Egyptian industry developed, several factors—mechanization, economies of scale, an intensified exploitation of labor, and an increased per capita productivity (in the modern capitalist sector)—led to a decrease in the number of workers required to produce the same commodities, while the purchasing power of the internal market did not expand rapidly enough to absorb the new productive capacity. The textile industry, in particular, was the scene of a sharp struggle over the introduction of new machinery, as workers were made to supervise a larger number of more highly mechanized looms, and consequently the loss of many jobs. This development was, of course, not

Formation of a Proletariat **263**

essentially different than the pattern of capitalist development anywhere else, including the advanced capitalist societies. It was, however, entirely contradictory to the hopes and projections of government officials, economists, and specialists who promoted industrialization in Egypt with the expectation that it would contribute substantially to solving the problem of overpopulation.

In fact, Patrick O'Brien has determined that although the annual rate of increase of industrial output was 6 percent from 1945 to 1957, and the share of manufacturing in the national output rose from 7 percent to 10 percent during that period, aggregate employment in manufacturing decreased 9 percent.[10] The drop was especially sharp in 1952–1957, by which time the economy could have been expected to recover from the effects of the war. Thus the expansion of industrial production that occurred during this period was primarily the result of increased capital, not labor. Therefore O'Brien concluded that industrial development, because of its capital intensive character, had actually contributed to increased unemployment.

Contradictory and Uneven Development

Although the overall growth of Egyptian industry in the 1930s and 1940s is unmistakable, it is necessary to examine the official statistics more closely to appreciate the contradictory nature and limits of this development. Certain statistics are particularly revealing. Over 12 percent of the 117,991 industrial enterprises enumerated in the *Industrial and Commercial Census* of 1947 are hairdressing and beauty salons, and over 4 percent engaged in building maintenance and cleaning. Only 3.6 percent of the enterprises employed ten or more persons, while nearly 49 percent employed no labor other than that of the proprietors and their unpaid families. Sixteen percent operated with no capital at all. Sixty percent of the establishments operated on capital of less than £E 50, while only 3 per cent could marshall capital of more than £E 1,000.

There were relatively few medium-sized enterprises situated between the two extremes—employing 5 to 9 workers with £E 50 to 10,000 in capital. This indicates the weakness of the Egyptian middle bourgeoisie. Indeed, large-scale mass production industry in Egypt was not, for the most part, created by the activity of an entrepreneurial petty bourgeoisie financing and expanding its activities out of its own profits. It was more commonly the product of the agrarian

10. Patrick O'Brien, "Industrial Development and the Employment Problem in Egypt, 1945–1965," *Middle East Economic Papers* (1962), pp. 97 ff.

264 Formation of a Proletariat

bourgeoisie's investments in Bank Misr, in other industrial stocks and bonds, or in foreign and *mutamassir* capital. In order to survive, Egyptian industry had to ally with foreign capital. This explains why Egyptian industrialists, who were among the first to rally to Egypt's national cause, became increasingly distant from the nationalist movement once industrial enterprises were actually established.

These conditions, typical of a subordinate capitalist social formation, must be recognized as the limiting factor which established the boundaries within which working class organization and consciousness developed. Until World War II, workers and independent owner-operators in small, low-capital enterprises constituted the bulk of the membership of the Egyptian trade union movement. This was particularly true in the 1920s and 1930s when trade unionism expanded beyond the transport, public utilities, and tobacco industries, where large numbers of workers and significant capital were concentrated. The organizational weakness of the trade union movement and its political subordination to nonworker patrons during this period was partly attributable to the dispersion of the working class among many small enterprises and the mixed class composition of many trade unions.

However, a contradictory tendency is also apparent in the growth of Egyptian industry in the 1930s and 1940s. While the overwhelming majority of industrial enterprises operated on little or no capital and employed few or no workers, manufacturing was dominated by a small number of firms controlling vast amounts of capital (by Egyptian standards) and employing large concentrations of workers. These included both foreign and Egyptian firms, the latter mainly controlled by Bank Misr and its associated companies. The high concentration of the Egyptian industrial work force is demonstrated in Table 5, which includes only those employed in the production of new commodities as defined by the *Census of Industrial Production*. According to these figures, 58 percent of all industrial production workers in 1947 were employed in only 583 enterprises, each of which employed at least fifty workers. These figures show that despite its overall underdeveloped and subordinate character, the expansion of capitalism in Egypt, as in advanced capitalist countries, led to the creation of a highly concentrated industrial working class. The tendency towards concentration developed very rapidly, as the 42 percent increase in the number of the largest firms (employing 500 and over), between 1944 and 1947 indicates. This is especially remarkable, as this was a period of contraction in total industrial employment as has already been noted.

Formation of a Proletariat **265**

Table 5   Concentration of the Egyptian Industrial Work Force

No. of Employees	No. of Enterprises 1944	1947	No. Employed 1944	1947
Under 10	18,874	23,362	79,000	96,000
10–49	2,778	2,798	58,000	58,000
50–499	523	519	77,000	76,000
500 and over	45	64	102,000	137,000
TOTAL	22,220	26,743	316,000	367,000

SOURCE: Charles Issawi, *Egypt at Mid-Century* (London, 1954), p. 157.
NOTE: These figures are based on the *Census of Industrial Production* for 1945 and 1948. Because the census forms were distributed in 1944 and 1947 respectively, Issawi gave those years as the dates in the table, and it has been left as he constructed it.

The working class of the postwar period therefore included, at one end of the spectrum, a large number of workers employed in very small enterprises producing in labor-intensive and capital-poor conditions where the distinction between employer and employee was often not very sharp; and at the other end, a large, and what is more important, growing number of workers in large-scale mass production industries. In addition to the industrial proletariat enumerated in Tables 4 and 5, many workers in transport, communications, construction, mining and extraction, and a smaller number of commercial workers also labored in enterprises with a high concentration of workers and capital. Although no figures are available, the pattern of dispersion and concentration in these economic sectors is similar to that of industrial manufacturing. The Cairo and Alexandria tramway and bus companies and the Egyptian State Railways, for example, together employed approximately 20,000 workers, by far the largest concentrations of transport workers, while the Shell and Socony Vacuum (Mobil) firms, which dominated the oil industry, employed several thousand workers each.

These contradictory trends of concentration and dispersion of labor and capital in the development of Egyptian capitalism were a consequence of the fact that the capitalist mode of production was introduced to Egypt by European colonialism and imperialism after it was already highly developed. In Europe, the intensification of production based on preindustrial techniques and social relations generally preceded the development of large-scale capitalist industry and helped provide the necessary capital accumulation to finance it. But in Egypt, complete modern capitalist factories were imported

266 Formation of a Proletariat

from Europe, and imposed production techniques and relations which had not developed organically and gradually.

This uneven development had a significant impact on the character of the Egyptian working class by accentuating its heterogeneity. Nominally independent craftsmen and artisans—owners of some means of production but structurally dependent on capital for their livelihoods—wage workers employed in small commodity production, and workers in a variety of informal and marginal occupations comprised the numerical majority of the working class. Their experiences in the under-capitalized, small-scale sector of the urban economy often lead these sectors of the working class to forms of organization and consciousness which denied that urban workers constituted a distinct class with their own interests in opposition to other classes in Egyptian society. The ethos of the artisanal workshop and other forms of petty commodity production was quite different from the consciousness of the emergent urban industrial working class rooted in large-scale mass production industry.

Although the consciousness of these sectors of the working class was an expression of the overall underdevelopment of Egyptian capitalism, there were other workers who were engaged in mechanized, large-scale production. As large-scale capitalist industry expanded, the urban industrial worker became more clearly visible and differentiated from the masses of urban working people, and consequently a shift occurred in the popular image of "the worker." Before World War II this had been a vague and indistinct term referring to all those who worked with their hands as well as many categories of white collar employees. After the war, the mechanical loom operator became the quintessential worker in the popular mind.

Massive postwar unemployment, especially in the textile industry, also contributed to a change in public consciousness about the meaning of the term "worker." Large-scale industry brought not only increased industrial employment, it also made periodic unemployment a regular part of the urban working experience. The term now assumed a problematic connotation as it became clear that the fluctuating requirements of the market played havoc with the security and conditions of employment for workers in modern capitalist industry. The persistence of chronic unemployment and underemployment despite the continuing growth of large-scale industry is an important factor in explaining the continuing unrest and militancy of Egyptian workers in the postwar period. As a consequence of this unrest the issues of industrial development, unemployment, and workers' welfare became major public questions.

"The Labor Question"

Any realistic discussion of the social conditions of Egyptian workers during the postwar period must be rooted in the aggravated impoverishment of the overwhelming majority of all of those considered workers. Workers were certainly poor during the 1930s, but during most of that decade there was almost no fluctuation in the cost-of-living index (Table 6). One of the salient economic effects of World War II was a protracted and dramatic increase in the cost of living. The financial counsellor of the British embassy correctly noted that the official cost-of-living figures indicated in Table 6 understate the extent of the increased cost of living because they are based on officially fixed legal prices rather than actually prevailing market prices.[11]

Any attempt to develop a reliable comparison of wages with the cost of living meets with a morass of statistical confusion and contradictions. Still, the overall conclusion that wages did not keep pace with prices from 1938 to 1945 is inescapable. According to the government's wage survey of 1936 referred to in Chapter II, the average

Table 6 Cost-of-Living Index, 1939–1954
(June–August 1939 = 100)

Year	Maximum for Year	Minimum for Year	Average for Year	Cost of Food Average for Year
1940	122	108	113	112
1941	156	123	138	141
1942	215	159	184	193
1943	257	222	242	263
1944	292	259	279	312
1945	298	290	293	325
1946	291	283	287	310
1947	285	276	279	298
1948	279	283	281	299
1949	273	281	278	302
1950	307	282	294	327
1951	328	312	319	355
1952	331	298	317	347
1953	299	296	296	324
1954	292	281	284	328

SOURCE: AS, 1951–1954.
NOTE: The cost of food represents 45 percent of the cost of living and includes fuel and soap.

11. FO 141/1136/1039/1/46.

268 Formation of a Proletariat

Table 7 Daily Industrial Wage Rates, 1937–1945

| | Daily Rates | |
Year	El-Mallakh	Anis
1937–39	7.7 piastres	7.76 piastres
1940	9	9
1941	11	11
1942	13.3	13.6
1943	12.8	15
1944	16.4	16.43
1945	16.4	16.43

SOURCE: Ragaei El-Mallakh, "The Effects of the Second World War on the Economic Development of Egypt" (Ph.D. diss., Rutgers University, 1954), p. 180; Mahmoud Anis, "A Study of the National Income of Egypt," *L'Égypte contemporaine*, no. 261–62 (November-December 1950), p. 805.

daily wage in industry was 7.8 piastres—8.4 for men and 5.5 for women. Table 7 shows the two most complete series of wage estimates for the war years, and indicates that daily wages increased some 113 percent during the war. The cost of living, however, increased by 193 percent during the same period so that there was, in fact, a substantial decline in real wages.

In July 1945 the government began publication of the semiannual *Statistics of Wages and Working Hours.* The wage rates in this series are based on projecting an average from a sample of one quarter of the industrial establishments covered by the survey. Because these figures include the wages of highly paid foreigners, managers, and proprietors of the enterprises, they are higher than the actual prevailing wages of Egyptian workers. According to these statistics the average weekly wage for a fifty-one hour week in July 1945 was 115 piastres.[12] If the daily rates for that year in Table 7 are multiplied by six, the result is approximately 98.6 piastres, though even the higher official figure would show a significant drop in real wages during the war.

Real wages recovered their prewar levels very slowly. Official Egyptian government statistics give the index of real wages as 86 in January 1949, and 88 in January 1950, using a base of 1938 equals 100.[13] According to a study done by the National Bank of Egypt, prewar wage levels had not yet been regained by 1955, though Charles Issawi disputes this conclusion and argues that wages had returned

12. Egypt, Ministry of Finance, Statistical Department, *Statistics of Wages and Working Hours* (July 1945).
13. Egypt, Ministry of Social Affairs, *The Labour Department* (Cairo, 1951), p. 45.

Formation of a Proletariat **269**

to their prewar level by 1951 or 1952.[14] In either case it is clear that wages failed to keep pace with inflation during, and for some time after, World War II.

The persistence of low wages and poverty among workers motivated several officials in the Labor Department of the Ministry of Social Affairs to express concern about what was widely becoming known as "the labor question" (*mushkilat al-'ummal* or *mas'alat al-'ummal*). Radi Abu Sayf Radi, the director of the Labor Department, authored a study reporting significantly lower wages than those given in Table 7. He used these figures to support his arguments in favor of further labor legislation and social welfare programs for workers because he believed such measures would promote greater productivity.[15] Zaki Badaoui, an inspector in the trade union section of the Labor Department, also expressed dismay about the debilitating effects of low wage levels on Egyptian workers and their families:

> In reality, wages in Egypt are a kind of individual bargain between the proprietor and the worker, always tending towards a small amount. The wage which results is thus insufficient for the workers' subsistence; nonetheless he must, in order to avoid dying of hunger, sell his labor at the price which is imposed on him. This state of affairs has resulted in continuing acute crises dominating the life of the worker and his family.[16]

Most workers in Egyptian industry, even the best paid, lived at or near subsistence levels. According to the United Nations, the minimum desirable number of calories to be consumed by an industrial worker is from 2,550 to 2,650 calories per day. Before World War II Egyptian industrial workers averaged only 2,199 calories per day, and in 1949–50 only 2,300, still well below the minimum recommended level.[17]

In 1945 a small number of the largest industrial enterprises began to provide cafeterias for their workers. These facilities were generally unpopular with workers, either because the food was too expensive

14. Charles Issawi, *Egypt in Revolution* (London, 1963), p. 193.
15. Radi, "Mushkilat al-'amil," p. 36. Radi reports an average wage of eight piastres per day in establishments employing five or more persons in 1941. Many categories of workers earned considerably less than the average. These included silk and wool hand loom workers, brass workers, barrel and plate makers, furniture and upholstery workers, carpenters and wood turners, metal workers, fitters, smelters, tailors of ready-made clothing, and hand loom weavers of carpets and kilims.
16. Zaki Badaoui, *Les problèmes*, p. 58.
17. El-Mallakh, "The Effects," pp. 36, 137.

270 Formation of a Proletariat

or of poor quality. At the Misr Dyeing Mill in Hilwan, south of Cairo, breakfast and lunch at the company-operated cafeteria might cost as much as 30 percent of the daily wage. Khaireya Khairy, who visited the mill as part of her research for a study of the nutritional standards of Egyptian workers, noted that on the day of her visit in 1945 a lunch consisting of potatoes, rice, and bread cost one piastre. Since wages in the mill ranged from eight piastres per day for a minor under fifteen years of age to fourteen piastres per day for an adult, it is clear why such a relatively expensive and nutritionally deficient meal would be unpopular.[18] Similarly, at the Misr Spinning and Weaving Company, most workers did not use the company cafeteria, and a report based on a survey of worker attitudes noted that, "It is apparent that a large number are not receiving proper diet because of low income and high number of dependents."[19]

Housing was generally unsanitary and overcrowded. In Cairo and Alexandria some workers' quarters had a density of over 50,000 inhabitants per square kilometer.[20] El-Gritly described the houses of industrial workers as "nothing but filthy hovels where masses of human beings are herded in utter disregard of hygiene or the dignity of man."[21] Such conditions prompted the uncharacteristically candid and blunt observation from the British embassy that, "The vast majority of Egyptian workmen live in conditions of degrading squalor."[22]

In Mahalla al-Kubra, Dr. 'Abd al-Wahid al-Wakil inspected workers' housing at the Misr Spinning and Weaving Company in the late 1930s and found that:

> The majority of these habitations, far from being habitable by man, is not suitable to shelter animals. Likewise it is the custom that each group of five or six workers rents a single room in a building in one of whose corners they set down their food which they have prepared in their villages; then they lay down together stretching out on the floor or on mats of the worst kind. The great majority of these houses are not equipped with toilets, running drinking water or bathrooms, and therefore they satisfy their needs outside. There results a pile of repugnant matter of every sort. In that manner they live in an atmosphere corrupted by nau-

18. Khaireya Khairy, "Nutritive Aspect," pp. 33–35.
19. William Carson, *The Mehalla Report* (Badr es-Sheyn, 1953), p. 3.
20. Badaoui, *Les problèmes*, p. 68.
21. A.A.I. El-Gritly, "Structure of Modern Industry in Egypt," *L'Égypte Contemporaine* no. 241–242 (November–December 1947), p. 533.
22. FO 371/41380/J2671 (1944) "Report on Conditions of Labour and Trade Unions in Egypt."

Formation of a Proletariat **271**

seating odors in which flies swarm; the room is also sometimes rented out to one group during the day and to another during the night.[23]

During and after World War II, Misr and a few of the other large companies began to provide housing for some of their workers. This new construction partly alleviated the overcrowding and squalor, but most workers considered it inadequate for their needs. Those who lived in company-provided housing also resented management's around-the-clock supervision and the loss of their personal independence.

Malnutrition and overcrowded and unhygienic housing resulted in a high rate of morbidity among workers. The most common diseases were parasites, tooth decay, anemia, and rickets. These maladies were compounded by unhealthy and unsafe working conditions. To all this one must add that the rate of industrial accidents doubled between 1933–34 and 1942, largely as a result of the increased use of machinery.[24] Industrial speedup may also have been a factor in increased accidents since employers sought to increase the pace of work to maximize the return on their capital investment. Zaki Badaoui confirms the prevalence of unsafe and unhealthy conditions in Egyptian industry:

Industries in Egypt are, in the main, unhealthy, dangerous and uncomfortable . . . the worker who performs his task under these conditions is the future victim of numerous maladies.[25]

The report of a visit to the Misr Spinning and Weaving mill, where working conditions were officially touted as among the most advanced in Egypt, noted that 90 percent of the 2,000 women employed there suffered from tuberculosis.[26] This was probably not untypical of the textile industry as a whole. Even the minimal health and safety regulations in effect were poorly, if ever, enforced. Occupational diseases were also endemic in tanneries and cotton ginning mills.[27]

A low level of literacy is the classical accompaniment to poverty, overcrowding, and disease, and Egypt is no exception in this regard. In 1937, 18.6 percent of all Egyptians over the age of five were literate,

23. "Report sur la situation des ouvriers de la Société Misr Pour la Filature et le Tissage à Mehalla El-Kebir," quoted in Badaoui, Les problèmes, pp. 68-69.
24. El-Gritly, "Structure of Industry," p. 542.
25. Badaoui, Les problèmes, p. 73.
26. Mustafa Kamil Munib, "Ahwal al-'amilat fi al-mahalla al-kubra," al-Tali'a, March 15, 1946, p. 12.
27. El-Gritly, "Structure of Industry," pp. 544–45.

272   Formation of a Proletariat

while in 1947 this figure rose to 22.8 percent.[28] In Cairo and Alexandria the proportion was about 50 percent. In 1944 the government enacted a law requiring all enterprises employing more than thirty workers, of whom half were illiterate, to provide classes for their instruction. According to Badaoui, this law was enforced only in the Giza Governorate,[29] probably a reference to the Eastern Tobacco Company where workers enjoyed a very high rate of literacy because their union had established literacy classes in cooperation with the company. In 1950 there were still 1,234 illiterates out of a work force of 3,357 at Eastern Tobacco, but by 1952 there were only 285 illiterates out of a total of 3,538 workers.[30] Badaoui insisted that this was exceptional, and estimated that only one in 120 industrial workers was literate.[31] Such a figure is not inconceivable in localities like Mahalla al-Kubra and Kafr al-Dawwar, though it seems too low for Cairo, Alexandria, and their suburbs. Still, literacy was unusual among industrial workers, even in these areas, and Taha Sa'd 'Uthman's estimate that 10 percent of the textile workers in Shubra al-Khayma could read is probably more representative of the truth.[32]

Although there is no way to measure it concretely, there can be no doubt that grinding poverty, malnutrition, poor living and working conditions, disease, and a lack of education took an enormous amount of energy and vitality out of the Egyptian working class, and considerably reduced its capacity to struggle in the trade union and political arena. In many cases the mere struggle for survival imposed the narrowest horizons on workers and absorbed all of their energies. Only a heroic minority was able to overcome these conditions and to participate regularly in trade union and political activity. For those activists, the material conditions of the working class were both a motive force and a constraint on the struggles which they waged.

Textiles: The Leading Sector

The growth of an urban proletariat expanded the potential for independent trade union organization and formation of a workers' movement no longer subject to the hegemony of political forces whose vision of the working class was informed by paternalism and corporatism. The first attempts to build such a movement after the de-

28. El-Mallakh, "The Effects," p. 148.
29. Badaoui, Les problèmes, p. 84.
30. Hussein Aly Orphy, "An Analysis of Welfare Programs in Egyptian Industries: A Tobacco Factory Case Study" (B.A. thesis, American University in Cairo, 1955), p. 21.
31. Badaoui, Les problèmes, p. 83.
32. Taha Sa'd 'Uthman, interview, October 28, 1980.

Formation of a Proletariat **273**

mise of the CPE and the CGT in 1924 have been described in Chapter VII. These efforts were the first steps in a process of transition which came to fruition during and after the last years of World War II. The weakness of the efforts of the late 1930s is at least partly attributable to the fact that a stable work force rooted in mass production enterprises was still in the process of formation. Although those recruited to work in the new large-scale industrial production enterprises during the late 1930s and 1940s often came from peasant backgrounds, they adapted to industrial life and began to participate in industrial struggle much more quickly than their employers imagined was possible. Workers in large-scale industry, particularly the textile industry, came to form the core of the Egyptian workers' movement. They were the bearers of a militant and politically independent trade unionism that became an increasingly powerful force within the workers' movement after the Second World War.[33]

As in many subordinate capitalist economies, the textile industry emerged as the leading sector in the expansion of Egyptian industry in the 1930s and 1940s. According to the *Census of Industrial Production* of 1945, 117,272 of the 316,144 employees in manufacturing enterprises were textile workers, and 9,425 of the 22,220 manufacturing enterprises were spinning and weaving mills. Thirteen of the forty-five enterprises employing over 500 workers were textile mills; the highest concentrations of industrial workers in Egypt were located in the textile sector. The largest of these by far was the Misr Spinning and Weaving Company in Mahalla al-Kubra established in 1927. By the end of World War II, this mammoth industrial agglomeration employed well over 25,000 persons. The work force of the Filature Nationale in Alexandria grew from around 1,200 after World War I to 8,000-10,000 during and after World War II. The Misr Fine Spinning and Weaving Company, established in Kafr al-Dawwar in 1938, employed some 9,000 workers by 1952. The Misr Bayda Dyers Company, also established in Kafr al-Dawwar in 1938 as a joint enterprise of Misr and the British Bradford Dyers Company, employed from 2,000 to 3,000 workers in the postwar period. The Sibahi Spinning and Weaving Company, established in 1937, employed 5,500 workers in three mills in Alexandria and Shubra al-Khayma. In 1947–48 these seven enterprises alone employed over 50,000, or somewhat less than half of all the textile workers in Egypt. Many other textile

33. There are some prominent exceptions to this generalization. The most significant are the Eastern Tobacco Company in Giza, the Cairo transport workers, and the Shell and Suez Canal Company workers. In each case there are particular reasons for the political character of the trade union leadership in the enterprise which will be discussed further on.

274 Formation of a Proletariat

firms in Alexandria, Shubra al-Khayma, and other Cairo suburbs employed from 1,000 to 2,000 workers during and after the war. The only other industrial establishments of comparable size were the sugar refinery at Hawamdiyya south of Cairo, the Eastern Tobacco Company in Giza, and the Shell refinery in Suez, each of which employed approximately 4,000 workers.

The precise number of workers in any textile mill fluctuated wildly with the ups and downs of the industry and the price of cotton. In addition, the progressive mechanization of the industry after the war continually reduced the number of workers required and made the insecurity of employment one of the major reasons for the high level of industrial conflict in this industry. Egyptian workers refused to accept the notion that profit and other market considerations were a legitimate reason to dismiss an employee from his job, and the successive waves of layoffs and dismissals in the textile industry in the postwar period led to extremely sharp struggles over job security and stability of wages. In 1947, of the 137 officially recorded strikes, eighty-eight (or 66 percent) occurred in the textile industry;[34] and in 1950, thirty-three of forty-nine officially recorded strikes (67 percent) were in the textile industry.[35] Official strike statistics for other years are not available, though the absolute number of strikes as well as the proportion of strikes in the textile industry was probably higher in 1945 and 1946.[36]

Textile workers comprised 39,500 of the 149,000 union members officially recorded in 1950; 32 percent of the industry was unionized.[37] But the figure for union members is far too low because it includes only those whose dues were fully paid and excludes workers whose unions were not officially recognized or had been dissolved by the government, such as the Shubra al-Khayma Mechanized Textile Workers Union. The only other sector of the economy where the number of unionized workers even approached the size of the textile industry was the much smaller transport and communications sector where 35,700 workers (89 percent of the industry) were union members.[38]

By the end of World War II, therefore, the textile industry had eclipsed transport and public utilities as the center of gravity of the Egyptian workers' movement. Transport workers remained a very im-

---

34. FO 371/80580/JE1735 (1950) "Translation and Summary of a Report by the Ministry of Social Affairs on its Work during the First Ten Years of its Existence, 1939–1949."
35. *The Labour Department*, p. 29.
36. See Chapter X for a discussion of strikes in Shubra al-Khayma in 1945.
37. *The Labour Department*, p. 36.
38. *Ibid.*

portant component of the movement, but they no longer provided the same overall leadership that had characterized their role up to the Cairo transport general strike of September 1941. This role was assumed by the textile workers concentrated in three main centers—the Delta, the Cairo suburbs, and Alexandria—each with a specific character resulting from the relations between labor and capital and the activity of political forces seeking to play a role in the workers' movement in each locale.

The Delta's textile industry was dominated by the giant mills of the Misr Company. During the period of the textile industry's rapid expansion in the 1930s, the Misr management consciously attempted to avert the possibility that large concentrations of urban workers might organize themselves and engage in economic and political struggles that might threaten the security of production and profit. The showpiece of Bank Misr's industrial empire, the Misr Spinning and Weaving Company in Mahalla al-Kubra, began operations in 1931 and within a few years was the single largest industrial enterprise in Egypt, employing 15,000 workers and capable of handling the entire textile manufacturing process from spinning to dyeing. The decision to locate this industrial complex in Mahalla was justified by such factors as climate, the availability of a cheap tract of land, and the town's long history as a center of handloom weaving. But more important was management's determination to control its work force by locating the factory far from the major urban centers and deliberately and selectively recruiting illiterate, unskilled peasants with no prior experience of industrial life rather than skilled and experienced factory workers who might be insubordinate and organize themselves to improve wages and working conditions. The same policy was applied at other factories such as Misr Fine Spinning and Weaving at Kafr al-Dawwar.

The Misr management was apparently quite willing to accept the lower efficiency that this policy entailed as the following comparison demonstrates. When the Misr factory at Mahalla was established, it employed eighteen to twenty-four workers per 1,000 spindles (fifteen to eighteen by the 1940s) in contrast to the United States and Europe where only five to eight workers were required. In pre-World War II Egypt the standard was one worker for every power loom, as opposed to one for every two, four, or even six looms abroad. During and after the war the disparity between Egyptian and international levels of labor intensity began to diminish. However, some textile mills continued to employ far more workers than were actually needed to offset the very high rates of turnover and absenteeism. Given the cheapness and abundance of labor in Egypt, this policy was not unfeasible, at

276 Formation of a Proletariat

least temporarily, because it made sense for many capitalists to seek to isolate their workers from the political turbulence and social currents of the time and offset lower productivity with a docile work force.[39]

In fact, peasants uprooted from their former social millieu did prove to be relatively docile for many years. Former peasants were grateful for a steady cash income, and in exchange were, at first, willing to accept the rigid and arbitrary discipline of the factory. Fikri al-Khuli, the son of a peasant family who began work at Misr Spinning and Weaving in Mahalla al-Kubra in 1929 at the age of 12, recorded the reactions of many of his fellow workers to the discipline of the factory in his autobiography:

> It is better here in spite of hard conditions, because one is sure of constant work and sure of earning a bit to give his mother and brothers. . . . If it weren't for the damned machines everything would be fine. When we were in the village we'd never have ten piastres in our hands all at once, or even five. It's true that we miss our home, but that is the way to make a living. Let's just pray that God keeps us all healthy and that everyone will get back safely to his family.[40]

On another occasion al-Khuli reported the response of his fellow workers to a new company regulation forbidding workers to resist physical abuse by their foremen. Some argued that workers should strike back if they were struck. Another responded:

> Anyone who can't put up with things as they are had better go back to his village before he comes to a sticky end. We've only come here to support our mothers and families and we've got to be prepared to be walked over for their sakes.[41]

39. William Carson, "The Social History of an Egyptian Factory," *Middle East Journal* 11 (1957):336; Frederick Harbison and Ibrahim Ibrahim, "Some Labor Problems of Industrialization in Egypt," *Annals of the American Academy of Political Science* 305 (May 1956):117–18; Eman, *Coton*, pp. 77, 101. Many years earlier Vallet had noted that despite their lack of experience and the need to watch them constantly, cotton gin operators "prefer casual laborers to experienced workers who would reject the low wages." *Contribution*, p. 94.
40. Quoted in Sawsan el-Messiri, "Class and Community in an Egyptian Textile Town" (Ph.D. dissertation, Hull University, 1980), p. 287. Fikri al-Khuli's autobiography is contained in a lengthy appendix to this dissertation. It was written while al-Khuli was in jail as a result of his activity in the communist movement and translated into English by el-Messiri.
41. *Ibid.*, p. 391

Formation of a Proletariat **277**

As long as those employed in the textile mills considered themselves to be temporary workers who had accepted industrial employment only to earn a certain sum of money after which they intended to return to their villages, the formation of trade unions and the growth of class consciousness made slow progress. At Misr Spinning and Weaving there was a 100 percent turnover in the work force between 1927 and 1943, while absenteeism averaged 10 percent per day during this period.[42] These are indications that it took several years before a relatively stable work force, which saw its future in industry, was formed.

The steady influx of former peasants without industrial experience into the ranks of the textile work force temporarily weakened the solidarity and cohesion of the workers as well as their capacity to resist the factory management. In many cases the new proletarians were easily manipulated and dominated by their employers until they gained enough experience to assert themselves and struggle for their interests. Village rivalries between workers from diverse and traditionally antagonistic localities were a common source of conflict among workers, dividing their ranks and inhibiting the growth of cohesive unity against the company. At Misr Spinning and Weaving, for example, peasants from the villages of Sharqiyya province across the Nile River from Mahalla al-Kubra were known as *sharqawiyya*, and were ostracized and looked down upon by the local workers known as *mahallawiyya*. Until the mid-1940s the *sharqawiyya-mahallawiyya* rivalry among the workers was the dominant social conflict in the mill.[43]

Workers at the Misr mills faced an additional obstacle to the development of collective organization and action not shared by those employed by foreign firms. Although Bank Misr and its associated industrial enterprises had substantially lost their "national" character by the end of the 1930s by allying themselves with both foreign and *mutamassir* capital, they were still widely regarded as the bulwark of Egyptian economic nationalism. Therefore, any disruption of production or other anticompany activity was unlikely to win the support of nationalist politicians or other nonworkers. This attitude was apparent in the response to the first major strike at Misr Spinning and Weaving, which occurred on July 18, 1938, in reaction to the introduction of a new work regime of three eight-hour shifts in place of

42. Ikbal Bahtimy, "The Mehalla el-Kobra Cotton Industry" (B.A. thesis, American University in Cairo, 1952), p. 17.
43. El-Messiri, "Class and Community," p. 262.

278 Formation of a Proletariat

two eleven-hour shifts. Since workers were paid by the piece, this amounted to a sharp wage cut. Some 1,500 weavers struck, demanding a raise in piece rates so that eight hours' production would yield the same wage as eleven hours' production at the old rate.[44] Many strikers were arrested, and fifty-five were brought to trial and convicted. The court's decision included the following admonition:

> The Correctional Tribunal of Mahalla al-Kubra finds that it must express its strong regret and its astonishment at this foolish action on the part of the weaving workers of the Misr Spinning and Weaving Company at Mahalla. It finds that they have departed from the fulfillment of their duty toward a company which helped them, supported them and opened a door for them which they might enter while they were still ignorant. . . . The workers must, in light of this situation, cooperate with the company for production and sacrifice every personal interest in order to serve the fatherland, develop its commerce, and not lose the fruits of that gigantic effort due to the influence of dangerous opinions which we do not like to see among the workers, whatever the reason. . . . Whatever the circumstances and causes—strikes and destruction have nothing to do with Egyptians. These acts are completely repulsive to them by virtue of their education, their circumstances and their religion, which is based on forgiveness, cooperation and nobility of character. This young company, one of the pillars of our current renaissance, did not overwork the workers and did not ask more than their capacity, wages being determined in accordance with output.[45]

The court's paternalistic assessment of the character of the Egyptian worker was soon shown to be quite mistaken. Despite the internecine feuding among the workers, the harsh discipline of the companies, and the appeals and threats in the name of nationalism, textile workers did come to feel and act based on their common interests. By the end of World War II, not even a myopic provincial judge could ignore the development of strong feelings of class solidarity and willingness to organize and act on these feelings on the part of many textile workers. Even at Mahalla al-Kubra, where pressures against the development of class-based organization and collective action were strongest, the *mahallawiyya-sharqawiyya* conflict receded in importance by the late 1940s. By 1952 Carson noted that,

44. According to *al-Ahram*, July 19, 1938, shifts were twelve hours before the strike.
45. Quoted in Eman, *Coton* pp. 183-84.

Formation of a Proletariat **279**

"Negative pressure has now created a feeling of solidarity and common cause in the labor force and antagonism toward the company."[46]

The Cairo suburb of Shubra al-Khayma, located on the road leading north to Banha, was another major textile center. Although it originally offered some of the same incentives for the location of mechanized textile mills as the Delta towns of Mahalla al-Kubra and Kafr al-Dawwar, the industry rapidly developed a radically different character there. In the early 1930s Shubra al-Khayma was a rural low-wage area with a large number of handicraft weavers in the vicinity. By the middle of the decade however, it was rapidly becoming an industrial center with a high concentration of mechanized textile mills: in 1937 there were ten factories (mainly textile mills), its population was approximately 250,000, and it was beginning to suffer a housing shortage and overcrowding due to the rapid growth of its wage labor force.[47] From this time forward, Shubra al-Khayma became clearly identified as a "social problem" whose origins were rooted in the industrial character of the area.

Shubra al-Khayma's proximity to Cairo and the persistently high level of industrial struggle in its textile mills projected it into the national consciousness as the exemplary expression of the contradictions created by the expansion of industrial capitalism in Egypt. This image was intensified because of the character of the textile industry there. Most of the mills were medium-sized, poorly capitalized enterprises, and a large proportion of the owners were foreigners and *mutamassirun*. Labor struggles against such enterprises were less susceptible to the nationalist admonitions employed against Misr employees. Therefore, local nationalist political figures and government officials often gave important support to the demands of the Shubra al-Khayma textile workers. The nationalist character of workers' economic struggles in Shubra al-Khayma enhanced the workers' organizational capacity and the national political impact of their activity.

There is no doubt that in some important respects Shubra al-Khayma and its workers were exceptional. Nowhere else was the working class so militant and so politically visible. No other group of Egyptian workers developed the same high level of sustained independent organization. Nowhere else was the struggle between competing ideological trends inside the labor movement so sharp and so fully documented. In all these respects there is a certain similarity between the Shubra al-Khayma textile workers and the metal workers

46. Carson, *The Mehalla Report*, p. 2.
47. *al-Balagh*, March 2, 1937; *Shubra*, May 5, 1938.

280 Formation of a Proletariat

of prerevolutionary Petrograd. In fact, Egyptian communists consciously envisaged the textile workers of Shubra al-Khayma and other Cairo suburbs such as Zaytun, Matariyya, Imbaba, Dar al-Salam, and Hilwan as the vanguard of the Egyptian working class. The communists linked up with leading trade union activists in Cairo's textile suburbs and devoted most of their efforts in working class organizing to the textile workers. The considerable, if temporary, successes they achieved, however, would not have been possible if the textile workers themselves had not begun to perceive themselves in more clearly class-based terms and to reject the paternalism and corporatism that characterized trade union organization during the interwar period. Nonetheless, regardless of certain similarities the analogy between Egyptian textile workers and Russian metal workers should not be pressed too far. Indeed, one of the failures of the Egyptian communists was precisely a tendency to rely on such mechanical analogies beyond the point of their usefulness.

Two institutions established in 1937 indicate the working class character of the Shubra area—the weekly newspaper *Shubra*, which appeared on March 25, 1937, and the Shubra al-Khayma Mechanized Textile Workers' Union (SKMTWU). *Shubra* was managed by political figures and did not, during its early years, express the views of any significant organized segment of the area's workers. Nevertheless, from its first issue the contents of *Shubra* indicated that the paper's editors were aware of the growing importance of industrial workers in the area. They attempted to appeal to them by writing about their complaints and grievances, and at least on the formal level, defending their interests. The contents of the paper reflected the existence of a clearly indentifiable worker constituency in Shubra al-Khayma with a distinct identity and interests.

'Isam al-Din Hifni Nasif, the socialist intellectual who had been a leading contributor to the leftist journal *Ruh al-'Asr* in 1930, was one of the regular contributors to the early issues of *Shubra*. He hoped to make *Shubra* into a vehicle of expression for workers of the area. But he was thwarted by the political intrigues of the paper's owner 'Abd al-Hamid 'Abd Allah who turned the paper into an instrument for promoting Prince 'Abbas Halim's efforts to reestablish himself as the leader (*za'im*) of the Egyptian workers. Nasif's objective was achieved only in 1942 when the SKMTWU took control of *Shubra* and began to publish it as the organ of the union.

The organization of the SKMTWU is the most important example of the changing consciousness among textile workers and the difference this made in trade union organization and political orientation. It is worth examining the experience of this union and its organizers in

Formation of a Proletariat **281**

some detail, not because it is typical, but because it highlights several analytically important aspects of the process of capitalist development and working class formation. Because of its high concentration of mechanized textile workers and its proximity to Cairo, Shubra al-Khayma was a vanguard region where contradictions, very much present elsewhere but for a variety of reasons less fully developed, received their fullest expression.

In the early 1930s an attempt to establish a mechanized textile workers union in the Shubra area failed. From this experience, activists learned that if a union were based on more than one mill and its leadership dispersed in more than one work place it would be more difficult to break the organization by firing its key leaders.[48] This was the beginning of the regional form of trade union organization that was to characterize the textile industry of suburban Cairo.

The first recorded mention of a regional trade union among Shubra area textile workers was in November 1937, when the Commission to Organize the Working Class (COWM) granted recognition to the SKMTWU.[49] Although the COWM was nominally under the leadership of Prince 'Abbas Halim, the driving force in the organization was Yusuf al-Mudarrik, whose primary commitment was to the principle of the independence of the trade union movement from all nonworker elements. Mahmud al-'Askari, the general secretary of the SKMTWU and its representative to the COWM executive committee, was a strong ally of al-Mudarrik within that organization. The two of them, along with Taha Sa'd 'Uthman who joined the SKMTWU in 1938, were to become the first effective communist worker leaders in Shubra al-Khayma. Thus from its inception, the SKMTWU was closely associated with tendencies in the workers' movement which sought to build trade unions as an expression of the class-based identity of workers. From very early on in their activities the organizers of the SKMTWU, developed the view that the ultimate efficacy and survival of their organization, as an expression of the needs of workers, required that they remain independent from nonworker political figures seeking to control the movement for their own interests. This was the basis for their early attraction to socialist ideas.

The nationalist component of the struggle of the Shubra al-Khayma workers is highlighted by the leading role of a significant number of educated and skilled Egyptian workers. The career of Taha Sa'd 'Uthman is in many ways typical of these leading worker activists in Shu-

48. Taha Sa'd 'Uthman, *Nidal 'ummal al-nasij al-mikaniki bi'l-qahira* (Cairo, 1946), pp. 6–8.
49. FO 141/660/357/8/37.

282 Formation of a Proletariat

bra al-Khayma.[50] In the early 1930s, most of the skilled workers and foremen in the Shubra al-Khayma mills were non-Egyptians. After 1936 the Egyptian government required the mill owners to begin hiring Egyptians for these positions, and it encouraged Egyptians to acquire the necessary skills by establishing tuition-free technical secondary schools. In January 1938, after graduating from such a school in Bani Suwayf, 'Uthman and four of his school mates became the first Egyptians to be employed as foremen at the Modern Textile Mill (Masna' Nasij al-Aqmisha al-Haditha) owned by Henri Pierre in Shubra al-Khayma, where Mahmud al-'Askari and several other SKMTWU leaders were already employed. At first 'Uthman and his mates showed no interest in joining the union and were prepared to cast their lot with management. Then the management reneged on a promise to increase the new foremen's wages after an initial training period. 'Askari approached the five and told them that if they threatened to strike they would receive the support of the other workers. They did threaten to strike and received their wage increases, and this convinced them to join the union. By the end of the year 'Uthman had become president of the union (a post he held until 1943); he subsequently served as treasurer, sergeant-at-arms, and secretary of the editorial board of *Shubra* after it was taken over by the union.

Incidents such as this made it clear to Egyptian skilled workers and foremen that they would not be accorded the pay or status given to foreigners in similar positions without a struggle. Consequently, they generally did not identify with management. They thought of themselves as workers and were accepted as such by other workers. Skilled workers and foremen were disproportionately represented among the leadership of the textile unions in Shubra al-Khayma and several other localities. They formed the backbone of the independent trend in the textile workers unions and were an important factor in building the leadership of the textile workers in the entire trade union movement.

The common nationalist sentiment uniting the original organizers of the Shubra al-Khayma textile workers is further highlighted by the fact that Taha Sa'd 'Uthman was not initially a leftist. Between 1935 and 1938 he was a member of the Society of Muslim Brothers. He was a prominent and capable organizer for the Society and a close personal friend of its founder and General Guide, Hasan al-Banna. After 'Uthman became active in the SKMTWU, Hasan al-Banna released him from his organizational responsibilities to the Brothers to free him to

---

50. Taha Sa'd 'Uthman's biography, unless otherwise indicated, is based on interviews recorded on October 28, November 5, and December 15, 1980.

Formation of a Proletariat **283**

carry out his trade union duties.[51] 'Uthman continued to share the world outlook of the Brothers until at least early 1943, when he began to draw close to the communist movement, and he maintained close personal relations with Hasan al-Banna until 1946.

The location of Shubra al-Khayma, the character of its textile industry, the existence of Shubra, and the quality of the textile workers' leadership all combined to make the SKMTWU one of the most militant, best organized, and politically independent trade unions in Egypt by the early days of World War II. This enabled the union to confront the textile mill owners successfully when workers' jobs were threatened because of economic pressures created by the war. Because of a shortage of raw material, many textile mills began laying off workers. At Henri Pierre an entire shift, including the SKMTWU leaders, was dismissed. In response, the union called a hunger strike. After four days, Prime Minister 'Ali Mahir issued a military order prohibiting further firings without government approval and restoring the jobs of the Henri Pierre workers.[52]

This successful hunger strike, undoubtedly inspired by the earlier hunger strike of trade union leaders led by Yusuf al-Mudarrik, fostered the rapid growth of the union. Despite a setback during the second half of 1940 and the first half of 1941 as a result of the dismissal of Taha Sa'd 'Uthman and thirteen other executive board members from their jobs, the union was well poised to resume and expand its activities in late 1941 and early 1942.[53]

Alexandria was the third center of Egyptian textile production in addition to suburban Cairo and the Delta. There the strength of independent trade unionism fell between the levels achieved in the other two centers. The nationalist motive was present in Alexandria, as it was in the Cairo suburbs, and conditions in the mills were sufficiently poor to motivate considerable discontent. For example, the Sibahi mill was commonly considered to have the worst working conditions in the industry. But the critical variable that explains the absence of the same high level of worker organization and struggle characterizing Shubra al-Khayma and the Cairo suburbs in general seems to be the lower concentration of conscious political forces playing a role in the workers' movement there. Alexandria is very much Egypt's "second city," and consequently political activists of all kinds paid less attention to it than to Cairo. This neglect also explains why there is relatively little information available about the

51. 'Askari, U, November 8, 1976.
52. *Ibid.*, November 1, 1976; *al-Ahram*, September 17, 1939.
53. Taha Sa'd 'Uthman, interview, October 28, 1980; 'Uthman, *Nidal*, pp. 10–11.

284 Formation of a Proletariat

workers' movement in Alexandria, although it is possible to form a general impression that the character of the textile workers' struggle there was more like that of Cairo than that of the Delta towns.

Despite the considerable variety in the experiences and the level of organization of textile workers in the three principal centers of the industry, it is nonetheless clear that taken as a whole they had emerged by the middle of the war as the leading force in the trade union movement. Although most Egyptian workers continued to be employed in small, under-capitalized shops, the demands and forms of organization of the textile workers set the tone and dominated the public image of the post-war workers' movement. Not surprisingly therefore, this industry was one of the key arenas of struggle among the political forces that emerged and contended for the leadership of the post-war workers' movement.

Chapter IX

The Struggle for the Trade Unions during the War

As a new war in Europe began to appear increasingly inevitable, Great Britain moved to safeguard exposed areas of its empire. The Middle East was a particularly vulnerable region. Militarily it was threatened by the Italian presence in Libya and Ethiopia. It was also politically insecure because the British had reneged on their promises of self-determination and independence made during and after World War I. Transjordan and Palestine remained subject to mandatory regimes sanctioned by the League of Nations. Egypt and Iraq exercised only a limited form of independence while remaining under British tutelage. France, Britain's closest ally, held Syria and Lebanon under mandate.

The Anglo-Egyptian treaty of 1936 was the cornerstone of the British effort to secure a stable internal situation in Egypt. The British had encouraged King Fu'ad to bring a Wafd government to power because the Wafd was the only party that could negotiate an agreement with Britain which might be accepted as legitimate by the Egyptian masses. All the traditional parties, except the Nationalists, had joined with the Wafd in negotiating the treaty, and they hailed it as the harbinger of full Egyptian independence. Although the treaty did achieve some political benefits for Egypt, it did not appreciably alter the fact that Britain remained the ultimate power in Egypt's political life, and the British ambassador, Miles Lampson, later Lord Killearn, retained extensive influence. Significant limitations on Egyptian sovereignty remained in effect. The British secured the right to maintain military bases along the Suez Canal for twenty years and continued to garrison troops in the heart of downtown Cairo until 1947. The treaty also preserved British rule over the Sudan, which many Egyptians re-

286 Struggle during the War

garded as an integral part of Egypt. Not surprisingly, most Egyptians regarded the treaty as unsatisfactory and well short of achieving full independence or national sovereignty. Though it remained the most popular party in Egypt, the Wafd's credibility was damaged permanently by criticism of the 1936 treaty, much of which came from pro-German political forces.

In the 1930s important sections of the intelligentsia in the colonial and semicolonial countries viewed fascism primarily as a militant form of nationalism. In Egypt some of the *effendiyya* abandoned the secularism and liberalism of the Wafd as a result of their dissatisfaction with the 1936 treaty and the continuing economic and social crisis of the country, and began to embrace more radical nationalist ideologies. Fascism also had a certain appeal, and because it was imported from Italy and Germany, the rivals of Egypt's British overlords, it seemed to those who despaired of the Wafd's failed liberal parliamentarianism an appropriate ideology to guide a resolute struggle against the British occupation. The relatively small Young Egypt (Misr al-Fatat) group led by Ahmad Husayn was the principal Egyptian political organization that attempted to translate fascism into an Egyptian idiom, but more diffuse pro-German sentiment was widespread at the outbreak of the war.

There was, therefore, an actual threat that some Egyptians, including Young Egypt and many in King Faruq's personal coterie who were attracted to the Germans as a means of ridding Egypt of British domination, might use the war as an occasion to press the demand for full independence. The Wafd, however, remained solidly committed to liberal and secular nationalism for several reasons. First, because it had been the chief Egyptian party to the 1936 treaty it felt obliged to support Britain in the war. Many Wafdists expected that in exchange for wartime cooperation with Great Britain, Egyptian demands for full independence would be given favorable consideration at the conclusion of the hostilities. Second, it was also firmly opposed to the king's attempts to enhance his own power at the expense of Parliament because the Wafd saw itself as the parliamentary party *par excellence*. The Wafd opposed the Germans both on ideological grounds and because its internal enemies, principally the Palace and Young Egypt, sought to ally with them. Thus despite its historic opposition to British domination, in the particular conjuncture of the Second World War the Wafd became the most pro-British force in Egypt. With Rommel's troops advancing across North Africa towards Egypt and King Faruq and his closest advisors harboring pro-German sentiments, the Wafd remained the only popular and reliably antifascist force with whom the British could cooperate to secure Egypt's internal front. Therefore, on February 4, 1942, British tanks surrounded the Royal Palace, while Lord Killearn delivered an ultimatum to King Faruq demanding that he dismiss the cabinet and ask Mustafa al-Nahhas to form a new Wafd government.

The approach of World War II also saw a new development in British policy toward labor movements throughout the empire. As part of the effort to ensure internal security before the impending conflict, British colonial policy makers began to experiment with influencing and coopting labor movements rather than opposing and repressing them. In 1938 the colonial secretary appointed a permanent labor advisor for the first time, Granville St. John Orde-Browne. These initiatives were further developed after the entry of Labor party ministers into the government. During the war the Trades Union Congress seconded British trade unionists to serve as labor advisors to the colonial governments of Nigeria, Sierra Leone, the Gold Coast, Trinidad, British Guiana, and Palestine. By the middle of the war labor departments had been established in the governments of many colonies and dependencies, and British colonial policy makers began to encourage the enactment of labor legislation, including the legalization of trade unions. Since Egypt was not formally a British colony, such measures could not be unilaterally undertaken there. Although there is no direct evidence available indicating a preponderant British role in the formulation and development of the Egyptian government's labor policy during World War II, there can be no doubt that the Wafd's approach to this question was substantively influenced by the new British attitude toward colonial labor movements.

Pro-Wafd and other nationalist writers tend to view the Wafd regime of 1942–1944 as the "real beginning" of the Egyptian trade union movement and all that preceded this period as prehistory.[1] These authors see the trade unions as a gift of the Wafd government to the workers who ought therefore to have been cooperative and reasonable in return. In fact, the history of the struggle for trade union independence from the Wafd (and 'Abbas Halim) in the 1930s should raise serious doubts about this interpretation of the relationship between the Wafd and the labor movement. The experiences of Wafd tutelage in the 1930s had made increasing numbers of trade unionists reluctant to accept Wafd control of the the labor movement in the 1940s. For similar reasons they were also unwilling to accept the patronage of Prince 'Abbas Halim and the British embassy. Although

1. Radi, Adwa', is the clearest example of this perspective. It is also implied more subtly in Abdel Raouf Abou Alam, The Labor Movement in Egypt (Washington, D.C., 1955). The author served as labor and social affairs attaché in the Egyptian embassy in Washington and was a member of a prominent Wafdist family.

288 Struggle during the War

the Wafd, the prince, and the British maintained some influence in the labor movement during and after World War II, more and more trade unions began to opt for independence from nonworker political parties and figures so that by the end of the war the independent trend was ascendent, though not entirely dominant.

When the Wafd returned to power on February 4, 1942, most of the trade union apparatus it had built up and supported in the 1930s was no longer functioning. Nonetheless, a majority of workers warmly supported the return of the Wafd. Muhammad Hafiz, president of the executive board of the Congress of Government Workers and a leader of the General Union of Royal Press Workers since its establishment in 1936, recalls in his memoirs:

> When the incident of February 4, 1942 occurred we didn't know that it was the English who returned al-Nahhas and we went out in demonstrations to support al-Nahhas Pasha. Afterwards we learned that what happened was an act of aggression against us and the King. Not the corrupt King, the King simply as a symbol of Egypt.[2]

Support for the Wafd in its capacity as Egypt's only mass nationalist party was still very widespread among workers at this time. The most organized and most solid base of support was among the government employees. This was the result of the concessions granted to these workers during the Wafd's previous tenure in office. Consequently, government workers, including contingents from the Maintenance Department, the Egyptian State Railway repair shops, and the Royal Press were prominent in the mass demonstrations that greeted the new government. Mustafa al-Nahhas and the new minister of finance, Makram 'Ubayd, addressed the workers, acknowledged their support, requested them to form delegations to make their grievances known to the government, and told them to return to work.[3] The Wafd was glad to have the support of the workers, but did not wish to see them mobilized and making demands on the government.

The Wafd and the Shubra al-Khayma Textile Workers

Just as the Wafd was returning to power the Shubra al-Khayma textile workers were in the midst of a sharp struggle to obtain for themselves the 10 percent cost-of-living allowance (COLA) the government of Hu-

2. "Mudhakkirat al-hajj Muhammad Hafiz, za'im 'ummal al-hukuma," quoted in Radi, *Adwa'*, p. 271.
3. *al-Balagh*, February 7, 18, 1942.

Struggle during the War **289**

sayn Sirri had enacted following the Cairo transport general strike.[4] All employers were legally required to pay the COLA, and large monopoly corporations generally obeyed the government's decree. But medium and small-sized firms, both Egyptian and foreign, including most of the Shubra al-Khayma textile mills, did not. Consequently, there were struggles at many individual enterprises over this issue.

At the Beso mill (Masna' Nasij al-Qahira), a Greek-owned enterprise employing nearly five hundred workers, the workers presented management with a list of demands, including the 10 percent COLA, and announced a fifteen-day deadline after which they would resort to "all methods of struggle." In response, Beso locked the workers out on January 1, 1942. Mahmud al-'Askari and seven Beso workers then installed themselves in the SKMTWU headquarters and announced a hunger strike, threatening to employ any means necessary to win their demands.

During the hunger strike the Wafd was returned to power, and along with most other workers, those from the Shubra al-Khayma textile mills welcomed the new government warmly. When 'Abd al-Hamid 'Abd al-Haqq, the new Wafd minister for social affairs, learned of the strike he quickly intervened on the side of the workers, and promised to protect their interests. Although the workers were favorably impressed with 'Abd al-Haqq's intervention, they did not leave the matter in his hands and continued the hunger strike. The "Committee of Hunger Strikers" then organized a march to the Wafd headquarters, the Sa'dist Club, in the Garden City section of Cairo on February 11 to press its demands. Textile workers from Shubra al-Khayma, Imbaba, Zaytun, Matariyya, 'Ayn Shams, and other suburban Cairo textile centers participated in the demonstration.

The list of demands the committee formulated reflects clearly the importance of the nationalist factor in the political orientation of the textile workers' leadership at this time. In addition to the 10 percent COLA, the marchers demanded equal pay and treatment for Egyptians and non-Egyptians. The demands explicitly applied to both production workers and supervisors, and included a call to replace foreign advisors with qualified Egyptians whenever possible. It is clear from these demands that discrimination against Egyptians in favor of foreigners was a major issue at all levels of employment in the textile mills of Shubra al-Khayma and suburban Cairo.

When the march reached the Sa'dist Club the workers occupied the

---

4. The account of this struggle is based on 'Askari, U, June 27 through September 5, 1977.

290   Struggle during the War

meeting room of the Wafd Executive Committee, and demanded to meet with Mustafa al-Nahhas. Al-Nahhas Pasha refused to meet the workers, claiming that he could not discuss matters with Mahmud al-'Askari amidst thousands of workers. Instead, he sent 'Abd al-Fattah al-Shalaqani as his surrogate; he was to become the deputy for Shubra al-Khayma in the parliament that convened on March 30, 1942. Al-Shalaqani brought with him the draft text of Military Order No. 239 of 1942, establishing Conciliation and Arbitration Committees, which the government proposed as the vehicle for resolving the workers' grievances. On the basis of commitments made by the Wafd leadership, the demonstrators left the Sa'dist Club, giving the government forty-eight hours to fulfill its promises. Al-Nahhas issued an order reopening the Beso mill, and the workers jailed in the course of the struggle were released. These workers returned to their jobs and received forty-five days back pay for the time of the lockout, and the 10 percent COLA was implemented.

This impressive victory enabled the SKMTWU to expand its activities and increase its membership. By April 1942 there were elected union stewards in at least sixteen mills, and a regional branch was established in the town of Mit Halfa.[5] This growth was reflected in the change of the name of the union to the General Union of Mechanized Textile Workers in Shubra al-Khayma and Cairo (GUMTWSKC).

The initiative in these events was in the hands of the textile workers, not the Wafd. Despite the strong nationalist feelings of the SKMTWU and the generally pro-Wafd sentiments of the majority of the textile workers and union members, the union was careful to maintain its independence from the Wafd. The fact that the Wafd depended on a popular majority for its strength, and always received it in any reasonably free election, made it more susceptible to mass pressure than other parties. This made a substantive difference in the outcome of many labor struggles. For example, the Conciliation and Arbitration Committees often ruled against the interests of workers, but in Qalyubiyya province (which included Shubra al-Khayma) the head of the committee was Fu'ad Shirin, a Wafdist. Under his administration, by virtue of a combination of his own nationalist sentiments and the independently organized strength of the textile workers, many of the demands raised in the demonstration of February 11, 1942, in addition to the COLA, were imposed on the textile mill owners.[6]

5. al-Wajib, April 6, 13, 20, 1942.
6. 'Askari, U, September 5, 1977.

The Legalization of Trade Unions

The Wafd did not intend to allow independently organized workers to determine its labor policy, and it implemented a number of prolabor measures designed to win the support of workers while taking the initiative back into its own hands. The most important of these was the enactment of Law 85 of (September) 1942 granting explicit legal recognition to trade unions for the first time in Egypt. The extent of trade union organization and activity prior to this time ought to leave no doubt that formal recognition did not provide the primary impetus for the growth of trade union activity in Egypt. However, because legal recognition had been a trade union demand for several years, the passage of this law was widely regarded as a workers' victory, and it was taken as an indication that the "people's ministry," as the Wafd dubbed its regime, was encouraging the formation of trade unions and taking the side of the workers in disputes with their employers. This impression was strengthened by the passage of Law 86 of 1942, which required large employers to provide accident insurance for their employees.

One of the most potent instruments of the Wafd's labor policy was the establishment of the Conciliation and Arbitration Committees referred to above. These committees went far beyond the nonbinding government mediation in labor disputes which had been an established practice since 1919, for now the government could use the force of martial law to impose binding arbitration. Moreover, because the committees were chaired ex *officio* by provincial governors, and their decisions had to be ratified by the Ministry of Social Affairs, the political element in the resolution of labor disputes became more prominent. Workers expected that decisions made by the "people's ministry" would reflect their interests. This expectation was most frequently met when workers' organizations were prepared to press their demands independently of the Wafd as in Shubra al-Khayma. These committees also occasionally ruled in favor of workers under non-Wafd governments when the level of labor militancy became too intense to manage without granting concessions, or when the government found it politically beneficial to pressure a foreign-owned enterprise, as in the cases of the Suez Canal Company and the Shell Oil Company discussed in Chapter XI.

The enactment of these measures represented the first substantial implementation of the Wafd's often repeated promises to workers. There were three reasons for this change in policy. First, because the Wafd was weakened and somewhat discredited by the 1936 treaty and the events of February 4, 1942, it needed more than ever before to

292 Struggle during the War

secure active popular support to fend off attacks from its rivals. The trade unions represented an important urban constituency that could be easily mobilized for demonstrations and other mass activities, and for this reason, the Wafd had always viewed trade unions as a strategic asset. Now unions became an even more important mass base for the party as its general popularity began to be threatened by the rise of new political forces. Second, in order to retain the confidence of the British, the Wafd had to prevent disruptions of production and communications vital to the allied war effort. In this regard the Wafd was helped by the new British policy toward colonial labor movements which made legal recognition and conciliation an acceptable strategy. Finally, increased pressure from workers, such as the demonstration organized by the Shubra al-Khayma textile workers, made it clear that the costs of not placating worker demands might be unacceptably high.

The Wafd's military orders and legislation succeeded in winning the support of most Egyptian trade unionists for the party, though the party abandoned neither its traditional view of the labor movement nor its attempts to contain and blunt the thrust of labor struggles and assert exclusive control over the movement. The announcement of the formation of the Conciliation and Arbitration Committees was accompanied by warnings that the government had noted that "nonworker elements" (a veiled reference to communists) were infiltrating the workers' movement and inciting the workers to disturbances and violations of public order. The Conciliation and Arbitration Committees were established explicitly to put an end to strikes and other industrial disorders, and the government sternly announced that workers now had no excuse to resort to strikes to obtain their demands. All complaints were now to be processed through the apparatus of the committees, and strikes would be dealt with harshly.[7]

The legalization of trade unions was hedged with qualifications limiting their effectiveness. Workers in a single enterprise were given the right to form unions, but federations of unions including workers in more than one enterprise were expressly forbidden. This latter point meant that most unions would remain fairly small and therefore organizationally and financially weak. The law also required that the police be notified of all meetings of union executive boards and all general assemblies of the membership. Furthermore, unions were prohibited from engaging in any political or religious activity. Agri-

7. *al-Ahram*, March 24, 1942; *al-Muqattam*, March 27, 1942; *al-Balagh*, March 24, 1942.

Struggle during the War **293**

cultural workers, personal servants, and government employees were not permitted to join unions at all. Law 85 was, therefore, a double-edged sword. It encouraged the formation of trade unions and permitted the trade union movement to expand into many previously nonunionized sectors of the economy. Simultaneously, it extended the government's direct control over the trade union movement and attempted to keep the movement weak, divided, and dependent.

Law 85 also gave the state extensive regulatory powers over the trade unions. All unions were to be registered and supervised by the Ministry of Social Affairs. This formal legal control was further expanded by the manner in which 'Abd al-Hamid 'Abd al-Haqq used his power as minister of social affairs. In September 1942 he established a fund to aid workers and their families in the event of the death or incapacity of a worker through accidents, illness, or old age,[8] and in March 1944 the ministry began granting direct subsidies to "qualified" trade unions.[9] Thus the Wafd's control of the government machinery overseeing trade unions and its prerogative to allocate the government's financial resources provided it with an unrivaled ability to dominate the many small and inexperienced trade unions.

The Wafd government was able to increase its influence over the unions of government workers simply by ignoring the legal prohibition on their existence. Indeed, the government circumvented its own law when the organizations of government workers called "clubs," were headquartered in a building provided by the Wafd, and united under the leadership of Muhammad Hasanayn, the Wafdist deputy for Bulaq.[10] Government workers also established a general federation called the Congress of Government Workers, headed by Muhammad Hafiz, one of the most loyal pro-Wafd trade union leaders.

Following the passage of Law 85, the trade union movement grew dramatically so that by May 1944, there were 350 registered trade unions with approximately 120,000 members.[11] These figures, like all official figures, tend to underestimate the number of union members because they include only fully paid-up members as reported to the government. In the absence of a dues check-off system, many union participants might not be counted. For example, the number of members attributed to the GUMTWSKC is 271, though according to newspaper reports 3,000 workers attended the union's general assembly of

8. *al-Yara'*, February 4, 1943.
9. FO 371/41379/J1562 (1944).
10. Radi, *Adwa'*, p. 108.
11. FO 371/41380/J2671 (1944) "Report by Mr. T. E. Evans, Second Secretary of H.M. Embassy in Cairo, on Conditions of Labour and Trade Unions in Egypt."

294 Struggle during the War

April 26, 1942, and 1,000 workers attended the April 1943 meeting.[12] These figures also do not include workers belonging to unions officially dissolved by the government. Still, despite the discrepancies, the general tendency indicated by the figures in Table 8 is undoubtedly accurate. Most of the newly established unions were based in relatively small enterprises. The law required a minimum of only fifty members to form a union, and in fact, nearly one-third of existing unions at the end of 1943 had fewer than 100 members. In many cases neither the leadership nor the membership of newly formed unions possessed any knowledge of trade union principles or practices.

Table 8 Union Membership as of December 31, 1943

Membership	No. of Unions	Membership	No. of Unions
Less than 100	96	600–699	3
100–199	87	700–799	4
200–299	48	800–899	7
300–399	19	900–999	4
400–499	14	Over 1,000	19
500–599	10	TOTAL	311

SOURCE: FO 371/41380/J2671 (1944).

Reassertion of Wafd Leadership over the Trade Union Movement

In addition to its ability to deploy the state apparatus to control trade unions, the Wafd was also able to offer organizational facilities most unions could not provide for themselves—an office, legal counsel, negotiating clout with employers, and access to the state. One of the most important tools of the Wafd in its attempt to reassert hegemony over the trade union movement was its sponsorship of a weekly workers' newspaper. The first such newspaper was *al-Wajib (The Task)*, which appeared briefly in late 1941 and early 1942 as a cooperative effort of the Shubra al-Khayma Mechanized Textile Workers' Union and the Egyptian General Printers' Union, whose leadership was closely identified with the Wafd. (The textile workers' union withdrew from this project in order to establish its own newspaper about which more will be said later.) On May 6, 1942, a new weekly, *al-Yara' (The Firefly)*, replaced *al-Wajib* as the Wafd labor organ; Zaki Abu Khayr, secretary of the Egyptian General Printers' Union, served as its managing editor. Its offices were located in a building rented by

12. *Shubra*, April 30, 1942; *al-Yara'*, April 24, 1943.

Struggle during the War **295**

the Wafd as a trade union center. In June 1942 the printers' union announced it was moving its union office to the premises of al-Yara' and assuming responsibility for publishing the paper.[13]

At the same time al-Yara' began displaying an increasingly open identification with the Wafd. For example, on June 15 'Abd al-Hamid 'Abd al-Haqq's picture appeared on the front page for the first time. This effort to promote the Wafdist leader most directly responsible for workers' affairs became a regular feature of subsequent issues. In the same issue Ahmad Farhat, a leader of the printers' union and a regular contributor to al-Yara', published an article entitled "The Workers' Nationalism" in which he declared that workers were firm supporters of the Wafd's principles. In a later article Farhat confirmed his identification with the Wafd's labor policies by denouncing evildoers who asserted that strikes were a legitimate means to protest and win workers' demands.[14]

Until the fall of 1942 there is almost no labor news of any substance in the pages of al-Yara' except for reports of the activities of several printers' unions: an absence that indicates the weakness of the Wafd's organizational influence in the trade union movement when it first came to power. The normal practice would have been for trade unions close to the Wafd and the editors of al-Yara' to report their activities in its pages, but even the announcement that al-Yara' would become a general Wafd labor newspaper, rather than an organ of the printers' union, did little to broaden trade union participation in its pages.

This situation changed however, as the Wafd's influence in the trade union movement grew dramatically in response to the passage of Law 85 recognizing trade unions. This enabled al-Yara' to embark on an intensive campaign to win labor support for the Wafd. The full text of the law was printed in three successive issues along with articles expressing more open and enthusiastic identification with the Wafd than ever before.[15] From October to December 1942, al-Yara''s pages contain many reports of the organization of new unions, the demands of various unions, and their routine organizational activities. The regular appearance of news of trade unions other than that of the printers indicated that after the enactment of Law 85 union leaders had become more willing to support and identify with the Wafd.

At the same time articles attacking "alien elements" in the workers'

13. al-Yara', June 22, 1942.
14. Ibid., August 3, 1942.
15. Ibid., September 21, 28, October 1, 1942.

296 Struggle during the War

movement began to appear with some regularity.[16] These articles are veiled in their accusations, and it is difficult to establish with certainty whom they are directed against. Because 'Abbas Halim was still under internment at this time, the most likely target would appear to be the revived Egyptian communist movement which was just beginning to become active among workers.

By February 1943, al-Yara' was publishing a regular column on "workers' affairs" featuring shop reports and summaries of executive board meetings from a large number of trade unions. Also reported were the activities of trade unions formerly associated with 'Abbas Halim, such as Muhammad Ibrahim Zayn al-Din's Chauffeurs' Union and Muhammad Hasan 'Amara's Cairo Barbers' Union.[17] There was broad support for the Wafd among the Alexandria trade unions. Sayyid Nada, president of the Filature Nationale union, which became the largest union in Alexandria after its reorganization in February 1943, expressed strong agreement with the Wafd's ban on strikes for the duration of the war.[18] Government employees continued their firm support of the Wafd.

The Wafd continued to strengthen its organizational control over the growing Egyptian trade union movement during the latter part of 1943 and 1944 through the creation of local trade union federations in a large number of provincial centers. The legal prohibition on establishing trade union federations was circumvented by calling these organizations "Workers' United Fronts." In any case the Wafd was not about to enforce the law against organizations designed to enhance its political strength. The Wafd was able to dominate these "Workers' United Fronts" by having the local Wafdist parliamentary deputy or a prominent Wafdist lawyer elected president. Fu'ad Siraj al-Din, who had replaced 'Abd al-Hamid 'Abd al-Haqq as minister of social affairs in June 1943, was generally elected honorary president of these federations "in his personal capacity." Regional trade union federations of this sort were established in Alexandria, Mansura, Daqahliyya, Damanhur, Sharqiyya, Port Said, Gharbiyya, Suez, Damietta, and Asyut.[19] Many of the provincial trade unions were composed of small numbers of workers in services or small-scale production. For them Wafd leadership offered access to resources which they could never have commanded on their own.

16. *Ibid.*, November 19, December 12, 1942; January 21, 1943.
17. *Ibid.*, February 4, 1943.
18. *Ibid.*, March 11, 1943.
19. *Ibid.*, December 19, 1943; March 2, 9, June 10, 19, 26, July 10, 31, August 21, September 25, 1944.

Resistance to Wafd Domination

Despite the overall success of the Wafd in entrenching itself in the trade union movement following the passage of Law 85 of 1942, there were also signs of dissent from the Wafd and its leadership methods at the very moment of its greatest strength. These dissenting voices were a reaction to the Wafd's insistence that the trade union movement should be organizationally and politically subordinated to it. Under Wafd leadership the working class was not allowed to develop any independent organizations or political perspective. The Wafd insisted on upholding its corporatist view of Egyptian society rejecting the existence of contradictory class interests between workers and employees.

We have already seen that although the GUMTWSKC was generally supportive of the Wafd, it was also careful to maintain its organizational and political independence. The union took a major step in consolidating this independence by establishing its own newspaper rather than continuing to collaborate with the Wafd in the publication of *al-Wajib* and *al-Yara'*. From the experience of publishing *al-Wajib*, Mahmud al-'Askari and the GUMTWSKC leadership became convinced of the value of a regular newspaper. The union arranged to rent the license to publish *Shubra* from its owner, 'Abd al-Hamid 'Abd Allah. The first issue of *Shubra* published by the GUMTWSKC appeared on April 30, 1942.

Shubra provided a stable, legal means of expression for the GUMTWSKC and served not only as an organizational tool for the union's internal affairs, but also as an instrument to broaden its political vision and extend its influence to other sectors of the working class. This broader political perspective was indicated on the masthead of *Shubra*, which after May 7, 1942, carried the subtitle "a weekly workers' political newspaper." Control of an independent newspaper enabled the union to express not only its general support for the Wafd, but also its reservations which would not have been possible to declare openly in the pages of *al-Yara'*.

The most important immediate difference between the GUMTWSKC and the Wafd concerned the *sine qua non* of trade union action, the right to strike. On June 25, 1942 *Shubra* published a "warning" to workers to beware of being misled by those who said that the strike weapon should not be employed so long as the Wafd was in power. Although they were not identified by name, the most prominent advocates of this view included the leading Wafd politicians attempting to guide the trade union movement, 'Abd al-Hamid 'Abd al-Haqq and

298 Struggle during the War

Muhammad Hasanayn.[20] The willingness to publish this statement, which challenged both the Wafd's short-term policy of outlawing strikes for the duration of the war and its more permanent policy of restraining worker militancy and expressions of class struggle, is a clear indication of the limited and conditional support the GUMTWSKC gave the Wafd. This support was not permitted to obstruct the workers' pursuit of their own interests as defined by their union leadership in light of their experience. The Wafd did not have the power to determine GUMTWSKC policy in the same way that it (and Prince 'Abbas Halim) had been able to manipulate the trade union federations of the 1920s and 1930s.

This point was further underscored by the GUMTWSKC's forthright protest against the removal of 'Abd al-Hamid 'Abd al-Haqq as minister of social affairs. 'Abd al-Haqq did not diverge from the traditional corporatism of the Wafd, and he fully supported the ban on strikes for the duration of the war. Nonetheless, he was popular among trade unionists and attentive to their concerns. Indeed, Mustafa al-Nahhas feared that 'Abd al-Haqq might be developing an independent mass base of support which he might use to vie for supremacy in the Wafd. Consequently, in June 1943 'Abd al-Haqq was transferred to the Ministry of Pious Foundations (*awqaf*), and Fu'ad Siraj al-Din became minister of social affairs. This change was widely perceived as an antiworker maneuver among trade unionists, especially because Siraj al-Din was a large landowner and one of the most conservative figures in the Wafd leadership. In response, the GUMTWSKC openly challenged the Wafd by calling for a national one-day strike of textile workers to protest 'Abd al-Haqq's removal.[21] There is no evidence to indicate the effectiveness of the strike, but it is clear that the sentiments of the GUMTWSKC were widely shared. Even *al-Yara'*, while welcoming Siraj al-Din to his new post, expressed regret at 'Abd al-Haqq's removal.[22] The issue remained a subject of concern among trade unionists for several months.[23]

Another indication of the Wafd's weakening position in the trade union movement was the reappearance of articles in *al-Yara'* warning against the influence of "alien elements" in the workers' movement.[24] Zaki Abu Khayr's description of the activities of these "alien elements" charged that they were joining political parties and benev-

20. For examples see their statements in *Shubra*, July 9, 1942 and *al-Yara'*, July 3, 1944.
21. 'Askari, *U*, October 3, 1977.
22. *al-Yara'*, June 10, 1943.
23. See for example, al-Nahhas' remarks on this subject at a gathering of representatives of Alexandria trade unions quoted in *al-Yara'*, September 7, 1943.
24. *al-Yara'*, September 7, 13, 1943.

Struggle during the War **299**

olent or cultural associations, and attempting to speak in the name of workers on some occasions and of intellectuals on others.[25] This accusation describes, in a crude and distorted form, the activities of communist intellectuals seeking to make contacts with workers at this time, and indicates that the Wafd was feeling increasingly threatened by these activities.

The Wafd suffered a serious defeat in the trade union movement when it attempted and failed to organize the workers at the Eastern Tobacco Company in Giza, the largest single enterprise in metropolitan Cairo. The Wafd-led Cairo Tobacco and Cigarette Workers' Union established a branch in Giza in order to organize the Eastern workers, but the pro-Wafd forces could not prevail.[26] The union was eventually organized by Fathi Kamil, a strong opponent of Wafd domination of the trade union movement, about whom more will be said further on.

The Wafd was particularly weak among the greater Cairo area trade unions. The April 24, 1943 issue of al-Yara' reported that thirty Cairo trade unions were headquartered in its offices, a clear indication that these unions were in the Wafd's organizational orbit. By the latter part of 1943, Cairo area unions were rarely mentioned in al-Yara''s trade union reports, and none of the largest unions in the Cairo area, except for the associations of government employees, were organizationally linked to the Wafd. The unions of the Shubra al-Khayma mechanized textile workers, Eastern Tobacco Company, the Cairo Tramway Company, the Egyptian General Omnibus Company (Thornycroft), and the Société Générale des Sucreries et de la Raffinerie d'Égypte in Hawamdiyya all kept their organizational distance from the Wafd. None of them accepted the free office space the Wafd provided on the premises of al-Yara'. The constraints entailed in such an arrangement were significant enough that these larger unions with sufficient funds to support their own offices chose to avoid dependence on the Wafd.

The Wafd's weakness in the Cairo area was not due to lack of effort, for as early as April 1943 Muhammad Hasanayn has been engaged in promoting himself as the titular head of the Cairo trade union movement though without success.[27] One year later, on April 28, 1944, Yusuf al-Mudarrik led a delegation of trade union presidents to meet with Fu'ad Siraj al-Din to convince him to help establish a Cairo Confederation of Trade Unions (Rabitat al-Niqabat). They suggested that

25. Ibid., September 13, 1943.
26. Ibid., August 23, 1943.
27. al-Muqattam, April 12, 1943.

300 Struggle during the War

Siraj al-Din would become honorary president of the confederation and that a worker would be chosen president. This was al-Mudarrik's way of attempting to ensure worker control over the proposed confederation while simultaneously ensuring the support and protection of the Wafd for an ostensibly illegal organization. At first Siraj al-Din accepted this proposal, but later changed his mind and insisted that Muhammad Hasanayn would have to be the president "because the president of the confederation would come into direct contact with government officials and a worker was not suitable for that."[28]

The news of the formation of the confederation and Muhammad Hasanayn's selection as president were announced simultaneously.[29] Consequently, what had originally been an initiative led by al-Mudarrik, who certainly had not intended to hand over the leadership of the Cairo area trade unions to the Wafd, was made to look like a Wafd-inspired proposal. However, opposition to Wafd domination was too strong for this maneuver to succeed. Only four trade union leaders attended the May 14 meeting of the Confederation of Trade Unions, which was packed by one hundred rank-and-file workers affiliated with the Wafd trade union center in the offices of al-Yara'. No independent unions were represented, and several large unions were conspicuously absent.[30] At its July 15 meeting attended by representatives of ninety-eight unions, the Cairo Confederation adopted a constitution that represented a victory for independents favoring greater freedom from Wafd control.[31] At a subsequent meeting Wafd supporters had to resort to rigged elections to secure the victory of their candidates.[32] British diplomatic reports as well as interviews with several trade union activists confirm that there was strong, widespread opposition among Cairo trade unions to the Wafd's attempt to dominate the confederation.

The decisive blow to Muhammad Hasanayn's attempt to control the Cairo area trade unions came on October 8, 1944 with the ouster of the Wafd from power. At this point, trade unions quickly abandoned the Wafd, and many unions and federations who had chosen Fu'ad Siraj al-Din as honorary president now substituted King Faruq.[33] In July 1944, T. E. Evans, second secretary of the British embassy in Cairo, reported that the Wafd-controlled trade unions had a membership of 47,000, whereas politically independent unions had

28. Mudarrik, *TU*, March 15, 1968.
29. *al-Yara'*, May 13, 1944.
30. FO 371/41319/J3702 (1944).
31. FO 371/41318/J2666 (1944).
32. FO 371/41318/J3024; FO 371/41318/J3099 (1944).
33. FO 371/41319/J3702 (1944).

Struggle during the War **301**

a membership of another 47,000, and unions loyal to 'Abbas Halim a combined membership of 3,750. Evans predicted that 25 percent of those unions loyal to the Wafd would drop their allegiance once the Wafd left office.[34] This percentage seems to be too conservative an estimate of the extent to which the Wafd's support in the trade union movement depended on its control of the government. Many unions continued to support the Wafd, and the Wafd's return to power, as an expression of their overall support for the national-democratic movement. After October 1944, however, there is no evidence of any trade union maintaining the kind of organizational link with the Wafd which had been typical of Wafd-union relations up to that point. Some less significant unions may have maintained such relations, especially in the provinces, but from this point on the Wafd's organizational role in the labor movement diminished dramatically.

Announcement of the Cadre for Government Workers[35]

The government employees who comprised one of the Wafd's strongest bases of support and whose leadership was deeply and sincerely committed to the Wafd quickly abandoned their open organizational affiliation to the Wafd, and demonstrated their support for the new government. Muhammad Hafiz expressed the problem in clear and instrumental terms:

> We had belonged to a federation headed by Muhammad Hasanayn Pasha, the Wafdist deputy for Bulaq. The meaning of this was that the federation would be attacked, as well as all the unions which belonged to it. And of course we would be attacked with it. So we went out congratulating the government of Ahmad Mahir. . . . In this way we made our [political] ideology one thing and our [economic] demands another.[36]

This assessment of the situation shows that Muhammad Hafiz remained loyal to the Wafd and to his nationalist convictions. He was also aware that as a leader of a relatively large group of strategically located workers he could wield significant bargaining power with the new government, which was in great need of popular support because it was composed entirely of minority parties with no mass base of any consequence.

34. FO 371/41380/J2671 (1944).
35. The French *cadre*, Arabized as *kadir*, refers to a standard schedule of job descriptions, pay scales, promotions, and benefits. Following the practice of British companies operating in Egypt, this is rendered in English as cadre.
36. "Mudhakkirat al-hajj Muhammad Hafiz" quoted in Radi, *Adwa'*, p. 277.

302 Struggle during the War

Muhammad Hafiz's task was made easier because Makram 'Ubayd had split with the Wafd to form a new party, the Wafdist Bloc. As minister of finance he had been responsible for dealing with government employees, and he had been one of the more popular Wafd leaders among workers. 'Ubayd retained the Ministry of Finance in the new government, and was able to use his personal prestige with government employees to facilitate the forging of a new relationship between Ahmad Mahir's government and its employees.

In exchange for their professions of loyalty, government workers won significant improvements in their wages and working conditions. On November 23, 1944, the government announced the promulgation of a cadre for its workers, setting down for the first time anywhere in Egypt a clearly defined set of job descriptions, wage rates, promotion schedules, and other benefits. In return the government received a tumultuous display of public support. On December 1, 1944, many thousands of government workers led by Muhammad Hafiz demonstrated in praise of the king, Ahmad Mahir, and Makram 'Ubayd, and celebrated the announcement of the cadre.[37] To capitalize on its success in winning the support of its employees, the government followed the issuance of the cadre with an immediate increase in the minimum wage to thirty piastres per day, an increased cost-of-living allowance, and other fringe benefits.[38] These measures were necessary because the cadre had only been approved in principle and had not been immediately implemented.

The government workers' success in using their organized strength to further their economic objectives represented a shift in the balance of power in the relationship between workers and their prospective patrons. Before 1942 the Wafd had been able to retain substantial strength in the trade union movement on the basis of promises of support for workers' economic demands. In 1942 it was compelled, for the first time, to make good on its promises, and by 1944, the government workers had recognized that their political support could be traded for economic benefits. Because they were organized in a large and viable federation which would not collapse if the Wafd withdrew its support, they were able to exchange their support for major economic gains. The Wafd understood this situation and did not criticize the actions of the government workers. The government workers had learned to play the patron-client game to their own advantage, just as earlier the Cairo transport workers had learned how to use Prince 'Abbas Halim to further their own objectives. This was the mildest

37. *al-Muqattam*, December 2, 1944.
38. Radi, *Adwa'*, pp. 166–69.

Struggle during the War **303**

form which trade union independence from nonworker political parties and figures assumed toward the end of World War II.

'Abbas Halim Returns to the Labor Movement

The Wafd's removal from power provided 'Abbas Halim the opportunity to launch his final attempt to play a role in the labor movement. Despite his internment during the war, the prince had maintained his relationship with the Cairo transport workers and other trade unionists who had been historically associated with him. But he no longer exercised real influence in the labor movement. After the fall of the Wafd government, 'Abbas Halim made a half-hearted attempt to resurrect his Labor party as a means of attracting worker support. In an interview with the Egyptian historian Ra'uf 'Abbas before his death, the prince acknowledged that his efforts to establish a Labor party in 1944 had been backed by King Faruq expressly to draw the loyalty of the working class away from the Wafd.[39] However, 'Abbas Halim's transparent alignment with the increasingly unpopular king had made it impossible to gain support for this endeavor. The Labor party was run by two of 'Abbas Halim's wealthy lieutenants, Mazhar Sa'id and Muhammad Sa'd, who had no standing in the labor movement, and who used the party principally as a vehicle to promote their unsuccessful candidacies in the parliamentary elections of January 1945.

Some of the trade union leaders who had been associated with the prince since the 1930s affiliated with the Labor party to use the royal protection 'Abbas Halim's name now offered to shield activities and opinions that were quite different than those the prince personally endorsed. This group included Muhammad Hasan al-'Amara, Kamil 'Izz al-Din, Labib Tadrus, and Sayyid Qandil. None of these individuals played a major role in the postwar labor movement, though even among this group of the prince's traditional clients, it is possible to see indications of a new sense of class identity and militance. For example, Sayyid Qandil began to promote his social democratic views with more combativeness and vigor. Yet at the same time he also published interviews with 'Abbas Halim in *al-Yara'* and generally served as his mouthpiece in the newspaper that had abandoned the Wafd and joined the prince's camp after the Wafd's ouster from power.[40] Although Qandil's socialism was gradualist and anticommunist, he

39. 'Abbas, *al-Haraka*, p. 214.
40. *al-Yara*, January 8, 16, 1945.

304 Struggle during the War

did on one occasion go so far as to announce: "We in Egypt, as Egyptian workers, believe in the call 'Workers of the world unite!' "[41]

British Attempts to Co-opt the Labor Movement

In the middle of World War II the British attempted, for the first time, to win Egyptian trade unions to their own conception of the appropriate goals and structure for a labor movement. In late 1943 or early 1944, the British embassy in Cairo began to explore the possibility of using the Egyptian trade movement as a way of spreading pro-British propaganda. Money from the British Ministry of Information was funneled to Egyptian trade unions through the Publicity Section of the Cairo embassy.[42] The conduit for British money and influence in the Egyptian trade union movement was Muhammad Ibrahim Zayn al-Din, who was described by Lord Killearn as being "employed by this Embassy for propaganda among trade unions in Egypt."[43] From March 9 to April 7, 1944 Zayn al-Din visited Palestine, Lebanon, Syria, and Iraq on behalf of the International Transport Workers' Federation, which acted as an intermediary between Zayn al-Din and the Ministry of Labor in London. At the conclusion of this trip Zayn al-Din prepared a "Report on Trade Unionism in the Middle East" for the British embassy in Cairo.[44] This was the first of several missions Zayn al-Din undertook for the British.[45]

Despite his close relationship with the British embassy and his access to funds to buy the support of Egyptian trade unions, Zayn al-Din was never able to win the leadership of any significant section of the trade union movement. This was partly the result of the Egyptian government's unwillingness to give adequate support for British proposals and programs designed by M. T. Audsley, labor counsellor in the Cairo embassy, to promote a nonpolitical trade union movement.[46] Ultimately the wealthy landowners and industrialists who dominated the governments of Egypt were too frightened of any form of

41. *Ibid.*, September 23, 1945.
42. FO 371/41379/J1695; FO/371/41379/J790 (1944).
43. FO 371/41379/J1704 (1944).
44. FO 371/41380/J2454 (1944).
45. For reports of other activities undertaken by Zayn al-Din for the British, see FO 371/53368/J146, FO 371/53327/J340, FO 371/53283/J613, FO 371/53368/J1447 and FO 371/53368/J4992 (1946).
46. Audsley was the chief architect of postwar British labor policy in Egypt. For his complaints about the lack of coöperation from the Egyptian government, see FO 371/80606/JE2181/1 (1950), FO 371/45978/J3264 (1945), and FO 371/80606/JE2181/2 (1950).

Struggle during the War **305**

working class organization to give the kind of encouragement necessary for Audsley's vision to succeed.

It was not only the lack of cooperation from the Egyptian government that prevented the realization of the British program. Few industrial enterprises in Egypt were financially secure enough to enable them to reach agreements with trade unions and still achieve large profit margins. Only relatively large and well-capitalized enterprises could afford to grant significant concessions to their workers. The majority of undercapitalized and internationally uncompetitive Egyptian industries simply could not afford to conciliate with trade unions. The nonpolitical business unionism the British sought to promote through Zayn al-Din and through pressure on the Egyptian government flourished in only one trade union of importance in Egypt, the Eastern Tobacco Company union led by Fathi Kamil.[47]

Eastern Tobacco was created by the British-American Tobacco Company, which in the 1920s had bought up many of the smaller Greek and Armenian tobacco enterprises and consolidated them under its ownership. By 1936, Eastern controlled 75 percent of the Egyptian cigarette and tobacco market. Because its profits were secure by virtue of its dominant position in the Egyptian market as well as significant exports, Eastern was able to adopt a conciliatory and cooperative attitude towards its union—a very rare posture for any company in Egypt at this time. Because of the prior history of trade union struggles at the former Matossian factory in Giza, now Eastern's main plant, there was a relatively high standard of working conditions even before the formation of Fathi Kamil's union: an eight-hour day had been in effect since the start of the company's operations. The original union of cigarette workers, first organized at this plant in 1908, was able to carry on only weak and sporadic activities in the 1920s before ceasing to exist entirely. In the 1930s there was some form of trade union organization in the Eastern plant, apparently in the form of separate unions in several individual departments of the plant, though it is unclear how many of the twenty-two departments of Eastern's operations were organized.[48]

In addition to the semimonopoly status of Eastern Tobacco and the history of trade union activity in the cigarette industry, the personal

47. Information on Fathi Kamil and the Eastern Tobacco Company is based, unless otherwise noted, on a series of interviews with him on November 29, December 3, 1979; October 13, 28, December 20, 1980; and February 14, 21, 1981. Much of this information is confirmed by Kamil's memoirs published several years after most of the research for this book was completed: *Ma'a al-haraka al-niqabiyya al-misriyya fi nisf qarn: safahat min dhikrayat Fathi Kamil* (Cairo, 1985).
48. Their existence is noted in *al-Jihad*, May 1, 1935.

306 Struggle during the War

history of Fathi Kamil, who emerged as the leader of the Eastern Tobacco workers in the 1940s, affected the character of the trade union in the plant. Kamil had a primary education certificate and some secondary education. His memoirs make it clear that he was motivated to enter the trade union movement because he was not granted the status he felt he deserved as an *effendi*.[49] Foreign employers treated him with the same disdain they showed Egyptian manual workers. In the late 1920s he was forced to work at manual labor unsuited to his educational qualifications before becoming a low-level bureaucrat in the Health Department, working in provincial posts between 1930 and 1938. By 1939, when Fathi Kamil began to work at Eastern, he had already been involved in discussions about trade unionism with Hasan al-'Amara, Sayyid Qandil, and others in their circle. His first job at Eastern was as a white-collar assistant clerk earning twenty-two piastres a day, a fairly high wage for that period. Nonetheless, he greatly resented the foreign supervisors who had authority over him, their abuses, and affronts to his sense of dignity. Urged on by Isma'il Sayyid Salama, an assistant foreman who had been a member of the first cigarette workers' union, Kamil proposed to Eastern's management that all of the company's 3,500 workers at the Giza plant be united into one union. This was accomplished in October 1943, in opposition to the Wafd's efforts noted earlier, to absorb the Eastern workers into a previously existing Wafd-dominated union.

The company did not resist the formation of the union. On the contrary, shortly after its formation the workers were granted a 20 percent wage increase, and as a result, over 80 percent of the workers joined the union. Eastern's extremely generous policy toward its new union, which was quite unusual, might best be explained as an effort to keep its work force out of the Wafd's sphere of influence. Within a few years Eastern workers were enjoying some of the best working conditions in Egypt: annual vacations of fifteen to forty-five days per year (depending on seniority); free medical care for workers and their families; sports teams; a musical troupe; and other social benefits. In 1946 Eastern established a cafeteria for workers, offering lunches costing fifteen milliemes for adults and ten milliemes for minors. (Approximately 10 percent of the workers were under eighteen, a very low percentage compared to other industrial establishments.) Union dues of five piastres a month were collected by a check-off system and the union used its funds to establish a consumer cooperative and a free night school to teach literacy. As late as 1955, social bene-

49. Kamil, *Ma'a al-haraka*, pp. 12, 23–29.

Struggle during the War **307**

fits comparable to those provided Eastern workers were available in only four other industrial enterprises in all of Egypt.[50]

Eastern's labor relations strategy was highly successful and resulted in nearly strike-free operations from 1943 to 1954. (Two brief minor work stoppages in April and June 1948 were opposed by the union.) Fathi Kamil, as a relatively well-educated white-collar employee, proved an ideal partner for the Eastern Company's labor strategy. He was strongly committed to nonpolitical business unionism, a commitment strengthened by Eastern's granting of additional fringe benefits to its workers. He had a mildly social democratic but firmly anticommunist political perspective, shared the corporatist view of social classes common to the Wafd and 'Abbas Halim, and saw the trade union movement, as they did, as one of the manifestations of Egyptian national revival.[51]

Eastern Tobacco's labor control strategy was possible primarily because it was a highly profitable multinational which could afford to pay higher wages and better benefits than almost all Egyptian-owned firms. Under these conditions Kamil's commitment to cooperative relations with the company was solidly supported by Eastern's workers. While more militant trade unionists often reproached him for his cozy relations with management, he could always defend himself easily by pointing to the extraordinary conditions members of his union enjoyed. What was not clearly understood by Fathi Kamil and the British officials who saw his union as a model organization was that it was impossible for workers in the textile industry, for example, to win the same conditions with the same strategy. For this reason, Eastern's workers remained relatively isolated from the militant political currents developing in the textile industry up to 1951, when the crisis of the old regime became so acute that even relatively privileged workers became part of the radical upsurge in the national and labor movements for the first time.

Because he was the leader of the largest union in metropolitan Cairo, it is not surprising that Fathi Kamil was wooed by many of the contending forces attempting to direct the Egyptian labor movement—the British, the Egyptian government, and 'Abbas Halim. In 1946 when Kamil was visiting England as a member of the trade

50. Orphy, " Analysis of Welfare Programs," p. 11.
51. Kamil, *Ma'a al-haraka*, pp. 60–61. See also *Mu'tamar al-Niqabiyin*, June 3–10, 1950, where Kamil refers to trade unions as "a tool of guidance and direction to ensure good relations between workers and employers, the advancement of industry and increased production. . . . We believe that we are performing a duty which is based on the highest principles of nationalism, that is, realizing the greatest solidarity between the various classes. . . ."

308 Struggle during the War

union delegation led by Muhammad Ibrahim Zayn al-Din, 'Abbas Halim, probably in an attempt to reinforce his position within the Labor party from which many of the trade union leaders had just split, announced that Kamil had joined his party. Similarly, the Egyptian government sought to win Kamil's support by appointing him to membership in the moribund Supreme Labor Advisory Council. While flirting with the British, the prince, and the government, Fathi Kamil was able to maintain his independence from them all. This was possible because the Eastern union was a large, well-organized, and financially independent organization that did not rely on any outside factor for its ability to secure benefits for its members. Despite Fathi Kamil's affinity with the corporatist view of trade unionism shared by the Wafd and 'Abbas Halim, he was able to keep his union relatively free of domination by outside forces.

When the Wafd returned to power on February 4, 1942, its prospects for reasserting control over the Egyptian workers' movement appeared extremely good. Between September 1942 and October 1944 the Wafd succeeded in extending its influence over much of the Egyptian trade union movement. As unions gained strength and experience, however, they became increasingly resistant to Wafd domination, though workers generally continued to give political support to the Wafd as Egypt's nationalist party. Many trade unionists were aware of the dangers of allowing their unions to be dominated by the Wafd, though in practice many unions were not strong enough to maintain their independence when the Wafd commanded the apparatus of the state in addition to its party machinery. Only the Cairo trade unions had enough strength to resist Wafd attempts to dominate them. The rapid shift in the loyalties of many trade unionists away from the Wafd after it was removed from power is an indication that these trade unionists were now using the Wafd to attain their own objectives rather than simply being used by the Wafd. After October 1944, the Wafd was never again able to play a major organizational role in the Egyptian trade union movement. Even when it returned to power for the last time in 1950, the Wafd was unable to restore the relationship it had established with the trade union movement in 1942–1944.[52]

Prince 'Abbas Halim had also lost most of his influence in the trade union movement by the end of the war. Although some trade unionists continued to attempt to use him as a cover for their activities, the prince and his Labor party were widely viewed as agents of an increasingly unpopular king.

52. FO 371/80606/JE2181/5 (1950).

Finally, the British attempts to promote a nonpolitical bread-and-butter trade union movement after World War II were stillborn. The succession of minority governments from 1944 to 1950 refused to accept the arguments of the British embassy that government encouragement of moderate trade unionists would lead to greater political and economic stability. Only a small number of firms were willing or able to develop cooperative relations with their unions, or provide the wages and benefits the British vision required for success. Among trade union leaders and rank-and-file workers, open cooperation with Britain was nearly unanimously rejected. The upsurge of the Egyptian national movement in the postwar period made such cooperation, regardless of its potential benefits, nearly impossible. Under the circumstances Muhammad Ibrahim Zayn al-Din had very little personal influence in the postwar workers' movement, and only the Eastern Tobacco Company union consciously adopted the British model of trade unionism.

The weakening influence of the Wafd and 'Abbas Halim and the failure of the British model of trade unionism are all negative phenomena indicating that the Egyptian workers' movement was passing beyond the stage of the patron-client trade unionism that had been the dominant mode of association in the prewar period. The dramatic increase in the number of unions, the growth in the size of the working class, particularly its industrial proletarian component, the upsurge in the nationalist movement in the postwar years, and the conscious assimilation of the accumulated political lessons of the prewar years by trade union leaders, all contributed to the emergence of a much stronger and politically independent trade union movement after the Second World War.

Chapter X

Communism and the Egyptian Workers' Movement, 1942–1948

Throughout the remainder of this book, communist activity in the working class receives relatively more attention than that given to other political forces. The reason for this focus, which may seem questionable in light of the communists' ultimate failure to maintain their influence in the working class, is that the communists were the most active and dynamic force in the workers' movement during this period. They successfully capitalized on the decline in influence of the Wafd and Prince 'Abbas Halim, the traditional patrons of the labor movement, by encouraging the demand of trade union activists to reorganize the movement on the basis of independence from non-worker personalities and parties. Communists were able to link up with trade unionists who had been fighting for this objective since the late 1930s, and by doing so they gained respect and legitimacy in significant working class centers.

Communist influence was partly the result of, and in turn accelerated, the decline of patron-client association and corporatist ideology in the workers' movement. The communists based their appeal to workers on their understanding of a reality which all the other political forces in contention for influence within the workers' movement denied: that class conflict was an unavoidable consequence of the growth of capitalist relations of production in Egypt, just as was the case in Europe. The growth of industry during the 1930s and the Second World War was not without its costs, and these were disproportionately borne by the working class. The communists championed workers' demands for equitable wages, security of employment, and a measure of control in the work place. Moreover, because they not only accepted but encouraged the intensification of class conflict,

Communism and Workers, 1942–1948 **311**

they were willing to employ militant methods of struggle and direct action—hunger strikes, protest marches, sit-ins, and of course, strikes—to achieve workers' demands, whereas all other political forces sought to restrain worker militancy and class conflict.

Because communist influence in the working class was based on the economic and social realities created by the development of capitalist industry it is not surprising that the textile industry, which was the leading sector in this development, was also the communists' main base of strength in the working class. Communist influence outside the principal strongholds in the textile industry and a limited number of other sectors of the urban economy was in most cases indirect, sporadic, and organizationally unconsolidated. Nonetheless, many of the working class struggles of the postwar period were characterized by a new sense of militance and confrontation that was encouraged and amplified by communists and their allies, though not always the direct result of communist influence.

Although the fundamental realities of capitalist development were the foundation for the communist presence and influence in the workers' movement, these alone might not have permitted the communists to become as important a factor in the working class and in national politics as they in fact were during the postwar period. The postwar conjuncture of a protracted economic crisis and the bankruptcy of Egypt's parliamentary system opened the way for radical forces on the right and the left to challenge the existing social and political order. The Wafd's loss of hegemony over the labor movement was only one of many symptoms of its general decline and of public disillusion with liberal nationalism. At the end of the war the central leadership of the Wafd, though still formally committed to achieving the full evacuation of British troops from Egypt, was unwilling to mobilize the masses to fight for this demand. The upper echelons of the Wafd had always been socially conservative: a tendency bolstered by the presence and influence of large landowners in the party leadership. After the war, Fu'ad Siraj al-Din's growing power within the party symbolized the ascendence of these elements. Forced to choose between maintaining social peace or mobilizing Egyptians for a militant struggle against the British and their supporters in the Palace, a struggle which could potentially have upset the prevailing social order, the Wafd's central leadership opted for social peace.

The timidity and conservatism of the Wafd leadership resulted in the formation of a left wing within the party based primarily on the youthful urban intelligentsia—the Wafdist Vanguard (al-Tali‘a al-Wafdiyya). These elements, whose leadership included the prominent literary figure and editor of the popular daily *al-Wafd al-Misri*

312 Communism and Workers, 1942–1948

(*The Egyptian Delegation*), Muhammad Mandur, embraced and popularized many of the ideas advanced by Egyptian Marxists. The most important of these ideas was the Marxist analysis of imperialism which for many was a plausible explanation of the complex alliances linking British rule in Egypt, the Palace, large landowners, and both foreign and local capital.

The continuing prominence of foreign capital and its alliance with local capital made it possible to link workers' demands for social justice with the central thrust of the Egyptian nationalist movement. On this basis militant workers and the radicalized urban intelligentsia formed an alliance which provided a new leadership and political direction to the postwar Egyptian nationalist movement. Militant working class action thus received nationalist legitimacy, and the communists were able to use their links to the intelligentsia to strengthen the workers' movement and broaden its demands and its political impact.

In addition, the communists not only provided nationalist legitimacy for Egyptian workers' militance, but gave it an international context as well. The resurgence of the Egyptian communist movement, the upsurge of labor militancy and the radicalization of a section of the nationalist movement in the postwar period were part of the widespread nationalist, labor, and socialist mobilization on an international scale. In the colonial and semicolonial countries these elements often combined, and though the mass movements that emerged in this conjuncture were frequently characterized by a lack of ideological clarity, they were no less substantial or significant on that account. These movements were propelled by the widespread feeling, like that after World War I, that the end of the war provided an opportunity to present accumulated demands and alter the international alignment of political forces. The impressive display of the Soviet Union's military capacity and heroism during the war brought that country to the attention of many Egyptians for the first time. Many Egyptians also felt a strong affinity for the Chinese revolutionary movement because they saw China as a country whose problems were similar to Egypt's—a semicolonial, mainly peasant land struggling for national liberation and economic and social progress. Thus communists offered a perspective that linked the Egyptian workers' movement to the demands of not only the national movement, but also to those of an international one that seemed to be marching inexorably forward. The resurgence of the Egyptian communist movement and its role in the workers' movement are, therefore, part of the broad postwar social movement for national liberation in the colonial and semicolonial countries, and this context must be borne in mind

Communism and Workers, 1942–1948   **313**

in order to assess the full significance of communist activity in the Egyptian working class.

In the mid 1930s the Egyptian petty bourgeoisie became politically radicalized as a result of Egypt's inability to free itself from British domination, disillusionment with the Wafd and especially the unsatisfactory treaty of 1936 it had negotiated with Great Britain, and disappointment with the failure of the formal structures of liberal democracy to achieve anything substantive. These political disappointments were further aggravated by substantial unemployment among intellectuals which contributed to the radicalization of the *effendiyya*. In the decade of rising fascism and German military power, many young anti-British Egyptians were attracted to openly fascist or fascist-influenced political movements such as Young Egypt or the Society of Muslim Brothers, both of whom employed fascist-style organizational methods and elements of fascist ideology. Even the Wafd had a paramilitary unit (the Blue Shirts) whose formation was inspired by fascist-style organizational methods. Pro-German sentiment, if only as an expression of hatred for Great Britain, was widespread.

Intellectuals who were disappointed with the Wafd's liberalism yet rejected a pro-German or fascist political orientation began to be attracted to communism in the mid 1930s. The young, radicalized intelligentsia, not the working class, revived the Egyptian communist movement and was always its strongest base. Despite repeated abortive attempts to reorganize a communist party, communism was, in effect, temporarily eliminated as a political force in Egypt following the defeat of the Alexandria workers' uprising in 1924.[1] There was no communist presence in the Egyptian workers' movement during the late 1920s and 1930s except for some personal contacts with former party members maintained by Yusuf al-Mudarrik and Sayyid Qandil. The first steps in the reorganization of the communist movement were taken by foreigners residing in Egypt, especially anti-fascist Italians and Greeks. They were soon joined by Egyptian Jews, for whom any association with pro-German, fascist influenced, or Islamic political trends was unimaginable. For Jews, communism was the only po-

---

1. Rif'at al-Sa'id, *al-Yasar al-misri, 1925–1940* (Beirut, 1972), argues for the historical continuity between the first and second communist movements in Egypt. There was, however, little continuity of personnel between the two movements and only a limited degree of intellectual continuity. The discussion of the Egyptian communist movement presented here treats only its relationship to the workers' movement. For a general history of the Egyptian communist movement during this period see Selma Botman, "Oppositional Politics in Egypt: The Communist Movement, 1936–1954" (Ph.D. diss., Harvard University, 1984).

314 Communism and Workers, 1942–1948

litical alternative to the declining Wafd that promised to protect their status in Egypt. This explains the disproportionately large role of Jews in the revival of the Egyptian communist movement.[2] These Jews, especially those fluent in Arabic in addition to European languages, provided a bridge between the foreign communists and the indigenous Egyptian intelligentsia and helped forge the link between communist intellectuals and the workers' movement.

New Dawn and the Shubra al-Khayma Textile Workers

In 1934 or 1935 a group of mainly foreign intellectuals led by a Swiss, Paul Jacot des Combes, established the Federation of Peace Partisans (Ittihad Ansar al-Salam), an antifascist democratic organization, among whose members were three Egyptian Jews—Ahmad Sadiq Sa'd, Raymond Douek, and Yusuf Darwish.[3] Darwish was a lawyer who had been educated in France in the early 1930s where he came into contact with Marxism; Sa'd was then a student at Cairo University. Following the outbreak of World War II, the Federation of Peace Partisans was dissolved, and a new organization, whose membership was also largely foreign, *La groupe d'études* (Jama'at al-Buhuth), took its place. In the course of their studies and discussions as members of this organization, Sa'd, Douek, and Darwish resolved to find a way to link themselves to the struggles of the masses.[4]

In 1940 they met a group of secondary school students who were conducting literacy classes in the Sabtiyya quarter of Cairo, and following their example, the three established the Youth Association for Popular Culture (Jama'at al-Shabab li'l-Thaqafa al-Sha'biyya). This association established two schools in the Bulaq quarter of Cairo (where Yusuf Darwish lived), one in Mit 'Uqba near Imbaba. Darwish served as director of these schools which had over 100 pupils each. The Association also made contact with similar schools in Tanta, Abu Sir, and al-Malaq near Bani Suwayf.[5]

During this period the trio made their first contact with workers.

---

2. This argument is based on many hours of discussion with Mohamed Sid Ahmed.

3. Marcel Israel, "Taqrir ila qiyadat al-hizb al-shuyu'i al-itali," translated into Arabic from the original Italian and reprinted in Sa'id, *1925–1940*, p. 263. Yusuf Darwish, "Letter to Jamal 'Abd al-Nasir," December 3, 1956 (Yusuf Darwish papers, Cairo); Ahmad Sadiq Sa'd, *Safahat min al-yasar al-misri fi a'qab al-harb al-'alamiyya al-thaniyya, 1945–1946* (Cairo, 1976), pp. 38–39.

4. Sa'd, *Safahat*, p. 42–43; Rif'at al-Sa'id, *Ta'rikh al-munazzamat al-yasariyya fi misr, 1940–1950* (Cairo, 1976), p. 170.

5. *Ibid.*, pp. 43–44; Darwish, "Letter to Jamal 'Abd al-Nasir," says that the organization was called the Committee for the Dissemination of Popular Culture (*Lajnat Nashr al-Thaqafa al-Sha'biyya*).

Communism and Workers, 1942–1948 **315**

Yusuf al-Mudarrik kept the books for a blacksmith's shop owned by Douek's brother, and it was he who introduced Douek to al-Mudarrik in 1939 or 1940, and later to Darwish.[6] Through al-Mudarrik, Darwish met Mahmud al-'Askari and the leadership of the Shubra al-Khayma textile workers' union. By this time Darwish had begun to assume the primary responsibility for organizing among workers. Douek and Sa'd eventually concentrated their political activity among intellectuals.

It is characteristic of the style of political activity developed by Darwish, Sa'd, and Douek that they did not formally establish a communist political organization at this time. The group continued to operate informally until early 1945 when they established a secret communist cell along with Ahmad Rushdi Salih, an intellectual who had been active with them in the Committee for the Dissemination of Modern Culture (Lajnat Nashr al-Thaqafa al-Haditha). Eventually the intellectuals were joined by Yusuf al-Mudarrik and Mahmud al-'Askari, who assumed responsibility for conducting political activities among workers.[7] The group had no formal name but was commonly known as New Dawn (al-Fajr al-Jadid) after the name of the semimonthly magazine (later weekly) which the intellectuals' section began to publish on May 16, 1945.

The New Dawn group focused most of the energies it devoted to working class organizing on the area of Shubra al-Khayma. Its concentrated industrial character and its proximity to Cairo made this a logical choice from the point of view of communist strategy. By this time there were some 20,000 industrial workers in Shubra al-Khayma, including 9,000 textile workers.[8] In 1942 an organic link between New Dawn and the Shubra al-Khayma textile workers was established when Darwish became legal counsel for the General Union of Mechanical Textile Workers in Shubra al-Khayma and Cairo.[9] Darwish was licensed to practice in the Mixed Courts which was a great asset to the union because many of the mill owners were foreigners.[10] This marked the first formal association of the union leadership with the communist movement.

6. Raymond Douek, interview, June 4, 1981.
7. Sa'd, *Safahat*, p. 48.
8. Taha Sa'd 'Uthman, *Min ta'rikh 'ummal misr: mudhakkirat wa-watha'iq*, al-kitab al-thani (Cairo, 1982), 2:78. Volume one of this work (*al-kitab al-awwal: kifah 'ummal al nasij*, Shubra al-Khayma, 1983) reached us too late to be used extensively.
9. Darwish, "Letter to Jamal 'Abd al-Nasir."
10. From 1875 to 1948 Egypt maintained a system of Mixed Courts which combined European and Egyptian jurisprudence. Because foreign nationals residing in Egypt could only be sued in such courts, legal cases involving Egyptian workers and foreign mill owners came under their jurisdiction.

316   Communism and Workers, 1942–1948

The fortunate encounter between Darwish and al-'Askari facilitated the rapid development of communist influence in this critical working class center, but the efforts of Darwish and his comrades could not have been successful if the GUMTWSKC's activities from 1937 to 1942 had not prepared the way for the rapid development of close ties between the union leadership and the communist intellectuals. In the struggle against domination of the trade union movement by 'Abbas Halim and the Wafd and in its early struggles against the mill owners the GUMTWSKC had developed its own style of working class radicalism without the benefit of any clearly formulated ideological system to support it. Independent organization and militant direct action were well established as fundamental elements of the union's identity and a source of its strength. What Darwish and his comrades who joined and supported the workers' struggles offered was a systematic world view which illuminated the structural connections between the union leaders' experiences and the broader framework of Egyptian politics. The communists also offered intellectual and organizational links to nonworkers which could prove important in mobilizing public support for workers' struggles. This was the basis for the original acceptance of these intellectuals into the confidence of the union leadership, despite the union's established principle of independence from nonworker political parties and figures.

The communist influence in the GUMTWSKC was amplified by the cohesion and stature of the union's leadership. Every Sunday, before the regular meetings, the members of the union executive board ate dinner at the home of one of their number.[11] These regular social gatherings strengthened the bonds of solidarity among the union leaders, brought the affairs of the union into the daily lives of their families and neighborhoods, and provided the occasion for the leadership to meet informally with representatives from a variety of political trends, such as Darwish and his comrades. Moreover, Mahmud al-'Askari, the general secretary of the GUMTWSKC, was a charismatic personality who wielded enormous personal influence among the textile workers.[12] Although some intellectuals later expressed reservations about his leadership methods, there is no doubt that he won the respect and loyalty of the textile workers and was able to carry a substantial portion of his followers into communist-led trade union and political action.

Under this dynamic leadership the union became an important in-

11. 'Askari, U, November 29, 1976.
12. Douek, interview, June 4, 1981.

Communism and Workers, 1942–1948   **317**

stitution in the lives of the area's textile workers. The GUMTWSKC attempted to make itself indispensible for earning a livelihood in the textile mills of the area. Among its major objectives was to establish a union hiring hall, which would ensure that laid-off members were rehired in an orderly manner through the union. One of its most important institutions was a welfare fund to provide financial aid to laid-off members to enable them to wait to be rehired through the union. The fund also paid benefits if a worker was dismissed as a result of activities authorized by the executive board, disabled, or if there was a death in a worker's family.[13] Such institutions made the GUMTWSKC a powerful social force in Shubra al-Khayma and permitted communist-inspired ideas to gain a wide audience, as we can see from the pages of the weekly newspaper *Shubra* during the nine-month period in which it was published by the GUMTWSKC (April 30, 1942–January 21, 1943). During this period the pages of *Shubra* demonstrate a nascent working class radicalism and the growing intellectual and cultural power of communist influence in Shubra al-Khayma.

This influence is particularly evident in the writing of Iskandar Sulayman Salib, *Shubra*'s social affairs editor, which displays a basic familiarity with general Marxist concepts and an inclination towards socialism. For example, in an article on the postwar economy Salib demanded that the government develop industry for the benefit of the public, and not for private gain, yet he called this program "nationalism in the economic and social arena," rather than socialism.[14] This is an early example of the manner in which, under the influence of Marxism, class demands became identified as national demands.

At the same time Taha Sa'd 'Uthman wrote a series of articles on "Labor and Work in Islam," which indicated his continuing commitment to an Islamic social and political orientation.[15] As was common among the proponents of this perspective, 'Uthman argued that Islamic law (*shari'a*) provided full guarantees for workers' rights and that Islam had great respect for workers because the *shari'a* regarded labor as the sole legitimate source of wealth. 'Uthman felt no contradiction between his commitment to Islam and his belief that workers could achieve their due if the *shari'a* were correctly implemented, on the one hand, and the general thrust of the union's activities at this time on the other. Political developments would later cause 'Uthman to reconsider this question.

Perhaps the most important concept *Shubra* promoted was a posi-

13. See the text of the union's constitution in *Shubra*, May 21, 1942.
14. *Shubra*, May 14, 1942.
15. *Ibid.*, December 17, 1942; January 8, 21, 1943.

318 Communism and Workers, 1942–1948

tive, militant self-image for workers. An article by 'Abd al-Hamid 'Abd Allah in the first issue of *Shubra* published by the GUMTWSKC, entitled simply "The Workers" is a panegyric to the positive characteristics of the working class—"strength," "the source of life," "humanity," "nationalists," and "the nerves of the state." Many other articles in a similar vein appeared in *Shubra*. The newspaper also provided a platform for the cultural and intellectual development and self-expression of workers. Many worker-intellectuals gained experience and confidence by writing in the pages of *Shubra*. Mahmud al-'Askari and Taha Sa'd 'Uthman are the most important figures in this group, and there were others whose long-term influence may have been less, but whose writings nonetheless reflected the political ferment among the Shubra al-Khayma textile workers during World War II. These authors addressed not only the major political issues of the day, but a broad range of political and social questions as well, such as the strategy for economic development after the war, women's liberation, and how workers should spend their leisure time.

Fathi al-Maghribi was one of the most articulate exponents of working class culture and identity during this period. He began his career working at the Misr Spinning and Weaving mill in Mahalla al-Kubra. By 1942, he was a well-established, popular literary figure. He wrote for *al-Wajib*, was a member of the editorial board of *Shubra* (from the first issue published by the GUMTWSKC) and even wrote for the Wafd's *al-Yara'*. Al-Maghribi wrote news items, short stories, and literary essays, but his favored medium was the *zajal* (pl. *azjal*) or popular colloquial poetry in strophic form. Many of his poems were published in *Shubra*, and he frequently recited his *azjal* at GUMTWSKC meetings. Often these poems commemorated struggles in which the union was engaged. In 1946 a collection of al-Maghribi's *azjal* entitled *I the Worker* was published with an introduction by Yusuf al-Mudarrik.[16] The title work had originally been recited at the April 26, 1942 general assembly of the GUMTWSKC. The political content of the other poems in the collection indicates that al-Maghribi was associated with the left wing of the workers' movement. One particular example captures well the emerging working class pride and self-consciousness al-Maghribi's poems both reflected and helped to form. This *zajal*, entitled "In All Pride We Are Workers," vividly expresses both working class national feeling and class pride in the realization that the workers are the real creators of the Egyptian national culture and heritage. Although the excerpts translated here do not do full justice to al-Maghribi's talent, they provide a concrete example of the way

16. Fathi al-Maghribi, *Ana al-'amil* (Cairo, 1946).

Communism and Workers, 1942–1948 **319**

workers in Shubra al-Khayma perceived themselves and their role in society.

In All Pride We Are Workers[17]

We are the Egyptian workers, we are the brave
A thousand salutes to you, oh Egypt, mother of all
. . .

Workers are the secret of the beauty of cities
Heroes guard the secrets of the crafts

We are the builders of your pyramids, oh sphinx
Workers, all of us your servants, as we all know

We are the builders of the Pharaohs' fleets
And all that is beautiful in this world
. . .

Besides providing a cultural and intellectual platform *Shubra* also gave the GUMTWSKC an important organizational tool that allowed it to extend its influence into other sectors of the working class. This extension of the union's influence beyond the boundaries of its immediate constituency began in 1941, after the victory at Beso in the struggle for the 10 percent cost-of-living allowance. At that time, delegations representing textile unions in Alexandria, Kafr al-Dawwar, Mahalla al-Kubra, Bani Suwayf, Damietta, Imbaba, and upper Egypt came to Shubra al-Khayma to consult with the GUMTWSKC leadership.[18] *Shubra* and the GUMTWSKC encouraged the formation of new unions among many previously unorganized workers: pharmaceutical warehouse workers in greater Cairo, linen weavers in Abu al-Ghayt, mechanized textile workers in Zaytun, and rubber shoe workers, ceramics workers, glass workers, and steamboat workers in Shubra al-Khayma.[19] By July 1942, *Shubra* was promoting the creation of federations of trade unions in various industries.[20]

Yusuf Darwish was intensely involved in these organizing activities which helped expand communist influence beyond the Shubra al-Khayma textile industry.[21] He assisted in the formation of several new unions, including the Shubra al-Khayma Steamboat Workers' Union and the Cairo Pharmaceutical Warehouse Workers' Union. By the end of the war, Darwish was serving as legal counsel for over twenty trade unions. As a result of his legal activities, Darwish be-

17. Published in *al-Yara'*, October 1, 1942.
18. 'Askari, U, September 5, 1977.
19. *Ibid.*, May 14, 25, June 18, July 2, 23, 1942; 'Uthman, *Min ta'rikh*, 2:78.
20. *Shubra*, July 30, 1942.
21. Darwish, "Letter to Jamal 'Abd al-Nasir."

320 Communism and Workers, 1942–1948

came widely known to the leadership of the Cairo-area trade union movement. A memorandum he submitted to the government concerning the Law of Individual Contracts (Law 41 of 1944) was endorsed by over sixty unions, and his pamphlet on work accidents, explaining the 1936 accident compensation law, was popular among trade unionists.[22] In February 1945 Darwish spoke at a conference of cafe, restaurant, and sweetshop workers convened by Rif'at Hasib (president of the Public Establishments Workers' Union)[23] to discuss the recent firings of large numbers of workers, another indication of broadening communist presence in the labor movement. As the lawyer for one of the unions participating in this conference, Darwish explained the laws relevant to the problem. Yusuf al-Mudarrik also addressed the conference, and his speech was well received.

Darwish and his comrades also tried to promote the political and educational development of the workers with whom they came into contact, though they never identified themselves publicly as communists. In 1942 and 1943 the GUMTWSKC, with Darwish's help, established a school for its members, and Darwish himself taught English and French. Other subjects including general social studies were also taught, sometimes by leftist intellectuals who were friends of Darwish.[24] Eventually secret Marxist study sessions were organized in which Mahmud al-'Askari, Taha Sa'd 'Uthman and others participated.[25]

Al-'Askari further advanced his political education during his arrest and detention from October 1943 to May 1944 as a result of the unsuccessful strike the GUMTWSKC called to protest the dismissal of 'Abd al-Hamid 'Abd al-Haqq as minister of social affairs and his replacement by Fu'ad Siraj al-Din.[26] In prison al-'Askari met a broad spectrum of dissident political elements including Anwar Kamil (a former editor of the short-lived socialist review *al-Tatawwur*), a large number of Greek communists, members of Young Egypt and the Wafdist Bloc, and several future members of the Free Officers Organization (including Anwar al-Sadat). He was especially influenced by 'Abd al-Mughni Sa'id, a functionary in the Labor Department with vaguely socialist views.[27] This prison experience apparently served to consolidate al-'Askari's political radicalism as he wrote in his memoirs:

22. Yusuf Darwish, *Sharh qanun isabat al-'amal* (Cairo, 1944).
23. *al-Jabha*, February 15, 1945.
24. 'Uthman, interview, October 28, 1980.
25. 'Uthman, *K*, July, 1971, p. 175.
26. 'Askari, *U*, December 12, 19, 1977; *al-Yara'*, May 27, 1944.
27. 'Askari, *U*, December 26, 1977.

Communism and Workers, 1942–1948 **321**

I emerged with the conclusion that the coming days carry the em-
bryo of a new society . . . which will herald a deep radical change
in Egyptian society that will be achieved as a result of the aspirations of these youth who are activated and impelled towards
achieving what the revolution of 1919 did not achieve.[28]

By this time al-'Askari almost certainly thought of himself as a socialist, yet his political point of departure in the passage above is the
unachieved goals of the 1919 revolution. Al-'Askari thus viewed the
radical social changes he anticipated as part of the unfinished nationalist agenda. This is an unusually clear example (perhaps because its
source is a highly self-conscious individual writing some thirty years
after the events) of the strong nationalist component in working class
political consciousness even among those workers most strongly influenced by communist ideas. Al-'Askari's account of his political
views in 1944 is only a short step away from the idea that the working
class, rather than the vague category of "youth" referred to above,
should assume the political responsibility for leading Egyptian society toward social reform and national independence.

**Beyond Trade Union Politics:
Workers in the Electoral Arena**

The dismissal of the Wafd government on October 8, 1944 provided
the opportunity for the GUMTWSKC to move beyond trade union and
working class political concerns and begin playing a role in the national political arena. After the ouster of the Wafd the union executive board published a statement affirming its independence from
"all nonworker organizations and personalities," and its intention to
continue operating within the limits of existing trade union legislation.[29] This statement was primarily a defensive measure designed to
avert any attacks on the union by the new anti-Wafd government. The
union had indeed been independent of the Wafd, despite its general
support of the Wafd government, and now that the Wafd was out of
power and had decided to boycott the parliamentary elections called
for January 1945 and had no hope of returning to power, the union
had all the more reason to continue in this manner. The implication
that in accordance with the law the union had been apolitical was
only formally correct, however, in the sense that it was not officially
linked to any party. In fact, under the slogan of "independence from
nonworker organizations and personalities" the GUMTWSKC had be-

28. *Ibid.*
29. *al-Yara'*, October 28, 1944.

322 Communism and Workers, 1942–1948

come the most politically conscious segment of the Egyptian working class.

A clear manifestation of this development was the union's decision to nominate a worker to run for the office of deputy for Shubra al-Khayma in the parliamentary elections. Some of those who supported this decision did so on the basis of social democratic political conceptions inspired by the example of the British Labor party. Others were influenced by the revolutionary Marxist political ideas propagated by Yusuf Darwish and his comrades, although the full import of these ideas was not widely known. The idea of running a workers' political campaign united both groups.[30] This was the first conscious and collectively organized attempt by Egyptian workers to compete for a share of state power, and therefore marks an important new stage in the development of the political consciousness of the Shubra al-Khayma textile workers.

The GUMTWSKC joined with the Greater Cairo Textile Foremen and Assistant Foremen's Union and the Cairo Handloom Weavers' Union to organize the electoral campaign. Mahmud al-'Askari was the GUMTWSKC's preferred nominee, but some members of the foremen's union objected to his candidacy because he was too radical and lacked formal education. The campaign organizers strongly believed in the need to maintain the unity of the foremen and the production workers if the campaign were to have any chance of success. This feeling was based on the supportive role played by many of the foremen in the union's shop floor struggles and the important role of foremen in the leadership of the GUMTWSKC. As a result, Faddali 'Abd al-Jayyid 'Abd al-Jawwad, a union activist since 1937 and president of the GUMTWSKC since January 1944, emerged as a compromise candidate. As a foreman at the Sibahi mill in Shubra al-Khayma and a graduate of a technical school, he possessed the status and education the foremen sought in a candidate. He had been the technical instructor of a large number of foremen in the area and was well-known and respected. Moreover, his standing among the workers was high because he was one of the many foremen who had not split away from the GUMTWSKC to form the foremen and assistant foremen's union in 1942. Faddali 'Abd al-Jayyid therefore was able to unite both the foremen and the production workers behind his candidacy, and won the nomination.[31]

When it became known that the workers of Shubra al-Khayma were preparing to enter the political arena independently of all the existing

30. 'Uthman, Min ta'rikh, 2:79.
31. Ibid., pp. 81 ff.; 'Askari, U, November 28, 1977.

political parties, Faddali 'Abd al-Jayyid was approached by representatives of the Sa'dist party to stand as their candidate, a proposal he and an overwhelming majority of the workers' electoral committee organized to manage the campaign rejected.[32] Instead, he ran as an independent on a comprehensive program that addressed all of the major political questions facing Egypt.[33]

This program is important because it reflects the development of a broad political vision among the textile workers' leadership. Its concerns extend far beyond the local arena of Shubra al-Khayma or the industrial working class. National political and economic questions, as well as rural issues, are treated in a manner that indicates a high degree of sophistication among those who adopted the program. The most prominent elements of the program are national demands: the evacuation of British troops, Egyptian sovereignty over the Sudan, a call for Arab unity on a popular basis (as opposed to the British-inspired maneuvers that had led to the formation of the Arab League), and the freeing of Egypt from foreign influence through the nationalization of foreign-owned monopolies and Egyptianization of major economic and cultural institutions. Secondary proposals included an extensive list of educational and social reforms for workers, peasants, and low-level white-collar employees.

There is no doubt that Yusuf Darwish, and perhaps other communist intellectuals, played a major role in the formulation of this program because it corresponds broadly to the immediate communist program for this period. Although it contains no explicit call for socialism, many of its elements point in that direction. It should be noted, in anticipation of future political developments, that there is nothing in it in the least bit critical of religion, nor anything devout Muslims could not support in principle.

Faddali 'Abd al-Jayyid lost his election bid: he received only 849 of 7,306 votes cast. However, these results cannot be taken as an accurate measure of popular sentiment in Shubra al-Khayma, for throughout Egypt these elections were among the least honest ever conducted under the constitution of 1923. Their results had been fixed beforehand by negotiations between the anti-Wafdist political parties.[34] In Shubra al-Khayma there were numerous electoral irregularities.[35] Election officials had refused to register new voters, or transfer workers' voting locales from the villages in which they were born to Shubra al-Khayma. At least 4,000 workers were deprived of the vote in

32. 'Askari, U, December 5, 1977.
33. A facsimile of the full text of the program appears in 'Uthman, Min ta'rikh, 2:283.
34. FO 371/41319/J4548; FO 371/41319/J4615 (1944).
35. 'Uthman, Min ta'rikh, 2:13–18, 106–112.

324 Communism and Workers, 1942–1948

this manner. In addition, there were the standard practices of bribery, intimidation, and destruction of ballots.

The outcome of the election, however, was less significant than the campaign attempt. The decision to enter a candidate was the clearest statement that the leadership of the Shubra al-Khayma textile workers had embraced the strategy of independent political action to further the interests of the working class as it understood them. The union continued to maintain a high level of political activity despite the electoral defeat. Marxist study activity became more intense, and the left tendency began to grow bolder and more active.[36] The union continued to exert political influence beyond the ranks of its own constituency to the extent that the British embassy considered it one of the six most important unions in the Cairo area.[37]

The months after the election, from January to April 1945, were marked not only by intensified political activity by the left, but also by an extraordinarily high number of strikes, none of which was reported in the daily press because of the continuing wartime censorship. The most probable reason for this high rate of strike activity is the slowdown in industrial activity, especially in the textile industry, brought about by the end of World War II. Many mills either closed down entirely or sharply reduced their work force. Workers faced with losing their jobs resorted to frequent strikes in an effort to save them. The high level of strike action seemed to validate the communists' analysis of the current situation in Egypt.

During this period of intense political and strike activity by the Shubra al-Khayma textile workers the New Dawn communist cell was formally established. Mahmud al-'Askari and Yusuf al-Mudarrik were the only workers who were actual members of the group. Taha Sa'd 'Uthman was a close associate of New Dawn, but only joined the organization when it was reorganized and renamed the Popular Vanguard for Liberation in September 1946. Other workers participated in activities inspired by New Dawn, but because of the extreme secrecy of the group they may not have known of its existence. The workers associated with New Dawn began issuing leaflets under the signature "Workers' Vanguard" (Tali'at al-'Ummal), and actively supported and advised the textile workers' strike movement. A Workers' Vanguard leaflet, dated March 28, 1945, urged striking workers to form strike committees and establish strike funds.[38] The agitation of the New Dawn group among the Shubra al-Khayma textile workers

36. 'Uthman, K, July, 1971, p. 175; Interview, December 2, 1980.
37. FO 371/45978/J1301 (1945).
38. FO 371/45978/J1791 (1945).

Communism and Workers, 1942–1948   **325**

extended beyond trade union questions. For example, Workers' Vanguard issued a leaflet calling for the celebration of May Day 1945.[39] This leaflet contained sharp political attacks on 'Abbas Halim, 'Abd al-Hamid 'Abd al-Haqq, and Fu'ad Siraj al-Din who had all acted as patrons of the workers in the past. It also warned against those advocating the immediate formation of a communist party which the New Dawn group regarded as premature.

In all probability the strong influence of communists and the high level of political activity contributed greatly to the government's decision to dissolve the General Union of Mechanized Textile and Preparatory Workers in Greater Cairo. But the official dissolution decree issued on April 28, 1945, justified the decision solely on the grounds that the union had incited or participated in over fifty strikes from January to April 1945, and had been attempting to organize a federation of textile workers' unions.[40] The union's latest name reflected its continuing effort to expand its constituency. Shortly before its dissolution, the union claimed nearly 15,000 members throughout greater Cairo,[41] making it the second largest union in Egypt. This represented a substantial mass base that had already engaged in a high level of militant working class economic and political struggle and was undoubtedly considered a dangerous threat by the government.

At the time of the dissolution of the union Taha Sa'd 'Uthman and several other union leaders were arrested briefly.[42] But the functioning of the union was not seriously impaired. A general committee of stewards, representing the various workplaces the union had organized, continued to meet regularly although secretly, and through its executive committee conducted the union's activities.[43] At the same time the union leadership became more intensely involved in political activity led by the New Dawn group.

The Egyptian Movement for National Liberation (EMNL)

New Dawn was the first Egyptian communist organization to strike roots in the working class during and after the Second World War. However, during the period from 1942 to 1954 the most influential and effective of the Egyptian communist organizations, among workers as well as among the general population, was the Democratic Movement for National Liberation (DMNL—al-Haraka al-Dimuqra-

39. FO 371/45978/J2001 (1945).
40. al-Waqa'i' al-misriyya, May 21, 1945, p. 6.
41. 'Uthman, Min ta'rikh, p. 78.
42. al-Jabha, August 22, 1945; 'Uthman, Min ta'rikh, p. 20.
43. 'Uthman, interview, October 28, 1980.

326 Communism and Workers, 1942–1948

tiyya li'l-Tahrir al-Watani). The DMNL had its origins in the Democratic Federation (al-Ittihad al-Dimuqrati), an association of intellectuals established in late 1938 or early 1939. Some of its leaders had been members of the Federation of Peace Partisans but decided to establish a new organization committed to establishing more contact with Egyptians.[44] The most prominent leaders of the Democratic Federation were three Egyptian Jews—Henri Curiel, Hillel Schwartz, and Marcel Israel. Between 1940 and 1942, the Democratic Federation split into what eventually became three rival communist organizations: People's Liberation (Tahrir al-Sha'b) led by Israel; Iskra led by Schwartz; and the Egyptian Movement for National Liberation (EMNL—al-Haraka al-Misriyya li'l-Tahrir al-Watani) led by Curiel.[45] People's Liberation and Iskra were composed almost exclusively of intellectuals. Only the EMNL succeeded in establishing contact with and recruiting significant numbers of workers. In 1945 and 1946 Iskra and the EMNL often cooperated in working class organizing, which helped lay the basis for their eventual fusion in 1947 into the DMNL.

In early 1942, before the actual formation of the EMNL, Henri Curiel began to publish a weekly magazine, *Hurriyyat al-Shu'ub (Peoples' Freedom)*, which by April featured a regular "Workers' Affairs" page. This was expanded to two pages in May, indicating the intention to become involved in the workers' movement. But its reports on trade union activity reflected an even greater distance from the day-to-day struggles of workers than the Wafd's *al-Yara'* for the same period. Many of the articles were theoretical or exhortatory in character, though there were some exceptions. Sayyid Qandil wrote regularly in *Hurriyyat al-Shu'ub* in 1942, and the magazine mentions the activities of a Federation of Company Workers' Unions (that is, private sector as opposed to government) led by Hafiz 'Abd Rabbuh.[46] However, there is nothing that gives the impression that Curiel or others around the magazine were in regular contact with a particular group of workers or trade unions at this time.

In January 1943 the EMNL was formally established after the conclusion of a cadres' school held on the agricultural estate of Curiel's father. Among the twenty-five students were three or four air force mechanics including Sayyid Sulayman Rifa'i, who later became one of the leaders of the EMNL workers' section and eventually general secretary of the DMNL.[47] These were the first worker recruits to the EMNL.

---

44. Marcel Israel, "Taqrir," in Sa'id, *1925–1940*, p. 266; "Mahdar niqash ma'a Hinri Kuriyal," in Sa'id, *1925–1940*, p. 278.
45. Sa'id, *1940–1950*, p. 180.
46. *Hurriyyat al-shu'ub*, May 16, 1942.
47. "Mahdar niqash ma'a Hinri Kuriyal," in Sa'id, *1925–1940*, pp. 280, 285, 289.

Communism and Workers, 1942–1948 **327**

Communist Factionalism and the Workers' Movement

The factional contention between the EMNL (and later the DMNL) and New Dawn (and its successors) dominated the history of the communist movement in Egypt from 1942 to 1958, when the unity of all the communist factions was briefly achieved with the establishment of the united Communist Party of Egypt. Other smaller organizations also participated in the factional disputes of this period, but none played a significant role within the workers' movement. However, the struggle between the EMNL and New Dawn had major repercussions within the workers' movement as early as 1944.[48]

Trade union leaders associated with the future New Dawn group as well as those linked to the EMNL were active in the formation of the Congress of Private Sector Trade Unions (CPSTU—Mu'tamar Niqabat al-Sharikat wa'l-Mu'assasat al-Ahliyya), which was established in the course of two meetings early in December 1944, shortly after the announcement of the promulgation of a cadre for government workers. The CPSTU's central demand was the application of the government workers' cadre to employees of companies of the private sector.[49] Muhammad 'Abd al-Halim, president of the Misr Press Workers' Union, was the primary initiator of the CPSTU, and was chosen president. Other trade unions in the original initiating group included the Heliopolis Tramway Company union (president, Husayn Ibrahim), the Cairo Water Company union (president, Sayyid Yasin),

48. The primary sources for the reconstruction of the history of communist activity in the workers' movement are the written and oral memoirs of political and trade union activists. All these memoirs reflect, to one degree or another, the factional loyalties that prevailed at this time, though both organizations have long since been dissolved. Many former participants in communist-led labor activities were reluctant to discuss their experiences with complete candor during the time the research for this study was undertaken because of fear of reprisals by the Egyptian government. Egyptian police records which might shed light on communist activity in the workers' movement from a perspective impartial to either faction (though hardly "unbiased") are currently unavailable. British diplomatic reports of communist activity are not very incisive. Rif'at al-Sa'id has written extensively on the history of the Egyptian communist movement, and his books have served an invaluable function by gathering and preserving documents, interviews, and accounts that might otherwise have been entirely lost. But it must be frankly noted that he writes from a perspective defending and upholding the line of the organization to which he belonged, the DMNL. These are the limiting conditions for the reconstruction of an account of the relationship between the communist and workers' movements.
49. 'Uthman, K, April, 1972, p. 141. This development was ominously foreseen by the minister for social affairs, Muhammad Husayn Haykal, who warned the cabinet that adoption of the cadre for government workers would be followed by demands for the same conditions from employees in the private sector, *Mudhakkirat fi al-siyasa al-misriyya*, 2 vols. (Cairo, 1951), 2:297.

328 Communism and Workers, 1942–1948

and the Cairo Electric Light Company Union (president, Hafiz 'Abd al-Rabbuh).[50] These unions were joined by three others where a considerable Marxist presence was already well established at the leadership level: the General Union of Mechanized Textile Workers of Shubra al-Khayma and Cairo (represented by al-'Askari and 'Uthman); the Cinema House Workers' Union (represented by Murad al-Qalyubi); and the International Union of Commercial Establishment Employees (represented by Da'ud Nahum).[51] Al-'Askari and 'Uthman were close to those who would soon form the New Dawn group; Nahum was a member of the EMNL; and al-Qalyubi was a member of Iskra.

In 1944 neither of the two emergent communist tendencies had yet developed a broad base of support within the Egyptian working class, though the two tendencies already manifested distinct political styles and perspectives in working class organizing. This difference was at least partially a reflection of the characteristics of the sectors of the working class where each tendency had made its original ties. The New Dawn group and its successors focused their activities on building an organizationally and politically independent workers' movement. This movement was to be led by workers themselves and not by intellectuals, no matter how sympathetic. In practice, this objective was modified by the reality that Yusuf Darwish provided important leadership for the workers grouped around New Dawn. Spreading explicitly Marxist ideas among workers and consolidating workers organizationally in an explicitly Marxist framework was of secondary importance. Through Yusuf al-Mudarrik and the leadership of the Shubra al-Khayma textile workers, New Dawn was linked to the most militant sectors of the trade union movement who had played an active role in advocating and establishing a certain degree of trade union independence from nonworker patrons since the late 1930s. This independent trend within the trade union movement had emerged as a force before communists had begun to play any role in the workers' movement. It was the product of the experiences and struggles of the trade union leaders themselves—an expression of the "self-directed bursting forth" (al-inbithaq al-dhati) of the Egyptian working class as one author has termed it.[52]

In contrast, the first contacts of the EMNL were with relatively privileged workers. The EMNL also paid more attention than New Dawn to the dissemination of Marxist ideology, and actively recruited mem-

50. 'Askari, U, January 9, 1978; 'Abbas, al-Haraka, pp. 119–120.
51. 'Askari, U, January 9, 1978; 'Uthman, K, April, 1972, p. 141.
52. 'Abd al-Samad Jad al-Mawla, Qadaya al-jabha al-wataniyya al-taqaddumiyya fi misr (Beirut, 1979), p. 51.

Communism and Workers, 1942–1948 **329**

bers from all classes of society. Because of the higher priority the EMNL placed on the assimilation of Marxism, the first workers who joined were more educated and influenced by European political ideas than workers in New Dawn's orbit. Da'ud Nahum, for example, was a member of one of the last unions in Egypt to include a large proportion of foreign workers: a union based on the clerks of the large and fashionable department stores in the European section of Cairo— Cicurel, Shimla, Sidnawi, 'Adas, and Benzion.[53] Nahum himself was Jewish and had friends and relatives active in the French left,[54] a personal situation most untypical for Egyptian workers. Murad al-Qalyubi's Cinema House Workers' Union was a small union of white-collar workers.

According to the EMNL, the immediate task of communists in Egypt was to organize a broad national front of workers and other "patriotic classes" (including the "national bourgeoisie"). This formulation was an application of the general line of the Comintern for communist parties in the colonial and semicolonial countries, and was also inspired by the EMNL's understanding of the course of the Chinese revolution, which was seen as a model for Egypt. New Dawn's perspective on this question was similar in many respects to that of the EMNL, but the EMNL's application of this strategy, though it retained the concept of the leading role of workers in the national front, tended in practice to place less emphasis on the development of a politically and organizationally independent workers' movement than New Dawn. As the EMNL grew and became the larger organization, the difference in the social base of the two organizations within the working class all but disappeared, though in the very early stages of their development this was an important factor exacerbating the factional conflict.

The CPSTU was based among workers employed by large and profitable monopoly or semimonopoly corporations, mainly owned by foreigners.[55] The members of these unions already enjoyed better wages and working conditions than most Egyptian workers. Mahmud al-'Askari saw the demand for the application of the government cadre to private sector workers as a narrow demand which could not possibly be won by the majority of Egyptian workers employed by less prosperous enterprises. He therefore urged the CPSTU to broaden its focus, expand its ranks, and include other unions not in a realistic

53. 'Askari, *U*, January 9, 1978.
54. FO 371/53368/J146 (1946).
55. See the list of member unions reported in *al-Jabha*, January 25, 1945, and those listed by 'Abbas, *al-Haraka*, p. 120.

330 Communism and Workers, 1942–1948

position to advance this demand.[56] Yusuf al-Mudarrik urged the CPSTU to delay pressing for this demand at least until the government cadre was irrevocably in place, fearing that private sector enterprises would press the government to rescind the cadre before it was implemented.[57]

Al-'Askari continued to attend meetings of the CPSTU until at least the second half of February 1945. During the three months he participated in its meetings, he could not convince the CPSTU to broaden its ranks.[58] Failing to win this point, al-'Askari and others sharing his perspective left the CPSTU. The trade unionists linked to the EMNL remained within the federation. Da'ud Nahum's Commercial Establishment Employees Union issued a pamphlet on May 1, 1946 claiming that during 1945 twenty-five Cairo area unions with a total membership of 15,000 were members of the CPSTU and seventy provincial unions were supporters of the federation.[59]

The Congress of the World Federation of Trade Unions (WFTU)

At its first meetings the CPSTU had raised the demand that an Egyptian worker be permitted to travel to London to attend the preparatory conference for the establishment of the World Federation of Trade Unions (WFTU) to be held on February 6, 1945.[60] Muhammad 'Abd al-Halim led a delegation to the Ministry of Social Affairs with a petition endorsed by sixty trade unions to make this demand, but the government rejected the unions' petition, and replied that the Egyptian ambassador in London could represent them.[61] Consequently, no Egyptian worker delegate attended the conference.

No other Arab representatives were present at the London conference. As a result, Walter Laqueur, who attended the meeting as the representative of the General Federation of Hebrew Workers in Palestine (the Histadrut), was named the Middle East representative on the WFTU Executive Committee.[62] The Palestinian Arab trade union leaders Bulus Farah and Mukhlis 'Amr had been in contact with Yu-

56. 'Askari, U, January 30, 1978.
57. Mudarrik, TU, May 1968. The cadre of government workers was not fully implemented until February 11, 1946.
58. For reports of al-'Askari's presence at meetings see al-Yara', February 26, 1945, and al-Jabha, February 22, 1945. See also 'Askari, U, January 30, 1978.
59. Quoted in 'Abbas, al-Haraka, p. 120. Note that "international" has now dropped from the union's name, an indication that the participation of foreign workers had ceased or become negligible.
60. 'Uthman, K, April, 1972, p. 141.
61. Ibid., pp. 172, 174; al-Jabha, January 25, 1945.
62. Mudarrik, TU, May 1968.

Communism and Workers, 1942–1948 **331**

suf al-Mudarrik before the London meeting and had urged the attendance of an Egyptian delegation precisely in order to avoid this development.[63] After the selection of Laqueur as Middle East representative, al-Mudarrik and his colleagues felt a greater urgency than before to attend the founding congress of the WFTU, which was to be held in Paris on September 25, 1945.[64]

The split in the CPSTU took place at about the same time that the government dissolved the Shubra al-Khayma textile workers' union. Under these circumstances the most politically conscious of the textile workers' leaders, al-'Askari and 'Uthman, along with al-Mudarrik and several other trade union leaders with whom they shared a common history of struggle for trade union independence, concentrated their activities on sending a workers' representative to the WFTU congress in Paris. Their efforts resulted in the establishment of the Preparatory Committee for an Egyptian Trade Union Representative to the WFTU Congress in early August 1945. Al-Mudarrik, al-'Askari, and 'Uthman were the leading personalities in this committee. Among the other prominent members of the preparatory committee were Rif'at Hasib, president of the Public Establishment Workers' Union, 'Abd al-Raziq 'Abd al-Rahman, president of the Cairo Pharmaceutical Warehouse Workers' Union, and Muhammad Madbuli Sulayman, president of the Shubra al-Khayma Steamboat Workers' Union.[65]

On August 29, 1945, al-Mudarrik convened a meeting of the preparatory committee attended by twelve Cairo area trade union leaders. They resolved to call a general conference of Cairo area unions the next day in order to choose a representative to the WFTU congress. The preparatory committee also drafted a program for its work which included the following points:[66] (1) Enactment of comprehensive labor legislation on a broad range of issues including the legalization of trade union federations, a forty-hour week, a minimum wage, a weekly day off, comprehensive social insurance, the providing of jobs for those dismissed by the Anglo-American armed forces, the defense of trade union freedoms and an end to intervention in trade union activity by the government, the recognition of the right to strike, the establishment of popular committees to provide food, clothing, and shelter for the needy and to supervise agricultural and industrial production; (2) Extension of the right to unionize to agricultural laborers and their inclusion in the scope of existing labor leg-

63. *Ibid.*, June 1968; 'Askari, *U*, February 6, 1978.
64. Mudarrik, *TU*, May 1968.
65. 'Uthman, *K*, September, 1971, p. 175.
66. *Ibid.*, p. 180; Mudarrik, *TU*, July 1968; *al-Fajr al-jadid*, September 16, 1945.

332 Communism and Workers, 1942–1948

islation; (3) Recognition of the right to work, education, and medical care for all; (4) Opposition to domination of the economy by monopoly corporations, and support for nationalization of heavy industry; (5) Evacuation of imperialist armies of occupation from all countries; (6) Abolition of the remnants of reaction and fascism and establishment of true internal democracy in Egypt; (7) Aiding Arab Palestine in its struggle against Zionism and imperialism; (8) Obligation of all national sections to uphold and carry out the decisions of the WFTU; (9) Representation of the WFTU at the Paris Peace Conference; (10) Acceptance of Arabic as an official WFTU language.

The presence of several national-political, as opposed to purely trade union, demands in this program indicates the dual functions of the preparatory committee. In the course of organizing representation to the WFTU congress, a purely trade union issue, it was also serving as a forum where trade union leaders organized around the broader political program of the New Dawn group. Thus the political direction established during Faddali 'Abd al-Jayyid's election campaign was being consolidated. There is no record of any objection by participants in the preparatory committee's activities to the inclusion of these national-political demands in the program of a trade union committee. In light of the prevailing political currents in the colonial and semicolonial countries after the Second World War and the widespread international mobilization around these issues, such demands did not seem out of place. They are a clear expression of the close link between the workers' movement and the postwar upsurge in the Egyptian nationalist movement. This parallel mobilization of the national and workers' movements followed the pattern established in the years 1907–12, 1919–24 and 1935–36. The difference on this occasion was that now a strategically located sector of the working class was organizing independently of the national movement and its leadership, although not in opposition to it.

On August 30, responding to the call of the preparatory committee, representatives of over fifty Cairo unions met to elect a representative to the WFTU congress.[67] The meeting was attended by trade unionists representing a broad spectrum of political views, and included Wafdists, supporters of 'Abbas Halim's Labor party, and the unions affiliated with the CPSTU. A large majority agreed on the importance of par-

---

67. The main features of the account of al-Mudarrik's election and the subsequent events are based on 'Uthman, K, September, 1971, pp. 175 ff. 'Uthman served as recording secretary of the preparatory committee, and he includes excerpts from his minutes in his memoirs. For a newspaper account of the August 30 meeting see al-Yara', September 6, 1945 (which gives the date of the meeting as September 1 and notes the attendance of only thirty-two unions).

Communism and Workers, 1942–1948   **333**

ticipating in the WFTU congress. The two nominees for delegate were Yusuf al-Mudarrik and Da'ud Nahum. Nahum's candidacy was supported by the CPSTU unions, but al-Mudarrik, who had a broader base of support because of his long personal history in trade union struggles and the backing of unions linked to Yusuf Darwish and the Shubra al-Khayma textile workers, won the election. Nahum and his supporters apparently accepted the results of the vote at this time because he agreed to serve on the propaganda committee chosen to publicize the WFTU congress and solicit additional trade union support for dispatching a delegate. The August 30 meeting also endorsed the preparatory committee's program.

The preparatory committee called a second meeting on September 5 at which representatives of twenty-nine additional unions, including provincial unions, endorsed Mudarrik's election. Taha Sa'd 'Uthman and Muhammad Madbuli Sulayman then travelled to the provinces to gather additional political and financial support for al-Mudarrik's trip. They were warmly received in most quarters, and at the end of the campaign received the endorsement of 102 unions representing 80,000 workers.

Sometime after al-Mudarrik's election, Nahum and his supporters reconsidered their original acceptance of the results of the election, and began a campaign to win counter endorsements for Nahum, Murad al-Qalyubi, and Muhammad 'Abd al-Halim as delegates. They succeeded in gaining the endorsement of sixty-two unions representing 60,000 workers. Most trade unionists were completely unaware of the existence, let alone the political content, of the sectarian contention between New Dawn and the EMNL. It does not appear that the rival campaigns for trade union endorsements even broached the issue of a competing delegate unless it was forced upon them.[68]

When the rival delegations arrived in Paris matters were further complicated by the presence of Muhammad Ibrahim Zayn al-Din and Ahmad al-Misri, who claimed to represent the Egyptian trade union movement. Neither of them had been present at the meetings in which al-Mudarrik had been elected delegate.[69] Zayn al-Din, as has already been noted, was a paid British agent whose trip had been financed by the British embassy in Cairo. He had no base of popular support in the trade union movement and represented no one but himself. Ahmad al-Misri attended the congress as a representative of

68. 'Uthman reports raising this issue only with 'Abd al-Hamid Sulayman, president of the Misr Spinning and Weaving Company union, because representatives of the opposing faction had already visited Mahalla al-Kubra and had attempted to gain the Misr Company union's support. See *K*, September 1971, p. 189.
69. 'Askari, *U*, March 27, 1978.

334 Communism and Workers, 1942–1948

the Labor party. He apparently had some standing among the Alexandria trade unions, which contributed £E 170 towards his trip. However, 'Abbas Halim personally contributed £E 400 to finance the trip.[70]

Only Nahum arrived in Paris in time for the opening of the congress. Al-Mudarrik arrived a few days later. Under pressure from the credentials committee of the WFTU and the other Arab delegates, they agreed to form a united delegation with al-Mudarrik as delegate (on the strength of his endorsement by a larger number of unions) and Nahum as deputy-delegate.[71] Zayn al-Din and al-Misri arrived in Paris after al-Mudarrik and refused to endorse the agreement negotiated between al-Mudarrik and Nahum. When the delegates returned from Paris, each claimed to have been the true representative. The official record of the proceedings of the congress contains contradictory indications of the status of the Egyptians,[72] though only al-Mudarrik was named as a member of the General Council of the WFTU, an indication that his status as a full delegate had been most generally recognized.

The proceedings and the decisions taken in Paris do not seem to have had any direct influence on the development of the Egyptian workers' movement. None of the Egyptians made a major contribution to the deliberations of the congress. The most important aspect of the congress for the Egyptian workers' movement was that a very large number of trade union leaders and rank-and-file workers wanted to participate in the congress and actively identified with it as an expression of an international movement with which they wished to affiliate. Sayyid Qandil expressed this sentiment most clearly in an article entitled "We Are Not Alone," in which he said that as a result of Egyptian representation at the WFTU congress, Egyptian workers had become "part of the world workers' milieu and that whoever attacks us attacks them."[73] It is important to bear in mind that Sayyid Qandil, although he considered himself a socialist, was consistently anticommunist. His support for Egyptian representation at the WFTU congress and the importance he attached to it are representative of the views of a large number of Egyptian trade unionists who, though they were not communists, saw affiliation with the WFTU as a way of building their movement and defending it against attacks from the government and the capitalists. One indication of the

70. FO 371/53368/J146 (1946).
71. 'Uthman, K, November, 1971, pp. 114–15; Mudarrik, TU, June 1968.
72. Fédération syndicale mondiale, *Rapport de la conférence-congrès syndicale mondiale 25 Septembre–8 Octobre 1945* (Paris, 1945).
73. *al-Yara'*, September 23, 1945.

Communism and Workers, 1942–1948 **335**

extent to which the masses of trade union members actively supported these views is that al-Mudarrik's trip had been financed largely by small contributions from workers. When he arrived in Paris he carried with him a satchel full of receipts for contributions, some as small as three or five piastres.[74]

When Yusuf al-Mudarrik returned from Paris in late October, the Ford Workers' and Employees' Union, which was then one of the leading forces in the Alexandria trade union movement, hosted a reception honoring him and the Syrian and Lebanese WFTU delegations who were stopping in Alexandria on their way home.[75] A second reception for Cairo trade unions was held at the Casino Lilas in Rawd al-Faraj on October 29. Trade union representatives from all over Egypt attended the Cairo reception and addressed the gathering of nearly 4,000 workers.[76] At this reception the Preparatory Committee for an Egyptian Trade Union Representative to the WFTU Congress was transformed into the Preparatory Committee for an Egyptian Trade Union Congress (PCETUC—al-Lajna al-Tahdiriyya li-Mu'tamar Niqabat 'Ummal Misr).[77] The strategy of the New Dawn group was to use the successful organization of al-Mudarrik's trip to Paris as a springboard for a wider campaign to unite the Egyptian trade union movement under al-Mudarrik's leadership.

Murad al-Qalyubi, Muhammad 'Abd al-Halim, and Da'ud Nahum did not attend the reception at the Casino Lilas. They were honored at a second reception on November 28 given by the CPSTU and attended by nearly 300 trade unionists from Cairo and the provinces.[78] The superficial unity imposed on the Egyptian trade union movement in Paris dissolved as soon as the delegates returned to Egypt as each of the rival communist tendencies continued their separate, competing trade union organizing activities.

The Workers' Committee for National Liberation (WCNL)

Trade unionists close to the New Dawn group had begun discussions on the establishment of a workers' political organization some time before the initiation of activities connected with the election of a delegate to the WFTU congress. This group decided on the formation of a public organization to be called The Workers' Committee for National Liberation—The Political Organization of the Working Class (WCNL

74. Douek, interview, June 4, 1981.
75. *al-Damir*, November 7, 1945.
76. *Ibid.*; Mudarrik, *TU*, September 1968.
77. 'Uthman, *K*, November, 1971, p. 125.
78. *al-Damir*, December 5, 1945.

336 Communism and Workers, 1942–1948

—Lajnat al-'Ummal li'l-Tahrir al-Qawmi, al-Hay'a al-Siyasiyya li'l-Tabaqa al-'Amila). The program of the WCNL was finalized in mid-September 1945 during a three-day meeting at the home of Yusuf Darwish. The participants, in addition to Darwish, included Yusuf al-Mudarrik, Mahmud al-'Askari, Taha Sa'd 'Uthman, Muhammad Madbuli Sulayman, Mahmud Qutb (a member of the stewards' committee of the Shubra al-Khayma textile workers), Mahmud Hamza (a leader of the Cairo Shoe Workers' Union), and Muhammad Wahid al-Din (a teacher). Because Darwish and Wahid al-Din were not workers they did not sign the WCNL program along with the other six members of the group,[79] a detail that expressed New Dawn's intention to build the WCNL as a purely workers' political organization that could exercise working class leadership of the Egyptian national movement.

Because the WCNL was to be a public and legal organization, it was also decided that it should have a regular newspaper, so al-'Askari arranged to rent the license of an already existing weekly newspaper, *al-Damir (The Conscience)*. Al-'Askari became its editor, and 'Uthman secretary of the editorial board.[80] The program of the WCNL was officially published on October 8, 1945, the first day after martial law had been lifted in Egypt. Prior to that date al-Mudarrik had carried English and French translations of the program to Paris, and had circulated them widely among the delegates to the WFTU congress. In Egypt, 15,000 copies of the program and 25,000 copies of an accompanying explanatory statement were distributed.[81]

New Dawn's strategic conception that it was the role of the working class to unite the popular classes into a broad nationalist front under its political leadership was clearly set forth in the preamble to the program:

> Citizens:
>
> The Workers' Committee for National Liberation believes that it is the duty of the working class, whose characteristics are in the process of maturing, to present to you a nationalist program that seeks the liberation of the popular classes, which are the great majority of Egypt's inhabitants, from the yoke of imperialism and the oppression of internal exploitation.[82]

79. 'Uthman, K, July, 1971, pp. 176–77.
80. Rif'at al-Sa'id, *al-Sihafa al-yasariyya fi misr, 1925–1948* (Cairo, 1977), p. 152, calculates that the date of the first issue of *al-Damir* published by the WCNL must have been September 26, 1945. But no one has located an issue dated earlier than October 17, 1945.
81. 'Uthman, K, July, 1971, pp. 176–77.
82. *Barnamaj lajnat al-'ummal li'l-tahrir al-qawmi* (Cairo, 1945).

The program presents a comprehensive list of political demands beginning with the total evacuation of all British occupation forces from Egypt. The other issues addressed include Egypt's foreign relations, the liberation of its economy from foreign influence, land redistribution and other measures to improve the lot of the peasants, health and educational reforms, the nationalization of all monopolies and development of the national economy, and internal political reforms such as voting rights for women, the abolition of the king's power to dissolve parliament, the abolition of the political police, and the expansion of civil liberties.

In this program the class demands of the working class and its allies in the national united front—land reform, nationalization of basic industry, extension of political and trade union freedoms—are presented as Egyptian national demands. No political distinction is made between class and national demands. The interests and objectives of the working class and its allies are presented as congruent with the full achievement of Egypt's national goals. The working class assumes the right and duty to lead the nation in the struggle for these national goals because of the failures of all alternative political and class forces since the 1919 revolution.

The publication of the program of the WCNL marks the beginning of a new stage in the Egyptian national movement, a stage in which the implicitly anticapitalist but not fully socialist demands it articulated became widely accepted as legitimate nationalist demands. In this period many of the WCNL's demands were also being raised by the student movement and the emerging left wing of the Wafd, the Wafdist Vanguard. Members of New Dawn, the EMNL, and Iskra were active in the Wafdist Vanguard and had a great impact on its political development. The influential daily newspaper of the Wafdist Vanguard, *al-Wafd al-Misri*, disseminated a left-wing nationalist perspective on the Egyptian national movement and its tasks to a broad audience.

The emergence of the WCNL, the growing militance of the student movement, and the progressive radicalization of the Wafdist Vanguard were part of the tremendous upsurge in the Egyptian national movement in late 1945 and early 1946. During this upsurge, for the first time since 1919, the old guard leadership of the Wafd was not at the head of the movement. The Wafd had been weakened and discredited by the 1936 treaty, the events of February 4, 1942 (which were now becoming widely known), and the attacks on the integrity of its leadership contained in the *Black Book* published by Makram 'Ubayd. New political forces—the WCNL, the National Students' Committee, the Wafdist Vanguard, and the young communist organiza-

338 Communism and Workers, 1942–1948

tions—had now come to provide the political and organizational leadership for the nationalist movement.

Although the WCNL's program was favorably received by many trade union activists, the founding members of the WCNL never recruited additional members even from among active supporters who agreed with it or distributed its literature. Rif'at Hasib and Hasan al-Sisi, two influential and politically aware trade union leaders, criticized the founding group for failing to include them in its activities. In his memoirs Taha Sa'd 'Uthman accepted this criticism, explaining that the WCNL had a "snail's view" of the political movement and inappropriately employed methods designed to protect a secret organization in a body intended to be public.[83] This organizational conservatism, characteristic of New Dawn's political style, was one of the major causes of its failure to maintain the leadership positions it had won within the workers' movement in the last half of 1945. Despite its failure to recruit new members and consolidate its position organizationally, nonetheless, the WCNL and its weekly al-Damir played an important role in spreading militant anti-imperialist and class consciousness among workers, particularly in the region of Shubra al-Khayma.

The convergence of the working class and national movements alarmed the Egyptian government, and it quickly took notice of the WCNL and al-Damir. On October 21, 1945, Prime Minister al-Nuqrashi called the members of the WCNL to his office to offer them financial support for al-Damir if they would agree to accept his nominee as editor. The WCNL members declined this offer and embarrassed the prime minister by publishing this conversation in the next issue of al-Damir.[84] When co-optation failed to control the activities of the WCNL, repression followed. In November Taha Sa'd 'Uthman was dismissed from his job at the Sibahi mill in Shubra al-Khayma. Blacklisted by the mill owners, he could no longer find work in the Cairo area and had to take a job as a teacher in a primary school for girls in Fayum.[85]

In mid-December the army and police began a virtual military occupation of Shubra al-Khayma. This led to a major confrontation between the government and the WCNL during a strike that idled nearly all of Shubra al-Khayma's textile workers from January 1 until January 9, 1946. The strike was a response to the continuing slowdown of the textile industry, as well as a protest against the armed occupation

---

83. 'Uthman, K, August, 1971, p. 181.
84. Ibid., p. 186; 'Askari, U, July 31, 1978; al-Damir, October 24, 1945.
85. 'Uthman, K, January, 1972, p. 138.

of Shubra al-Khayma. The workers' demanded that all the plants in the area be reopened, the workers rehired, and the police and army be withdrawn.[86] Officials viewed the WCNL as the instigator of the strike and were particularly apprehensive about al-'Askari's growing prestige and influence among textile workers beyond the metropolitan Cairo area.[87] On January 2, al-Mudarrik, al-'Askari, and 'Uthman were arrested. Six hundred other workers were arrested in the course of the strike and released on January 18, but the three WCNL leaders remained in jail until May 30, 1946.[88]

In a joint statement the CPSTU and the PCETUC denounced these arrests. The joint statement also listed and protested the following incidents of repression the trade union movement had suffered from late 1945 to early 1946:[89] The Cairo Water Company had fired the president and members of the executive board of its union, charging them with incitement to strike. The Egyptian General Omnibus Company had fired sixty-eight workers including the president and secretary of its union. The Shubra al-Khayma textile workers' union had been dissolved by government order. Trade union meetings had been proscribed in Fayum, Port Said, Kafr al-Shaykh, and Damanhur. Meetings of the CPSTU and the PCETUC had been banned. The annual meeting of the Egyptian General Omnibus Company Workers' Union had been prohibited. The Ford union in Alexandria was threatened with dissolution because of its leading role in the local trade union movement. A military occupation of Shubra al-Khayma had been in effect since mid-December 1945. Muhammad 'Abd al-Halim had been fired from his job at the Misr Press for attending the WFTU Congress. Hundreds of workers' homes had been searched and tens of workers arrested. During a strike at the Cairo Water Company, even strikers' wives had been arrested and held captive in the company offices in order to force an end to the strike.

There is no doubt that the Egyptian government was alarmed by the power to unite the social and national questions the WCNL represented, or the government would not have acted so severely to repress the Shubra al-Khayma textile workers, destroy the organized working class radicalism they supported, and block similar developments elsewhere. The government's repressive actions did destroy the WCNL as an organized body with a mass following, but the upsurge in the workers' movement continued under new leadership. The arrest

86. *WM*, January 2, 4, 1946.
87. FO 371/53327/J1565 (1946).
88. *al-Ahram*, January 19, 1946; *WM*, May 31, 1946.
89. *Bayan mushtarak min al-lajna al-tahdiriyya wa-mu'tamar niqabat al-sharikat wa'l-mu'assasat al-ahliyya* (Yusuf al-Mudarrik papers, Cairo).

340 Communism and Workers, 1942–1948

of the three WCNL leaders crippled the activity of the WCNL and the New Dawn group within the workers' movement. This might not have occurred if sympathetic workers had been recruited to the WCNL or New Dawn and given adequate political training. Because al-Mudarrik and al-'Askari were the only formally affiliated worker members of New Dawn, the group's influence in the working class was heavily dependent on their personal roles. Following their arrest *al-Damir* had to suspend regular publication.[90] After January 1946 the EMNL became the more influential communist organization in the working class.

The National Committee of Workers and Students (NCWS)

Shortly before the outbreak of the Shubra al-Khayma textile strike, on December 20, 1945, the Egyptian government had sent a memorandum to Great Britain suggesting that the 1936 treaty be renegotiated on the basis of maintaining the military alliance between the two countries. When the contents of this memorandum and the British reply became known to the public, the response was mass outrage at the very willingness of the Egyptian government to negotiate with Great Britain while British troops still occupied Egypt, let alone to consider maintaining the alliance and a possible continuation of British military presence in the country. Public confidence in the government's ability to win Egypt's national demands, principally the total evacuation of British troops, evaporated.

The Shubra al-Khayma strike served to intensify the confrontation between the regime and the nationalist opposition. The Wafdist Vanguard's daily, *al-Wafd al-Misri*, actively supported the striking textile workers, and despite its tendency to minimize the political implications of the strike, the alignment of political forces was clear. The nationalist movement led by left-wing political forces was supporting both workers' economic demands and national political demands opposed by the government, its large landowning and industrialist supporters, the Palace, and Great Britain. Throughout January and February the political crisis escalated until it was brought to a head by developments in the student movement.[91]

90. The first issue of *al-Damir* published after the arrest of the three which has been located is dated June 24, 1946. It bears the numbering volume 8, no. 9, so it is possible that eight earlier issues were published in 1946, but even if this were the case, publication could only have been very sporadic.
91. For a detailed account of these events, see Jean-Pierre Thieck, "La journée du 21 février dans l'histoire du mouvement national égyptien" (Mémoire de D.E.S., Université de Paris, VII, 1973).

Communism and Workers, 1942–1948   **341**

On February 9, 1946, several thousand students held a conference at Cairo University in Giza. Resolutions were adopted demanding the termination of negotiations with Britain, abrogation of the 1936 treaty and the 1899 agreement on the Sudan, and the immediate evacuation of British troops from Egypt and the Sudan. The students then marched to 'Abdin Palace to present their resolutions to King Faruq. As the demonstration crossed the 'Abbas Bridge spanning the Nile River, the Egyptian police and army opened the bridge and attacked the procession. Several marchers fell into the river and many were injured. This incident provoked an upswelling of popular anger throughout Egypt which resulted in an acceleration in the tempo of nationalist agitation and demonstrations from February 10 to March 4.

The climax of the nationalist agitation and the clearest expression of its new class content and political direction was the formation of the National Committee of Workers and Students (NCWS—al-Lajna al-Wataniyya li'l-'Ummal wa'l-Talaba). The NCWS was formed on February 18 and 19 after a series of meetings in which representatives of the General Nationalist Committee of Shubra al-Khayma workers, Cairo tram workers, printers, the CPSTU, the PCETUC, and the Association of Egyptian Working Women (Rabitat al-'Amilat al-Misriyya) participated.[92] Among the prominent worker members of the NCWS were Sayyid 'Ali, secretary of the Misr Press Workers' Union; Murad al-Qalyubi and Husayn Kazim of the Cinema House Workers' Union; Najib Sus, secretary of the Cairo Tramway Workers' Union; Husayn Nassar, secretary of the Egyptian General Omnibus Company Workers' Union; Mahmud al-Dumrani and Sayyid Khudayr, members of the stewards' committee of the Shubra al-Khayma textile workers; and Kamil al-Najjari, a waiter.[93] These trade union figures represented many of the important sectors of the working class in the greater Cairo area. The textile workers of Shubra al-Khayma were especially prominent in the working class component of the NCWS.

The NCWS called for a general strike on February 21, which was designated as "Evacuation Day." On that day in Cairo a crowd of from 40,000 to 100,000, which included a contingent of 15,000 workers from Shubra al-Khayma, rallied at Queen Farida (now Opera) Square.[94] Following the rally four British armored vehicles crossing the street in front of the Qasr al-Nil British army barracks (currently the site of the Nile Hilton Hotel) drove into a crowd of demonstrators

92. 'Abd al-Mun'im al-Ghazzali, "Mawqi' 21 fibrayir 1946 min al-ta'rikh," al-Tali'a 2 (February 1966):54. Al-Ghazzali was an active participant in these events as a student.
93. FO 371/53368/J1447 (1946).
94. al-Ahram, February 22, 1946.

342 Communism and Workers, 1942–1948

and killed or injured several of them. The crowd attacked the vehicles, set them on fire, and by the end of the day 23 demonstrators were dead and 121 wounded. General strikes and demonstrations were also conducted in a dozen provincial cities on February 21. Such widespread militant nationalist mobilization had not been witnessed in Egypt since the 1919 revolution.

As a memorial to the Cairo demonstrators who died on February 21, the NCWS called for a second general strike on March 4, which was designated as "Martyrs' Day." The demonstration in Cairo was small that day; but in Alexandria a clash between the large crowd and British troops left 28 demonstrators dead and 342 wounded. Newspapers, factories, stores, and schools closed in protest throughout the country. The largest strike was a Mahalla al-Kubra where 25,000 workers stopped work at the Misr Spinning and Weaving Company.[95]

February 21, 1946: Problems and Prospects

In *What Is To Be Done?* Lenin counterposes the spontaneous character of economic and political mass movements to the theoretically informed consciousness that, he argued, the leadership of such movements required if they were to achieve any but the most immediate goals. In this sense the formation of the NCWS was a spontaneous phenomenon: the product of an upsurge of popular participation and militancy in the nationalist movement unparalleled since 1919. The pace of the development of the mass movement in early 1946 far outstripped the capacity of any existing or potential leadership to direct or provide it with a stable organizational form. The creation of the NCWS was the result of the desire for unity among the leadership of the left wing of the nationalist movement based among the radicalized intelligentsia and workers. However, this leadership was unable to overcome its internal divisions and lack of experience sufficiently to carry out the tasks it faced. Shuhdi 'Atiyya al-Shafi'i, who participated in the NCWS as a Cairo University campus activist and member of Iskra, specifically mentions the divisions among its leadership as one of the factors that weakened the NCWS and diminished its effectiveness.[96]

A second weakness mentioned by al-Shafi'i was the undemocratic structure of the NCWS. Because the NCWS was formed hastily and without advance preparation in the midst of a mass movement in

95. *WM*, March 5, 1946.
96. Shuhdi 'Atiyya al-Shafi'i, *Tatawwur al-haraka al-wataniyya al-misriyya*, pp. 108–109.

Communism and Workers, 1942–1948   **343**

rapid motion, its leaders did not have the opportunity to establish regular procedures for consulting the mass organizations they were ostensibly representing. This tended to isolate the committee members from their constituencies and weaken the representative character of the NCWS. The NCWS did not establish local branches in factories, neighborhoods, or schools which might have provided roots for the coalition of forces achieved at the national leadership level.

The New Dawn group, especially its worker organizations, the WCNL and the PCETUC, were less active in the NCWS than the EMNL, the CPSTU, and Iskra. This was because of the incarceration of the three most prominent worker-leaders of the WCNL during most of the period that the NCWS was in existence and because New Dawn and the WCNL had failed to recruit new members during this period of mass radicalization. Because of their weaker position within the NCWS, New Dawn supporters were somewhat more sensitive to the flaws in its internal structure, and in particular, to the domination of the NCWS by the student element.

This was indicated by the PCETUC's letter to the NCWS charging that workers were not fairly represented on the committee because the number of student and worker representatives was equal, and students had a majority of votes in the secretariat and financial committee.[97] As a corrective measure, the PCETUC suggested that no decision be adopted without the agreement of at least half the worker members of the NCWS. In addition, the proposed political program of the NCWS was criticized for failing to indicate sufficient confidence in the struggle of the Egyptian working class. According to the PCETUC, the role of students in this period was not to lead the national movement, but to help the working class express its goals and demands. The PCETUC also wanted the NCWS to become a purely representative body whose members were bound by the decisions of their constituent organizations which, it argued, would improve both the mass mobilization capacity and the level of internal democracy within the NCWS. The PCETUC was especially insistent that the organizational and political independence of workers' organizations not be subordinated to non-workers.

The PCETUC's letter identified substantive weaknesses. Though its criticisms reflected the political perspective of the New Dawn group and New Dawn's emphasis on building the organizational and political independence of the working class, they should not be considered merely sectarian carping. The PCETUC's letter, although it is more detailed and much more sensitive to the question of the relationship

97. Quoted in 'Uthman, K, May, 1972, pp. 153 ff.

344 Communism and Workers, 1942–1948

between the class forces within the NCWS, identified the same basic weaknesses as al-Shafi'i's summation of the activity of the NCWS written from a competing political perspective. The NCWS was neither sufficiently united politically nor deeply rooted enough among the Egyptian people to carry out simultaneously the tasks of mobilizing and leading both the national and workers' movements. The political and organizational immaturity of the NCWS leadership prevented it from fully exploiting the enormous political opportunity before it.

Despite these weaknesses the events of February 21, 1946 irreversibly infused the Egyptian national movement with a new and more radical social content. These events marked the Wafd's effective loss of leadership over the national movement and the sharp contention between the left and the Muslim Brothers to provide an alternative identity and ideology for that movement. Although the left failed to consolidate itself as a new nationalist leadership, it would henceforth always be a political factor to be considered, representing possibilities all the other political forces in Egypt desperately sought to avoid.

The Attempt to Establish Trade Union Unity

The success of the mass mobilizations of February 21 and March 4, the recurrent attacks on the trade union movement, continuing plant closings, the steady increase in the number of unemployed workers, and the arrests of al-Mudarrik, al-'Askari, and 'Uthman all created pressure for establishing greater unity in the workers' movement. However, the arrests of the PCETUC leaders on January 2, 1946 critically weakened that organization, and it was therefore the CPSTU which emerged as the center of leadership as the movement struggled to achieve unity. Because most rank and file trade unionists were unaware of the ideological dispute which underlay the division between the CPSTU and the PCETUC, it was not difficult for the CPSTU to step into the vacuum left by the arrest of the PCETUC's leadership. One clear indication that most workers did not distinguish between the two rival communist trends was the election of Muhammad Shatta, a member of the EMNL, as chairman of the stewards' committee of the Shubra al-Khayma Textile workers[98] which had formerly been the main base of support for the WCNL.

The CPSTU took advantage of the relative inactivity of the PCETUC

98. Sa'id, 1940–1950, p. 247, says that Shatta was elected in late 1945 and after the strike. However, the strike did not take place until January 1, 1946. The first time Shatta's name appears at the head of a list of stewards' signatures is in al-Ahram, January 7, 1946. It seems reasonable to assume that his election was related to the arrest of al-'Askari and 'Uthman.

Communism and Workers, 1942–1948 **345**

and seized the opportunity provided by the upsurge in the nationalist movement and the growing desire for trade union unity to expand its ranks beyond its original constituency. This intention was signaled on May 1, 1946 by announcing that the organization was henceforth to be known as the Congress of Egyptian Trade Unions (CETU—Mu'tamar Niqabat 'Ummal Misr).[99] Husayn Kazim, president of the Cinema House Workers' Union and a member of the EMNL, was elected general secretary of the CETU. Among its constituent unions was the Association of Egyptian Working Women, the first organization of women workers in Egypt, led by Hikmat al-Ghazzali, a textile worker in Shubra al-Khayma and a member of the EMNL.

An additional incentive for the consolidation of trade union unity was the outbreak of a major strike of Shubra al-Khayma textile workers on or around May 12. The events of this strike are difficult to reconstruct because shortly after it began the government imposed censorship on press coverage. The strike appears to have begun over the refusal of the Nasr Textile Company to pay workers their wages and the management's threat to close the mill and move it to Alexandria. The workers occupied the mill and refused to leave until management and the government assured them that the two Nasr mills in Shubra al-Khayma would remain open.[100] The strike spread quickly and eventually at least nineteen mills in Shubra al-Khayma went out—a nearly total regional strike of the textile industry.[101] The main issue, as it had been for a year in most of the labor struggles of the area, was the threat of closure of the mills and unemployment. The mill owners and the government recognized the critical nature of this struggle and mounted a major campaign, enlisting the aid of the Society of Muslim Brothers, to break the strike, the organization of the Shubra al-Khayma textile workers, and the strength of the left within the workers' movement. (For more on the role of the Muslim Brothers in the strike, see Chapter XI.)

On May 15, just days after the Shubra al-Khayma strike began, Muhammad Madbuli Sulayman, as secretary of the PCETUC, sent a letter to Murad al-Qalyubi offering to unite the two trade union federations because of the continuing attacks on the trade union movement.[102] The offer of unity was immediately accepted, and the May 18 issue of al-Mu'tqmar (The Congress), an irregular newspaper published by the CPSTU and then the CETU, carried the new name of the united trade

99. This date is written in by hand on a copy of Mashru' la'ihat al-nizam al-asasi li-mu'tamar niqabat 'ummal misr (Yusuf al-Mudarrik papers, Cairo).
100. WM, May 12, 28, 1946.
101. IM, June 2, 1946.
102. Text quoted in 'Uthman, K, March, 1972, p. 145.

346 Communism and Workers, 1942–1948

union federation on its masthead—the Congress of Trade Unions of Egypt (CTUE—Mu'tamar Niqabat 'Ummal al-Qatr al-Misri).[103]

The factional contention was not, however, so easily resolved. On May 30 a mass meeting was held in Cairo to endorse the decision to unify the two factions.[104] Rank and file workers and trade union leaders, particularly those from the provinces, exerted considerable pressure on the partisans of both factions to confirm the decision to unite. At one point in the meeting Sayyid 'Ali, secretary of the Misr Press Workers' Union, ripped up the minutes taken by Taha Sa'd 'Uthman declaring that they revealed too much dissension. The majority of those attending the meeting warmly supported this action. Finally, an uneasy ratification of unity was achieved on the basis of representing both factions in the leadership of the new trade union federation. However, most of the active figures in the CTUE leadership were members or supporters of the EMNL.

The May 30 meeting also endorsed the program of demands that had been adopted by the CETU on May 1:[105] (1) the immediate and total political, military, and economic evacuation of Great Britain from the Nile Valley; (2) the application of the government workers' cadre to all workers; (3) a campaign against unemployment by government takeover of all plants threatening to close; (4) the return of unemployed workers to their jobs; (5) the release of all workers jailed for trade union activities; (6) an end to the firings and banishment of Shubra al-Khayma workers; (7) a forty-hour work week; and (8) recognition of May Day as an official holiday. June 10 was set as a deadline for the government to reply favorably to these demands after which the CTUE threatened a nation-wide general strike. Subsequently, both the deadline and date for the general strike were postponed to June 25.

The prominence of the demand for British evacuation at the head of a list of trade union demands indicates the extent to which the events of late 1945 and early 1946, had fused the connection between their economic struggle and the national political struggle, in the minds of Egyptian worker-leaders. Perhaps because of this, the CTUE leadership had an exaggerated sense of its own strength. Taha Sa'd 'Uthman's attempt to warn the May 30 meeting that it was unrealistic to expect to achieve British evacuation within ten days, and that the

103. No copies of this publication appear to have survived, so this account relies on 'Uthman, K, April, 1972, p. 142.

104. The account of this meeting is based on 'Uthman, K, July, 1972, pp. 148–49. 'Uthman served as recording secretary of the meeting which he attended with al-'Askari and al-Mudarrik only hours after the three were released from jail.

105. WM, May 5, 1946; Sa'id, *1940–1950*, p. 255.

Communism and Workers, 1942–1948   **347**

CTUE was not strong enough to lead the proposed general strike were dismissed as defeatism and an expression of his fear of returning to jail.[106]

The CTUE's decision to call for a general strike was not an entirely overoptimistic evaluation of its capacities. There was an unmistakable popular upsurge affecting many sectors of the working class during May and June 1946. This upsurge was linked to the continuing high level of nationalist mobilization, but it was also rooted in the independent class demands of the working class. The most important of these, and this is clearly indicated in the program of the CTUE, was the demand to reduce the level of unemployment and improve job security. This demand was consistently supported by the Wafdist Vanguard and *al-Wafd al-Misri*, which portrayed the question of unemployment as part of the national question.[107]

The impending unification of the Egyptian trade union movement and the outbreak of the strike in Shubra al-Khayma sparked a wave of strikes, political protests, and declarations of support for the CTUE. Trade unions in Alexandria, Banha, Mahalla al-Kubra, Damietta, Port Said, Damanhur, Mansura, Zaqaziq, Manfalut, and Shubra al-Khayma affiliated to the CTUE, in addition to the Cairo affiliates.[108] The issue of mass unemployment, particularly in the textile industry, which the Shubra al-Khayma strike highlighted, was taken up by workers in other textile centers. On May 23 several workers attempted to commit suicide in the Alexandria Labor Office as a protest against unemployment.[109] On May 26 unemployed workers held a conference in the Nubar Gardens of Alexandria. Police surrounded the meeting and arrested 400 workers.[110] There were two strikes during June at the Misr Spinning and Weaving Company in Mahalla al-Kubra organized by secret workers' committees in opposition to the recognized union.[111] The workers raised demands related to firings and layoffs.

Another expression of both the radicalization of the working class and the desire for unity within the labor movement caused by the events of the first half of 1946 was the split in Prince 'Abbas Halim's Labor party. Members of the WCNL and other independent-minded trade unionists infiltrated the barely functioning party and appear to have been among the forces instigating the split. The trade union

---

106. 'Uthman, K, July, 1972, p. 151.
107. See, for example, WM, April 17, 1946.
108. *Ibid.*, May 5, 1946.
109. *Ibid.*, May 24, 1946.
110. *Ibid.*, May 27, 1946.
111. *Ibid.*, June 12, 1946; al-Ghazzali, *Ta'rikh*, p. 220.

348 Communism and Workers, 1942–1948

leaders who had been affiliated with the party denounced the leadership of the prince's lieutenants and demanded that the party become a popular democratic front which would not cooperate with reactionary capitalist or landholding interests. Among the specific complaints of the trade unionists was 'Abbas Halim's failure to support the Shubra al-Khayma strike.[112] After the split the trade union leaders formed the short-lived Socialist Labor party.

The mobilization and radicalization of the labor movement did not go unnoticed by the government. Isma'il Sidqi had been brought to power on February 17 in an effort to stem the tide of the nationalist upsurge. Sidqi was particularly unpopular with workers who recalled his harsh repression of the trade union movement during his previous term as prime minister in 1930–1933. During its first months in office the Sidqi government was unable to do more than monitor the mass nationalist upsurge, but the CTUE's brash call for a general strike allowed the government and its allies to deploy their strength and influence and demonstrate the limits of the power of the workers' movement. For example, the Cairo Tramway Workers' Union, headed by Shaykh 'Abd al-Zahir al-Shahid, a sympathizer of the Muslim Brothers, was persuaded to withdraw its support from the CTUE and the general strike.[113] The inability to halt public transportation in Cairo sharply diminished the potential impact of the threatened general strike. Another sector of the trade union leadership was removed from the impending confrontation on June 21 when the delegation of Egyptian trade unionists led by Ibrahim Zayn al-Din and Fathi Kamil left for London—a trip, arranged by the British labor attaché in Cairo, M. T. Audsley. Finally, the government, in conjunction with the Muslim Brothers and the mill owners, unleashed a campaign of repression and intimidation against the Shubra al-Khayma textile strike, which had become the symbol of postwar worker militancy and the new political role of the workers' movement.

The internal disunity of the CTUE and its organizational weakness which were due to its recent formation combined with the government's efforts to blunt the proposed general strike left the CTUE unable to implement its threat. On June 25 there was a partial strike of Suez Canal workers in Port Said and a full strike at the Filature Nationale in Alexandria.[114] The weakening strike at Shubra al-Khayma continued, but the general strike was almost a complete failure. In the days following June 25, many of the CTUE leaders were arrested for

112. WM, June 9, 1946; 'Abbas, al-Haraka, pp. 331-34.
113. 'Uthman, K, July 1972, p. 157.
114. WM, June 26, 1946.

Communism and Workers, 1942–1948   **349**

inciting to strike. Among those jailed were the two CTUE secretaries, Husayn Kazim and Taha Sa'd 'Uthman, two of the leaders of the stewards' committee of the Shubra al-Khayma Textile workers, Sayyid Khudayr and Mahmud al-Dumrani, Ibrahim 'Abd al-Salim, secretary of the Alexandria Shoemakers' Union, Yusuf al-Mudarrik, Mahmud al-'Askari, and Murad al-Qalyubi.[115]

Following the failure of the general strike and the arrest of the CTUE leaders, the government launched a comprehensive attack on the Egyptian communist movement and the entire left wing of the national movement which had been cooperating with the communists since the beginning of the nationalist upsurge. On July 11, all of the leftist and labor newspapers, magazines, and associations in Egypt were closed. A large number of intellectuals and workers were arrested and charged with spreading communism, and the CTUE was officially dissolved. A new anticommunist law was submitted to the parliament. July 11, 1946 marked the decisive defeat of the mass upsurge of late 1945 and early 1946 and brought a close to a period in which the possibility of a social and political revolution, though unrealistic in retrospect, had been taken seriously by all sides in the confrontation.

Repression and Reorganization

The harsh repression unleashed by the Sidqi government inflicted a major setback on both the nationalist and workers' movements. The radical intelligentsia and the working class which had led the mass movement of late 1945 and early 1946 were not strong enough or sufficiently well organized to defeat the government and its British allies. At the very least the movement would have had to establish a strong alliance with the peasantry in order to have made this a realistic prospect. However, although the government succeeded for the moment in preserving the regime and destroying many of the opposition organizations, it was not prepared to carry out substantive social reforms to eliminate the conditions that had given rise to the mass movement. This guaranteed that as soon as the repression was eased, the opposition movement would reassert itself.

The memorandum of explanation accompanying the anticommunist law proposed in July 1946 noted the rapid growth of communism in Egypt, "especially among our quiet and gentle working classes."[116] Despite the government's open admission that communism had be-

115. *Ibid.*, June 29, 1946; FO 371/53327/J3793 (1946).
116. *al-Ahram*, July 10, 1946.

350 Communism and Workers, 1942–1948

come an important factor in the working class, it refused to believe that this was the result of causes other than the satanic manipulations of "outside agitators." The prevailing political theory of those representing landholding and industrial interests still did not imagine that any Egyptian workers could come to see themselves as a class whose interests were opposed to those of the Egyptian ruling classes and their British allies. Hamid al-'Abd, director of the Labor Department, expressed this traditional view of the Egyptian ruling classes in an interview with *al-Ahram* on July 23, 1946 in the wake of the government's crackdown on the left. Egyptian workers, he asserted, were not prone to violence and were immune to communism because communist ideology contradicted their religion.

Despite Hamid al-'Abd's assertion of Egyptian workers' docility, the government was sensitive enough to social reality to make at least a token effort to placate worker militancy. In early July 1946, a ministerial committee was formed to investigate workers' demands. The only worker representatives on the committee who had participated actively in the CTUE were Muhammad 'Abd al-Halim, one of the few leading figures not arrested, and Shaykh 'Abd al-Zahir al-Shahid, who had shown his pliability by removing his Cairo Tramway Workers' Union from participation in the general strike. The committee held several meetings throughout the summer of 1946, but nothing ever came of its discussions or decisions. One of the more creative actions of the workers' movement during the lull created by the Sidqi repression was the publication of the minutes of the meetings of the ministerial committee. Textile workers were represented on the ministerial committee by 'Abd al-Fattah Husayn, president of the Textile Foremen and Assistant Foremen's Union, and he secretly gave Taha Sa'd 'Uthman copies of the minutes of the meetings. 'Uthman then published them so that this officially sanctioned description of wages and working conditions and the suggested improvements raised in the committee meetings could be used to support workers' demands.[117] The minutes of the discussions revealed that low wages, unsafe and unhealthy working conditions, and insecurity of employment were characteristic features of Egyptian industry, particularly in the textile sector.

The Sidqi repression succeeded in cutting the personal and organizational link between the workers' movement and the left wing of the national movement by arresting most of the individual leaders

---

117. *Mahadir wa-taqarir al-lajna al-wizariyya al-'ulya al-mukawwana fi yulyu 1947* [i.e. 1946] *li-bahth matalib al-'ummal* (Cairo, 1946); 'Uthman, interview, January 22, 1981.

Communism and Workers, 1942–1948 **351**

who had connected the two movements through their political activity and organizational affiliations. The arrest of leading militants naturally led to a decline in both trade union and nationalist struggle. The number of strikes and other worker protests dropped sharply as the working class withstood the impact of the repression. The tide of the nationalist movement also began to recede as a result of the repression and the opening of the Sidqi-Bevin negotiations to revise the 1936 treaty. The second half of 1946 and the first half of 1947 was a period of relative inactivity, regroupment, and reorganization for the workers' movement. Still, the Sidqi repression was unable to destroy the mutually reinforcing relations between the workers' movement and the nationalist movement and the new social content this imparted to the nationalist movement. On the contrary, the pattern of parallel ebb and flow between the two became more pronounced and persisted throughout the postwar period until the military coup of July 23, 1952.

The failure of the Sidqi-Bevin negotiations exhausted the political credit of the regime and allowed the nationalist movement to begin to recover some of the momentum it had lost during the period of demobilization produced by the repression. However, the resurgence of the mass movement was temporarily contained by the government's request that the United Nations Security Council consider Egypt's demand for full independence and British evacuation. By late summer 1947 it became apparent that the council would not resolve the question to Egypt's satisfaction. This realization sparked a renewal of nationalist activity that was accompanied by a strike wave from September 1947 to April 1948.

The organization that appears to have suffered most heavily from the Sidqi repression was New Dawn/Workers' Vanguard. In September 1946 the group was reorganized and renamed the Popular Vanguard for Liberation. It had perhaps twenty-five or thirty members at this time, which, though still a small number, represented a 500 percent growth in membership.[118] Despite this growth, the organization appears to have become closed in on itself as a result of the repression, and it grew even more security-conscious and wary of open communist political activity than ever before. Its working class section, already damaged by the blacklisting and arrest of its leading cadres, was further weakened by the repeated and lengthy arrests of Yusuf Darwish (from November 1948 to November 1949 and from November 1950 to April 1953).[119] Consequently, most of the Popular

118. Rif'at al-Sa'id, *Munazzamat al-yasar al-misri, 1950–1957* (Cairo, 1983), p. 306.
119. Darwish, "Letter to Jamal 'Abd al-Nasir." According to *al-Ahram*, November 3,

352 Communism and Workers, 1942–1948

Vanguard's activities after 1946 were conducted within the framework of the Wafdist Vanguard. All these factors—the overly security-conscious attitude of the organization, the blacklisting of veteran worker-leaders, such as al-'Askari and 'Uthman, and the arrest of key cadres—resulted in a virtual end to the visible and leading role that workers associated with New Dawn and the WCNL had played in 1945 and 1946, though the Popular Vanguard continued to wield some influence among both workers and intellectuals.

The EMNL and Iskra originally suffered organizational damage that may have even exceeded the impact of the Sidqi repression on the Popular Vanguard for Liberation. The number of EMNL cadres in Shubra al-Khayma fell from 120 to 20 during the repression.[120] But these organizations, unlike the Popular Vanguard, quickly reestablished themselves, and in June 1947 merged to form the Democratic Movement for National Liberation (DMNL), whose 1,600 members included a majority of intellectuals and a significant number of foreigners and mutamassirun.[121] The workers' section of the organization was composed almost entirely of former EMNL members.[122] The unity of Iskra and the EMNL was achieved without full discussion and agreement by the cadres of each organization, and for this reason the DMNL began to fracture in late 1947 and early 1948. By July 1948 several splits had occurred which resulted in the formation of a number of smaller groups. Recriminations against the heavily Jewish leadership of the DMNL and its endorsement of the partition of Palestine and the establishment of a Jewish state played an important part in the factional conflict within the DMNL. Despite these splits, the DMNL continued to be the largest and most influential communist organization and the only one with broad working class support. As Tariq al-Bishri has suggested, its influence and importance in both the working class and the broader Egyptian political movement far exceeded its relatively small membership.[123]

The early success of the DMNL was due largely to the quality of its weekly newspaper, al-Jamahir (The Masses), which was first issued by Iskra on April 7, 1947, but then became the organ of the DMNL. Its circulation has been variously estimated to have been from 8,000 to

1950 a key textile worker activist, Fu'ad 'Abd al-Mun'im Shihtu, was arrested with Darwish in November 1950, another blow to the organization's influence in the textile industry.
120. Sa'id, 1940–1950, p. 411.
121. Ibid., p. 389.
122. Ibid., FO 371/69250/J1890 (1948).
123. Tariq al-Bishri, al-Haraka al-siyasiyya fi misr, 1945–1952 (Cairo, 1972), p. 74.

Communism and Workers, 1942–1948   **353**

12,000.[124] Even the smaller figure would have represented a substantial number for a weekly newspaper in a country where the overwhelming majority of inhabitants were illiterate. *Al-Jamahir* was particularly important for the working class organizing of the DMNL because in 1947 there were no large trade unions under communist leadership and communist activity in the working class had to be conducted outside, and even in opposition to, the trade unions in the large industrial enterprises.[125] The DMNL used *al-Jamahir* effectively as an organizing tool. Free copies of the paper were distributed to workers in large industrial enterprises. In order to make contacts in these work places, *al-Jamahir* regularly devoted its centerfold to "factory exposures" of the kind described by Lenin in *What Is to Be Done?* Detailed articles and photographs displaying a high journalistic standard were published on the Shubra al-Khayma textile industry, the Misr Spinning and Weaving Company in Mahalla al-Kubra, the Filature Nationale in Alexandria, the Hawamdiyya sugar refinery, Eastern Tobacco Company, the Cairo Tramway Company, the Suez Canal Company, the textile industry of the Zaytun and Matariyya suburbs of Cairo, and many other large industrial enterprises. Each article provided a history of the enterprise, or group of enterprises, and the labor struggles that had occurred there. Current conditions were summarized and a program of demands for the workers was suggested. Using this method the DMNL was able to make contacts and win the support of workers in many of these enterprises during late 1947 and early 1948.

Strike at Misr Spinning and Weaving Company

Al-Jamahir seems to have been the main instrument used by the DMNL to organize workers at the Misr Spinning and Weaving mill. The centerfold of the June 2, 1947 issue contained an exposé of the mill that described the history of the 1938 strike, the links of the Misr Company to the government, and called on workers to reform the union and oust its procompany leadership. The next issue announced that "a group of Mahalla workers" had made a financial contribution to support *al-Jamahir*—a detail that indicates that *al-Jamahir*'s exposé was favorably received by some Misr workers. According to British diplomatic reports, twelve DMNL members came to Mahalla al-Kubra from Cairo and hired on at the Misr mill under false

124. FO 371/69250/J1890 (1948); Sa'id, *al-Sihafa al-yasariyya fi misr, 1925–1948*, pp. 177–78.
125. FO 371/63046/J645 (1947).

354 Communism and Workers, 1942–1948

names.[126] A DMNL branch was established in the city led by Muhammad Hamza, a textile worker. All indications point to him as the leader of the secret strike committees that organized the massive workers' uprising which broke out in the mill in September 1947.[127] Tension had been building among the workers in the mill for nearly a year. There had been a short work stoppage in January 1947 prompted by rumors that 3,000 workers (according to some reports 8,000) and 250 clerical employees were to be dismissed as a result of the introduction of new machinery.[128] A large number of workers had been dismissed during the summer which led workers to the conclusion that the company was attempting to dismiss veteran workers and replace them with new hires at lower wages.[129] On September 2, the Misr management posted a new schedule of disciplinary regulations with accompanying fines for violators in the mill. Complaints against the harsh and arbitrary methods of management had long been a major grievance of the workers, and the new regulations and fines, though insignificant in themselves, unleashed years of pent-up hatred and frustration. Some recently dismissed workers read the regulations aloud to a large crowd of workers about to begin a new shift which provoked a spontaneous demonstration against the new measures. When company security officials arrived, one fired his weapon and thereby instigated a riot.[130] Workers set fire to the cafeteria, damaged some of the workers' housing built by the company, and destroyed company property worth £E 20,000. Four workers were killed, nineteen wounded, and fifty-seven arrested as a result of the riot.

The Misr Company proudly advertised its deep concern for the welfare of its workers and provided them with a cafeteria, housing, recreational activities, clubs, a store, a clinic and many other facilities. The destruction of the cafeteria and housing in the September 1947 workers' uprising indicates that workers scorned these services as inadequate, self-serving, or otherwise faulty.[131] The violence of the

126. FO 371/69250/J1890 (1948).
127. Sa'id, *1940–1950*, p. 404; Sa'id, *al-Sihafa al-yasariyya, 1925–1948*, p. 205. Hamza's name also appears as one of the signatories to the list of workers' demands published in *al-Jamahir*, September 6, 1947.
128. Mudarrik, *TU*, May 15, 1969; *al-Ahram*, January 14, 1947; *al-Misri*, September 6, 1947.
129. *Sawt al-umma*, September 5, 1947.
130. Mudarrik, *TU*, May 15, 1969, insists that the discharge of the weapon preceded the riot.
131. This is the overwhelming indication of the results of the survey research conducted by William Carson in 1952, and there is no reason to believe that conditions or attitudes were substantially different in 1947. See Carson, *The Mehalla Report*.

Communism and Workers, 1942–1948   **355**

rebellion manifested workers' rejection of the company's paternalism and its attempt to create a controlled environment in which no aspect of workers' lives would be free of company influence. When, as punishment for the riot, the company closed the mill until September 10, the locked-out workers responded with demands that further expressed their desire for a measure of autonomy and control over their working lives: (1) dissolve the current union because it is dominated by company agents; (2) elect a new union leadership; (3) abolish the fine schedule; and (4) stop the dismissals of workers.[132]

As the company had no intention of meeting these demands, labor unrest in the mill continued. On September 16, after the mill reopened, some 1,000 workers declared a strike and demanded payment of their wages for the time of the lockout. The next day the strike spread to all the mill's 26,000 workers. The government dispatched troops to Mahalla al-Kubra, and the workers occupying the mill were expelled by force. Fifty white-collar employees and a large number of workers were fired for instigating the strike.[133] The mill reopened on October 4 after the Labor Department agreed to hold elections for a new union. The workers' other demands were ignored.

The lockout and strike at Misr Spinning and Weaving had a tremendous impact on the workers' movement. Expressions of solidarity and support for the Misr workers poured into Mahalla al-Kubra from a large number of other workers.[134] On September 5 there were solidarity strikes at several Shubra al-Khayma textile mills. The strike at Misr also received widespread political support beyond the communist and labor movements. A delegation of lawyers from Cairo travelled to Tanta to provide legal aid to the arrested Misr workers, and many of the merchants of Mahalla al-Kubra supported the workers.[135] The left Wafdist daily *Sawt al-Umma (Voice of the Nation)*, which took the place of *al-Wafd al-Misri* after it was closed down by the Sidqi repression, supported the strike and opened its pages to messages of solidarity from workers. The Labor party and the Socialist Labor party both issued statements of support.[136] But Salah Harb, president of 'Abbas Halim's Labor party, tried to end the strike and attacked its leadership for extremism, although he agreed that the union was unrepresentative.[137]

132. *al-Jamahir*, September 6, 1947.
133. *Sawt al-umma*, September 17, 18, 26, 1947.
134. See the letters and statements published in *Sawt al-umma*, September 6, 7, 8, 1947.
135. Mudarrik, *TU*, July 15, 1969.
136. *al-Ahram*, September 22, 1947; *Sawt al-umma*, September 8, 1947.
137. Salah Harb's speech to the workers is quoted in Berque, *Egypt*, pp. 625–26, with

356 Communism and Workers, 1942–1948

The Muslim Brothers took an equivocal position: they refrained from openly supporting the strike, chastised the workers for initiating the violence, but announced their support of the workers' demands for payment of wages during the lockout and election of a new union. They also declared that the schedule of fines which had precipitated the workers' demonstration and the subsequent violence on September 2 was "prejudicial to their rights, a violation of their honor and threatening to their future."[138] (For more on the role of the Muslim Brothers in this strike see Chapter XI.)

The strike at the Misr Company was the first in the strike wave of September 1947 to April 1948. The most important of the strikes which followed was a seventeen-day strike (from September 26 to October 13) of nearly 10,000 workers at the Filature Nationale and its subsidiary Egyptian Textile Company in Alexandria.[139] The key demand of the strike was an eight hour day with eleven hours' pay—a demand that had actually been accepted by the company in a 1919 agreement with the workers, but ignored in the 1920s when the union's strength declined. In September 1947 the Labor Department began to enforce the law limiting the working day to nine hours. In response, the company reinstituted the eight-hour day, but it also cut wages. The dispute was not fully resolved until a collective bargaining agreement between the company and the union was signed on February 2, 1949.[140]

There was also a rash of smaller strikes in the wake of the Misr and Filature Nationale strikes. Textile workers in Imbaba, 'Abbasiyya, and Shubra al-Khayma held one-hour solidarity strikes in support of the Misr and Filature Nationale workers on September 30.[141] On September 22, 8,000 handloom weavers in Qalyub province struck for higher wages.[142] There were also strikes at the Nile Textile Company, Egyptian Oil and Cake Mills, and Bata Shoes in Alexandria in the first week of October, and a strike of telegraph operators later that

---

no mention of the original source. Berque's description of these events differs sharply from the one offered here because, as he acknowledges, he relies principally on the reportage of *al-Ahram*, which was generally unfavorable to the labor movement.

138. *IM*, September 4, 19, 1947.

139. FO 371/62994/J5855 (1947).

140. The background to the strike is contained in the preamble to the contract: *Sharikat al-ghazl al-ahliyya al-misriyya wa'l-sharika al-misriyya li-sina'at al-mansujat, 'aqd al-'amal al-mushtarak wa-qararat al-lajna al-'ulya li-tawhid shurut al-'amal wa'l-ujur bi-masani' al-nasij* (s.l., February 1949). See also a report of the struggle in *IM*, January 1, 1948.

141. *Sawt al-umma*, October 1, 1947.

142. *Ibid.*, September 23, 1947.

Communism and Workers, 1942–1948   **357**

month.[143] In the Suez Canal Zone, workers at the Shell refinery at Suez and the Suez Canal Company struck in September 1947 and thereby initiated struggles which were to continue until the spring of 1948. (See Chapter XI for further details.)

As a result of the Misr strike and the subsequent strike wave, the DMNL was able to extend its influence, particularly in the textile industry. In late September textile union representatives from Shubra al-Khayma, Mahalla al-Kubra, Cairo, Alexandria, and Damietta met and resolved to form a national federation of textile workers.[144] Those endorsing the call to form this federation included both DMNL members and noncommunist trade unionists, an indication that the DMNL had been able to overcome its isolation from the trade union leadership and unite with other trade union leaders around a program to defend workers' rights. (The federation did not, however, come into existence at this time.) One final development pointing to an increased DMNL influence in the trade union movement was the marked increase in both the volume and range of labor news in *al-Jamahir* after September 1947.

Following the Misr strike communist labor leaders tried to summarize its lessons in a way that would encourage further struggle. Yusuf al-Mudarrik wrote a pamphlet explaining the causes of the strike, defending the workers' actions, and exposing working conditions at the Misr mill.[145] Wage cuts, speedups, mandatory fees for work clothes and identity cards, overcharging by the company store, crowded conditions in company housing, excessive and arbitrary fines, harsh disciplinary measures for lateness and arbitrary firing of workers are among the grievances cited. According to al-Mudarrik, the main achievement of the strike was the Misr Company's loss of influence over the union executive board where its supporters had functioned as a fifth column. In addition, he argued, the workers had learned that they needed an organization rather than a spontaneous uprising to achieve their objectives, and that promanagement white-collar employees could not be allowed to lead the union.

While the Mahalla workers may indeed have drawn these conclusions from their experience, the combination of the Misr Company's propaganda campaign and government repression proved too strong to enable them to actually implement their new understanding. After the strike there was a sharp struggle of ideas between the company and the advocates of a union free of company domination. Al-Mudar-

143. FO 371/62994/J5855 (1947).
144. *al-Jamahir*, September 28, 1947.
145. Yusuf al-Mudarrik, *Hawla mushkilat 'ummal al-mahalla* (Cairo, 1947).

358 Communism and Workers, 1942–1948

rik's pamphlet was distributed widely among the Misr workers as a weapon in this struggle. The procompany union executive board, which the Labor Department had permitted to remain in office pending new elections, also mounted its own propaganda campaign: an irregular magazine, 'Amil al-Mahalla (The Mahalla Worker) carried a vicious mix of anticommunism and anti-Semitism—the communists were identified as Jews—combined with enthusiastic support for the Misr Company, the government, and King Faruq. Several articles attacked al-Mudarrik's pamphlet explicitly and offered refutations of his charges against the company.[146] The magazine's editor, 'Abd al-'Alim al-Mahdi, was not a worker at all. He had formerly served as editor of the short-lived organ of 'Abbas Halim's Labor party, al-'Amal (Labor), and appears to have retained his affiliation with the Labor party while orchestrating the propaganda for Misr's anticommunist campaign. The government relied on the police rather than the power of ideas to bring the Misr workers into line. On January 20, 1948, just before the new union elections were to be held, over eighty Misr Spinning and Weaving Company workers were arrested and charged with possession of illegal literature.[147] Over 200 workers were interrogated and searched in their homes. Those arrested were released from jail too late to file nominating petitions for the union election. M. T. Audsley, the British labor attaché, noted approvingly that the Misr Company "neatly timed the introduction of the improved wage scales to coincide with a ruthless police clean-up of the communist elements."[148] As a result of these measures, the company was able to secure the victory of its candidates in the elections for the new union executive board.

Despite the ultimate defeat of the strike and the workers' inability to establish a truly representative union, the struggle at Misr Spinning and Weaving was a major turning point in the development of the postwar workers' movement. The Misr workers dared to challenge the power of the largest agglomeration of industrial capital in Egypt, and having done so were supported by a broad campaign of workers and other sympathetic Egyptians. The Misr Company's image as a nationalist institution was severely damaged, and the formerly widespread assumption that workers should not strike against Egyptian-owned enterprises was, in practice, discredited. These events had a radicalizing effect on the entire workers' movement,

146. 'Amil al-Mahalla, December 13, 1947.
147. IM, January 23, February 6, 1948; al-Balagh, February 18, 22, 1948; al-Jamahir, January 25, February 8, 1948. According to al-Jamahir the total number arrested was 300.
148. FO 371/73474/J3567 (1949).

Communism and Workers, 1942–1948 **359**

which experienced a new "openness of thought" (al-tafattuh al-fikri), as Yusuf al-Mudarrik described it.[149] British diplomatic observers concurred that the strike created a favorable atmosphere for the spread of communist ideas among workers.[150]

The Strike Wave Continues

The strike wave ebbed in November and December 1947, but resumed following the announcement of the government's proposed wage scale for the textile industry in January 1948. This wage scale was merely a recommendation and not obligatory. Nonetheless, it had an important impact because it proposed minimum wages, an eight-hour day, and a six-day work week.[151] The wage scale, as reported in the daily press, appeared to be fairly high because it included all of the cost-of-living allowances granted during World War II, a 20 percent increment for dangerous work, and an additional 20 percent increment in lieu of social services in the mills of Shubra al-Khayma, Alexandria, and Kafr al-Zayyat, which did not provide housing, food, or recreation facilities as the Misr Company did at Mahalla al-Kubra and Kafr al-Dawwar. Still, the recommended minimum wages were half of the prevailing average wage according to al-Jamahir,[152] and a British evaluation notes obliquely that the introduction of eight-hour shifts and a "revised wage structure" resulted in labor disputes in the textile industry, especially at the Filature Nationale and Sibahi mills in Alexandria.[153] In response to the published wage scale both enterprises witnessed recurrent violent strikes from February to April accompanied by solidarity strikes and demonstrations of support by other textile workers.[154]

Even if we accept the most improbable assumption that the wages recommended by the government were adequate, and even if the government had been willing to enforce these recommendations energetically, the government report would still have been insufficient to quell workers' unrest in the textile industry. The real crisis in the textile industry was not the low level of wages per se. Although far from

149. Mudarrik, TU, August 1, 1969.
150. FO 371/69282B/J5425 (1948).
151. The text of this report is unavailable. For a detailed account of the contents see al-Asas, January 9, 1948.
152. al-Jamahir, February 8, 1948.
153. FO 371/73474/J3567 (1949).
154. See al-Jamahir, February 22, 29, March 7, 22, 1948; IM, March 17, 18, 1948; al-Ahram, March 19, 26, April 1, 9, 1948. The two Sibahi mills in Shubra al-Khayma were especially active in support of the Alexandria Sibahi workers.

360 Communism and Workers, 1942–1948

adequate to support a decent standard of living, wages in the larger textile mills were higher than in many other industries, and urban workers were certainly better off than the large number of rural landless. The central issue in the textile industry was the volatility of the market for all but the most common textiles (known as "popular cloth") and the introduction of more labor-efficient machinery into the industry. These had been the issues in the background of the strike at Misr Spinning and Weaving. As a result of the unstable market for fine textiles, large numbers of workers who had staked their futures on leaving the countryside and finding permanent urban employment were being dismissed from their jobs or working only sporadically. Moreover, because the unavailability of agricultural land and the large and growing number of landless peasants made a return to the countryside economically impossible, textile workers were left with little choice but to struggle for job and income security.

The rebellion at Misr Spinning and Weaving and the continuing unrest in the textile industry followed immediately on the failure of one more attempt to achieve a negotiated withdrawal of British troops from Egypt. Popular confidence in the government was rapidly eroding and a feeling of general social crisis was becoming widespread. This atmosphere encouraged other workers, even many who had never before shown the slightest inclination towards militant industrial action, to follow the lead of the textile workers. Engineers in the Irrigation Department of the Ministry of Agriculture struck on January 1, 1948.[155] Petroleum distributors in Cairo struck on February 12, closing all the gas stations in the city.[156] There was a two-hour warning strike of Suez Canal Company workers on March 22 in support of their case, which was under adjudication by the Labor Conciliation Board[157] (see Chapter XI). As mentioned earlier, there were strikes at the Eastern Tobacco Company in April and June (see Chapter IX).

In early April the strike movement reached a crescendo and threatened a complete breakdown of public order. The authority of the government was openly challenged in illegal strikes by the police on April 5 and 6, and by 1,500 male nurses in the Qasr al-'Ayni hospital in Cairo on April 7.[158] The nurses' strike was especially violent. Police attempting to break up the strike were met by a barrage of oxygen cylinders, pieces of steel, and tree stumps. Over 400 nurses were arrested and charged with illegal assembly and inciting an illegal

155. *IM,* January 1, 1948.
156. *Ibid.,* February 13, 1948.
157. *al-Ahram,* March 23, 1948.
158. *Ibid.,* April 6–8, 1948.

Communism and Workers, 1942–1948 **361**

strike.[159] The striking nurses demanded higher pay and shorter hours. A British assessment of the nurses' pay scale offered the blunt judgement that their rates of pay were "disgraceful (270 PT/month)."[160] (This strike was one of the few strikes outside the textile industry during this period in which it can definitively be established that communists played an organizing role.)[161] A further disruption of public order was threatened when the 7,000 workers of Cairo's public transportation network (buses, trams, and metro) announced on April 7 that they would strike on April 25 unless they received their share of the one millieme fare increase that had been instituted specifically to fund higher wages.[162]

The strike wave of late 1947 and early 1948 was marked by increasingly sharp challenges to the authority of the state. The violent incidents at Mahalla al-Kubra, the Filature Nationale, the Sibahi mills in Alexandria, and the Cairo nurses' strike brought workers into repeated confrontations with the police. Civil servants struck frequently during this period, demonstrating the inability of the government to control its own bureaucracy. The police strike showed that the government was losing its authority even among those who were directly charged with enforcing it. There was a rapidly accelerating radicalization within the ranks of the trade union movement during this period. The assistant labor attaché in the British embassy desperately reported general deterioration in labor relations.[163]

The intensity of the strike wave was only one of many indications that the government was entering a crisis period in which its fundamental legitimacy was gradually but unmistakably being undermined by its double failure to achieve full national independence or improve the progressively deteriorating economic conditions of the vast majority of the people. However, before the regime entered its death throes, it was granted a remission by the outbreak of the Palestine war. Although the Palace attempted to manipulate the war for its own benefit, the Palestine cause was, at first, genuinely popular in

159. *IM*, April 18, 1948.
160. FO 371/69210/J2765 (1948).
161. FO 371/69250/J1435 (1948).
162. *Ibid.*, *IM*, April 8, 1948. This strike was averted because of 'Abbas Halim's intervention "ôn behalf" of the Cairo transport workers, the only significant group of workers with whom he retained any influence. The reason for the persistence of his influence long beyond the time when other unions had broken their ties with the prince is not clear. It may simply have been a remnant of the close relations built up in the 1930s and early 1940s, or it may have been due to 'Abbas Halim's good relations with the management of the public transport companies. This link between the Prince and the Cairo transport workers persisted until 1950 or 1951.
163. FO 371/69210/J2724 (1948).

362 Communism and Workers, 1942–1948

Egypt. This tended to increase feelings of national cohesion and moderate class antagonisms. But the government was not willing to rely on national feeling alone to stem the tide of mass discontent. Martial law was proclaimed on May 13, two days before the official entry of Egyptian troops into Palestine. The strike wave and the radicalization of the trade union movement came to an abrupt halt, and virtually all political activity was subjected to harsh repression. Some 3,000 communists, Wafdists, Muslim Brothers, and other political activists were rounded up and held in detention camps.

The communist movement suffered from both repression and loss of political credibility. Attacks on the communist movement had begun to intensify even before the official start of the Palestine war, as the arrest of a large number of Trotskyists in February 1948 shows.[164] In March *al-Jamahir* was closed down. Arrests of communists continued to be reported throughout 1949.[165] The DMNL in particular, and the communist movement in general, suffered a serious erosion of influence because it followed the lead of the Soviet Union and endorsed the partition of Palestine and the establishment of the state of Israel.

The Palestine war brought an end to the social unrest of late 1947 and early 1948, just as the Sidqi repression had stopped the mass upsurge of 1945–1946. During both periods of mass mobilization and collective action, social and national demands had been inseparably linked in the popular consciousness as the ruling classes well understood. The Palestine war extended the life of the regime by justifying the complete repression of political activity from the second half of 1948 through 1949. But after the war the government's utter failure in Palestine would intensify popular dissatisfaction and grievously alienate the officer corps of the army. When the political prisoners began to be released from the detention camps in late 1949 and early 1950, it was only a matter of time until the dynamic of 1945–1946 and 1947–1948 reasserted itself once again.

164. FO 371/69250/J1435 (1948).
165. For example, *al-Asas*, April 29, June 24, 1949, which report the arrest of the DMNL cell in Mahalla al-Kubra; *Akhbar al-Yawm*, April 2, September 24, 1949, report the arrest of the DMNL Central Committee.

Chapter XI

The Muslim Brothers and the Egyptian Workers' Movement

Since the mid-1970s there has been a revival of interest in Islamic political activism in Egypt and elsewhere. But Islam is hardly a new phenomenon in the political life of Egypt. It has long been a factor shaping political consciousness and political debate. During the interwar period secular liberalism and bourgeois nationalism derived from the political traditions of Western Europe were the preeminent cultural and political values of Egypt's ruling classes and the professional urban middle class. However popular these values may have been among the Egyptian elite, they did not strike deep enough roots to eliminate popular attitudes and practices identified with Islam. Islam continued to play an important role in the daily lives and world outlook of the rural and urban masses as well as the traditional urban middle class.

The Society of Muslim Brothers was founded in 1928 by Hasan al-Banna in the city of Isma'iliyya.[1] At first it was simply one of the many Islamic associations established during this period. The proliferation of these associations was one of the consequences of disappointment with the achievements of secular liberalism in Egypt and a symptom of the political disillusionment and consequent radicalization of the urban middle classes referred to previously. The Islamic associations based their appeal on the obvious failure of the Egyptian form of parliamentary liberalism to achieve full political independence or improve the standard of living of the people. They also op-

---

1. The best comprehensive work in English on the Muslim Brothers remains Richard P. Mitchell's pathbreaking study *The Society of the Muslim Brothers* (London, 1969).

364 The Muslim Brothers

posed the dominance of Western political power, capital, and culture in Egypt from a standpoint that made none of the concessions to the West which a liberal nationalist political perspective implied. Although these associations were based mainly in the traditional urban middle class, they had adherents in almost all sectors of society because they employed an Islamic idiom that had broad legitimacy to articulate widely felt grievances and objectives.

At first the Muslim Brothers, like the other associations, had an inward focus emphasizing personal piety, mutual aid, and Islamic renewal, but by the end of the 1930s, as a result of their active support for the Palestinian Arab revolt of 1936–1939 and their participation in Palace-sponsored intrigues against the Wafd, the Muslim Brothers became increasingly committed to political activism. Their political program, however, was always vague, and relied on general Islamic slogans—"God is our King. The Qur'an is our constitution. The Prophet is our Leader,"—to convey their belief that the shari'a was a sufficient, indeed the only, basis for a just ordering of society.

The Muslim Brothers represent a continuation of the movement for Islamic revival (the salafiyya) whose origins are often traced to the teachings of Muhammad 'Abduh (1849–1905). His disciple and biographer, Rashid Rida, had a great influence on the thought of Hasan al-Banna. 'Abduh was one of the earliest advocates of Islamic reform and revival to comment on the phenomena we associate with the spread of capitalism in Egypt and its effect on workers. Rida reports that 'Abduh argued that excessive accumulation of wealth created a "social problem" (mas'ala ijtima'iyya), and that strikes and labor unrest were the consequence of this development.[2]

This chain of authority establishes the historical and intellectual roots of the Muslim Brothers' ideas about labor and its role in society. However, to understand the actual role the Muslim Brothers played in the workers' movement, it is necessary to give primary attention not to the abstract content of their ideas, but to the concrete activities of the Society and its supporters and their relationship to other political forces involved in the workers' movement. The Muslim Brothers entered the labor movement in the 1930s motivated by genuine sympathy for the plight of workers and sought to improve their spiritual and material condition. They attempted to implement their understanding of the shari'a by providing mutual financial aid for unem-

---

2. Rashid Rida, *Tafsir al-qur'an al-karim.* 12 vols. (Cairo, 1367 H.), 3:107–09. In this passage the term *riba* (usurious interest) is employed, and not capitalism. But the sense is that *riba* can be construed as a metaphor for the kind of capitalist development Egypt was experiencing.

The Muslim Brothers **365**

ployed or disabled workers who joined the Society. After the Second World War the Muslim Brothers began to advocate distinctive political positions in the workers' movement as part of their attempt to promote a comprehensive vision of Egypt's future and an alternative to both continuing British domination of Egypt and the secular nationalism of the Wafd. The decisive moment in this development was Hasan al-Banna's arrest in 1943 and his final rupture with the Wafd. Following these events the Brothers' press adopted a noticeably more popular and activist tone. This was shortly followed by a more assertive political stance in the workers' movement.

The Muslim Brothers' new orientation brought them into conflict with the Wafdist Vanguard/communist alliance that mobilized the post-World War II nationalist upsurge. Within the workers' movement this resulted in a sharp confrontation with communists wherever they had any influence or following. The Muslim Brothers became increasingly opposed to the communists' encouragement of trade union independence from nonworker patrons and greater labor militancy which they saw as sowing conflict and social discord among Muslims. Consequently, the Society actively attempted to defeat all expressions of communist influence through countermobilization and propaganda. Therefore Shubra al-Khayma, and the textile industry in general, became one of the principal arenas of contention between Islam and Marxism in the workers' movement, an organizational contest of strength whose outcome had a major impact on the direction of the entire postwar nationalist movement.

Although the Brothers' theories about labor and its role in society were rooted in concepts embraced by Muhammad 'Abduh and many others before him, they were articulated and developed into a practical program of action only after the clash with the communists in Shubra al-Khayma. Thus, while the Brothers' stance in this confrontation accurately reflects the Society's absolute aversion to engaging in or supporting workers' actions which would exacerbate class tensions among Egyptians, it does not constitute a full picture of their role in the workers' movement. Workers in certain situations found the Muslim Brothers' explanations of the causes of Egypt's social problems plausible and attractive, and the general appeal to Islamic sentiment found widespread acceptance. Nonetheless, the concrete conditions of the working class and the character of the Muslim Brothers' actions among workers put a clear limit on the efficacy of Islamic politics in the Egyptian workers' movement during the period under study.

366 The Muslim Brothers

Muslim Brothers and Communists in
Shubra al-Khayma

The first recorded mention of the Muslim Brothers' involvement with working class issues *per se* is a report in *Shubra* that a "group of educated workers" met in the Society's headquarters and decided to hold a workers' conference on August 22, 1938 to discuss the poor condition of the workers' movement and the possible formation of a workers' party. Apparently such a party was formed and headquartered in the Society's offices, though it appears to have been a very insignificant and short-lived affair inspired by the Palace and other anti-Wafd elements with no prominent trade unionists among its leadership.[3] According to Muhammad Sharif, former head of the Workers' Section of the Society of Muslim Brothers, a workers' committee was established by the society in Shubra al-Khayma in the late 1930s.[4] This may have been the activity he was referring to.

In the late 1930s the Muslim Brothers were among the forces active in the formation of the Shubra al-Khayma Mechanized Textile Workers' Union through Taha Sa'd 'Uthman who had been a member of the Society before becoming involved in the textile workers' union. He remained sympathetic to the Society until at least 1943. Relations between the Brothers and committed, independent trade union radicals, like Mahmud al-'Askari were cooperative during the late 1930s and early 1940s.[5] During this period the Brothers' activity seems to have been confined to providing a social solidarity framework and mutual aid. The Brothers' meetings provided a congenial and familiar framework of association for workers amidst the strangeness of factory life, and the financial support given to unemployed members was undoubtedly a powerful inducement to affiliate.

The very first issue of the Society's magazine, *al-Ikhwan al Muslimun (The Muslim Brothers)*, which appeared on August 29, 1942, reported the establishment of a Social Affairs Section within the Society, the first indication of the Brothers' increased concern with social issues. But the articles on "social reform" from that date until the magazine temporarily suspended publication in January 1944 were general and abstract discussions of the Islamic perspective on social questions. None of the articles explicity mentioned labor issues, and the Brothers apparently had no distinctive views on specific questions of trade union tactics and strategy at this time. However, when the magazine resumed publication in December 1944, its articles

3. *Shubra*, August 18, 25, September 15, 1938.
4. Muhammad Sharif, interview, October 28, 1980.
5. *Ibid.*

The Muslim Brothers **367**

were written in a more popular language and with an openly political tone.

This change was accompanied by a concentrated effort to exert more direct influence in the workers' movement. During 1944 the Workers' Section of the Society of Muslim Brothers was established,[6] and two clearly identified members of the Society, 'Abd al-Mun'im 'Isawi and Muhammad Abu Talib, were elected to the executive board of the Shubra al-Khayma textile workers union.[7] 'Isawi's memoirs reveal a deep hostility to ward Yusuf Darwish and his influence over some members of the executive board,[8] but despite this evidence of their increasing opposition to communist influence in the union, serious factional activity by the Muslim Brothers only began to develop after the union was formally dissolved by the government in April 1945.[9] The Brothers may well have felt that the government's action gave them an opening which they might not have had so long as the union executive board, with its strong communist presence, had legal recognition.

As the political and ideological contention between the Brothers and the Marxists intensified in Shubra al-Khayma during 1945, the Brothers' distinctive views on labor and trade union questions became more clearly articulated. With the issue of June 28, 1945 al-Ikhwan al-Muslimun began to publish a regular "workers' page" initiated by reprinting an excerpt from the memoirs of Hasan al-Banna. The General Guide recalled that the Brothers had always been involved with workers because the founding members of the first branch of the Society in Isma'iliyya had been workers. The same article also contained the first confirmation of the existence of a Workers' Section in the Cairo general headquarters of the Society. Its modestly defined objectives were not to interfere in trade union affairs or compete with workers' organizations but simply to "bring the good news [da'wat al-khayr] to these noble souls." This may be understood as an indication that the Brothers' position in the working class was not yet well-established. Another indication of the Society's organizational weakness among workers at this time is the relatively mild and veiled anticommunism of this article compared to the virulent tirades that were to become common in less than a year.

The break between the Brothers and the Shubra al-Khayma textile

6. Sharif, interview, December 3, 1980.
7. al-Yara', January 13, 1944. Their membership in the Society was confirmed by 'Uthman, interview, December 15, 1980.
8. 'Abd al-Mun'im 'Isawi, "Safha mutawwala min ta'rikh niqabat 'ummal al-nasij," al-Thaqafa al-'ummaliyya, May 1, 1969, p. 12.
9. 'Uthman, interview, October 28, 1980.

368 The Muslim Brothers

workers was still not decisive at this point. When Faddali 'Abd al-Jayyid died, Taha Sa'd 'Uthman used his good personal relations with the Brothers to persuade them to publish a memorial pamphlet at their publishing house in order to circumvent the censors. *Al-Ikhwan al-Muslimun* also printed a favorable account of Faddali 'Abd al-Jayyid's funeral.[10]

However, this same issue of *al-Ikhwan al-Muslimun* also contains the Brothers' first overt attack on socialism:

> Those who speak about the workers with these beautiful words [i.e., who use the phrases socialism and social justice] and who call for socialism are the wealthy of the country and its rulers. They are the leaders of opinion and the possessors of influence. And what have they done for the workers?

This article can be considered a public declaration of war against communist influence in the working class. As the center of communist influence in the working class at this time was the leadership of the Shubra al-Khayma textile workers' union, this also marked the beginning of the open struggle against the union leadership. The importance of anticommunism as a motive for the activity of the Muslim Brothers should not be underestimated. The Brothers viewed the communists as "a group of traitors who have betrayed God and his prophet."[11] Thus, no activities in which communists were involved could have any legitimate purpose or outcome. As the Brothers considered the communists to be "neither Egyptian nor nationalist, but entirely Russian,"[12] they saw no nationalist basis on which to cooperate with them. Muhammad Sharif personally confirmed that anticommunism was one of the two principal motives animating the organizing activities of the Muslim Brothers in the working class. The other was, of course, spreading the call of Islam.[13] The Brothers made Shubra al-Khayma a center of their interest precisely because communist influence was strongest there.

This anticommunism explains the Society's response to the arrest of Yusuf al-Mudarrik, Mahmud al-'Askari and Taha Sa'd 'Uthman following the outbreak of the Shubra al-Khayma textile strike on January 1, 1946. The Brothers pointed out that they were members of communist cells headed by Jews.[14] The Society was critical of the government's action, not because it opposed the arrest of commu-

10. *IM*, August 30, 1945.
11. *Ibid.*, August 10, 1946.
12. *Ibid.*, February 25, 1948.
13. Sharif, interviews, October 28, December 3, 1980.
14. *IM*, January 5, 1946.

The Muslim Brothers **369**

nists, but because the government's tactics in the fight against communism were ineffective. Only a return to Islamic values would effectively combat the spread of communism, the Brothers argued. The Brothers' failure to support this strike and their anti-Semitic red-baiting marked an important turning point in the relationship between the Society and the textile workers' leadership and led 'Uthman to cut his remaining ties to the Society.[15]

The Great Confrontation

The sharpening antagonism between the Muslim Brothers and the leadership of the Shubra al-Khayma textile workers was only one manifestation of the Brothers' stand against the communist/Wafdist Vanguard coalition that led the upsurge in the Egyptian nationalist movement in late 1945 and the first half of 1946. The Shubra al-Khayma textile workers participated actively in this upsurge through the formation of the General Nationalist Committee of Shubra al-Khayma, which was represented on the National Committee of Workers and Students. On February 21, 1946, 15,000 Shubra al-Khayma workers attended the demonstration in Cairo called by the NCWS.

The Muslim Brothers also participated in the general strike and demonstrations of February 21, 1946, but soon afterwards they split from the NCWS and formed a rival National Committee (al-Lajna al-Qawmiyya). This was a conscious attempt to combat the growing influence of the communist/left Wafd leadership within the nationalist movement. The National Committee also included the right-wing nationalist Young Egypt, the Nationalist Party, and other anti-Wafd and anticommunist elements. The left wing of the nationalist movement frequently excoriated this coalition, whose Islamic-nationalist ideological tone might best be described as romantic-reactionary, as antinationalist and fascist. One of the best illustrations of how the left wing of the nationalist movement saw the activities of the Muslim Brothers during the nationalist upsurge of 1945–1946 is a statement issued by the EMNL-led Congress of Private Sector Trade Unions after the formation of the National Committee:

> Since the dawn of the current national renaissance the Society of Muslim Brothers has persisted in spreading intrigues and planning plots aimed in their totality at thwarting the nationalist movement or diverting it from its objectives in a manner which

15. 'Uthman, interview, December 15, 1980. The Brothers' activities in the strike of May–June 1946, discussed below, were another reason that 'Uthman gave for breaking with the Brothers.

370 The Muslim Brothers

serves nothing but imperialism. The NCWS is the legitimate committee representing students and workers and [white-collar] employees, elected in free and democratic elections, and the organizer of the struggle of [all] sections of the people for the abolition of imperialism. But they have formed an imaginary committee for workers and students issuing statements against the legitimate NCWS. They have also formed a National Committee, which is not supported by a popular base and therefore died the day it was born.

Today the naked intentions of this Society have been exposed to the people: from calling for [religious] sectarianism aimed at splitting the ranks of the people for the benefit of imperialism to fighting the Students' General Executive Committee with fascist methods using their sticks. They used the same methods against the workers of Shubra al-Khayma.

In light of this, the CPSTU announces its denunciation of these abominable aggressions against sincere student and worker nationalists. The CPSTU also announces that it and other workers' organizations throughout the country support only the NCWS and warn worker colleagues against joining any committee formed by the Muslim Brothers. A worker who joins any of their committees represents no one but himself.

Long live the NCWS
Down with fascism
Down with imperialism[16]

The Brothers had warmly welcomed the government of Isma'il Sidqi,[17] which was brought to office on February 17 in an effort to stem the tide of the nationalist upsurge, while most politically conscious workers saw Sidqi as a historic enemy. The Sidqi government supported the National Committee as an "alternative" nationalist political center, and tried to use it to foil the communist/Wafdist Vanguard coalition. To enhance the impact of their anticommunist message, the Brothers were granted a license to turn *al-Ikhwan al-Muslimun* into a daily newspaper.[18] These developments, in addition to the Muslim Brothers' attacks on the strike of January 1946, crystalized the rift between the Brothers and the communist/left Wafd wing of the nationalist movement. The leadership of the Shubra al-Khayma textile workers fully identified with the political line of the NCWS, and their enmity towards the Brothers deepened as they continued to

16. Quoted in al-Ghazzali, "*Mawqi' 21 fibrayir*," p. 59.
17. *IM*, February 26, 1946.
18. FO 371/53330/J1184 (1946).

The Muslim Brothers **371**

participate in both the continuing mass upsurge of the nationalist movement and the efforts to strengthen the left wing of the trade union movement through the tentative unification of the New Dawn and EMNL-led trade union federations.

After splitting with the NCWS, the Brothers began a full- scale organizing campaign to attempt to supplant the left as the leading force among the workers of Shubra al-Khayma. In March the Society announced the formation of committees in each of the Shubra factories and mills as well as a Higher Committee of Factory Representatives.[19] This organization paralleled the structure of the stewards' committee, the effective embodiment of the now dissolved union, and was therefore a direct challenge to its leadership. The stewards' committee issued a sharply worded statement denying that the Muslim Brothers' committees had actually been established, accusing the Brothers of "speaking in the language of the imperialists and the bosses" and announcing their unqualified opposition to the Brothers' attempts to organize such committees.[20] Several of the stewards signing this statement were members and supporters of the EMNL.

Throughout the spring of 1946 the Brothers pressed forward with their campaign to recruit workers in Shubra al-Khayma. During this campaign the Brothers were not adverse to using coercion and relying on the power of the state and the mill owners to achieve their objectives. On one occasion a foreman at the Nile Company, who was a member of the Society, attempted to recruit Ahamd al-Shinawi, a member of the stewards committee. When al-Shinawi refused to join he was dismissed from his job. Subsequently workers occupied the mill demanding that he be rehired. The local police and the director of the Labor Department, Hamid al-'Abd, promised that he would be rehired. But sixty days after his original dismissal al-Shinawi was still out of work.[21]

The alignment of forces represented in this incident and the tactics the Muslim Brothers were willing to use against the communists prefigure the major confrontation between the communists, the Wafdist Vanguard, and their allies on the one hand, and mill owners, the government, the Muslim Brothers, and their allies on the other which occurred during the May–June 1946 strike of the Shubra al-Khayma textile workers. This confrontation was particularly intense because both sides realized that this battle would have decisive repercussions

19. *IM*, March 19, 1946.
20. This statement is reprinted as an appendix to Muhammad Hasan Ahmad, *al-Ikhwan al-muslimun fi al-mizan* (Cairo, 1946), pp. 93–99. Muhammad Hasan Ahmad is a pseudonym for a group of EMNL members.
21. *WM*, May 21, 1946.

372 The Muslim Brothers

not only for the workers' movement, but for the political direction of the entire nationalist movement as well. The government of Isma'il Sidqi saw the strike as a communist-led conspiracy. Hamid al-'Abd contacted Muhammad Sharif to enlist the aid of the Muslim Brothers in combatting the communists and ending the strike. Muhammad Sharif describes his role as mediating the dispute.[22] However, it seems clear that rather than mediation, what the Brothers set out to do was to break the strike and its leadership entirely. According to reports in *al-Wafd al-Misri* which are confirmed by personal accounts of participants in the strike, the Muslim Brothers informed the police of the names and addresses of members of the strike committee, and as a result over one hundred workers were arrested.[23] The Brothers also urged the workers to return to work immediately and to sign the no-strike pledge the mill owners and the Labor Department demanded. The Society expressed the hope that after the return to work the government would act to resolve the workers' problems.[24]

As the strike progressed, *al-Ikhwan al-Muslimun* and *al-Wafd al-Misri* exchanged daily charges and countercharges about the strike: *al-Ikhwan al-Muslimun* published a report that a delegation of workers had announced their intention to return to work;[25] *al-Wafd al-Misri* countered with a statement of denial from the stewards who further denounced the Brothers' role in the strike and repeated the accusation that they were spying for the police.[26] The Brothers defended themselves by denying they were agents of capitalism. They pointed to their long-standing ties with workers, and recalled that workers had been among the founders of the Society. They called those who slandered the role of the Society in Shubra al-Khayma "professional agitators."[27] As the weeks passed and most of the workers continued to refuse to sign no-strike pledges, the conflict between the workers and the Society intensified. Members of the Society attacked a group of workers with sticks to force them to return to work and accept the no-strike pledge.[28]

By the middle of June, Mahmud al-Dumrani and Sayyid Khudayr, stewards representing the Shubra al-Khayma textile workers in the leadership councils of the Congress of Trade Unions of Egypt, argued that the strike should be ended because most of the workers had given

22. Sharif, interviews, October 28, December 3, 1980.
23. *WM*, May 31, 1946.
24. *IM*, June 2, 1946.
25. *Ibid.*
26. *WM*, June 3, 1946.
27. *IM*, June 3, 1946.
28. *WM*, June 16, 1946.

The Muslim Brothers **373**

up hope of winning. The leadership of the CTUE urged the continuation of the strike. There was still a great deal of suspicion and distrust between the two factions of the CTUE. New Dawn supporters accused EMNL supporters of sabotaging the workers by prolonging the strike beyond the point where it could be won.[29] The inability of the two factions to work together and discuss their assessments of the strike without recrimination weakened the ability of the workers themselves to persevere in the strike.

The CTUE's call for a national general strike on June 25 was motivated in part by a desire to rally national support for the ongoing Shubra al-Khayma strike. The mill owners tried to block the potential impact of the general strike in Shubra al-Khayma by issuing an ultimatum that those who failed to sign no-strike pledges by June 22 would be dismissed.[30] The failure of the national general strike and the subsequent arrest of many of the textile worker leaders further weakened and discouraged the strikers and by the beginning of July, 75 percent of them had signed no strike pledges.[31] In the face of concerted opposition from the mill owners, the government and the Muslim Brothers, those who had not been arrested, fired, or expelled from Shubra al-Khayma returned to work.

The failure of the textile strike, the defeat of the CTUE's call for a national general strike, and the government's campaign of repression against the left dealt a severe blow to the communists' position of leadership in Shubra al-Khayma. The Muslim Brothers, continuing their conscious effort to supplant this communist leadership, announced the formation of a new Shubra al-Khayma Textile Workers' Union.[32] Legal appeals against the government's dissolution of the GUMTPWGC were still in the courts. The New Dawn group persistently opposed the establishment of a new union in order not to allow the court an excuse to avoid dealing with the suit against the dissolution of the former union. They feared that the existence of a new union would allow the court to declare the case moot. The Brothers' establishment of a union was therefore a new direct attack on the former union and its leadership.

The only concrete activity of the Brothers-sponsored union reported in the now daily *al-Ikhwan al-Muslimun* was to send a telegram of protest to the minister of social affairs, the prime minister, and the head of the Royal Cabinet protesting a particularly sharp increase in unemployment because of seasonal pressures in the textile

29. 'Uthman, K, July, 1972, pp. 157–58.
30. *WM*, June 25, 1946.
31. *Ibid.*, July 1, 1946.
32. *IM*, July 5, 1946.

374 The Muslim Brothers

industry during early 1947.[33] The telegram was signed by representatives of nine Shubra al-Khayma mills and the secretary of the union, 'Ali Ibrahim Pasha, whose title certainly indicated he was neither a worker nor a foreman. None of the nine representatives had ever been mentioned previously in any context as having participated in the struggles in the textile industry. According to DMNL sources, this union had a total membership of only 200 workers.[34] One indication of the union's lack of influence on the Shubra al-Khayma workers was its warning to the director of the Labor Department that if the government did not resolve the unemployment problem, the union could not take responsibility for the workers' actions.[35] This might be interpreted as a veiled threat, but the union failed to issue a strike warning or take any other forceful action over this issue. Therefore it appears that its leadership was seeking to avoid responsibility for potentially militant actions because it was not sure it could restrain workers' anger.

The most important activity of the Muslim Brothers in Shubra al-Khayma during this period was the establishment of a textile mill, the Muslim Brothers' Spinning and Weaving Company. The decision to establish the mill was taken in May 1946 by the Brothers' Shubra branch "to protect *its members* from unemployment"[36] (emphasis added). It was capitalized by selling 1,950 shares with a total value of £E 6,000. The mill began operations in December 1947 under the management of Muhammad Sharif, head of the Workers' Section of the Society. With less than sixty workers and fourteen looms it was among the smaller mills in the area.[37]

The Muslim Brothers established the mill as a working demonstration of the viability of Islamic principles in the management of an industrial enterprise. The mill's objectives were to apply these principles in its operation, encourage popular technical education, distribute profits to the largest number of Egyptians, encourage the habit of saving money (so that workers in the mill could buy shares), promote industrial cooperation among workers, and encourage Egyptians to buy locally manufactured products. All workers in the mill were required to buy at least one share. The Brothers reasoned that if workers owned shares in the enterprise the conflict between labor and management would be eliminated, since all parties would have a stake in the success of the enterprise. This was the concrete expres-

33. *Ibid.*, April 28, 1947.
34. *al-Jamahir*, May 5, 1947.
35. *IM*, April 28, 1947.
36. *Ibid.*, May 13, 1946.
37. *Ibid.*, September 5. 1948

sion of the Brothers' view that there was no class conflict in a justly ordered Islamic society.

Despite the mill's small size, it proved extremely profitable, returning 15 percent on investment by July 1948 according to the Society's claims.[38] However, it certainly did not constitute a major contribution to reducing unemployment among textile workers because the size of its work force was simply too small to make an impact given the large numbers of unemployed. Moreover, it is very unlikely that many unemployed workers could afford the approximately £E 3 required to purchase even one share in the company. The Muslim Brothers' mill ceased operations early in 1949 when the government sequestered the Society's assets following its official dissolution. Despite the small size and short-term operation of this enterprise, Muhammad Sharif considered it an unqualified success and felt that this experience thoroughly demonstrated the viability of running an enterprise according to what he considered Islamic principles.[39]

The defeat and repression of the left, the alliance of the Muslim Brothers with the Sidqi government, and the mill owners' active efforts to eliminate communist influence enabled the Brothers to gain influence in Shubra al-Khayma in 1946–1948. During this period all of the elected stewards who had continued the activity of the GUMTPWGC in late 1945 and 1946 were dismissed, and many were banished to their villages.[40] Shubra al-Khayma itself declined somewhat in importance as a textile center after the strike of 1946 as some of the mills were moved to other suburban Cairo locations, or even as far away as Alexandria to avoid the high level of industrial struggle that characterized Shubra al-Khayma.

Although the Muslim Brothers do not appear to have gained as great a following in Shubra al-Khayma in 1946–1948 as the communists had earlier established, their presence there was an effective obstacle to the reestablishment of a communist center in the area until after the conclusion of the Palestine war. During this period the communist movement went into decline throughout the country, though the defeat of the strike in Shubra al-Khayma in June 1946 was an important factor in this general decline. Continuing factional contention and disunity also severely impeded efforts to rebuild a communist presence.

38. *Ibid.*
39. Sharif, interview. October 28, 1980.
40. Murad al-Qalyubi, *Mashru' qanun bi-sha'n al-tawfiq wa'l-tahkim fi munaza'at al-'amal* (Cairo, 1948), p. 33.

376 The Muslim Brothers

The Muslim Brothers' Vision of a "Moral Economy"

The confrontation between the communists and the Muslim Brothers in Shubra al-Khayma was exceptionally sharp and bitter, and the actions of the Muslim Brothers in that confrontation played an important role in determining the relations between the Society and the left throughout the postwar period. The antiunion and anticommunist activities of the Brothers in Shubra al-Khayma illustrate the concrete role of Islamic politics, as interpreted by the Society of Muslim Brothers, in the social struggles of postwar Egypt. But they do not give any indication of the content of the Brothers' own social program, nor do they explain why the Brothers were able to attract a significant number of workers to their banner in the postwar period.

As the liberal political principles of the Wafd appeared to be incapable of providing the basis for achieving Egypt's national objectives, the Muslim Brothers and the communists posed two diametrically opposed alternative visions for Egypt's future. In opposition to the communists' theory, which divided society into contending classes with contradictory interests, the Muslim Brothers counterposed the ideal of society structured as an organically interdependent unity. The various social strata of society were envisioned as functionally differentiated corporate bodies, and not classes in mutual opposition. Their relations were to be governed by the principle of "mutual social responsibility" (*takaful ijtima'i*). The application of this principle to relations between employers and employees has been succinctly summarized by Richard P. Mitchell in his study of the Muslim Brothers:

> Islam has established certain rights and duties for the worker. His relationship with his employer is governed by the principle governing all human relations—"a mutuality of duties and rights" based on mutual "respect and sympathy" and ordered by the "spirit of brotherhood." He has the right to a healthy and clean home, wages adequate to provide the needs of life and "punctually" paid, and limited hours of work. The worker is forbidden to "allocate any part of his wages" to his leaders. In return for these rights he shall "perform his work faithfully," thus respecting the rights of management and fulfilling his own responsibilities.[41]

The Brothers also insisted that a properly functioning Islamic state must provide each member of society with a certain degree of social security by organizing mutual social responsibility so that the needs

41. Mitchell, *The Society*, p. 253.

The Muslim Brothers 377

of all are provided for. The principal method of providing for the poor and needy was to be through the traditional practice of giving alms (*zakat*) regulated and directed by the state which could further tax the wealthy to support the poor when necessary. Particularly important in the context of massive postwar unemployment was the Society's view that an individual's right to work must be guaranteed by the state, and that if work were not available or wages insufficient to support a worker and his family, the state should supplement incomes through alms.[42] The Society was very sensitive to the general economic crisis of postwar Egyptian society and the insecurities it created. It was especially concerned with the issue of unemployment, and articles on the "problem of the unemployed" and a variety of proposed solutions appeared regularly in the pages of *al-Ikhwan al-Muslimun*.

The concept of mutual social responsibility stands in stark contradiction to the capitalist notion that workers can be hired and fired according to the fluctuating requirements of production and profitability. The Brothers rejected the view that employers were not responsible for workers after they were dismissed. Most often the Brothers appealed to the Egyptian state to remedy the unemployment problem, and they considered the government morally bound to find work for the unemployed because it had taken them from their villages to work in the war industries.[43]

Although the Brothers upheld an individual's right to private property as a basic human desire, they opposed the materialist values and greed that, they argued, capitalism promoted. Foreign-owned enterprises bore the brunt of the Society's attacks on capitalism. They were seen as imperialist companies exercising an economic occupation of Egypt, "exploiting its national wealth, humiliating its labor force . . . and the spirit of its people."[44] From 1944 to 1948, Egyptian-owned capitalist enterprises were very rarely criticized. As M. T. Audsley noted, "Hasan al-Banna was willing to support workers against foreign employers, but not against Moslem ones."[45] The restriction of the Society's criticism of capitalism to foreign-owned enterprises in this period allowed this criticism to merge easily with the general upsurge in the postwar nationalist movement as did the workers' struggles against the mainly foreign and *mutamassir* textile mill owners in Shubra al-Khayma. One of the most frequent criticisms the Society raised against foreign-owned companies was that they dismissed

42. *Ibid.*, p. 274.
43. *IM*, May 7, 1946.
44. *Ibid.*, December 6, 1948.
45. FO 371/73474/J3567 (1949).

378 The Muslim Brothers

Egyptian workers and replaced them with foreigners, and paid foreign workers higher wages than Egyptians performing the same work.[46] These issues were especially sharp at the Suez Canal Company and at the Shell Oil Company and its subsidiary, Anglo-Egyptian Oil Fields. It is therefore no accident that the unions in these enterprises, and throughout the Suez Canal Zone generally, were the strongest centers of Muslim Brothers' strength in the Egyptian workers' movement.

The Muslim Brothers' attack on foreign capitalists and their vision of an economic and social order governed by principles of Islamic brotherhood and mutual responsibility corresponded with a widely shared, if imprecisely articulated, popular and traditional definition of social justice in Egypt. A large number of Egyptians identified with the Islamic idiom of the Brothers (despite the novelty of many of their interpretations of Islam) much more easily than with the theoretical concepts and style of the communists or the Wafdist Vanguard. Moreover, the Brothers' criticism of foreign economic domination and of the impersonal and materialistic values and practices of the large foreign monopoly corporations, particularly the dismissal of workers during periods of recession, resonated with many workers' sense of what was wrong with the postwar Egyptian society and economy. In this sense the Brothers' vision of a just Islamic society bears a similarity to the concept of a "moral economy" which E. P. Thompson has used to describe the social consciousness of the eighteenth-century English crowd.[47] This vision held a strong attraction for many workers—recent arrivals in Cairo, the Canal Zone or other urban centers, wrenched from their rural and preindustrial social networks, and confronted with the harsh regime of industrial discipline dominated by what appeared to be specifically European rather than simply capitalist values and norms. This vision also appealed to small independent artisans and craftsmen whose markets and very livelihoods were under attack from commodities produced by large-scale capitalist methods.

In addition to helping workers overcome their social isolation and alienation by providing organized activity in a customary Islamic framework, the Society also provided a degree of economic security for its worker-members through establishing a form of unemployment insurance. The Workers' Committee of the Brothers' Shubra al-Khayma branch paid full salaries to members who lost their jobs.[48]

46. *IM*, June 17, August 15, December 13, 1946; August 12, 1947.
47. E. P. Thompson, "The Moral Economy of the English Crowd in the Eighteenth Century," *Past and Present*, no. 50 (1971), pp. 76–136.
48. *IM*, May 13, 1946.

The Muslim Brothers **379**

Membership in the Society also provided access to political protection. Muhammad Mutawalli al-Sha'rawi, a trade union militant at the Misr Fine Spinning and Weaving Company in Kafr al-Dawwar, recalled that in 1948, when his union activities brought him into conflict with the company, he joined the Society and paid dues for two months in order to obtain legal aid and protection from the company.[49]

In opposition to the impersonal character of factory life, the Brothers upheld the importance of personal relations and individual conduct. Their message to the worker was: "Fulfill your obligation as a worker. Be a moral example and an exemplary worker."[50] Personal charity and other forms of individual action were important forms of social melioration for the Muslim Brothers. For example, *al-Ikhwan al-Muslimun* approvingly reported a story about a worker dismissed from one of the Shubra al-Khayma mills without his severance compensation who received a loan of five pounds from a Society member. This gesture was lavishly praised as an illustration of exemplary Islamic interpersonal responsibility and brotherhood, and *al-Ikhwan al-Muslimun* appeared much more concerned about this aspect of the story than the quite common injustice of a worker being dismissed without severance pay.[51]

Methods of Trade Union Struggle

The Society's relationship with Egyptian workers was characterized by the same patron-client pattern that had governed the relations of the Wafd and Prince 'Abbas Halim with their trade union supporters. In an explanation of their role in the Shubra al-Khayma strike, the Brothers stated that they had established a "committee to oversee [ra'aya] the affairs of the workers of this area."[52] The use of the term *ra'aya*, with its paternalistic connotation of guardianship, stands in direct opposition to the theory and practice of independent trade unionism that had characterized the development of the Shubra al-Khayma textile workers' union from its origins. Neither Muhammad Sharif nor any other leading figures of the Society's Workers' Section were, in fact, workers and there is no evidence that the Society made

49. Muhammad Mutawalli al-Sha'rawi, interview, April 3, 1981. The instrumental nature of this affiliation is highlighted by the fact that al-Sha'rawi was already on his way to becoming one of the leading leftists in Kafr al-Dawwar.
50. Sharif, interview, October 28, 1980.
51. *IM*, August 23, 1945. At the same time this article makes no comment on the injustice of the dismissal or the lack of severance compensation.
52. *Ibid.*, June 18, 1946.

380 The Muslim Brothers

any effort to promote workers to positions of responsibility within the Workers' Section. The Society's efforts on behalf of workers followed a traditional pattern of intercession by social betters pleading for social justice for their social inferiors. The Society consciously saw its task as conveying workers' demands to the authorities rather than organizing workers themselves to achieve these demands.[53]

The characteristic mode of the Society's activity on behalf of workers was for *al-Ikhwan al-Muslimun* to print an exposé of the poor working conditions in a particular enterprise along with a list of demands by the workers. The paper would either explicitly indicate its editorial support for these demands or imply it by the manner in which the article reporting them was constructed. Then the article would urge the company and the government to look into these demands at the same time that it urged the workers not to strike, or to return to work if a strike were in progress. The Muslim Brothers never explicitly supported a strike by workers from 1944 to 1948, though in some cases they gave veiled or implicit support to strikes against foreign-owned enterprises.

This was the stance of the Brothers regarding the strike of the Cairo tramway workers which began on October 5, 1946. While the strike was in progress *al-Ikhwan al-Muslimun* editorialized:

> We continue to appeal to the authorities to reinvestigate the workers' affairs and to treat them decisively and justly so that there will be no room for concern by the workers . . . and they will agree to work in a quiet and orderly manner. . . . We continue to urge that the government invite representatives of the union and come to an amicable understanding with them . . . which will result in equity [*insaf*].[54]

In the course of this strike the government had arrested the union president, Shaykh 'Abd al-Zahir al-Shahid, twelve members of the union executive board, and over sixty other workers.[55] Houses of union members and the union headquarters itself were searched by the police, and union papers were confiscated. The Brothers reported that the unions of the Hawamdiyya sugar refinery, the Alexandria tramway, and the Shubra al-Khayma textile workers, all unions in which they had considerable influence, supported the demands of

53. Sharif, interview, December 3, 1980. See also the article by Muhammad Sharif containing an exposé of the workers' poor conditions and suffering addressed explicitly "to the responsible authorities in general and the Labor Department in particular," in *IM*, April 29, 1947.
54. *IM*, October 8, 1946.
55. For details of this strike see *ibid.*, October 6–9, 1946.

The Muslim Brothers **381**

the Cairo tramway workers and protested the arrests. They also reported that the workers had asked 'Abbas Halim to intercede and negotiate for them, and though the prince was, by this time, discredited among most trade unionists, the Brothers offered no criticism of his participation in this dispute. In fact, there appears to have been considerable cooperation between the Brothers and the prince in labor matters at this time.[56] 'Abbas Halim personally ended the strike before its demands were met by driving the first tram out of its depot as he had done in the Cairo transport general strike of 1941.

The Brothers' ambiguous attitude toward the strike was evident in an unsigned article (entitled "The Brothers and the Workers' Strike") in *al-Ikhwan al-Muslimun* that argued that the workers' demands were just, and that the company and the government should not deal harshly with the workers. Still, they refrained from explicitly endorsing the strike, despite the fact that its leadership was sympathetic to the Society.[57] After the strike, the prince and the Society continued to press the workers' demands to the government and the company. Eventually these demands were partially satisfied when the new government of Mahmud al-Nuqrashi decided to implement a cadre for all of Cairo's transport workers on January 1, 1947.

The Muslim Brothers' approach to the tramway workers' strike demonstrates that it was not necessarily support for workers' demands *per se* that motivated the Society, but the connection between the tramway workers' struggle and broader political developments. Toward the end of 1946, the Society's original warm endorsement of the Sidqi government gave way to increasingly sharp criticism stimulated by reports of the unsatisfactory progress of the Sidqi-Bevin negotiations. The eventual failure of these negotiations led the Brothers to use workers' demands as a vehicle to criticize the government. Even the Brothers' equivocal support for the Cairo tramway strike was an attack on the Sidqi regime because the strike threatened social stability. The new al-Nuqrashi government was ultimately able to capitalize on the strike because the decision to impose the transport workers' cadre on the foreign-owned metro and tramway companies was a popular nationalist act, while imposing the same cadre on the bus company owned by the Wafd supporter Ahmad 'Abbud struck a blow against an opponent of both the government and the Society of Muslim Brothers.

In the tramway strike the Brothers' criticism of the government was

56. This can be inferred from the frequent favorable mention of 'Abbas Halim's activities in the pages of *IM* during 1946 and 1947.
57. *IM*, October 6, 1946.

382 The Muslim Brothers

implicit, but a more militant stance was evident in the conference of over 1,000 workers organized by the Workers' Section of the Society in Port Said two days after Sidqi returned to Egypt with a draft of a new Anglo-Egyptian treaty. The resolutions adopted at this meeting reflected the general Egyptian nationalist consensus at this time: (1) complete British evacuation of Egypt and the Sudan; (2) the unity of Egypt and the Sudan under the Egyptian crown; (3) abrogation of the 1936 Anglo-Egyptian treaty; (4) no alliance with Great Britain until after military evacuation; (5) full payment of Britain's wartime debts to Egypt.[58] These resolutions were a sharp repudiation of Sidqi's conduct in the negotiations. The Brothers' ability to convene such a large meeting of workers in Port Said opposing the government's policy on the most critical issue of the day indicates substantial strength among workers in the Suez Canal Zone. However, the lack of reports of similar meetings organized by the Muslim Brothers elsewhere suggests that this strength was based on the local factors to be examined below.

After breaking with Sidqi, the Brothers began to criticize the government much more openly and sharply on questions of labor policy. Only a month after al-Nuqrashi Pasha's government took office the Society launched a comprehensive attack on the Ministry of Social Affairs and its Employment Bureau for failing to resolve the unemployment crisis. The Brothers correctly pointed out that most existing labor legislation was poorly enforced and that the bureaucracy charged with supervising labor affairs was ineffective and understaffed.[59] The Society also charged that the Shubra al-Khayma Labor Office was operating in complicity with the mill owners and failing to enforce the law that prevented factories from dismissing more than 10 percent of their workers during a six-month period.[60] Despite this increasingly sharp criticism of the government and its labor policies, the Muslim Brothers still refrained from actively organizing workers to demand their rights.

The Muslim Brothers' attitude towards the massive September 1947 strike at the Misr Spinning and Weaving Company, the most significant industrial action of the strike wave of late 1947 and early 1948, reveals continuing ambiguity and opposition to any form of workers' direct action. As has already been noted, *al-Ikhwan al-Muslimun* was sympathetic to the workers' demands, but the key role of communists in organizing the strike made it virtually certain that the

58. *Ibid.*, October 27, 1946.
59. *Ibid.*, January 14, 1947.
60. *Ibid.*, February 25, 1947.

The Muslim Brothers **383**

Brothers would not effectively support it. Towards the end of the strike the left-Wafdist daily *Sawt al-Umma* published two statements by a group of Misr workers accusing the Muslim Brothers of denouncing fifty white-collar employees who had participated in organizing the second work stoppage. The fifty subsequently lost their jobs. The statements also charged the Brothers with breaking the unity of the workers' ranks, and recalled their strike-breaking activity in Shubra al-Khayma.[61]

The majority of the following of the Muslim Brothers in the Misr mill was drawn from the ranks of management and the white-collar employees rather than from the blue-collar workers.[62] There were also very close links between the local leadership of the Society and the Misr Company management. Both the director of the personnel department and the assistant director of the weaving department were on different occasions identified as leading members of the Society of Muslim Brothers in Mahalla al-Kubra.[63] This may explain why the local branch of the Society took an active role in opposing the strike, if the charges printed in *Sawt al-Umma* are credible, despite *al-Ikhwan al-Muslimun*'s support for the workers' demands. This internally contradictory stand was characteristic of the Brothers' lack of consistency regarding labor matters; and while this example is particularly blatant, there were numerous other occasions on which different elements within the Society adopted opposing positions in labor disputes. What is unusual in this incident is that the central leadership appeared to be more favorable to the workers than the local leadership.

The Brothers' stand regarding the Misr strike was seen by the communists and the Wafdist Vanguard as simply a continuation of the position the Society had adopted in Shubra al-Khayma in 1946. The charges of informing on strike leaders, especially those engaged in joint action with communists, are consistent with the Brothers' fundamental approach to achieving workers' demands, which did not change during the period 1944–1948, despite the Society's increasing opposition to the government after the summer of 1946. The Society

61. *Sawt al-umma*, September 28, October 1, 1947.
62. Carson, "Social History," p. 369.
63. *al-'Amal*, October 24, 1946, contains a letter from the clerks of the personnel department complaining that their director was attempting to recruit them into the Society by giving preferential treatment to those who joined. *Al-Tahrir*, November 30, 1954, in an "exposé" of the Muslim Brothers' activities in Mahalla al-Kubra after the attempted assassination of Jamal 'Abd al-Nasir, identifies the assistant director of the weaving department as the head of the Society in the city and notes other close connections to the Misr management.

384   The Muslim Brothers

offered numerous proposals to the government to resolve the unemployment problem and other social questions affecting workers. But if the government failed to act on the Society's proposals, it was not prepared to organize workers to fight for them. Throughout the period 1944–1948 the Muslim Brothers, as a matter of principle, were unwilling to organize workers for direct action to win their demands or to lend active support to workers who did so on their own. To do so, the Brothers argued, would exacerbate social conflicts and disturb social peace.

Even during the most active period of the Workers' Section from 1944 to 1948, labor organization, as opposed to propaganda and agitation, was the Society's weak point.[64] Its newspaper, *al-Ikhwan al-Muslimun*, was a much more active force among workers than the Society as an organization. The paper reported on many labor struggles where the Brothers had no organizational presence. The Society consciously defined the main goals of its activity among workers as conducting education and propaganda (that is, spreading the call of Islam and anticommunism) rather than building a stable organization and conducting struggle. However, because the Muslim Brothers promoted a popularly shared vision of social justice articulated in an Islamic idiom with unassailable legitimacy for most Egyptians, many trade unionists who were not actual members of the Society identified with it in a general sense. It is therefore possible to speak of an Islamic trend within the trade union movement which looked to the Society and its charismatic General Guide, Hasan al-Banna, for leadership, without being organizationally tied to the Society or under the discipline of its central leading bodies. Among those trade union leaders who could be considered part of this Islamic trend without being formally members of the Society were Shaykh 'Abd al-Zahir al-Shahid, president of the Cairo Tramway Workers' Union, Shaykh Muhammad 'Abd al-Salam, president of the Hawamdiyya sugar refinery workers' union and 'Abbas Zaki Muhammad, a member of the executive board of the Filature Nationale union.

Local Strength in the Canal Zone

There were two major exceptions to this pattern of organizational weakness. The first was the Shubra al-Khayma textile workers' union organized by the Muslim Brothers in a sustained organizational effort

---

64. This point was stressed repeatedly by Jamal al-Banna, the brother of the founder and General Guide of the Society of Muslim Brothers and Labor Editor of *al-Da'wa*, in interviews on December 22, 1980 and January 3, 1981. Jamal al-Banna also identified the trade union leaders who were supporters but not members of the Society.

The Muslim Brothers **385**

in opposition to the communist stronghold there. This was a short-lived affair because by 1950 the Brothers' textile workers' union had become inactive and the communists had begun to rebuild their strength in Shubra al-Khayma. The second exception was in the Suez Canal region where the Brothers succeeded in maintaining a long-term, well-organized presence and direct organizational control over at least one of the most important unions in the area, the Shell and Anglo-Egyptian Oil Fields Employees' and Workers' Union.

One reason for this success may have been that Isma'iliyya, along the Suez Canal, was not only the birthplace of the Society but the city's alien character, dominated by foreign enterprises such as the Suez Canal Company, the shipping and warehousing firms servicing the canal traffic, and the blatantly European atmosphere of Isma'iliyya and the Suez Canal area made the region particularly receptive to Hasan al-Banna's message and contributed to the rapid growth of the Society. The Society transformed this popular support in the cities along the Suez Canal into a solid base of organizational strength in the trade unions of the region during the course of two major labor struggles at the Suez Canal Company and the Shell refinery which received widespread national attention in late 1947 and early 1948.

The key demands of the Egyptian workers at both companies were equal wages, promotion opportunities, job security for Egyptian and foreign workers, and an increase in the percentage of Egyptian workers and white-collar employees. The demands of Egyptian white-collar employees, who suffered discrimination at the hands of foreign management, were an important element in these struggles, just as the demands of foremen had been prominent in the struggles of the Shubra al-Khayma textile workers. The Egyptian government fully supported the demands of the Egyptian workers and employees against both foreign companies. On June 5, 1947, the Port Said Labor Conciliation Board issued a decision affirming the Suez Canal Company's obligation to grant equal rights and wages to foreign and Egyptian employees. The company refused to implement this decision, and went through a year-long process of appeal during which there were several two-hour warning strikes and strike threats. As in the case of the Cairo tramway workers' strike, the Muslim Brothers fully supported the workers' demands, but did not openly encourage or support their strikes. Finally, after all appeals had been exhausted the Labor Conciliation Board granted the workers' demands in full on March 27, 1948. The decision was ratified by the Ministry of Social Affairs, and the Suez Canal Company was required to pay wages to

386 The Muslim Brothers

Egyptians amounting to nearly four times the prevailing rate in the Canal Zone.[65]

At Shell the struggle took a very similar course. A five-day strike of 4,000 workers occurred at the Suez refinery in late September 1947 during which demands the workers advanced were supported by the Labor Department, and in November the Ministry of Social Affairs ratified the decision of the Labor Conciliation Board granting the workers' main demands.[66] But once again, the final resolution was delayed by an extended appeal process until, on April 20, 1948, the Labor Conciliation Board finally required the company to grant most of the workers' demands.[67] The final wage settlement with Shell was not as punitive as the settlement with the Suez Canal Company, partly because the Shell management had adopted a less arrogant tone towards the Egyptian government, but in the end Shell was still required to pay wages up to double the prevailing level.[68] Some of the settlement's other provisions included the transfer of some of the higher grade Egyptian supervisors and skilled workers from daily-paid to monthly-paid status, which gave them much greater job security; the transfer of all other Egyptians to monthly-paid status after five years of service; and restrictions on the dismissal of workers and the use of contract labor. In addition, Shell was also required to submit a statement to the governor of Suez describing its plans to provide promotion opportunities for Egyptian workers.

The year-long struggles of the Suez Canal Company and Shell workers exemplify the main themes of the postwar workers' movement—the demands for higher wages, job security, and an end to discrimination against Egyptian workers. In both cases *al-Ikhwan al-Muslimun* popularized these demands to its national audience, attacked the companies as exploitative imperialist enterprises, and highlighted their discrimination against Egyptian workers. Despite their reticence to encourage strike action, the Muslim Brothers' support for the workers' demands, especially in the Shell struggle, enabled them to gain prestige and support among the workers of the Canal Zone. This led to the extension of the Brothers' direct influence over the Shell workers' union.

Several days after the announcement of the Labor Conciliation

65. FO 371/69181/J4474 (1948).
66. *al-Ahram*, September 30, 1947; *IM*, November 12, 1947.
67. The text of this decision is one of the few remnants of the archives of the Labor Department. These are currently located in the Ministry of Labor Power and Training. Maslahat al-'amal, qalam al-mahfuzat, Dossier 11/4/5/5.
68. FO 371/69181/J4474 (1948).

The Muslim Brothers **387**

Board's decision, the Shell union held its general assembly, and chose Anwar Salama, an ardent member of the Muslim Brothers, as the new president of the union. Several other Brothers were elected to seats on the executive board in what appears to have been a political coup because all of the members of the former executive board were denounced by the general assembly, and none were reelected.[69] This victory entrenched the Muslim Brothers in the leadership of the Shell union. Several union leaders who were Muslim Brothers were arrested when the government dissolved the Society in December 1948,[70] but Anwar Salama retained his position as president of the union and enhanced his prestige by negotiating a series of labor agreements that gave the workers and employees of Shell and its subsidiaries extraordinarily good wages and working conditions by Egyptian standards.[71]

The decisions of the Labor Conciliation Board in the Suez Canal Company and Shell cases set the standard for labor settlements at several other European-owned shipping and warehousing companies for the remainder of 1948 and 1949.[72] There is no direct evidence for the Muslim Brothers' involvement in these cases, but it is reasonable to assume that since the Society had been a prominent force in supporting the original demands at the Suez Canal Company and Shell, it was able to increase its strength among workers who benefited from the improved wages and working conditions first won at those firms then spread throughout the Canal Zone.

The British embassy in Cairo was outraged at the decisions of the Labor Conciliation Boards in the Canal Zone. Embassy officials claimed that these judgments were punitive and discriminatory measures directed against large and prosperous foreign-owned firms that reflected the government's attitude that such firms should pay higher wages. The British claimed that the local governors who presided over the Boards of each city or Governorate had allowed the cases to be decided against foreign companies to maintain social peace and enhance their own popularity.[73] These charges were substantially correct, though there is more than a little hypocrisy in British complaints about discrimination.

69. *IM*, April 25, 1948.
70. FO 371/73474/J3567 (1949).
71. For the texts of several Shell contracts see Maslahat al-'amal, idarat al-buhuth al-fanniyya wa'l-ihsa', qism al-tasjil, Dossier 11/4/3/5/ pt 1.
72. Maslahat al-'amal, qalam al-mahfuzat, Dossier 11/4/6/4 pt 1 "Ittifaqiyyat bi-ma'rifat maktab al-'amal—maktab bur sa'id."
73. FO 371/69181/J4474 (1948).

388 The Muslim Brothers

The complaints of the British embassy characterize the almost unique local circumstances that enabled trade unions in the Suez Canal Zone to achieve their demands without the same kind of protracted struggle that had characterized the textile industry and especially Shubra al-Khayma. Shell Oil and the Suez Canal Company could afford to pay higher wages and benefits than any other enterprises in Egypt because of their extraordinary profits. The workers did not need to rely on their independent organization to win their demands, because the Egyptian government saw support for the workers' cause as an easy way to gain much-needed public approval. In these circumstances the ideology of the Muslim Brothers, which attributed the evils of the corporations to their non-Muslim character, advocated the solidarity of all-Muslims—workers and their government—and rejected militant direct action provided an appropriate and effective organizational framework for workers. Anwar Salama, a capable leader and clever politician, was thus able to win the leadership of the Shell union. Similar conditions obtained at only one other large-scale, industrial enterprise in Egypt—Eastern Tobacco Company. There too, a noncommunist trade unionist was able to win the leadership of the workers because the company was willing and financially able to conciliate with the union rather than attempt to break it. The extraordinary profitability of multinational capital divided the industrial working class in ways that made the communist labor strategy of independent trade unionism and industrial militance unnecessary in both these cases.

The Muslim Brothers' successful participation in the campaign against the Suez Canal Company and Shell represented the high point in the Society's activity in the labor movement. After the outbreak of the Palestine war, the declaration of martial law, and the official entry of Egyptian troops into Palestine on May 15, 1948, the Muslim Brothers' interest in labor affairs declined sharply as they devoted all their efforts to mobilizing popular support and material aid for the Palestinian cause. The Brothers did try to mobilize workers to support Palestine by collecting contributions at various factories, but their other organizational efforts among workers seem to have ceased after the outbreak of the war. After June 1948 the "workers' news" section of *al-Ikhwan al-Muslimun* was dropped, and there were only scattered reports of trade union and labor activity in the second half of 1948. By the end of the year, M. T. Audsley judged that "the Brotherhood . . . had little influence in labour matters."[74]

74. FO 371/73474/J3567 (1949).

The Muslim Brothers **389**

Dissolution, Reformation, and Radicalization

During 1948 the Muslim Brothers committed a series of terrorist acts against the Jewish community of Cairo. Several of its arms caches were discovered by the government, and the Society was implicated in assassination attempts on several political figures. A large collection of documents accidentally captured by the Cairo police disclosed the existence of a "secret apparatus" within the Society.[75] The government concluded that the Muslim Brothers were planning a revolution, and on December 8, 1948, it dissolved the Society. In retaliation, on December 28, 1948, Brothers assassinated Prime Minister al-Nuqrashi. Hasan al-Banna was in turn assassinated on February 12, 1949, by secret police agents acting on behalf of the new prime minister, Ibrahim 'Abd al-Hadi.

These events marked the conclusion of an entire period in the Society's development. The death of Hasan al-Banna led to sharp factional disputes among the remaining leaders of the Society, and its organizational coherence was seriously impaired. Previously disputes had been settled by the fiat of the General Guide. After his death no decisive and final authority was universally recognized by the membership. One consequence of Hasan al-Banna's death was that many of the potentially radical and even revolutionary tendencies in the Brothers' world view began to develop and become explicitly articulated. These radical tendencies were not apparent while the Brothers continued their activities on a reduced level as an illegal underground organization during 1949. Only after the Wafd returned to power for the last time in January 1950 and the Society began to reemerge cautiously until it was again granted legal recognition on May 1, 1951 did the new radical current of thought become readily apparent in some of the Society's publications.

The Muslim Brothers' world view was articulated in conservative Islamic terms and called for the establishment of an ideal society modelled on the early Muslim community. Although couched as a call to restore traditional Islamic values, this appeal had a profoundly radical effect because it denied the moral legitimacy of both British imperial domination of Egypt and the secular nationalist movement that had arisen to challenge it. Some of the Society's leaders were interested only in the conservative aspect of the Society's message, but many of the Society's rank-and-file members who had been attracted by the emphasis on social solidarity, mutual aid, nationalism, and the vision of a "moral economy" were quite open to the radical interpre-

75. For a discussion of these events and their aftermath see Mitchell, *The Society*, pp. 58 ff.

390 The Muslim Brothers

tations of the Society's doctrine, which began to gain influence and widespread attention even beyond the ranks of the Muslim Brothers. Some Brothers were impelled by their radicalism into the ranks of the communist movement, retracing the ideological journey of Taha Sa'd 'Uthman. In early 1949 Prime Minister 'Abd al-Hadi reportedly said that half of the Brothers sent by the Society's leadership to spy on the communist organizations were ultimately recruited into those organizations.[76] When the Society was dissolved, many Brothers were rounded up and placed in detention camps together with communists, many of whom had been interned since the declaration of martial law. This experience, too, seems to have had a radicalizing effect on many of the Brothers. A number of communist veterans of these detention camps recalled that some of the Brothers were deeply impressed by the egalitarian social relationships among the communist prisoners.

The radical tendency within the Society of Muslim Brothers was best articulated in the writings of Sayyid Qutb, Muhammad al-Ghazzali, al-Bahi al-Khuli, and some of the articles in the "workers' page" of *al-Da'wa (The Call)*, the weekly magazine of what may loosely be termed the Society's left wing in 1951–1954.[77] Sayyid Qutb and Muhammad al-Ghazzali were not official spokespersons for the Society when they first published their major works on social questions, whereas al-Bahi al-Khuli's book, *Islam . . . Not Communism and Not Capitalism*, was an official publication of the Workers' Section, which was reestablished when the Society was reconstituted in 1951. As such it represents the fullest official theoretical exposition of the Society's views on labor, its role in society, and the rights and obligations of workers.

The bulk of the book reiterates and amplifies the basic views of the Muslim Brothers on mutual social responsibility explicated previously and repeats criticisms of the government's labor policy. Both communism and capitalism are attacked as materialistic ideologies emanating from the West, in opposition to which it is necessary to uphold and affirm the Islamic heritage. The novel and revolutionary implications of al-Khuli's exposition are contained in the final sections of the book where he relates an oral tradition attributed to the Caliph 'Umar according to which an employer complained to 'Umar that his workers stole from him. 'Umar replied that if the workers repeated

76. FO 371/73476/J1937; FO 371/73476/J3502 (1949).
77. Sayyid Qutb, *al-'Adala al-ijtima'iyya fi al-islam* (Cairo, 1949) and *Ma'rakat al-islam wa'l-ra'smaliyya* (Cairo, 1954); Muhammad al-Ghazzali, *al-Islam wa-manahij al-ishtirakiyya* (Cairo, 1951); al-Bahi al-Khuli, *al-Islam . . . la shuyu'iyya wa-la ra'smaliyya* (Cairo, 1951).

The Muslim Brothers **391**

this offense the employer's hands would be cut off because it meant the wages paid the workers were insufficient. The employer therefore bore the responsibility for the workers' act and should receive its appropriate punishment. Al-Khuli went on to argue that those who do not work have no right to a share of society's wealth, though in contemporary Egypt the rich and idle were systematically oppressing those who worked. Exploitative monopoly companies and big landowners were held responsible for this situation. Al-Khuli attacked both foreign and Egyptian companies for their treatment of workers. The conclusion of the section of the book devoted to urban labor contains an appeal to improve workers' conditions based on the concepts of "human rights" and "natural rights." Al-Khuli warned that if these rights are not secured, the result will be a violent and destructive social upheaval. This is not the outcome which he desired. Therefore he urged workers to retain their self-control and rally round Islam.[78] This call seems to contradict the moral stand implied in the oral tradition attributed to 'Umar, and may have been inserted to satisfy the more conservative members of the Society's leadership or the requirements of government censorship. It is also possible that at the very last moment al-Khuli was unable to embrace the ultimate conclusions of his own argument, or break completely with the Brothers' long-standing aversion to exacerbating social tensions.

Expressions of militant anticapitalist sentiment in the pages of *al-Da'wa* were less ambiguous. Muhammad al-Fuli, a labor lawyer who served as counsellor for several unions in the Alexandria area, contributed a regular column offering legal advice to workers and expounding the Islamic point of view on labor questions. His opposition to capitalism was unequivocal, and rather than calling on workers to restrain themselves, he urged them to unite and struggle against the capitalists, not only for day-to-day economic demands in the factories, but for a workers' ideology (*fikra 'ummaliyya*).[79] He warned the capitalists against the righteous wrath of the workers:

> Oh tyrannical capitalists . . . the sword of justice is unsheathed against you. Either you grant the workers their rights or justice will conquer. And the day that it will triumph you will have neither existence nor power.[80]

The radicalization of a section of the Muslim Brothers made possible the establishment of a limited, sporadic, and unstable national

78. al-Khuli, *al-Islam* . . . , p. 106–18.
79. *al-Da'wa*, October 2, 1951.
80. *Ibid.*, August 21, 1951.

392 The Muslim Brothers

united front that included some elements of the Society and the largest of the communist organizations, the DMNL. This united front functioned briefly in the second half of 1951 in opposition to the increasingly discredited Wafd regime, and again in 1953 after the Wafd, the DMNL, and some of the Brothers turned against the military regime of the Free Officers.

In some localities and industries this united front extended into the trade union movement. At the Misr Fine Spinning and Weaving Company a coalition led by communists, but embracing adherents of all the political tendencies within the workers' movement, successfully removed the company-dominated union and replaced it with a union freely chosen by the workers. When this victory was finally achieved in March, 1953, after several years of struggle, Muhammad Mutawalli al-Sha'rawi, a DMNL supporter, was elected president of the union, and Muhammad al-Fuli was chosen as its legal counsel. This alliance was exceptionally stable because neither the Brothers nor the communists had a strong base among the workers. Moreover, Muhammad al-Fuli's commitment and involvement—he had been employed at the mill as a white-collar clerk before obtaining his law degree—in this struggle were especially strong. Even at Kafr al-Dawwar there was a certain amount of contention within the framework of a de facto alliance as indicated by the fact that Muhammad Mutawalli al-Sha'rawi's opponent in the union's presidential election of 1953 was a member of the Muslim Brothers.[81]

During the period of the 1953 united front an important change took place in the attitude of some elements of the Society toward strikes. Jamal al-Banna, who became labor editor of *al-Da'wa* that year, partially endorsed a program of trade union rights formulated by the DMNL and presented to the government. He tentatively advanced a "labor compact" that included a demand that the government permit peaceful strikes.[82] Several months later *al-Da'wa* editorially endorsed this demand.[83] This new attitude received concrete expression in the August 1953 strike at the Shurbaji textile mill in Imbaba which was supported by the national united front.[84]

81. al-Sha'rawi, interview, April 3, 1981; *al-Da'wa*, April 14, 1953.
82. *al-Da'wa*, January 13, 1953.
83. *Ibid.*, April 14, 1953.
84. Because of press censorship, there are no reports of the details of this strike. Several references to the role of communists appear in Sa'id, *1950–1957*, passim. Several references to the Shurbaji workers in *al-Da'wa*, though without mention of a strike, are the only indications of the Muslim Brothers' involvement in this incident. However, Taha Sa'd 'Uthman confirmed that the Muslim Brothers played an important role in this union.

The Muslim Brothers **393**

Despite the fact that some sections of the Muslim Brothers adopted a much more radical proworker stance in both theory and practice from 1951 to 1954 than the Society as a whole had officially embraced in 1944–1948, the Brothers' organizational links with the workers' movement were weaker in the 1950s than in the 1940s.[85] Muhammad Sharif did not resume his position as head of the Workers' Section when it was reformed in 1951. He cited the diminished effectiveness of the section as his reason for abandoning his position.[86] His opposition to the new radical direction of some elements in the Workers' Section seems likely to have been a factor in this decision, and it is possible that policy differences between socially conservative and more radical elements may have contributed to weakening the Workers' Section.

The Muslim Brothers' consistently weak organizational presence in the workers' movement was the mirror image of the broad popularity of the Society's appeal for a moral economy. This moral appeal was not consistently developed into an effective program for workers' political action. Most often the Society simply propagandized for its vision, called on the state to mend its errant ways, and when this failed, resorted to terror (as in 1948) or continued propagandizing. Most of the Society's writings on labor affairs suffered from ambiguity, inconsistency, and programmatic unclarity.

The ambiguity of its position enabled a large number of workers and others to identify with the Society. But it also made it difficult for the Society to galvanize its supporters for a prolonged campaign of political action. Its rapidly shifting political alliances—for and against Sidqi, the Wafd and the national fronts of 1951 and 1953—made the Society an unreliable leader of trade union struggles where consistency, programmatic clarity, and stable long-term alliances are the keys to success. Because the Society's actions were guided by criteria external to the labor movement, it was not easy to predict its stands on vital trade union matters. For example, in 1948 when Fathi Kamil, a secularist not sympathetic to the Muslim Brothers, was president of the Eastern Tobacco Company union, the Society sharply criticized the union for being subservient to management.[87] Yet the very same week the Brothers had nothing but praise for the management of the Misr Spinning and Weaving Company, which was notorious for handpicking the leadership of its union.[88] But in 1952, after the Brothers had gained considerable influence within the Eastern

85. Jamal al-Banna, interview, December 22, 1980.
86. Sharif, interview, December 3, 1980.
87. *IM*, April 22, 1948.
88. *Ibid.*, April 20, 1948.

394 The Muslim Brothers

Company union, they were very supportive of both management and the union.[89]

Pro-Wafd or procommunist workers were unlikely to forget or forgive the charges of strikebreaking made against the Muslim Brothers in Shubra al-Khayma and Mahalla al-Kubra. These same workers saw the Brothers' withdrawal from the NCWS and their campaign against the popular upsurge of the nationalist movement in 1946 as antinationalist acts of collaboration with imperialism. These negative impressions could only have been overcome by a clear and consistent record of unimpeachable trade union and national political activity from 1951 to 1954. Instead, the sporadic and uncertain participation of the Society in the national united fronts of 1951 and 1953, which was the result of internal division among the Brothers, reinforced the Society's image as an unreliable political ally easily given to sudden reversals in policy.

The Muslim Brothers were, with the exception of the Wafd, the largest mass movement in postwar Egypt. However, without organizational and programmatic coherence, size alone, even when augmented by the undeniable sincerity and militance of many individual members and supporters, was insufficient to make the Brothers an effective political force. The Muslim Brothers posed a fundamental ideological challenge to British hegemony and to secular nationalism. But a programmatically unspecific and vague moral denunciation of British imperialism and secularism, no matter how popular and potentially radical, was not the same as, and perhaps was even an obstacle to, becoming an effectively organized force within the Egyptian workers' movement, and ultimately, within the broader nationalist political movement.

89. *al-Da'wa*, February 26, November 25, 1952.

Chapter XII

The Labor Movement and the Crisis of the Old Regime

By the end of the Palestine war it was becoming increasingly apparent that the coalition of class forces that had ruled Egypt since the end of the First World War was incapable of offering a solution to the political and economic crisis of Egyptian society. The large landowners who dominated both the Wafd and the opposition political parties clung tenaciously to their privileges, and were unwilling to concede even minimal reforms in the vital areas of land tenure, ground rent, and the taxation of agricultural property. The large landowners were well-integrated into the world market for cotton and other agricultural products, and on that basis can be considered an agricultural bourgeoisie, though many remnants of precapitalist social relations continued to form an integral part of rural economy and society. The social status and political power of the landed pashas was intimately associated with attitudes and practices commonly identified in Egypt as "feudal." Consequently, the large landowners as a class (Wafd supporters as well as others) remained the bastion of social conservatism, while the king (who was the single largest landowner) and the landed magnates linked to the Palace embodied blind reaction.

The Egyptian industrial bourgeoisie and its representatives in Parliament, often identified with the Sa'dist party, acknowledged the need for agrarian reform, a more equitable distribution of wealth, and accelerated industrial development, though in practice, because the industrialists were closely linked to large landowning interests by family and social ties and derived much of their capital from agrarian interests, they shared the same social conservatism and fear of unleashing the anger of the impoverished rural and urban masses. Many proposals for economic and social reform were blocked by this fear.

396 Crisis of the Old Regime

The industrialists did not comprise an independent and self-confident class prepared to challenge the hegemony of the agrarian bourgeoisie. Egyptian industry did not, and still has not, transcended the limitations created by its original formation under the domination of European capital. In order to survive, Egyptian industrialists had to conciliate and ally with both the large landowners and the West to obtain capital and political support.

The peasants who comprised the majority of the population remained unorganized on a national scale, and hardly participated in political life beyond delivering their votes to whichever party happened to dominate the local constellation of forces. The Wafd had the greatest support in the countryside, but this was based on its appeal to "rich" peasants and village headmen who in turn influenced the poorer villagers. Indeed, no political party ever succeeded in establishing a mass base among the poor peasantry.

The urban *effendiyya*, who provided the activist core for all of the political trends in the country, continued to struggle actively for national independence, but the political loyalties of this stratum were fragmented. The Muslim Brothers, Young Egypt (reorganized as the Socialist party after 1950), the Wafdist Vanguard, and the various communist organizations all had adherents among the *effendiyya*. The political fragmentation of the *effendiyya* was due to the division between the traditional and modern sectors within this stratum, the diversity of individual members' interests, and their varied relations and alliances with other social strata. This made the *effendiyya* incapable of providing the social base for a unified political movement that could topple the old regime.

The social and political paralysis of the agrarian and industrial bourgeoisie led the Workers' Committee for National Liberation, one of the the the first expressions of the emergence of the working class as an independent political force on a national scale, to propose that the working class should carry out the national and democratic tasks that had been accomplished by the bourgeoisie in the West. In the upsurge of industrial and nationalist struggle in 1945–1946, it briefly seemed possible that this perspective might provide the solution for Egypt's crisis. The working class and the radical intelligentsia did provide new leadership and social content to the nationalist movement, but the working class was too small, too fragmented by the uneven character of Egyptian capitalism, and too politically inexperienced to unite the nationalist movement under its hegemony.

Because no force in Egyptian society possessed the strength or flexibility to resolve the social and political crisis, a political gridlock was created. Everyone understood that the old regime was dead, but

Crisis of the Old Regime **397**

no one knew precisely how to bury it. This political stalemate gave
the Wafd a final opportunity to return to power and attempt to salvage
the regime by resolving the crisis. In this conjuncture the organized
working class, under the leadership of a renewed communist movement, again engaged in intensified industrial struggle linked to an upsurge in the nationalist movement.

The political organizations of the radical intelligentsia and the urban working class had been badly battered and disorganized by the
repression of 1946 and the period of martial law and detention in
1948–1949. Political and trade union activity began to revive slowly
at the end of 1949 and the beginning of 1950, as prisoners began to be
released from the detention camps. Although the nationalist and populist appeal of the Wafd had been badly tarnished by the Anglo-Egyptian treaty of 1936, the incident of February 4, 1942, and the scandals
revealed in Makram 'Ubayd's *Black Book* both the communists and
the Muslim Brothers supported the Wafd in the elections of January
1950 in the hope that a Wafd victory would end martial law and permit resumption of normal political activity. When a modicum of political freedom was restored, the DMNL was able to reorganize and expand rapidly. It was by far the most dynamic force in the workers'
movement in the last years of the old regime and its influence on the
national political scene was much greater than its limited membership might have implied.

Despite its declining popularity, the Wafd returned to power in
1950 because no other legal political party could claim as much historic or popular legitimacy. The low turnout (only 56 percent) in the
elections revealed widespread public cynicism toward the Wafd and
the entire political system. In Cairo, voter participation was only 15
percent, and it was only slightly higher in Alexandria. The Wafd received only 40 percent of the popular vote, the lowest percentage ever
in a reasonably free election, and the British embassy judged even
this modest success to have been the result of the ineffectiveness of
the other parties.[1]

The most conservative elements of the Wafd, led by the minister of
the interior, Fu'ad Siraj al-Din, dominated the government. None of
the younger figures associated with the Wafdist Vanguard were given
cabinet posts. Moreover, the Wafd government of January 1950 to January 1952 displayed more respect and acceptance of the monarchy
than any previous Wafd administration, for its central leadership
understood that the regime was in deep crisis and wished to preserve
it. But the Wafd's inability to overcome the conservative tendencies

1. FO 371/96874/JE1018/104 (1952).

398 Crisis of the Old Regime

of its central leadership and its failure to implement a clear program of political and economic reforms ensured that it would ultimately fall with the monarchy.[2]

King Faruq had become increasingly unpopular since his capitulation to the British ultimatum of February 4, 1942. The defeat of the Egyptian army in Palestine was a further severe blow to the prestige of the monarchy because it was so closely associated with the army. Perhaps more than anything else, Faruq's ostentatious display of corruption and debauchery rendered him an object of public mockery and scorn.[3] The legitimacy of the Wafd was further diminished by its conciliating attitude toward the king, for it did nothing to protest or restrain his public profligacy. Moreover, Siraj al-Din defended the Palace when the magazine *Ruz al-Yusuf* published a series of articles charging personalities in the king's retinue with responsibility for supplying faulty weapons to the Egyptian army during the Palestine war. The exposure of this scandal finally destroyed the legitimacy of the monarchy in the eyes of the Egyptian people and resulted in widespread disaffection in the ranks of the army.

Faced with a fundamental crisis of the entire political system it could not resolve, the Wafd oscillated between the radical tendencies of its left wing and the deeply conservative character of its leadership. The Wafd did allow greater political freedom and tolerated the activities of both the communists and the Muslim Brothers, but it was inconsistent in this regard. In May 1950 it attempted to enact a law restricting the activity of "politically suspicious" persons, and in August 1951 it attempted to legislate press censorship. Both measures were defeated by campaigns of mass public pressure, evidence that the Wafd was still somewhat responsive to popular opinion. Nonetheless, the Wafd did not hesitate to undertake strong anticommunist measures when it appeared that communist strength was becoming too great. Henri Curiel, the principal leader of the DMNL, was deported to Italy in August 1950.[4] The weekly newspaper *al-Bashir* (*The Herald*), which began the year as a left Wafd journal supporting the government and gradually became an unofficial organ of the DMNL, was banned in December 1950. A second unofficial DMNL weekly, *al-Malayin* (*The Millions*), began publication in May 1951, but was also closed down by the government in December 1951.

2. For a perceptive discussion of Wafd-Palace relations during this period see al-Bishri, *al-Haraka al-siyasiyya*, pp. 302 ff.
3. For an evocative account of Faruq's personal degradation see Berque, *Egypt: Imperialism and Revolution*, pp. 660–61.
4. Curiel's family had Italian citizenship, but he was born in Egypt, had renounced his Italian citizenship, and become an Egyptian citizen on reaching his majority.

The Labor Movement and the Final Wafd Regime

The Wafd's desperation and its lack of a clear political direction was expressed in its labor policy. The Wafd did not try to organize a trade union federation (the first time it failed to do so while in control of the government), though it is unlikely that the Wafd would have been able to retain control over such an organization had it tried. Too many trade unions had by now adopted a stance of political nonalignment. To contain labor unrest the Wafd enacted labor legislation improving the standards of occupational health and safety and authorizing unions to sign collective agreements for their members. The government's most important labor initiative was Military Order No. 99 of February 20, 1950, which established a daily minimum wage of 12.5 PT for adult workers, and what was more important, required private employers to follow the government's lead in increasing the cost-of-living allowance added on to basic wages since 1944 by 50 percent. This military order was an attempt to alleviate the persistent gap between wage levels and the continually rising cost of living.

However, after announcing this regulation, the government failed to enforce it consistently. As a result, sharp industrial struggles broke out over how to apply the military order. Many employers made no distinction between the base wage and the cost-of-living increment, so it was often unclear what proportion of the wage was to be increased by 50 percent. Smaller enterprises that could not afford higher wages resorted to a variety of evasive tactics, such as dismissing veteran workers and rehiring new workers at lower pay rates. Even some larger firms cut annual bonuses and fringe benefits in order to reduce their wage costs.[5] There were strikes and protests in all sectors of the economy over the cost-of-living allowance: in March the Cairo tramway workers protested by not collecting fares; and in April dockers in Port Said and Alexandria struck for three days.[6]

One of the largest strikes, at the Hawamdiyya sugar refinery formerly under French control but now owned by the Egyptian magnate Ahmad 'Abbud, demonstrated the constraints on the Wafd's labor policies. 'Abbud resisted paying the cost-of-living increase throughout 1950 and demanded that the government reduce the excise duty on sugar as compensation for the increased wage bill. 'Abbud had substantial leverage over the Wafd government because he was one of the party's major financial backers, and had close personal relations with al-Nahhas Pasha and Ahmad Husayn, who was both minister of

5. FO 371/80606/JE2181/5 (1950).
6. *Ibid.*

400 Crisis of the Old Regime

social affairs and the brother of 'Abbud's son-in-law.[7] This network of personal and political patronage relations clearly illustrates why the Wafd found it difficult to implement social reforms, or enforce the legislation it had enacted. Following a two- hour warning strike to demand the cost-of-living increase on December 7, ninety-two sugar workers, among them the entire union leadership, were arrested. Finally, the 4,000 workers struck from December 18, 1950, to January 6, 1951. The government refused to support the strike, even though its principal demand was that 'Abbud comply with a government decree. This enabled the pro-Palace newspapers *al-Zaman* and *Le Journal d'Égypte* to launch a campaign of support for the strike in an attempt to discredit and embarrass the Wafd and enhance Faruq's public image.[8] But the Palace gained little support from workers for these efforts because it was well known that the editor of these papers, Edgar Jallad, was paid by the king.

Nonetheless, a large number of trade unions and prominent individuals did support the sugar workers, and this broad labor solidarity encouraged other sectors of the working class to press their demands with greater intensity. This high level of solidarity was an indication that many trade unionists were now willing to identify their interests with those of other workers, despite the government's obvious antipathy for the strike: a development that was especially remarkable because the communists, who would ordinarily have been the main promoters of class-wide solidarity, did not participant significantly in this strike. In the end the Wafd was thoroughly embarrassed by having allowed a major industrial enterprise to flaunt the law for a full year. The sugar refinery workers only received their cost-of-living allowance in February 1951 when the government agreed to compensate the sugar company for its increased wage bill with a subsidy on sugar.

Textile workers continued to play a central role in the trade union movement, and the struggle to implement Military Order No. 99 was very sharp in the textile industry. In Shubra al-Khayma only three of the smallest textile mills, employing a total of 310 workers, granted the cost-of-living allowance, and 150 workers from various mills were dismissed for demanding the implementation of Military Order No. 99.[9] Throughout 1950 several textile mills in Shubra al-Khayma and the other suburban Cairo textile centers repeatedly dismissed workers, cut wages, and maneuvered to avoid paying the increased

7. FO 371/90231/JE2182/4 (1951).
8. *al-Zaman*, December 18, 1950 to January 8, 1951.
9. *al-Bashir*, May 2, 9, 1950.

Crisis of the Old Regime **401**

cost-of-living allowance.[10] The union established by the Muslim Brothers in Shubra al-Khayma was no longer active, and no new union had been organized to take its place.[11] As a result, the workers were unable to effectively resist the tactics of their employers. In desperation, eight textile workers in Rawd al-Faraj (the district adjacent to Shubra al-Khayma) went on a hunger strike to protest their employers' failure to pay the increased cost-of-living allowance.[12] *Al-Bashir* continually urged the Shubra al-Khayma workers to unite and reorganize,[13] but despite the persistent efforts of Muhammad Shatta and other DMNL organizers, it proved impossible to reorganize the Shubra al-Khayma textile workers until 1951. Even then, the government succeeded in blocking the convening of a general assembly which was a legal requirement for the formal recognition and reestablishment of the union.

However, a strong textile workers' union was established under the leadership of the DMNL in the neighboring Cairo suburb of Zaytun, where several thousand workers were employed in approximately fifteen textile mills. This Greater Cairo Mechanized Textile Workers' Union (GCMTWU) became the first important center of DMNL strength in the trade union movement after the revival of communist activity in 1950. The union had been organized in 1946 by Muhammmad 'Ali 'Amir, who considered himself a left Wafdist at that time.[14] 'Amir and his union had been active in the events of February 21, 1946, and in supporting the Misr Spinning and Weaving Company strike in September 1947. In 1947 and 1948 'Amir was associated with a Trotskyist group, and was arrested with many of its members in February 1948. After his release from jail he joined the DMNL.

'Amir was not only the president and the dominant figure of the GCMTWU, he was also a popular political leader in Zaytun and Matariyya with deep roots in the local community. He had a reputation as a "tough character" and commanded respect for his physical strength and oratorical ability. 'Amir had been a political and trade union activist since the 1930s, first as a partisan of 'Abbas Halim, and later as a Wafd militant.[15] He was an organizer of the Wafd Blue Shirts (a par-

10. *Ibid.*, July 8, 15, August 5, September 2, 16, October 21, November 11, 18, 1950.
11. *Ibid.*, July 8, 1950.
12. *al-Ahram*, December 18, 1950.
13. *al-Bashir*, August 5, September 16, 30, November 18, 1950.
14. Details of Muhammad 'Ali 'Amir's biography, unless otherwise noted, are based on interviews of November 27, December 5, 9, 1980.
15. *al-Jihad*, April 30, 1936, reports that Muhammad 'Amir, nicknamed "al-nims" ("the weasel," a name denoting physical prowess), supported the Wafd against 'Abbas Halim in the split that occurred in the trade union movement that year.

402 Crisis of the Old Regime

amilitary formation) in the late 1930s, and by the end of World War II, he was the head of all the Wafd Youth Committees in the area. After joining the DMNL, in addition to his trade union activity, 'Amir played a leading role in the Egyptian branch of the Partisans of Peace organization and its campaign to obtain signatures on a petition for world peace—one of the DMNL's most important efforts in its attempt to form a broad national united front in 1951.

The establishment of a center of DMNL strength among the Zaytun and Matariyya textile workers precipitated a confrontation with the Muslim Brothers just as it had in Shubra al-Khayma. However, on this occasion Muhammad 'Ali 'Amir's personal popularity and authority, in addition to the Brothers' questionable record in trade union struggles, enabled the DMNL forces to prevail easily.[16] The dispute began in 1950 when the owner of a small textile mill in Cairo who was a member of the Muslim Brothers invited Jamal al-Banna to advise and instruct workers on how to manage their union, which was affiliated to the GCMTWU. Because of his involvement with the workers at this mill, al-Banna became known to the leadership of the GCMTWU, which, although al-Banna was not a worker, invited him to join the executive board of the union because he was a proficient accountant and could manage the union's finances. 'Amir approved this without knowing that al-Banna was the brother of the founder of the Society of Muslim Brothers, for at the time Jamal al-Banna was known as Ahmad Jamal al-Din.

The union executive board elections of June 18, 1950 resulted in the victory of two DMNL members, Muhammad 'Ali 'Amir and Fikri al-Khuli (whose autobiographical accounts of his early experiences at Mahalla al-Kubra are cited in Chapter VIII) and two supporters of the Muslim Brothers, Jamal al-Banna and 'Abd al-Mun'im 'Isawi (who had earlier served on the executive board of the Shubra al-Khayma textile workers' union). Shortly after the election, al-Banna prepared to publish a new magazine, independent of the union, to be called *al-Niqaba (The Union)*. 'Amir perceived this as an attempt to undermine his leadership of the GCMTWU and establish a competing center of Muslim Brothers-inspired influence within the union. Very shortly thereafter Jamal al-Banna was ousted from the union executive board,

16. This incident is obliquely referred to in *al-Bashir*, October 7, 14, 1950. This account has been supplemented by interviews with Jamal al-Banna on October 5, 1980, Muhammad 'Ali 'Amir on December 5, 1980, and fragments of the union's papers made available by Jamal al-Banna, who asserts he was not a member of the Society of the Muslim Brothers at this time. This may well be formally correct, but there is no doubt that he identified with and was seen as a representative of the Islamic trend in the trade union movement referred to in Chapter XI.

Crisis of the Old Regime   **403**

and the GCMTWU remained solidly under the leadership of Muhammad 'Ali 'Amir and the DMNL for the next several years.

The Sibahi mill in Alexandria was the scene of exceptionally sharp struggle during 1950. There were strikes in February, June and August over implementation of the increased cost-of-living allowance, late payment of wages, and other minor issues.[17] The June strike was especially violent, and was marked by the deaths of four workers who drowned in the Mahmudiyya Canal which ran by the mill. Although management was widely believed to have been responsible for these deaths, no charges were ever brought to court. The Sibahi mills were notorious for their poor treatment of workers. Both *al-Bashir* and British diplomatic reports concur that the Sibahi management was one of the worst in Egypt.[18] Following these strikes the Sibahi management, with cooperation from prominent Alexandria Wafdists, dismissed over 1,000 workers in order to weed out all the trade union militants in the mill, and a blacklist was compiled to prevent these workers from being employed elsewhere.[19]

Faced with the consequences of the intensifying social contradictions the struggles in the textile industry exemplified, the Wafd, in practice, aligned itself with the dominant social classes in an effort to maintain social peace. It did not offer any fundamental solutions to the underlying social issues of employment security and low wages which caused explosive incidents such as the one at Sibahi, nor did it consistently enforce the short-term measures it had enacted, such as Military Order No. 99. Consequently, the dissatisfaction of the working class grew, and increasingly greater numbers of workers and trade union leaders came under the influence of the DMNL.

Broadening Communist Influence in the Workers' Movement

The Cairo transport workers played a key role in the revival of trade union activity in 1950–51. During this period 'Abbas Halim finally disappeared from the scene. Members and supporters of the DMNL began to gain influence in the Cairo transport unions, and the transport industry became the second most important concentration of DMNL strength in the labor movement, after the textile industry. The principal DMNL leaders among the transport workers were two Cairo taxi drivers, Hasan 'Abd al-Rahman and Sayyid Khalil Turk.

Hasan 'Abd al-Rahman had been a member of a Cairo taxi drivers'

17. FO 371/80606/JE2181/5 (1950); *al-Ahram*, June 24, 25, August 18, 1950; *al-Bashir*, September 30, 1950.
18. *al-Bashir*, July 1, 1950; FO 371/80606/JE2181/5 (1950).
19. *al-Bashir*, November 11, 25 1950.

404 Crisis of the Old Regime

union since 1942.[20] There was a split in the union in 1947 or 1948, and he formed a separate union and became its president. He became a member of 'Abbas Halim's Labor party in 1947 or 1948, but by early 1951 he had joined the DMNL. In late 1950 'Abd al-Rahman began to campaign for the unification of the four unions of Cairo taxi drivers.[21] This unity was achieved in January 1951 when 'Abd al-Rahman was elected president of the 5,000 member Cairo United Drivers' Union.[22]

Continuing to broaden his efforts to unite transport workers, 'Abd al-Rahman called for a national conference of transport workers. Representatives of thirty-four transport workers' unions met in Cairo on January 17–19, 1951, and adopted a list of demands covering all sectors of the transport industry—taxis, trucks, buses, and tramways. Among the main demands were improving the pay and working conditions of Cairo bus and tramway workers to bring them up to the standard achieved by the Alexandria Joint Transport workers, and a 40 percent increase in taxi fares.[23] Alexandria taxi drivers had already announced that they would strike on February 5 to protest the government's refusal to approve the requested fare increase.[24] The Cairo conference endorsed this strike deadline and thereby threatened a national transport general strike. However, on February 1 some of the more conservative union leaders, especially those of the Cairo bus and tramway unions, called off the strike, claiming that the government was about to grant the transport workers' demands.[25]

These demands were not met, and consequently 'Abd al-Rahman convened a second meeting of representatives of the transport

20. Details of Hasan 'Abd al-Rahman's biography, unless otherwise noted, are based on an interview on December 7, 1980.

21. al-Muqattam, October 21, 1950.

22. Ibid., January 6, 20, 1951. There are, however, persistent subsequent reports of efforts by Ibrahim Zayn al-Din to continue the existence of his chauffeurs' union. Although this union was very weak and inactive at this time, financial support from the British enabled Zayn al-Din to maintain a presence among the transport union leaders.

23. Ibid., January 20, 1951; al-Misri, January 20, 1951. Taxi drivers who did not own their own vehicles were paid 25 percent of total receipts.

24. al-Muqattam, January 13, 1951.

25. Ibid., February 3, 1951. For a very different account of the January 1951 transport conference, see FO 371/90231/JE2182/5 (1951). E. A. Chapman-Andrews reported that the demands of the conference were met, and gave a different version of the demands as well. If this report were correct, the subsequent activities of the transport workers' unions could not be understood. This inaccuracy can be explained by the fact that the British embassy's source of information was undoubtedly Ibrahim Zayn al-Din, who tried but failed to use this conference to enhance his own position among the transport workers. Chapman-Andrews, who was not the regular labor attaché, may have been somewhat more gullible than Audsley who understood Zayn al-Din's isolation in the trade union movement. See FO 371/90231/JE2182/11 (1951).

Crisis of the Old Regime **405**

unions. The Congress of Egyptian Joint Transport Drivers' and Workers' Unions met on June 2, 1951 and elected 'Abd al-Rahman its president and Sayyid Khalil Turk its general secretary. Other members of the executive committee represented transport workers from Alexandria, Port Said, Isma'iliyya, Damietta, and Upper Egypt. The following demands were adopted: a 40 percent taxi fare increase, wage increases for tramway and bus drivers, the application of labor legislation to all drivers, and a requirement that vehicle owners purchase insurance for the drivers and passengers. The meeting denounced the leadership of the Cairo tramway and bus unions, and Ibrahim Zayn al-Din was specifically attacked as a British agent and identified as having opposed the call for a general strike.[26] Subsequently the Cairo Joint Transport Federation (JTF) issued a statement that Zayn al-Din alone had been responsible for sabotaging the strike of February 5.[27] Because Zayn al-Din personally commanded the loyalty of very few workers at this time, it is unlikely that this was entirely true, but scapegoating him permitted the reestablishment of a reasonable degree of unity among the Cairo transport workers' leadership. In accordance with its objective of establishing a national united front, the DMNL was striving to establish the broadest possible unity within the trade union movement. By agreeing to unite with the Cairo bus and tramway union leaders after they denounced Zayn al-Din, the DMNL was able to increase its influence among the transport workers. 'Abd al-'Aziz Mustafa, the president of the Cairo Tramway Workers' Union, was especially friendly and cooperative with the DMNL in late 1951 and 1952, though he never joined the organization.[28] Two DMNL members were active in the tramway workers' union, Mahmud al-Farghali, who served as a shop steward and then secretary of the union, and Sayyid Mustafa.

The continuing and intensifying political crisis of the Egyptian regime provided fertile ground for the rapid growth of the communist movement during 1951. According to Walter Laqueur, the DMNL had only 100 or 200 members in February 1950, but by the end of 1952 its ranks (including both workers and nonworkers) numbered 2,000 or 3,000.[29] Tariq al-Bishri accepts these figures and supplements them with the estimate of former DMNL leader Zaki Murad that in November 1951 nearly 1,500 workers were members, candidates, or close supporters of the organization.[30] DMNL supporters and members were

26. *al-Malayin*, May 27, June 3, 1951.
27. *Ibid.*, June 17, 1951.
28. Ahmad Taha, interview, December 2, 1979.
29. Laqueur, *Communism and Nationalism*, p. 46.
30. al-Bishri, *al-Haraka al-siyasiyya*, p. 422.

406 Crisis of the Old Regime

elected to official positions in several unions during 1951. Among the most prominent union officials who were also DMNL members (in addition to those already mentioned) were Ahmad Taha, secretary of the Marconi Wireless Company union, Anwar Maqqar, secretary of the Cairo Restaurant and Hotel Workers' Union, 'Atiyya al-Sirafi, president of the Zifti and Mit Ghamr Bus Workers' Union, Muhammad 'Abduh Nuh, head of the Alexandria seamens' union, and Yasin Mustafa, head of the Cairo shoemakers' union. DMNL influence was also strong in the Alexandria Joint Transport Federation and the union of the Coca Cola Company, where Sayyid Khalil Turk had once been employed.

Toward a National Trade Union Federation

Even more significant than the increase in the number of workers and trade union officials affiliated with the DMNL was the growing trend towards unity within the trade union movement. By encouraging this unity the DMNL was able to assume the leadership of a large section of the trade union movement by late 1951 in the context of a massive mobilization of the Egyptian nationalist movement. As in February 1946, there was a convergence of the national and workers' movements that allowed the communists to assume a prominent position in both movements and exert an influence far stronger than their limited numbers would have suggested was possible.

However, although the DMNL was unquestionably the leading force in the trade union movement in late 1951, the influence of the communists in the nationalist movement was not as broad as it was in 1946. Other forces, such as the Muslim Brothers, the Socialist party, and ultimately the army, were more prominent in that arena. This was at least partially attributable to the intensified factionalism within the communist movement. Communist factionalism was much more strongly felt among intellectuals who had greater leisure and inclination to take an interest in theoretical issues than among workers, where none of the other communist organizations were as active or as successful as the DMNL. Another issue limiting the nationalist appeal of the communists was their support for the partition of Palestine and the creation of the Jewish state which had not been a factor in 1946. This question also appears to have been more significant among intellectuals than among workers.

The impetus for the nationalist upsurge in late 1951 was the slow progress of the negotiations between the Wafd and the British over revision of the 1936 treaty. Negotiations had begun in March 1950, but the British now offered less favorable terms to the Wafd than they had

Crisis of the Old Regime **407**

proposed to Sidqi in 1946. Public pressure for suspending the treaty talks and unilateral abrogation of the treaty mounted throughout 1951. The trade union movement was active in the nationalist mobilization, just as it had been in 1946, and began to raise nationalist demands frequently. For example, on August 26, 1951, thousands of workers, among them the traditionally pro-Wafd Royal Press, railroad, and Abu Za'bal government workshop workers, demonstrated denouncing the 1936 treaty.[31] The Cairo JTF began a campaign for the nationalization of Cairo's public transport system, which was still mainly owned and operated by foreign concessionaires.[32] Faced with growing popular pressure and his own declining popularity, Prime Minister al-Nahhas made one last attempt to restore the prestige of the Wafd and the viability of the regime by announcing, on October 8, 1951, Egypt's unilateral abrogation of both the 1936 treaty and the 1899 Anglo-Egyptian Condominium Agreement, which regulated the administration of the Sudan. This proclamation unleashed a storm of popular nationalist fervor which expressed itself dramatically in the organization of guerilla operations against British military and economic installations in the Suez Canal Zone.

In the labor movement, al-Nahhas Pasha's declaration was enthusiastically welcomed. Textile workers in Zaytun and Matariyya joined by members of the Partisans of Peace demonstrated and rallied for two days in support of the cancellation of the treaties. Slogans were raised calling for the extension of democratic liberties, the abolition of the political police, and a treaty of friendship with the Soviet Union.[33] There were also workers' demonstrations in Shubra al-Khayma, and in Alexandria ten percent of the Marconi Wireless Company employees refused to handle traffic to the British military base in the Suez Canal Zone. At the Cairo Marconi office, workers staged a complete strike in support of an employee dismissed for destroying telegrams for the British base. All traffic to the Canal Zone was stopped.[34] Dockers in Port Said went on strike from October 8 to the middle of February 1952, and were joined by dockers in other Suez Canal ports as well as by Suez Canal Company workshop workers.[35]

The most massive labor action in response to the abrogation of the treaty was the resignation of most of the workers employed by the British military installations in the Suez Canal Zone. The Muslim Brothers, the Socialist party, and the communists all called on the

31. *al-Ahram*, August 27, 1951.
32. *al-Malayin*, August 19, 1951.
33. *Ibid.*, October 21, 1951.
34. FO 371/90211/JE1431/5 (1951); FO 371/90211/JE1431/6 (1951).
35. FO 371/97073/JE2183/3 (1952); FO 371/97073/JE2183/4 (1952).

408 Crisis of the Old Regime

workers to leave their jobs, while the government promised to find them employment at wages equal to those offered by the British. According to British records there were 51,000 Egyptian workers employed directly by the British forces in the Canal Zone and 20,000 employed indirectly through labor contactors. By November 10, ninety percent of the directly-employed workers and all of the contracted workers had left their jobs. But the Ministry of Social Affairs reported that over 80,000 workers had registered to obtain new jobs.[36] Apparently several thousand workers who had never been employed by the British attempted to take advantage of the government's promise of high-paying jobs. Although some workers were employed by already overstaffed government offices, many did not find new jobs, and there were demonstrations for work and food in Cairo.[37] Wafdist ministers had known that this would be the result of withdrawing workers from the Canal Zone and had told the British earlier in 1951 that they had no intention of creating this problem for themselves.[38] But the government had been overwhelmed by the mass demand to actively confront the British occupation. While the withdrawal of workers was popular, and workers were proud to have made a significant contribution to the nationalist struggle, the immediate effects of this measure served to exacerbate Egypt's economic crisis.

Some of the prominent noncommunist trade union leaders cooperated with a spurious campaign launched by the Egyptian government accusing the British of forcibly detaining workers in the Canal Zone and employing forced labor. 'Abd al-'Aziz Mustafa, Anwar Salama, and Mahmud 'Abd al-Majid Rajab, president of the Federation of Sugar Workers' Unions (a minor federation under company control since the Hawamdiyya strike) sent telegrams to the International Labor Organization and the British Trades Union Congress requesting that they support Egyptian workers and charging the British with using forced labor.[39] The International Labor Organization's investigation did not substantiate the Egyptian government's charges. Anwar Salama, now president of the Petroleum Workers' Federation, apparently attempted to play both sides of this conflict. While he signed the letter protesting British actions, he was also sent around in a Shell Company car asking Egyptian workers not to stop working for Shell.[40] M. T. Audsley spoke very highly of Salama during this period, and

36. FO 371/97072/JE2181/67 (1952); FO 371/97078/JE2188/3 (1952).
37. FO 371/90231/JE2182/31 (1951).
38. FO 371/90155/JE1053/1 (1951).
39. FO 371/90232/JE2182/42 (1951).
40. FO 371/97070/JE2181/28 (1952).

Crisis of the Old Regime **409**

the British seem to have accepted his claim that he was no longer affiliated with the Muslim Brothers.

Within a week of the abrogation of the treaties, the DMNL initiated the formation of the Preparatory Committee for a General Federation of Egyptian Trade Unions (PCGFETU—al-Lajna al-Tahdiriyya li'l-Ittihad al-'Amm li-Niqabat 'Ummal Misr). Ahmad Taha was chosen its general secretary and Muhammad 'Ali 'Amir, Hasan 'Abd al-Rahman, and 'Atiyya al-Sirafi occupied positions on its executive committee. The formation of the PCGFETU was made possible by the increased activity and influence of the DMNL in the trade union movement throughout 1950 and 1951, but because it appeared at this particularly intense moment in the nationalist struggle, it assumed the dual character of a trade union federation and an expression of working class nationalism. These two functions were not necessarily mutually exclusive, and undoubtedly contributed to the PCGFETU's rapid growth, though even within the ranks of the DMNL leadership there was confusion about its primary role. Ahmad Taha, representing the view that the PCGFETU's trade union function was primary, declared in an interview with *al-Malayin* that "The political struggle should be carried out by political parties and not the trade union movement."[41] The very next week an article in *al-Malayin* celebrating the formation of the PCGFETU and discussing its significance argued that the federation

> is considered the basic organizer of the Egyptian working class, and indeed the entire people in its role as the backbone of the organization of all the various sectors of the popular nationalist forces.[42]

By serving as the organizer of working class nationalist expression, the PCGFETU was able to attract trade union leaders who had never before been willing to unite with communists on any basis whatsoever. One of the most important of these figures was Fathi Kamil. He had always been considered a leader of the right wing in the trade union movement by the DMNL, and he was frequently denounced in the pages of *al-Jamahir* and *al-Bashir* for his flirtations with 'Abbas Halim and the British, and for adopting a conciliatory attitude in his relations with the management of the Eastern Tobacco Company. Since late 1946 Kamil had been president of the Congress of Trade Unionists (Mu'tamar al-Niqabiyyin), a loose grouping of trade union leaders many of whom had been affiliated with 'Abbas Halim in the

---

41. *al-Malayin,* October 14, 1951.
42. *Ibid.,* October 21, 1951.

410 Crisis of the Old Regime

past. Sayyid Qandil 'Abd al-'Aziz Mustafa, and Kamil 'Izz al-Din, were among the prominent figures and 'Abd al-Hamid 'Abd al-Haqq, vice-president of 'Abbas Halim's Labor party served as its counselor.[43] The organization maintained a friendly relationship with the prince and had its offices in the same building as the Labor party, but according to Fathi Kamil, 'Abbas Halim had no voice in its affairs. Scattered issues of an irregular publication of the Congress of Trade Unionists indicate that it espoused mildly social democratic ideas, loyalty to the monarchy, and a corporatist view of the functions of trade unions.[44]

During late 1950 or early 1951 Fathi Kamil made a decisive break with the British and with Ibrahim Zayn al-Din. The British now complained that Kamil was "flirting with known communists" and suggested he had supported Hasan 'Abd al-Rahman's organizing efforts among taxi drivers.[45] During this period some of the members of the Congress of Trade Unionists, notably Fathi Kamil and 'Abd al-'Aziz Mustafa, began cooperating with trade union activities led by the DMNL. Hasan 'Abd al-Rahman, 'Atiyya al-Sirafi, and possibly other DMNL members belonged to both organizations and helped radicalize some of its members.[46] Fathi Kamil's break with the British and his association with communists is a further indication of the extension of a class-based conception of solidarity to elements of the labor movement which had previously resisted this perspective as had been apparent in the campaign of support for the Hawamdiyya sugar workers' strike.

In the atmosphere of political crisis which deepened during 1951, organizational affiliations tended to become blurred as a vaguely de-

---

43. See FO 371/73466/J9007 (1949) for a report that dates the founding of this organization to 1949. According to Fathi Kamil, Ma'a al-haraka, pp. 71 ff., the Congress of Trade Unionists was established in 1946 after his return from England. At that time the organization consisted of Kamil, Sayyid Qandil, 'Abd al-'Aziz Mustafa, Mahmud Ibrahim al-'Ajami, president of the union of government Road Department workers, and presidents of one or two other unions (possibly Ibrahim Zayn al-Din and Kamil 'Izz al-Din). It is easy to understand why Fathi Kamil may have wanted to forget Ibrahim Zayn al-Din. In any case, the Congress of Trade Unionists had no public presence until 1950 when the group began publishing a newspaper. Soon afterwards it began cooperating with the DMNL in the PCGFETU. Kamil claims (p. 75) that he and the Congress of Trade Unionists intitiated and led the PCGFETU—an "alteration" of history that reflects the difficulty of crediting communists with anything positive in Egypt during the 1970s and 1980s.

44. Mu'tamar al-niqabiyyin, June 24, September 7, 23, October 20, 1950. Copies of this publication were kindly provided by Professor Ra'uf 'Abbas.

45. FO 371/90231/JE2182/11 (1951).

46. 'Abd al-Rahman, interview, December 7, 1980; 'Atiyya al-Sirafi, interview, December 29, 1980.

Crisis of the Old Regime **411**

fined "revolutionary current" emerged within the trade union movement. The broadening sense of class solidarity was the basis for this current which was generally identified with a willingness to undertake militant industrial action and support workers who did so. The "revolutionary current" also demanded immediate and unconditional British evacuation of Egypt and the Sudan and was prepared to take up arms to win this demand. In the midst of an intense nationalist struggle in late 1951 the militant nationalism of this revolutionary current may have been the more important component of its political identity. By initiating the PCGFETU, the DMNL was able to place itself at the head of this trend within the trade union movement and to unite a very substantial portion of the movement under its leadership. Fathi Kamil's willingness to join the PCGFETU and to serve on its executive committee is the clearest indication of this development. By December 1951, 104 unions with a membership of nearly 65,000 workers, representing approximately 50 percent of all union members and 20 percent of all existing unions, were affiliated with the PCGFETU.[47] This number continued to increase in late December and early January 1952.

In preparation for the formal establishment of a general trade union federation, efforts were made to strengthen individual trade unions, establish industry-wide federations, and expand the membership of the PCGFETU. The Founding Committee for a Union of Mechanized Textile and Preparatory Workers of Shubra al-Khayma and its Suburbs had been acting as a union executive committee throughout 1951. During this period the political police repeatedly prevented the convening of a general assembly to formally reconstitute the union. In late October the founding committee made one more attempt to hold a general assembly and achieve legal recognition for a union, but this too was thwarted by the police.[48] A Congress of Egyptian Textile Workers was established under the leadership of Muhammad 'Ali 'Amir, and it convened a national conference of textile workers in Cairo on January 5, 1952.[49] The Congress of Egyptian Joint Transport Drivers' and Workers' Unions also scheduled a national conference in Cairo on January 5, but it was prevented from meeting by the political police. Each week additional trade unions declared their affiliation with the PCGFETU. The culmination of all these organizational efforts was the announcement that a founding congress for a General

47. Laqueur, *Communism and Nationalism*, p. 53. These figures are based on an article by Hasan 'Abd al-Rahman which appeared in a Russian periodical.
48. *al-Malayin*, October 28, 1951; *al-Nas*, October 31, 1951.
49. *al-Malayin*, December 26, 1951.

412 Crisis of the Old Regime

Federation of Egyptian Trade Unions would be held in Cairo on January 27, 1952.

From the Cairo Fire to the Military Coup

The congress was never held. On January 25 British forces attacked an Egyptian police station in Isma'iliyya because they believed that the police and gendarmes had been aiding the guerrilla attacks against British installations in the Suez Canal Zone. Over fifty police and gendarmes were killed and some one-hundred wounded. In reaction to what was popularly perceived as a massacre and a violation of Egyptian sovereignty, the masses of Cairo exploded in anger. On the following day, January 26, in the course of tumultuous demonstrations and riots, fires broke out all over Cairo which destroyed large sections of the Europeanized central business district and many prominent symbols of British colonial rule. The riots and the fires unmistakably demonstrated the outrage and despair of the Cairene masses at the continuing British occupation of Egypt as well as the bankruptcy of the monarchy and the entire established order.

Although it is widely acknowledged that the fires were deliberately set, no fully satisfactory determination of responsibility is generally accepted, and the question remains a topic of fierce debate in Egypt today. Many believed that the Socialist party was responsible for the fire, and in fact, this was the conclusion of the British embassy's committee of enquiry which investigated the causes of the fire.[50] In May 1952 Ahmad Husayn, the leader of the Socialist party, and five others were indicted for inciting to riot, but the charges were dropped after the military coup. In the immediate aftermath of the fire, the government accused the communists of setting the fire and even tried to implicate the PCGFETU directly, though British diplomatic reports repeatedly quote high officials in the Ministry of the Interior, and the minister himself, saying that the police had "no evidence whatever" of direct communist responsibility for the fire and riots.[51] Ahmad Taha and many others argue that agents of the Palace and British intelligence set the fire to prevent the founding of a national trade union federation.[52] However, the tone of the British embassy committee's report on the fire leaves no doubt that the embassy officials who investigated the matter were surprised by the fire and alarmed that Brit-

50. FO 371/96873/JE1018/86 (1952), "Report of the British Embassy Committee of Enquiry into the Riots in Cairo on the 26th of January 1952, M. T. Audsley, Chairman."
51. FO 371/96875/JE1018/156 (1952); FO 141/1455/1016/3/52a (1952).
52. Ahmad Taha, interview in Jamal al-Sharqawi, *Hariq al-qahira* (Cairo, 1976), pp. 866–69.

Crisis of the Old Regime **413**

ish interests had been a major target of those setting the fires. If the British did have a hand in the fires, the embassy was not aware of it. The Palace, perhaps acting with Ahmad Husayn, remains a likely suspect. Although ultimate responsibility for the organized aspect of the fires remains undetermined, once the fires and rioting were underway, adherents of many political tendencies tried to assert their leadership over this spontaneous outburst of mass outrage.

The immediate result of the fire was to end the popular upsurge of the nationalist movement, as well as the activities of the PCGFETU. On the night of the fire martial law was proclaimed, and a large number of communists, among them many PCGFETU leaders, were arrested. The next day the Wafd government was dismissed. The new government of 'Ali Mahir put an end to the guerrilla movement in the Canal Zone. The fire also increased the number of urban unemployed, for the establishments destroyed in the fire employed, according to British estimates, from 15,000 to 30,000 clerks, shop assistants, bookkeepers, waiters, and accountants.[53]

The repressive measures abruptly halted the activities of the nationalist mass movement and put an end to virtually all popular political activity. Government repression was effective, just as it had been in 1946, despite the broad, deeply-felt popularity of the nationalist cause and its principal objectives of complete independence and full British evacuation. This apparent contradiction is explained not only by the harshness of the government's repressive measures, but also by the lack of organization and unity among the nationalist political forces, none of which commanded support broad enough or sufficiently well-organized to enable them to effectively challenge the regime on their own. The guerrilla fighting in the Canal Zone, for example, was not a coordinated campaign, but a series of separate efforts by a variety of political forces.

The DMNL understood the need for organization and unity, and this was the basis for its effort to build a broad national united front. However, the DMNL was itself based mainly among the urban intelligentsia and the urban working class. Although these new class forces were strategically located to play a major role in Egyptian political life, their ability to do so depended on their establishing firm links to the peasants and the traditional urban middle class. The sharp divisions between the active political forces in the nationalist movement—the Muslim Brothers, the Socialist party, the left wing of the Wafd, and the communists—prevented the establishment of such links. The central leadership of the Wafd, which still had a mass constituency,

53. FO 371/96957/JE1123/1 (1952).

414 Crisis of the Old Regime

was frightened by the guerrilla fighting and the chaotic political situation prevalent before the Cairo fire because the Wafd wanted independence but not an end to the old regime. The disunity of the more militant nationalist forces meant that the field of political action was left open to the one force in Egyptian society sufficiently well organized and united to undertake the task of ending the old regime—the army. Meanwhile, the Cairo fire extended the lifespan of the monarchy for an additional six months until the military coup of July 23, 1952 delivered the long-expected terminal blow to the old regime and signaled the end of the era of colonialism in Egypt.

In the aftermath of the Cairo fire the PCGFETU adopted a semiunderground mode of operation, and no public actions of a mass character were undertaken. Its general secretary, Ahmad Taha, and some other leaders who escaped arrest met on January 27 as scheduled, and changed the name of the body to the Founding Committee for a General Federation of Egyptian Trade Unions (FCGFETU—al-Lajna al-Ta'sisiyya li'l-Ittihad al-'Amm li-Niqabat 'Ummal Misr).[54] The legal status of the FCGFETU during the last months of the old regime was ambiguous. Leading communist trade unionists continued to be arrested during the last months of the old regime, and some remained in jail even after the military coup when all political prisoners but seventeen communists were released.

In this confused period there were several attempts to replace the PCGFETU/FCGFETU as the central leading body of the workers' movement. On February 12 an American-sponsored Committee on Egyptian Labor Affairs met in the headquarters of the Socony-Vacuum Employees Union at the invitation of the union's president, Mahmud 'Abd al-Khaliq.[55] Among those attending were the labor attaché of the American embassy, P. Lunt, the director general of the Labor Department of the Ministry of Social Affairs, Fathi Kamil, Anwar Salama, 'Abd al-'Aziz Mustafa, and Mahmud 'Abd al-Majid Rajab. The meeting was an attempt by the Egyptian government, in cooperation with the American embassy, to split the noncommunist trade union leaders in the FCGFETU from their coalition with the DMNL by creating an alternative center of trade union leadership. The reactivation of the Supreme Labor Advisory Council, which had not met for two years, was a further effort by the government to coopt and control the movement for a national trade union federation. Fathi Kamil and 'Abd al-'Aziz Mustafa, two of the most prominent non-DMNL members on the executive committee of the FCGFETU, were appointed to this body to-

54. Taha, interview in al-Sharqawi, *Hariq*, p. 868.
55. FO 371/97078/JE2188/4 (1952); Sa'id, *1950–1957*, p. 68.

Crisis of the Old Regime **415**

gether with four other more conservative trade union officials and six representatives of management.[56]

There seem to have been some tactical differences between the communist and noncommunist trade union leaders about how to ensure the survival of the FCGFETU under martial law. Fathi Kamil and 'Abd al-'Aziz Mustafa announced the actual formation of a general federation of trade unions without receiving legal authorization from the government, and Mustafa was named president of the temporary executive committee.[57] Perhaps the noncommunists thought that the government would allow the federation to function if communists were eliminated from leading positions, but this was not the case. The government was unable to exploit any tactical differences that might have existed among the trade union leaders to gain any real advantage because it was unwilling to concede the basic demand for a national trade union federation. When the Supreme Labor Advisory Council convened its first meeting after its reorganization, Fathi Kamil requested that it authorize the formation of a general federation of trade unions, but Radi Abu Sayf Radi, the minister of social affairs, refused to consider the request, arguing that it was not on the agenda.[58] Thus the government lost what appears to have been an opportunity to isolate the communists from other trade union leaders.

The participation of the American labor attaché in the February 12 meeting was one of many indications that the American embassy, which was well aware of the extent of the crisis of the Egyptian regime, was taking an increasingly active interest in social affairs. During 1951 the assistant secretary of state for Middle Eastern affairs, the secretary of labor, and the American ambassador, Jefferson Caffery, had all undertaken tours of Egypt during which visits to the textile mills at Mahalla al-Kubra and other industrial establishments had been prominent. In the same year Ibrahim Zayn al-Din undertook a five-month visit to the United States on a "town hall" mission. After his return he seems to have abandoned his former British sponsors and adopted a pro-American perspective.[59]

Zayn al-Din's transfer of allegiance did not relieve his isolation within the trade union movement, but it was a clear indication of the shift in imperial power underway in Egypt as in many other British imperial outposts. One consequence of the decline of British power

56. *al-Ahram*, February 24, 1952. Anwar Salama, who never joined the FCGFETU, was another of the trade union leaders appointed.
57. *Ibid.*, February 13, 1952. The formation of a general federation of trade unions was still illegal under the terms of Law 85 of 1942.
58. *Ibid.*, April 10, 1952.
59. FO 371/90231/JE2182/11 (1951); FO 371/97078/JE2188/3 (1952).

416 Crisis of the Old Regime

in Egypt was a deterioration in the quality of British information. During the mass movement for abrogation, it became unacceptable among trade unionists to maintain contacts with the British embassy. After the abrogation of the Anglo-Egyptian treaty in October 1951, M. T. Audsley complained that he had lost all direct contact with Egyptian trade unionists.[60] By 1952 British reports were frequently based on information provided or confirmed by the American embassy.

The only continuation of the high level of mass activity that had characterized the trade union movement before the Cairo fire was the convening of a conference of representatives of 20,000 workers employed by twenty-five provincial bus companies on July 13, 1952 to demand that they be granted the same conditions and wages accorded to the Cairo and Alexandria transport workers. The central issue in the provincial transport industry was the inability of workers to preserve rights and conditions won from former employers as smaller companies were gradually bought out by larger ones who disregarded existing labor agreements or traditionally established practices. The conference also demanded that Cairo transport workers be given their share of the one-millieme fare increase that had been in effect in 1944–1945 and that Cairo tramway workers be granted the same cadre that governed Cairo and Alexandria bus workers. These demands broadened the base of the conference and won it support from Cairo and Alexandria unions, which endorsed the call for a transport general strike on July 27 if these demands were not met.[61] The military coup took place before the strike deadline, and therefore the strike threat was not implemented.

Two themes of special importance in the postcoup period emerge from an examination of trade union activities during the last months of the old regime. The first is the attitude of noncommunist trade union leaders towards the government. Despite the progress made towards the building of a trade union movement independent of nonworker patrons and political parties, some of the most prominent noncommunist supporters of these concepts, such as Fathi Kamil and 'Abd al-'Aziz Mustafa, still looked to the government as the ultimate source of adjudication in labor disputes. They were willing to cooperate with a government that had imposed martial law, abandoned the guerrilla struggle against the British in the Canal Zone, and imprisoned the leadership of the labor movement. The second theme is the importance of transport workers in the trade union movement.

60. FO 371/97979/JE2188/6 (1952).
61. *al-Misri*, July 14, 17, 1952.

Crisis of the Old Regime **417**

Because the Cairo and Alexandria tramway and metro companies were owned by major foreign monopolies, the government was often willing to support the demands of their workers, as it had supported the demands of the Shell and Suez Canal Company workers, as a way of appealing to nationalist sentiment. In contrast, textile workers were increasingly less able to appeal to nationalist sentiment as more of the mills came to be owned by Egyptians. The government's willingness to support their demands gave the transport workers power and influence within the trade union movement, and reinforced the idea that the government, rather than class struggle, was the best arbiter of labor disputes. These themes were rarely explicit in the discussions of labor activists, for the intertwining of the labor and national movements made it almost impossible to articulate such issues. Still, they would become critical in determining the character of the relations between the labor movement and the government after the military coup.

Chapter XIII

The Free Officers and the Labor Movement

The Revolutionary Command Council (RCC—Majlis Qiyadat al-Thawra) which took power on July 23, 1952 did not have a well-developed plan for managing the government after the military coup. It also lacked a clearly articulated ideological platform other than militant Egyptian nationalism with only the vaguest "antifeudal" social content. The young junior officers who constituted the Free Officers' Organization and their real leader, Jamal 'Abd al-Nasir, presented General Muhammad Najib as leader of "the revolution," though he had had no part in the actual planning or execution of the military coup. Najib was well liked and respected by the public as one of the few commanders who had performed credibly during the Palestine war, and his senior rank gave the regime stature and authority.

Soon after taking power the RCC announced a six-point program advocating: (1) the purification of political life; (2) the establishment of democracy; (3) the promotion of social justice; (4) the abolition of the remnants of feudalism; (5) the creation of a strong national army; and (6) the assertion of full Egyptian independence and sovereignty. On the basis of this program, which addressed, albeit vaguely, the central issues of postwar Egyptian society, the RCC received enthusiastic support from nearly all quarters, a consequence of the widespread belief that the leadership of the agrarian bourgeoisie no longer offered any hope for resolving the pressing questions of national independence and social justice. The Wafd had proved itself ultimately unable to resist domination by the large landowners, while all the other legal political parties had always been under their control. The existing parliamentary system therefore offered no solution to the crisis of the old regime, whereas the army movement had distinguished itself by

Free Officers and Labor **419**

bringing a decisive end to the unpopular monarchy. Perhaps it could deal as decisively with the other issues facing Egypt.

The broad spectrum of political views represented among the leadership of the Free Officers made it possible for both the DMNL and the Muslim Brothers to claim the movement as "their own." Both organizations were seriously mistaken in their judgment, though the Brothers had somewhat more justification for their claim. The RCC included members and supporters of the DMNL and the Muslim Brothers: Yusuf Siddiq was a member of the DMNL and Khalid Muhyi al-Din, who had briefly been a DMNL member in 1947, remained a sympathizer; Ahmad Hamrush, though never a member of the RCC, was a prominent Free Officer who was also a DMNL member; Ahmad Fu'ad was a military judge and a member of the DMNL, and served as liaison between it and 'Abd al-Nasir, who was known as "comrade Maurice" to the DMNL leadership. The Free Officers' leaflets had been printed on the DMNL printing press since the Cairo fire, and the DMNL knew of the coup the night before it occurred and distributed leaflets supporting it the next morning.[1] 'Abd al-Mun'im 'Abd al-Ra'uf was the leading proponent of the Muslim Brothers within the ranks of the Free Officers, and RCC members Kamal al-Din Husayn and Husayn al-Shafi'i were also members of the Society. RCC member Anwar al-Sadat was a sympathizer of the Muslim Brothers and had acted as a liaison between discontented army officers and the Brothers in 1940–1942. The Brothers had also received advance notice of the coup and actively organized mass support during the first few days of the new regime.[2] Jamal 'Abd al-Nasir was in touch with both the DMNL and the Muslim Brothers as well as other civilian-based political forces, but his ultimate commitment was only to his own Free Officers' Organization, which he refused to commit to a permanent alliance with any civilian-dominated political forces.

Workers, like most other sectors of society, were quick to express confidence in the new regime on the basis of its nationalist appeal, its

---

1. Ahmad Hamrush, *Qissat thawrat 23 yulyu*. 5 vols. (Cairo, Beirut, 1977–1981), 1:287–88. Hamrush tends to overstate the influence of the left in the RCC, as in his contention that Khalid Muhyi al-Din was still a DMNL member in 1952 which Muhyi al-Din himself denied in his interview with Hamrush in volume four, p. 145. Hamrush's account of DMNL-RCC relations has been modified on the basis of an interview with Mohamed Sid-Ahmed on July 25, 1985. Despite this flaw, this combination memoir-history is one of the most valuable sources of information on post-1952 Egypt, especially the interviews with a wide range of political personalities contained in volume four (subtitled *Shuhud yulyu*) which have been extensively used in this chapter.
2. Mitchell, *The Society*, pp. 96–98 ff.

420 Free Officers and Labor

attacks on the privileges and corruption of the old regime, and perhaps above all, its promise to establish social justice. As an act of confidence in the new regime the transport workers called off their threatened general strike.[3] On July 31, 1952, the FCGFETU met and issued a statement supporting the army movement as an expression of the people's hopes and as a means to realize social justice.[4] The signatures on this statement indicate that the coalition between the DMNL and important noncommunist trade unionists was still in effect and had even been broadened to include several figures not previously identified with the FCGFETU.

The FCGFETU statement also indicated the trade unionists' apprehensions about military rule when it urged the army to defend the constitution, restore parliamentary life as soon as possible, repeal martial law and all repressive legislation, and abolish the political police. Thus the FCGFETU (and the DMNL) expressed general support for the military while also demanding the rapid restoration and extension of democratic liberties. These two positions soon became impossible to reconcile however. The one political principle to which the Free Officers quickly became committed was the impermissibility of any organized political challenge to the regime. This implied an effort to destroy or co-opt the anticorporatist and antipaternalist trend within the workers' movement, which had been developing since the late 1930s, and was a potential social and organizational base of opposition to the regime. The elimination of communists from positions of leadership in the trade union movement was an essential component of this effort. Thus a clash between the RCC and the DMNL was almost inevitable despite the DMNL's original enthusiastic support of the Free Officers.[5]

3. *al-Misri*, August 8, 1952.
4. *al-Ahram*, August 2, 1952.
5. The DMNL was the only communist organization to support the military regime. The Communist Party of Egypt denounced the new regime as a pro-American fascist dictatorship and remained underground and in complete opposition until after the conclusion of the arms purchase agreement with Czechoslovakia in September 1955. It had little influence in the trade union movement and no role in the PCGFETU/FCGFETU because it advocated only secret trade union work. Workers' Vanguard (formerly New Dawn) was at first guardedly critical of the military regime and then became antagonistic after the events of Kafr al-Dawwar. It also did not participate in the PCGFETU/FCGFETU because it opposed the establishment of a national trade union federation before completing the consolidation of progressive leadership in individual unions. None of the DMNL's splinter groups shared its positive evaluation of the regime, but with a few minor exceptions, they had no influence among workers.

Free Officers and Labor   **421**

Kafr al-Dawwar: A Turning Point

Less than a month after the Free Officers came to power their relations with the trade union movement were seriously strained by the regime's response to a violent strike and demonstration at Kafr al-Dawwar, a textile center fifteen miles south of Alexandria.[6] The Misr mills at Kafr al-Dawwar were closely associated with the monarchy, for Hafiz 'Afifi, a former head of the royal cabinet, was director of the Misr Company's textile operations, and Elias Andraos, a favorite of the former king, was manager of the Misr Bayda Dyers company. Andraos was closely linked to local officials in Kafr al-Dawwar, and was allegedly paying salaries to the local ma'mur and police commander.[7] At the largest of Misr's three mills, Misr Fine Spinning and Weaving, which employed over 9,000 workers, a company-dominated union had been in existence since 1943.[8] The general conditions of employment, the company's paternalism, and its disciplinary and social welfare policies were similar to those at Mahalla al-Kubra. Since 1948 a group of workers, including partisans of all the political currents in the workers' movement, had periodically attempted to win seats on the union executive board and turn out the procompany elements. Muhammad Mutawalli al-Sha'rawi and Ahmad al-Yabani, who were close to the DMNL, were among the leaders of the union reform movement. But the DMNL presence at Kafr al-Dawwar was not very strong. Despite the nationwide growth of militance and independent organization in the trade union movement in 1951, the union reform movement at Misr Fine Spinning and Weaving was so weak that it did not contest the union elections that year.

At the Bayda Dyers Company (a joint enterprise of Misr and the British Bradford Dyers Association, as was Misr Fine Spinning and Weaving) the 3,000 workers were not represented by any union. On August 9 the Bayda workers struck, declared their support for Muhammad Najib and the new regime, and demanded representation by a union and the removal of five managers associated with Elias Andraos, who had already been removed following Faruq's abdication. Economic demands for an increased annual bonus and reinstatement of some dismissed workers are mentioned in British accounts of the

6. This account of the events in Kafr al-Dawwar, unless otherwise noted, relies on the reports of al-Misri, August 14–19 and September 7–8, 1952, which include extensive excerpts from the trial testimony, and interviews with Muhammad Mutawalli al-Sha'rawi on January 7 and April 3, 1981.

7. FO 371/96880/JE1018/317 (1952); FO 371/96880/JE1018/319 (1952).

8. Harbison and Ibrahim, "Some Labor Problems," p. 120 confirms the procompany character of the union.

422 Free Officers and Labor

strike, but they did not seem to be a major issue.[9] Clearly the Bayda workers saw the fall of the monarchy as a good opportunity to remove disliked supervisors associated with a friend of the former king and to win union recognition. The workers' demands were met quickly, and the strike did not last long. On August 11, four workers at the third Misr establishment in Kafr al-Dawwar, the Misr Rayon Company, which also did not have a union, were arrested for inciting to strike, probably in order to demand union recognition.

These worker actions at the two nonunionized mills in Kafr al-Dawwar undoubtedly made the authorities in the area anxious about the possible direction that continued strikes and other workers' collective actions might take. They also encouraged the union reform forces at Misr Fine Spinning and Weaving to renew their activity. The leadership of the group, which still included representatives of the entire spectrum of political tendencies, met and formulated a program of demands to be sent to Muhammad Najib and other government officials. The possibility of an immediate strike was discussed, but the group decided to wait the legally required fifteen days after the submission of demands for the government to respond before considering a strike.

On the night of August 12, some 500 workers at Misr Fine Spinning and Weaving began a sit-down strike and locked themselves inside the mill. Shortly thereafter fires were set to some of the auxiliary buildings inside the complex. The strike was not organized by the union reform group, which was still awaiting the expiration of the fifteen-day period before deciding on any strike action. Both Muhammad Mutawalli al-Sha'rawi and Ahmad al-Yabani were meeting with a company official on their own time when the sitdown and the fire began. At 3:00 a.m. on August 13, troops arrived from Alexandria, and were met by two demonstrations, one outside the walls of the mill on the road to Alexandria, the other inside the walls near the workers' housing. The demonstrators shouted their support for the revolution and for Najib, and raised demands for: (1) the removal of several company officials considered particularly abusive and repressive; (2) a freely elected union; (3) moving the union office out of company owned premises; (4) equal bonuses for clerical and blue-collar workers; (5) wage increases; and (6) amnesty for the strikers. Shots of disputed origins were fired in the vicinity of the demonstration outside the walls of the mill. The army returned the fire, and in the exchange two soldiers, one policeman, and four workers were killed and many others wounded.

9. FO 371/96882/JE1018/393 (1952).

Free Officers and Labor **423**

The military authorities moved quickly to contain the unrest at Kafr al-Dawwar and arrested 545 workers, charging twenty-nine with various offenses including premeditated murder, arson, destruction of property, theft of police weapons, and resistance to officers performing their duty. A military tribunal was convened and held its first session on the evening of August 15. The three principal defendants were Mustafa Khamis amd Muhammad al-Baqari, who were rumored to be members of an illegal communist organization, and Muhammad Shihab, a Muslim Brother. The trial began so quickly that Khamis, who was tried first, did not have time to engage a lawyer. The court refused to allow Khamis to defend himself and appointed Musa Sabri, a journalist covering the trial for the notoriously right-wing daily al-Akhbar and who happened to have a law degree, as Khamis' attorney. By August 16 Khamis was found guilty, and on August 18 he was sentenced to death by hanging. Shortly thereafter al-Baqari was also convicted and sentenced to death. Muhammad Shihab received a sentence of thirteen years at hard labor, but this was reduced to nine years by General Najib. Ten other workers received jail sentences. On September 7 Khamis and al-Baqari were executed. Khamis' final words were, "I am wronged. I want a retrial."

Considerations of space and the lack of definitive historical sources make it impossible to construct a comprehensive defense brief for the workers.[10] However, there is more than enough evidence to justify a reasonable doubt about the guilt of Khamis, al-Baqari, and the other principal defendants in the case. This evidence points to the conclusion that the decision to execute Khamis and al-Baqari was taken because of fear of the political effects of the strike rather than their personal responsibility for acts of arson or other violence. Significant exculpatory evidence was presented to the military tribunal but was ignored. Musa Sabri's summation statement in defense of Khamis pointed out that: (1) Khamis was a participant in the demonstration inside the walls of the mill, whereas the shots were fired in the other demonstration; (2) according to most witnesses Khamis was arrested before the shots were fired; and (3) according to all but one of the witnesses the demonstrators were shouting "Long live Muhammad Najib," indicating there was no intention to oppose the new regime.[11]

Twenty-nine years later Musa Sabri insisted in an interview that

10. During 1979–1981, when research for this book was carried out in Egypt, a young Egyptian lawyer, who must remain unnamed, was preparing a comprehensive brief arguing the defendants' innocence. We have lost contact with him, and his work has apparently not been published.

11. Parts of Sabri's plea are contained in a bowdlerized transcript of the trial published to justify the regime's actions, *Muhakamat kafr al-dawwar* (Cairo, n.d.), pp. 51–55.

424 Free Officers and Labor

the court's primary consideration in determining the guilt of Khamis and al-Baqari had been their alleged membership in illegal communist organizations.[12] No evidence was presented at the trial proving that they were members of such organizations, nor was any evidence presented that communist organizations were responsible for the riots. According to Ahmad Sadiq Sa'd, Khamis had been a member of Workers' Vanguard some time before the military coup, but had lost contact with the organization before the strike.[13] British sources describe Khamis as head of the local Wafd Committee, though there was no evidence that the Wafd had been involved in the riots.[14] Muhammad Mutawalli al-Sha'rawi asserted that neither Khamis nor al-Baqari were members of the DMNL. Al-Sha'rawi regarded Khamis as a "class conscious worker" while al-Baqari had no well-developed political views and was arrested and drawn into the case because he assaulted a company security official with whom he had a long-standing personal dispute.[15]

The court did not consider the suspicious circumstances that implicated others in the responsibility for the events. Hafiz 'Afifi, the chairman of the Misr Company board of directors, had visited Kafr al-Dawwar on the day of the strike and fire. His son, Amin Hafiz 'Afifi, who was employed by the Fine Spinning and Weaving Company, the commander of the local police, and the ma'mur were all arrested at the time of the violence, but released without being charged. The DMNL accused them of responsibility for setting the fires and pointedly asked why the police did not intervene when the incident began on the night of August 12, but waited until the army arrived early the next morning before acting. The DMNL suggested that Amin Hafiz 'Afifi and the local police commander had been acting on behalf of those who wished to see a clash between the workers and the army in order to strengthen the hand of the civilian prime minister, 'Ali Mahir, and weaken popular support for the military.[16] This was also the original assessment of the director of military intelligence, who saw

12. Musa Sabri, interview, April 11, 1981.
13. Ahmad Sadiq Sa'd, interview in 'Abd al-'Azim Ramadan, *'Abd al-Nasir wa-azmat maris* (Cairo, 1976), p. 299.
14. FO 371/96882/JE1018/393 (1952). This could be consistent with Sadiq Sa'd's claim that Khamis had been a member of Workers' Vanguard because of the close ties between the left wing of the Wafd and that organization.
15. al-Sha'rawi, interview, January 7, 1981.
16. *Bulletin d'études et d'information sur l'Égypte et le Soudan*, no. 17 (August 1952). This was an official DMNL publication issued in Paris under the direction of Henri Curiel. Articles from this and other issues are reprinted in the "Annexes" to Marie-Dominique Gresh, "Le P.C.F. et l'Égypte, 1950–1956" (Mémoire de maîtrise, Université de Paris, I, 1976–77).

the Wafd, rather than adherents of the former king, as the most likely instigators of the riot.[17] However, the American embassy's labor attaché, who visited Kafr al-Dawwar immediately after the riot, reported that there was no information indicating either communist or Wafdist responsibility for the events.[18]

The composition of the military tribunal that tried the case and its extraordinary zeal for bringing the proceedings to a rapid conclusion leave room to doubt the purity of the motives of the judges. 'Abd al-Mun'im Amin, who volunteered to serve as presiding judge, was one of the most pro-American of all the Free Officers and in close contact with the American ambassador in Cairo, Jefferson Caffery. After the trial Amin assumed responsibility for labor affairs in the Ministry of Social Affairs. In this capacity he presented proposals to the RCC urging that strikes be outlawed and employers be given full freedom to dismiss workers. These measures were necessary, Amin argued, in order to attract foreign capital to invest in Egyptian industry. When they were presented to the RCC, Amin's proposals were partially blocked only by Khalid Muhyi al-Din's threat to resign if they were implemented.[19]

Despite some members' doubts about the guilt of Khamis and al-Baqari, the RCC certified the military tribunal's death sentence and thereby indicated that the regime would resolutely oppose any expression of autonomous working class organization and collective action. Clearly, the majority of the RCC perceived the events at Kafr al-Dawwar as a communist-inspired political challenge to the military. Khalid Muhyi al-Din believed this was a political decision not motivated by the facts of the case,[20] and Muhammad Najib mentioned "reports that informed us of the dangers of workers' movements" as one of the principal motives for his vote to sustain the tribunal's sen-

17. FO 371/96880/JE1018/317 (1952)

18. FO 371/97079/JE2188/6 (1952). This is Audsley's most complete report on Kafr al-Dawwar. He did not visit Kafr al-Dawwar, but drew his information from interviews with government officials in Cairo. Although his conclusions were the same as those of the American labor attaché, his American colleague's on-the-spot assessment indicates a much more aggressive American presence, and is a further indication of the decline of British influence.

19. Khalid Muhyi al-Din, interview in Hamrush, Qissat, 4:151; 'Abd al-Mun'im Amin, interview in Hamrush, Qissat, 4:252. A facsimile of Muhyi al-Din's letter of resignation and an article explaining its circumstances were published in al-Ahali, July 24, 1985.

20. Muhyi al-Din, interview, May 19, 1981. Most reports concur that Muhyi al-Din, Yusuf Siddiq, and 'Abd al-Nasir were the only members of the RCC who voted against sustaining the death sentence. Under these circumstances Muhyi al-Din's assessment of the political character of this decision might ordinarily be suspect. However, it is supported by Musa Sabri's judgement cited previously, which is based on an opposing political perspective.

426 Free Officers and Labor

tence.[21] Najib was obviously not entirely convinced by the evidence in the case, because after the RCC had already voted to certify Khamis' sentence he agreed to interview him to determine if there were grounds for clemency. In the interview Najib pressed Khamis to confess that he was a member of a communist organization and to reveal the names of those who had encouraged him to undertake his actions, but Khamis admitted nothing. Najib therefore agreed to the execution because of "the possibility of the spread of these strikes and Mustafa Khamis' refusal to declare anything that would justify reducing his sentence."[22]

The widespread, though unproven, assumption that communists were responsible for inciting the workers of Kafr al-Dawwar to rebellion against the new regime strengthened the hand of the already considerable anticommunist elements among the Free Officers. After Kafr al-Dawwar, the RCC began to take measures to isolate the communists in its own ranks and remove them from all positions of power. In late September, Ahmad Hamrush, who had been appointed editor of a new proregime magazine, al-Tahrir (Liberation), was removed from his position and arrested. A number of other DMNL members and sympathizers on the staff were also removed. On October 16 a decree granting amnesty to those accused of political offenses from the date of the signing of the Anglo-Egyptian treaty on August 26, 1936 to July 23, 1952 deliberately excluded communists.[23]

The Muslim Brothers, who were still on very friendly terms with the new regime, participated in the anticommunist campaign promoted by the preponderant forces in the RCC. For al-Da'wa the events of Kafr al-Dawwar illustrated the increased potential for spreading communist propaganda created by the revolution. In a remarkably violent article on its workers' page, al-Da'wa called on workers to take vigilante action to eliminate communist propaganda from their midst: "We must strike these communists who want to use this opportunity with an iron hand so that they are driven to their dens."[24] It should be recalled that the third defendant in the Kafr al-Dawwar trial was himself a Muslim Brother and that Brothers had cooperated with DMNL members in the union reform movement—a glaring inconsistency that further indicates the Brothers' contradictory views on concrete questions of trade union tactics, and particularly, on the permissibility of joint action with communists.

21. Muhammad Najib, interview in Hamrush, Qissat, 4:431.
22. Ibid.
23. Hamrush, Qissat, 1:291–92.
24. al-Da'wa, August 15, 1952.

Free Officers and Labor **427**

Trade Unions and the Military Regime after Kafr al-Dawwar

The RCC's reaction to the events of Kafr al-Dawwar was the result of the anticommunism and the fear of working class collective action that gripped the majority of its members. Although the DMNL and the FCGFETU were aware of these sentiments, they continued to support the RCC hoping to alter the balance of forces within the regime. With the encouragement of the DMNL, the FCGFETU issued a statement denouncing the violence at Kafr al-Dawwar as motivated by pro-imperialist interests.[25] On August 18, after Khamis' sentence was announced, the FCGFETU held a meeting in Alexandria attended by representatives of ninety-five unions.[26] It was still possible for the FCGFETU to meet in Alexandria because Ahmad Hamrush was stationed there, and the military commander of the city was a DMNL sympathizer. Following this meeting members of the FCGFETU and the DMNL-led Preparatory Committee for an Egyptian Student Federation mounted loudspeakers on vehicles provided by the army and circulated in working class neighborhoods in Alexandria and Kafr al-Dawwar urging workers to remain calm and not to riot in response to Khamis' sentence. The future labor historian, 'Abd al-Mun'im al-Ghazzali, was among the DMNL cadres who organized this activity.[27] He later explained that the DMNL's position in regard to Kafr al-Dawwar was that the workers' demands were legitimate and just, but that the use of the strike weapon at this time would only benefit reactionaries.[28] According to DMNL leader Zaki Murad, the execution of Khamis and al-Baqari strained the relations between the DMNL and the RCC, though the DMNL continued to support the regime because it felt that announcing its opposition would have aided 'Abd al-Mun'im Amin and those who wished to see a schism between the regime and the working class.[29]

The DMNL's reluctance to openly denounce the regime after the executions of Khamis and al-Baqari contributed to disaffection and, eventually, splits within the organization which would reduce its influence in the working class. Two members of the DMNL's Central Trade Union Bureau, Muhammad 'Ali 'Amir and Muhammad 'Abduh Nuh, publicly protested the executions and were jailed as a result.[30] Nonetheless they remained loyal to the DMNL. But another

25. *al-Ahram*, August 15, 1952. For the role of the DMNL, see Rif'at al-Sa'id, *Munazzamat al-yasar al-Misri, 1950–1957* (Cairo, 1983), p. 65.
26. *al-Misri*, August 19, 1952.
27. *Ibid.*
28. 'Abd al-Mun'im al-Ghazzali, interview in Ramadan, *'Abd al-Nasir*, p. 347.
29. Zaki Murad, interview in Ramadan, *'Abd al-Nasir*, p. 337.
30. al-Said, *1950–1957*, p. 117.

428 Free Officers and Labor

member of the bureau, Sayyid Khalil Turk, became one of the leaders of the splinter DMNL Revolutionary Trend, which was established in June 1953 on the basis of rejecting the DMNL's original favorable analysis of the military regime.[31] The DMNL did not openly repudiate and criticize its position on the Kafr al-Dawwar incident until September 1953.[32] By then the organization was underground and seriously weakened.

The FCGFETU's continued expressions of support for the regime made it possible for it to take over the weekly newspaper *al-Wajib* on September 10, 1952. Under the editorial direction of Ahmad Taha, *al-Wajib* attempted to advance the FCGFETU's organizing activity and the preparations for the official establishment of a national trade union federation. Representatives of two hundred trade unions had planned earlier in the summer to hold a congress to establish such a federation on September 14 and 15, but two days before the meeting was to have convened, the Ministry of Social Affairs, fearful that the left would be prominent in the event, announced, without previously consulting the trade unions, that the meeting was postponed. Instead, the unions were instructed to purge their ranks after which the ministry promised to reschedule the congress in three months.[33] The congress was not held until January 1957.

At the end of October *al-Wajib* reported that the Ministry of the Interior had banned meetings of the FCGFETU and was undertaking a campaign to have communists expelled from trade union leadership positions.[34] During this period communists were ousted from positions of influence among the Cairo transport workers. Hasan 'Abd al-Rahman's United Taxi Drivers' Union, for example, was infiltrated by the police, and opponents of the new executive board (and 'Abd al-Rahman himself) were dismissed from their jobs. Moreover, the executive board refused to call new elections despite appeals from over 300 union members.[35] The DMNL also appears to have lost influence in the Cairo Tramway Workers' Union and began to issue leaflets criticizing the union's leadership. It is possible that understanding the balance of political forces, 'Abd al-'Aziz Mustafa became reluctant to

31. *Ibid.*, pp. 112, 137. Al-Sa'id appears to suspect Turk's integrity on the basis of his rapid rise to prominence and departure from the DMNL, but no conclusive evidence that he was a police agent is offered.

32. *Ibid.*, pp. 113, 117, 415.

33. FO 371/97078/JE2188/7 (1952); *al-Ahram*, September 17, 1952.

34. *al-Wajib*, October 29, 1952.

35. *al-Mu'arada*, October 16, 1952.

Free Officers and Labor **429**

continue cooperating with the DMNL.[36] The Cairo Printers' Union, too, was infiltrated by the political police.[37] Muhammad 'Abduh Nuh and Muhammad 'Ali 'Amir remained in jail because of their protest against the executions of Khamis and al-Baqari, and other leading textile workers were also arrested.[38] Fathi Kamil was forced out of his position as president of the Eastern Tobacco Company union when Muslim Brothers won a majority of the seats on the executive board and installed one of their own as president.[39]

The regime continued to make clear its absolute opposition to strikes by workers regardless of their motivation. Twenty-five workers charged with inciting to strike at the Filature Nationale and Sibahi textile mills were tried by a military tribunal in Alexandria.[40] A Cairo military court sentenced two workers to six months in jail for leading a work stoppage at the Marconi Wireless Company on December 4, 1952.[41] This strike had been motivated by the company's delay in paying a semi-annual bonus and lasted only four hours. Earlier the Marconi workers had actively supported the nationalist upsurge of late 1951 by refusing to relay telegrams to the British forces on the Suez Canal. Now, the workers argued that Marconi was an imperialist company because it was foreign-owned, and therefore exempt from the laws prohibiting strikes against public utilities. The court rejected the workers' nationalist defense and did not take into account the previous patriotic activity of the Marconi workers in assessing their guilt. The court's unwillingness to show leniency may have been influenced by the fact that Ahmad Taha was the head of the Marconi union, although he had long since been dismissed by the company.

When the FCGFETU was banned its place was immediately taken by the Trade Union Committee for the Defense of Liberties (TUCDL—al-Lajna al-Niqabiyya li'l-Difa' 'an al-Hurriyyat), which continued to press the RCC to adopt a more friendly and supportive attitude towards the trade union movement. The TUCDL proposed a "trade union covenant" that included both national, political, and trade union demands. The covenant called for: (1) the complete evacuation of British troops from Egypt and the Sudan; (2) prompt elections for a new parliament; (3) the abolition of martial law; (4) self-determina-

36. This conclusion is based on several DMNL leaflets made available by Dr. Rif'at al-Sa'id and Professor Ra'uf 'Abbas.
37. al-Wajib, October 29, 1952; al-Mu'arada, October 30, 1952.
38. al-Wajib, November 12, December 18, 1952.
39. al-Da'wa, November 25, 1952.
40. al-Misri, September 25, 1952.
41. al-Akhbar, February 5, 6, 12, 1953.

430 Free Officers and Labor

tion for the Sudan after British evacuation; (5) limiting the access of foreign capital to Egypt in order to protect Egyptian industry; (6) a minimum wage law; (7) comprehensive unemployment, accident, health and retirement insurance; (8) the cancellation of the ban on the FCGFETU and permission to convene a trade union congress; (9) revision of all labor laws in consultation with trade union leaders; and (10) the extension of democratic rights and especially the abolition of all limitations on the right to strike.[42]

This covenant was intended to demonstrate the contention of the TUCDL (and the DMNL) that there was no antagonism between the general demands of the Egyptian nationalist movement and the particular demands of the working class. It also indicated the TUCDL's belief that it was still possible for the regime to evolve in a progressive, democratic, and prolabor direction. Soon after the covenant was formulated it became apparent that the RCC intended to adopt decidedly undemocratic policies, assert state control over all trade union activity, and supervise the labor movement closely. During the last month of its publication *al-Wajib* appealed desperately to the Free Officers to permit freedom of trade union organization and activity. In a heavily censored call "From the Working Class to the Free Officers and Soldiers," Ahmad Taha recalled and reaffirmed the FCGFETU's support of the Free Officers' program and the working class' solidarity with the army on July 23. He strongly implied in a vaguely worded passage that the workers of Kafr al-Dawwar had been incited by imperialist agents, but offered no specific criticism of 'Abd al-Mun'im Amin (who was still a member of the RCC) or the executions of Khamis and al-Baqari.[43] These omissions, which are especially striking in light of the fact that this is the only reference to Kafr al-Dawwar in *al-Wajib* during the entire time it was published under FCGFETU/TUCDL auspices, show how far the TUCDL and the DMNL were willing to bend in order to find a basis for conciliation and cooperation with the RCC, even as their own freedom of political expression was becoming sharply restricted.

Despite the fact that the Free Officers permitted the publication of *al-Wajib* during the last four months of 1952 and the first half of January 1953, it is evident that the DMNL and its supporters and allies in the trade unions were engaged in a rearguard action throughout this period. The DMNL kept relying on its friends among the Free Officers to effect a change in the regime's labor policy. Hoping that through internal maneuverings among the Free Officers they could isolate

42. *al-Misri*, November 16, 1952.
43. *al-Wajib*, December 10, 1952.

Free Officers and Labor **431**

those elements most antagonistic to the left, the DMNL refrained from public criticism of the regime and did not organize any mass actions to protest the executions of Khamis and al-Baqari, the arrests of the trade union leaders, or the progressive restriction of freedom of trade union activity.

In retrospect it is easy to judge that this policy was doomed to failure, but in the political circumstances of postcoup Egypt there were few viable alternatives. The trade union movement, even if it had remained solidly under the leadership of the DMNL, could not possibly have challenged the political power of the army on its own. Any open challenge to the army would have encouraged the RCC to increase its reliance on the Muslim Brothers as an organized source of popular support and intensified the anticommunist sentiments within the RCC. Moreover, the Wafd, the monarchists, and other reactionary civilian political forces would have benefitted from any criticism of the new regime. Since they could not challenge the regime on their own and did not wish to risk increasing the influence of reactionaries, the TUCDL and the DMNL had little choice but to conduct a defensive holding action in the hope that in a still unstable political situation the balance of forces might shift in their favor.

The RCC's Labor Policy: Corporatism and Paternalism

Despite the political shifting that did occur within the RCC, the majority of the body never wavered from the stand it established towards the workers' movement by approving the executions of Khamis and al-Baqari. The efforts of Khalid Muhyi al-Din, Yusuf Siddiq, Ahmad Hamrush, and others sympathetic to the DMNL who argued for permitting freedom of trade union action and the right to strike were dismissed by the majority of the RCC. The official slogan of the new regime, "Unity, Order, and Labor," succinctly expressed its vision of workers' tasks in the new order. Such a vision left no room for initiatives from popular forces outside the regime's control. The RCC's response to the events of Kafr al-Dawwar clearly indicated the absolute hostility of most of the Free Officers towards independent action by the working class, even when taken in support of the army.

The RCC eventually developed the ad hoc measures that had characterized its early stance toward the working class into a policy informed by the corporatist conception of Egyptian society shared by all the postwar political forces with the exception of the communists and the Wafdist Vanguard. This policy was a logical accompaniment to the vague nationalism and social reformism that constituted the Free Officers' political platform. Corporatism combined easily with

432 Free Officers and Labor

the paternalistic attitude towards the working class which had been the common outlook of most of the political currents active in the Egyptian workers' movement since its origins. By choosing to isolate and then eliminate the communists who were the leading dissidents from corporatism and paternalism, the majority of the RCC was embracing the dominant social attitudes of Egyptian political culture as it had developed since the early part of the century.

The successful implementation of this corporatism and paternalism required not only that the RCC eliminate the communists from positions of influence in the working class, but also that it establish a significant base of active support for the regime within the trade union movement. The RCC's first initiative in this regard was to undertake a thorough revision of all existing labor legislation. On December 8, 1952, without prior consultation with representatives of trade unions or other workers' organizations, the government enacted comprehensive, new labor legislation in three separate acts.[44] The new Law of Individual Contracts granted workers significantly improved material benefits—increased severance compensation, longer annual vacations, free transportation to factories in remote areas, and free medical care. The most important provisions of this law were the establishment of higher levels of severance compensation to be paid by employers to dismissed workers, and the right to appeal dismissals for no cause (that is, layoffs due to economic conditions). These provisions were further strengthened by Decree 165 of April 1953, which made it a very expensive and bureaucratically cumbersome undertaking to dismiss a worker without cause. In enacting this measure the regime granted the single most important economic demand of the postwar workers' movement—job security—and in doing so the army won the support of many workers and trade union leaders who saw this measure as a significant concrete demonstration of the army's commitment to social justice.

The workers, however, had to pay a high price for this victory: a military order issued concurrently with the new legislation banned all strikes. Moreover, the provisions of the other two laws significantly reduced the scope of permissible trade union action. The Law of Arbitration and Conciliation in Labor Disputes imposed compulsory arbitration on all labor disputes, and the new Law of Trade Unions formally gave unions much more freedom to organize their af-

---

44. For a detailed description of all the provisions of Laws 317, 318, and 319 of 1952, see 'Ismat al-Hawari, *al-Tatawwur al-ta'rikhi li-tashri'at al-'amal fi al-jumhuriyya al-'arabiyya al-muttahida, Kitab al-'amal*, no. 35 (January 1967), pp. 25–27; For a British evaluation of the effects of the new measures see FO 371/102931/JE2183/3 (1953) and FO 371/102931/JE2183/6 (1953).

Free Officers and Labor **433**

fairs and allowed agricultural workers to join trade unions for the first time. Still, a petition of the Cairo Printers' Union objecting to several provisions of this law indicated that some conscious and articulate trade unionists felt many of its provisions weakened rather than strengthened trade unions.[45] The law entrenched the practice of establishing separate unions in each individual enterprise rather than on an industrial basis, and also required membership in unions if three-fifths of the workers in an enterprise were already union members. This provision allowed an employer to establish a union under his tutelage and require his recalcitrant employees to join once three-fifths of them had done so. This law also permitted the establishment of separate unions for blue-collar and white-collar workers in a single enterprise, and thus divided the membership base of unions and made it more difficult to unite workers in a given enterprise. The right of unions to initiate litigation against employers on behalf of their members was weakened. Despite these negative aspects of the new legislation and the accompanying military decree outlawing strikes, a large sector of the labor movement embraced the government's labor program.

The earlier enactment of land reform legislation on September 9 as well as the labor legislation of December 8 secured the regime substantial popular support from peasants and workers, and with its flanks thus protected, the army now moved against all potential sources of political opposition. On January 17, 1953, all political parties were dissolved, and 101 political figures arrested. As usual the communists suffered the brunt of the political repression; forty-eight of those arrested were communists, and all the left newspapers, including *al-Wajib*, were closed. Yusuf Siddiq resigned from the RCC in protest, but to no avail.[46]

Only at this point, after it had already lost most of its positions of political strength, did the DMNL adopt a policy of opposition to the regime. Despite the fact that the Muslim Brothers were the only political organization excluded from the January 17 decree, the DMNL endeavored to include them, along with the Wafd, elements of the Socialist party and some army officers in a National Democratic Front in opposition to the regime. Eventually only the Wafd and the DMNL reached a formal agreement on the formation of the front, and those elements of the Socialist party and the Muslim Brothers who participated did so on an informal and individual basis.

45. Niqabat 'ummal al-matabi' bi'l-qahira, *Mudhakkira bi-talab ta'dil qanun al-niqabat* (Cairo, n.d.).
46. *al-Misri*, January 20, 1953; Hamrush, *Qissat*, 1:293.

434 Free Officers and Labor

Because of the influence of the DMNL in the National Democratic Front, the front included upholding the freedom of trade union organization as a programmatic principle of unity, and endeavored to organize opposition to the regime within the trade union movement.[47] There are two clear examples of cooperation between the DMNL and some elements of the Muslim Brothers in the labor movement which apparently resulted from establishing the National Democratic Front. In the first, Muhammad Mutawalli al-Sha'rawi and Muhammad al-Fuli cooperated to provide leadership for the Misr Fine Spinning and Weaving Company union after March 1953. The second was al-Da'wa's endorsement of the demand for workers' right to strike (see Chapter XI).

In the Cairo suburb of Imababa there seems to have been both limited cooperation and contention between the DMNL and the Muslim Brothers in the textile workers' union established there in October 1952. Members of this union employed at the Shurbaji Textile Company engaged in the most significant demonstration of labor militancy since the events of Kafr al-Dawwar. The Shurbaji management announced that about one-third of its workers were to be dismissed because of production cutbacks. In response, the National Democratic Front organized a strike in late August 1953. The strike was still in progress on September 7, the anniversary of the executions of Khamis and al-Baqari. The DMNL chose this as the occasion to repudiate publicly its previous position on the executions and made a public display of its opposition to the regime by encouraging escalation of the Shurbaji strike. On September 7 the workers barricaded themselves in the factory and shouted slogans against the government. Some machinery was apparently burned, although it is not clear how. The army attacked the sit-in with tanks and between 350 and 500 workers were arrested.[48] This strike and sit-in provide evidence that, despite the regime's efforts to court workers, some trade unionists were unwilling to go along with the the government's labor policy, and it also indicates continuing communist influence in the textile industry, even as communist influence in other industries was sharply diminished.

47. Zaki Murad, interview in Ramadan, 'Abd al-Nasir, p. 340.
48. Ibid., p. 341; al-Sa'id, 1950–1957, pp. 114–15; FO 371/102931/JE2183/19 and FO 371/102931/JE2183/20 (1953) For reports on the Imbaba union, the dispute at Shurbaji, and Jamal al-Banna's intervention, see al-Da'wa January 6, May 12, and August 11, 1953. No strike is mentioned, and because of press censorship the details of this incident and the roles of the political forces involved are not clear. The accounts cited are all vague, partial, and contradictory.

Free Officers and Labor **435**

The exact extent of cooperation between the Muslim Brothers and the DMNL in the trade union movement is impossible to determine based on currently available information. Whatever it may have been, it is clear that *al-Da'wa* was the single most important and virtually only regular legal source of labor news during the latter part of 1953. On November 3, 1953, Muhammad Shatta, Ahmad Taha, and all the other leaders of the National Democratic Front were arrested. It is probably no coincidence that the only labor news to appear in *al-Da'wa* from this point until its closure in March 1954 consists of relatively harmless legal advice explaining the details of the new labor laws and their practical application.

By January 1953 many of the forces favoring a trade union movement independent of the regime had been stripped of their positions in the unions, and by the end of the year virtually all of the most important communist labor leaders were in jail. The FCGFETU and the TUCDL had been completely suppressed. The labor legislation of December 8, 1952, had established a substantial base of popular support for the RCC among trade union members and leaders. It remained only for the army to organize this support. For this purpose the Liberation Rally (Hay'at al-Tahrir), was established as the political organization of the RCC, more particularly of its effective leader Jamal 'Abd al-Nasir, after the abolition of political parties was decreed.

'Abd al-Nasir assumed the position of general secretary of the Liberation Rally while the day-to-day organizational and political direction of the organization was in the hands of its deputy secretary, Major Ibrahim al-Tahawi, and its director of trade union affairs, Major Ahmad 'Abd Allah Tu'ayma. Because it was an organization imposed from above that permitted no opportunity for political initiatives by its rank-and-file members, the Liberation Rally never fully succeeded in accomplishing its mission of mobilizing popular political support for the regime. However, the Liberation Rally was able to establish close links with a number of trade union leaders. Trade unions were a special object of the attention of Majors al-Tahawi and Tu'ayma for the same reason that the Wafd had sought to organize trade unions in the 1920s and 1930s: workers constituted a relatively easily mobilizable and highly concentrated mass located in politically strategic urban areas. The Liberation Rally was most successful in building a close relationship with the leadership of one of the most strategically placed groups of Egyptian workers, the Cairo transport workers.

One of the Liberation Rally's first public activities was a meeting attended by several hundred trade union leaders in Cairo, at which al-Sawi Ahmad al-Sawi, the recently elected president of the Cairo

436 Free Officers and Labor

Joint Transport Federation (JTF), was one of the principal speakers.[49] Al-Sawi had occupied various leadership positions among the Cairo transport workers since 1948 when he became a member of the executive board of the bus company union. Still, he seems to have been only a minor figure in the trade union movement because his name is not mentioned in any of the newspaper reports of the activities of the transport workers until his election as president of the Cairo JTF in November 1952 shortly after the attacks on the left in the Cairo transport workers unions.[50] These circumstances strongly suggest that al-Sawi owed his position in the trade union movement to his willingness to cooperate with the regime.

The RCC was less successful in other efforts to ingratiate itself with noncommunist trade union leaders during 1953. Fathi Kamil was appointed as labor representative to the labor and workers' committee of the body selected to draw up a five-year plan for economic development and was singled out for praise by Muhammad Najib as "the best trade unionist who represents all sectors of the workers."[51] Kamil was also sent to the International Labor Organization's conference in Geneva on June 4, 1953 as the only worker-representative in the Egyptian delegation.[52] Kamil however, remained unconvinced by the regime's efforts, and he did not support its labor policies. On his return from Europe, the Cairo Tramway Workers' Union, which was the only one of the Cairo transport unions whose leadership did not fully support the regime, gave a reception in his honor attended by a large number of trade unionists from all over Egypt.[53] Kamil's obliquely worded address to the assembled suggested that the very fact of convening such a group of trade union leaders constituted an act of opposition to the regime's policy of throttling the independence of the trade unions. In the absence of communist trade union figures, Kamil became the leading proponent of the demand for trade union freedom of action. Yet, Kamil kept his opposition within boundaries acceptable to the regime, and never took the step of actively organizing against the RCC, perhaps hoping that he could use his official positions to further his trade union objectives.

Although it made an effort to co-opt trade union leaders like Fathi Kamil, the RCC continued to oppose any attempts to organize workers which it did not itself initiate. In the summer of 1953 Muhammad

49. *al-Misri*, January 19, 1953.
50. For reports of the election see *Ibid.*, November 25, 1952. For further details on al-Sawi's trade union career see 'Abd Allah, *al-Wa'y*, pp. 40–41.
51. *al-Ahram*, March 1, 1953.
52. *al-Akhbar*, May 26, 1953.
53. *al-Ahram*, September 5, 1953; *al-Zaman*, September 9, 1953.

Free Officers and Labor   **437**

Mutawalli al-Sha'rawi and several other textile union leaders from Alexandria and Cairo attempted to establish a national federation of textile workers' unions, but the regime persistently blocked this effort for over a year (probably because of strong communist influence within the textile unions) despite the fact that it was carried out in accordance with the new labor legislation.[54] A national organization of textile workers represented too great a potential for explosive political and economic struggle that might threaten the relationship the RCC was seeking to establish with the trade union movement.

The Crisis of March 1954

Because the Free Officers were not a unified political organization and did not have a well-developed political program, the stability of the military regime was dependent on maintaining a delicate balance among its own internally contradictory elements. By early 1954 it was becoming impossible to contain the contradictions within the regime. A broad-based popular challenge to the legitimacy of military rule and the suspension of parliamentary democracy began to develop as a result of a crisis in the relations between the RCC and the Muslim Brothers, the largest mass membership organization in Egypt at this time (most of the Wafd's more numerous supporters were never active members). On the formal level the Brothers had maintained cordial relations with the RCC throughout 1953, and in return had been granted a privileged political position in the new regime: the Society was the only political organization active during the old regime which remained legal because of the RCC's decision that the Muslim Brothers were not a political body. This formal cordiality, however, masked sharp divisions within the Society over the issue of continued support for the regime.[55]

In late 1953 and early 1954 General Guide Hasan Hudaybi and General Muhammad Najib had discussed the possibility of overthrowing 'Abd al-Nasir and placing real power in Najib's hands.[56] On January 12, 1954, the Brothers led a memorial rally at Cairo University honoring students who had fallen in the guerrilla fighting on the Suez Canal in 1951–52. Some speakers at the rally denounced 'Abd al-Nasir as a pro-American dictator, and the demonstration clashed violently with supporters of the Liberation Rally. Probably acting on the basis of knowledge of the Najib-Hudaybi contacts, the RCC responded

54. al-Sha'rawi, interview, January 7, 1981.
55. Mitchell, *The Society*, pp. 105 ff.
56. Ramadan, *'Abd al-Nasir*, pp. 142–44.

438 Free Officers and Labor

by declaring the Brothers a political organization and dissolved the Society in accordance with the decrees of January 1953. Driving the Muslim Brothers into total opposition meant that the RCC was now opposed by every organized civilian political force from the precoup period.

The clash between the RCC and the Muslim Brothers provoked a crisis within the RCC pitting 'Abd al-Nasir against Najib, who now demanded effective powers commensurate with his formal offices of chairman of the RCC, prime minister and president of the republic. Because Najib had never been a member of the Free Officers, he served as a focal point for all of the political forces opposed to military rule. Najib saw the RCC's attack on the Brothers as a blow against his own base of support and a strengthening of military rule in the face of popular demands for the restoration of parliamentary democracy and the return of the army to its barracks. On February 24, Najib resigned from all of his posts and thereby brought the crisis within the RCC to the public's attention. When 'Abd al-Nasir assumed both the premiership and the presidency, mass demonstrations of support for Najib and the restoration of parliamentary democracy erupted with the participation of the Muslim Brothers, Socialists, Wafdists, and communists. Even a section of the army (cavalry officers led by Khalid Muhyi al-Din) threatened to rebel. In the face of this massive display of support for Najib, the RCC was obliged to reinstate Najib as president of the republic while 'Abd al-Nasir remained prime minister. On March 4 and 5 the RCC voted to convene a constituent assembly by July, to lift martial law by June, and to rescind press censorship immediately. On March 9 Najib once again assumed the posts of prime minister and chairman of the RCC.

Najib's ostensible return to power and the lifting of press censorship resulted in the unleashing of a torrent of criticisms and protests against the regime from every quarter including workers and trade union leaders. Labor news had all but disappeared from the press since the closure of *al-Wajib* (except for *al-Da'wa*'s workers' page), but after the lifting of press censorship, the pro-Wafd daily *al-Misri* (*The Egyptian*) initiated a weekly page featuring workers' news, grievances, and demands from a large number of trade unions and groups of workers.[57] Mursi al-Shafi'i, who had been jailed for his role in the Shurbaji strike, contributed a column entitled "The Worker" in which he noted that a large number of those detained on political charges were workers who deserved to be released. Nonetheless, al-Shafi'i and other workers remained incarcerated throughout March,

---

57. This feature appeared on March 10, 17, and 24, 1954.

Free Officers and Labor **439**

and the number of political prisoners, including workers, actually increased during this time.[58]

The climax of this short-lived revival of the workers' movement was the convening of a meeting of twenty-one trade union leaders to discuss the nomination of workers' candidates for the announced elections for a Constituent Assembly.[59] The meeting was initiated by Mahmud Ibrahim al-'Ajami, president of the union of the government Road Department workers. Fathi Kamil was now serving as counsellor of this union. These circumstances seem to indicate that Kamil's views on trade union independence from the regime still had significant support among trade unionists. Communists would certainly have supported Kamil's stand, but no communists attended this meeting because almost all the prominent communist trade union leaders were still in jail.

On March 25 the RCC adopted resolutions permitting the establishment of political parties and declared that it would disband itself without forming a political party on July 24, 1954, the date for the convening of the Constituent Assembly. 'Abd al-Nasir himself introduced these resolutions, and it is entirely possible that he fully intended to instigate the chaos their announcement created, for elements of the army immediately protested the decisions and demanded that the RCC remain in power. The Muslim Brothers, who had supported Najib against 'Abd al-Nasir, now withdrew their support for the democratic movement because they opposed the formation of political parties and because the decisions of March 25 meant that the Wafd was most likely to be returned to power on July 24, 1954.

On March 26, massive pro-Najib demonstrations supporting a return to democracy took place all over Cairo. In the industrial suburbs of Shubra al-Khayma and Hilwan, demonstrators took complete control of the streets for most of the day.[60] According to Ahmad Sadiq Sa'd, Workers' Vanguard participated actively in these demonstrations.[61] When the pro-'Abd al-Nasir forces began to counter the mas-

---

58. *al-Misri*, March 3, 1954 reports the arrest of 118 political opponents of the regime, among them forty-five Muslim Brothers, twenty Socialists, five Wafdists, four communists, and fifteen workers.

59. *Ibid.*, March 24, 1954.

60. *Ibid.*, March 27, 1954.

61. Ahmad Sadiq Sa'd, interview in Ramadan, *'Abd al-Nasir*, p. 301. The other communist organizations were not as active as Workers' Vanguard during the crisis. The DMNL was suffering from internal organizational turmoil because of a policy dispute between the leadership in jail and the cadres outside over supporting the military regime in light of its recent neutralist and anti-American foreign policy initiatives. See Ramadan, *'Abd al-Nasir*, pp. 95–99. The Communist Party of Egypt was not a signifi-

440 Free Officers and Labor

sive popular expressions of support for Najib and a return to parliamentary democracy, the trade union connections established through the efforts of the Liberation Rally proved critical in enabling the army to mobilize its own mass support. The Cairo transport workers' general strike of March 27–28 was a decisive contribution to the RCC's ability to turn back the tide of popular opinion, consolidate the power of 'Abd al-Nasir, and confirm the continuation of military rule. The only currently available evidence indicating how this was accomplished consists of contradictory memoirs by the leading participants in these events. Such sources make it impossible to render a detailed account of the developments with complete certainty, but they are sufficient to reconstruct the main outlines of the story.

According to al-Sawi Ahmad al-Sawi, on March 10 and again on March 17 Yusuf Siddiq suggested organizing a strike in support of Najib to force the RCC to relinquish power even before July 24. Siddiq offered to pay £E 10,000 in compensation for the material losses the workers might suffer as a result of a strike, and had planned to coordinate the workers' strike with actions by university students.[62] Siddiq vehemently denied this account before his death and claimed never to have met al-Sawi, though he offered nothing to support his denials.[63] Al-Sawi's story is corroborated by Majors al-Tahawi and Tu'ayma who claim that al-Sawi reported Siddiq's offer to them.[64] According to al-Tahawi, his conversation with al-Sawi occurred on March 21, that is, before the RCC's decision to permit the establishment of parties and liquidate itself was taken. On that day al-Tahawi and al-Sawi decided to organize a transport general strike in support of 'Abd al-Nasir and the RCC which suggests 'Abd al-Nasir may well have known in advance that he could still command the streets after the RCC's decisions of March 25. Al-Tahawi asserts, however, that 'Abd al-Nasir refused to sanction the strike once he was informed of it.[65] In contrast, Khalid Muhyi al-Din recalls that after the events 'Abd al-Nasir personally told him that the total cost of the demonstrations and general strike of March 27–28 was no more than £E 5,000, most

---

cant actor in the crisis because it supported neither Najib nor 'Abd al-Nasir in this confrontation.

62. al-Sawi Ahmad al-Sawi, interview in 'Abd al-'Azim Ramadan, *al-Sira' al-ijtima'i wa'l-siyasi fi misr mundhu qiyam thawrat 23 yulyu 1952 ila nihayat azmat maris 1954* (Cairo, 1975), p. 118.

63. Ahmad Hamrush, "Yusuf Siddiq al-muftara 'alayh," *Ruz al-yusuf*, March 24, 1975, p. 68.

64. Ahmad 'Abd Allah Tu'ayma, interview in Ramadan, *'Abd al-Nasir*, p. 304; Ibrahim al-Tahawi, interview in Ramadan, *'Abd al-Nair*, p. 292; Ibrahim al-Tahawi, interview in Hamrush, *Qissat*, 4:17.

65. al-Tahawi, interview in Hamrush, *Qissat*, 4:17.

Free Officers and Labor **441**

of which was paid personally to al-Sawi.[66] This suggests that though 'Abd al-Nasir may have been reluctant to assume direct responsibility for the strike, he was more than simply an innocent beneficiary.

Kamil al-'Uqayli, president of the Cairo Federation of Taxi Drivers, provides a second version of the origins of the general strike which is corroborated by Muhammad Nuh, president of the Cairo Tramway Clerical Employees' Union.[67] They assert that they and Zaki Mukhaymar, president of the Cairo Tramway Workers' Union, and Sayyid Khallaf, president of the Cairo Store Clerks' Federation, were called to the offices of Major Tu'ayma at the Liberation Rally on March 26, and informed of the RCC's decisions of the previous day. In response al-'Uqayli suggested organizing a general strike in support of continuing the revolution. Al-Sawi was then chosen in absentia to lead the strike because it had been rumored that the Cairo transport workers were going to participate in demonstrations supporting Najib called by the Bar Association for March 28. In addition, al-Sawi's leadership would provide the strike with the broadest base of support among strategically placed workers.

These two versions of the origins of the strike can be reconciled by presuming that al-Sawi, al-Tahawi, and Tu'ayma had, in fact, agreed before March 26 that a strike should be organized, but had not announced their intentions because they were uncertain of the possible response to it, or the most appropriate moment for it. Al-'Uqayli need not necessarily have been apprised of this decision when he made his suggestion. The idea of a general strike was widespread on both sides of the political divide. Al-'Uqayli claims he had not discussed a strike with Tu'ayma before March 26. Still, the willingness of al-'Uqayli and others to organize a strike in support of 'Abd al-Nasir and the RCC may well have been what Tu'ayma was seeking in order to carry out the plan devised earlier with al-Sawi.

On the evening of March 26 the Cairo transport union leaders gathered in the offices of the JTF and called for a workers' general strike while they themselves proclaimed a hunger strike. Their demands, broadcast on the radio before any workers began to strike, urged: (1) no legalization of political parties; (2) maintaining the RCC in power until the complete evacuation of British troops had been achieved; (3) the formation of a National Assembly which would include the representatives of all trade unions and other public associations to serve as a consultative body for decisions and measures the RCC wished to

66. Khalid Muhyi al-Din, interview in Hamrush, *Qissat*, 4:159. In Ramadan, *'Abd al-Nasir*,.p. 323, Muhyi al-Din gives the figure of £E 4,000.
67. Kamil al-'Uqayli, interview in Ramadan, *al-Sira'*, p. 120; Muhammad Nuh, interview in Ramadan, *al-Sira'*, p. 119.

442 Free Officers and Labor

implement; and (4) no elections.[68] According to the radio these demands were endorsed by the Cairo JTF, the Federation of Store Clerks and Workers, the Cairo General Union of Taxi Drivers, the Federation of Agricultural Workers, the Cairo Printers' Union, and unnamed textile workers' unions.

The response to the call for a general strike was mixed. The Cairo bus, taxi, and metro workers participated fully, and on March 27 public transportation in Cairo was paralyzed. The Cairo tramway workers, however, did not participate in the strike despite the fact that the presidents of the unions of both the blue-collar and the clerical employees were among the hunger strikers in the headquarters of the Cairo JTF. Mahmud al-Farghali, secretary of the tramway workers' union, led the tramway workers' resistance to the call for a general strike. He was assaulted by workers and police who then forced some of the trams to stop running.[69] The Cairo Printers' Union announced that it did not, in fact, endorse the demands broadcast on the radio, and that its name had been incorrectly used.[70] The strongest trade union resistance to the call for a general strike was in Alexandria where many union leaders convened to issue a statement calling for: (1) abolishing martial law; (2) dissolving the RCC; (3) guaranteeing democratic liberties; (4) freedom for all jailed workers and reconstituting all administratively dissolved unions; (5) establishing a general federation of trade unions; and (6) denouncing all attempts to split the ranks of the workers. These demands were endorsed by members of the executive boards of the unions of the Alexandria Joint Transport Federation, several textile mills, merchant seamen, cinema workers, and others.[71] A number of Cairo unions issued a "Patriotic Statement" supporting the RCC's decisions of March 25 and raising the same demands as the Alexandria unions. Among the unions endorsing this statement were the General Union of Spinning, Weaving, Knitting, Dyeing, and Associated Workers of Greater Cairo, the Cairo Shoe Workers Union, and the unions of candy makers, newspaper distributors, tailors, elevator operators, iron and building ornamentation workers, carpenters, and the national federations of shoe workers and building trades workers.[72] In Kafr al-Dawwar, the Misr Fine Spinning and Weaving Company union adopted a resolution sup-

68. al-Misri, March 28, 1954.
69. Ibid., Ramadan, al-Sira', p. 113; Ramadan. 'Abd al-Nasir, pp. 206–207. Farghali had earlier been a member of the DMNL, and it is not clear to which communist organization he belonged at this time.
70. al-Misri, March 28, 1954.
71. Ibid.
72. Ibid.

Free Officers and Labor **443**

porting the restoration of parliamentary democracy and rejecting the call for a general strike. Army units entered the mill and shut down the machinery while Muhammad Mutawalli al-Sha'rawi and others attempted to keep it running.[73] A similar confrontation apparently occurred at the Filature Nationale and its subsidiary Egyptian Textile Company in Alexandria because both a strike and union resolutions supporting the RCC decisions of March 25 were reported.[74]

On March 27 and 28, the ranks of the trade unions were clearly divided for and against Najib, and the restoration of parliamentary democracy, but by March 29 a large number of trade unions had either been persuaded or coerced to join the general strike. On that day the streets of Cairo were filled with demonstrators shouting "No parties, no democracy." Meanwhile, 'Abd al-Nasir had organized his supporters among the junior army officers while Najib vacillated and failed to mobilize his own forces. On the evening of March 29, the RCC met and announced it would delay implementing its decisions of March 5 and March 25 until January 1956. Although Najib was not finally removed from the scene until November 1954, it was clear within a few weeks that 'Abd al-Nasir and the RCC had triumphed decisively: the army was to remain in power. Directly after the announcement of the RCC's decisions, 'Abd al-Nasir and RCC members Salah Salim and Kamal al-Din Husayn visited the headquarters of the Cairo JTF where al-Sawi and other executive board members were addressing a crowd.[75] This visit symbolized the forging of the alliance between a section of the trade union leadership and the RCC and recognized the critical role of al-Sawi and the Cairo transport workers in preserving the rule of the RCC and elevating 'Abd al-Nasir to uncontested power.

March 1954: An Assessment

Was March 1954 a victory for the working class, the beginning of a new "revolution of workers and peasants," as 'Abd al-'Azim Ramadan suggests?[76] It is certainly true that the Free Officers broke the economic and political hegemony of the large landowners, the dominant class in Egypt since the era of Muhammad 'Ali, through the land reform, the dissolution of the political parties of the old regime, and the RCC's decision of April 15, 1954 to deprive the leaders of the Wafd, the Liberal Constitutionalist, and Sa'dist parties of all political rights

73. al-Sha'rawi, interview, January 7, 1981.
74. al-Misri, March 28, 1954.
75. Hamrush, Qissat, 1:348–49.
76. Ramadan, 'Abd al-Nasir, p. 220.

444 Free Officers and Labor

for ten years. Although recent developments make these measures appear less definitive now than they did when they were taken, it can still be said that the era of the RCC and 'Abd al-Nasir substantially altered the structure of economic and political power in Egypt. But did the working class, by virtue of the fact that a number of important trade union leaders had supported "continuing the revolution," come any closer to achieving political power? The answer is definitely no. The working class provided a significant proportion of the shock troops in the battle to eliminate the political power of the old ruling class, but it did not thereby inherit it.

The trade union leaders who cast their lot with 'Abd al-Nasir made a bargain on terms that were unmistakably clear, even though they may not have been explicit. They agreed to support a military dictatorship that had repeatedly demonstrated its unalterable opposition to a free trade union movement, the right to strike, and any form of independent initiative and action by workers. In exchange the regime confirmed them in their positions of trade union leadership and agreed to preserve and extend the economic gains that had already been achieved, especially the all-important guarantee of job security. This bargain was sustained by a significant section of the working masses not only because of the economic gains achieved under the rule of the RCC but also because the RCC represented the only viable vehicle for achieving the demands of the Egyptian nationalist movement. The Wafd, and certainly all the other political parties, had repeatedly proven incapable of forcing a total evacuation of British troops from Egypt, whereas the RCC was on the verge of accomplishing this objective.

The motives of al-Sawi and al-'Uqayli, the principal candidates for the title of "initiator of the general strike," may be discerned by recalling their personal histories. The former did not become a leading figure in the trade union movement until after the military coup, and the latter had been president of one of the four rival Cairo taxi drivers' unions before Hasan 'Abd al-Rahman's campaign to unify the unions. Al-'Uqayli had been among those responsible for calling off the transport general strike announced for February 5, 1951, and his leadership was later repudiated when Hasan 'Abd al-Rahman and Sayyid Khalil Turk assumed the leadership of the Cairo JTF in June 1951. Both al-Sawi and al-'Uqayli therefore owed their prominent positions to the fact that the regime had jailed or otherwise repressed their predecessors and rivals. The president of the Cairo Tramway Workers' Union, Zaki Mukhaymar, had not played a major role in the precoup trade union movement although he had been an officer of the union since 1939. In contrast, the tramway union leaders 'Abd al-

'Aziz Mustafa and Mahmud al-Farghali, who had actively participated in the PCGFETU and the conferences of transport workers in
1952, opposed the call for a general strike.

Ramadan has suggested an economic motive for the failure of the
Cairo tramway workers to support the call for the general strike in arguing they were more privileged than other transport workers.[77] This
assertion is contradicted by the fact that at the transport workers' conference of July 13, 1952, the Cairo tramway workers advanced the demand to be granted the same cadre as Cairo and Alexandria bus workers. Moreover, Alexandria transport workers, who strongly opposed
the general strike, enjoyed slightly better wages than their Cairo counterparts. In any event, it is much more likely that political consciousness was the decisive factor in determining workers' responses to the
general strike call. Unions with a significant communist presence in
their leadership generally opposed the strike, and Ramadan himself
points out that many of the Cairo tramway union leaders, not only
Mustafa and Farghali, were either Wafdists or communists.[78] This
was also the case in the textile industry, where sentiment was
strongly against the strike. Other unions led by communists or other
proponents of an independent trade union movement, such as the Alexandria Merchant Seamen's Union and the Cairo Shoe Workers'
Union, also cpposed the strike.

Not all who had supported the demand for an independent trade
union movement opposed the strike. Although the slogan of "trade
union independence from political parties" was widespread by 1954,
it is doubtful many trade unionists fully grasped its meaning. Supporters of the Wafd and Prince 'Abbas Halim had long used it to mean
independence from their respective rivals. Communists and other
leftists were also partly responsible for the slogan's lack of clarity. Although the communists campaigned for independence from the
Wafd, 'Abbas Halim, the Palace, and the minority parties, they were
sometimes sectarian and undemocratic, especially before 1950, in
their dealings with each other and with those like Fathi Kamil who
advocated independence from the various communist political organizations as well. Although Kamil's admiration for the British Labor party's brand of social democracy brought him precariously close
to collaboration with the occupation in 1946, he strongly opposed the
general strike of March 1954 on the grounds that a trade union movement could not flourish without democracy. Many other noncom-

77. *Ibid.*, pp. 186–87. For a comparison of Cairo and Alexandria transport workers'
wages in 1952, see FO 371/97078/JE2188/2 (1952).
78. Ramadan, *'Abd al-Nasir*, p. 187.

446 Free Officers and Labor

munists who had supported the slogan of "trade union independence from political parties" had a different understanding of its import, and this allowed them to give their allegiance to the RCC, which was not a political party of course, without feeling they had violated the slogan's intent.

Even as the military regime imposed its tutelage and control over the trade union movement, it had undeniably provided some significant economic gains for workers. Therefore, the question of whether to continue supporting the regime or not, despite its increasingly undemocratic character, was a political issue to be decided on the basis of the trade union leadership's vision of the role and ultimate objectives of the movement. The leading activists in the efforts to establish an independent trade union movement also tended to support a return to democracy, and these included many communists or those influenced by them. These activists shared a vision of the workers' movement as a leading component in the broad, anti-imperialist political movement for national liberation. Their opposition to continued rule by the RCC was heavily influenced by its clear refusal to allow the workers' movement to play such a role in the new regime. Those who had not actively supported the political independence of the trade unions, or who used the slogan of independence primarily for partisan ends, tended to emphasize the trade union movement's more narrowly economic objectives, and for this reason saw no harm in accepting the tutelage of a regime that had significantly advanced these objectives. In most cases it appears that the rank-and-file members of the unions followed the decisions of their leaders on this question.

The considerable self interest al-Sawi and al-'Uqayli had in maintaining the RCC in power does not necessarily detract from the sincerity of their conviction that it provided the best guarantee of maintaining and advancing the economic position of their constituency. The restriction of the employers' right to dismiss workers without cause was widely hailed as a major workers' victory. Indeed, al-Tahawi mentions that preservation of this gain was al-Sawi's main concern when he visited him to report Yusuf Siddiq's overtures.[79]

It was not, as has already been noted, a victory without a certain price. Unwillingness to pay this price explains why a large number of textile workers' unions, which were the most advanced in their commitment to an independent trade union movement, refused to support the general strike, despite the fact that their members were potentially among the major beneficiaries of the restrictions on

79. al-Tahawi, interview in Hamrush, *Qissat*, 4:17.

dismissing workers enacted by the RCC. Those trade union leaders and workers who supported the general strike were willing to accept the consequences of the victory of the RCC: a trade union movement dominated by the government and shorn of the right to strike and a political system which stripped workers of their right to organize independently of government control. This was, in essence, a development of the patron-client model of trade union organization with the state in the guise of patron. A few years later this would lead to the institutionalization of the corporate conception of society when the trade unions were absorbed into the apparatus of the state.

Chapter XIV

Conclusion

This book has demonstrated the political role of urban workers in twentieth century Egypt and the importance of understanding that role in class terms. In the early part of the twentieth century urban workers began to cohere into a new social class which, by the end of the Second World War, was a highly visible and politically significant force in Egyptian society. As a result of their collective participation in both economic struggles in the workplace and in the nationalist political movement, many of these workers eventually came to see the working class as a distinct and independent political force in society. Two closely related factors defined the matrix within which the working class was formed, organized, and engaged in struggle: the structure of Egyptian capitalism itself, and Egypt's domination by British colonialism. The conjuncture of these two factors forged an inextricable link between the workers' movement and the nationalist movement.

The development of capitalism in Egypt was stimulated by the country's integration into the world market in the course of the nineteenth century, mainly through the export of cotton and other agricultural products to Europe. In the second half of the nineteenth century, and especially after the British occupation in 1882, there was a large-scale influx of foreign capital concentrated primarily in the agricultural sector, though some foreign and *mutamassir* capital was invested in services, transport, and to a very limited degree in industry as well. After the First World War an indigenous Egyptian industrial bourgeoisie dominated by the Misr group began to emerge, deriving its capital in large part from segments of the Egyptian agrarian bourgeoisie. The Misr group self-consciously sought to establish an

Conclusion **449**

indigenously owned and managed industrial economy in Egypt, but the power of foreign and *mutamassir* capital ultimately compelled this nascent industrial bourgeoisie to abandon the dream of independence. By the mid-1930s the Misr group had entered into an alliance with foreign and *mutamassir*, capital and lost its "national" character.

During the 1930s and 1940s indigenous, *mutamassir* and foreign industrialists all promoted considerable industrial development, especially of a large-scale mechanized textile sector. Despite significant industrial growth during this period however, the dominant share of capital invested in Egypt remained committed to agriculture and controlled by a reactionary and parasitical class of large landowners linked to the European and *mutamassir*-dominated cotton market. After the Second World War, industrialists were unable to continue their earlier advances because the state did not effectively provide adequate capital and credit, direct the investment of capital into productive areas, increase the purchasing power of the local market, or limit the wasteful expenditures of the local ruling class on conspicuous consumption of luxury imports. Thus the externally induced industrial boom came to a halt at the end of World War II when the temporarily expanded market for locally produced industrial goods collapsed. The loss of this market and the economic crisis of the postwar period exposed the continuing structural weakness of Egyptian industry, especially its lack of capital and overdependence on the textile sector.

The evolving structure of the working class reflected the uneven development of Egyptian capitalism. Because of the weakness of industrial capital, the majority of urban workers were employed in small, under-capitalized, and unmechanized shops where many elements of precapitalist production and social relations remained in force. Such workers must be considered part of the working class, and they did participate in trade unions and other forms of collective action. But workers employed in large-scale mechanized transport and industry eventually became the most active forces in the labor movement. The early concentration of large numbers of workers in transport, public utilities, and service enterprises was largely the result of European capital's primary interest in the extraction of cotton from Egypt. Until the mid-1930s the largest concentrations of workers were in transport enterprises, and these workers constituted the center of gravity of the labor movement. With the growth of large-scale mechanized industry their leading position was eclipsed by textile workers.

By the Second World War the working class included a large num-

450 Conclusion

ber of industrial workers in large-scale mass production industries, though not all of them embraced the politically independent outlook and militant industrial strategy that characterized the textile workers. In firms like Shell Oil, the Suez Canal Company, and Eastern Tobacco, the extraordinary profits of multinational capital and the presence of skillful anticommunist trade union leaders resulted in workers' support for corporatist and paternalist trade unions. Thus the uneven development of capital in Egypt tended to fragment politically even some of the most highly concentrated sectors of the working class. Nonetheless, it is impossible to deny the leading role of the textile workers in shaping the political character of the postwar workers' movement.

The processes of capital accumulation and capitalist development brought into existence a mass of urban wage laborers and created the possibility of a workers' movement, trade unions, and other forms of organization and struggle. The development of capitalism and the emergence of a working class did not however, automatically determine that workers would adopt certain forms of consciousness and assume a predetermined political role in Egyptian society. The specific character of the Egyptian workers' movement was shaped by the facts that from 1882 to 1956 Egypt was subject to British colonial domination and that until the late 1930s nearly all of the large-scale employers were also foreigners whose economic power was enhanced and protected by the British occupation. Under these conditions economic demands and demands for greater autonomy and respect in the workplace were seen as part of the nationalist struggle. The historical point of reference for the Egyptian labor movement was the nationalist revolution of 1919, in which the demands of the emergent working class merged with the political movement for national independence in a mutually reinforcing pattern. Subsequently there was never, in the minds of most worker activists, a clear distinction between the economic demands of workers and the political demands of the nationalist movement. Both were perceived as part of the same struggle for Egyptian self-determination.

In this context the bourgeois nationalism of the Wafd emerged as the hegemonic ideological and organizational force within the labor movement. The Wafd regarded the workers as simply one of many components of the national movement it led, and sought to bring the trade unions under its control. The Wafd's relationship to the trade unions was characterized by corporatism, paternalism, and patron-client organizational forms. Government workers, workers employed by large foreign monopolies, such as the Cairo tramway workers, and workers employed in small workshops, where social relations were

Conclusion **451**

still influenced by precapitalist relations of production, all found reasons to accept the patron-client structure of the trade union movement in the interwar period. The role and political perspective of Prince 'Abbas Halim differed somewhat from that of the Wafd and allowed more opportunities for the working class to assert its own identity and interests. But ultimately, the Wafd and the prince shared the same basic outlook toward the working class.

On the basis of this early pattern of Wafdist domination of the labor movement, some scholars, notably Marius Deeb, have concluded that Egyptian workers were largely passive and that the trade unions were simply instruments of the Wafd and other nonworker political forces.[1] However, even in the 1920s there were numerous instances in which workers and their unions rejected domination by nonworker patrons. By the end of that decade, a debate had begun within the labor movement over whether workers should organize themselves and struggle for their demands independently of the Wafd. Because of the failure of the Wafd and 'Abbas Halim to achieve either the economic or national political demands of the workers, those workers most able to do so, mainly those employed in large-scale enterprises, embarked on an independent course of action. In the 1930s the proponents of a politically independent workers' movement and trade unions independent of nonworker political parties and personalities began to gather strength.

The newly-formed Egyptian communist organizations became the leading force in this tendency within the workers' movement and achieved their greatest strength and influence during the high points of the post-World War II nationalist mobilizations of January to June 1946 and October 1951 to January 1952. The emergence of a left wing within the workers' movement was symbolized by the creation of a new political point of reference—February 21, 1946—the day on which the most politically advanced sectors of the workers' movement emerged as a major component of the revived nationalist movement, and thereby infused the nationalist movement with a more radical social program.

In the postwar period a new political force, the Society of Muslim Brothers, emerged as a rival to both Wafdist bourgeois nationalism and communism within the workers' movement as well as in Egyptian society as a whole. The workers' movement was a major arena of contention between the Muslim Brothers and the communists. Yet despite some local and partial successes, the Brothers were not able

1. Deeb, "Labor and Politics." See also, for example P. J. Vatikiotis, *The History of Egypt* (Baltimore, 1980), pp. 334–42.

452 Conclusion

to establish a stable base in the working class. In many respects the Muslim Brothers' approach to the working class was rooted in the same paternalistic and corporatist social vision which shaped the outlook of the Wafd and 'Abbas Halim.

In both the period of domination by nonworker patrons and in the period of the emergence of an independent class-based workers' movement, the consciousness and organized struggle of the workers' movement were rooted in a set of demands and a political perspective which united economic issues in the workplace with broader national political demands. This did not mean that workers were unwilling to struggle against representatives of Egypt's "national" bourgeoisie. The economic struggles of Egyptian workers from as early as 1938 demonstrated a concrete repudiation of the argument that national unity of capitalists and workers was required so long as full Egyptian independence was not established. However, given the predominance of the national question in Egyptian politics during the first half of the twentieth century, nationalism remained a central component of the consciousness of Egyptian workers, and class questions were most often perceived in national terms.

Even the political practice of the communists, who were the most consistent in insisting on the importance of asserting the independent interests of the working class, combined the advancement of these interests with active participation in a broad national front that included bourgeois forces. It is instructive to recall that when the WCNL presented its political program, it justified doing so on the basis that all other political forces had failed to achieve Egypt's national goals. In fact, the failure of the old guard of the Wafd to provide adequate leadership for the mass nationalist upsurges after the Second World War contributed substantially to the growth of communist influence. Both Workers' Vanguard and the DMNL consistently argued that Egypt was not ripe for a socialist revolution and that a national democratic revolution similar to the one advocated by Mao Tse-tung in China was the next item on Egypt's political agenda. The communists however, expected that even a national revolution could not occur without the leadership of the working class.

The organizations and struggles of the working class have had a significant influence on the course of Egyptian social and political history and on the shaping of the country's economic and political agenda. The presence of this new social class was manifested in a variety of direct and indirect ways over the three decades before the collapse of the old regime in 1952. For example, from the 1920s onward the Wafd and its rivals competed for the leadership of the trade union movement because all the competing political forces feared the po-

Conclusion   **453**

tential for social instability which even an embryonic working class movement represented. At the same time, a controlled workers' movement could potentially provide a readily mobilizable source of support in key urban concentrations. This required that all the political forces, even the most reactionary, at least recognize and pay lip service to workers' demands. Thus even in the 1920s and early 1930s, when the workers' movement was still in its formative stages, the potential which such a movement represented, as much as its actual achievements, imposed itself on the political and economic agenda of the country.

The existence of a workers' movement also influenced industrial policy. The decision of the Misr company to locate its principal textile mills in the Nile Delta and to rely on untrained workers was a direct response to the history of working class organization and collective action in Cairo and Alexandria, where the textile mills would normally have been located on the basis of economic considerations other than the need to control the labor force. The Misr company's adoption of paternalism as a strategy of labor control was likewise related to its fear of labor militancy. While this strategy was successful for a limited time, the violence and intensity of the strikes at Mahalla al-Kubra in 1947 and Kafr al-Dawwar in 1952 demonstrated the workers' rejection of paternalism and contributed to the adoption of a new industrial strategy after 1952.

In Shubra al-Khayma, medium-sized textile mills could not afford such an elaborate structure of labor control, because there was constant pressure on the owners to cut the cost of labor in order to remain competitive in a volatile market. Strikes and other forms of collective action were less violent than those against the Misr Company, but they were more organized and sustained. Shubra al-Khayma thus became a testing ground for political currents that posed alternatives to the impotence of the Wafd's liberal nationalism—principally the communists and the Muslim Brothers. The outcome of the contest in Shubra al-Khayma had far-reaching ramifications for the national political scene.[2]

2. This analysis contradicts the argument of Robert Tignor in his recent study of the development of Egyptian capitalism, *State, Private Enterprise, and Economic Change in Egypt,* which disregards the role of workers in shaping the course of industrial development. Moreover, insofar as he does deal with the working class, Tignor is often misleading and inaccurate. This may be the result of his uncritical reliance on European language sources, which are hostile to the working class and contain tendentious accounts of labor history. In a recent article Tignor also argues that Egyptian workers were passive and did not take the initiative in demanding economic equity in the postwar period, except when encouraged by nationalist politicians. The account presented in this book differs sharply with that view. See "Equity in Egypt's Recent Past: 1945–

454 Conclusion

The strikes at Shubra al-Khayma and Mahalla al-Kubra were the most forceful manifestations of the recurrent upsurges of militant working class protest in the post-World War II period and made the "labor question" a pressing item on the national economic and political agenda. By this time the existence of a working class and the need to ameliorate its conditions by action in the political arena were recognized by many politically conscious Egyptians across a wide range of ideological orientations and party affiliations. The political paralysis of the regime blocked effective action on this issue. Many other urgent reforms widely regarded as essential, such as land reform, were also not implemented as the old regime tottered toward its final collapse. But there is no doubt that the "labor question" was an important component of the social crisis that brought the monarchy to an end and set the political agenda for the regime of the Free Officers.

If it is true that the working class had become a significant factor in Egyptian society and was increasingly asserting itself as an independent political force in the years before 1952, how then can we explain the voluntary abdication of that independent political role by a significant section of the trade union leadership in the course of the crisis of March 1954 and its eventual acquiescence to incorporation into the state apparatus under the regime of Jamal 'Abd al-Nasir? The traditional explanation of "orthodox" Marxists has emphasized the "betrayal" of the trade union leaders. As already pointed out, if personal aggrandizement may have been a factor in the actions of certain trade union leaders, this can not fully explain the success of the general strike that confirmed Jamal 'Abd al-Nasir and the RCC in power. Moreover, throughout the Nasirist era the working class did not repudiate the terms of the bargain struck in March 1954. Despite sporadic strikes and other manifestations of collective action, there was nothing comparable to workers' participation in the mass movements of 1946 or 1951. These facts suggest that the events of March 1954 and their consequences must be explained by something more fundamental than the personal betrayal of trade union leaders.

The military coup of July 23, 1952 surprised and disoriented all the political forces in Egypt. Despite the communists' efforts to continue organizing workers around independent class-based demands, the nationalist appeal of the Free Officers, the economic benefits and job security of the new labor legislation, and a generous dose of repression created the conditions for the "historic compromise" of March 1954. The regime agreed to grant many of the economic demands of

---

1952," in Gouda Abdel-Khalek and Robert Tignor, eds., *The Political Economy of Income Distribution in Egypt* (New York, 1982), p. 40.

Conclusion **455**

the trade union movement and the trade union leadership agreed to accept the regime's tutelage.

The experience of March 1954 created a new point of reference for the political activity of the working class. Because the RCC clearly would not tolerate independent political initiatives from below of any sort, continued militant mass action would have resulted in repression and isolation of the working class. Moreover, the political successes of the new regime, especially the evacuation of British troops from the Suez Canal Zone and the nationalization of the Canal, made the state the leading actor in the national movement, and confronted the workers' movement with a historic choice: to press its independent demands in opposition to the limits imposed by the state and risk becoming isolated from the nationalist movement that had provided the overall context for working class political activity throughout the twentieth century, or to accommodate itself to the new conditions. Given the overwhelming importance of nationalist demands in the broader political arena as well as for the workers' movement itself, the relatively small size of the working class, the internal divisions among the leaders of even the most highly concentrated sectors of industrial and transport workers, the lack of a firm alliance with the peasantry, the political immaturity of the trade unions, and the lack of a unified political leadership the option of sustained opposition to the state in the name of the independent demands of the working class was not a viable political orientation.

The "historic compromise" of March 1954 thus reflects both the strength and the weakness of the Egyptian workers' movement as it had developed up to that point. Its principal strength was that by fusing the demands of the working class with those of the broader national struggle, any political force aspiring to address the national question was also compelled to address the demands of the working class. However, the framework of the nationalist movement was for a long time defined principally by the leadership of the Wafd in bourgeois-liberal terms that did not promote the independent demands and interests of the working class. The Wafdist Vanguard and communist forces attempted to alter the social character of the national movement by promoting such concepts as the leading role of the working class within the national movement. These ideas did reach a broad audience, and there is no doubt that the Marxist left had extensive influence on postwar Egyptian political thought, even within the ranks of the RCC. But 'Abd al-Nasir and the RCC were unalterably committed to the leading role of the military and of the state as fundamental political principles. Eventually the RCC's nationalist successes enabled it to impose this statist perspective on the national movement

456 Conclusion

and on political life after 1954. The weaknesses of the workers' movement noted above made it impossible for the working class to resist the new political current. In the absence of a strong and widespread ideological commitment to political independence per se, most workers and their trade union leaders accepted the government's control, particularly once the RCC had made good on its economic and political promises.

The decline of working class collective action after March 1954 might appear to indicate an end to its significance in modern Egypt. But it is not possible to properly understand the apparent passivity of the working class after March 1954 without appreciating that the concrete outcome of working class struggle up to that date created the conditions for a new pattern of relations between labor, capital, and the state which gradually emerged in the late 1950s and 1960s.

Adam Przeworski has argued that "Classes are organized and disorganized as outcomes of continuous struggles."[3] This should not be interpreted as an argument that political struggle alone can create or destroy the potential for class-based organization and action. This potential is brought into existence by the objective processes of capital accumulation and the expansion of capitalist relations of production, and it cannot be reversed. But it does suggest that class consciousness and collective action are shaped by what workers perceive to be the requirements and possibilities of the struggles in which they are currently engaged, and by the outcomes of actual past struggles. In this sense the Egyptian working class was "disorganized" as a historical actor by the partial success of its struggles up to 1954, the government's assumption of responsibility for improving the standard of living of workers and peasants, and its concrete, albeit limited, achievements in this regard.

As a result of the workers' history of organization and struggle, the RCC could not deal with them by offering empty promises as the Wafd had done in the 1920s, or by using naked repression as Sidqi had done in the 1930s. Repression was, of course, employed, in Kafr al-Dawwar, Imbaba, and elsewhere, and many of the government's commitments were more rhetorical than real. But the continued stability of the new government was heavily dependent on its making real concessions to workers far beyond what any previous Egyptian government could have envisioned. It quickly implemented legislation improving wages, job security, and social benefits.

Beyond these measures, the new regime moved to institutionalize the labor movement by establishing a General Federation of Egyptian

---

3. Przeworski. "Proletariat into a Class," p. 371.

Conclusion **457**

Trade Unions under government auspices in 1957, and a Ministry of Labor in 1959. Anwar Salama became the first president of the General Federation of Egyptian Trade Unions and later minister of labor. Since that time the trade unions have been fully integrated into the apparatus of the Egyptian state. Many politically inclined workers and trade union officials have acquired official positions with government-paid salaries in the vast bureaucracies of the General Federation of Egyptian Trade Unions and the Ministry of Labor (now the Ministry of Manpower and Training). Bureaucratization of the trade union leadership was, of course, a central component in the strategy of labor control under the regimes of both Jamal 'Abd al-Nasir and Anwar al-Sadat. Nonetheless, official recognition of the importance of the trade union movement has also enhanced the economic and social status of the Egyptian workers.

This process was further developed during the 1960s when "Arab socialism" became the official ideology of the state. Arab socialism, although it explicitly rejected the concept of class struggle within Egyptian society, recognized the legitimacy of class as a valid social and political category. According to the theory of Arab socialism, Egypt's revolutionary transformation was to be led by a "bloc of popular forces" that included workers, peasants, soldiers, intellectuals, and "national capital." In reality, the social strata referred to in this slogan did not equally exercise state power, or ultimately share the same interests, nor was the regime's refusal to acknowledge this the result of willful ignorance. Although the regime promoted a significant amelioration in the living and working conditions of workers and peasants, it required that they remain in a subordinate role within the Nasirist state. Whatever its political rhetoric, the regime of 'Abd al-Nasir was engaged in building a state capitalist economic system.

Despite the ultimate failure of "Arab socialism," government action inspired by this slogan did establish the working class as a recognized force in the institutions of state and society. In the 1960s, legislation was enacted requiring that workers constitute at least 50 percent of the management committees of public sector enterprises, and that workers and peasants comprise 50 percent of the membership of the National Assembly. These years also witnessed a modest redistribution of income in favor of regularly employed workers, white collar employees, and middle peasants. The standard of living of urban workers employed in the formal sector of the economy continued to rise until 1965–1966. During this period the concerns and conditions of the working class became a central feature of official political discourse, and intellectuals received official encouragement to

458 Conclusion

investigate the history of the workers' movement as the pioneering secondary works cited in this study illustrate.

The relative success of Nasirist Arab nationalism during the 1950s and 1960s also helped keep the workers' movement quiescent and within the boundaries of the nationalist movement as defined by the regime. In November 1954 an Anglo-Egyptian agreement on the complete evacuation of British troops from Egypt was reached. Although there was some popular criticism of the terms of the agreement and the failure to obtain Egyptian sovereignty over the Sudan, the agreement was considered a substantial success and received wide support. The nationalization of the Suez Canal in 1956 was also extremely popular, and increased the promotion opportunities and jobs open to Egyptians at the Suez Canal Company.

In 1956, mainly as a result of the regime's foreign policy reorientation toward "positive neutralism" and militant anti-imperialism, many communists and other former advocates of trade union independence, such as Fathi Kamil, joined ranks with the government and participated actively in the formation of the International Confederation of Arab Trade Unions, which promoted Arab nationalist sentiment among Egyptian and Arab workers. Moreover, the tripartite aggression of 1956 served to confirm, for the politically conscious Egyptian public, that the main political question of the day was still the struggle against imperialism and neocolonialism, now augmented by Zionism as a result of Israel's attack on Egypt.

Throughout the era of 'Abd al-Nasir, these issues rather than the internal class struggle dominated Egyptian politics. The official ideologues did refer to the struggle against "reaction," but as often as not this slogan meant opposition to regional Arab adversaries such as Jordan, Saudi Arabia, and Iraq. The struggle against internal reaction in Egypt was not comprehensive and thorough, though the worst abuses of the old regime were substantially eliminated.[4] Until 1967 'Abd al-Nasir appeared to be highly successful in waging the struggles he defined as central to the Egyptian and Arab political agenda. The workers' movement, under the tutelage of the government, was politically oriented toward nationalist issues, and there was virtually no explicit political opposition to this orientation. Some of the Egyptian communists spoke out against the internal deficiencies of the Nasirist regime, especially its undemocratic character, but both major tendencies in the communist movement indicated their willingness to

4. For an example of the regime's reluctance to undertake a continuing struggle against internal reaction see the discussion of the "Kamshish affair" of 1966 in Leonard Binder, *In a Moment of Enthusiasm: Political Power and the Second Stratum in Egypt* (Chicago, 1978), pp. 341 ff.

Conclusion   **459**

accept the terms of the Nasirist political agenda by voluntarily dissolving the two communist parties in the spring of 1965.

It should also be said that significant repression was directed against those who rejected the government's view of the appropriate role for workers in the new regime: many communist trade unionists spent long years in jail during the 1950s and 1960s; unions were supervised by government security agencies, and the government invalidated the election of opposition union officials. Repression is a factor in explaining the relative quiescence of the working class since 1954, but it has not been severe or comprehensive enough, except in 1959–1964, to be the major factor. Repression would not have succeeded had it not been for the improved material and social conditions of the working class and the continuing ideological hegemony of nationalism as defined by Jamal 'Abd al-Nasir.

When viewed in historical perspective, the crisis of March 1954 allowed the working class to realize some very significant gains, and began the process of consolidating working class support for the regime which was augmented by the nationalization of the Suez Canal, the tripartite aggression and its outcome, the nationalizations of 1960–1961, and the regime's emphasis on the expansion of modern industry. The working class grew in size, gained political legitimacy and status, and the standard of living of the organized sector of the working class continued to rise for more than a decade. The consciousness of the working class was remade by these experiences, and this explains why the bargain struck in March 1954 was sustained by the majority of workers.

The economic strategy of Nasirism was based on capital-intensive development of industry, economic planning, and a certain amount of income redistribution in favor of the poorer sectors of the population. Maintaining a high level of consumption among the poorer strata contributed greatly to the legitimacy of the regime and its stability, and was partly rooted in the desire to prevent the recurrence of the labor unrest that had characterized the years before the military coup. This economic strategy began to falter as early as 1965 because the economy could not sustain simultaneously high levels of investment and consumption. The failure of this strategy eventually led to its replacement by the "open door" economic policy. The first tentative steps toward this policy were initiated cautiously by 'Abd al-Nasir in the late 1960s and then enthusiastically elaborated by Anwar al-Sadat, especially after 1974. A comprehensive analysis of the open door policy can not be offered here, and many competing interpretations are readily available, though most would agree that its adoption

460 Conclusion

represents an abandonment of the political and economic commitments embodied in the historic compromise of March 1954.

Nonetheless, despite the government's considerable efforts to dismantle much of the Nasirist economic apparatus during the open door era, it has continued to maintain the institutionalization of the labor movement established in the 1950s and 1960s. This has helped contain the threat of potential working class protest while the nationalist movement, having achieved the evacuation of British troops and the Egyptianization of the economy and society, has receded in importance as a political factor. Nationalism alone can no longer provide a context for working class political action. The era of the open door has also coincided with the massive migration of Egyptian labor to the oil-rich Arab countries which has partially shifted the locus of contradiction between labor and capital away from Egypt and provided a critical infusion of cash that has offset the negative effects of the open door on workers' standard of living. All these factors have perpetuated the disorganization of the working class.

Despite this continuing disorganization, it is clear from the scanty evidence currently available that there was a working class response to the open door policy. There was an upsurge of strikes, sit-ins, demonstrations, and other manifestations of working class collective action during 1975 and 1976. Most of these actions were sporadic and unorganized. The textile workers of Shubra al-Khayma and Mahalla al-Kubra, the Cairo transport workers, and the approximately 10,000 workers at the Hilwan iron and steel mill were prominent in this period. The workers of Hilwan, the site of many related and subsidiary industries in addition to the iron and steel mill, as well as the older textile mills, appear to have been exceptionally well organized in contrast to the overall lack of organization of the working class outside the channels of the official trade union movement. It is important to note that the emergence of Hilwan as an industrial center, and especially the iron and steel works, is a product of Nasirist economic policy. The upsurge in working class activism culminated in substantial working class participation in the food riots of January 18–19, 1977, which began in the Hilwan factory area. The importance of the mass struggles of the mid-1970s should not be exaggerated: with some local exceptions, notably in Hilwan, no viable political or organizational framework for sustained struggle was established. Nonetheless, the continuing presence of the working class as a historical actor is evident.

After 1977 the crisis of the Egyptian economy was to a limited extent alleviated by a massive infusion of American aid provided as a result of Egypt's peace treaty with Israel. In addition, Egypt enjoyed

Conclusion **461**

relatively high revenues from massive remittances from workers employed abroad, the export of oil, fees from the use of the Suez Canal, and increased tourism. Still, none of these sources of income derived from the economy's increased productivity: the industrial sector in particular contributed little to economic growth in the 1970s and early 1980s—an indication that the basic structural crisis of the economy has not been resolved.

Under these conditions, the Egyptian working class can not be written out of the historical process. The strike and riot of textile workers in Kafr al-Dawwar in September 1984 may signal an end to the period of relative economic peace and labor quiescence. But whether or not this occurs, these events are an important reminder that the working class remains a factor to be reckoned with in Egyptian society. Both because of and despite its experiences in the Nasir period, it has grown in size, self-confidence, and organizational capacity. Even though presently unorganized and relatively inactive, the working class retains a potential for mobilization and collective action which will insure it a part in shaping Egypt's future.

Bibliography

Unpublished Materials

I. Interviews
II. Private Papers
III. Government Documents
    Belgium
    Egypt
    France
    Great Britain
IV. Labor Materials
V. Trades Union Congress
VI. Unpublished Dissertations

Published Materials

I. Newspapers and Periodicals
II. Egyptian Government Documents
III. British Government Documents
IV. Trade Union and Political Documents
V. Memoirs and Writings of Labor Activists
VI. Books and Articles in Arabic
VII. Books and Articles in English, French, and Hebrew

Unpublished Materials

I. Interviews (recorded in Cairo in Arabic by Joel Beinin and Ellis Goldberg, except as noted)

Ḥasan 'Abd al-Raḥmān (December 7, 1980).
Muḥammad 'Alī 'Āmir (November 27, December 5, and 9, 1980).
Jamāl al-Bannā (September 18, October 5, December 22, 1980, and January 3, 1981).

464 Bibliography

Raymond Douek (Paris, June 4, 1981, by Joel Beinin, in English).
Muhammad Jād (February 16 and 28, 1981).
Fathī Kāmil (November 29 and December 3, 1979, by Joel Beinin; October 13, 28, and December 20, 1980, February 14, and 21, 1981).
Khālid Muhyi al-Dīn (May 17, 1981, by Joel Beinin).
'Abd al-'Azīz Mustafa (January 23, 1980, by Zachary Lockman, unrecorded).
Mūsā Sabrī (April 11, 1981, by Joel Beinin, in English).
Ahmad Sādiq Sa'd (February 10, 1981).
Muhammad Mutawallī al-Sha'rāwī (Kafr al-Dawwār, January 7, 1981, and Cairo, April 3, 1981).
Muhammad Sharīf (October 28, by Joel Beinin; and December 3, 1980, unrecorded).
'Atiyya al-Sīrafī (Mit Ghamr, December 29, 1980).
Ahmad Tāhā (December 2, 1979, May 1, 1981, by Joel Beinin).
Muhammad Kāmil al-'Uqaylī (February 14, 1981, by Joel Beinin, unrecorded).
Taha Sa'd 'Uthmān (October 28, November 5, December 15, 1980, and January 22, 1981).

II. Private Papers

Jamal al-Bannā (materials relating to the Cairo textile workers, etc.)
Yūsuf Darwīsh (materials on communist activities among workers).
Yūsuf al-Mudarrik (trade union documents and publications, in the possession of Prof. Ra'ūf 'Abbās).
Rif'at al-Sa'īd (Cairo transport workers' leaflets, etc.)

III. Government Documents

Belgium. Archives du Ministère des Affaires Étrangères, Brussels; files marked "AF 10" and others (in French).
Egypt. Mahfūzāt majlis al-wuzarā', nizārat al-dākhiliyya (in the Dār al-Wathā'iq, Cairo) "taqārīr al-amn":
(1) "Rapports du jour" from Branch B, Public Security Department, Commandant of the Alexandria City Police, to Sa'īd Pasha Dhū al-Faqār, Grand Chamberlain of the Royal Dīwān, June 1923 to April 1929 (in French).
(2) Reports from the Office of the Commandant, Cairo City Police, to the Undersecretary of State for Public Security at the Ministry of the Interior, July 1923 to November 1924 (in French).
(3) Reports from the Special Branch, Cairo Police, to Sa'īd Pasha Dhū al-Faqār, Grand Chamberlain of the Royal Dīwān, designated *sirrī siyāsī* ("secret/political"), August 1926 to November 1926 (in Arabic).
(4) Reports from the Special Branch, Cairo Police, to the Undersecretary of State for Public Security at the Ministry of the Interior, February 1940 to December 1941 (in Arabic).
Egypt. Mahfūzāt majlis al-wuzarā', nizārat al-ashghāl, maslahat al-sikka al-hadīd (in the Dār al-Wathā'iq, Cairo), "mawdū'āt mutanawwa'a": cartons marked "28 February 1910–November 1923" and "2 January 1882–22 December 1918" (in Arabic).
Egypt. Maslahat al-'amal (Archives in the Ministry of Manpower and Training, Heliopolis, in Arabic).
"Milaff 'uqūd al-'amal al-mushtarik—al-suways." Dossier 11/4/3/5 pt. 1.
" 'Uqūd al-'amal al-mushtarik—al-qanāh." Dossier 11/4/3/4.
"Ittifāqiyyāt bi-ma'rifat lijān al-tawfīq—muhāfazat al-suways." Dossier 11/4/5/5.

Bibliography **465**

"Ittifāqiyyāt bi- maʻrifat lijān al-tawfīq—mudīriyyat al-gharbiyya." Dossier 11/4/5/8.
"Ittifāqiyyāt bi-maʻrifat maktab al-ʻamal—maktab būr saʻīd." Dossiers 11/4/6/4 pt. 1 and pt. 2.
"Ittifāqiyyāt bi-maʻrifat maktab al-ʻamal—maktab al-suways." Dossier 11/4/6/8.
"Ittifāqiyyāt bi-maʻrifat maktab al-ʻamal bi-dimyāt." Dossier 11/4/6/12.
"Maḥkamat istiʼnāf al-qāhira. hayʼat al-taḥkīm." Decisions—1952–53.
France. Archives of the French Embassy in Cairo.
Great Britain. Foreign Office (Archives in the Public Record Office, London).
FO 141
FO 371   FO 633
FO 407   FO 921
FO 423   FO 922

IV. Labor Materials

Memoirs of ʻAbd al-Raḥmān Fahmī Pasha, in the Dār al-Wathāʼiq, Cairo (in Arabic).
Minutes of meetings of the Executive Board of the Cairo Tramway Workers' Union, November 1939–August 1942; found at the offices of the Cairo tramway and trolleybus workers' union committee (in Arabic).

V. Trades Union Congress

File T1903, "Egypt," in the TUC Archives, London.

VI. Unpublished Dissertations

ʻAbd al-ʻAzīz, Nawāl. "al-Ḥaraka al-ʻummāliyya wa-atharuhā fī taṭawwur al-taʼrīkh al-siyāsī fī miṣr, 1899–1930." M.A. thesis, Cairo University, 1972–73.
Abdel Messih, Fouad. "The Labor Policy of the Anglo-Egyptian Oilfields Company." B.A. thesis, American University in Cairo, 1952.
ʻAshmāwī, al-Sayyid Muḥammad. "Taʼrīkh al-fikr al-siyāsī al-miṣrī, 1945–1952." Ph.D. diss., Cairo University, 1977.
Bahtimy, Ikbal. "The Mehalla el-Kobra Cotton Industry." B.A. thesis, American University in Cairo, 1952.
Botman, Selma. "Oppositional Politics in Egypt: The Communist Movement, 1936–1954." Ph.D. diss., Harvard University, 1984.
El-Mallakh, Ragaei. "The Effects of the Second World War on the Economic Development of Egypt." Ph.D. diss., Rutgers University, 1954.
Goldschmidt, Arthur. "The Egyptian Nationalist Party." Ph.D. diss., Harvard University, 1968.
Gresh, Marie-Dominique. "Le P.C.F. et L'Égypte: 1950–56." Mémoire de Maîtrise, Université de Paris I, 1976–77.
Hussein, Mona Tewfik. "Regional Industrial Wage Differentials in Egypt: 1943–1948." M.A. thesis, American University in Cairo, 1979.
Ibrāhīm, Muḥammad al-Saʻīd. "al-Wafd waʼl-ḥaraka al-ʻummāliyya fī miṣr." Ph.D. diss., Cairo University, 1979.
Kamel, Ibrahim Ahmed. "The Impact of Nasser's Regime on Labor Relations in Egypt." Ph.D. diss., University of Michigan, 1970.
Khairy, Khaireya. "The Nutritive Aspects of Egyptian Labor." B.A. thesis, American University in Cairo, 1946.
el-Messiri, Sawsan. "Class and Community in an Egyptian Textile Town." Ph.D. diss., Hull University, 1980.

466 Bibliography

Nagi, Mostafa H. "Demographic and Socio-Economic Analysis of the Egyptian Labor Force, 1937–85." Ph.D. diss., University of Connecticut, 1970.
Orphy, Hussein Ali. "An Analysis of Welfare Programs in Egyptian Industries: A Tobacco Factory Case Study." B.A. thesis, American University in Cairo, 1955.
el-Tatawy, Nadia Abdel Moneim. "Cotton Textile Industry and Industrial Development in Egypt." M.A. thesis, American University in Cairo, 1972.
Thieck, Jean-Pierre. "La Journée du 21 février 1946 dans l'histoire du mouvement national égyptien." Mémoire de D.E.S., Université de Paris VIII, 1974.
Williams, Neil V. "Factory Employment and Family Relationships in an Egyptian Village." Ph.D. diss., University of Michigan, 1964.

Published Materials

I. Newspapers and Periodicals (published in Cairo and available in the Dār al-Kutub, Cairo, except as noted).

al-Ahrām
al-Akhbār
Akhbār al-yawm
al-'Alamayn (1944)
'Āmil al-mahalla
    (1947–49, Mahalla al-Kubrā)
al-'Āmil al-miṣrī (1930)
al-'Amal (1946–47)
al-Asās
al-Balāgh
al-Bashīr
    (1950, Rif'at al-Sa'īd papers)
La Bourse Égyptienne
    (Alexandria)
al-Ḍamīr
    (1945–46, Yūsuf al-Mudarrik papers)
al-Da'wa (1951–54)
L'Égypte Industrielle
The Egyptian Gazette
al-Fajr al-jadīd (1945–46)
Ḥurriyyat al-shu'ūb (1942–45)
Ibn al-balad (1933–34)
al-Ikhwān al-muslimūn (1942–48)
Ittiḥād al-'ummāl (1924–25)
al-Jabha (1945)
al-Jamāhīr (1947–48)
al-Jihād
al-Kutla

Majallat 'ummāl al-sikka
    al-ḥadīd (1909)
al-Malāyīn (1951)
Minbar al-sharq
al-Mu'āraḍa (1952)
al-Mu'ayyad
al-Mugaṭṭam
al-Mustaqbal (1950)
Mu'tamar al-niqābiyyīn
    (1950, Yūsuf al-Mudarrik papers)
al-Nahār (1941)
Nahḍat al-'ummāl (1937–51, Tanta)
al-Nās (1951)
Rūḥ al-'aṣr (1930)
al-Ṣafā' (1931)
Ṣawt al-umma
al-Shabbān al-wafdiyyūn
    (1936–38)
al-Shu'a' (1938)
Shubrā (1937–39, 1942–43, Shubra)
al-Siyāsa
al-Taḥrīr
al-Ṭalī'a (1945–46)
al-Taṭawwur (1940)
al-'Ummāl (1924)
Umm durmān (1945–46)
al-Wafd al-miṣrī
al-Wājib (1942, 1952)
al-Yarā'
al-Zamān

II. Egyptian Government Documents

Amīn, Aḥmad Ḥilmī. "Taqrīr maṣlaḥat al-'amal 11 yūlyū 1939." Reprinted in al-Thaqāfa al-'ummāliyya, June 1967.

Bibliography **467**

Egyptian State Railways. *Report of the Egyptian State Railways and Telegraphs for 1907.* Cairo, 1908.
Lajnat al-tijāra wa'l-ṣinā'a. *Taqrīr.* Cairo, 1916.
Majmū'at maḍābit majlis al-nuwwāb. Cairo, 1926.
Ministère des Finances. *Annuaires Statistiques.* Cairo.
Ministère des Finances. *Statistique des sociétés anonymes par actions travaillant principalement en Égypte au 31 décembre 1911.* Cairo, 1913.
Ministère des Finances. *Statistique des sociétés anonymes travaillant principalement en Égypte juillet 1940.* Cairo, 1940.
Ministry of Finance. *Almanac 1939.* Cairo, 1939.
Ministry of Finance. *The Census of Egypt Taken in 1907.* Cairo, 1909.
Ministry of Finance. *The Census of Egypt Taken in 1917.* Cairo, 1921.
Ministry of Finance. *Census of Industrial Production 1950.* Cairo, 1953.
Ministry of Finance. *Index Numbers of Wholesale Prices in Egypt 1930–1935.* Cairo, 1936.
Ministry of Finance. *Industrial and Commercial Census 1927.* Cairo, 1931.
Ministry of Finance. *Industrial and Commercial Census 1937.* Cairo, 1942.
Ministry of Finance. *Industrial and Commerical Census 1947.* Cairo, 1955.
Ministry of Finance. *Statistics of Wages and Working Hours in Egypt (1945–1950).* Cairo, 1946–1951.
Ministry of Social Affairs. *The Labour Department.* Cairo, 1951.
Sa'īd, 'Abd al-Mughnī. "Ziyāra ta'rīkhiyya li-'ummāl al-manājim (10 ayyām fī al-baḥr al-aḥmar: aghusṭus 1946)." Reprinted in *Kitāb al-'amal,* no. 201 (November 1980).
al-Waqā'i' al-miṣriyya. April 1945.
Wizārat al-dākhiliyya. *Taqrīr 'an ḥālat al-amn al-'āmm fī al-qaṭar al-miṣrī fī al-mudda min sanat 1930 ila sanat 1937.* Cairo, 1939.
Wizārat al- shu'ūn al-ijtimā'iyya wa'l-'amal. *Taqwīm al-niqābāt wa'l-ittiḥādāt al-'ummāliyya fī jumhūriyyat miṣr.* Cairo, 1956.
Wizārat al-tijāra wa'l-ṣinā'a. *Taqrīr lajnat baḥth al-wasā'il al-kafīla li-musā'adat ṣinā'at al-ghazl wa'l-nasīj wa-tashjī'ihā.* Cairo, 1950.

III. British Government Documents

Department of Overseas Trade. *Report of the United Kingdom Trade Mission to Egypt, February–March 1931.* London, 1931.
Reports by His Majesty's Agent and Consul-General on the Finances, Administration, and Condition of Egypt and the Soudan in 1904. Egypt no. 1 (1905), C. 2409.
Reports by His Majesty's Agent and Consul-General on the Finances, Administration, and Condition of Egypt and the Soudan in 1905. Egypt no. 1 (1906), C. 2817.
Report of His Majesty's Agent and Consul-General on the Administration, Finances, and Condition of Egypt and the Soudan in 1906. Egypt no. 1 (1907), C. 3394.

IV. Trade Union and Political Documents

Bureau des Questions Syndicales. *Le mouvement syndicale en Égypte.* Cairo, May 1948.
Ḥizb al-'amal al-ishtirākī. *Barnāmaj.* Cairo, 1949.
Ḥizb al-'ummāl. *Dustūr ḥizb al-'ummāl.* Cairo, n.d.
Kādir 'ummāl al-trām bi-ḥukm hay'at al-taḥkīm: yūlyū 1949. Cairo, 1949
al-Lajna al-taḥdīriyya li'l-ittiḥād al-'āmm li'l-niqābāt al-miṣriyya [wa-]mu'tamar niqābāt àl-sharikāt wa'l-mu'assasāt al-ahliyya. *Bayān mushtarik.* Cairo, February 4, 1946.

468 Bibliography

al-Lajna al-taḥdīriyya li'l-ittiḥād al-ʿāmm li'l-niqābāt al-miṣriyya. *Lā'iḥat al-niẓām al-asāsi li'l-ittiḥād al-ʿāmm li'l-niqābāt al-miṣriyya.* Cairo, n.d.
al-Lajna al-waṭaniyya li'l-ʿummāl wa'l-ṭalaba. *Bayān.* Cairo, 1946.
Lajnat al-ʿummāl li'l-taḥrīr al-qawmī. *Barnāmaj lajnat al-ʿummāl li'l-taḥrīr al-qawmī.* Cairo, 1945.
Mashrūʿ lā'iḥat al-niẓām al-asāsī li-mu'tamar niqābāt ʿummāl miṣr. Cairo(?), n.d.
Niqābat ʿummāl al-maṭābiʿ bi'l-qāhira. *Mudhakkira bi-talab taʿdīl qānūn niqābāt al-ʿummāl.* Cairo, November 1953.
Niqābat ʿummāl al-maṭābiʿ bi'l-qāhira. *Mulāḥaẓa ʿalā qānūn ʿaqd al-ʿamal al-fardī.* Shubra, 1950.
Niqābat ʿummāl sharikat asmint būrtland bi-ḥilwān. *Qānūn.* Cairo, 1943.
Niqābat ʿummāl sharikat sāfūn al-handasiyya. *Lā'iḥat al-niẓām al-asāsī . . . wa'l-lā'iḥa al-dākhiliyya wa-mā ḥaṣalat ʿalayhi al-niqāba min matālib mundhu tasjīlihā fī 19/3/1944 ḥattā ākhir 1949.* n.p., n.d.
Niqābat ʿummāl wa-mustakhdimay al-sharika al-sharqiyya li'l-dukhān wa'l-sijāyir. *Niqābatuka fī ʿashar sanawāt.* Cairo, 1953.
Sharikat al-ghazl wa'l-nasīj al-ahliyya al-miṣriyya wa'l-sharika al-miṣriyya li-ṣināʿat al-mansūjāt. *ʿAqd al-ʿamal al-mushtarik.* Alexandria, 1948.
Sharikat al-ghazl wa'l-nasīj al-ahliyya al-miṣriyya wa'l-sharika al-miṣriyya li-ṣināʿat al-mansūjāt. *ʿAqd al-ʿamal al-mushtarik wa-qarārāt al-lajna al-ʿulyā li-tawḥīd shurūṭ al-ʿamal wa'l-ujūr bi-masāniʿ al-ghazl wa'l-nasīj.* Alexandria, 1949.

V. Memoirs and Writings of Labor Activists

ʿAbd Allāh, ʿAbd al-Wārith ʿAbd al-Ḥalīm. *al-Waʿy al-niqābī fī miṣr.* Cairo, 1957.
ʿAlī, Muḥammad Zakī. *Taqrīr ʿan ḥālat ʿummāl al-trām bi'l-qāhira maʿa kalima ʿan al-ʿummāl.* Cairo, 1945.
ʿAllām, Husayn. *Niqābāt al-ʿummāl.* Cairo, 1945.
ʿAmāra, Muḥammad Ḥasan. "Min mudhakkirāt niqābī qadīm," serialized in *al-Thaqāfa al-ʿummāliyya,* October 1975 to May 1976. Also in a slightly variant typewritten form, titled "Taṭawwur al-ḥaraka al-ʿummāliyya fī miṣr," obtained from Mu'assasat al-Thaqāfa al-ʿUmmāliyya, Cairo.
Anon. "Mudhakkirāt kumsārī trām," serialized in *al-Nīl,* March–April 1924.
al-ʿArābī, Maḥmūd Ḥusnī. *Mā hiya al-niqāba?* Cairo, 1931.
———. *89 Shahr fī al-manfā.* Cairo, 1938.
al-ʿAskarī, Maḥmūd. "Min ta'rīkh al-ḥaraka al-ʿummāliyya al- miṣriyya." Serialized in *al-ʿUmmāl,* June 9, 1975 to October 23, 1978.
———. "Liqā' al-mufakkirīn al-ishtirākiyyīn al-miṣriyyīn bi-ḥarakat al-ṭabaqa al-ʿāmila wa-niqābātihā marra ukhrā." *al-Thaqāfa al-ʿummāliyya,* September 15, 1968.
———. "Taʿlīq ʿalā ṣafḥa maṭwiyya min ta'rīkh niqābat ʿummāl al-nasīj." *al-Thaqāfa al-ʿummāliyya,* May 15, 1969.
al-Bannā, Jamāl. "al-Ḥaraka al-niqābiyya al-miṣriyya mā bayna shāriʿ najīb al-rihānī wa-shāriʿ al-jalāʿ." *al-Thaqāfa al- ʿummāliyya,* November 1, 1973.
Boulad, Emile. *Les Tramways du Caire en 1919.* Cairo, 1919.
Darwīsh, Yūsuf. *Sharḥ qānūn iṣābāt al-ʿamal.* Cairo, 1944.
Faraḥat, Aḥmad. *Ḥayat al-ʿāmil al-miṣrī.* Cairo, 1939.
Ghānim, Amīn al-Ḥusaynī. *al-Ḥaraka al-ʿummāliyya fī miṣr wa-sirr tadahwuriha.* Cairo, 1934.
Ghunaym, Fu'ād. *al-ʿĀmil wa'l-niqāba fī al-ʿahd al-dhahabī.* Cairo, 1944.
Ḥalīm, ʿAbbās. *al-ʿUmmāl al-miṣriyyūn.* Cairo, 1934.

Bibliography **469**

———. "al-'Ummāl al-miṣriyyūn fī al-'ishrīn sana al-mādīyya." *al-Majalla al-jadīda* 3 (November 1934).

Ḥusayn, Ḥasan. *Qaḍīyat al-'ummāl fī miṣr wa-'alājihā.* Cairo, 1937.

'Īsawī, 'Abd al-Mun'im. "Ṣafḥa maṭwiyya min ta'rīkh niqābāt 'ummāl al-nasīj." *al-Thaqāfa al-'ummāliyya*, May 1, 1969.

Kāmil, Anwar. *Mashākil al-'ummāl fī miṣr.* Cairo, 1941.

Kāmil, Fatḥī. *Ma'a al-ḥaraka al-niqābiyya al-misriyya fī niṣf qarn: ṣafaḥāt min dhikrayāt.* Cairo, 1985.

al-Maghribī, Fatḥī. *Ānā al-'āmil.* Cairo, 1946.

al-Miṣrī, Aḥmad. *Miṣr fī al-mu'tamarāt al-'ummāliyya al- duwwaliyya.* Alexandria, 1945.

al-Mudarrik, Muḥammad Yusuf. *Dalīl al-ta'ārif al-niqābī.* Cairo, 1947.

———. *Ḥawla mushkilat 'ummāl al-maḥalla: taḥqīq 'ummālī.* Cairo, 1947.

———. *Khiṭāb al-zamīl Muḥammad Yūsuf al-Mudarrik, murashshakh al-'ummāl 'an dā'irat shubrā al-khayma.* n.p., 1949.

———. "Ṣafḥa min ḥarakat al-'ummāl qabla al-thawra." Serialized in *al-Thaqāfa al-'ummāliyya*, August 15, 1967 to September 1, 1969.

———. *al-Tarbiyya al-niqābiyya.* Cairo, 1948.

Munīb, Muṣṭafa Kāmil. "Aḥwāl al-'āmilāt fī al-mahalla al-kubra." *al-Ṭalī'a* 1 (March 15, 1946): 7–12.

———. *I'ānat ghilā' al-ma'īsha wa-taḥdīd al-ujūr.* Cairo, 1950(?).

Nuṣayr, Ibrāhīm. *Ṣayḥat al-'ummāl li-ilghā' qānūn 'aqd al-'amal al-fardī.* Cairo, 1952.

al-Qalyūbī, Murād. *Mashrū' qānūn bi-sha'n al-tawfīq wa'l-taḥkīm fī munāza'āt al-'amal.* Cairo, 1948.

Qandīl, Sayyid. *al-'Āmil wa'l-niqāba.* Cairo, 1948.

———. *Kayfa nuḥarrir anfusanā?* Cairo, 1946.

———. *Niqābiyyatī—al-risāla al-'ummāliyya al-ūlā.* Cairo, 1938.

Sa'īd, 'Abd al-Mughnī. *Niḍāl al-'ummāl wa-thawrat yūlyū.* Cairo, 1968.

al-Shāfi'ī, 'Abd al-Mun'im Nāṣir. *Ba'ḍ mashākil al-'amal fī miṣr.* Cairo, 1939.

al-Shantanāwī, Ḥusnī, ed. "al-'Amal wa'l-'ummāl fī miṣr." Special issue of *Majallat kulliyyat al-ḥuqūq* 8 (January 1935).

al-Ṣīrafī, 'Aṭiyya. *'Askarat al-ḥayāh al-'ummāliyya wa'l-niqābiyya fī miṣr.* Cairo, 1983.

'Uthmān, Ṭaha Sa'd. *Maḥāḍir wa-taqārīr al-lajna al-'ulyā al-mukawwana sanat 1947* [i.e., 1946] *li-baḥth maṭālib al-'ummāl.* n.p., 1946.

———. *Min ta'rīkh al-ṭabaqa al-'āmila al-miṣriyya: mudhakkirāt wa-wathā'iq.* 2 vols. Cairo, 1982 (al-kitāb al- thānī); Shubrā al-Khayma, 1983 (al-kitāb al-awwal: kifāḥ 'ummāl al-nasīj).

———. "Mudhakkirāt wa-wathā'iq min ta'rīkh al-tabaqa al- 'amila." Serialized in *al-Kātib* 11 (July 1971) to 12 (July 1972).

———. *Niḍāl 'ummāl al-nasīj al-mīkānīkī bi'l-qāhira.* Cairo, 1946.

VI. Books and Articles in Arabic

'Abbās, Ra'ūf. *al-Ḥaraka al-'ummāliyya fī miṣr, 1899–1952.* Cairo, 1967.

———. *al-Ḥaraka al-'ummāliyya al-miṣriyya fī ḍaw' al- wathā'iq al-barīṭāniyya, 1924–1937.* Cairo, 1975.

'Abd al-Ḥalīm, Maḥmūd. *al-Ikhwān al-muslimūn: aḥdāth ṣana'at al- ta'rīkh, ru'ya min al-dākhil.* Alexandria, 1979.

Aḥmad, Kamāl Maẓhar. *al-Ṭabaqa al-'āmila al-irāqiyya: al-takawwun wa-bidāyat al-taḥarruk.* Baghdad, 1981.

Aḥmad, Muḥammad Ḥasan (pseud.). *al-Ikhwān al-muslimūn fī al-mizān.* Cairo, 1946.

470 Bibliography

Amīn, Muḥammad Fahīm. *Ta'rīkh al-ḥaraka al-niqābiyya wa-tashrī'āt al-'amal bi'l-iqlīm al-miṣrī.* Cairo, 1961.

Anīs, Muḥammad. *4 fibrāyir 1942 fī ta'rīkh miṣr al-siyāsī.* Beirut, 1972.

——. *Dirāsāt fī wathā'iq thawrat 1919, I: al-murāsalāt al-sirriyya bayna Sa'd Zaghlūl wa-'Abd al-Raḥmān Fahmī.* Cairo, 1963.

'Aryān, Malīka. *Markaz miṣr al-iqtiṣādī.* Cairo, 1923.

al-Bannā, Ḥasan. *Mudhakkirāt al-da'wa wa'l-da'īya.* Cairo, n.d.

Barakat, 'Alī. *Taṭawwur al-milkiyya al-zirā'iyya fī miṣr, 1813–1914.* Cairo, 1977.

Bayūmī, Zakariya Sulaymān. *al-Ikhwān al-muslimūn wa'l-jamā'āt al-islāmiyya fī al-ḥayāh al-siyāsiyya al-miṣriyya, 1928–1948.* Cairo, 1978.

al-Bishrī, Ṭāriq. " 'Āmm 1946 fī al-ta'rīkh al-miṣrī." *al-Ṭalī'a* 1 (February 1965):50–58.

——. *al-Ḥaraka al-siyāsiyya fī miṣr, 1945–1952.* Cairo, 1972.

——. "Miṣr wa'l-thawra al-ijtimā'iyya, 1947–1948." *al-Kātib* no. 82 (January 1968): 101–119.

al-Disūqī, 'Āṣim Aḥmad. *Kibār mallāk al-arāḍī al-zirā'iyya wa-dawruhum fī al-mujtama' al-miṣrī, 1914–1952.* Cairo, 1975.

——. *Miṣr al-mu'āṣira fī dirāsāt al-mu'arrikhīn: dirāsa fī al-kamm wa'l-kayf.* Cairo, 1977.

——. *Miṣr fī al-ḥarb al-'ālamiyya al-thāniyya, 1939–1945.* Cairo, 1976.

Ghandūr, 'Abd Allāh al-Sayyid. *Ḥuqūq al-'aduw wa-wājibātuh fī al-niqāba wa'l-zamāla wa'l-ta'mīnāt al-ijtimā'iyya.* Cairo, 1981.

al-Ghazzālī, 'Abd al-Mun'im. *25 'Āmman min ḥayāt ittiḥād al-'ummāl al-'arab.* Beirut, 1981.

——. "al-Ḥaraka al-niqābiyya wa'l-'ummāliyya al-miṣriyya ba'da al-ḥarb al-'ālamiyya al-thāniyya." *al-Ṭalī'a* 4 (February 1968):94–102.

——. "Mawqi' 21 fibrāyir 1946 min al-ta'rīkh." *al-Ṭalī'a* 2 (February 1966):51–60.

——. *Ta'rīkh al-ḥaraka al-niqābiyya al-miṣriyya, 1899–1952.* Cairo, 1968.

al-Ghazzālī, Muḥammad. *al-Islām wa'l-manāhij al-ishtirākiyya.* Cairo, 1954.

Ḥabīb, Sa'd 'Abd al-Salām. *Mashākil al-'amal wa'l-'ummāl.* Cairo, 1951.

Ḥamdī, Ḥusayn. *Mashākil al-baṭāla: baḥth wa-dirāsa muqārina.* Cairo, 1944.

Ḥamrūsh, Aḥmad. *Qiṣṣat thawrat 23 yūlyū.* 5 vols. Beirut, 1974–81.

Ḥanna, 'Abd Allāh. *al-Ḥaraka al-'ummāliyya fī sūriyya wa-lubnān, 1900–1945.* Damascus, 1973.

Ḥarb, Ṭal'at. *Majmū'at khuṭub Ṭal'at Ḥarb.* Cairo, 1939.

Ḥasan, Aḥmad 'Āṭif. *Ta'rīkh al-ḥaraka al-niqābiyya al-miṣriyya: dirāsa taḥlīliyya.* Cairo, 1981.

Ḥasanayn, Jamal Majdī. "al-Mumayyizāt al-'āmma li'l-tarkīb al-ṭabaqi fī miṣr 'ashyat thawrat yūlyū 1952." *al-Ṭalī'a* 7 (April 1971):51–69.

al-Hawārī, 'Iṣmat. "al-Taṭawwur al-ta'rīkhī li-tashrī'āt al-'amal fī al-jumhūriyya al-'arabiyya al-muttaḥida." *Kitāb al-'amal,* no. 35 (January 1967).

Haykal, Muḥammad Ḥusayn. *Mudhakkirāt fī al-siyāsa al-miṣriyya.* 2 vols. Cairo, 1951–53.

Īsā, Ṣalāḥ. *al-Burjwaziyya al-miṣriyya wa-uslūb al-mufāwaḍa.* Cairo, 1980.

'Izz al-Dīn, Amīn. "Ba'kūkat Maḥjūb Thābit." *al-'Arabī* (May 1975).

——. "Maḥjūb Thābit." *al-Hilāl* (June 1969).

——. *Shakhṣiyyāt wa-marāḥil 'ummāliyya.* Cairo, 1970.

——. *Ta'rīkh al-ṭabaqa al-'āmila al-miṣriyya mundhu nash'atihā ḥattā thawrat 1919.* Cairo, 1967.

——. *Ta'rīkh al-ṭabaqa al-'āmila al-miṣriyya, 1919–1929.* Cairo, 1970.

——. *Ta'rīkh al-ṭabaqa al-'āmila al-miṣriyya, 1929–1939.* Cairo, 1972.

Bibliography **471**

Jād al-Mawlā, 'Abd al-Ṣamad. *Qaḍāya al-jabha al-waṭaniyya al-taqaddumiyya fī miṣr.* Beirut, 1979.

Jirjis, Fawzī. *Dirāsāt fī ta'rīkh miṣr al-siyāsī mundhu 'aṣr al-mamālīk.* Cairo, 1958.

Kāmil, Anwar. *Mashākil al-'ummāl fī miṣr: baḥth iqtiṣādī muqaddam ilā wizārat al-shu'ūn al-ijtimā'iyya.* Cairo, 1941(?).

Kaylānī, Muḥammad Sayyid. *Trām al-qāhira.* Cairo, 1946.

Khallāf, Ḥusayn. *Niqābāt al-'ummāl fī miṣr.* Cairo, 1946.

al-Khūlī, al-Bāhī. *al-Islām lā shuyū'iyya . . . wa-lā ra'smāliyya.* Cairo, 1951.

al-Kitāb al-tadhkārī 'an ḥayāt al-duktūr Maḥjūb Thābit. Cairo, 1946.

Lāshīn, 'Abd al-Khāliq. *Sa'd Zaghlūl wa-dawruhu fī al-siyāsa al-miṣriyya.* Cairo, 1975.

Maḥmūd, Ḥāfiẓ, et al. *Ṭal'at Ḥarb.* Cairo, 1936.

al-Manṣūrī, Muṣṭafa Ḥasanayn. *al-Madhāhib al-ishtirākiyya.* Cairo, 1915.

al-Maṣīlḥī, Ḥasan. *Qiṣṣatī ma'a al-shuyū'iyya.* Cairo, 1979.

Muḥākamāt kafr al-dawwār. Cairo, n.d.

Muḥammad, Muḥammad Sayyid. *Kifāḥ al-'ummāl fī al-jumhūriyya al-'arabiyya al-muttaḥida.* Cairo, n.d.

Mūsā, Salāma. ''Ḥarakat al-'ummāl fī miṣr.'' *al-Majalla al-jadīda* (February 1935).

Mutawallī, Maḥmūd. *Miṣr wa'l-ḥaraka al-shuyū'iyya khilāla al-ḥarb al-'ālamiyya al-thāniyya: dirāsa wathā'iqiyya ta'rīkhiyya.* Cairo, 1979.

―――. *Ta'rīkh miṣr al-iqtiṣādī wa'l-ijtimā'ī khilāla al-ḥarb al-'ālamiyya al-thāniyya, 1939–1945.* n.p., n.d.

―――. *al-Usūl al-ta'rīkhiyya li'l-rāsmāliyya al-miṣriyya wa-taṭawwurihā.* Cairo, 1974.

Naḥḥas, Yūsuf. *al-Fallāḥ: ḥālatuh al-iqtiṣādī wa'l-ijtimā'ī.* Cairo, 1926.

al-Nassāj, Sayyid Ḥāmid. ''Ḥarakat al-fikr al-taqaddumī fī miṣr ba'da al-ḥarb al-'ālamiyya al-thāniyya.'' *al-Kātib,* no. 172 (July 1975): 18–37.

al-Nukhaylī, Sulaymān Muḥammad. *al-Ḥaraka al-'ummāliyya fī miṣr wa-mawqif al-ṣaḥāfa wa'l-sulṭāt al-miṣriyya minhā min sanat 1882 ilā sanat 1952.* Cairo, 1967.

―――. *Ta'rīkh al-ḥaraka al-'ummāliyya fī miṣr.* Cairo, 1963.

Qurrā'a, Sanīyya. *Nimr al-siyāsa al-miṣriyya.* Cairo, 1950(?).

Quṭb, Sayyid. *al-'Adāla al-ijtimā'iyya fī al-islām.* Cairo, 1980.

―――. *Ma'rakat al-islām wa'l-ra'smāliyya.* Cairo, 1951.

Rāḍī, Nawāl 'Abd al-'Azīz. *Adwā' jadīda 'alā al-ḥaraka al-'ummāliyya al-miṣriyya, 1930–1945.* Cairo, 1977.

Rāḍī, Rāḍī Abū Sayf. ''Mushkilat al-'āmil.'' *Majallat al-shu'ūn al-ijtimā'iyya* 3 (March 1942):33–42.

al-Rāfi'ī, 'Abd al-Raḥmān. *Fī a'qāb al-thawra al-miṣriyya.* 3 vols. Cairo, 1969.

―――. *Muḥammad Farīd: ramz al-ikhlāṣ wa'l-tadḥiyya.* Cairo, 1948.

―――. *Thawrat sanat 1919.* 2 vols. Cairo, 1946.

Ramaḍān, 'Abd al-'Aẓīm. *'Abd al-Nāṣir wa-azmat māris.* Cairo, 1976.

―――. *al-Ṣirā' bayna al-wafd wa'l-'arsh, 1936–1939.* Cairo, 1979.

―――. *al-Ṣirā' al-ijtimā'ī wa'l-siyāsī fī miṣr mundhu thawrat 23 yūlyū 1952 ilā nihāyat azmat māris 1954.* Cairo, 1975.

―――. *Ṣirā 'al-ṭabaqāt fī miṣr, 1837–1952.* Beirut, 1978.

―――. *Taṭawwur al-ḥaraka al-waṭaniyya al-miṣriyya, min sanat 1918 ilā sanat 1936.* Cairo, 1968.

―――. *Taṭawwur al-ḥaraka al-waṭaniyya fī miṣr min sanat 1937 ilā sanat 1948.* 2 vols. Beirut, n.d.

Riḍā, Rashīd. *Tafsīr al-qur'ān al-karīm.* 12 vols. Cairo, 1367 H.

472 Bibliography

Rifā'ī, 'Abd al-'Azīz. *al-'Ummāl wa'l-ḥaraka al-qawmiyya fī miṣr al-ḥadītha, 1900–1952*. Cairo, n.d.

Sa'ātī, Ḥasan. *al-Taṣnī' wa'l-'umrān: baḥth midānī fī al-iskandariyya wa-'ummalīhā*. Alexandria, 1962.

Ṣa'd, Aḥmad Ṣādiq. *Ṣafaḥat min al-yasār al-miṣri fī a'qāb al-ḥarb al-'alāmīyya al-thāniyya, 1945–1946*. Cairo, 1976.

al-Sa'īd, Rif'at. *Aḥmad Ḥusayn: kalimāt wa-mawāqif*. Cairo, 1979.

———. *Ḥasan al-Bannā: matā . . . kayfa . . . wa-li-mādha?* Cairo, n.d.

———. *'Iṣām al-Dīn Ḥifnī Nāṣif*. Cairo, 1970.

———. *Kitābāt fī al-ta'rīkh*. Cairo, 1981.

———. "Miṣr bayna mu'āhadat 1936 wa-intifāḍat 1946." *al-Ṭan'a* 8 (December 1972):81–92.

———. *al-Mu'allafāt al-kāmila*, I, including: *Ta'rīkh al-fikr al-ishtirākī fī miṣr, Thalātha lubnāniyyīn fī al-qāhira, Niqūlā Haddād*, and *'Iṣām al-Dīn Ḥifnī Nāṣif*. Cairo, 1978.

———. *Munazzamāt al-yasār al-miṣrī, 1950–1957*. Cairo, 1983.

———. *al-Ṣiḥāfa al-yasāriyya fī miṣr, 1925–1948*. Cairo, 1977.

———. *al-Ṣiḥāfah al-yasāriyya fī miṣr, 1950–1952*. Beirut, 1981.

———. *Ta'rīkh al-munazzamāt al-yasāriyya al-miṣriyya, 1940–1950*. Cairo, 1976.

———. *al-Yasār al-miṣrī, 1925–1940*. Beirut, 1972.

Sayyid Aḥmad, Muḥammad 'Abbās. "Ḥarakat al-ta'rīkh al-miṣrī bayna laylat 4 fibrāyir 1942 wa-laylat 23 yūlyū 1952." *al-Tali'a* 1 (March 1965):86–95.

al-Shāfi'ī, Shuhdī 'Aṭiyya. *Taṭawwur al-ḥaraka al-waṭaniyya al-miṣriyya, 1882–1956*. Cairo, 1957.

Shafīq, Aḥmad, Ḥawliyyāt miṣr al-siyāsiyya. Cairo, 1926–1931.

Shanūda, Emile Fahmī Ḥannā. *Ta'rīkh al-ta'līm al-ṣinā'ī ḥattā thawrat 23 yūlyū 1952*. Cairo, 1967.

al-Sharqāwī, Jamāl. *Ḥarīq al-qāhira*. Cairo, 1976.

Shawqī, Zākī Muḥammad. *al-Ikhwān al-muslimūn wa'l-mujtama' al-miṣri*. Cairo, 1980.

Ṣidqī, Ismā'īl. *Mudhakkirātī*. Cairo, 1950.

al-Silkāwī, Aḥmad Ibrāhīm Aḥmad Ramaḍān. *Nahḍat al-'ummal al-miṣriyyīn fī al-'aṣr al-ḥadīth: 'ashar sanawāt ma'a al-'ummāl*. Cairo, 1952.

al-Sūdānī, Ṣāliḥ 'Alī 'Īsā. *al-Asrār al-siyāsiyya li-abṭāl al-thawra al-miṣriyya wa-āra' al-duktūr Mahjūb Thābit*. Cairo, 19-16(?).

Yūsuf, Muṣṭafa al-Naḥḥas Jabar. *Siyāsat al-iḥtilāl tijāha al-ḥaraka al-waṭaniyya, 1906–1914*. Cairo, 1975.

VII. Books and Articles in English, French, and Hebrew

Abbas, Raouf. "Labor Movement in Egypt, 1899–1952." *The Developing Economies* 11 (1973):62–75.

Abdel-Fadil, Mahmoud. *The Political Economy of Nasserism: A Study in Employment and Income Distribution Policies in Urban Egypt, 1952–1972*. Cambridge, U.K., 1980.

Abdel-Malek, Anouar. *Egypt: Military Society*. New York, 1968.

———. *La Formation de l'idéologie dans la renaissance nationale de l'Égypte (1805–1892)*. Paris, 1969.

Abou Alam, Abdel Raouf. *The Labor Movement in Egypt*. Washington, D.C., 1955.

Abrahamian, Ervand. *Iran Between Two Revolutions*. Princeton, 1982.

Bibliography   473

———. "The Strengths and Weaknesses of the Labor Movement in Iran, 1941–1953." In *Modern Iran: The Dialectics of Continuity and Change*, edited by Michael Bonine and Nikki Keddie, pp. 211–32. Albany, 1981.

Abu Lughod, Janet. *Cairo: 1001 Years of the City Victorious*. Princeton, 1971.

———. "Migrant Adjustments to City Life: The Egyptian Case." *American Journal of Sociology* 67 (1961):22–32.

———. "Urbanization in Egypt: Present State and Future Prospects." *Economic Development and Cultural Change* 13 (1963):313–43.

Agwani, M. S. *Communism in the Arab East*. Bombay, 1969.

Ahmad, Eqbal. "Trade Unionism." In *State and Society in Independent North Africa*, edited by Leon Carl Brown, pp. 146–91. Washington, D.C., 1966.

Althusser, Louis, *For Marx*. New York, 1970.

Anderson, Perry. *Arguments within English Marxism*. London, 1980.

Anis, Mahmoud Amin. "A Study of the National Income of Egypt." *L'Égypte contemporaine*, no. 261–62 (November–December 1950).

Arminjon, Pierre. *La Situation économique et financière de l'Égypte*. Paris, 1911.

Artin, Yacoub. *Essai sur les causes du renchérissement de la vie matérielle au Cairo dans le courant du XIXe siècle*. (1800 à 1907). Cairo, 1907.

Audsley, M. T. "Labour and Social Affairs in Egypt." *St. Antony's Papers* 4 (1958):95–106.

Badawi (Badaoui), Ahmad Zaki. *La Législation du travail en Égypte*. Alexandria, 1951.

———. *La Question ouvrière*. Alexandria, 1954.

———. *Les Problèmes du travail et les organisations ouvrières en Égypte*. Alexandria, 1948.

Baer, Gabriel. *Egyptian Guilds in Modern Times*. Jerusalem, 1964.

———. *Studies in the Social History of Modern Egypt*. Chicago, 1969.

el-Barawy, Rashed. *The Military Coup in Egypt: An Analytical Study*. Cairo, 1952.

Barbour, K. M. *The Growth, Location and Structure of Industry in Egypt*. New York, 1972.

Bashear, Suliman. *Communism in the Arab East, 1918–1928*. London, 1980.

Batatu, Hanna. *The Old Social Classes and the Revolutionary Movements of Iraq*. Princeton, 1978.

Beinin, Joel. "Formation of the Egyptian Working Class." *MERIP Reports*, no. 94 (February 1981):13–23.

Beling, Willard A. *Pan Arabism and Labor*. Cambridge, Ma., 1961.

Berg, Elliot J., and Butler, Jeffrey. "Trade Unions." In *Political Parties and National Integration in Tropical Africa*, edited by James S. Coleman and Carl G. Rosberg, pp. 340–81. Berkeley, 1964.

Berque, Jacques. *Egypt: Imperialism and Revolution*. London, 1972.

——— "The Establishment of the Colonial Economy." In *Beginnings of Modernization in the Middle East*, edited by W. R. Polk and R. L. Chambers, pp. 223–44. Chicago, 1968.

Binder, Leonard. *In a Moment of Enthusiasm: Political Power and the Second Stratum in Egypt*. Chicago, 1978.

Bonnell, Victoria. *Roots of Rebellion: Workers' Politics and Organization in St. Petersburg and Moscow, 1900–1914*. Berkeley, 1983.

Bourdieu, Pierre. *Travail et travailleurs en Algérie*. Paris, 1963.

Braverman, Harry. *Labor and Monopoly Capital*. New York, 1974.

Brinton, Jasper. *The Mixed Courts of Egypt*. New Haven, 1930.

474 Bibliography

Carson, William Morris. *The Mehalla Report.* Badr es-Sheyn, 1953.

———. "The Social History of an Egyptian Factory." *Middle East Journal* 11 (1957):361–70.

Charles-Roux, J. *L'Isthme et le canal de Suez.* Paris, 1901.

Chesneux, Jean. *The Chinese Labor Movement, 1919–1927.* Stanford, 1968.

Clarke, John, Critcher, Chas., and Johnson, Richard, eds. *Working Class Culture: Studies in History and Theory.* London, 1979.

Clawson, Patrick. "The Development of Capitalism in Egypt." *Khamsin*, no. 9 (1981): 77–116.

———. "Egypt's Industrialization: A Critique of Dependency Theory." *MERIP Reports*, no. 72 (November 1978):17–23.

Clerget, Marcel. *Le Caire: Étude de géographie urbaine et d'histoire économique.* 2 vols. Cairo, 1934.

Clegg, Ian. *Workers' Self-Management in Algeria.* New York, 1971.

Cohen, Robin. *Labor and Politics in Nigeria, 1945–1971.* New York, 1974.

———. "Michael Imoudou and the Nigerian Labor Movement." *Race and Class* 18 (1977):345–62.

———, Gutkind, Peter, and Brazier, Phyllis, eds. *Peasants and Proletarians: The Struggles of Third World Workers.* New York, 1979.

Colombe, Marcel. *L'Evolution d'Égypte, 1924–1950.* Paris, 1951.

Congrès National Égyptien. *Oeuvres du Congrès National Égyptien ténu à Bruxelles le 22, 23, 24 septembre 1910.*

Cooper, Mark. "Egyptian State Capitalism in Crisis: Economic Policies and Political Interests, 1967–1971." *International Journal of Middle East Studies* 10 (1979):481–16.

———. *The Transformation of Egypt.* Baltimore, 1982.

Couland, Jacques. *Le Mouvement syndical au Liban (1919–1946).* Paris, 1970.

———. "Regards sur l'histoire syndicale et ouvrière égyptienne (1899–1952)." In *Mouvement ouvrier, communisme et nationalismes dans le monde Arabe*, edited by René Gallisot, pp. 173–201. Paris, 1978.

Crouchley, Arthur E. *The Economic Development of Modern Egypt.* London, 1938.

———. *The Investment of Foreign Capital in Egyptian Companies and Public Debt.* New York, 1977.

Cuno, Kenneth. "The Origins of Private Ownership of Land in Egypt: A Reappraisal." *International Journal of Middle Eastern Studies* 12 (November 1980):245–75.

Davies, Ioan. *African Trade Unions.* Middlesex, U.K., 1966.

Davis, Eric. *Challenging Colonialism: Bank Misr and Egyptian Industrialization, 1920–1941.* Princeton, 1983.

De Cosson, A.F.C. "The Early History of the Egyptian Railway." *Egyptian State Railways Magazine* 1 (no. 11, November 1932).

———. "Further Notes on the Early History of the Egyptian Railway." *Egyptian State Railways Magazine* 2 (no. 6, June 1933).

Deeb, Marius. "Bank Misr and the Emergence of the Local Bourgeoisie in Egypt." *Middle Eastern Studies* 12 (1976):69–86.

———. "Labor and Politics in Egypt: 1919–1939." *International Journal of Middle Eastern Studies* 10 (1979):187–203.

———. *Party Politics in Egypt: The Wafd and Its Rivals, 1919–1936.* London, 1979.

De Jong, F. *Turuq and Turuq-Linked Institutions in Nineteenth Century Egypt.* Leiden, 1978.

De Saint-Omer, Henri. *Les Enterprises belges en Égypte.* Brussels, 1907.

Bibliography   **475**

D'Hestroy, le Baron E. de Gaiffier. *Égypte: Situation économique, financière et commerciale en 1907*. Brussels, 1908.

Dorra, Albert J. "L'Industrie égyptienne et ses possibilités et développement." *L'Égypte contemporaine*, no. 214 (November 1943) 1: 410–23.

Ducruet, Jean. *Les Capitaux européens au Proche Orient*. Paris, 1964.

Eman, André. *L'Industrie du coton en Égypte: étude d'économie politique*. Cairo, 1943.

Fanon, Frantz. *The Wretched of the Earth*. New York, 1968.

Farouk-Sluglett, Marion, and Sluglett, Peter. "Labor and National Liberation: The Trade Union Movement in Iraq, 1920–1958." *Arab Studies Quarterly* 5 (1983):139–54.

Fawzi, Saad ed Din. *The Labour Movement in the Sudan, 1946–1955*. London, 1957.

Fédération égyptienne de l'industrie. *Livre d'or de La Fédération égyptienne de l'industrie*. Cairo, 1948.

Fédération syndicale mondiale. *Rapport de la Conférence-congrès syndicale mondiale, 25 septembre–8 octobre*. Paris, 1945.

el-Gammal, A.A.K. *A Modern Transport Problem: Rail versus Road (with particular reference to Egypt)*. Cairo, 1939.

Gaulis, B.-G. *Le Nationalisme égyptien*. Paris, 1928.

Goldberg, Ellis. "Bases of Traditional Reaction: A Look at the Muslim Brothers." *Peuples méditeranéens-Mediterranean Peoples*, no. 14 (January–March 1981):79–95.

———. *Tinker, Tailor, and Textile Worker: Class and Politics in Egypt, 1930–1954*. Berkeley, 1986.

Gran, Peter. "Modern Trends in Egyptian Historiography: A Review Article." *International Journal of Middle Eastern Studies* 9 (1978):367–71.

El-Gritly, A.A.I. "The Structure of Modern Industry in Egypt." *L'Égypte contemporaine*, no. 241–42 (November–December 1947).

Gutkind, Peter. *The Emerging African Urban Proletariat*. Montreal, 1974.

Handley, W. J. "The Labor Movement in Egypt." *Middle East Journal* 3 (1949):277–92.

Hansen, Bent. *Prices, Wages, and Land Rents: Egypt, 1895–1913*. Working Paper no. 131, Department of Economics, University of California, Berkeley, October 1979.

———. *Wage Differentials in Italy and Egypt: the Incentive to Migrate before World War I*. Working Paper no. 164, Department of Economics, University of California, Berkeley, October 1982.

Harbison, Frederick, and Ibrahim, Ibrahim A. "Some Labor Problems of Industrialization in Egypt." *Annals of the American Academy of Political Science* 305 (May 1956):114–24.

Harris, Christina. *Nationalism and Revolution in Egypt*. The Hague, 1964.

Hartmann, Paul, ed. *L'Égypte indépendante*. Paris, 1938.

Helmy, Mahmoud Abdel Moneim, Helmy, Abbas, and Baraghit, Mohammad Ibrahim. *Egyptian Railways in 125 Years: 1852–1977*. Cairo, 1977.

Heyworth-Dunne, James. *Religious and Political Trends in Modern Egypt*. Washington, D.C., 1950.

Hodgkin, Thomas. *Nationalism in Colonial Africa*. New York, 1956.

Hourani, Albert. *Arabic Thought in the Liberal Age, 1798–1939*. London, 1970.

———, and Stern, S. M., eds. *The Islamic City*. Oxford, 1970.

Hussein, Mahmoud. *Class Struggle in Egypt, 1945–1970*. New York, 1977.

Ibrahim, Ibrahim A. K. "Socio-Economic Changes in Egypt, 1952–1964." In *Industrial Relations and Economic Development*, edited by A. M Ross, pp. 115–33. London, 1966.

476 Bibliography

Issa, Hossam. M. *Capitalisme et sociétés anonymes en Égypte: essai sur le rapport entre structure sociale et droit.* Paris, 1970.

Issawi, Charles. "Assymetrical Development and Transport in Egypt, 1800–1914." In *Beginnings of Modernization in the Middle East,* edited by W. R. Polk and R. L. Chambers, pp. 383–400. Chicago, 1968.

———, ed. *The Economic History of the Middle East, 1800–1914.* Chicago, 1966.

———. *Egypt at Mid-Century.* London, 1954.

———. *Egypt in Revolution: An Economic Analysis.* London, 1963.

Jankowski, James. *Egypt's Young Rebels: "Young Egypt," 1933–1952.* Stanford, 1975.

———. "The Egyptian Blue Shirts and the Egyptian Wafd, 1935–1938." *Middle Eastern Studies* 6 (1970):77–95.

Jones, Gareth Stedman. *Languages of Class: Studies in English Working Class History, 1832–1982.* Cambridge, U.K., 1983.

Kilson, Martin. " Nationalism and Social Change in British West Africa." *The Journal of Politics* 20 (1958):368–87.

Kraiem, Mustapha. *Nationalisme et syndicalisme en Tunisie, 1918–1929.* Tunis, 1976.

Lacouture, Jean. *Egypt in Transition.* New York, 1958.

Landes, David. *Bankers and Pashas: International Finance and Economic Imperialism in Egypt.* Cambridge, MA, 1979.

Lane, E. W. *Manners and Customs of the Modern Egyptians.* 1836. Reprint. London, 1978.

Laqueur, W. Z. *Communism and Nationalism in the Middle East.* London, 1956.

Laraoui, Abdallah. *The Crisis of the Arab Intellectual.* Berkeley, 1976.

Lazreg, Marnia. *The Emergence of Classes in Algeria.* Boulder, CO, 1976.

Lecarpentier, G. *L'Égypte moderne.* Paris, 1925.

Legrand, F. *Les Fluctuations de prix et les crises de 1907 et 1908 en Égypte.* Nancy, 1909.

Lockman, Zachary. "Notes on Egyptian Workers' History." *International Labor and Working Class History,* no. 18 (Fall 1980):1–12.

Longuenesse, Elisabeth. "La classe ouvrière au Proche Orient: La Syrie." *La Pensée,* no. 197 (January–February, 1978) 120–32.

———. "The Syrian Working Class Today." *MERIP Reports,* no. 134 (July–August, 1985):17–24.

Lord Lloyd. *Egypt since Cromer.* London, 1933.

Lugol, Jean. *Egypt and World War.* Cairo, 1945.

Mabro, Robert. *The Egyptian Economy, 1952–1972.* Oxford, 1974.

———, and Radwan, Samir. *The Industrialization of Egypt, 1939–1973.* Oxford, 1976.

Manchester Chamber of Commerce. *Report of the Manchester Chamber of Commerce Mission to Egypt.* Manchester, 1937.

el-Maraghi, Aziz. *La Législation du travail en Égypte.* Paris, 1937.

Marsot, Afaf. *Egypt's Liberal Experiment.* Berkeley, 1977.

Martin, Germain. *Les Bazars du Caire et les petits métiers arabes.* Cairo, 1910.

Mazuel, Jean. *Le Sucre en Égypte.* Cairo, 1937.

McCarthy, Justin A. "Nineteenth-Century Egyptian Population." *Middle Eastern Studies* 12 (October 1976):1–39.

McLennan, Gregor. *Marxism and the Methodologies of History.* London, 1981.

Mead, Donald. *Growth and Sturctural Change in the Egyptian Economy.* Homewood, IL, 1967.

Menouni, Abdeltif. *Le syndicalisme ouvrier au Maroc.* Casablanca, 1979.

Messeri, Michael. "Tnu'at hapo'alim bazira hapolitit bemitzrayyim, 1919–1936." 3 parts. *ha-Mizrah he-hadash* 12 (nos. 2–4, 1971).

Bibliography **477**

Métin, Albert. La Transformation de l'Égypte. Paris, 1903.

Meynaud, Jean, and Bey, Anisse Salah. Trade Unionism in Africa: A Study of Its Growth and Orientation. London, 1967.

Mitchell, Richard P. The Society of the Muslim Brothers. London, 1969.

Morris, Morris David. The Emergence of an Industrial Labor Force in India: A Study of the Bombay Cotton Mills, 1854–1947. Berkeley, 1965.

Moseley, Sydney. With Kitchener in Cairo. London, 1917.

Musa, Salama. The Education of Salama Musa. London, 1961.

Nagi, Mostafa H. Labor Force and Employment in Egypt: A Demographic and Socioeconomic Analysis. New York, 1971.

Nassef, Abdel-Fattah. The Egyptian Labor Force: Its Dimensions and Changing Structure, 1907–1960. Philadelphia, 1970.

Naus, Henri. Recueil des discours prononcés à la Fédération Égyptienne des Industries. Cairo, 1939.

O'Brien, Patrick. "Industrial Development and the Employment Problem in Eygpt, 1945–1965." Middle East Economic Papers (1962):90–120.

————. The Revolution in Egypt's Economic System: From Private Enterprise to Socialism, 1952–1965. London, 1966.

————, and Mabro, Robert. "Structural Changes in the Egyptian Economy, 1937–1965." In Studies in the Economic History of the Middle East, edited by M. A. Cook, pp. 412–27. London, 1970.

Owen, Roger. "The Attitudes of British Officials to the Development of the Egyptian Economy." In Studies in the Economic History of the Middle East, edited by M. A. Cook, pp. 485–500. London, 1970.

————. Cotton and the Egyptian Economy, 1820–1914. London, 1969.

————. "Lord Cromer and the Development of Egyptian Industry, 1883–1907." Middle Eastern Studies 2 (1966):282–301.

————. The Middle East and the World Economy. London, 1981.

Petras, James. Critical Perspectives on Imperialism and Social Class in the Third World. New York, 1978.

Politis, Athanase. L'Hellénisnme et l'Égypte moderne. 2 vols. Paris, 1930.

Poulantzas, Nicos. Political Power and Social Classes. London, 1978.

————. Social Classes in Contemporary Capitalism. London, 1978.

Przeworski, Adam. "Proletariat into a Class: The Process of Class Formation from Karl Kautsky's The Class Struggle to Recent Controversies." Politics & Society 7 (1977):343–401.

Quraishi, Zaheer M. Liberal Nationalism in Egypt: Rise and Fall of the Wafd Party. Allahabad, 1967.

Radwan, Samir. Capital Formation in Egyptian Industry and Agriculture, 1882–1967. London, 1974.

Raymond, André. Artisans et commerçants au Caire au XVIIIe siècle. 2 vols. Damascus, 1973–1974.

Riad, Hassan. L'Égypte Nassérienne. Paris, 1964.

Richards, Alan. Egypt's Agricultural Development, 1800–1980: Technical and Social Change. Boulder, CO, 1982.

————. "Primitive Accumulation in Egypt: 1789–1882." Review 1 (1977):3–49.

Rothstein, Theodore. Egypt's Ruin. London, 1910.

Russell, Thomas. Egyptian Service, 1902–1946. London, 1949.

el-Saaty, Hassan, and Hirabayashi, Gordon K. Industrialization in Alexandria: Some Ecological and Social Aspects. Cairo, 1959.

Sabel, Charles. Work and Politics. Cambridge, U.K., 1982.

478 Bibliography

Safran, Nadav. *Egypt in Search of Political Community*. Cambridge, MA, 1961.

Samuel, Raphael, ed. *People's History and Socialist Theory*. London, 1981.

Sandbrook, Richard, and Cohen, Robin, eds. *The Development of an African Working Class*. Toronto, 1975.

Sembene, Ousmane. *God's Bits of Wood*. New York, 1970.

Seth, Ronald. *Russell Pasha*. London, 1966.

Sewell, William H. *Work and Revolution in France: The Language of Labor from the Old Regime to 1848*. Cambridge, U.K., 1980.

Shorter, Edward, and Tilly, Charles. *Strikes in France, 1830–1968*. London, 1974.

Socolis, Georges. *Notes sur l'Égypte et son histoire économique depuis 30 ans*. Paris, 1903.

Soliman, Ali. *L'Industrialisation de l'Égypte*. Lyons, 1932.

Stichter, Sharon. "Workers, Trade Unions and the Mau Mau Rebellion." *Canadian Journal of African Studies*, 9 (1975):259–75.

Stock Exchange Year-Book of Egypt. Cairo, 1943.

Thompson, E. P. *The Making of the English Working Class*. New York, 1963.

―――. "The Moral Economy of the English Crowd in the Eighteenth Century." *Past and Present*, no. 50 (1971):76–136.

―――. *The Poverty of Theory and Other Essays*. New York, 1979.

Tomiche, Fernand J. *Syndicalisme et certains aspects du travail en République arabe unie (Égypte) 1900–1967*, Paris, 1974.

Tignor, Robert L. "Dependency Theory and Egyptian Capitalism, 1920 to 1950." *African Economic History*, no. 9 (1980):101–18.

―――. "The Egyptian Revolution of 1919: New Directions in the Egyptian Economy." *Middle Eastern Studies* 12 (1976):41–67.

―――. "Equity in Egypt's Recent Past: 1945–1952." In *The Political Economy of Income Distribution in Egypt*, edited by Gouda Abdel-Khalek and Robert Tignor, pp. 20–54. New York, 1982.

―――. *Modernization and British Colonial Rule in Egypt, 1882–1914*. Princeton, 1966.

―――. *State, Private Enterprise and Economic Change in Egypt, 1918–1952*. Princeton, 1984.

Vallet, Jean. *Contribution à l'étude de la condition des ouvriers de la grande industrie au Caire*. Valence, 1911.

Vatikiotis, P. J. *The History of Egypt*. 2nd ed. Baltimore, 1980.

Warren, Bill. *Imperialism, Pioneer of Capitalism*. London, 1980.

Waterbury, John. *The Egypt of Nasser and Sadat: The Political Economy of Two Regimes*. Princeton, 1983

Weiner, Lionel. *L'Egypte et ses chemins de fer*. Brussels, 1932.

Weiss, François. *Doctrine et action syndicales en Algérie*. Paris, 1970.

Wilmington, Martin. *The Middle East Supply Centre*. Albany, NY, 1971.

Ziadeh, Farhat. *Lawyers, the Rule of Law and Liberalism in Modern Egypt*. Stanford, CA, 1968.

Index

'Abbas Halim: arrest (1934), 207; arrest and internment (1942), 250, 296; conception of working class, 199, 451; and COWM, 226-27, 281; and CTWU, 242-46, 248, 251-52, 381, 403; employment scheme, 208; and Fathi Kamil, 307-308, 409-10; and GFLUKE, 232-33; and Hawamdiyya strike (1936), 221-22; and hunger strike (1939), 236; and independent trade unionism, 214-15, 287-88, 310, 325, 445; and Labor party (1931), 203-204, 226; and Labor party (1944), 303, 308, 309, 334, 347-48, 355, 358, 404, 410; and Muhammad 'Ali 'Amir, 401; and Muslim Brothers, 381; and NFTUE, 195-217; popularity, 196, 198; return to labor politics (1937), 226-27, 280; unions loyal to, 246, 296, 301, 361n; withdrawal from labor politics (1936), 213; and Young Egypt, 210
'Abbud, Ahmad, 11, 202, 381, 399-400
al-'Abd, Hamid, 350, 371, 372
'Abd Allah, 'Abd al-Hamid, 280, 318
'Abd al-Halim, Muhammad, 327, 330, 333, 335, 339, 350
'Abd al-Haqq, 'Abd al-Hamid, 289, 293, 295-98, 320, 325, 410
'Abd al-Jayyid, Faddali, 322-23, 332, 368

'Abd al-Khaliq, Mahmud, 414
'Abd al-Nasir, Jamal, 3, 163, 418, 419, 425n, 435, 437-41, 443, 444, 454, 455, 457-59
'Abd al-Rabbuh, Hafiz, 326, 328
'Abd al-Rahman, Hasan, 403-405, 409, 410, 428, 444
Abu Khayr, Zaki, 294, 298
'Afifi, Amin Hafiz, 424
'Afifi, Hafiz, 421, 425
Agha, Ahmad Muhammad, 178, 180, 185-86
'Ajami, Mahmud Ibrahim, 439
'Ali, Sayyid, 341, 346
'Ali Shawqi Pasha, 175, 177, 178, 180
al-'Amal, 358
'Amara, Muhammad Hasan, 193, 197, 199, 225, 296, 303, 306
'Amil al-Mahalla, 358
al-'Amil al-Misri, 190-91, 194
Amin, 'Abd al-Mun'im, 425, 427, 430
'Amir, Muhammad 'Ali, 401-403, 409, 411, 427, 429
'Anabir (Cairo railway workshops) workers: activism (1920-21), 155-56; agitation during 1919, 103, 118; and GUW, 167, 175; links with Wafd, 156-57; and MTWU model, 124; and 1919 revolu-

480 Index

'Anabir (*cont.*)
tion, 95, 97-98; and 1930 unrest, 190;
and 1931 elections, 201-202; pre-1914
activism, 72-76; rehiring of (1936),
223; and Wafd (1937), 229
Andraos, Elias, 421
Anglo-Egyptian treaty of 1936, workers'
response to abrogation, 407-409, 411,
416
anticommunism, 140n, 143, 144, 150-51,
160-61, 303, 349-52, 368-69, 370, 376,
398, 425-27, 433
al-'Arabi, Mahmud Husni: and CPE, ESP,
141-51; exile (1930), 194; and fourth
Comintern congress, 143-44; and nationalism, 142; and *Ruh al-'Asr*, 191;
trial (1924), 151. See *also* Bolshevism,
Communist Party of Egypt, Egyptian
Socialist party, socialism
Arab socialism, 457, 459
al-'Askari, Mahmud: arrest (January
1946), 339, 343, 344, 368; arrest (June
1946), 349; and Beso strike, 289; and
COWM, 226, 281; and CPSTU, 328-30;
and *al-Damir*, 336; and election campaign (1944), 322; at Henri Pierre, 282;
and Muslim Brothers, 366; and New
Dawn, 315-16, 324, 340, 352; radicalization, 320-21; and *Shubra*, 297, 318;
and WCNL, 336; and WFTU Congress,
331
Audsley, M. T., 304-305, 348, 358, 377,
388, 404n, 416, 425n
al-Azhar, 91, 97, 101

Badaoui, Zaki, 269, 271, 272
Bank Misr, 10, 11, 114, 244, 259, 264
al-Banna, Hasan, 282-83, 363-65, 367,
377, 384, 385, 389
al-Banna, Jamal, 384n, 392, 402, 434n
al-Baqari, Muhammad, 423-25, 427, 429,
430, 431, 434
al-Bashir, 398, 401, 403, 409
Bolshevism, 108, 112, 139-40. See *also*
communist movement (after 1924);
Communist Party of Egypt; Egyptian
Socialist party; socialism
Bourse de Travail, 112-13
British labor movement, 71, 143, 200,
408
Butler, Harold, 204-205

Caffery, Jefferson, 415, 425
Cairo Confederation of Trade Unions,
299-300
capitalism, development of, 8-12, 28, 34,
48-49, 257-59, 263-66, 448-49
child labor, 26, 45, 205, 306
cigarette workers: early activism, 49-53;
as labor elite, 39; and mechanization,
53, 125-26; Muhammad Kamil Husayn
and 'Aziz Mirham as counsellors of,
127; strikes of 1917-18, 85-87; and
Wafd, 299. See *also* Eastern Tobacco
Company workers; Matossian cigarette
factory
cinema workers, 328, 341, 345, 442
coal heavers (Port Said), 23, 27-31, 108,
126
Coca Cola Company workers, 406
des Combes, Paul Jacot, 314
Committee (later Commission) to Organize the Workers' Movement (COWM):
and CTWU leaders, 242; core of
GFLUKE, 232; establishment, 225-27;
and Shubra al-Khayma textile workers,
226, 281
communist movement (after 1924): 310-
62, 401-407, 451, 452, 455; and Free
Officers, 419, 424-26, 430-31, 433, 439,
454; and Muslim Brothers, 365-76,
378, 382-83, 390, 402-403, 426, 433-
35, 451; Rafiq Jubbur group (1925),
151; role of foreigners and Jews, 313-
15, 352, 368, 445-46. See *also* Bolshevism; Communist Party of Egypt;
Egyptian Socialist party; socialism
Communist Party of Egypt (CPE, 1922-
24): 141-54; and Comintern, 141; and
nationalism, 142-43; reasons for failure, 152-53; shift in line, 144; suppression (1924), 147-49, 313. See *also* Bolshevism; communist movement (after
1924); Egyptian Socialist party; socialism
Communist Party of Egypt (CPE, 1949-
57), 420n, 439-40n
Communist Party of Egypt (CPE, 1958-
65), 327, 458-59
Conciliation and Arbitration Committees: 290-92; and Shell workers, 386-
87; and Suez Canal Company workers,
360, 385, 387

Index **481**

Confédération Générale du Travail (CGT), 139, 141-51
Congress of Egyptian Trade Unions (CETU), 345
Congress of Private Sector Trade Unions (CPSTU), 327-30, 339, 341, 343, 344, 369-70
Congress of Trade Unionists, 409-10
Congress of Trade Unions of Egypt (CTUE), 346-49, 372-73
cooperatives, 62
corporatism, 7, 163, 198-99, 297, 307, 431-32
Curiel, Henri, 326, 398, 424n

al-Damir, 336, 338, 340
Darwish, Yusuf, 314-16, 319-20, 322, 323, 328, 333, 336, 351, 367
al-Da'wa, 390-92, 426, 434, 435, 438
deference: and Cairo tramwaymen, 243-44, 251-52; decline of, 180; and tutelage of notables, 81, 166
Democratic Movement for National Liberation (DMNL), 325-27, 352, 413, 452; expansion of influence, 357, 397, 405-406; and Free Officers, 419, 420, 426-28, 433, 439n; and Misr Fine Spinning and Weaving workers, 392, 421, 424; and Misr Spinning and Weaving workers, 353-54; and Muslim Brothers, 392, 433-35; and PCGFETU, 409-11; and transport workers, 404-405; and Wafd, 398. *See also* Egyptian Movement for National Liberation
Democratic Movement for National Liberation—Revolutionary Trend, 428
dockers, 407
Douek, Raymond, 314-15
Dumrani, Mahmud, 341, 349, 372

Eastern Tobacco Company workers, 126, 174, 240, 272, 274, 299, 305-308, 360, 388, 393-94, 429, 450. *See also* Matossian cigarette factory
effendiyya, 6, 10, 13, 66, 89, 179, 210, 220, 286, 313, 396
Egyptian Federation of Industries (EFI), 184, 193
Egyptian Movement for National Liberation (EMNL), 325-30, 333, 337, 343-46,

352, 369, 371, 373. *See also* Democratic Movement for National Liberation
Egyptian Socialist party (ESP, 1921-22), 139-41. *See also* Bolshevism; communist movement (after 1924); Communist Party of Egypt; socialism
Egyptian Workers' Union (EWU), 174, 177
Fahmi, 'Abd al-Rahman: arrest and resignation (1924-25), 168-69; and GUW, 157; report to Zaghlul on unions, 104; secretary of Wafd in Cairo (1919), 93n; and Shafiq Mansur, 168-69; and Wafd's labor federation (1924), 158-61; warning to government, 164

al-Fajr al-jadid, 315
al-Farghali, Mahmud, 405, 442, 445
Farid, Muhammad: and "European disease," 55; and Keir Hardie, 71; and labor legislation, 67; on unions, 70, 79-80
Faruq (King), 227, 234, 300, 303
fascist influence, 221, 313
Federation of Company Workers' Unions, 326
Filature Nationale workers: 147-48, 220-21, 273, 296, 348, 356, 359, 361, 384, 429, 443
Ford Workers' and Employees' Union, 335, 339
foreign capital, 7-9, 11, 23, 48-49, 258-59, 448-50
foreign workers: 35-37, 39, 43; Armenians, 35; Eastern Europeans, 35, 146; Greeks, 35, 50-54, 106; Italians, 35, 36, 107, 109, 111-12; Jews, 35, 146; labor activism among, 37, 53-54, 106-10, 111-13; relations with Egyptian workers, 41-42, 54-55, 109-10, 112, 166; at Suez Canal (1919), 106-10
Founding Committee for a General Federation of Egyptian Trade Unions (FCGFETU), 414-15, 420, 427-30, 435
Free Officers, 12, 320, 418-47, 454-56
Fu'ad (King), 174-75, 177, 186
Fu'ad Ahmad, 419
Fuda, Salim, 244-50
al-Fuli, Muhammad, 391, 392, 434

482 Index

General Federation of Egyptian Trade Union, 456-57
General Federation of Labor Unions (1928), 185, 186, 193
General Federation of Labor Unions in the Kingdom of Egypt (GFLUKE, 1938-41), 232-41
General Federation of Labor Unions in the Nile Valley (1924), 158-59, 164-69
General Union of Mechanized Textile and Preparatory Workers of Greater Cairo (GUMTPWGC). See textile workers (Shubra al-Khayma)
General Union of Mechanized Textile Workers in Shubra al-Khayma and Cairo (GUMTWSKC). See textile workers (Shubra al-Khayma)
General Union of Workers (GUW), 157, 167-68, 175, 177, 182
al-Ghazzali, 'Abd al-Mun'im, 427
al-Ghazzali, Hikmat, 345
al-Ghazzali, Muhammad, 390
government policy toward workers: attitudes of British officials, 63-64, 78, 108-109, 112, 115, 117, 130, 206-207, 209, 287, 304-305, 348; creation of Labor Office, 194; Cromer (1896), 30-31; role of Egyptian officials, 63, 78, 117, 371, 372. See also Graves; Keown-Boyd; labor legislation; Labor Office; Sidqi; Wafd
government workers, 288, 293, 301-302, 360, 439, 450. See also 'Anabir workers; railway workers
Graves, R. M., 194, 209, 212, 228
guilds, 9, 28-29, 32-35

Hafiz, Muhammad, 288, 293, 301-302
Hamrush, Ahmad, 419, 426, 427, 431
Harb, Salah, 355
Harb, Tal'at, 114
Hasanayn, Muhammad, 293, 298-301
Hasib, Rif'at, 320, 331, 338
Hawamdiyya sugar refinery workers: 126, 274, 299, 380, 384; harassment of union (1931), 199; in 1919 revolution, 98-99; seasonal employment of peasants, 25; strike (1936), 221-22; strike (1950-51), 299-400, 408, 410; workers' club (1924), 161

Hilwan workers, 270, 439, 460
Hurriyat al-Shu'ub, 326
Husayn, 'Abd al-Fattah, 350
Husayn, Ahmad, see Young Egypt; Socialist party
Husayn, Muhammad Kamil: and Cairo tramwaymen (1919), 110, 113-15; and Cairo tramwaymen (1920-21), 128-35; and Cairo unions (1921), 127; end of career, 133-35; and Liberal Constitutionalist party, 134; and Nationalist party, 100

Ibrahim, 'Ali, 374
al-Ikhwan al-Muslimun, 366-68, 370, 372, 373, 377, 379, 380, 382-84, 386, 388
industrial bourgeoisie, 10-11, 114, 258, 259, 394-95
industrial schools, 34-35, 282
International Confederation of Arab Trade Unions, 458
International Federation of Trade Unions, 185, 193, 201, 204
International Labor Office (later Organization), 185, 204-205, 408, 436
'Isawi, 'Abd al-Mun'im, 367, 402
Iskra, 326, 328, 337, 342, 343, 352. See also Democratic Movement for National Liberation (DMNL)
Isma'il, Ahmad, 185, 186, 193
Israel, Marcel, 326
Ittihad party, 173, 175
Ittihad al-'Ummal, 158, 166-67
'Izz al-Din, Kamil, 303, 410

al-Jamahir, 352-53, 357, 359, 362, 409
Joint Transport Federation (Alexandria), 404, 406, 442
Joint Transport Federation (Cairo—JTF), 247-48, 405, 407, 435-36, 441-44

Kamil, Anwar, 320
Kamil, Fathi, 240, 299, 305-308, 348, 393, 409-10, 411, 414-16, 429, 436, 439, 445, 458
Kazim, Husayn, 341, 345, 349
Keown-Boyd, Alexander, 144, 148, 149, 183, 206-207, 209, 212
Khallaf, Sayyid, 441

Khamis, Mustafa, 423-27, 429-31, 434
Khudayr, Sayyid, 341, 349, 372
al-Khuli, al-Bahi, 390-91
al-Khuli, Fikri, 276, 402
Kom Ombo workers, 159, 164. *See also*
sugar workers

Labor Conciliation Board: and CGT, 144,
145; establishment, 116-17; inactivity
of (1929), 186; replacement by local
boards (1924), 163; and unemployed
cigarette workers, 125
labor contracting, 25, 28, 31; at Suez
Canal, 40-41, 109, 190
labor legislation: accident compensation
law (1936), 223, 320; accident insurance, 291; Butler report, 204-205; establishment of LCB, 116-17; Graves' attitude, 209; hours of labor, 356; Law of
Individual Contracts (1944), 320; law
of 1909, 45, 67n; laws on women's and
children's labor (1933), 205; limitation
on dismissals, 383; minimum wage,
399; opposition by SLAC, 223; promised by Nahhas (1937), 229; promised
by Wafd (1924, 1936), 163, 219; of
RCC, 432-33, 435; recognition of trade
unions, 116-17, 223, 235-36, 291-94;
union demands for, 183-85, 192, 230,
234; vagrancy law, 145, 223
Labor Office (from 1936 Labor Department): enforcement of nine-hour day,
356; establishment, 184, 194; inade-
quacy of inspection services, 205; and
Misr Spinning and Weaving strike,
358; and Shubra al-Khayma textile
workers, 371, 372, 374; workers' complaints against, 206
Labor party: of 1931, 203-204, 210, 226;
of 1944, 303, 332, 334, 347-48, 355,
358, 404, 410; and Wafd, 224-25, 228-
29
Laqueur, Walter, 330-31
Lenin, V. I., 342, 353
Liberal Constitutionalist party, 134, 168,
186, 193
Liberation Rally, 435, 437, 439, 441
literacy, 67, 272, 314

al-Maghribi, Fathi, 318-19

al-Mahdi, 'Abd al-'Alim, 358
Mahir, 'Ali, 213, 236, 246, 250
Mahmud, Muhammad, 186, 236
al-Malayin, 398, 409
Mandur, Muhammad, 312
Manual Trades Workers' Union
(MTWU): and Alexandria railway
workers in 1919, 95-96, 98; at 'Anabir
in 1909-14, 73-76; branch at Filature
Nationale, 147; breakaway to form
GUW, 157-58; decline after First
World War, 124-25; disavowal of com-
munism, 150; and Nationalist party,
67-68, 76, 81; pre-1914 character and
composition, 67-72, 81-82; reappear-
ance at end of First World War, 87-88
Mansur, Shafiq, 135, 158, 167, 169
Mao Tse-tung, 452
Maqqar, Anwar, 406
Marconi Wireless Company workers,
405, 407, 429
Marun, Antun, 141, 144, 147-49, 151
Matossian cigarette factory, 50, 52, 305.
See also Eastern Tobacco Company
workers
Middle East Supply Center, 258
military workers, 260-61, 407-409
Mirham, 'Aziz: and Cairo cigarette workers, 127; and CTWU, 230, 242; as
Wafdist labor leader, 181-82, 184, 192,
209-10, 224, 227
Misr Bayda Dyers Company workers,
273, 421-22
Misr Fine Spinning and Weaving Company workers, 46, 273, 275, 359, 379,
392, 420n, 421-26, 430, 434, 442-43,
453, 456, 461
Misr Rayon Company workers, 422
Misr Spinning and Weaving Company
workers: 46, 270-73, 275-79, 359, 453-
54, 460; strike of 1938, 277-78; strike
of March 4, 1946, 342; strikes of June
1946, 347; strike of 1947, 352-59, 361,
382-83, 401
al-Misri, 438
al-Misri, Ahmad, 333, 334
al-Mudarrik, Muhammad Yusuf: 313,
318, 320; arrest (January 1946), 339,
343, 344, 368; and Cairo Confederation of Trade Unions, 299-300; and

484 Index

al-Mudarrik, Muhammad Yusuf (cont.) COWM, 225, 281; and CPSTU, 330; in GFLUKE, 238; and Misr Spinning and Weaving strike, 357-59; and New Dawn, 315, 324, 328, 340; and 1939 hunger strike, 235-36, 283; and WCNL, 336; and WFTU Congress, 330-35
Muslim-Christian relations, 102, 113
Muhyi al-Din, Khalid, 419, 425, 431, 438, 440
Mukhaymar, Zaki, 441, 444
Muslim Brothers, see Society of Muslim Brothers
Mustafa, 'Abd al-'Aziz, 405, 408, 409, 414-15, 416, 428, 444-45
al-Mu'tamar, 345
mutamassirun, 9, 11, 23, 41, 352, 377

Nafi', Hasan, 127, 158, 177, 182
al-Nahar, 238-39
al-Nahhas, Mustafa, 228-29, 288, 290
Nahum, Da'ud, 328, 329, 333-35
Najib, Muhammad, 418, 421, 423, 425-26, 436-41, 443
Nasif, 'Isam al-Din Hifni, 191, 280
Nassar, Husayn, 341
National Committee, 369-70
National Committee of Workers and Students (NCWS), 340-44, 369-70, 394
National Democratic Front, 391-92, 433-35
National Federation of Trade Unions in Egypt (NFTUE), 197-217, 232
Nationalist party: 66-67, 218; conception of workers, 69-71, 77; and MTWU, 67-72; people's night schools, 67; and workers before 1914, 76-81; and workers in 1919, 100-101; and Wafd, 147. See also Manual Trades Workers' Union
New Dawn (organization), 315, 324-25, 327-29, 333, 335, 337, 338, 340, 343, 351, 352, 371, 373. See also Workers' Vanguard; Popular Vanguard for Liberation
1919 Revolution: Cairo tramway workers' role in, 91-95; patterns of worker participation in, 98-100; railway workers' role in, 95-98; socioeconomic con-

text, 84, 90-91
Nuh, Muhammad, 441
Nuh, Muhammad 'Abduh, 406, 427, 429
al-Nuqrashi, Mahmud, 381
nurses, 360-61

Palestine war, 361-62, 375, 388
Partisans of Peace, 407
paternalism: of 'Abbas Halim, 198-99, 451-52; of Free Officers, 431-37; of Misr Company, 453; of Muslim Brothers, 379-80; of Wafd, 135, 159-63, 451-52
peasant workers: 24-27, 31, 98-99; at Hawamdiyya sugar mill, 221-22; strikes by, 56, 126, 164, 203; in textile industry, 275-77
Peers, Robert, 260
People's Liberation, 326
petty bourgeoisie (urban): 6-7, 263; transformation of, 32-35; and working class 6-7, 38-39, 240-41, 266
pharmaceutical workers, 319, 331
Pizzuto, Giuseppe, 111-13
police, 360, 361
Popular Vanguard for Liberation, 324, 351-52. See also New Dawn, Workers' Vanguard
Preparatory Committee for a General Federation of Egyptian Trade Unions (PCGFETU), 409-14, 445
Preparatory Committee for an Egyptian Representative to the WFTU Congress, 331-35
Preparatory Committee for an Egyptian Trade Union Congress (PCETUC), 335, 339, 341, 343-44, 345
printers, 53, 78, 111-12, 288, 294-95, 327, 341, 346, 429, 433, 442
public utility workers, 65, 128, 144, 146, 246, 327, 328, 339
al-Qalyubi, Murad, 328, 329, 333, 335, 341, 345, 349

Qandil, Sayyid, 191, 225, 240, 303-304, 306, 313, 334, 410
Qutb, Mahmud, 336
Qutb, Sayyid, 390

Radi, Radi Abu Sayf, 269, 415

railway workers: activism (1906-1908), 72-73; in Alexandria MTWU (1919), 88; and Mahjub Thabit, 100; in 1919 revolution, 95-97; segmentation of labor force, 40; unrest in Alexandria (1924), 147; and Wafd, 103, 156-57, 229. *See also* 'Anabir workers; Manual Trades Workers' Union
Rajab, Mahmud 'Abd al-Majid, 408, 414
Ratib, Da'ud, 193, 194, 196-97
repressive legislation, 78, 144-45, 246, 349, 398, 413
restaurant and hotel workers, 111, 320, 331, 406
Revolutionary Command Council (RCC), *see* Free Officers
Rida, 'Abd al-Rahman, 184-85
Rifa'i, Sayyid Sulayman, 326
Rosenthal, Joseph, 138-39, 141, 143, 151. *See also* Bolshevism; Communist Party of Egypt (1922-24); Confédération Générale du Travail; Egyptian Socialist party; socialism
Ruh al-'Asr, 191-92, 194, 225, 280

Sabri, Musa, 423
Sabri, Zuhayr, 178-80, 182-83, 212, 223, 224
Sa'd, Ahmad Sadiq, 314-15, 424
Sa'd, Muhammad, 303
Sa'dist party, 227, 232
Sa'id (Upper Egypt), 26-31
Sa'id, 'Abd al-Mughni, 320
Salama, Anwar, 240, 387, 388, 408-409, 414, 415n, 457
Salama, Isma'il Sayyid, 306
Salib, Iskandar Sulayman, 317
Salih, Ahmad Rushdi, 315
al-Sawi, al-Sawi Ahmad, 435-36, 440-41, 443, 444, 446
Sawt al-Umma, 355, 383
Sayf al-Nasr, Ahmad Hamdi, 211, 212, 224
al-Sayyid Pasha Abu 'Ali, 174, 177
Schwartz, Hillel, 326
seamen, 406, 442, 445
al-Shafi'i, Mursi, 438
al-Shafi'i, Shuhdi 'Atiyya, 342-44
al-Shahid, 'Abd al-Zahir, 348, 350, 380, 384

Shahin, 'Ali, 242, 245
Shalaqani, 'Abd al-Fattah, 290
al-Shanadi, Ahmad al-Damardash, 232
al-Shantanawi, Husni, 190
al-Sha'rawi, Muhammad Mutawalli, 379, 392, 421, 422, 424, 434, 436-37, 443
Sharif, Muhammad, 366, 368, 372, 374, 375, 379, 380n, 393
Shatta, Muhammad, 344, 401, 435
Shell Oil Company workers, 265, 274, 357, 378, 386-87, 388, 408, 417, 450
Shihab, Muhammad, 423
Shirin, Fu'ad, 290
shoe workers, 6, 336, 349, 406, 442, 445
Shubra, 280, 297, 317-19, 366
Shubra al-Khayma Mechanized Textile Workers Union (SKMTWU), *see* textile workers (Shubra al-Khayma)
Shubra al-Khayma Steamboat Workers' Union, 319, 331
Shurbaji textile workers, 392, 434, 438, 456
Sibahi Spinning and Weaving Company workers, 273, 359, 361, 403, 429
Siddiq, Yusuf, 419, 425n, 431, 433, 440, 446
Sidqi, Isma'il, 194, 204-205, 348-52, 355, 362, 370, 372, 375, 381, 382, 456
al-Sirafi, 'Atiyya, 406, 409, 410
Siraj al-Din, Fu'ad, 13, 296, 298-300, 320, 325
Skouphopoulos, Dr., 109, 125, 138
socialism: formation of ESP, 139; Greek workers' familiarity with, 51; influence of *Ruh al-'Asr*, 191-92; pre-First World War influence of, 71; politics of Italian radicals, 111-12; and Salama Musa, 139; transformation of ESP into communist party, 141. *See also* Bolshevism; Communist Party of Egypt (1922-24); Egyptian Socialist party
Socialist Labor party, 348, 355
Socialist party, 396, 406, 407, 412-13, 433, 438. *See also* Young Egypt
Society of Muslim Brothers: 344, 348, 363-94, 396, 406, 407, 413, 451-52; and Eastern Tobacco workers, 393-94, 429; economic enterprises, 208-209, 374-75; and Free Officers, 419, 426, 433, 437-38, 439; and Isma'il Sidqi, 370,

486 Index

Society of Muslim Brothers (*cont.*)
375, 381-82; and Misr Fine Spinning
and Weaving workers, 392, 423, 426;
and Misr Spinning and Weaving workers, 356, 382-83, 393, 394; and 1939
hunger strike, 236; and Shubra al-
Khayma textile workers, 345, 365-79,
383, 394; and Suez Canal Zone workers, 382, 384-88; and Taha Sa'd 'Uthman, 282-83, 366, 368, 390; Workers'
Section, 366, 367, 379, 382, 384, 390,
393
Socony-Vacuum workers, 265, 414
store clerks, 111, 328, 330, 441, 442
strike, Arabic terms used for, 55
students: and Nationalist party, 66; and
NCWS, 341-43, 370; and New Dawn,
314; 1935 uprising, 212-13; and people's night schools, 67; Wafd's loss of
support among, 227
Suez Canal Company workers: 450, 458;
and abrogation of 1936 treaty, 407; activism in 1919, 106-10; activism in
1930, 190; and CGT, 146; foreign immigrants among, 36; labor dispute of
1947-48, 357, 360, 378, 385-88, 417;
structure of workforce, 40-41
sugar workers, 26, 126, 174, 274, 408.
See also Hawamdiyya sugar refinery
workers
Sulayman, Muhammad Madbuli, 331,
333, 336, 345
Supreme Council (of the NFTUE), 210-
12, 224, 233, 242
Supreme Labor Advisory Council
(SLAC), 205, 223, 228, 308, 414-15
Sus, Najib, 341

Taha, Ahmad, 406, 409, 412, 428-30, 435
al-Tahawi, Ibrahim, 435, 440-41, 446
taxi drivers, 92, 193, 404, 410, 428, 441,
442, 444
textile workers: leading role, 7, 241, 272-
75, 279-80, 417, 446-47, 449; national
federations, 357, 411, 437
textile workers (Alexandria): 274, 283-
84, 359, 403, 442. *See also* Filature Nationale workers; Sibahi Spinning and
Weaving Company workers
textile workers (Kafr al-Dawwar), *see*

Misr Fine Spinning and Weaving
Company workers
textile workers (Mahalla al-Kubra), *see*
Misr Spinning and Weaving Company
workers
textile workers (Shubra al-Khayma): 237,
274, 279-83, 355, 356, 383, 407, 439,
453-54, 460; Beso strike, 289-90, 319;
and COWM, 226, 281; and cost-of-living allowance, 288, 319, 400-401; and
CPSTU, 328; and DMNL, 344, 401,
411; dissolution of union, 325, 331,
339, 373; growth of union, 290, 293-
94; literacy, 272; and Muslim Brothers,
365, 366-76, 378-80, 384-85, 401; and
NCWS, 341, 369; and New Dawn, 314-
21, 324-25; and 1944 elections, 321-24;
and *Shubra*, 297-98; stewards' committee, 325, 344, 349, 371, 375; strike
of January 1946, 338-39; strike of May-
June 1946, 345, 347, 348, 371-73; and
Wafd, 288-90, 299, 321; and *al-Wajib*,
294
textile workers (Zaytun, Matariyya, and
greater Cairo), 401-403, 407, 442. *See
also* Shurbaji textile workers
Thabit, Mahjub: and Alexandria MTWU,
100; and 'Anabir workers, 156; and
communism, 150; election to Parliament, 181; and EWU, 177; health care
for workers, 68; and Mahmud regime,
186-88; and Rida commission, 184;
role in labor movement, 181
Thornycroft (Egyptian General Omnibus
Company) workers: 202, 206, 339, 404-
405, 416; and 'Abbas Halim, 208, 246,
247, 361n; and NCWS, 341; and Wafd,
299
Trade Union Committee for the Defense
of Liberties (TUCDL), 429-31, 435
trade unions: among foreign workers, 53-
54; government recognition of, 116-17,
183, 234, 235-36, 291-93; leadership,
188-89, 238-41; numbers and membership of, 78, 119, 123-24, 179-80, 210,
274, 293-94; question of independence
of, 180, 187-89, 192, 216, 225-27, 233-
34, 238-41, 252-53, 287-88, 297-301,
308-309, 445-46
tramway workers (Alexandria): counsel-

Index   **487**

lors of, 127, 180; and early unrest among, 56; and Muslim Brothers, 380; in 1919 revolution, 98; strike of 1911, 64-65; strike of August-October 1919, 111, 113, 118; strike of 1936, 220-21; and wage cuts (1933), 215
tramway workers (Cairo—CTWU): and 'Abbas Halim, 242-44, 245-46, 361n, 381, 450; activism in 1920-24, 128-37; and 'Ali Shawqi Pasha, 175, 176; and DMNL, 405, 428-29; formation of union in 1919, 103; and Free Officers, 436, 441, 442, 444-45; and general strike of June 1946, 348, 350; and Muslim Brothers, 380-81, 384; and NCWS, 341; and Nationalist party, 62-63; and NFTUE, 208; pre-First World War activism, 57-66; revival in 1918, 87; role in 1919 revolution, 91-95; strike of August-October 1919, 110-11, 113-18; strike of September 1941, 248, 289; strike of October 1946, 380-81; and Wafd, 134-35, 230, 242-43, 250, 299, 399
tramway workers (Heliopolis), 111, 246, 247, 327
transport workers: cadre, 381; and DMNL, 403-405; and Free Officers, 435-36, 440-43; JTF (1941), 247-48; national organizations, 404-405, 411, 445; in provinces, 406, 416; role in labor movement, 274-75, 416-17, 449; threatened strike (1948), 361, 361n; union membership, 274
Tu'ayma, 'Abd Allah, 435, 440-41
Turk, Sayyid Khalil, 403, 405, 406, 428, 444

'Ubayd, William Makram, 135, 143, 158, 228, 288, 302
al-'Ummal, 158, 166-67
unemployment, 46, 84, 123, 208, 237, 260-63, 266, 324, 360, 373-74
union, Arabic terms used for, 55, 68-69, 100
al-'Uqayli, Kamil, 441, 444, 446
'Uthman, Taha Sa'd: 240, 281-83, 325, 328, 350, 352; arrest (January 1946), 339, 343, 344, 368; and CTUE, 346, 349; and al-Damir, 336; and Muslim

Brothers, 282-83, 366, 368, 390; and New Dawn, 324; radicalization, 320; and Shubra, 317-18; and WCNL, 336, 338, 369; and WFTU Congress, 331, 333

Wafd: and Cairo Confederation of Trade Unions, 299-300; and CGT, 139; and communist movement, 143, 150, 161, 295-96, 298-99, 392, 397; conception of working class, 157-63, 297, 450-51; and Free Officers, 431, 433, 438, 439; in Gharbiyya, 228, 230-31; and government workers, 156-57, 228, 288, 301; and independent trade unionism, 287-88, 300-301, 308, 309, 310, 311, 445; and Labor Department, 228; and recognition of trade unions, 291-95; in 1924, 154, 157-70; role of Wafdists in labor movement, 101-105, 135, 154-55, 157-59, 177-78, 181-82, 192-93, 294-301, 332, 401-403, 424-25, 445; and sabotage in 1919, 93; and workers, 7, 104, 121, 132, 135-36, 172-74, 177-79, 187, 189, 192, 197, 209-12, 216, 219-20, 222-25, 227-29, 231, 399-403, 456
al-Wafd al-Misri, 311-12, 337, 340, 347, 355, 372
Wafdist Vanguard, 311-12, 337, 340, 347, 352, 365, 369, 370, 371, 378, 383, 396, 397, 431, 454
wages and working conditions: before First World War, 39-40; during depression of 1930s, 189-90; in interwar period, 43-47, 49, 270-71; in 1917-18, 84-85; in 1920s, 123-24; and Second World War, 237, 267-69; after Second World War, 268-70, 272, 399; in sugar mills, 26; in textile mills, 270-71, 359-60
al-Wajib, 294, 297, 428, 430, 433, 438
women workers: Association of Egyptian Working Women, 341, 345; in cigarette factories, 50, 174; at cotton ginning and baling plants, 26; in labor press, 166-67; in peasant families, 31; in pre-First World War working class, 39; in textile mills, 271; in unskilled factory jobs, 45

488 Index

Workers' Committee for National Liberation (WCNL), 335-40, 343, 348, 352, 396, 452
Workers' Vanguard, 324-25, 351, 420n, 424, 439, 452. *See also* New Dawn; Popular Vanguard for Liberation
working class: conceptions of, 6-8, 38-39, 42, 69-71, 77, 100, 159-63, 184-85, 198-99, 266, 291-92, 297, 376-80, 431-32, 445-47, 449-51, 456; and depression of 1930s, 46, 189-90; and First World War, 83-85; formation and structure of, 5-8, 23-24, 37-47, 257-66, 272-75; and nationalism, 7-8, 14-18, 66, 80-81, 90, 99, 105, 109-10, 118-19, 136-37, 282, 288, 301, 317, 321, 332, 336-37, 340-41, 362, 396, 409, 450, 451, 452; and non-Egyptian managers

and owners, 41-43, 279; and petty bourgeoisie, 6-7, 179-80, 240-41, 266; and Second World War, 237, 259-62
World Federation of Trade Unions, 330-35

al-Yabani, Ahmad, 421, 422
al-Yara', 294-96, 297, 299, 326
Young Egypt, 210, 219-20, 222, 236, 396. *See also* Socialist party

Zaghlul, Sa'd, 134, 143, 148, 149-50, 160, 163
Zayn al-Din, Muhammad Ibrahim, 193, 197, 200-201, 296, 304, 305, 308, 309, 333, 334, 348, 404n, 405, 410, 415
Ziwar, Ahmad, 173-74, 176, 205, 223